T0134681

Lecture Notes in Computer Science 10920

Commenced Publication in 1973
Founding and Former Series Editors:
Gerhard Goos, Juris Hartmanis, and Jan van Leeuwen

More information about this series at http://www.springer.com/series/7409

Aaron Marcus · Wentao Wang (Eds.)

Design, User Experience, and Usability

Users, Contexts and Case Studies

7th International Conference, DUXU 2018
Held as Part of HCI International 2018
Las Vegas, NV, USA, July 15–20, 2018
Proceedings, Part III

 Springer

Editors
Aaron Marcus
Aaron Marcus and Associates
Berkeley, CA
USA

Wentao Wang
Baidu Inc.
Beijing
China

ISSN 0302-9743   ISSN 1611-3349 (electronic)
Lecture Notes in Computer Science
ISBN 978-3-319-91805-1   ISBN 978-3-319-91806-8 (eBook)
https://doi.org/10.1007/978-3-319-91806-8

Library of Congress Control Number: 2018944301

LNCS Sublibrary: SL3 – Information Systems and Applications, incl. Internet/Web, and HCI

Printed on acid-free paper

This Springer imprint is published by the registered company Springer International Publishing AG
part of Springer Nature
The registered company address is: Gewerbestrasse 11, 6330 Cham, Switzerland

Foreword

The 20th International Conference on Human-Computer Interaction, HCI International 2018, was held in Las Vegas, NV, USA, during July 15–20, 2018. The event incorporated the 14 conferences/thematic areas listed on the following page.

A total of 4,373 individuals from academia, research institutes, industry, and governmental agencies from 76 countries submitted contributions, and 1,170 papers and 195 posters have been included in the proceedings. These contributions address the latest research and development efforts and highlight the human aspects of design and use of computing systems. The contributions thoroughly cover the entire field of human-computer interaction, addressing major advances in knowledge and effective use of computers in a variety of application areas. The volumes constituting the full set of the conference proceedings are listed in the following pages.

I would like to thank the program board chairs and the members of the program boards of all thematic areas and affiliated conferences for their contribution to the highest scientific quality and the overall success of the HCI International 2018 conference.

This conference would not have been possible without the continuous and unwavering support and advice of the founder, Conference General Chair Emeritus and Conference Scientific Advisor Prof. Gavriel Salvendy. For his outstanding efforts, I would like to express my appreciation to the communications chair and editor of *HCI International News*, Dr. Abbas Moallem.

July 2018   Constantine Stephanidis

HCI International 2018 Thematic Areas and Affiliated Conferences

Thematic areas:

- Human-Computer Interaction (HCI 2018)
- Human Interface and the Management of Information (HIMI 2018)

Affiliated conferences:

- 15th International Conference on Engineering Psychology and Cognitive Ergonomics (EPCE 2018)
- 12th International Conference on Universal Access in Human-Computer Interaction (UAHCI 2018)
- 10th International Conference on Virtual, Augmented, and Mixed Reality (VAMR 2018)
- 10th International Conference on Cross-Cultural Design (CCD 2018)
- 10th International Conference on Social Computing and Social Media (SCSM 2018)
- 12th International Conference on Augmented Cognition (AC 2018)
- 9th International Conference on Digital Human Modeling and Applications in Health, Safety, Ergonomics, and Risk Management (DHM 2018)
- 7th International Conference on Design, User Experience, and Usability (DUXU 2018)
- 6th International Conference on Distributed, Ambient, and Pervasive Interactions (DAPI 2018)
- 5th International Conference on HCI in Business, Government, and Organizations (HCIBGO)
- 5th International Conference on Learning and Collaboration Technologies (LCT 2018)
- 4th International Conference on Human Aspects of IT for the Aged Population (ITAP 2018)

Conference Proceedings Volumes Full List

1. LNCS 10901, Human-Computer Interaction: Theories, Methods, and Human Issues (Part I), edited by Masaaki Kurosu
2. LNCS 10902, Human-Computer Interaction: Interaction in Context (Part II), edited by Masaaki Kurosu
3. LNCS 10903, Human-Computer Interaction: Interaction Technologies (Part III), edited by Masaaki Kurosu
4. LNCS 10904, Human Interface and the Management of Information: Interaction, Visualization, and Analytics (Part I), edited by Sakae Yamamoto and Hirohiko Mori
5. LNCS 10905, Human Interface and the Management of Information: Information in Applications and Services (Part II), edited by Sakae Yamamoto and Hirohiko Mori
6. LNAI 10906, Engineering Psychology and Cognitive Ergonomics, edited by Don Harris
7. LNCS 10907, Universal Access in Human-Computer Interaction: Methods, Technologies, and Users (Part I), edited by Margherita Antona and Constantine Stephanidis
8. LNCS 10908, Universal Access in Human-Computer Interaction: Virtual, Augmented, and Intelligent Environments (Part II), edited by Margherita Antona and Constantine Stephanidis
9. LNCS 10909, Virtual, Augmented and Mixed Reality: Interaction, Navigation, Visualization, Embodiment, and Simulation (Part I), edited by Jessie Y. C. Chen and Gino Fragomeni
10. LNCS 10910, Virtual, Augmented and Mixed Reality: Applications in Health, Cultural Heritage, and Industry (Part II), edited by Jessie Y. C. Chen and Gino Fragomeni
11. LNCS 10911, Cross-Cultural Design: Methods, Tools, and Users (Part I), edited by Pei-Luen Patrick Rau
12. LNCS 10912, Cross-Cultural Design: Applications in Cultural Heritage, Creativity, and Social Development (Part II), edited by Pei-Luen Patrick Rau
13. LNCS 10913, Social Computing and Social Media: User Experience and Behavior (Part I), edited by Gabriele Meiselwitz
14. LNCS 10914, Social Computing and Social Media: Technologies and Analytics (Part II), edited by Gabriele Meiselwitz
15. LNAI 10915, Augmented Cognition: Intelligent Technologies (Part I), edited by Dylan D. Schmorrow and Cali M. Fidopiastis
16. LNAI 10916, Augmented Cognition: Users and Contexts (Part II), edited by Dylan D. Schmorrow and Cali M. Fidopiastis
17. LNCS 10917, Digital Human Modeling and Applications in Health, Safety, Ergonomics, and Risk Management, edited by Vincent G. Duffy
18. LNCS 10918, Design, User Experience, and Usability: Theory and Practice (Part I), edited by Aaron Marcus and Wentao Wang

19. LNCS 10919, Design, User Experience, and Usability: Designing Interactions (Part II), edited by Aaron Marcus and Wentao Wang
20. LNCS 10920, Design, User Experience, and Usability: Users, Contexts, and Case Studies (Part III), edited by Aaron Marcus and Wentao Wang
21. LNCS 10921, Distributed, Ambient, and Pervasive Interactions: Understanding Humans (Part I), edited by Norbert Streitz and Shin'ichi Konomi
22. LNCS 10922, Distributed, Ambient, and Pervasive Interactions: Technologies and Contexts (Part II), edited by Norbert Streitz and Shin'ichi Konomi
23. LNCS 10923, HCI in Business, Government, and Organizations, edited by Fiona Fui-Hoon Nah and Bo Sophia Xiao
24. LNCS 10924, Learning and Collaboration Technologies: Design, Development and Technological Innovation (Part I), edited by Panayiotis Zaphiris and Andri Ioannou
25. LNCS 10925, Learning and Collaboration Technologies: Learning and Teaching (Part II), edited by Panayiotis Zaphiris and Andri Ioannou
26. LNCS 10926, Human Aspects of IT for the Aged Population: Acceptance, Communication, and Participation (Part I), edited by Jia Zhou and Gavriel Salvendy
27. LNCS 10927, Human Aspects of IT for the Aged Population: Applications in Health, Assistance, and Entertainment (Part II), edited by Jia Zhou and Gavriel Salvendy
28. CCIS 850, HCI International 2018 Posters Extended Abstracts (Part I), edited by Constantine Stephanidis
29. CCIS 851, HCI International 2018 Posters Extended Abstracts (Part II), edited by Constantine Stephanidis
30. CCIS 852, HCI International 2018 Posters Extended Abstracts (Part III), edited by Constantine Stephanidis

http://2018.hci.international/proceedings

7th International Conference on Design, User Experience, and Usability

Program Board Chair(s): **Aaron Marcus, USA**
and Wentao Wang, *P.R. China*

- Sisira Adikari, Australia
- Claire Ancient, UK
- Jan Brejcha, Czech Republic
- Silvia De los Rios Perez, Spain
- Marc Fabri, UK
- Chao Liu, P.R. China
- Judith A. Moldenhauer, USA
- Jingyan Qin, P.R. China
- Francisco Rebelo, Portugal

- Christine Riedmann-Streitz, Germany
- Kerem Rizvanoglu, Turkey
- Elizabeth Rosenzweig, USA
- Patricia Search, USA
- Marcelo Márcio Soares, Brazil
- Carla G. Spinillo, Brazil
- Manfred Thüring, Germany
- Xuemei Yuan, P.R. China
- Paul Michael Zender, USA

The full list with the Program Board Chairs and the members of the Program Boards of all thematic areas and affiliated conferences is available online at:

http://www.hcl.international/board-members-2018.php

HCI International 2019

The 21st International Conference on Human-Computer Interaction, HCI International 2019, will be held jointly with the affiliated conferences in Orlando, FL, USA, at Walt Disney World Swan and Dolphin Resort, July 26–31, 2019. It will cover a broad spectrum of themes related to Human-Computer Interaction, including theoretical issues, methods, tools, processes, and case studies in HCI design, as well as novel interaction techniques, interfaces, and applications. The proceedings will be published by Springer. More information will be available on the conference website: http://2019.hci.international/.

General Chair
Prof. Constantine Stephanidis
University of Crete and ICS-FORTH
Heraklion, Crete, Greece
E-mail: general_chair@hcii2019.org

http://2019.hci.international/

Contents – Part III

Emotion, Motivation, and Persuasion Design

Player Behavior Influence by Visualizing the Game Sound Landscape 3
Daniel Paz de Araujo and Renan Bonin

Design of a Task-Management APP to Avoid Procrastination 16
Cayley Guimarães and Danielly J. P. Lazaro

Conformed Thought: Consolidating Traces of Memories 28
Silvia Laurentiz

Research on Service Process Design of Mobile Medical Platform
Based on Patient's Emotional Demand 41
Yingying Miao, Tong Cui, and Bin Jiang

PosiTec – How to Adopt a Positive, Need-Based Design Approach 52
*Kathrin Pollmann, Nora Fronemann, Anne Elisabeth Krüger,
and Matthias Peissner*

Do You Eat This? Changing Behavior Through Gamification,
Crowdsourcing and Civic Engagement 67
*Rejane Spitz, Francisco Queiroz, Clorisval Pereira Jr.,
Leonardo Cardarelli Leite, Marcelo P. Ferranti, and Peter Dam*

Research on Image Emotional Tag Generation Mechanism
Based on the "Cloud Pet Keeping" Phenomenon 80
Chen Tang, Ke Zhong, and Liqun Zhang

Persona Design for Just-in-Time Adaptive and Persuasive
Interfaces in Menopause Self-care 94
Amaury Trujillo, Caterina Senette, and Maria Claudia Buzzi

Comparing User Experience in Interactions with Different
Types of Digital Products 110
Lemeng Xu, Dede Ma, and Pengyi Zhang

Conceptual Framework for Affective and Cognitive Product Design 124
Sol Hee Yoon, Young Woo Kim, and Yong Gu Ji

Research on Information Recommendation Optimization Mechanism
Based on Emotional Expression and Cognition 133
Ke Zhong, Liqun Zhang, and Xiaolei Guan

DUXU and Children

The Importance of User-Centered Design in Performing Background
Checks in Child Care   149
    Fuad Abujarad, Allissa Desloge, Kristina Carlson,
    and Sarah J. Swierenga

Song of Red Pine Woods - Design and Study of Digital Picture
Books for Preschool Children on iPad   158
    Qi Cao, Jing-Hua Han, Yu-Yi Ding, Shi Huang, and Chao Liu

A Study on Application of AR Three-Dimensional Touch
Interaction in Children Education   170
    Yu-Yi Ding, Jing-Hua Han, Qi Cao, and Chao Liu

Bridging the Gulfs: Modifying an Educational Augmented
Reality App to Account for Target Users' Age Differences   185
    Hannah Klautke, John Bell, Daniel Freer, Cui Cheng,
    and William Cain

How Animation Improve Children's Cognition in User Interface:
A Study of the Kids VOD Application   196
    Wei Li, Xuan Zhang, and Yi Shen Zhang

An Interactive Digital Storytelling to Identify Emotions
and Consequences in the Elementary School Child   218
    Erick López-Ornelas and Rocío Abascal-Mena

Lessons Learned in Designing a Digital Therapeutic Game to Support
the Treatment and Well-Being of Children with Cancer   231
    Kamila R. H. Rodrigues, Daniel B. F. Conrado,
    and Vânia P. A. Neris

DUXU in Automotive and Transport

Investigating the Effect of Different Autonomy Levels on User Acceptance
and User Experience in Self-driving Cars with a VR Driving Simulator   247
    Jana Helgath, Philip Braun, Andreas Pritschet, Maximilian Schubert,
    Patricia Böhm, and Daniel Isemann

Improving Deaf Driver Experience Through Innovative
Vehicle Interactive Design   257
    Jingpeng Jia, Xueyan Dong, Yanjuan Lu, Yingjie Qian, and Dai Tang

Interactive Car Parking Simulation Based on On-line Trajectory
Optimization.   270
    Jungsub Lim, Hyejin Kim, and Daseong Han

Exploring Potential User Experience Design for Traditional Chinese
Service Station: A Case Study in Guangzhou, China   285
    Zhen Liu, Yifan Meng, Di Xu, Jun-en He, Xiusheng Gu,
    Lijun Jiang, Xiaohua Li, Shaoxin Wu, and Zhengquan Li

Extraction of Key Factors and Its Interrelationship Critical to Determining
the Satisfaction Degree of User Experience in Taxi Passenger
Service Using DEMATEL   299
    Chunrong Liu, Yi Jin, and Xu Zhu

What Sensory Desires Make Young Chinese Users Prefer One Instrumental
Panel Form of Passenger Car to Another?   314
    Chunrong Liu, Yang Xie, and Yi Jin

Young Chinese Consumers' Perception of Passenger Car Form
in Rear View   329
    Chunrong Liu, Yi Jin, Xiaoguo Ding, and Yang Xie

A Method of Car Styling Evaluation Based on Eye Tracking   342
    Zhaolin Lu, Shaobing Xu, and Bo Cheng

The Analysis of Visual Communication Design of Commonweal
Information Through Interactive Design Thinking - Public Commonweal
Information Design and Communication in Urban Traffic Spatial
Environment as an Example   351
    Shi Peng, Chao Liu, and Wentao Wang

Interaction Design of Autonomous Vehicle Based on Human Mobility   363
    Jingyan Qin, Zeyu Hao, and Shujing Zhang

Design Process of a Mobile Cloud Public Transport
Application for Bus Passengers in Lima City   375
    Juan José Ramírez, Juan Arenas, and Freddy Paz

Factor Model for Passenger Experience in the Aircraft Cabin Design.   389
    Siyu Ren, Xinyi Tao, and Ting Han

Smart Flashlight: Navigation Support for Cyclists   406
    Bing Jing Wang, Cheng Hung Yang, and Zhen Yu Gu

Smart Information Service Design Based on Autonomous Vehicles   415
    Qiong Wu, Long Qin, Yin Shuai Zhang, and Jie Chen

Acceptance and Effectiveness of Collision Avoidance System
in Public Transportation   424
    Xiaonan Yang and Jung Hyup Kim

A Design for a Public Transport Information Service in China   435
DanDan Yu, MuRong Ding, and Cong Wang

Research on User Needs of Digital Consumption Services
in Communicating Vehicles Context   445
Di Zhu

DUXU, Culture and Art

Study on Display Space Design of Off-line Experience Stores
of Traditional Handicraft Derivative Product of ICH Based
on Multi-sensory Integration.   459
Bingmei Bie, Ye Zhang, and Rongrong Fu

Artelligent: A Framework for Developing Interactive Computer
Artwork Using Artificial Intelligent Agents   471
Francisco de Paula Barretto and Suzete Venturelli

Conceptual Framework for Supporting the Creation of Virtual Museums
with Focus on Natural User Interfaces   490
Guilherme Corredato Guerino, Breno Augusto Guerra Zancan,
Tatiany Xavier de Godoi, Daniela de Freitas Guilhermino Trindade,
José Reinaldo Merlin, Ederson Marcos Sgarbi, Carlos Eduardo Ribeiro,
and Tércio Weslley Sant'Anna de Paula Lima

Rethink of Urban Arts: AR Technology with Participatory
Experience of New Urban Arts.   503
Ziyang Li, Hao He, and Xiandong Cheng

Study on Introducing Digitalization in Folk Art: Taking Beautiful!
Chinese New Year Paintings as an Example.   515
Song Lu

The Integration of New Media Art and Chinese Traditional Culture   524
Yunqiao Su

The "Living State" Research of China Non-material Cultural Heritage
on Digital Age: Taking the Nanjing Jinling Sutra Office as an Example.   535
Xiaoxian Wang and Hao Liu

Formation and Influence of New Media Art Form in Public Space   550
Lili Zhang and Yunqiao Su

DUXU Case Studies

Compliance with Static vs. Dynamic Warnings in Workplaces such
as Warehouses: A Study Using Virtual Reality   563
Ana Almeida, Francisco Rebelo, and Paulo Noriega

Blue-Collars/Tough Designs: UX Within Fire Service Occupational
Safety and Health Programs   573
    Timothy R. Amidon and Tiffany Lipsey

Peruvian Public Universities and the Accessibility of Their Websites   589
    Fanny Dolores Benites Alfaro
    and Claudia María Del Pilar Zapata Del Río

Co-design with Raspberry Pi: Developing and Hosting Sustainable
Community Application   608
    Salomao David and Esperança Muchave

Research on the Adaptability of Underground Soft Guidance
and Culture Based on Memorability   620
    Yang Du, Chao Liu, and Ye Zhang

A Preliminary Study on Design for Different Social Classes   635
    Jiong Fu and Chenhui Shi

Investigation on the Correlation Model Between Display
Height and Tilt Angle   648
    Huimin Hu, Yahui Bai, Chaoyi Zhao, Yinxia Li, Na Lin,
    and Zhongting Wang

Short Paper: How Do People Choose a Means for Communication
in Disaster Situations? Surveys After the Great East Japan
Earthquake and the Kumamoto Earthquake   657
    Masayuki Ihara and Hiroshi Watanabe

A Platform to Connect Swiss Consumers of Fair Trade Products
with Producers in Developing Countries: Needs and Motivations   664
    Julia Klammer and Fred W. G. van den Anker

Little Big Choices: Customization in Online User Experience   682
    Marco Neves and Maria Reis

The Influence of Short Text Ad. on Consumer Purchase Intention:
An Empirical Study   693
    Jia Qu and Can Huang

Expected User Acceptance of an Augmented Reality
Service for a Smart City   703
    Francisco Rebelo, Paulo Noriega, Tiago Oliveira, Daniela Santos,
    and Sabrina Oliveira

The Design of the SaiteBooker: An Authoring Tool for E-books
for Health Distance Learning Courses in Brazil   715
    Carla G. Spinillo, Claudio H. Silva, Ana Emília F. Oliveira,
    Dilson José L. Rabêlo Jr., and Aldrea M. O. Rabelo

Tourism and Virtual Reality: User Experience Evaluation
of a Virtual Environment Prototype.   730
    Yanick Trindade, Francisco Rebelo, and Paulo Noriega

Evaluating the Benefit of Accordion Web Elements for Low
Literacy Populations   743
    Shannon Tucker, Kathryn Summers, Tim McGowan,
    and Chris Klimas

Research on Interface of Large-Scale Equipment Network Management
System Based on User Experience   756
    Lei Wu, Lijun Mou, and Yao Su

Design of Human-Machine Interface System in Inverter Spot Welding.   768
    Yancong Zhu and Wei Zhou

Author Index   779

Emotion, Motivation, and Persuasion Design

Player Behavior Influence by Visualizing the Game Sound Landscape

Daniel Paz de Araujo[1(✉)] and Renan Bonin[2]

[1] PUC-Campinas – CEATEC, Rod. Dom Pedro I, Km 136, Campinas, SP, Brazil
daniel.araujo@puc-campinas.edu.br
[2] UNICAMP – Instituto de Artes, Rua Elis Regina 50, Campinas, SP, Brazil

Abstract. Historically games have been present in daily human life for centuries, reflecting and shaping behaviors. Technological evolution has also provided advances in games, having relevance in the digital context with the emergence of video games. They are a relevant form of entertainment but do not always offer good experiences to the deaf player, limiting their play behavior. Often the sound landscape is an important feedback information provider, thus causing frustration for non-listeners. This work presents the development of an interface that aims to make the universe of audio games more accessible to deaf people through the visualization of the sound landscape. To achieve this objective, the project was based on understanding the deaf culture and understanding the pains of the user, so that tools could be created that assertively softened the main problems encountered. In this way, deaf players are expected to be able to experience richer experiences in digital games.

Keywords: Accessibility · Game design · Sound landscape

1 Introduction

There was a time of human behavioral disruption, particularly during the period of digital convergence, when all types of media migrated from their different physical support to a unique computational platform, digitally based. In this way, mostly visual (space-based), audio (time-based) media; and the audiovisual (space-time based) discontinued to inhabit their traditional physical devices and began to be created or converted to the digital universe. Digital games were also influenced by this change, as they are entirely based on space, time and space-time media, increased by interactivity.

Ruled by their own rules, games create their universe. For Huizinga [6] "any thinking person can see at a glance that play is a thing on its own, even if this language possesses no general concept to express it". Since the digital systematization of the games, new experiences could be designed, redefining the behavior and the relationship of the player to the game. The experiences created by games can outweigh the player's interest in the real world. As McGonigal [9] explains, the real world just does not offer up as easily the carefully designed pleasures, the thrilling challenges, and the powerful social bonding afforded by virtual environments.

Technological developments have brought improvements to accessibility issues. People, who were once marginalized, find themselves increasingly immersed in the media that were previously difficult to access. But this evolution is not perfect and is still restrictive in some cases, moving away and segregating diverse groups. Such an event can be seen in games, where universes are created, but people are excluded because some interactions are not accessible to all people. Some problems faced by the deaf are often ignored by the listener. Either by the lack of knowledge of the pains of these people or by not being able to understand their difficulties.

Game designers have explored new possibilities for interaction, creating interactive mechanics that make use of different media. There are cases where visuals and audio impact the formal structure of a game and should be considered part of the rules [14]. However, players with visual or sound limitations often have their experience impaired, because the designer has not taken due care of the accessibility. The visual restrictions, in this case, are more critical, since a video game, as the name shows, is a game used through a video. So, depending on the visual restraint level, it may be impractical for the disabled to play the game. On the other hand, individuals who are hearing impaired, even on severe levels, can play a video game, but their experience is also limited and yet made complicated by the lack of accessibility. It happens because sound art is usually included in the game as background music or sound effects. The audio itself is a relevant part of the game experience and can be a decisive factor in situations an element is heard but is out of view field. Audio is an essential component of aesthetics and sound effects help to tell the story too [15].

The pursuit of entertainment through games by deaf users can be somewhat painful. These people usually need to adapt to an interface, rather than the other way around. Since games hardly offer tools for them to be fully exploited by a deaf person. Taking this into account, there is a latent demand for a feature that solves problems encountered by deaf people while playing. There is an opportunity to create something that softens these issues while bringing visibility to a recurring and often overlooked problem.

In this sense, the objective of this research is to influence the player behavior by enhancing the experience of digital games for the hearing impaired, so they can act in the universe of the video game with similar or same potential of other players. By offering access to the hearing impaired, it is expected that the player will have the ability to own, within the universe of the game, the same behavior as a fully trained player. The improved game experience can extrapolate the sound limits of the interaction, allowing the designer's dynamics to be fully enjoyed by the player.

This project aims to improve the behavioral experience for deaf gamers. To achieve this objective, the research is based on the visualization of the sound landscape through a radar that allows the audio of the game to be represented visually in real time, allowing the player to perceive what is around him, but out of his field of vision. At first, this project will be focused only on gamers who play on the computer. Such a decision was made, taking into account the difficulty of integrating a program into the consoles since the user needs to be with other software running parallel to some game, to take advantage of the tools.

The overall goal of the project is to alleviate problems that deaf gamers encounter during their game plays. To achieve this, the following specifics objectives will be sought [1]:

- Provide a tool that allows the deaf player to have a visual mapping of the audio emitted by the games, mainly sound effects;
- Create an environment where the deaf gamer feels comfortable in being;
- Encourage discussion of accessibility in games;
- Allow the deaf gamer to know the nuances of a game, taking into account accessibility, before buying it.

The research is on classic and contemporary bibliographical references, as well as documentary analysis. Interviews will be conducted with game players and designers and the hearing impaired to identify critical points in the gaming experience. Based on the information collected will be proposed a series of practices that could be considered by the designer to provide accessibility in games that are still being created. For the existing games will be made a prototype as a proof of concept to support the visualization of the game sound landscape. The results obtained will be made available to the community interested in the accessibility of digital games.

2 Cognition and Heuristics

The digital tools shall to have fluid navigation and natural understanding for the user. So, it is possible for him to get the best out of it and have behavioral satisfaction by his interaction. It was necessary to use a method to check the quality of navigation and whether it met the objectives. For this reason, the cognitive path method was chosen.

The cognitive pathway is an analytical method, and its primary objective is to evaluate the learning facility of the system [1]. In this way, the choice for such an approach was focused on the exploration of a system and it's learning. This method allows the deductions and analysis to come from the researcher himself, as long as he has enough information and content to understand the user and his needs.

To support the cognitive course, this project relied on the best practices found in developing systems through Nielsen heuristics. The Nielsen [10] heuristics evaluation is a method to find usability problems in interfaces and add points to a basic set of heuristics, which are:

- Visibility of system state: the interface should always inform the user about what is happening.
- Correspondence between the system and the real world: the language of the interface must be compatible with that of the user, avoiding technical terms.
- Control and freedom of the user: the user must always be able to undo or go back a step, if there is no possibility, he must be informed of the reason.
- Consistency and standardization: a command, function, text, and icon must have the same purpose during navigation throughout the system.
- Error prevention: the interface should anticipate a possible user error and not allow it to happen.

- Recognize, do not remember: the user should not be forced to remember some interface factor. It should not need to decorate some information from one area, to be used in another.
- Help users diagnose and recover errors: the error message needs to accurately indicate the problem that has occurred and, in a clear way, the ways to correct it.
- Help and documentation: an interface needs to be simple to the point where the user does not need outside help, but it is still necessary to create documentation that can be accessed by the user in case of doubt.
- Flexibility and efficiency of use: the interface must be functional for a beginner, but also provide shortcuts so that the more experienced can accelerate their flow.
- Aesthetic and minimalist design: avoiding irrelevant information is necessary for the user to focus on what is interesting to him.

3 Deafness

3.1 Deafness and Entertainment

Deafness is characterized by total or partial loss of listening ability. The causes are diverse, being able to be genetic or by external factors, like by physical traumas. It has several ways of being understood and can be analyzed from a cultural, health and even educational point of view [3].

The history of deaf education has, in general, been perpetuated through discriminatory situations. During Antiquity, more specifically in the Middle Ages, the deaf were considered "stupid" and "untrained" people, even being persecuted by extremist religious groups; those who learned to read and write were regarded as miraculous. It was only in the early sixteenth century that teaching methods began to be adapted for the deaf [8]. According to Lacerda [8], the data are uncertain regarding the pedagogical methods for the education of the deaf, because, at that time teachers worked autonomously, mainly for noble families or with much purchasing power, in this way, the professionals did not they shared methods with each other.

According to Soares [16], deafness in itself does not necessarily imply the inability or difficulty of learning of the individual. These, in turn, are symptoms of society and conventional pedagogical methods, which are not apt to include the deaf in education. According to the author, even if there are laws, they are hardly fulfilled comprehensively. The education of the deaf is often focused on oralization, and the majority of teachers are not bilingual, that is, they do not teach their students in their first language, which makes it difficult for the student to understand since it has variations of spoken.

In this way, deaf students, instead of being included in regular schools to live in a community, were deprived of education and not only that, but their behavior was also deprived because they were in schools mainly listening, their culture reduced and stereotyped, with significant efforts to be a listener. Therefore, it is necessary for the State and society to understand that the deaf subjects have a different identity, language, and culture than those of the listener. Therefore, there is an extremely thin line between inclusion and exclusion, since cultural aspects are rarely mentioned or remembered, which excludes the social identity of the deaf subject. Finally, understanding the history of the education of the deaf and understanding the effects on the development of these people is a crucial point for the evolution of this project.

Authors such as Bisol and Valentine [2] discuss the lack of cultural content and entertainment for deaf people. Although technological developments help to democratize entertainment and include deaf people in places where they were once inaccessible, it is still not fully exploited. It thus generates latent demand. Still, according to the authors, there are significant differences between the listener culture, about the deaf culture. This is mainly due to the difference in sign language for oralized language.

Also, the deaf population often have different references to people, artists, behaviors, writers, fables, plays, musicality, among other elements, all belonging to their own culture. A study by Thoma [17] found that there is a deficiency of representation of the deaf population in the media in general. In movies, for example, there are few films with deaf actors or that approach deafness as a theme. Therefore, it is still complex, but very necessary, to evaluate the conditions of the media that are an available deaf community, considering its totality, as well as its identity.

Regarding television, according to Crepaldi and Mendonça [4], the issue is even more critical, since this is the main means of communication and information of the population currently. In this way, guaranteeing the deaf the right to information, as well as entertainment, is also the duty of the media. There are different types of accessibility tools for need bearers, such as audio description, which is about narration describing programming, usually for blind or blind people and the Closed Captions often used by deaf people. The latter, in turn, is only the programming legend. However, it still has many weaknesses, since there are several text errors and there is the difficulty of understanding since not all deaf people were literate.

Musicality, on the other hand, is much discussed among the deaf community, as it is also a form of entertainment, it is also a way of reproducing and experiencing the art that the deaf often cannot appreciate due to the lack of resources. However, in the contemporary world, some resources have been used to include music in the lives of the deaf, such as the interpretation of music in sign language; as well as multisensory features, such as vibration, colors, and formats. Thus, deaf people can enjoy music, transforming it into a physical-motor experience and not just sound, as listeners are accustomed to [13].

Also, there are theater groups, focused on the deaf population. Theater plays are often used as an educational form. However, there are also theater groups with deaf actors. All this contributes to the experimentation of art and also as a form of entertainment for the deaf population, which respects and keeps alive the culture of this population. According to a study carried out by Barbosa [1], with the improvement of technology and the Internet, it is possible to use several resources for the education of deaf people, including elementary education. One of the alternatives would be online games, for example, since they have colors, shapes, and images that can be used as play tools in the teaching-learning process. Also, they can be used as entertainment. Nonetheless, Barbosa [1] considers that there are weaknesses in this method, since many auditory resources are used in such games.

In this way, it is possible to consider that through technology, communication and entertainment resources would guarantee the inclusion of deaf people in society.

However, there is still a lack of investment, both on the part of the Government and on the part of the big media companies, making it difficult for the deaf population to access the various types of entertainment.

3.2 Deaf Gamer

The game industry, which is continually growing, is also of great importance to deaf people, even if significant difficulties are encountered in this environment, especially in online games. To verify the possible sounds present in the games, several games were experienced and compared when played with and without sound aid. This experience was not based on empathy (since, as a listener, there was already a previous memory of the games and would not be a correct method), but to note important points during the game that were demonstrated only through sound, with no visual resources of support.

The game Left 4 Dead 2 [7], developed by Valve Corporation, stood out against other titles used for this research. The survivor horror game (a sub-genre of action games, when it is set in horror scenes and features elements of survival games) is set in a world during a zombie apocalypse. The goal is to go from point A to point B on a map full of enemies. The player has three other survivors for the match; these can be controlled by other people when played online or through BOT's (robot short). Important details were noted during the playing the game with sounds and were transcribed:

- At first, I hear zombies. Despite being in a quiet place, where you cannot see any, I know there are nearby enemies.
- Next, to the first door seen in the game I start to hear grunts and knocks on the door from the other side.
- There are special zombies that offer more danger to the player, and each one has a distinctive sound that sets them apart from all other enemies.
- When some important element or moment of the game is about to happen, there is a warning sound.
- Apart from enemies, there are other elements that inflict damage to the character, such as fire and gas. If I am suffering damage from something like that, there is a specific sound for each one.

Other important details were noted during the playing the game without sounds and were transcribed:

- The beginning of the game would not be possible to know of the presence of nearby enemies.
- I often ended up meeting special enemies as I had no clue that they were close.
- I opened doors and came across a horde of enemies, even if I thought I was in a quiet area of the game.
- I went to places with fire and only realized after having taken damage because a change occurs in the interface.
- When I'm on fire, even when I leave the danger area, flames appear in the lower corner, showing that the character is losing a life. The only problem is not knowing where the fire was coming from.

There was a sense of frustration every time the character died from some danger that was not being shown at the interface. When researching on a deaf gamers analysis, however, was found compliments to the closed captions feature, which was disabled until then. It needs to be enabled in the options menu, as shown in Fig. 1, and can only function as a caption of the characters' speeches or as a textual translation of almost all the sound effects that take place in the game.

Fig. 1. Audio configuration of Left 4 Dead game [7].

With this feature, the experience is entirely different, as it is possible to anticipate enemies and create strategies, as shown in Figs. 2 and 3. It is possible to demonstrate the difference of when the feature is disabled and activated. Each type of sound has a different color, just as it is for each character.

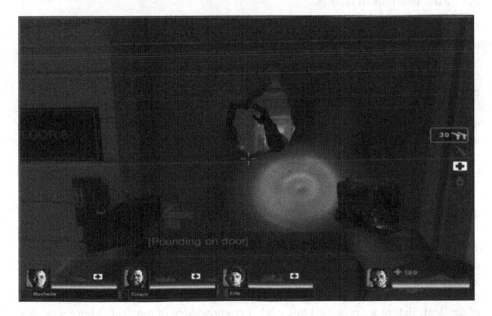

Fig. 2. Left 4 Dead [7] gameplay with sound visualization.

Fig. 3. Left 4 Dead [7] gameplay with sound visualization.

In addition to color separations, brackets are used to identify when a sound is not verbal, such as a special enemy approaching or sound of flames near the player.

3.3 Modifications in Games

With the discovery of the possibility of closed captions in a game, a search was made to find out which other games have such functionality. Unfortunately, there are not many titles that have the application. However, during the research, it was possible to find something is very present in the world of games: the modifications. Many games or even consoles have undergone some unofficial modification.

The documentary series Paralelos [11] deals in its last chapter on the historical value of the modifications to the Brazilian gamer community. Modifications to football games were more successful than the original game. The modifier community grew along with the gaming market. When a blockbuster game does not provide Portuguese subtitles, it is possible to find several translation projects, which are freely available to the public.

4   Sound Landscape

The project was born facing one problem encountered by deaf gamers: the lack of visual clues that represent the sound. When analyzing the complaints in various forums and groups, it was evident the need for a tool that would improve the behavioral experience of these players. Much of the beginning of the project was useful to know the universe of the deaf. Before we proposed this work, my knowledge of the deaf culture was very limited.

Although the project's inspiration came from the memory of a deaf childhood friend who then played some online games with me, we did not have any other interactions with the deaf community until this project. With that, in the first few weeks, we tried to understand the interactions between the deaf community and to know a little of its history. Before any direct contact, we had to know who we would be talking to and the pains they often face would miss something in games.

The user will access the radar through the game page or a link sent by someone from the community. The player can save a radar as a favorite, so it stays highlighted. It will be possible to search for radars in the community itself and, if you wish, to customize it to your liking. Most of the sounds created by gamers designers are geared towards some feedback to the player. Many of these sounds are not represented graphically in the game interface. There are several items that build the sound landscape in a game. Huiberts [5] formulates the model IEZA (acronym interface, effect, zone, and affection). His model brings theoretical tools for the development of the sound design.

The diegetic axis at Fig. 4 represents the sounds that occur in the fictional world of the game, the sounds the character could hear. The non-diegetic refers to sounds that are outside the fictitious environment, such as a soundtrack. The other axis represents if the sound that happens through the direct action of the player or caused by the game, but being part of the narrative or if it happens as an effect of ambiance. Therefore:

- Interface: sounds out of the fiction that communicates some activity of the game;
- Effect: sounds within the fiction that communicate some activity of the game;
- Zone: ambient sound, within the fictional world;
- Affection: Sound that emotionally characterizes an environment, not being within the fictional world.

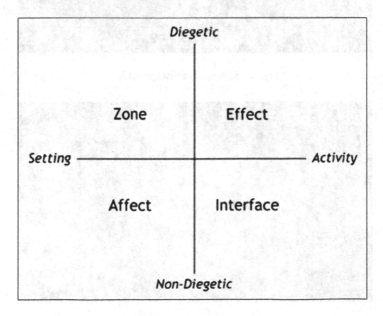

Fig. 4. IEZA Framework [5].

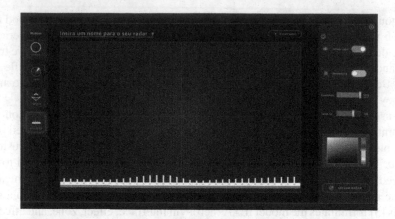

Fig. 5. 2d Sound landscape setup.

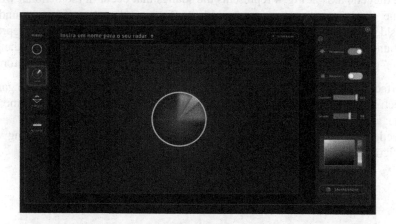

Fig. 6. 3d Sound landscape setup.

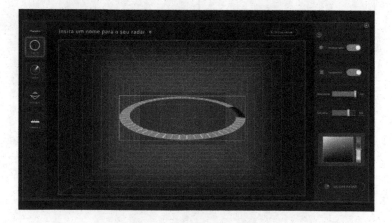

Fig. 7. 3d Sound landscape setup.

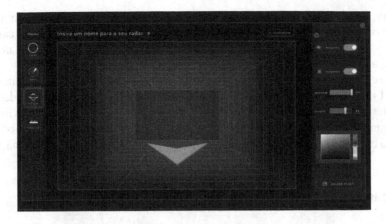

Fig. 8. 3d Sound landscape setup.

Knowing these specifications, it was possible to understand the limitations that the radar would have. Although graphically representing the direction of a sound, it could not correctly represent, for example, zone and effect sounds, as shown in Figs. 5, 6, 7 and 8.

This could be solved if the sound representation was made specifically for a particular title, where the sound landscape could be studied and graphically represented. The limitation was taken into account, but it was not a deciding factor for a change of plans, as this project seeks to help as many deaf gamers as possible and this would not happen if the focus were on a single title.

5   Conclusions

This project defined ways to bring accessibility to the deaf gamers behavior, based on the knowledge acquired through research. As a result, an interface has been obtained that allows greater integration of the deaf with games, as well as providing opportunities to soften the limitations that the games bring when they do not offer enough visual clues of the sound landscape that can be used by these people.

The functionalities were built through an evolutionary process. It was possible to cross-check observation, qualitative, interview and find the same problems being reported. Some of these problems are solved by the community itself, which, through unofficial modifications made to the games, improves the experience and usability. The sound landscape can enhance the game experience for deaf players, allowing them to play similar to hearing players.

By exploring applications opportunities, even hearing players could benefit from this research goals. They can be able to have a different behavioral experience by seeing the sound landscape instead of only hearing it.

Considering the evolutionary process of the project, it is also possible to think about future improvements. For example, the creation of a cam chat functionality to simplify entertainment consumption, taking into account the growth of platforms such as

Twitch.tv, where people play live games daily while interacting with the community. Another possibility of creation would be to automate the creation of closed captions, through a Machine Learning process, in which the main sounds of a sound landscape could be represented in a more automatic way.

This research work allows knowing a culture that was once far off. This situation led to reflect on how often was negligent a specific group of people during the design of some interface. However, being an antithesis, it also allowed me to know ways in which design can solve impasses created by some medium that does not provide accessible means to be used. It was a process of project evolution, accompanied by personal development.

References

1. Barbosa, S., Silva, B.: Interação Humano-Computador: Projetando a Experiência Perfeita. Rio de Janeiro, Campus (2010)
2. Bisol, C., Valentini, C.: Cultura Surda. Objeto de Aprendizagem Incluir – UCS (2011). http://www.grupoelri.com.br/Incluir/downloads/OA_SURDEZ_Cultura_Surda_Texto.pdf Accessed 19 Jan 2018
3. Carvalho, M., Nascimento, M., Garcia, J.: História e Memória da Deficiência Auditiva no Brasil Id on Line Revista de Psicologia, vol. 9, no .27. pp. 194–204 (2015). ISSN 1981-1189
4. Crepaldi, A., Mendonça, J.: Acessibilidade na TV: modelo de closed caption para surdos. Revista Advérbio **9**(18), 48–66 (2017). http://www.adverbio.fag.edu.br/ojs3/index.php/ojs3/article/view/138/140 Accessed 19 Jan 2018
5. Huiberts, S., Tol, R.: IEZA: A Framework for Game Audio (2008). http://www.gamasutra.com/view/feature/131915/ieza_a_framework_for_game_audio.php. Accessed 19 Jan 2018
6. Huizinga, J.: Homo Ludens: A Study of the Play Element In Culture. Routledge and Kegan Paul, London (1944)
7. Kyra: Left 4 Dead has some of the best subtitles in any game. https://www.resetera.com/threads/left-4-dead-has-some-of-the-best-subtitles-in-any-game-more-games-need-to-do-this.16496. Accessed 19 Jan 2018
8. Lacerda, C.: Um pouco da história das diferentes abordagens na educação dos surdos. Cadernos Cedes 46, vol. 46, pp. 68–80. UNICAMP/Papirus, Campinas (1998)
9. McGonigal, J.: Reality is broken: Why Games Make Us Better and How They Can Change The World. Penguin, London (2011)
10. Nielsen, J.: Usability Engineering. Kaufmann, Amsterdam (2010)
11. Paralelos: Direção e Produção de Hugo Haddad e Pedro Falcão (2016). https://www.redbull.com/br-pt/serie-paralelos-narra-pirataria-de-games-no-brasil. Accessed 19 Jan 2018
12. Prates, R., Barbosa, S.: Avaliação de Interfaces de Usuário - Conceitos e Métodos. In: Jornada de Atualização em Informática, Congresso da SBC, 2003, Belo Horizonte: UFMG, (2003). http://homepages.dcc.ufmg.br/~rprates/ge_vis/cap6_vfinal.pdf. Accessed 19 Jan 2018
13. Rodrigues, I., Gattino, G.: Música, Musicoterapia e surdez: uma revisão literária. Nupeart, vol. 14, pp. 56–73 (2015). http://revistas.udesc.br/index.php/nupeart/article/view/6333/4895. Accessed 19 Jan 2018
14. Salen, K., Zimmerman, E.: Rules of Play: Game design fundamentals. MIT Press, Cambridge (2004)
15. Schell, J.: The Art of Game Design: A book of lenses. CRC Press, Boca Raton (2014)

16. Soares, M.: Novas Práticas de leitura e escrita: letramento na cibercultura. Educação e Sociedade, Campinas, vol. 23, no. 81, pp. 143–160, dez. (2002) http://www.scielo.br/pdf/es/v23n81/13935. Accessed 19 Jan 2018
17. Thoma, A.: O cinema e a flutuação das representações surdas – "Que drama se desenrola neste filme? Depende da perspectiva...", Porto Alegre (2002). http://hdl.handle.net/10183/37838. Accessed 19 Jan 2018

Design of a Task-Management APP to Avoid Procrastination

Cayley Guimarães[✉] and Danielly J. P. Lazaro

UTFPR, R. Lourenço Pinto 410, Curitiba, PR 80.010-160, Brazil
cayleyg@utfpr.edu.br

Abstract. Procrastination (the delay of execution of important tasks and decision-making) is a habit due to multiple reasons: lack of interest and motivation, distraction, lack of management skills among others. Procrastination is known to be the cause of dire consequences: anguish, guilty, social and work failures, among others. Currently, the use of Information and Communication Technologies may be a source of procrastination due to the attention-grabbing and distracting activities. On the other hand, the very same technology is an ally in habit formation - a feature that can be used to inform the design of App's that help the user to manage their activities to avoid procrastination. Existing applications present several inadequacies (i.e. lack of good information design, lack of usability among others). Such inadequacies compromise the use of the application, and thus are detrimental to its efficiency. This article addresses such issues in order to inform the design of a task-management app to track the execution of task and help avoid procrastination.

Keywords: Procrastination app · Task management · Habit formation

1 Introduction

Procrastination, defined by Stober and Joorman (2001) as the deliberate delay of execution of important tasks, has long been a problem for individuals. Procrastination brings sever consequences to the human being (such as anguish, guilty, social and work failures, among other), according to Brito and Bakos (2013). Procrastination occurs due to multiple reasons: some people claim that in order to start a task, they need certain conditions (e.g. I have to wash the car before I go to the supermarket) - some of these conditions are never attained. Mostly, people procrastinate due to task aversion (when the task is considered boring); impulsivity (need for instant gratification); low awareness of the impacts; lack of management skills (manifested in distractions, lack of organisation and lack of action, according to Steel (2007).

Dyden and Sabelus (2012) tell us that as much as 80% of students procrastinate - an unexpected high number when one considers that the technologies allow for simultaneous tasks to be performed everywhere, anytime. In the current society, however, the use of technologies distracts our attention away from important tasks (Oulasvirta et al. 2012) - on one hand, the technologies aide us in performing complex tasks automatically, fostering interactions and playing important role on social activities (Royo 2008; Pantzar

© Springer International Publishing AG, part of Springer Nature 2018
A. Marcus and W. Wang (Eds.): DUXU 2018, LNCS 10920, pp. 16–27, 2018.
https://doi.org/10.1007/978-3-319-91806-8_2

2010). On the other hand, they can be a distraction, excessively dictating a person's life and behaviour (Lowry and Moskos 2005; LaRose et al. 2003).

Fortunately, technologies are our best allies in habit formation, a feature that can be used to inform the design of applications that help us manage our activities, in a process that is conducive of task management to avoid procrastination (Jones et al. 2015). However, existing applications present several inadequacies (e.g. lack of good information design, lack of good interaction and usability among others). Such inadequacies compromise the use of the application and are, thus, detrimental to its efficiency. The use of an adequate application to minimize procrastination would benefit individuals, especially those who are disorganised, and need reminders and task completeness visualisation, among other features. Such application would help the individual to set goals, initiate action and keep track of progression, thus leading to a healthier approach to their daily lives.

Digital intervention for healthy habit forming depends of several aspects, such as context of use (Perry et al. 2012), good interaction and usability, an easy to use and understand information organisation, among others (Bonsiepe 2011). The literature has several studies providing mechanisms to aide habit formation (Bai et al. 2013), mood assessment (Ma et al. 2012), health control (Stawarz et al. 2014), motivation (Haynes et al. 1976), to help maintain focus (Park and Kidder 1996). As for task management tool, the studied tools were found to be inadequate, and lacking some features, that became user requirements - annex insertion (such as pic, notes, videos) and comments; easy visualisation of task progress and sub-tasks; warnings of important milestones; possibility to work offline; general reminders and alarms; filters to allow independence of task organisation; gamification and over all look and feel.

This article uses Design Thinking to inform the design of a task management app to track the execution of task to avoid procrastination. Heuristic Evaluation concluded for the usability; and evaluation via Technology Acceptance Model (Venkatesh et al. 2003) conclude for the use of the proposed application. The remainder of the article briefly discus the theory, presents the development process and the evaluation.

2 Procrastination and the Use of Technology

The use of mobile technologies (such as tablets, smartphones etc.) permeates modern life. Oulasvirta et al. (2012) tells us that such technologies impact habit formation among users. And Jones et al. (2015) tells us that the use of these technologies may bring unforeseen consequences. On one hand, this use may help the user to perform complex tasks; on the other hand, the user may loose control of time management and be distracted (Lowry and Moskos 2005; Marlatt et al. 1988; Towers et al. 2006). Boomer et al. (2011) points to a fragmentation of use, for example, due to constant checking of multiple applications.

In order to inform the design of an application to help procrastination and habit formation there are several models (Padovani et al. 2017). They allow for simplification of tasks (Oliveira and Almeida 2001); they focus on context, content, communication, customisation and control (Tung et al. 2014); they use gamification (Farias and Teixeira,

2014) and focus on specific groups (Anjos and Gontijo 2015) and adaptation of web applications (Sanches and Sniker 2012).

The proposed application uses gamification, for example, in order to value the motivation, facilitate the perception of the task as fun, to give clear goals to achieve to complete the task, to allow for an immersion in which the user feels comfortable, for example.

2.1 Procrastination

Procrastination, defined by Stober and Joorman (2001) as the deliberate delay of execution of important tasks, has long been a problem for individuals. Procrastination brings sever consequences to the human being (such as anguish, guilty, social and work failures, among other), according to Brito and Bakos (2013). Procrastination occurs due to multiple reasons: some people claim that in order to start a task, they need certain conditions (e.g. I have to wash the car before I go to the supermarket) - some of these conditions are never attained. Mostly, people procrastinate due to task aversion (when the task is considered boring); impulsivity (need for instant gratification); low awareness of the impacts; lack of management skills (manifested in distractions, lack of organisation and lack of action, according to Steel (2007).

Additionally, Steel (2007) points out that task aversion, especially when the task is considered boring and burdensome; low understanding of the importance of the task; lack of self-regulation; increase of external factors that cause distractions; lack of organisation; low motivation and lack of action are some of the causes of procrastination. According to the author, the further in time an event is, the lower the impact it has on the decision making process of the individual - this mechanism of immediate gratification seeking leads to procrastination. This is aggravated by the multiple pleasurable tasks that compete to one's attention.

People who procrastinate due to lack of management skills are seldom hostages of a self-fulfilling situation that keeps them from initiating actions to perform important tasks (Brito and Bakos 2013). Some of the consequences os procrastination are: insurmountable worry in general about one's ability to perform socially, anguish, anxiety, feelings of guiltiness, depression, among others (Stober and Joorman 2001; Brito and Bakos 2013). Instead of acting, people get caught up in anxious contemplation of the consequences of no executing the task. Steel (2007) tells us that simple management actions, such as the planning of how, when, where a task should be performed estimulantes its completion - a clear call for a task-management app.

2.2 Related Work

Digital intervention for habit formation requires attention to the context of use (Perry et al. 2012) and accessibility (Macedo 2013). Bonsiepe (2011) tells us that information organisation and presentation for interaction is paramount, and the lack thereof is detrimental in use. Coates and Ellison (2014) reinforce this need of information design. Bai et al. (2013) present a predictive model of habit formation for health concerns, and Ma et al. (2012) present a model for daily mood assessment. Stawarz et al. (2008) emphasise memory mechanisms aimed at educating the user to change attitudes and behaviours regarding medication intake. Haynes et al. (1976) reminds us that even motivated people forget, and that time alarms do not take into account action-based tasks (Park and Kidder 1996).

2.3 Cognitive Behaviour Therapy

Cognitive behaviour therapy is psycho-social theory that aims at helping the individual to develop strategies for solving unhelpful patterns in thoughts, attitudes, beliefs, behaviours among others. It is focused on a problem, and oriented towards action. It helps inform the design of an application that addresses procrastination (Beck 2011). In general, the idea is to have the user view the situation through three prisms: thoughts, feelings and behaviours: thoughts and feelings affect behaviour. The application was designed to help the user replace any negative thoughts and feelings and lack of action that leads to procrastination into motivations and actions to avoid procrastination.

As pointed out earlier, some users procrastinate because they feel overwhelmed, because they require certain conditions to happen before taking action, because they lack management skills. Some think that they won't be able to succeed because they don't see a clear path to execute their tasks, for example. The application was designed to provide the user with coping mechanisms to overcome these negative traps, and initiate action. It helps the user to stop procrastinating by offering aide so people can understand how procrastination impacts their lives, and how it can be avoided. Then, it allows for the planning of the important tasks, and to create strategies to achieve them, as well as means to track progress, motivation to finish, and alternatives to take when the task is delayed. This way, for example, instead of giving up half-way through a task that is incomplete, the user can plan a path to success.

3 Application Development

This research followed the Design Thinking process to inform the design of the application. In total, 5 designers and 3 undergraduate students, potential users, participated in all the development phases.

3.1 Survey and Persona

In order do get to know the user better, a survey with undergraduate students of a federal university in Brazil was conducted. The Survey used an open tool, and was available for two weeks during the fall semester. The link to the survey was broadcast in a social media group, and the students volunteered to participate. There were 46 respondents, from 18 to 26 years of age. All respondentes volunteered that they were procrastinators, even though 75% of the respondents said that they used some sort of task-management tool. The respondents claimed that the reason they procrastinate is due to overwhelming amount of social and school work so that they can not keep up with the demand.

The most common problem the respondents had with the tools they used was the learning curve: the complexity of managing a task meant that they would stop using the tool because it wasn't helping, and it was taking even more time to feed the tool than to actually performing the task.

The respondents were the basis for the creation of personas (Ambrose and Harris 2011), as seen in Fig. 1. Camila is a 22 year old Engineering student who teaches math in high school, and would like to pursue a research career. She lives alone and uses bike of bus. She likes to read, to watch movies and technologies. She travels frequently to her parent's house. She considers that she procrastinates because she lives alone, and has little time to juggle work, studies and personal life.

Fig. 1. Persona camila.

Figure 2 shows another persona created to represent the user during the design process:

Fig. 2. Persona lucas.

Figure 2 shows Lucas, a 23 years old Communications student who works as writer in a local newspaper. Lucas lives with his family, including his dog. He has his own car. He loves to go out and make new friends. He wants a tool to balance his social, student and work life in order to be able to do the activities that interest him the most.

3.2   Briefing/Requirements

The development of the application was geared towards young adults (18 to 26 years old), undergraduate students who use technologies extensively in their daily lives, including task-management systems. The system was designed to be used anywhere, anytime, including offline. Figure 3 shows some sketches of scenarios of use (Carroll 2003):

Fig. 3. Scenarios of use.

Figure 2 shows the user using the application in several situations: at work, going to bed, studying.

As for the requirements, they were compiled from the analysis of similar products and from two brainstorming sessions, each lasting three hours.

The most important requirements were related to the possibility to insert anexes to the task (pics, links, reminders etc.); the possibility to insert additional comments. This would allow the user to better categorise the activity, and to plan for actions.

One of the visual aides that the application provides is a progress graph and a check button. This allows the user to have a sense of accomplishment and success. Additionally, typography was also designed to better adapt to digital technology (Babich 2016).

Another important visual tool was a colour-coded hierarchy of information for easy viewing of related and precedented tasks, priorities, task categories etc.

These features were coupled with the possibility of applying several filters to allow to organise tasks by category.

Additionally, the application was designed for open integration with existing social media platform, and the possibility to view progress via a dashboard with percentual progress indication.

The information design followed Lipton (2007) principles: consistency (similarities among the items); proximity (spacial relations among elements, such as the tool bar); segmentation (grouping of functions); alignment and hierarchy; balance and reading flow and clarity (use of real work concepts and words). Figure 4 shows a sketch of how the requirements were incorporated into the design:

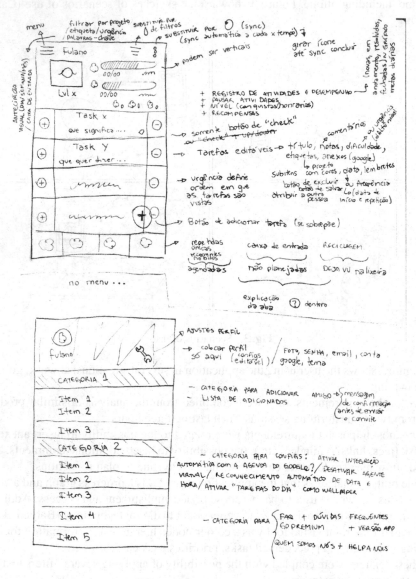

Fig. 4. Sketch of the application incorporating the requirements.

The app was developed with minimalist design, with help and tutorial for first time users. Confirmation messages were required upon insertion and deletion; backtracking of actions was allowed; multiple types of views (e.g. daily, weekly, most recent etc.); sub-task attribution (in the case where the completion of a task is dependent on actions of others) among other. These requirements were designed to increase motivation, promote action, give a sense of achievement and aide the user in their task management activities to minimize procrastination.

Additional requirement was to provide emotional interaction, to emphasise the link with the application. The development of the task-helper, the virtual agent named Paco, the red Alpaca, took into consideration its ability to thrive in the most harsh environments, typically mountains with several obstacles - to motivate the user to see minor set-backs as course adjustments towards achieving the goal (Miller 2004; Norman 2004). Figure 5 shows the design of the virtual character:

Fig. 5. The virtual character, Paco the Alpaca.

Figure 4 shows the design studies of the virtual character that was an interface of the system with the user, designed to impart information, help with the use of the application, provide feedback among other features.

Figure 6 shows the application in different shades of colours (a feature that allows the user to customize her application).

Fig. 6. The logo.

The logo for the application was about emotions, designed to impart motivation - Stamina is related to the theme of the effort to complete tasks, and to the virtual character, Paco.

3.3 Development

The development was iterative, and wireframes were used to get the consensus among designers (Garrett 2011). Figure 7 shows a sketch of a task entry operation.

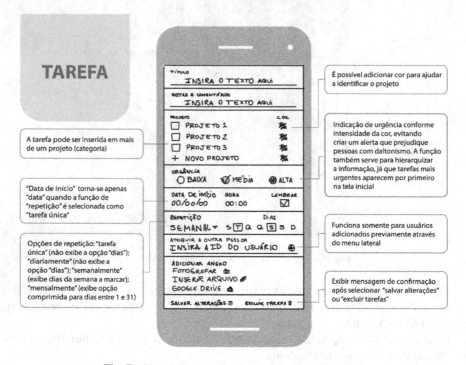

Fig. 7. Sketch for entering a task into the application.

Each task can be entered in more than a category or project. A task date is initiated when it is entered or is set to a later day, and remains on until the completion of the task. A task may be a one time activity, last for a period of time, or be a repetitive (e.g. weekly, everyday, monthly etc.) task. After entering a task, a confirmation is displayed. If a task is to be performed with another person or a group, this can be set. A color code informs the user of the urgency of the task. This also serves to provide a visual clue as to the hierarchy of the task.

Each task may be divided up into sub tasks, intermediate steps to help the user to achieve their goal by breaking a seemingly difficult task into smaller, attainable activities. The application allows for links to other social media application.

4 Validation

A heuristic evaluation was performed (Nielsen and Mack 1994) for usability (Barbosa 2010) and other aspects. The expert evaluator has 10 plus years of experience as both a professional and a professor in a public university in Brazil. Additionally, the evaluator has extensive experience in digital art and habit formation applications.

Regarding the visibility of the state of the system, it was considered that the virtual character helps to motivate the user, and to keep track of their tasks. It also helped the user to situate within the application and navigate through the operations required to use the application. The navigation icons also helped to keep the user informed of their location.

Regarding the correspondence with the real world, some terms, such as "saved tasks" did not convey their actual meaning - a better term in this example would have been tasks accomplished. Other terms include: "remember" for "attribute task".

The application allowed for control and flexibility by allowing the user to rearrange the tasks using multiple filters (by date, by category etc.). The application was consistent.

The suggestions that were implemented: a new screen that summarised a task, the remaining time for its completion and its progress. Removal of a sync function, given that most applications already performs the synchronisation automatically. Replication of the research bar in all screens (not only on the first screen), among other suggestions.

Habit changing is a very complex enterprise. Results may appear only after months of use of the proposed application. In order to further validate the feelings, thoughts and intentions to act about procrastination, the researchers used the Technology Acceptance Model to validate the relationship between perceived usefulness (the belief that the use of an application would enhance performance), perceived ease of use (the belief that the use of an application would be simple) and system use (Davis 1989).

Ten (10) students of a Bachelor's program in Design agreed to participate in the validation process, that took place in the university, and lasted for 2 h. They all considered themselves procrastinators. Four of the participants had tried other applications to avoid procrastination, but didn't succeed. Each participant received a copy of the application and was allowed to familiarize with it.

The respondents were asked to respond questions about the usefulness and easy of use, using a Likert scale (1 - totally disagree to 5 - totally agree). The alternative hypothesis being that the proposed application was not perceived to be of help in their attempt to avoid procrastination (0.025, t test).

As for usefulness, the mean was 4.52, with a standard deviation of 0.744, $t = 3.20$, $p = 0.0001$. As for easy of use, the mean was 4.58, standard deviation 0.722, $t = 3.01$,

$p = 0.0001$. The results indicated that the users felt the application was useful and easy to use, and that they would adopt it.

5   Final Considerations

Procrastination is a behaviour that affects most students. It can be traced back to many causes such as task aversion, when the task is considered boring or troublesome; it is also related to a low understanding of the importance of a given task, and how the act of not performing it can bring negative consequences. Additionally, one of the main factors of procrastination is the lack of self-regulatory skills, an increasing in distracting and competing digital tasks, self of management skills, low motivation and a low desire for action. Additionally, some people procrastinate because they consider to be hostage of insurmountable obstacles (Brito and Bakos 2013).

The most common problems that procrastination brings are worries, anguish, anxiety, stress, depression, guilty, among others. This research designed an application to help users to break away from procrastinatory cycles.

References

Ambrose, G., Harris, P.: Design Thinking. Bookman, Porto Alegre (2011)

Anjos, T.P., Gontijo, L.A.: Recomendações de usabilidade e acessibilidade para interface de telefone celular visando o público idoso. Production **25**(4), 791–811 (2015)

Babich, N.: XD Essentials: typography in mobile apps. Adobe Creative Cloud (2016)

Bai, Y., Xu, B., Jiang, S., Cui, J.: Can you form healthy habit? Predicting habit forming states through mobile phone. In: BODYNETS, pp. 144–147 (2013)

Barbosa, S.D.J., Silva, B.S.: Interação humano-computador. Elsevier, Rio de Janeiro (2010)

Beck, J.S.: CBT: Basics and Beyond. The Guilford Press, New York (2011)

Boomer, M., et al.: Falling asleep with Angry Birds, Facebook and Kindle. In: Proceedings of the 13th International Conference on HCI with Mobile Devices and Services, pp. 47–56 (2011)

Bonsiepe, G.: Design, cultura e sociedade. Bucher, São Paulo (2011)

Brito, F.S., Bakos, D.G.S.: Procrastinação e terapia cognitivo-comportamental: uma revisão interativa. Revista Brasileira de Terapias Cognitivas **9**(1), 34–41 (2013)

Carroll, J.M.: Scenario-Based Design. John Wiley, New York (2003)

Coates, K., Ellison, A.: An Introduction to Information Design. Lawrence King Publishing, Londres (2014)

Davis, F.D.: Perceived usefulness, perceived ease of use, and user acceptance of information technology. MIS Quarterly **13**(3), 319–340 (1989)

Dyden, W., Sabelus, S.: The perceived credibility of two rational emotive behaviour therapy rationales for the treatment of academic procrastination. J. Ration.-Emot. Cogn.-Behav. Ther. **30**(1), 1–24 (2012)

Farias, B.S.S.; Teixeira, M.M.: Análise de elementos visuais em jogos digitais: a função da navegação, instrução, comunicação em dispositivos portáteis. In: Anais do USIHC - ErgoDesign 2014. Univille, Joinville (2014)

Garrett, J.J.: The Elements of User Experience: User-Entered Design for the Web and Beyond. New Riders, Berkeley (2011)

Haynes, R.B., et al.: Improvement of medication compliance in uncontrolled hypertension. The Lance **307**(7972), 1265–1268 (1976)

Jones, S.L., et al.: Revisitation analysis of smartphone app use. In: UBICOMP, pp. 7–11 (2015)

LaRose, R., Lin, C.A., Eastin, M.S.: Unregulated internet usage: addiction, habit or deficient self-regulation? Media Pshychol. **5**(3), 225–253 (2003)

Lipton, R.: The Practical Guide to Information Design. Wiley, Hoboken (2007)

Lowry, D., Moskos, M.: Hanging on the mobile phone. In: Critical Management Studies Conference: Flexibility, pp. 1–19 (2005). Working paper 153

Ma, Y., et al.: Daily mood assessment based on mobile phone sensing. In: BSN, pp. 142–147 (2012)

Macedo, C.M.S.: Diretrizes de acessibilidade em conteúdos didáticos. Revista Brasileira de Design da informacao. **10**(2), 123–136 (2013)

Marlatt, et al.: Addictive behaviors: ethology and treatment. Annu. Rev. Psychol. **39**(1), 223–252 (1988)

Miller, C.H.: Digital Storytelling. Elsevier, Burlington (2004)

Nielsen, J., Mack, R.L. (eds.).: Usability Inspection Methods. John Wiley, New York (1994)

Norman, D.: Emotional Design. Basic Books, New York (2004)

Oulasvirta, A., et al.: Habits make smartphone use more pervasive. Pers. Ubiquit. Comput. **16**, 105–114 (2012)

Oliveira, V.N.P., Almeida, M.B.: Um roteiro para avaliação ontológica de modelos de sistemas de informação. Perspectivas em Ciência da Informação. **16**(1), 165–184 (2001)

Padovani, S., Puppi, M.R., Schlemmer, A.: Modelo descritivo para interfaces de aplicativos em smartphones. Revista Brasileira de Design da Informação. **17**(1), 123–143 (2017)

Pantzar, M.: Future shock: discussing the changing temporal architecture of daily life. J. Future Stud. **14**(4), 1–22 (2010)

Park, D.C., Kidder, D.P.: Prospective memory and medication adherence. In: Brandimonte, M., Einstein, G.O., McDaniel, M.A. (eds.) Prospective memory: theory and applications, pp. 369–390. Lawrence Erlbaum Associates, Boston (1996)

Perry, G.T., Eichler, M.L., Resende, G.: Avaliação de usabilidade do Mobiteste, um aplicativo educacional para dispositivos móveis. Revista Brasileira de Design da Informação. **9**(2), 70–87 (2012)

Royo, J.: Design digital. Edições Rosari, São Paulo (2008)

Sanches, T.Z., Sniker, T.G.: Design da informação e conteúdo para dispositivos móveis: projeto de website para Instituição de Ensino Superior, IES, adaptado para iPad. Revista Brasileira de Design da Informação. **9**(2), 100–109 (2012)

Stawarz, K., Cox, A.L., Blandfor, A.: Don't forget you pill! designing effective medication reminder apps that support users' daily routines. In: CHI2014 (2014). https://doi.org/10.1145/2556288.2557079

Steel, P.: The nature of procrastination: a meta-analytics and theoretical review of quintessential self-regulatory failure. Psychol. Bull. **133**, 65–94 (2007)

Stober, J., Joormann, J.: Worry, procrastination, and perfectionism: differentiating amount of worry, pathological worry, anxiety and depression. Cogn. Ther. Res. **25**(1), 49–60 (2001)

Towers, I., Duxbury, L., Thomas, J.: Time thieves and space invaders: technology, work and the organiston. Management. **19**(5), 593–618 (2006)

Tung, T., Jai, T.M., Burns, L.D.: Attributes of apparel tablet catalogs: value proposition comparisons. J. Fash. Mark. Manage. **18**(3), 321–337 (2014)

Venkatesh, V., Morris, M.G., Davis, G.B., Davis, F.D.: User acceptance of information technology: toward a unified view. MIS Q. **27**(3), 425–478 (2003)

Conformed Thought: Consolidating Traces of Memories

Silvia Laurentiz[✉]

University of Sao Paulo, São Paulo, SP, Brazil
silvialaurentiz@gmail.com

Abstract. For Gestalt, the performance of a task depends on previous performances, and the concept of memory traces is an attempt to explain this dependence. It is not easy to distinguish an innate process from an acquired one, but the interesting point is that *"an experienced tennis player has not learned to perform a small number of specific moves, but to hit the ball properly in the multivariate situations of the game"* (Koffka 1975, p. 516). That is mean, in the learning process we create systems of traces of a type, we consolidate and make them increasingly accessible, whether in repeated or new situations. (Idem, idem, p. 533). Thus, learning is defined by traces of learned, consolidated and available memories that modify processes and, consequently, behaviors. They also consider that traces can be transformed through interaction with other traces and processes. At that early moment of Gestalt theory, psychologists questioned improvement the practice and effect of repetition (ibid., p. 562). Therefore, the idea that we can exercise cognitive abilities and make them accessible to new functions, through a learning process, was already studied in that period. In previous work, we have established relationships between experiences of the senses and the representational aspects of experiences (Laurentiz 2015). At this moment, we will be focused on how these cognitive abilities acquired through conformed thoughts (patterns, codes and set of codes, algorithms) reflect in aesthetic experience, by the intrinsic condition of the relationship between experience, sensations and thought.

Keywords: Sensations · Model · Cognition · Thought

1 Introduction

Studies on video games and the development of cognitive abilities (Laurentiz 2017; Gong et al. 2015), point out that games - especially action games - increase our ability to spatial distribution of attention, cognitive control and emotional regulation, and thus, contribute to the formation of our symbolic thinking, learning and knowledge, as well as sensory capabilities. In previous research, we conclude that many skills are developed by game players: improvements in reaction time, concentration, improvement of peripheral vision, precision, control in hesitation and timing in the spatial resolution of vision, attention, cognitive control and emotional regulation, multisensory temporal processing skills, manual motor coordination, contrast sensitivity, oculomotor performance and

© Springer International Publishing AG, part of Springer Nature 2018
A. Marcus and W. Wang (Eds.): DUXU 2018, LNCS 10920, pp. 28–40, 2018.
https://doi.org/10.1007/978-3-319-91806-8_3

body movement, selective attention, and attentional blinking. We still need to know how cognitive abilities are acquired by patterns, conformed thoughts, and how they will reflect in the aesthetic experience.

Our hypothesis is we are training thought forms from conformed thoughts, which will consolidate traces, as defined by the Gestalt, and they are not a response to direct stimuli by things of the world. We are training thought forms through simulations, models, patterns, and algorithms, and these are the core of what we call conformed thought. This will cause significant changes in our thinking, and consequently, behavior.

To better present the concept that we have developed, we will observe the diagrams below.

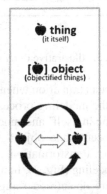

Fig. 1. Illustrative diagram

Fig. 2. Illustrative diagram

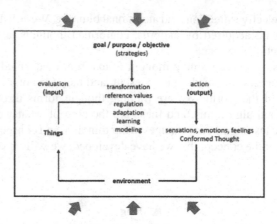

Fig. 3. Illustrative diagram

As we can see, there is an important transition when the image of something becomes the model of this something and the modeling process itself. From the outset we can perceive a difference between 'thing in itself' and model (Figs. 1 and 2), where models are formed by things that have been made objects, contextualized, conceptualized, inserted in a process of evaluation, transformation, comparison to reference values, adaptation, coding, and finally, modeling (Fig. 3). In models, on the other hands, which are made up of objects (which are objectified things), the structure of relationship between objects, and the analogous internal relations of objects and objectified things, are also replicated. Models and objects are part of the modeling process.

Clearly there is a tension between 'thing in itself' and object (or something objecti-fied) (Fig. 1), that already triggers significant consequences in the sign process. We will not need to review this step because it has been too much explored. However, we are interested in explaining the passage from an object to a model.

Above all, it should be made clear that the very definition of object is something that cannot be explained by its separate parts. Therefore, we must consider that it is not possible to define an object only by the effects it causes, nor even by the context in which it is inserted. Denying the existence of objects, considering only their qualities of exis-tences does not seem to us also insightful, once that would be very reductive disregard the complexity of their formative parts, effects and context.

In this way, the concept used in this work for objects is 'objectified thing', where aiming is to give expression, either to an abstract notion, a feeling, an ideal, or anything, in a form that can be experienced by others. Therefore, the formative characteristics, the effects caused, the context in which it is inserted, and its qualities of existence will be considered, in a cohesive whole, that immerses beyond its subcomponents, and which cannot be explained in its separate parts.

Thus, it is evident that an apple (thing) and the image of this [apple] (objectified thing, therefore, object) already carry the historical questions of the sign, which have already been much discussed, but which will also provide impetus to our next steps (Fig. 1). According to the diagram, from the image of something, we move to a next level of abstraction when we have the explanation (or concept) of that image, and with an image of this explanation we have a model of something (Flusser 2010, p. 117–118) (Fig. 2). A process of third-degree abstraction, according to Vilém Flusser, is one that *"abstracts one of the dimensions of the traditional image to result in texts (second-degree abstraction), then reconstitutes the abstracted dimension to result in an image again"* (Flusser 2011, p. 13). It is crucial to understand that all this happens in a context that feeds the system and that, as already mentioned, there are processes of evaluation, transformation, comparison to reference values, adaptation, coding (as graphically shown in Fig. 3).

Explained in this way, we will pass to the analysis of two cases to perceive cognitive abilities that are acquired through conformed thoughts (patterns, codes and set of codes, algorithms) which, from these initial settings, will reflect in aesthetic experience, by intrinsic condition of the relationship between experiences, sensations and thought.

2   Case Analysis: The Game Flow Free

[1]Flow Free is a free iOS application, which allows players to solve puzzles by connecting pipes according to their color. It is a board puzzle game, what means it involves problem solving through logic, strategy, pattern recognition and sequencing. In other words, it is a logic game, such as Tetris, Maze, Jigsaw.

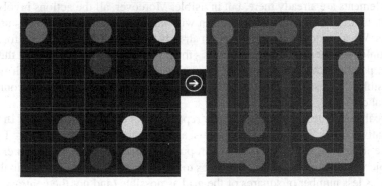

Fig. 4. Flow Free game illustration image. Flow Free game screenshots.

Flow Free is a simple game: connect the matching colors through a pipe to create a flow. Match all the colors by filling in every square of the board – grid - to solve each puzzle (Fig. 4). The only rule is that the pipes intersected or overlapped will be broken, and you lose the game. The goal is to fill all squares of the grid using the pipes.

---

[1] Flow Free® by Big Duck Games LLC in http://www.bigduckgames.com/.

As soon as we complete the grid, a sense of accomplishment through some creative ability seems to take our mind, generating a sense of satisfaction that leads us wanting to move on to the next level[2].

There are several different levels of 'Flow Free', the first level is the most basic and is very simple. It serves to introduce the player in the game, familiarizing him/her as much as its gameplay. Although Flow Free does not induce high levels of stress initially, when the player progresses to higher levels, according to his/her abilities and interests, he/she can provoke hedonic, cardiac and excitement reactions. This is described in a survey carried out on the potential of smartphone applications as a solution for stress reduction (Dillon et al. 2016), considering stress level, mood changes and anxiety, measured by detecting physiological signals such as heart rate, breathing, muscle activity, or skin temperature before and after the participants played the game. These demonstrated changes reinforce our argument about the intrinsic condition of the relationship between experience, sensations and thought. That is, even in practice of conformed thoughts there is an important sensorial participation in the decision making and learning.

1. Another important factor is that the player can play the game in different positions, locations, time, even performing other tasks, due to the mobility of the smartphone and the ease of gameplay[3].

Analysis: In fact, nothing very creative is required, despite the resulting sensation. All the elements are already there, but invisible. Moreover, all the actions involved are expected, nothing surprising or unforeseen will happen. And this also guides us in our decisions. What we do is to make visible an already predetermined grid. Therefore, there is an initial grid, where the trajectory lines - the pipes - were erased, and only the initial and final points of these lines appear. Once the predetermined path is confirmed and made visible, the mission is successfully completed. That is, it is a game of connecting the digital dots.

We realize that decisions are driven by repetitions of previous actions and that there is no creative act involved in the process, just a predetermine problem-solving. To reach a creative stage, it would be necessary to propose alternatives to the game. For example, in the objectives were included possibilities to fill the lines of the initial and final points by using as less number of squares of the grid as possible (and not the contrary, where the total grid fill was previously predetermined). Thus, it would complete the game the one who follows the standard model, but someone who could complete the pipes using the least number of grid squares would gain extra bonuses. In this way, we would add a creative and innovative factor to the game (of course, this possibility should be foreseen, which is not currently). There are variations of this game on the internet already, some more creative than others.

2. The 'game with time' experience (Timed mode) leads to a record breaking, but there is a mechanical problem that is prevented from overtaking. It is necessary to solve

---

[2] The reports about this game were made from a proposal to perform daily puzzles for a year, with at least the execution of a challenge per day.

[3] In addition, under stress, boredom, waiting time, this game can help control anxiety.

as many of the puzzles as possible, before the timer has set runs out. The touch screen responds at machine and application speed. Therefore, the performance of the game will depend on the interface and application. Another interesting fact is that, after a period of experience, the touch of the finger on the screen participates in the game, and the body begins to think the movements and participates in the cognitive and sensorial process.

Analysis: After a while, the frame settings are memorized, and the mind follows automatically, by reflex, depending on the mechanical agility of the process. Adding something creative in this step could be introducing random changes during the game, which would lead to a change of route of the player over time. This implementation in the game destabilize the acquired habits and could cause changes in the results. Currently we already have intelligent learning programs, and these could establish new strategies during the game, from the recognition of tendencies of each player.

3. After some levels, the player learns trends, formats, rules, and acquires greater perform-ance (although still depending on the performance of the interface, as mentioned). From this point on, we play with the patterns, what we call conformed thinking (using conformed thought), and react from these configurations that have been acquired, memorized, even without full control over them. For example, someone naturally tries first to draw the largest and outer lines, and then to solve the central lines. Dots that are both far apart and resting on the very edges of the grid are a sure-fire clue to draw a big line around the edge of the board to join them together. Pairs of different colored dots in these positions can often be another clue to create concentric circles of lines on the grid. We try to find recognizable blocks - what we could call meaningful blocks -, contours, paths and repeated configurations in previous plays. You are looking for easy-to-solve moves first (those of obvious solution, because they are positioned in situa-tions with no other outputs[4]) and complete the grid with the most difficult decisions from them. These are strategies generated by a thought that was acquired from the repetition of the goals acquired (Figs. 5, 6, 7 and 8).

Fig. 5. Flow Free game screenshot. The larger pipe is connected first and then the internal ones are solved.

---

[4] For example, dots that are within three spaces of each other are a clue to draw them together.

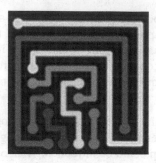

Fig. 6. Flow Free game screenshot. Here, it is difficult to reach the solution of the yellow pipe before the solution of the green, even if one has the initial idea of starting at the ends. (Color figure online)

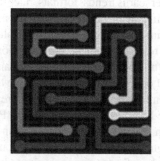

Fig. 7. Flow Free game screenshot. In this case, there is no way to solve by the formula of starting with the external lines and then solving the internal ones, since most of them have external and internal points.

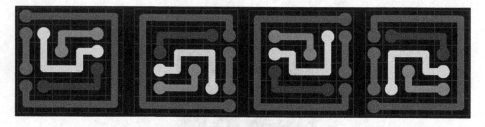

Fig. 8. Flow Free game screenshot. In these challenges is noticed that the red pipe has a single solution, the decision to solve it initially is immediate. It does not depend on place or direction, the red pipe (or even pipes of other colors) is recognized as a pattern and easily identified. (Color figure online)

Analysis: The same memorization mentioned in item 2 gains complexity at this moment. The framework is considered as a whole in itself, and the strategies - traces of memories - begin to guide the actions of the players. The creation of variations of the model (expansion packs) in Hexes, Warps, Bridges, Rainbow, Interval, Garden, Tower, Party, etc. already offers an alternative for breaking the monotony of the models. It is a determining factor where the passage from one format to another is naturally received, without any detailed explanation about the changes, since they follow the fundamental principles of the original, and the changes are explained by the internalization of the system acquired. Thus, body and mind will already have acquired the performance of that task and will be able to perform them in new situations.

An even more radical variation, which would apply a creative motivation to the game, would be the model to be self-constructed from a rhizomatic structure with random rules or by the application of an intelligent agent that would participate with the player in the construction of the space structure and timing of the game. This would be an implementation that would add a creative action to the game (Fig. 9).

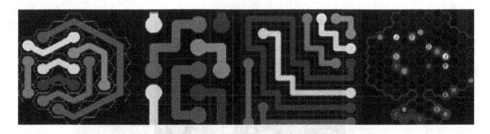

Fig. 9. Variations of the model of Flow Free game.

Nowadays, there are numerous digital games that present themselves with the figure of flows, tubes and pipes. If they really represent tubes, flows or pipes is not the point. If they are indeed flows and pipes does not matter for this moment. But they are tasks that require strategies and logical reasoning, and that will be exercised and repeated, over and over again.

They are exercises to connect points, despite the figures. The implementations that we are suggesting are only proposals to add non-premeditated actions to the game, as this is a property of digital environments that can be exploited. Unlike a physical game, where matter carries the physical limits of the game, the digital one can explore other spatiality and temporalities[5]. But the point is: repeating an abstraction[6] also generates traces of memories and can trigger cognitive and sensory experiences and behavior changes.

These graphic patterns that we present could be drawn on a simple sheet of paper. The point here is to perform the same task to exhaustion, which would not be possible using only paper and pencil, because of the limits and difficulties of doing this with paper and pencil, as opposed to the ease of performing these procedures in the digital

---

[5] Besides, the player can gameplay while riding the bus to work, while commuting on the subway, or simply while he/she is relaxing at home. This is another reason for new temporal and spatial experiences.

[6] Considering the levels of abstraction of Vilém Flusser, as presented previously.

environment. In addition, the recording of all experiences are also opportunities for comparisons, references, identification and recognition of blocks of meaning, and all of this will potentiate the process. Moreover, the assessment of learning, in response to the correct and mistaken practices, is merely immediate and automatic mechanical action. Now, multiply by the countless logic games of today. We are training these conformed thoughts all the time, and everywhere. And this will cause effects on us.

3   Case Analysis: Online Tennis Game

Sports games simulate traditional physical sports. They can emphasize playing the sport or the strategy behind the sport.

Tennis for two[7] and *Pong*[8] are of the first computer games that look like tennis (Fig. 10).

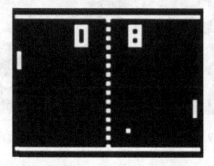

Fig. 10.   Image to represent Pong game.

When we play a virtual tennis game[9] between players in different locations on a digital platform, the racket and ball are just pixels on the computer screen. The actions performed are transmitted via computer-network, which trigger a complex sequence and generate several updates of the records corresponding to the positions of the racket and the ball on the screen of each of the players. An additional fact is that a programmer could update these logs directly, without even visualizing racket and ball. Therefore, despite the impression that we are playing a match with the same single ball, there are two: one in the computer of the first player and another in the computer of the opponent, which are updated from the transmission of the coordinate changes, in response to the commands of each.

Analysis: Although the perception be a game of tennis with a single ball in the match, in fact, we will have interfaces, each one with a ball, causing an effect of the same reality to us, from a *"perception through the user interface multimodal"* (Hoffman 2008).

---

[7] *Tennis for Two* is a sports video game developed in 1958, which simulates a game of tennis, and was one of the first games developed in the early history of video games, by the American physicist William Higinbotham.

[8] Pong was originally developed by Allan Alcorn and released in 1972 by Atari corporations.

[9] There are several games currently available, for this study we will not analyze a specific case.

Neither the racket nor the ball sends signals to the computer, the racket and the ball only show on screen the output of the actions that were triggered by a data complex sequence - but hidden inside the computer -, resulting in adequate updating of records corresponding to the racket and ball positions (ibid., p. 96). We are led to believe that we are in one and same game, with one and unique ball. This means that we believe that we are playing a game of tennis, but it is a simulation, and therefore, an algorithm simulates certain actions, without being an actual tennis match. It is an algorithm and an interface that leads us to believe that we are playing, that is, a conformed thought guides us to act as if it were a conventional tennis match. There are objects (ball, racket, scenery, avatars, interface...) from a model (simulation of a match, with a relationship structure between the objects in the scene), responding based on parameters as if they were a tennis match. But they react under certain aspects of a game and not in all its aspects. Just remember that the speed of the engine can be decisive for the outcome of the game where the ball on the screen will be updated at a speed while the ball on the opponent's screen may be updating in another. Besides, as we have already said, there are two balls in fact, appearing to be just one.

Another point to note is that we are always armored, we will never get a ball or a racquet right at our face, we will not get hurt with a deviation, or a fall, common in a tennis game. That is, our reflexes will be performed solely and exclusively in response to calculations and the interface, whether a joystick, mouse, or other device specially created for the game, which means that we will be repeatedly training actions from models, algorithms, thoughts conformed. It is interesting because there are many currently simulators that are being used in learning processes but being in the face of the simulated action itself differs from practicing the action itself, by the various presented points. Currently we have very well-developed interfaces to simulate the game of tennis, but surely, they are not able to simulate all the characteristics of playing tennis. Returning to our initial argument, that for Gestalt, the performance of a task depends on previous performances, and that "*an experienced tennis player has not learned to perform a small number of specific moves, but to hit the ball properly in the multivariate situations of the game*" (Koffka 1975, p. 516), we are, in this case, training other motions and in different situations by the simulation of the same game, and that, after all, will cause completely different effects exactly because their characteristics are immaterial and moved by conformed thought.

4 Final Considerations

Charles Darwin has already said in 1871 that "*a long and complex train of thought can no more be carried on without the aid of words, whether spoken or silent, than a long calculation without the use of figures or algebra*" (Darwin 1871, p. 57). The author further states that "*as the voice was used more and more, the vocal organs would have been strengthened and perfected through the principle of the inherited effects of use*" (idem, ibidem). He argues there is no doubt that continued use of language would have reacted in some way in the mind, allowing and encouraging it to hold long thoughts (idem, ibidem).

In the same way that Darwin has recognized, the complexity of thought, at from a moment, started to need words, just as the calculations need numbers and algebra, today, patterns, models and algorithms are needed to deal with the complexity of our current thought.

This doesn't mean we are saying that learning develops only through training through repetition. Repeating certain patterns means that we will internalize a system of rules, consolidating traces of memories, and this is one factor that determines a thought, but not the only one. There are several factors involved in complex mental acts.

There is also the hypothesis that from this interaction something unexpected arises that, according to Noam Chomsky, "*to the best of our knowledge, the possession of human language is associated with a specific type of mental organization, not simply more intelligence*" […]. "*This poses a problem for the biologist, since if it is true, it is an example of real emergence - the appearance of a qualitatively different phenomenon at a specific stage of the complexity of the organization*" (Chomsky 2006, pp. 61–62).

Therefore, different thought organization can make different phenomena emerge, in other words, we may be at an earlier stage of the emergence of a new language (even through something premeditatedly programmed), or of an organizational transformation in response to specific abstraction exercises, such as we have seen in the analyzed cases.

From the proposition of conformed thought, that resulting from third-degree abstraction, we can consider that we are thinking today through these patterns, and if this means that we are moving further away from the things of the world (as shown in Figs. 1, 2 and 3), in a reverse way, we will be establishing new models, which when objectified will carry a new sensible and cognition dimension. Since we understand that mental image is an internal representation that functions as a "*weak form of perception*" (Kosslyn et al. 2015, p. 590), a model formed by objects (objectified things) can cause sensory effects (aesthetic experience), although we are not in front of the materialized object, even in lesser power, just as things in the world affect us. Thus, considering that mental images function as a weak form of perception, they will feed back the cognitive and sensorial system, so the thought (Fig. 11).

It remains the question whether objectified models will replace objects that in turn substitute things (object in the sense of being an expression in a form that can be experienced by others), and how these levels of abstraction will cause effects in our thought organizational structures. And, if learning is defined by memory traces, and these will modify behaviors, how will we act in the future if our impacts and frictions will be between immaterial data and will we have only the confrontations with multimodal interfaces? How to think without attrition, gravity and rubbing?

Finally, when we 'play' with the patterns, that we call conformed thinking (using conformed thought), and react from these configurations that have been acquired, memorized, we are been affected by them and their interface-things. The digital system appropriates our experiences but is guided by models and patterns that guide the outcome. For example, when using the mechanical typewriter, every mistake made is the reason for redoing a whole process or applying correctives because they were definite marks left on paper. Today, text-based programs recognize errors and are capable of automatically correcting them, even before we account for them. Programs recognize patterns and trends and automatically correct any slippage in our memory traces or even

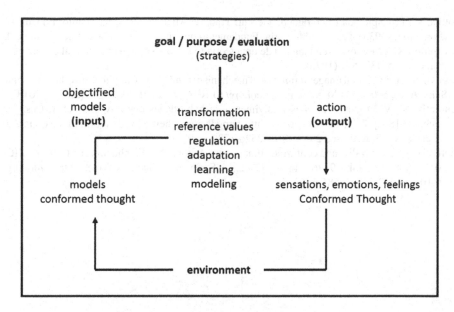

Fig. 11. Final graphic

our reflexes. Therefore, comparisons and deviations are readjusted and rearranged by the computer. This means there are decision-makings that are not just individual ones, the computer can have programmed actions that re-evaluate our activities and change them according to a pattern, an algorithm, a conformed thought. And sophisticated smart programs will be generating their own templates and patterns, which will automatically cause us new memory traces. Thus, the relationship with the 'things' of the world is transformed, our interactions with the interfaces alter our perception, cognition and sensoriality, and our decision-making is relating to computer(s) and/or device(s).

References

Chomsky, N.: Language and Mind, 3rd edn. Cambridge University Press, Cambridge (2006)

Darwin, C.: The Descent of Man, and Selection in Relation to Sex. Princeton University Press, New Jersey (1871)

Dillon, A., Kelly, M., Robertson, I.H., Robertson, D.A.: Smartphone applications utilizing biofeedback can aid stress reduction. Front. Psychol. **7**, 832 (2016). https://doi.org/10.3389/fpsyg.2016.00832. Accessed 2018

Flusser, V.: O Mundo Codificado. Cosac Naify, São Paulo (2010). (2ª reimpressão, 1ª ed. 2007)

Flusser, V.: Filosofia da caixa preta: ensaios para uma futura filosofia da fotografia. Annablume, São Paulo (2011)

Gong, D., He, H., Liu, D., Ma, W., Dong, L., Luo, C., Yao, D.: Enhanced functional connectivity and increased gray matter volume of insula related to action video game playing. Sci. Rep. 5, Article number: 9763 (2015). https://doi.org/10.1038/srep09763. Accessed 16 Apr 2015

Hoffman, D.D.: Conscious realism and the mind-body problem. Mind Matter **6**(1), 87–121 (2008). http://www.cogsci.uci.edu/~ddhoff/ConsciousRealism2.pdf. Accessed 2018

Koffka, K.: Princípios da Psicologia da Gestalt. Trad. de Álvaro Cabral, São Paulo: Ed Cultrix. (Prefácio de 1935). Cap X – Memória: Fundamento de uma teoria do traço. Seção teórica. E capítulo XI – Memória: fundamento de uma teoria to traço – seção experimental e conclusão da teoria, pp. 433–537 (1975)

Kosslyn, S., et al.: Mental imagery: functional mechanisms and clinical applications. Trends Cogn. Sci. **19**(10), 590–602 (2015). http://dx.doi.org/10.1016/j.tics.2015.08.003. Accessed 2018

Laurentiz, S.: Videogames e o desenvolvimento de habilidades cognitivas. DAT J. Des. Art Technol. [S.1.] **2**(1), 80–90 (2017). http://ppgdesign.anhembi.br/datjournal/index.php/dat/article/view/45. Accessed 2018. ISSN 2526-1789

Laurentiz, S.: Sensoriality and conformed thought. In: Antona, M., Stephanidis, C. (eds.) UAHCI 2015. LNCS, vol. 9176, pp. 217–225. Springer, Cham (2015). https://doi.org/10.1007/978-3-319-20681-3_20

Research on Service Process Design of Mobile Medical Platform Based on Patient's Emotional Demand

Yingying Miao$^{(\boxtimes)}$, Tong Cui, and Bin Jiang

School of Design Arts and Media,
Nanjing University of Science and Technology,
200, Xiaolingwei Street, Nanjing 210094, Jiangsu, China
398991222@qq.com, 617885531@qq.com, 631603555@qq.com

Abstract. At present, the development of medical and health system in our country is unbalanced and the cost of obtaining medical and health services is high. Therefore, how people in different regions can enjoy the same quality treatment has become a problem to be solved urgently. Many Internet companies rely on their own advantages in Internet technology, mobile payment and big data. Begin to join the ranks of mobile medical platform layout. In the case of having numerous mobile medical platform, it is pivotal for mobile service platform to enhance the user experience by grasping the most urgent emotional needs of patients, so as to find out the best fit for patients' needs. This paper through adopting the qualitative research and the quantitative research methods takes mobile medical platform service as the research object, starting from the patient's emotion demand to analyze the process design of mobile medical platform service, which provides theoretical basis for how to meet the needs of patients and improve the user experience.

Keywords: Mobile medical platform · Emotional needs
Service process design

1 Introduction

As an industry closely related to people's health, traditional medical treatment has many doctor-patient disputes due to asymmetric information. The introduction of mobile Internet technology can open up broad market prospects for the future development of medical industry and boost the service level of the whole industry. The application of mobile medical platform can not only realize the rational allocation of medical resources, but also improve the quality of medical service. Therefore, how to design the medical platform to best meet the needs of patients is particularly important. In the design of the mobile medical platform, it is divided into many functional modules, such as provide health information, common sense of life, interactive communication, online medical service and so on. Among them, the online medical service is the most central medical service function in the mobile medical platform, and the link of patients in the use of mobile medical platform directly feeling the quality of service. The physiological origin design of mobile medical platform is closely related to users'

© Springer International Publishing AG, part of Springer Nature 2018
A. Marcus and W. Wang (Eds.): DUXU 2018, LNCS 10920, pp. 41–51, 2018.
https://doi.org/10.1007/978-3-319-91806-8_4

physical and psychological needs. Based on this, this paper studies the theory of emotion, investigates and surveys the mobile medical service to come up with a reliable basis for constructing the service design of mobile medical platform in the future.

2   The Connotation and Theoretical Analysis of Emotional Needs

2.1   The Connotation of Emotional Demand

Emotion is a kind of psychological activity in which people make subjective evaluation of objective things, which mainly reflects the relationship between objective things and people's subjective consciousness. Emotional demand is also a kind of emotional satisfaction, a kind of psychological identity, it comes from people's spiritual pursuit, and has a close relationship with the satisfaction of the subject's needs. The higher the degree of satisfaction, the stronger the emotion, which is the demand of spiritual level and a process of psychological identity. Emotion is an important element of human psychological cognitive system.

2.2   The Emotional Needs of Patients

For patients, functional needs are the basis for the development of emotional needs. After the functional needs are satisfied, patients will germinate yearning for emotional needs. The needs of patients with using mobile medical platform are not only at the functional level, but also in pursuit of more advanced emotional needs. Patients expect the service design of mobile medical platform to conform to their own physiology, behavior, thinking, etc. The development of judgment needs to achieve a perceptual identity and a good comprehensive experience. People want to use applications that are not only practical, but also humanized. Interactive, emotional and experiential, able to design and make based on the user's emotional needs. At that time, the design of mobile medical platform is no longer a simple visual design and information presentation. The interaction between the system and the user and the experience in the process become particularly important.

Through reading the literature and reading the survey report, the motivation of patients using the mobile medical platform for medical consultation followed by "get doctor's help", "reduce the number of visits to the hospital," "share access to medical information," "reduce anxiety," " Increase self-confidence to cure the disease "and" the medical treatment process is more private. 'It is not hard to find that when patients use the medical platform to reduce anxiety, increase self-confidence, access to privacy has exceeded some functional needs and become the patient's use of this mobile medical platform, an important incentive for medical treatment, and these motivations are exactly patient's psychological response to the mobile medical platform is an important manifestation of emotional needs.

3   Analysis of Current Situation of Mobile Medical Platform

The mobile medical platform is the medical application based on the mobile communication terminal. After 2014, the mobile medical platform is even more explosive. According to statistics, there are more than 2,000 APP related to the market at present. Various types of mobile medical APP have sprung up in front of consumers and health care workers. The most numerous and most used functions are consulting medical services, the main purpose of which is to help consumers with health management. And provide a more convenient way to communicate with doctors.

Data show that in 2014, the market size of mobile medicine in China was close to 3 billion yuan, while the total investment in mobile medicine reached 690 million US dollars, 2.5 times that of the past three years. It is expected that by end of 2018, The scale of China mobile medical market will exceed 10 billion yuan, reaching 12.53 billion yuan. At present, there are more than 2,000 kinds of medical care APP products in our country, and the fierce competition is intensified. Under this background, research on the service design strategy of mobile medical platform is carried out. It has deep practical significance.

4   Service Design

Service design, like system design, focuses on the context of the service system. The International Service Research Association defines service design as: Service design is to set up a service from a customer's perspective, the purpose of which is to ensure a service interface. From the user's point of view, to do service design is useful, usable and easy to use; from the service provider in terms of service design to be effective, efficient and distinctive.

The quality of interaction and user experience between service providers and service recipients to be considered in service design. Its purpose is to closely around the user in the service design process, in the system design and testing process, there must

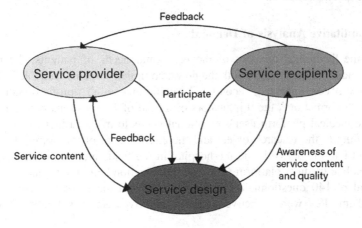

Fig. 1. Service design relationship model

be user participation, and timely access to user feedback, according to user needs and feedback information, continuous improvement of the design until satisfied. Service design in the relationship between the various models shown in Fig. 1.

5 Study of Patients' Emotional Needs Extraction

5.1 Qualitative Study of Patients' Emotional Needs

(1) Literature research content analysis
At the stage of literature research, the main method used in this paper is coterm analysis, which is mainly by analyzing the co-occurrence of key words and terms in the relevant literature. To examine the relationship between different factors under a certain theme. Based on the "emotional needs", "patient's medical feeling" and "patient's emotional needs", the author searched the domestic medical industry and service industry for the past seven years. The use of ChinaNet's knowledge information export function, first export all the relevant data and information needed for this study, and then saved into NoteFirst format. Then, the Bicmb2.0 bibliography is used. Analysis software, to extract the key words to aggregate analysis, merge the same meaning of repetitive keywords. Then the cumulative frequency of about 40% times of the high frequency words for interception and analysis, it can effectively reflect the emotional needs of patients in the field of medical care in China in the past seven years. Seven emotional evaluation indexes, including "reliable", "assured", "immediacy", "convenience", "economy", "communication" and "professionalism", are obtained.

(2) Interview content analysis
After studying the literature, select patient users on the mobile medical platform for real-time online communication (20 interviews) to understand the actual feelings of patients in the use of mobile medical platform, The experience of mobile medical platform service flow. According to the record of interview, the requirement of "privacy" and "information" is obtained from the two aspects of existing problems and patients' expected function.

5.2 Quantitative Analysis of Demand

Through the theoretical analysis of the emotional needs of patients, the results of previous studies and interviews with the news, compiled contains "reliable", "assured", "immediacy", "convenience", "economy", "communication", "professionalism", "privacy" and "information", the 9 indicators of a total of 25 questions a questionnaire to the mobile medical platform user's emotional needs to make further extraction.

According to the research object and the environment of this topic, the questionnaire is put into the network and the hospital in the field, and the questionnaire is put into the mobile medical platform in the communication community and the hospital.

A total of 140 questionnaires were sent out, and the recovery rate was 100%. Among them, 121 were effective and the effective rate was 86.4%. The invalid questionnaire was mainly empty or non-standard (such as multi-selection, empty selection or full volume selection of the same answer).

Through the previous research, we put forward a number of emotional needs, through the survey of the proportion of users' emotional needs, we get the order of importance. At the same time, the indexes of emotional needs are screened. The emotional needs obtained by data screening are as follows: "reliable", "immediacy", "information ", "convenience" and "communication".

6 Typical Mobile Medical Platform Service Process Extraction

By selecting more than 1,300 consumer-oriented mobile medical apps from Apple's iTunes Store and Google Market (Android Market), 40 scored, high-profile and mobile healthcare platforms launched by the hospitals were finally selected as samples Conduct evaluation and analysis on the practicality and usage of the platform, etc., and extract and summarize the service process of each mobile medical platform. By extracting and summarizing the service flow of the mobile medical platform can be summarized as the following three kinds. The basic service process shown in Fig. 2.

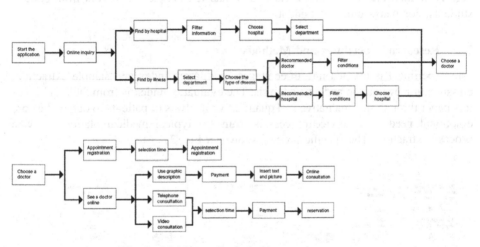

Fig. 2. Mobile medical platform service process

7 Service Process Research Based on Patient's Emotional Needs

7.1 Research Objectives and Methods

At present, both the developed and the developing countries, the medical service reform has become an important topic. How to improve efficiency and reduce costs under the premise of rational utilization of medical resources is a hot issue in the world. However, the advantages of low cost, high efficiency and quickness of mobile medical services has become an important solution to this problem, and mobile medical services are changing the traditional medical model at an unprecedented rate. China's mobile medical industry is still in its infancy. With the advancement of medical information in our country, the enormous social and economic benefits demonstrated by mobile medical care deserve further promotion and research. Therefore, this paper studies the emotional needs of patients in the use of mobile medical platform, and different service processes to meet the emotional needs. And the results of the data analysis to explore different service processes for different emotional satisfaction, and emotional needs of patients in receiving services for the latter part of the mobile medical service platform to provide a reference for the design process.

7.2   The Test Population Positioning

According to the usage of mobile medical platform in real life, this experiment made more objective screening conditions for the experimental participants. (1) 20 to 50 years old (2) Using a smartphone: (3) Being able to use the app independently of your smartphone; (4) Having Internet or self-service registered device experience and watching the internet.

All in all, a total of 30 people participated in their experiment at a sex ratio of 1:1. Age is divided into three stages, each stage has ten people. Surveyors from college students, company staff and residents.

7.3   Research Procedures and Methods

The experiment is divided into three stages: evaluation index and sample extraction, classification evaluation and data analysis. The evaluation index is from the first half of this paper through the qualitative and quantitative analysis of patients to obtain the core emotional needs, the service process is from the typical medical platform service process extraction. The specific process shown in Fig. 3.

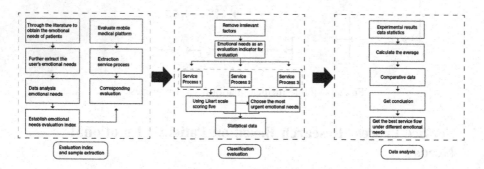

Fig. 3.   Test procedure

In the stage of classification evaluation, in order to avoid the influence of extra variables on the experimental results, different service processes are made into style with the same vision, and the visual factors are removed. The variables were controlled

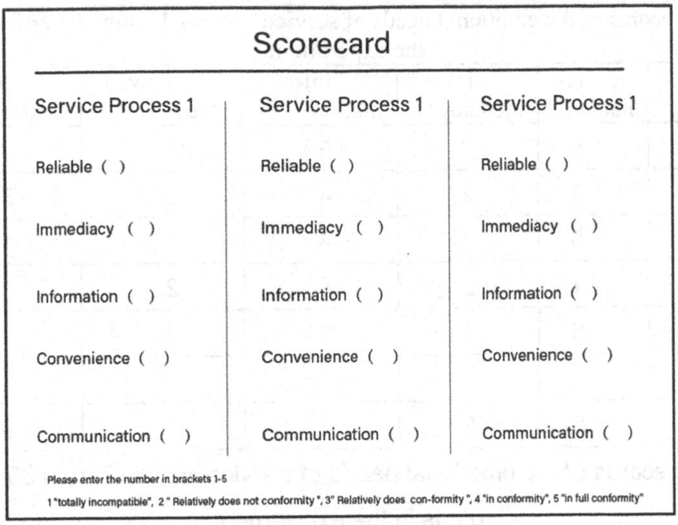

Scorecard

Service Process 1	Service Process 1	Service Process 1
Reliable ( )	Reliable ( )	Reliable ( )
Immediacy ( )	Immediacy ( )	Immediacy ( )
Information ( )	Information ( )	Information ( )
Convenience ( )	Convenience ( )	Convenience ( )
Communication ( )	Communication ( )	Communication ( )

Please enter the number in brackets 1-5

1 "totally incompatible", 2 " Relatively does not conformity ", 3" Relatively does con-formity ", 4 "in conformity", 5 "in full conformity"

Fig. 4. Score table

in the service process itself. The participants scored each group of service processes according to the evaluation index. At the end of the scoring, the data were counted to get the score of the process under each evaluation index. Each evaluator selected the emotional needs that they considered the most important in the service process. In the data analysis stage, the participants of the experiment were scored on the evaluation indexes. By calculating the average value of this process in the various emotional indicators of the final score to assess the comparison, access to this service process performance under various emotional needs. Statistics on the emotional needs of the participants selected, access to emotional needs of patients in the service process.

7.4 Experimental Process and Data Statistics

The testing process of this experiment is divided into three steps, allowing participants to operate different service processes and then scoring whether the process satisfies the listed emotional needs and choosing what they need in the process emotion. The consent of the patient must be obtained before the test begins, and the patient voluntarily participates in the investigation with full understanding of the content. The scorecard is recycled on the spot, and the researcher conducts a comprehensive inspection of the scorecard to ensure the integrity of the data. Data entry with excel, repeated verification, to ensure accuracy. Before statistical analysis, make sure the data is accurate again.

The steps are as follows:

Step 1: Participants in the experiment scanned the given QR code to obtain the apk (Android) or ipa (Apple) used in the experiment, which consisted of three different service processes.

The scores of the emotional needs of service process 1 from 30 participants in the experiment					
partic-ipants	re-liable	im-mediacy	infor-mation	conven-ience	communi-cation
1	4	3	5	2	3
2	3	2	4	1	3
3	5	1	4	1	4
4	4	2	5	2	3
5	5	1	3	3	5
....	...	...	...	...	...
30	5	2	4	2	3
The scores of the emotional needs of service process 2 from 30 participants in the experiment					
partic-ipants	reliable	im-mediacy	infor-mation	conven-ience	communi-cation
1	4	4	3	4	4
2	3	3	2	3	2
3	2	3	3	5	5
4	2	4	4	2	4
5	3	5	2	4	3
....	...	...	...	...	...
30	5	4	3	5	4
The scores of the emotional needs of service process 3 from 30 participants in the experiment					
partic-ipants	re-liable	im-mediacy	infor-mation	conven-ience	communi-cation
1	2	5	2	5	5
2	1	4	3	5	4
3	3	5	2	5	4
4	1	5	2	4	4
5	1	5	1	3	5
....	...	...	...	...	...
30	2	3	1	5	5

Fig. 5. Score statistics

Step 2: The experiment participants operate on the mobile phone and score on the score card after use. Scores from 1 to 5 are expressed as "totally incompatible", " Relatively does not conformity", " More in conformity", "in conformity", "in full conformity". The score card is shown in the following Fig. 4:

Step 3: Participants in the experiment choose their emotional needs in the online medical service process. The option is double selection.

The experiment statistics collected 30 participants to the three groups of service flow five evaluation indicators a total of 450 points, 60 emotional needs vocabulary selection, the statistical results are detailed in the table (due to the length of the article, only partial statistics are provided here) (Figs. 5 and 6).

30experiment participants' choice of emotional needs				
relia-ble	imme-diacy	infor-mation	con-venience	communi-cation
25	8	20	10	7

Fig. 6. Statistical emotional needs of choice

By describing the above data, we can get the satisfaction of different processes to different emotional needs and patients' expectations. Shown in Figs. 7, 8 and 9.

	Sample size	Average value	Theoretical median
Reliable	30	4.5	3
Immediacy	30	3	3
Information	30	5	3
Convenience	30	2	3
Communication	30	3	3

Fig. 7. Service Process 1 score analysis

From the above table, we can draw the conclusion of this service process evaluation test:

The design of service process 1 is through more steps to allow patients to have a deeper understanding of the hospitals and doctors they choose. This way you can get more comprehensive information and equal information. More information will give patients more trust. Relatively speaking, this cumbersome procedure makes convenience less than median, and patients' emotions of wanting to quickly communicate

	Sample size	Average value	Theoretical median
Reliable	30	4	3
Immediacy	30	4	3
Information	30	3	3
Convenience	30	3.5	3
Communication	30	4	3

Fig. 8. Service Process 2 score analysis

	Sample size	Average value	Theoretical median
Reliable	30	2	3
Immediacy	30	4.5	3
Information	30	1.8	3
Convenience	30	5	3
Communication	30	4.5	3

Fig. 9. Service Process 3 score analysis

with their doctors are difficult to meet. Process 2 has two operating paths to choose from. This process is designed to average all the scores in this process without any fraction below the median. Better to take into account the various emotions, but did not highlight its strengths. Process 3 will automatically match the appropriate doctor for patients, better meet the needs of patient convenience, but the obvious drawback of this service model is that patients can not have a comprehensive understanding of the doctor. This process led to the process of reliability and information than the average low.

It can be seen from the table of the statistics of the patients' emotional needs that for the participants, the mobile medical platform should first provide patients with enough sense of security and information to meet the other emotional needs of patients.

8   Conclusion

Nowadays, in the mobile medical platform, most of them are a consultation service platform for public health. Its functional framework has been basically formed. The mobile medical APP is different from the APP in other industries. The need to meet the emotional needs of users is more unique. In the network era, the establishment of product viscosity and reputation depends more on the user experience brought by the product itself and the user-centered design of mobile medical product service. Pay more attention to the user's spiritual needs and emotional experience in the system, which is based on material satisfaction and usability.

In the design of mobile medical platform service flow, users should be given sufficient security. The number and level of doctors greatly affect the user experience. Patients can consult quickly through the platform anytime, anywhere, can reduce the cost of time, space and money. Under this premise, developers can according to their own brand characteristics. Select the appropriate service flow for your own use with the desired direction of development.

References

1. Cai, K.: Analysis of the Components of Product System Design. Wuhan University of Technology, Wuhan (2008). CAI
2. Li, S., Gu, Z.: Interaction Design. China Water Power Press, Beijing (2012)
3. Hu, W., Bi, Y.L., Wu, S.: Mobile medical - the sunrise industry of medical services. In: The Second National Medical Devices Academic and Industrial Forum Proceedings, pp. 41–42 (2003)
4. Chen, H.: System Design Principles. Wuhan University of Technology Press, Wuhan (2003)
5. Lin, S., Lei, H.: Research on the evolution trend of China's medical services marketization: marketization index and its application. Chin. Hosp. (12), 21–24 (2013)
6. Wang, J., Han, L., Yang, X., et al.: Analysis of internet-based mobile medical clinic program and design. China Digit. Med. (8), 21–24 (2015)
7. Meng, Z.: Emotional Psychology. Peking University Press, Beijing (2005)
8. Zhao, X., Yao, H., Liu, X., et al.: Expand and refine the mobile medical technology clinical services. China Digit. Med. (4), 10–12 (2014)
9. Fei, D.: Relational emotion dependence and rationality, reasoning. Chin. Soc. Sci. (8), 31–47 (2012)

PosiTec – How to Adopt a Positive, Need-Based Design Approach

Kathrin Pollmann[1(✉)], Nora Fronemann[2], Anne Elisabeth Krüger[2],
and Matthias Peissner[2]

[1] Institute of Human Factors and Technology Management IAT,
University of Stuttgart, Stuttgart, Germany
kathrin.pollmann@iat.uni-stuttgart.de
[2] Fraunhofer Institute for Industrial Engineering IAO, Stuttgart, Germany

Abstract. In User Experience (UX) design many approaches emphasize that a positive UX can be promoted by addressing basic human needs. However, in practice UX design needs are scarcely considered. We believe that this is due to a lack of adequate methods and guidelines and present a methodological toolkit to support designers in adopting a need-cantered design approach. The toolkit is a collection of innovative user research methods, combined in a guided process to make sure that user needs are taken into account in all steps of the human-centered design process. We propose Experience Interviews as a basis to extract and further interpret the user needs of the target group. The interpretation is realized with the Needs Profile method and fed into an ideation brainstorming. First design solutions of this brainstorming are evaluated and further developed using the co-creation tool UX Concept Exploration. The concrete application of the proposed methods is illustrated based on the example of designing a technical product to promote positive aging of older adults.

Keywords: User Experience · Need-based design · User needs
Experience Interviews · Needs profiles · User Experience Concept Exploration
Positive aging

1 Motivation for a Need-Based Design

User Experience (UX) has become an important factor in product design. The human-centered design process (DIN EN ISO 9241-210) [1] suggests to involve potential users in all design stages to develop products that promote a positive experience for their users (Fig. 1).

Although, so far, the UX community has not been successful in establishing one definition of UX, many approaches emphasize the close relationship between UX and basic human needs [2, 3]. They describe that positive UX can be promoted by designing products that satisfy human needs such as competence (i.e. to accept and master a challenge) or connectedness (feeling close to loved ones). A summary of the relationship between user needs, UX and product use is provide by the *UXellence®-Framework* [2]: Positive experiences with a product can be deliberately evoked by satisfying user needs,

© Springer International Publishing AG, part of Springer Nature 2018
A. Marcus and W. Wang (Eds.): DUXU 2018, LNCS 10920, pp. 52–66, 2018.
https://doi.org/10.1007/978-3-319-91806-8_5

which, in the long run, increases product bonding and the motivation to keep using the product. While this approach seems reasonable from a theoretical perspective, comprehensible, hands-on methods for integrating this need-based approach into the human-centered design process are still missing.

To design for positive experiences it is first necessary to identify those needs which are associated with the use of the product. However, it appears to be especially challenging to initially assess the users' needs, as the abstract concept of needs is often difficult to grasp and users find it hard to verbalize their needs. The same is true for the design team who finds it often difficult to take needs into account for their product design. This is mainly due to difficulties in developing an understanding of the abstract concept of needs as well as a lack of methodological guidance for systematically involving needs in the design process.

In this paper, we present a methodological toolkit to support designers in adopting a need-centered design process. The toolkit is a collection of innovative user research methods, combined in a guided process to make sure that user needs are taken into account in all steps of the human-centered design process. The goal is to arrive at design solutions that address relevant user needs of the target groups and can be tested with users. The concrete application of the proposed methods is illustrated based on the example of designing a product to promote positive aging of older adults.

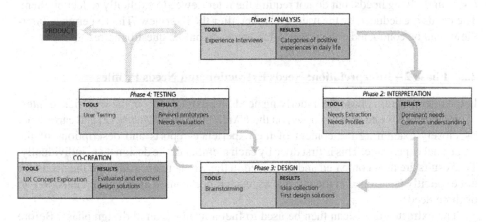

Fig. 1. Human-centered design process including the tools and results of the PosiTec toolbox for need-based design that is based on the phases of the human-centered design process (Analysis, Interpretation, Design and Testing). A co-creation phase is added to involve users in early design decisions.

2   Need-Based Design Approach and Toolkit

Our need-based design approach proposes concrete methods to involve user needs in every step of the human-centered design process (Fig. 1). It comprises a methodological toolkit to help the design team to better understand user needs and consider them in design decision during the different phases of product design. The proposed toolkit is sufficient to cover the phases of analysis, interpretation and design, but should ideally be combined with other user research and design methods. We add a phase of co-creation after the first iteration of the design phase that extends the design phase but also offers an initial evaluation of the design ideas. This allows us, to involve users in early design decisions, thus ensuring that their needs are taken into account for all further design solutions. The testing phase is not included in the present paper.

2.1 Phase 1 – Analysis: Experience Interviews

In the analysis phase, we propose to conduct *Experience Interviews* to learn more about trigger events of positive experiences in everyday life and the underlying needs. An experience interview is a semi-structured interview during which the interviewee is asked to report a positive experience they had in the past two weeks in a certain context. The method was first proposed by Zeiner et al. [4] who investigated positive experiences in the work environment. It is important that the interviewees do not only reports the facts and setting of the positive experience, but also describe their emotions in detail. In addition, it can be assessed whether other people or technology were involved in the experience. We suggest Experience Interviews as a good starting point to identify potential sources and key events of positive experiences for your user group as well as to take an indirect approach to user needs assessment. They contain implicit information about underlying needs, but do not require the interviewee to explicitly reflect on them. The needs are deduced by the user researcher after the interview. The Experience Interviews can be conducted either face-to-face or as an online questionnaire.

2.2 Phase 2 – Interpretation: Needs Extraction and Needs Profiles

In the interpretation phase the underlying needs are extracted from the Experience Interviews. The needs extraction is based on the *UXellence®-Framework* [2] and carried out by closely examining the content of the experience reports and descriptions of the emotional experience. This is first done by each member of the design team individually. The results are then compared and discussed in the whole team. Although the needs are not explicitly mentioned in the interviews, each report can on average be related to two or three needs.

The extracted needs can then be used to fuel a need-centered design phase. Before developing the first design solutions, it is, however, important to fully understand the extracted needs with all their relevant aspects and characteristics, as user needs are sensitive to context and can be ambiguous. Therefore, it is crucial to develop are shared understanding within the design team. To do so, elements of the *Needs Profile* method was used [5]. To generate a common understanding and to highlight the relevant aspects of the needs, all team members together build a representation of each relevant need with Lego®-bricks (based on the metaphoric building approach of the Lego® Serious Play® method). Building the model requires them to exchange their point of views on the specific needs and thereby they arrive at an understanding of the need that incorporates a part of everybody's individual perspective. The process of building also promotes an intuitive understanding of the rather abstract needs and activates implicit knowledge [6, 7], which is relevant because a main part of the information about needs is stored here [8, 9]. They then develop personified representations of the needs, the so-called *Needs Persona*, with the help of an *Empathy Map*. Needs Personas are personifications of the needs and vividly describe a representative of the user group who has an especially strong stamping of one of the needs [5, 10]. The characteristic actions, habits, quotes, thoughts and motivations are noted down on a revised Empathy Map template [5, 11, 12] along with the personal profile of the persona including a name, age, profession and hobbies. The personification of the needs makes the needs even easier to grasp and enhances the empathy for the user group within the design team. The personification of the needs can be used to deduce user requirements and inspire ideas for the initial proto-type of the product to be developed.

2.3   Phase 3 – Design: Brainstorming

In the design phase ideas for an initial product concept are brainstormed, taking into account the Needs Personas. The core question of this brainstorming is which charac-teristics regarding functionality, interaction and visual design the product should have, in order to address the relevant user needs. Ideas are collected for each relevant needs and the three categories functionality, interaction and visual design independently in consecutive silent brainstorming session. The ideas are then clustered by the design team within the three categories. Similarities within the requirements across the needs can be interpreted as basic product features. Those requirements that differentiate the needs from each other can be marked as need-related features. A prototype of the product needs to incorporate all the basic product features and provide variants that take into account the need-related features.

2.4   Phase 4 – Co-creation: User Experience Concept Exploration

It is advisable to also involve users in the design process, especially regarding the need-related features. We therefore propose to include a period of co-creation that can be regarded as a transition from design to testing phase. Thus, through different design stages it can be assured that the product really addresses the needs of the target group. We propose to use of the method of *User Experience Concept Exploration* [2] that enables users to evaluate ideas developed by the design team and create their own design solution in a real-life context of use. Over a week, participants are asked to carry out daily tasks during which they reflect on how they can integrate the product into their daily routines and add new aspects that enrich their positive experience with the product.

The method comprises three phases: an initial workshop to present the product concept based on the results of the ideation, five days of individual tasks to come up with new ideas for the product be completed by the participants and a closing workshop. The workshops can be conducted individually or in groups of participants to promote the heterogeneity of the co-creation process. In the initial workshop participants are introduced to the product idea and asked to elaborate on it by building their own repre-sentation of the product which also serves as a remembrance token for the following phase, during which it should remind participants to carry out their daily individual task.

When the week is over, the task results of all participants are gathered together and compared. In the closing workshop participants are confronted with a summary of their own as well as other participants' ideas and evaluate and discuss them together.

The results from User Experience Concept Exploration and the brainstorming within the design team are combined to create a first testable design solution for the product which can then be evaluated together with users in the testing phase.

3   Practical Example: Need-Based Design of a Virtual Companion to Promote Positive Aging

We applied the need-based design approach and methodological toolkit in a project aimed at designing a product that promotes positive aging. This example shows how the proposed methods can be used in practice and how they add up to arrive at novel, need-related design solutions.

As the world population is growing older with prognosis that the number of adults aged 60 or above will more than double by 2050 [13], the question of how people can maintain independence and self-determination as long as possible becomes more important. Technology can provide solutions to support people in remaining active and pursuing an independent life style [14]. However, there is a strong focus on developing technical products to reduce negative implications of aging such as health issues and social isolation. Little emphasis has been put on positive aspects of aging and how to promote the overall well-being and flourishing of older adults as they age, as proposed by the *positive design* approach.

It has been shown that the experience of positive emotions can broaden peoples' minds and resourcefulness, which makes them more resilient and better at coping with negative situations [15]. Levy et al. [16] support the assumption that older adults would benefit strongly from a boost of positive emotions in their lives with their study about the relationship between positive self-perception and aging. They discovered that people with a positive perception of themselves lived on average 7.5 years longer than those with a less positive perception. The present project is thus aimed at developing a technical product that promotes *positive aging* which we define as "a process of growing older which is predominantly characterized by the experience of positive emotions and a high level of overall well-being" [17].

It needs to be considered that older adults are a heterogeneous target group with differing abilities and affinity towards technology [18]. They are not naturally inclined to accept additional technical products in their private homes, so it is important to address the users' specific capabilities, desires and necessities to provide a real benefit for them [19]. To do so, it is crucial to involve the users in the development process as much as possible and especially consider their needs, which is why we decided to take a need-based design approach.

3.1   Phase 1 – Analysis: User Study with Experience Interviews

Experience Interviews were conducted to identify aspects of daily life that are experienced as positive by older adults and then deduce the need which guide the design of the product to be developed.

Participants and Procedure. The Experience Interviews were carried out both face-to-face and through an online survey. 63 older adults took part in the study (25 females, 29 online). In accordance with the definition of the World Health Organization we defined older adults as adults with a minimum age of 60 years [20]. This is also the retirement age in most European countries. Participants were between 60 and 95 years old (M = 70.88, SD = 9.14). The majority of participants was retired (74.6%). 12.7% (8 participants) had full-time jobs, 11.1% (7 participants) were working part-time and 1.6% (1 participant) were unemployed. The professional background was very diverse, ranging from engineering over teaching and therapeutic professions to sales.

Before the interview started, participants gave their informed consent. The interview was semi-structured and the main part of the interview was the experience report for which participants were asked to describe a positive experience they had in the past two weeks, including their emotions during the experience and the involvement of other people and technical products/technology.

Results. The face-to-face interviews were transcribed and analyzed together with the data of the online survey. In total, we received 81 experience reports, as some participants reported more than one experience. All experience reports were read by all member of the design team and then clustered into experience categories (as proposed by Zeiner et al. [4]) that summarize key aspects of positive experiences in older adults' daily lives.

The experience reports were very diverse describing situation from different areas of daily life or special events. The clustering of the experience reports resulted in 18 experience categories which could be further grouped into three superior experience themes: people-oriented experiences, self-oriented experiences and goal-oriented experiences. Some experiences were very detailed and could be related to more than one experience category. Those were split up into smaller segments and then categorized based on the most prominent aspect.

88% of the described experiences were related to other people: 62% family members, 15% friends and 23% other people such as former students or colleagues. Only a small amount of experiences was experienced by the participant alone (12%). In 44% of the experience reports other people were named as the cause of the positive experience. Given the social nature of humans [21] those results do not come as surprise. They are also in accordance with the study by Zeiner et al. [4] who found that around 80% of positive experience in the work environment are related to other people.

Technology was less frequently mentioned in the experience reports. 28% of the experiences involved technical products or internet services, especially mobile phones and computers. This was to be expected as older adults are generally considered as having a rather low affinity for technology. Still, even in the work environment similar results were obtained. Although the general use and availability of technical products is high in this context, technology was only mentioned on 36% of the experience reports.

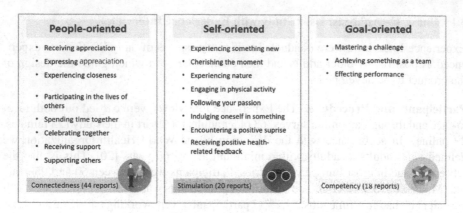

Fig. 2. Overview of experience themes, categories and related needs.

It could hence be concluded that technology is generally only weakly associated with positive experiences. One goal of a need-based design approach should therefore be to make sure that the use of technical products which are helpful or necessary for older adults is as comfortable and enjoyable for them as possible and to promote positive experiences with technical products.

3.2 Phase 2 – Interpretation: Needs Extraction and Needs Profiles

Procedure. The interpretation of the results of the experience interviews consisted of two steps: First, we examined the experience reports with regard to the underlying needs. Each member of the design team matched each experience report with the underlying needs. The results were then merged in a round of discussion with the whole team. Most experience reports were related to two or three needs. There were only few experiences that could only be linked to one single need. After the needs extraction, the Needs Profile-method [5] was used to explore the three needs that were mentioned most in detail.

Needs Extraction Results. The experience reports could be related to eight of the needs included on the UXellence® framework. Only the needs collecting the meaningful and competition could not be associated with any experience report. The following needs were found to be most intensively expressed: connectedness (44 experience reports), stimulation (20 reports) and competence (18 reports). We discovered a close connection between these needs and the experience themes derived from the Experience Interviews (Fig. 2).

Having a strong need for connectedness means being very satisfied when spending time with and being liked by people you like. *Connectedness* is hence strongly associated with people-centered experiences. Someone with a strong need for stimulation finds fulfillment in experiencing and trying out new things. *Stimulation* is therefore mainly underlying self-oriented experiences. People with a strong need for *competence* enjoy facing and mastering a challenge. It can thus predominantly be found in the goal-oriented experience reports.

Two experience reports could not be related to any need. Although they clearly describes self-oriented experiences (tasting fresh cassis fruits from the garden, observing a dear in the forest), the positive emotions were mainly created by the mindful perception of the situation. The participants themselves were not involved in active interaction with the environment and needs underlying such rather passive activies are not included in the UXellence® framework.

Needs Profiles Results. In a first step, the team built one Lego model for each needs in which they visualized the most important aspects of the respective need. As an example, Fig. 3 shows a picture of the model that was built for the need *stimulation*. The model associates the need for stimulation with the following aspects: a constant search for new trends and adventures (1); the wish to explore and engage in various activities (2), the desire to meet new people (3); the urge to try something new every day (4); the willingness to takes new paths, discovers unknown lands (5), the attempt to leave boring stuff behind (6), and a certain restlessness, being always on the move (7).

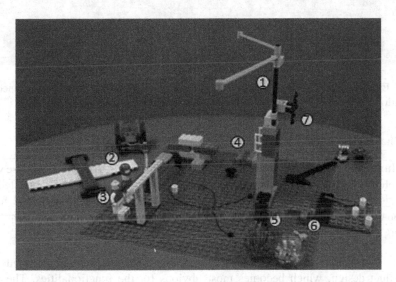

Fig. 3. Lego® model to characterize the need for stimulation together in the design team [5].

To make the established shared understanding of the needs even more concrete, three Needs Personas were developed in a second step: Luna Love (*connectedness*), Carl Clever (*competence*) and Nancy New (*stimulation*). Figure 4 presents the empathy map for Nancy New. In short, she is characterized as a very active, curious older lady, a former travel agent at the age of 76. She is constantly on the search for new ideas and activities and, for that purpose, uses apps like Pinterest or Tripadvisor on the smartphone that she received as a gift from her family. She also enjoys travelling to different places, trips into nature and photography. She likes to take part in the cultural events of her town and recently joined a club which organizes meeting and trips to get to know new people. Nancy lives the spirit that you are never too old for adventures.

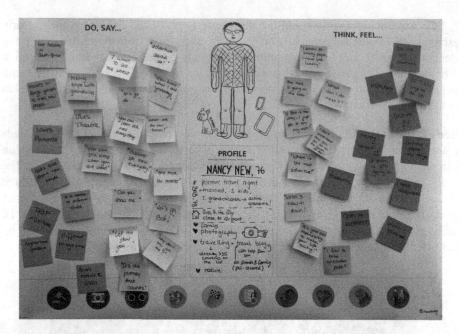

Fig. 4. Empathy Map for the persona Nancy New, an older lady with a strong need for stimulation [5].

3.3 Phase 3 – Design: Brainstorming

Procedure. Based on the personas the design team proceeded to the design phase where we developed first ideas for a product that takes into account the needs of connectedness, stimulation and competence to promote positive aging. Ideas were collected for the functionalities, interaction strategies and visual design of the product in a silent brainstorming and then clustered according to the three categories and needs.

Results. The results clearly showed that each need poses individual requirements upon the product design, which becomes most obvious for the functionalities. The need-specific functionalities voted by the design team as most interesting for a need-base design were:

- for *connectedness*: sharing pictures and experiences, shared calendars, documentation of shared experiences, helping others
- for *stimulation*: self-orientation: physical activity, suggestions for new things and events, discovery trip
- for *competence*: planning projects, further education.

In addition, the following general requirements and basic features were defined: The product should be portable or mobile, so that it can be used both inside and outside the home. It should be a haptic product that users can manipulate and not just a virtual representation. The product should be intuitive to use with no expert knowledge required for set-up, usage and maintenance. Taking into account the strong need for connectedness in the target group, the product should enable a natural interaction and support the user in developing a relationship with it, in order to increase acceptability. This might best be realized by giving the product some kind of personality or personified representation. Last, it should be assured that the user maintains control over the product at all times.

Considering these requirements we came up with the concept of a virtual personalized, personified companion for older adults that promotes positive experiences by offering a customized set of functionalities that is tailored to the user's needs. It also encourages the user to carry out activities that help them maintain a healthy and independent living to, in the long run, contribute to positive aging. The functionalities and requirements named above could be transformed into a first low-fidelity prototype right away. However, we decided to not specify the design of companion further to leave more space for participants' input during the follow-up co-creation phase.

3.4   Phase 4 – Co-creation: User Study with UX Concept Exploration

A User Experience Concept Exploration [2] study was conducted in order to evaluate and extend the idea of a virtual companion together with older adults. The functionalities and requirements that resulted from the design phase were used as a basis for the study.

Participants and Procedure. Four participants from the initial Experience Interviews (2 females, mean age: 65.75 years) were asked to evaluate the developed solutions based on User Experience Concept Exploration. In the initial workshop we explained the participants the general idea of the companion and the main insights of the ideation phase. They were then asked to build their own personal companion with Play Doh®. An example is depicted in Fig. 5. On the one hand, this self-build representation of the companion serves as a remembrance token for the following phase, during which it should remind participants to carry out their daily individual task. On the other hand, the task of building the companion already provides first requirements regarding the technical features and interaction strategies of the companion. Participants were then asked to come up with an everyday situation during which the companion provides them with a positive experience and to visualize this situation with an assorted Lego® Serious Play® set (see Fig. 5). This was the same task that participants were to carry out on a daily basis in the subsequent phase. After participants described their Lego model and the situation of positive experience, we explained the needs of the UXellence framework to them and asked them to select the underlying needs for the described situation. At the end of the workshop participants received an instruction card that contained a detailed description of the daily tasks as well as the main insights from the ideation to inspire participants.

For the five days of individual tasks, participants took the Play Doh® model of their personal companion home together with the instruction card that guided them to reflect on how the proposed companion could enrich their daily life. Every day, participants sent their results to our design team via a private Whatsapp chat where they could also ask questions or advice if needed. The concrete instruction included the following steps:

Fig. 5. Example of Play Doh® model of the personal companion and positive experience visualized in a Lego® model: the companion encourages the participant to master the challenge of the difficult physical exercise.

Report your current mood, build the Lego model of a positive experience with the companion, take a video of the model and describe it, describe how you would improve your initial version of the companion, select the related need(s) and report the added value of the described new functionality.

The task results of all participants were gathered together and compared. In the closing workshop participants first received a summary of their *week with their personal companion* including the situations of positive experiences they came up with. They were then presented with the whole set of ideas taken from all participants and asked to mark their favorite three ideas of the other participants. We also showed them the initial Play Doh® models of the other participants and had them elaborate on which technical aspects and interaction strategies would add benefit to their own present idea of the companion.

Results. To analyze participants' results, we drew up an overview of the described situations and related need for each participants. Then we clustered those situations that were rather similar across all participants. We also checked whether participants' selected needs for each situation were in accordance with our understanding of the needs based on the UXellence®-Framework [2]. Afterwards we quantitatively assessed how often the different needs were mentioned. This overview of the results was supplemented by the ideas generated during the closing workshop.

Participants came up with diverse situations during which they could benefit from their virtual companion. During the closing workshop the following activities were, with three votes each, rated as most promising by the participants:

- Storing memories to share with family members later on,
- motivating and facilitating physical exercising at home,
- support in mastering challenges,
- and taking over organizational household tasks.

These activities further detail and extend the functionalities of the coach developed during the ideation workshop. It became clear that participants saw great potential in the motivational character of the companion to promote positive experiences. They were less interested in letting the companion carry out things for them like a slave. On the contrary, the were rather intrigued by the idea that the companion would help them accomplish things that they struggled with or were hesitant to do on their own.

The needs that appeared most often in the described situations were, with nine mentionings each, *self-expression* and *security*, closely followed by *physical wellbeing* (8 mentionings) and *stimulation* (7 mentionings). With three and four mentionings, respectively, *connectedness* and *competence* were only of minor interest for the participants. These findings suggest that the situations in daily life which are self-oriented and connected with *stimulation* and *self-expression* are the ones where participants saw the most potential for promoting more positive experiences through a virtual companion.

Security appeared in about 30% of the described situations, in contrast to the Experience Interviews (analysis phase), in which it was only mentioned once. Still, in the described situations, *security* was mainly understood as a feeling of self-confidence which was caused by the motivating nature of the companion. This finding is hence well in line with the focus on self-orientation we uncovered in the described situations.

While *connectedness* was the most prominent need in the Experience Interviews, it nearly disappeared in UX Concept Exploration. This might be explained by the fact that three out of four participants were living together with their partners. All participants had regular contact with friends and family and therefore might have a needs profile which is more self- and less people-oriented. It should be noted that the relationship status, social network and living situation might be important factors to take into account when conducting UX Concept Exploration. Moreover, *competence* was mentioned rather often by one particular participant, but not by the others, which is why it scored rather low. These inter-individual differences highlight the need for individualizing the companion and tailoring it to the user's specific needs profile.

To sum up, the data obtained in the co-creation phase suggests to focus the functionality of the companion on facilitating and motivating self-oriented activities related to *stimulation* and *self-expression*. It also yields some extensions to the requirements we defined during the ideation phase which help us to narrow the requirements down to more concrete design guidelines (see Table 1). The data also shows that all suggested requirements were confirmed by participants' comments during the individual tasks and closing workshop. The results of the UX Concept Exploration study serve as input for the next design phase.

Table 1. Requirements derived from ideation, verified by participants during UX Concept Exploration.

Initial requirements retrieved from ideation	Extensions during UX Concept Exploration	Verifications during UX Concept Exploration
Promotion of positive experiences	Should be realized through motivational character of companion	Usefulness of companion was confirmed by all participants
Portability/Mobility	It should be possible to carry companion around	Confirmed by 3/4 participants
Haptic product	Companion's appearance should be a physical one and customizable	All participants imagined a haptic representation of companion
Intuitive use	Interaction with Companion should be realized by voice control (most natural interaction) and possibly extended by light signals	Perceived as a given by all participants. Voice control was perceive as the most natural way of communication
Personality	Companion should be motivating and rather active, approaching user with new ideas and suggestions	3/4 participants gave their companion a name and/or a motivating attitude
User is in control	–	All participants want to decide themselves when to use the companion and when to shut it down

4   Conclusion and Future Work

The practical example shows that the proposed methodological toolkit can aid designers to adopt a need-based approach in UX design. The Experience Interviews proved to be a good starting point to uncover underlying needs with little effort for both, interviewee and user researcher. Through the interpretation and design phases interesting, need-related solutions could be developed that were appropriate for a consecutive co-creation phase. The User Concept Exploration study served its purpose of both, verifying existing ideas and extending them with new design aspects and features.

More work needs to be done to provide guidance for designers to develop products that address multiple needs at the same time. It is also planned to extend the need-based design approach with methods for the testing phase, so that the full human-centered design process can be covered.

References

1. ISO: Ergonomics of human-system interaction – Part 210: Human-centred design for interactive systems. Beuth, Berlin (2010). **13.180; 35.180** (ISO 9241-210)
2. Fronemann, N., Peissner, M.: User experience concept exploration. User needs as a source for innovation. In: Roto, V. (ed.) Proceedings of the 8th Nordic Conference on Human-Computer Interaction: Fun, Fast, Foundational, Helsinki, Finland, 26–30 October 2014, pp. 727–736. ACM, New York (2014)
3. Hassenzahl, M.: User experience (UX): towards an experiential perspective on product quality. In: Proceedings of the 20th International Conference of the Association Francophone d'Interaction Homme-Machine, pp. 11–15. ACM, New York (2008). https://doi.org/10.1145/1512714.1512717
4. Zeiner, K.M., Laib, M., Schippert, K., Burmester, M.: Identifying experience categories to design for positive experiences with technology at work. In: CHI 2016. Extended Abstracts (2016)
5. Krüger, A.E., Kurowski, S., Pollmann, K., Fronemann, N., Peissner, M.: Needs profiles - sensitising approach for user experience research. In: OzChi, Brisbane, Australia (2017)
6. Harel, I., Papert, S.: Constructionism: Research Reports and Essays, 1985–1990. Ablex Pub. Corp, Norwood (1991)
7. Schön, D.A.: The Reflective Practitioner. How Professionals Think in Action. Basic Books, New York (1983)
8. Krüger, A.E., Peissner, M., Fronemann, N., Pollmann, K.: Building Ideas. In: Björk, S., Eriksson, E. (eds.) Proceedings of the 9th Nordic Conference on Human-Computer Interaction. NordiCHI, Gothenburg, Sweden, pp. 1–6. ACM, New York (2016). https://doi.org/10.1145/2971485.2996750
9. Sanders, L., Stappers, P.J.: Convivial Design Toolbox. Generative Research for the Front End of Design. BIS, Amsterdam (2012)
10. Krüger, A.E., Fronemann, N., Peissner, M.: Das kreative Potential der Ingenieure. menschzentrierte Ingenieurskunst. In: Binz, H., Bertsche, B., Bauer, W., Roth, D. (eds.) Stuttgarter Symposium für Produktentwicklung (SSP). Entwicklung smarter Produkte für die Zukunft, Stuttgart, p. 40 (2015)
11. Ferreira, B., Silva, W., Oliveira, E., Conte, T.: Designing personas with empathy map. In: The 27th International Conference on Software Engineering and Knowledge Engineering, 6–8 July 2015, pp. 501–505. KSI Research Inc. and Knowledge Systems Institute Graduate School (2015). https://doi.org/10.18293/seke2015-152
12. Osterwalder, A., Pigneur, Y., Clark, T., Smith, A.: Business Model Generation: A Handbook for Visionaries, Game Changers, and Challengers. Wiley, Hoboken (2010)
13. United Nations, Department of Economic and Social Affairs, Population Division: World Population Prospects: The 2015 Revision. Key Findings and Advance Tables, Working Paper No. ESA/P/WP.241 (2015). Accessed 11 Aug 2016
14. Mynatt, E.D., Rogers, W.A.: Developing technology to support the functional independence of older adults. Ageing Int. **27**, 24–41 (2001). https://doi.org/10.1007/s12126-001-1014-5
15. Fredrickson, B.L.: The role of positive emotions in positive psychology. The broaden-and-build theory of positive emotions. Am. Psychol. (2001). https://doi.org/10.1037//0003-066X.56.3.218
16. Levy, B.R., Slade, M.D., Kunkel, S.R., Kasl, S.V.: Longevity increased by positive self-perceptions of aging. J. Personal. Soc. Psychol. **83**(2), 261 (2002)

17. Fronemann, N., Pollmann, K., Weisener, A., Peissner, M.: Happily ever after. In: Björk, S., Eriksson, E. (eds.) Proceedings of the 9th Nordic Conference on Human-Computer Interaction. NordiCHI, Gothenburg, Sweden, pp. 1–6. ACM, New York (2016). https://doi.org/10.1145/2971485.2996740
18. Eisma, R., Dickinson, A., Goodman, J., Syme, A., Tiwari, L., Newell, A.F.: Early user involvement in the development of information technology-related products for older people. Univ. Access Inf. Soc. **3**, 131–140 (2004). https://doi.org/10.1007/s10209-004-0092-z
19. Hirsch, T., Forlizzi, J., Hyder, E., Goetz, J., Stroback, J., Kurtz, C.: The ELDer project. Social and emotional factors in the design of eldercare technologies. In: Thomas, J.C., Scholtz, J.C. (eds.) CUU 2000 Conference Proceedings, pp. 72–79. Association for Computing Machinery, New York, (2000). https://doi.org/10.1145/355460.355476
20. World Health Organization: Health statistics and information systems. Definition of an older or elderly person
21. McAdams, D.P.: The person: an introduction to the science of personality psychology, 5th edn. Wiley, Hoboken (2009)

Do You Eat This? Changing Behavior Through Gamification, Crowdsourcing and Civic Engagement

Rejane Spitz[1(✉)], Francisco Queiroz[1,2], Clorisval Pereira Jr.[1], Leonardo Cardarelli Leite[1], Marcelo P. Ferranti[1], and Peter Dam[2]

[1] Laboratório de Arte Eletrônica, Departamento de Artes & Design, PUC-Rio, Rio de Janeiro, Brazil
rejane@puc-rio.br
[2] TecGraf, Institute of Technical-Scientific Software Development, PUC-Rio, Rio de Janeiro, Brazil

Abstract. The current excessive use of artificial additives by the food industry, the side effects of these potentially harmful ingredients and their impact on public health should be more widely acknowledged by consumers and further disclosed and discussed by citizens. Governments should develop stricter regulations on food additives, promote better labeling, apply taxes on miscreant food and conduct tighter industry surveillance. In parallel, broader behavior change towards nutrition habits might also be fostered through social innovation and citizen participation. In this paper, we present the design process for creating Dyet (Do you eat this?), a gamified app devised for collecting data and informing on the presence of such additives in commercially available food products. We argue that information on food ingredients and artificial additives should not only be accessible and legible, but also intelligible and personally meaningful to citizens. Through gameplay, we expect to foster the habit of reading ingredients lists, encouraging users to better inform themselves about what they eat and drink. Our overall goal is to change consumer's potentially unsafe eating habits by bringing visibility to the excessive intake of artificial additives and on harmful food industry practices, making it possible and easier for everyone to make healthier dietary choices.

Keywords: Interface design · Gamification · Crowdsourcing

1 Introduction

Today, eating "fresh, healthy, homemade food" has become an extremely rare commodity, especially in the big cities around the world. Scientific research and technological innovation in the field of food engineering have led to a major increase in the world production and consumption of industrially processed food products. Thanks to that, today the food industry does much – and, in many cases, more - of the work of preparing and cooking what we eat and drink.

Consumer demand for processed foods continues to grow globally: highly processed food items often smell good and look fresh, come in well-designed packages, and in general cost less than non-processed food items. They are usually ready or semi-ready

© Springer International Publishing AG, part of Springer Nature 2018
A. Marcus and W. Wang (Eds.): DUXU 2018, LNCS 10920, pp. 67–79, 2018.
https://doi.org/10.1007/978-3-319-91806-8_6

to be consumed, and have a much longer shelf life than "in natura" products, making storage much easier. All these attributes seem to bring a solution to the busy life in the big cities: food-engineered products have cut the time needed to prepare a meal, making food preparation easier and faster.

To achieve such attractiveness, practicality, durability and low cost, the food industry makes use of artificial food additives - colorings, preservatives, flavorings, acids, solvents, emulsifiers, thickeners, sweeteners, chelators, anti-caking agents, antioxidants, glazing agents, improvers, bleaching agent, among many others. Per definition, artificial food additives are synthetic substances produced by chemical or bacterial synthesis. They have absolutely no nourishing attributes, and are increasingly being added to most industrialized food products with the sole intent to modify their physical, chemical, biological or sensory characteristics, making them more appealing to consumers. Chemical additives of all kinds are being carefully and incessantly devised by engineering processes to make food items look, smell and taste better, last longer on the shelf, and cook faster [1, 2].

But all this comes at a high price. Although each country has its own food regulations, and they all may require some form of evidence that each substance is safe at its intended level of use before it may be added to foods [3, 4], scientific studies indicate that when consumed excessively, artificial food additives can produce adverse reactions and lead to irreversible, long-term illnesses such as obesity, diabetes, allergies and cancer [5–12]. Today, over 6,000 artificial additives are routinely employed by food manufacturers and their excessive use by the food industry has become a major concern for public health – an issue that should be further disclosed and discussed.

In this paper, we present the design process for creating Dyet, a gamified app devised for informing and collecting data on the presence of such additives in commercially available food products. Through Dyet, we expect to crowdsource a database of products carrying dangerous additives, and to inform users about risks associated to those ingredients. More importantly, with Dyet we intend to foster the habit of reading the ingredients list, encouraging users to better inform themselves about what they eat and drink. This paper is structured as follows: in *Related Work*, we briefly discuss similar initiatives regarding gamification of healthy eating habits. Then, in *Methodological Aspects*, we contextualize our project and present goals, challenges, and particular issues it addresses. Next, *Design Process* presents the evolution of the project, from ideation to experimental gameplay, providing an overview of Dyet's design rationale. Finally, in *Discussion and Concluding Remarks*, we summarize our findings from the design process and experimental gameplay session, comparing results to initial expectations.

2   Related Work

When researching other mobile applications which could possibly resemble or be similar to our project, we found out several other apps (such as Foodeducate, MyFitnessPal, Foodsmart and Weight Watchers) that tell you about the substances and additives that industrialized foods contain after you scan their barcodes. However, no one of those apps makes use of gamification techniques. Interestingly, some authors remind us that the link between food and playfulness has been traditionally explored by food industry marketing campaigns to promote potentially harmful dietary habits by focusing on fun rather than nutrition [13, 14].

There are, nevertheless, several applications and studies on gamified approaches to eating and health issues: Greenify presents missions for its players such as buying organic food [15]. The Improver rewards users points and badges for entering data such as food intake and physical activities, allowing users to post results in social media [16]. Edufitment, a web-based system containing health education games and a gamified health habits tracker, attempts to address issue of child obesity in the southern United States [17]. Azhar [18] has developed an online game to raise awareness about heart disease causes among Malaysian children. Child obesity was also tackled by González et al. [19], who developed a training program combining school and home activities such as motor play, commercial Nintendo WiiFit games, custom made exercise video game and educational online multiplayer game. My Plate Score was developed to support nutrition counseling by providing quantifiable metrics and food intake tracking [20]. Hungry Panda is an eating game that uses a sensor-equipped fork to track eating behavior in children [21]. HappyInu allows users to 'feed' virtual pets by uploading daily photos of their (real-life) breakfasts [22]. Users are rewarded, with both virtual points and real cash, for healthy food habits.

On a critical note, Maturo and Setiffi [23] have highlighted that health apps tend to frame health improvement and weight loss as individual issues rather than addressing social and political causes for such issues. Dyet is an attempt at addressing those issues by informing users about harmful practices perpetrated by the food industry with the connivance of lenient governmental bodies.

3   Methodological Aspects

The project "Dyet" (Do you eat this?) is a gamified citizen science collaborative project which is currently being developed by Laboratório de Arte Eletrônica (LAE), an inter-disciplinary lab in the Department of Art and Design - with the support of the Institute of Technical-Scientific Software Development (TecGraf) - at PUC-Rio University, Brazil.

The idea of this project – for which we received a research grant from Fundação de Amparo à Pesquisa do Rio de Janeiro (FAPERJ) in 2016 - originated from our desire to combine diverse academic interests of our research group, so that everyone could contribute to the development of a new project without detracting from their individual areas of interest. At the time, the projects, dissertations and theses being conducted by team members encompassed the fields of game design and gamification, crowdmapping, intelligent citizenship and civic technologies, mobile applications and audio-visual-haptic interface design.

At Laboratório de Arte Eletrônica (LAE) a team of faculty members, undergraduate and graduate students research, create and produce projects at the intersection of the domains of art, design, science and technology. We are especially interested on the study of social, cultural and environmental implications of the use of digital technologies, and on devising digital media projects which address those concerns. Since its very beginning, in 1992, Laboratório de Arte Eletrônica has adopted a unique work methodology: all team members participate in all phases of the projects, and - although each one has a predefined role, according to his/her core expertise - we encourage all team members to perform diverse activities and contribute, as much as possible, to different areas. At our meetings, musicians may have a say in the choice of colors, animators can end up discussing codes, and programmers may help create images [24]. Such a methodological approach offers team members a more holistic view of the project and entices more exchange and collaboration among them.

Once we defined the focus of the project - the increasing and excessive use of chemically-produced, artificial additives in food products by the industry - we then approached the researchers at Fundação Oswaldo Cruz (Oswaldo Cruz Foundation, known as Fiocruz), the most prominent science and technology health institution in Latin America, attached to the Brazilian Ministry of Health, and asked for their guidance on the information content that should be crowdsourced by our project. They suggested a list of ingredients and additives which can cause serious health problems, and specially highlighted the risks of artificial food dyes – which can impair children's behavior and cause serious health diseases but are commonly found in candies, cookies, soft drinks, chewing gums, jellies and other food products marketed to children and teenagers, as discussed above. Based on their advice and after reviewing related scientific literature [5–11], we then established several major categories of artificial food additives we were going to include in our project, which are: antioxidants, colorings, flavorings, preservatives, emulsifiers, sweeteners, stabilizers and thickeners.

The use of gamification in our project is fair and justifiable, especially when considering two main strategies: (a) users are constantly alerted of issues and motivations within the gamified tasks (i.e.: food safety) – in fact, we argue that those issues and motivations can be intrinsic motivators for user participation; (b) users should benefit from performing tasks by learning about products they consume and, hopefully, by making better decisions about their nutrition habits – in that sense, we expect that users goals would be aligned with ours.

With Project Dyet, we aim at: (1) Entice the public to search for food additives in the ingredient lists on products packaging, scan and upload barcode information to our database; (2) Invite the public to share information about food additives on social media. (3) Build and maintain a database of harmful additives and products containing them; and (4) Raise awareness about food additives among the general public, also presenting associated risks and types of products that usually carry them.

Ultimately, the overall goal for Dyet is to change consumer's potentially unsafe food habits by bringing visibility to harmful food industry practices.

There are three major challenges related to this goal. First, information about food additives is not easily approachable, since there is not a global open database on healthcare issues regarding food additives, and therefore, the project needs to research, curate, assemble and present such information in a clear and compelling manner. Second, gathering information about individual food products and their ingredients is a task that cannot be easily automated – hence the need for crowdsourcing the retrieval of such data, thus the challenge is engaging the public and fostering participation. This is particularly important for two main reasons: (a) ingredients lists often present poor legibility due to size, typography, or placement, which makes it a difficult task.; (b) building the database with as many different products as possible is a tedious and repetitive task; gamification then, as in many cases of crowdsourced activities, makes such tasks more compelling. Third, there is the challenge regarding the ethical use of gamified volunteer work, and the team believes that gamification and data crowdsourcing should not be exploitative towards participants and should be ethically grounded.

4   Design Process

4.1   Initial Concepts and Layouts

Initial design decisions for the application's usability and visual style were conceived according to the team's perception of its target audience. Aiming at users between 13 and 30 years old, but also considering a more diverse user base that might include older adults, we concluded that Dyet's user experience should combine user interface characteristics of utility and productivity apps with videogame-like design elements and aesthetics. From the very beginning, we have envisioned that the application should also be a location-based game, along the lines of Niantic's Pokemon Go, in which players are challenged to actively search for objects by moving around in the real world [Fig. 1].

Fig. 1.   Scanning the barcode

In respect to the game dynamics, we initially proposed the following sequence of steps and phases: (1) players are presented visually compelling information about a harmful ingredient that must be searched for; (2) players look, in the real world, for products including that ingredient; (3) players scan the barcode of such products; (4) players enter additional information about that product; (5) players send the gathered information to a database of products containing harmful ingredients; (6) players are virtually rewarded for their contribution.

We also proposed that the game provides opportunities for self-expression (there will be a section in which players can share their personal view on products they contribute with), socialization (information generated can be shared through social media), and we also expect the game to foster a mild competition, since the results accomplished by each player will be compared to the average between all participants.

With these conceptual goals in mind, we started to brainstorm and sketch some initial ideas and possible design alternatives [Fig. 2].

Fig. 2. Brainstorming and initial sketches

A first storyboard was conceived, summarizing all the ideas initially selected for the project and providing a basic narrative of all steps involved in the app's user experience [Fig. 3]. Such a narrative enabled all team members to visualize the entire process of the app.

Fig. 3. Storyboarding the user experience

Given the plurality of visions and backgrounds of the participants, we then resorted to Playgen's Adding Play gamification framework to assist with the process. Using Adding Play's card system, we have organized the game goals, motivation, design elements and mechanics [Fig. 4].

At that point, we decided that Dyet should combine characteristics commonly found across gamified applications, such as Missions, Scores and Social Interactions. Also, the gameplay should empower the project's main objectives: it should raise awareness of food and health issues in a similar way to eating habits and healthcare apps; it should crowdsource a database of potentially hazardous food additives as well as present those additives in an informative manner, similar to citizen science projects; and, finally, it should promote civic engagement and public awareness, hopefully fostering a debate on the need for new policies regarding the use food additives by the industry.

Fig. 4. Game design organized in playgen's adding play framework

We then developed a journey map for the application's interaction phases, giving us a holistic idea of the entire user experience and pointing to all the necessary design elements [Fig. 5].

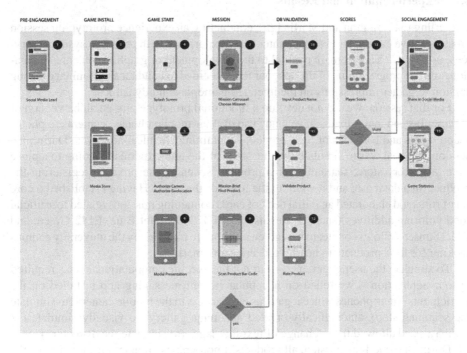

Fig. 5. Project diet - app's user journey

After establishing the conceptual ideas, discussing technological and methodological issues and having a clear picture of the application's complete user journey, we started working on graphical user interface layouts in order to explore the look and feel of the app [Figs. 6 and 7].

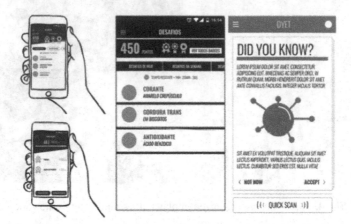

Fig. 6. Screen design elements and navigation alternatives for project dyet's app

4.2　Experimentation and Results

According to Hanington and Martin [25], conducting an experience prototyping session "fosters active participation to encounter a live experience with products, systems, services, or spaces". Therefore, in parallel to the development of graphic elements, navigation, and the programming of the app, our team decided to conduct a preliminary testing session to gather impressions on the intended gameplay and dynamics.

For that session, we did not develop a functional prototype, nor an alpha version of the app. Instead, participants have made use of their mobile phones' cameras to photograph labels and barcodes of food products containing chemical additives. During the session, the goal was to simulate specific steps of the user experience: going to a place – i.e. a grocery store; searching for a product; scanning the product; registering the product on a database; and rewarding the user for the entry. Having established a core set of rules and elaborated an initial deck of cards containing missions related to artificial food coloring additives (such as, for instance, E133 Brilliant Blue, E142 Green, and E110 Sunset Yellow) - our team was given one hour to roam freely the university campus looking for food products in nearby groceries and markets.

To simulate the user experience – but not the specific computational tasks required by our application – we relied on a popular instant messaging app installed on the participants' smartphones, since it gave us easy access to the mobile camera (to simulate the scanning step), automatically created an image gallery (to visually simulate the database) and allowed the exchange of text messages (to simulate the data entry).

During the one-hour session, all products' photographs, along with a text listing the names of the product and additive(s) they contained, were posted on a group created in the instant messaging app. The team registered a little over one hundred industrialized food products, such as beverages, condiments, candies, chips, cereal, among others. An

Fig. 7. Graphic layouts for project dyet's app

arbitrary point system was used to symbolically reward the pair with the highest first-time entries count, since our intended reward system will gratify these kinds of entries the most.

Rules for the gameplay testing session were:

- *Twelve participants were divided into six groups of two.* Although the app is intended for individual use, we have made that decision for two reasons: first, it would compensate for the extra steps needed for product submission, such as the manual typing of additives' names and the process of attaching photographs to messages; second, it could foster discussions between participants, offering an opportunity for reflection and insight during the process. Three of this paper's authors were among the twelve participants. The group comprised four senior members of the lab and eight undergraduate collaborators - two of them formally enlisted as junior researchers within the lab.

- *The length of the test session was established at sixty minutes.* Given the need to move geographically across streets nearby in search of stores and markets, the time length was considered enough for a typical intended game session.
- *All participants (with one exception) joined a dedicated instant message group.* The group was not intended for conversations, but exclusively for the upload of products' photographs and data.
- *Participants were sent eighteen individual image files containing the name, description and illustration of different food additives.* The goal of the proposed game was to win as many points as possible by reporting products containing those additives.
- *Groups were set free to search for food products and report their findings through the instant messaging app.* Participants were free to leave the lab premises for the session time length. Messages were later be used to compute the points awarded by each group.
- *Participants were told to return to the lab at the end of the one-hour session.* Messages sent after the session length were not computed.

In approximately 60 min, the participants made a total of 122 valid submissions identifying 103 unique products. A total of 15 of the 18 food additives presented were identified. Some products had as much as 6 of the presented additives in their ingredients list. Artificial food dyes were found in 87 of the 103 identified products (approximately 84%). In total, 168 unique associations between products and additives were established.

5   Discussion and Concluding Remarks

After the session, all participants joined a discussion, while points were manually computed by junior members of the lab. The goals of the discussion were to compare personal impressions and expectations and to establish next steps in the app's design and development. The discussion was mostly focused on fun, gameplay, and how they could affect the database crowdsourcing process. Several valid insights which derived from that conversation will influence design decisions in future iterations, such as:

- *The importance of implementing a QuickScan mode allowing for the selection of multiple additives at once.* During the test session, participants occasionally sent messages with more than one ingredient - which was not explicitly forbidden in that session but did not replicate the intended gameplay. This strategy, we believe, should be beneficial for entering more data points to the database.
- *The possibility of submitting generic categories.* Some food products' labels listed unspecified additives under the name of their categories (e.g.: "preservatives") – a worrying practice that should be registered.
- *The advantages of limiting the number mission cards.* Some players have expressed their difficulty in concentrating on many additives at once. Allowing them to pursue a limited number of missions per session could help them focus on the task. Additionally, it could encourage them to search for less popular/memorable substances that would otherwise be ignored.

- *The advantages of attributing different scores to different additives.* One of the strategies of the group with the higher score was submitting a large number of products carrying common – and not particularly hazardous – additives. In terms of both awareness and database population, it would be advisable to encourage players to search for more diverse and dangerous substances.
- *The importance of feedback.* Most participants claimed to have felt motivated by following, through the messaging channel, the performance of the other players. In this case, it seemed advisable to offer ways for the player to follow in real time the number of submissions to the database, including and the number of submissions made by the user's friends. Such improvement, could have a bigger impact on player's performance than the mere inclusion of global rankings.
- *Time matters.* Although most players have expressed they had fun during the testing session – especially during the initial minutes – some of them reported tiredness after the first thirty to forty-five minutes. Based on those reports, two suggestions were made: (a) the inclusion of a progress bar to both recommend a minimum target and to measure the player's daily performance; and (b) a time-based game mode initiated either by the game system or the player himself. These features could potentially help to sustain players' medium to long-term commitment to the game.

Overall, the gameplay experimental session has confirmed some of our expectations, most pronouncedly a sense of fun in performing the tasks proposed and an improved awareness of potential side effects of artificial food additives and risks associated to specific products. Additionally, the desire for quicker methods for populating the database was also corroborated by participants.

On the other hand, the session suggested some possibilities for adjusting gameplay and improving engagement in ways that we had not anticipated: this is particularly true for the proposal of real-time feedback on total submissions to the app – which indicates a higher potential for competitive gameplay than we had initially foreseen. Another unanticipated issue was the need for generic entries by categories (rather than specific food additives).

Finally, the session helped us make design decisions we were hitherto undecided about, namely the limitation of active mission cards; the inclusion of time-based gameplay missions; and the attribution of different number of points to different substances.

Next steps for the project include the deployment of an alpha version, currently being developed for Android and iOS platform with the Unity game engine.

We believe this project will bring visibility to people's excessive and increasing intake of artificial additives, inform on the danger they can cause to their health, trigger a debate on harmful food industry practices, hopefully contributing to promote consumers' behavior change in terms of their dietary choices and nutrition habits. Moreover, we believe this project can contribute to the field of gamification and crowdsourcing, identifying ways of balancing gameplay, engagement, and information in a fun, ethical and sustainable manner.

Acknowledgements. The authors would like to thank the student volunteers of Laboratório de Arte Eletrônica for their invaluable work, as well as the Department of Art and Design and Tecgraf Institute of Technical-Scientific Software Development at PUC-Rio, for their academic and technical support. This study is part of a research project supported by Fundação de Amparo à Pesquisa do Rio de Janeiro (FAPERJ).

References

1. Lambert, C.: The way we eat now: ancient bodies collide with modern technology to produce a flabby, disease-ridden populace, May–June 2004. https://harvardmagazine.com/2004/05/the-way-we-eat-now.html. Accessed 05 Feb 2018
2. Blythman, J.: Swallow This: Serving Up the Food Industry's Darkest Secrets. Fourth Estate, London (2015)
3. Agência Nacional de Vigilância Sanitária (ANVISA). Legislação sobre aditivos alimentares e coadjuvantes de tecnologia. http://portal.anvisa.gov.br/aditivos-alimentares-e-coadjuvantes. Accessed 19 Feb 2018
4. United States of America Food and Drug Administration. Overview of Food Ingredients, Additives and Colorings. https://cspinet.org/new/201601191.html. Accessed 08 Feb 2018
5. Stevens, L.J., Burgess, J.R., Stochelski, M.A., Kuczek, T.: Amounts of artificial food dyes and added sugars in foods and sweets commonly consumed by children. Clin. Pediatr. **54**(4), 309–321 (2014)
6. Center for Science in the Public Interest. The Science Linking Food Dyes with Impacts on Children's Behavior (2016). https://cspinet.org/sites/default/files/attachment/science%20linking%20food%20dyes.pdf Accessed 11 Feb 2018
7. Rosenthal, E.: Some food additives raise hyperactivity, study finds. The New York Times, Research, 6 September 2007. http://www.nytimes.com/2007/09/06/health/research/06hyper.html. Accessed 11 Feb 2018
8. Nascimento, D.S.S., Teles A.R.S., de Góes, C.A., Barretto, L.C.O., dos Santos, J.A.B.: Aditivos de Alimentos e sua Relação com as Mudanças de Hábitos Alimentares. In: Congresso Brasileiro de Ciência e Tecnologia de Alimentos CBCTA, Outubro de 2016, FAURGS, Gramado (2016)
9. Center for Science in the Public Interest. Seeing Red: Report Finds FDA Fails to Protect Children in Light of New Evidence on Food Dyes (2016). https://cspinet.org/new/201601191.html. Accessed 28 Jan 2018
10. Fai, A.E.C., Oliveira, A. de M., de Paiva, E.P., Soares, D. de S., Mitchell, T.C.C., Stamford, T.L.M.: Aspectos legais do uso de aditivos químicos em alimentos - legal aspects of the use of chemical additives in food. Hig. Aliment. **22**(166/167), 194–199 (2008)
11. Prado, M.A., Godoy, H.T.: Corantes artificiais em alimentos. Alim. Nutr. Araraquara **14**(2), 237–250 (2003)
12. Grier, S.A., Mensinger, J., Huang, S.H., Kumanyika, S.K., Stettler, N.F.: Fast-food marketing and children's fast-food consumption: exploring parents' influences in an ethnically diverse sample. J. Public Policy Mark. **26**, 221–235 (2007). https://www.researchgate.net/publication/228638749. Accessed 25 Jan 2018
13. Elliott, C.: 'Big Food' and 'gamified' products: promotion, packaging, and the promise of fun. Crit. Public Health **25**(3), 348–360 (2015)
14. Jones, S., Thom, J.A.: Advergames play with nutrition by making fast food rewarding. The Conversation, pp. 1–4, 6 December 2013

15. Lee, J.J., Matamoros, E., Kern, R., Marks, J., de Luna, C., Jordan-Cooley, W.: Greenify: fostering sustainable communities via gamification. In: CHI 2013 Extended Abstracts on Human Factors in Computing Systems, pp. 1497–1502. ACM (2013)
16. De Mesmaeker, D., Provo, J., Abeele, V.V.: Improving physical health via social media and gamification principles (2012)
17. Richards, C., Thompson, C.W., Graham, N.: Beyond designing for motivation: the importance of context in gamification. In: Proceedings of the First ACM SIGCHI Annual Symposium on Computer-Human Interaction in Play, pp. 217–226. ACM (2014)
18. Azhar, A.M.: The implementation of gamification in health awareness. Universiti Teknikal Malaysia, Melaka (2015)
19. González, C.S., Gómez, N., Navarro, V., Cairós, M., Quirce, C., Toledo, P., Marrero-Gordillo, N.: Learning healthy lifestyles through active videogames, motor games and the gamification of educational activities. Comput. Hum. Behav. **55**, 529–551 (2016)
20. Palmer, J.A.: Gamification of nutrition-based wellness counseling with my plate score©. J. Acad. Nutr. Diet. **116**(9), A64 (2016)
21. Kadomura, A., Li, C., Chen, Y., Tsukada, K., Siio, I., Chu, H.: Sensing fork: eating behavior detection utensil and mobile persuasive game. In: CHI 2013 Extended Abstracts on Human Factors in Computing Systems, pp. 1551–1556. ACM (2013)
22. Luhanga, E.T., Arakawa, Y., Hippocrate, A.A., Suwa, H., Yasumoto, K.: Happyinu: exploring how to use games and extrinsic rewards for consistent food tracking behavior. In: 2016 Ninth International Conference on Mobile Computing and Ubiquitous Networking (ICMU), pp. 1–7 (2016)
23. Maturo, A., Setiffi, F.: The gamification of risk: how health apps foster self-confidence and why this is not enough. Health, Risk Soc. **17**(7–8), 477–494 (2016)
24. Spitz, R.: Teaching computer graphics in Brazil: social commitment, creativity and passion - against all odds! In: SIGGRAPH 2000 Conference Abstracts and Applications, Computer Graphics Annual Conference Series, ACM SIGGRAPH, New York (2000)
25. Hanington, B., Martin, B.: Universal Methods of Design: 100 Ways to Research Complex Problems, Develop Innovative Ideas, and Design Effective Solutions (Kindle Locations 2116 2117). Creative Publishing International Kindle Edition (2012)

Research on Image Emotional Tag Generation Mechanism Based on the "Cloud Pet Keeping" Phenomenon

Chen Tang, Ke Zhong, and Liqun Zhang[✉]

Institute of Design Management, Shanghai Jiao Tong University, Shanghai, China
zhanglliqun@gmail.com

Abstract. In Chinese UGC background, the "Cloud Pet Keeping" phenomenon that social media users keep eyes on certain pets' growth by viewing the photos and texts released by pet bloggers is rising. Users obtain emotional resonance through browsing pet photos shared and are happy to contribute the consuming behavior. However, there are still large amount of people can't find their favorite pets through searching. The emotional tags' lack can be a possible reason, which causes the bad user experience. This research tried to purpose an approach based on "cloud pet keeping" phenomenon by using neural networks to develop the image emotional tag generation mechanism. In this experiment, cats' photos are taken as the example to construct the model. This mechanism is used to predict the emotional categories of images. When users uploading the images, the mechanism will automatically generate emotional tags based on its prediction. This is a positive way to solve the problem in the lack of image emotional tags. It is foreseeable that the theory can be applied to other fields, such as industrial product and so on.

Keywords: Image emotional tags · Neural network
"Cloud pet keeping" phenomenon

1 Background

The advent of Web 2.0 technologies has enabled the creation and distribution of user-generated content (UGC), bringing a lot of new phenomenon in social medias. "Cloud Pet Keeping" is a phenomenon rising in Chinese UGC background that social media users keep eyes on certain pets' growth by viewing the photos and texts released by pet bloggers. With the accelerated pace of modern living and limited conditions, more and more urbanites in china choose to browse amusing pet photos shared by bloggers and are willing to praise, forward these information, and contribute the consuming behavior for these contents to get emotional resonance. Emotion is an essential part of attitude. Research shows that there is established relationship between attitude and behavior and indicate attitude serves as a mediating factor between the use and creation of UGC. [1] While, a great deal of users complain about can't find optimal content, resulting in difficulties in finding pets' information that is in line with their preference. The main possible reason is the difference between emotional expression tags input by users and bloggers. This indicates the lack of

© Springer International Publishing AG, part of Springer Nature 2018
A. Marcus and W. Wang (Eds.): DUXU 2018, LNCS 10920, pp. 80–93, 2018.
https://doi.org/10.1007/978-3-319-91806-8_7

appropriate emotional tags. While, it is not practical to label the pictures by manual work. Therefore, to find a way to generate the accurate emotional image tag is quite necessary for improving the user experience. Most research methods of emotional experience based on images are feature analysis [2], user knowledge architecture [3, 6], and quantitative study [4, 5]. These methods focused more on how to describe the user's emotional experience preference. There is less research on study how to propose a method to generate emotional tags to improve the user experience.

With the rapid development of image acquisition equipment, the cost of obtaining image data is getting lower and lower. And with the continuous expansion of data scale and computing power brought by the development of information and communication technology, it is becoming more and more common for people to process data and explore based on these data resources. Faced with the large amount of image data currently available in social networks, this paper tries to put forward a set of mechanisms using neural network to help improve the lack of emotional tags in actual use based on the "Cloud Pet Keeping" phenomenon.

The rest of the paper is organized as follows. The concepts and methods needing explanation are sorted out in Sect. 2. Section 3 presented the mechanism how to generate emotional tags for photos. In order to verify the maneuverability of the mechanism, experiments with cats' photos have been done is in Sect. 4. Section 5 is the summary and Sect. 6 is the conclusion.

2   Concepts and Methods

2.1   Concepts

Image.   The image in this article means photos that is taken by a camera, a mobile phone and other devices.

Digital Image.   If the scene in real world wants to be processed, identified, and stored by the computer, the image must be transformed into a format that can be recognized by the computer. In the computer, image is stored in the digital form. Therefore, the image is also called the digital image.

The digital expression of image is divided into four steps:

- Scanning: divided the image into M x N grids and each of grid is called a sampling point.
- Color separation: the color of the sampling point of the colorful image is decomposed into three basic colors (RGB)
- Sampling: measuring the brightness of each component of each sampling point
- Quantization: the analog quantity is represented by the digital quantity to realize the A/D conversion of the luminance value.

Image Tag.   Tags are the keywords added by users to describe the image contents. [8] In particular, tags are not only the labels, but also can be the keywords in the topics, texts, stickers, comments and so on. Tags, as the image features, are necessary for people to retrieve key information.

2.2 Methods

Emotional Tags Cluster Analysis. Cluster analysis is a common tool for data analysis. Correlation Score. Professionals grade the correlation between any two of these tags. They score on a 9-point scale ranging from 'significant negative correlation' to 'significant positive correlation'. Smaller the value is, higher the similarity. (see Fig. 1.) This method calculates the Euclidean distance (1) between these emotional tags in a multi-dimensional space and classifies them following the closest distance principle.

$$Euclidean\ \text{distance} = \sqrt{(x_1 - x_2)^2 + (y_1 - y_2)^2 + \ldots + (y_n - y_n)^2} \qquad (1)$$

Word\Word	T1	T2	T3	T4	T5	...	Tn
T1	1	4	7	9	2	...	6
T2	4	1	3	5	4	...	5
T3	7	3	1	8	...	...	...
T4	9	5	8	1	...	...	...
T5	2	4	...	...	1	...	...
...	...	...	...	...	...	1	...
Tn	6	5	...	...	...	...	1

Fig. 1. Semantic correlation matrix of emotional tags

Smaller the distance, higher similarity between the two tags. At the beginning, each tag is regarded as a cluster. Combine two nearest clusters at a time. Until finally only one cluster is left (see Fig. 2).

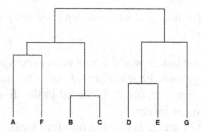

Fig. 2. Hierarchical clustering

Emotional Tags Multidimensional Scaling Analysis. Multidimensional scaling analysis reduces tag classes in multi-dimensional space to the low-dimensional space to locate, analyze and classify.

By combining these two analysis results, researchers conclude and extract emotional expression Vocabularies in a more scientific way.

Grayscale Images

In photography, computing, and colorimetry, a grayscale or grayscale image is one in which the value of each pixel is a single sample representing only an amount of light, that is, it carries only intensity information. [9]

The image can be converted to the grayscale one by the following methods:

$$Gray = (R + G + B)/3 \tag{2}$$

Mean Value Method. The formula is simple, so it is easy to maintain and optimize. However, from the perspective of human eyes, the gray shadow and brightness of the picture are not good enough.

$$Y' = R * 299/1000 + G * 587/1000 + B * 114/1000 \tag{3}$$

Psychology Method. For images in color spaces such as Y'UV and its relatives, which are used in standard color TV and video systems such as PAL, SECAM, and NTSC, a nonlinear luma component (Y') is calculated directly from gamma-compressed primary intensities as a weighted sum, which, although not a perfect representation of the colorimetric luminance, can be calculated more quickly without the gamma expansion and compression used in photometric/colorimetric calculations. [10]

$$Gray = G: only\ take\ green/red/blue \tag{4}$$

One Channel Method. It is a quicker way to make gray images, without doing any calculation, and taking the value of a channel directly as a gray value. It is difficult to predict the result of this transformation, so this algorithm is mostly used for artistic effects.

In practical applications, considering that human eyes have different degrees perception to different colors' light, researchers also want to avoid low speed floating-point operations, therefore, grayscale photos in this experiment are processed with python to converse from "RGB" mode to "L" mode according to the formula:

$$Y' = R * 299/1000 + G * 587/1000 + B * 114/1000 \tag{5}$$

Artificial Neural Network

Deep learning discovers intricate structure in large data sets by using the backpropagation algorithm to indicate how a machine should change its internal parameters that are used to compute the representation in each layer from the representation in the previous layer [7]. Among the deep learning field, artificial neural (ANN) networks are the main choice in many data classification tasks [8]. Another commonly used classification method is k-NearestNeighbor (KNN), which is classified according to the distance of the pixel. But it is very slow in the test stage of the model, and the distance measurement information on the image is not quite large enough, so this method is not used this time.

The artificial neural network is also referred to as the connection model. The traditional expert system is the idea of a series of "if" rules of the statement, classification of things go from the top down, and the neural network is the transmission, let the machine to explore the classification rules. As the computing power of the computer is rapidly enhanced, the neural network can be better implemented.

The steps of neural network based on classification are as follows:

- collect data and matches the data with the corresponding classified labels
- use neural network to train a classifier
- use the trained classifier to predict the class of new pictures.

Classifier - Architecture of Artificial Neural Networks

For classification problems, the input layer is used to accept data, the hidden layer seeks the characteristics of the data, and the output layer is used to predict the category. There are multiple inputs on each node. These inputs are assigned random weights at the initial time, and then decide whether the nodes will continue to transmit information back and forth by mathematical functions. The system error is obtained by the forward propagation of the input to the output, and then the weight is adjusted by the output to the input back propagation, and the error is reduced. The neural network continuously trains the weights between different levels through a large number of data cases. Finally, the accuracy of the machine prediction is tested by the data in the test set. If the performance is over 0.80, the neural network can be considered successful.

> **Input layer**—The leftmost layer is called input layer. It contains nodes that receive input information from the given on which network will learn or do other process.
> **Output layer**—The rightmost layer is called output layer. It contains nodes that respond to the information about how it's learned any task.
> **Hidden layer**—The middle layer of nodes is called the hidden layer. These nodes' values are not observed (see Fig. 3).

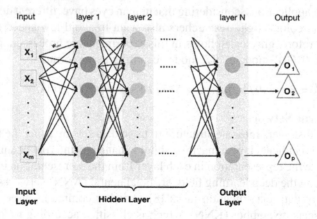

Fig. 3. Structure diagram of neural network

The Use of the Neural Network. A successful neural network can be used as a classifier. When having a new image, it can be read, and the machine can automatically predict the emotional tag of the image.

3 Image Emotional Tags Generation Mechanism

The whole image emotional tags generation mechanism has three parts: (see Fig. 4).

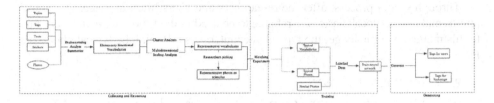

Fig. 4. Image emotional Tags generation mechanism

3.1 Method for Filtering Typical Images

Emotion means the subjective feelings or experiences of the individual [11]. There must be difference existed when people see the same picture. Emotional experience is about the individual subjective experience of emotions [12]. Different emotional experience will influence people's emotional expression. In order to ensure the accuracy of pictures' emotional category labels, we use the method (see Fig. 5) to screen and extract image categories to get the most the approximate emotional expression vocabularies and typical photos.

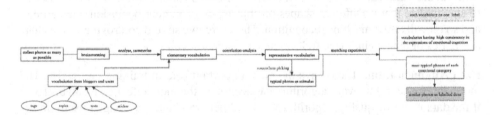

Fig. 5. Method for filtering experimental photos

The method for filtering experimental photos involves three parts.

Collection and Analysis. Collect vocabularies and photos which is about the object of the phenomenon from bloggers and users as many as possible from social medias. Then professional researchers brainstormed, analyzed, summarized and correlated all the emotional expression vocabularies, and extracted representative vocabularies according to the correlation score matrix through the multi-dimensional scale and cluster analysis by SPSS.

Filtering. Researchers filter representative photos from social networks according to these presentative vocabularies as stimulus.

Matching Experiments. By calculating Euclidean distance and statistical methods with data from multi matching experiments of emotional expression vocabularies and stimulus, vocabularies that having high consistency between users and bloggers and most typical photos of each emotional category are obtained.

Through such a process, after the researchers and users filtering twice, the typical photos and typical vocabularies are reliable to be used in the following part. According to this method, we finally get the typical vocabularies set W and the typical photos set P.

$$W = \{W1, W2, W3, \dots .WN\}$$

$$P = \left\{P_{W1}^1, P_{W1}^2, P_{W1}^3 \dots ., P_{W1}^M; P_{W2}^1, P_{W2}^1, P_{W2}^3 \dots ., P_{W2}^X; P_{WN}^1, P_{WN}^2, P_{WN}^3 \dots ., P_{WN}^Y\right\}$$

3.2 Artificial Neural Network

The second part of the Mechanism is using the artificial neural network to train a classifier.

Data Collection. The typical vocabularies and typical photos obtained from the last step is the key data for the neural network. The typical photos are used as the labelled data for neural network to learn and test. The number of the typical vocabularies N decides the number of nodes in hidden layers.

Standardize Images. As the size of collected images is quite different, it is necessary to standardize them. Different shapes of objects, environment occlusion, background and so on will affect machine recognition. Therefore, we should control the single characteristics of objects in image to learn and classify.

Data Augmentation. Data plays the most important role in training the model. The more data an neural network algorithm has access to, the more effective it can be. Even if the data is of low quality, algorithms can still perform better, as long as useful information can be extracted by the model from the original data set [13]. Data augmentation, which no matter is guided by expert knowledge [14], or generic [13], and has shown effective in image classification [14].

In this experiment, several methods are applied as follows:

Scaling: Different scaled object in the image is an important part of image diversity. For real users, the object in their photos can be large or tiny.

Rotating: According to different requirements, it is necessary to rotate the photos at diverse angles. Users prefer to try different angles while taking photos of the object they love. However, this method probably adds background noise when the background color can't blend with the image (black or white). The network may consider that as a feature to learn.

Adding Salt-and-Pepper Noise: Salt-and-pepper noise is sparsely addition of white and black pixels in the image. For real users, most of them are not professional photographer. There is high possibility existing that photos taken by them are fuzzy with a large amount of white and black dots.

Changing Lighting Condition: Photos with different lighting condition will help the network to learn properly the object and also the diverse scenario of the images.

Translation: Translation means to shift the object to various parts of the image. This method also may bring background noise. This method can make the network learn the invariant features.

3.3 Tags Generating

The value of output nodes shows the possibility of each emotional class. They can be ranked from height to low. Tags of high possibilities can be used to add to the photo. There are two ways to use the prediction results as follows:

Provided to the User. After ranking the value of predictions to each class, tags of high possibilities can be shown for the user to choose. This is a good way to improve the accuracy of prediction with more and more data are collected.

Added by Backstage Automatically. When the user uploads a image, the backstage automatically predicts the category of emotional labels that match the image. Also, each emotional category contains many emotional vocabularies with high correlation. Backstage can add these tags all, this will greatly improve the efficiency of the user's search.

4 Experiment

4.1 Experimental Images and Categories Preparation

For cats are the most popular pet in china social media, cats' photos are chosen from social networks as experimental material.

Collection and Analysis. More than 700 photos are collected from Weibo and Lofter, the most famous social platforms. 92 supplementary emotional expression vocabularies are collected form several different sources. Through experts' analysis, brainstorming, summarize, the final number of vocabularies to be analyzed is 46. Three professionals are invited to grade the correlation between any two of these 46 vocabularies. Three professionals are invited to grade the correlation between any two of vocabularies. Finally, 14 vocabularies are extracted from 46 vocabularies as indicators for later experiment. The vocabularies are *Happy, Naughty, Adorable, Disgusted, Serious, Tsundere, Calm, Focused, Lazy, Curious, Shocked, Angry, Dazed, Sad.*

Filtering. Based on the 14 emotion cognition vocabularies. 70 stimuli photos are obtained.

Matching Experiments. Ranking the value the consistency between bloggers and users' choosing, vocabularies that having a high level of consistent with bloggers emotional cognition: *Angry, Curious, Naughty, Lazy, Sad, Shocked, Happy, Serious.*

The typical photos of each category are obtained (see Fig. 6).

Fig. 6. Typical photos of each category

4.2 Processing of Experimental Photos

Data Collection. According to the results of the mechanism for filtering experimental images, 8 adjectives with relatively small deviation are obtained. These typical vocabularies are as follows:

Angry, Curious, Naughty, Lazy, Sad, Shocked, Happy, Serious.

Fig. 7. Similar photos picked by researchers according to typical photos

From analyzing the typical photos' features, researchers filtering similar photos. Take *shock* as an example, the features of typical photos are: the cat's eyes are round and the mouth is triangular (see Fig. 7). Through these typical features, researchers screened other images that represent the shocking emotional expression.

4.3 Processing of Experimental Photos

Standardize Images. In order to eliminate the influence of the ornaments on the cat's body, this experiment cut the cat's head in each picture as the final experimental material. And the cats' photos in *Naughty* category are mainly featured with the body movement and gesture. Therefore, in final experiment, 7 emotional expression tags as 7categories are retained, they are *Angry, Curious, Lazy, Sad, Shocked, Happy, Serious.*

Because colors of the picture have no obvious influence on the users' emotional cognition of the picture, so this research used grayscale images for the experiment.

Photos collected were processed into grayscale, and resized to 127pixel * 127 pixel. A 127 * 127 size matrix that can describe the whole image with the gray value of each pixel in the image. By transforming the matrix, a matrix of size 16129*1, (16129 = 127 * 127) is finally obtained. For now, the image is represented by the array (see Fig. 8).

Fig. 8. Processing of experimental images

Data Augmentation. Through the various methods mentioned above, each typical image was rotated, zoomed, added salt-and-pepper noise, translated, changed different level lighting conditions and so on (see Fig. 9).

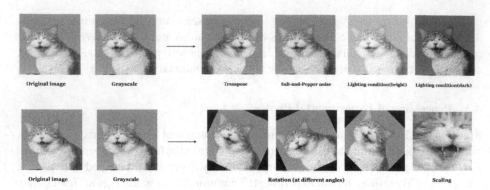

Fig. 9. Example photos of data augmentation

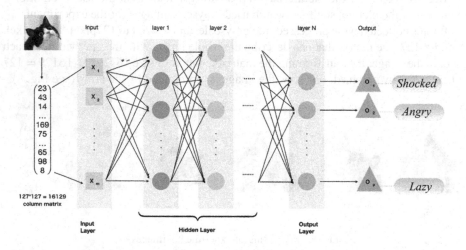

Fig. 10. Structure diagram of this experiments' neural network

Train. The size of the matrix of the image pixel decides the number of nodes in input layers.

In this experiment, the input layer has $127*127 = 16129$ nodes, $X_1, X_2\ldots$ is the gray-scale value of each pixel. The output layer has 7 nodes, corresponding to 7 typical emotion expression vocabularies. Examples for each emotional expression vocabulary, and explanation of how we represent the labels (see Fig. 11).

Training Set: 4802 pictures (127 by 127 pixels) of emotional tags
Test Set: 964 pictures (127 by 127 pixels) of emotional tags.

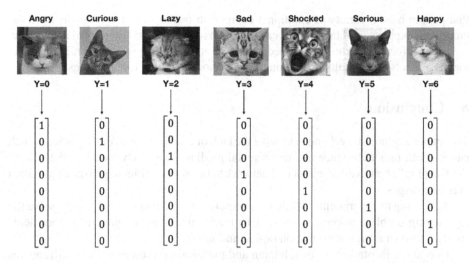

Fig. 11. Examples for each emotional expression vocabulary, and explanation of how we represent the labels

The value of each nodes in output layer is the neural network's prediction. Therefore, the vocabulary corresponding to the largest value between O1, O2.... is the predictive result of the neural network (see Fig. 10).

The final performance is 0.87, which is basically satisfactory. The result shows the program can effectively predict the emotional class of the photo of cat's head. When the user uploads a image, the backstage automatically predicts the category of emotional labels that match the image. Also, tags of high possibilities can be generated for the user to choose. With more and more data are collected, the accuracy of prediction will improve a lot.

5   Summary of Research Methods

Based on the "Cloud Pet Keeping" phenomenon, which is the new phenomenon rising in Chinese UGC background,as the example, this article tries to explore a mechanism to provide emotional tags for photos to help users to retrieve more accurate information.

Future Direction The possible future direction of improvement in experiment are summarized as follows:

- **Use colorful images.** The color contains lots of information, which will have a certain influence on people's mind when observing the image, thus affecting the emotional expression.
- **Use the whole body image of the target.** Body language and gesture may lead to a different interpretation of the object's emotions.

Consider the Special Effects of the Image.   There are more and more people that are accustomed to use various filters to process images before uploading them. The indicates that people have a variety of emotional expression needs. Learning to understand the emotional expression of these filters can also help to know users' emotional experience.

More information can be obtained by incorporating more factors. While, this also means a much larger scale of computation and more complex rules settings.

6   Conclusion

This paper explores a mechanism to solve the lack of emotional tags of the photos, which causing bad user experience in today's social medias. This study based on the "Cloud Pet Keeping" phenomenon, use neural network to build a classifier to generate emotional tags for images.

According to experiment's result, the generation mechanism can positively solve the tag-lacking problem at certain extent. This mechanism can be applied to other fields such as product design, information design and so on.

Due to the limitation of time, human and materials and there must be differences existed in culture and emotional expression of each country, this study is just an exploratory experiment. Researchers can consider perfecting the mechanism by expanding the data amount, enriching the data types and so on to make the mechanism to adapt to a broader situation.

References

1. Daugherty, T., Eastin, M.S., Bright, L.: Exploring consumer motivations for creating user-generated content. J. Interact. Advert. **8**(2), 16–25 (2008)
2. Liang, N., Zhong, J., Wang, D., Zhang, L.: The Exploration of user knowledge architecture based on mining user generated contents – an application case of photo-sharing website. In: Marcus, A. (ed.) DUXU 2016. LNCS, vol. 9748, pp. 180–192. Springer, Cham (2016). https://doi.org/10.1007/978-3-319-40406-6_17
3. Wang, D., Liang, N., Zhong, J., Zhang, L.: Mining and construction of user experience content: an approach of feature analysis based on image. In: Marcus, A. (ed.) DUXU 2016. LNCS, vol. 9748, pp. 223–234. Springer, Cham (2016). https://doi.org/10.1007/978-3-319-40406-6_21
4. Xie, M., Zhang, L., Liang, T.: A Quantitative study of emotional experience of Daqi based on cognitive integration. In: Marcus, A., Wang, W. (eds.) DUXU 2017. LNCS, vol. 10288, pp. 306–323. Springer, Cham (2017). https://doi.org/10.1007/978-3-319-58634-2_24
5. Liang, T., Zhang, L., Xie, M.: Research on image emotional semantic retrieval mechanism based on cognitive quantification model. In: Marcus, A., Wang, W. (eds.) DUXU 2017. LNCS, vol. 10290, pp. 115–128. Springer, Cham (2017). https://doi.org/10.1007/978-3-319-58640-3_10
6. Zhong, J., Wang, D., Liang, N., Zhang, L.: Research on user experience driven product architecture of smart device. In: Marcus, A. (ed.) DUXU 2016. LNCS, vol. 9748, pp. 425–434. Springer, Cham (2016). https://doi.org/10.1007/978-3-319-40406-6_41
7. LeCun, Y., Bengio, Y., Hinton, G.: Deep learning. Nature **521**(7553), 436 (2015)
8. Johnson, S.: Stephen Johnson on Digital Photography. O'Reilly, Sebastopol (2006). ISBN 0-596-52370-X
9. 邓铸, 朱晓红. 心理统计学与 SPSS 应用[M]. 华东师范大学出版社 (2009)

10. Poynton, C.: The Magnitude of Nonconstant Luminance Errors in Charles Poynton, A Technical Introduction to Digital Video. WIley, New York (1996)
11. Fox, E.: Emotion Science Cognitive and Neuroscientific Approaches to Understanding Human Emotions. Palgrave Macmillan, Basingstoke (2008)
12. Carstensen, L.L., Pasupathi, M., Mayr, U., Nesselroade, J.R.: Emotional experience in everyday life across the adult life span. J. Personal. Soc. Psychol. **79**, 644 (2000)
13. Perez, L., Wang, J.: The effectiveness of data augmentation in image classification using deep learning (2017)
14. Vasconcelos, C.N., Vasconcelos, B.N.: Increasing deep learning melanoma classification by classical and expert knowledge based image transforms. CoRR, abs/1702.07025 (2017)
15. Marchesi, M.: Megapixel size image creation using generative adversarial networks. ArXiv e-prints, May 2017
16. Xu, Y., Jia, R., Mou, L., Li, G., Chen, Y., Lu, Y., Jin, Z.: Improved relation classification by deep recurrent neural networks with data augmentation. CoRR, abs/1601.03651 (2016)

Persona Design for Just-in-Time Adaptive and Persuasive Interfaces in Menopause Self-care

Amaury Trujillo[1,2(✉)], Caterina Senette[1], and Maria Claudia Buzzi[1]

[1] IIT-CNR, 56124 Pisa, Italy
{amaury.trujillo,caterina.senette,claudia.buzzi}@iit.cnr.it
[2] Dipartimento di Informatica, Università di Pisa, 56127 Pisa, Italy

Abstract. Despite the recent increase in research and development of mobile self-care tools, there are very few solutions regarding the prevention of negative health effects of menopause. Moreover, most of these solutions are not based on well-founded user models, such as personas, and fail to seize the potential of persuasive mobile technology, which results in a user experience that is neither engaging nor adaptive. In this paper, we describe how we designed personas during the development of a mobile application for menopause self-care. For this design, we used the principles of the Persuasive Systems Design model and the Just-in-Time Adaptive Interventions framework, along with participatory techniques and demographic data analysis. This approach is not limited to menopause, as it could be used to reliably represent users in the interaction design of mobile self-care solutions in other health-related domains.

Keywords: Personas · Self-care application · m-Health

1 Introduction

The world population is aging rapidly, especially in the most economically developed countries. This demographic shift implies significant changes at the societal and economic levels, and has already begun to have a negative impact on public healthcare systems. For these reasons, there has been increasing interest in healthy aging and personal self-care, particularly by means of innovative Information and Communication Technology (ICT). The plethora of available health and fitness smartphone applications (apps), as well as related research initiatives, are a prime example of this phenomenon. However, most of these apps are merely trackers that do not adapt to users' health status and behavior, and many do not apply best practices to human-computer interaction (HCI), with both factors leading to poor user adherence. These issues are particularly true for the few available apps for women that focus on menopause and its effects.

Menopause is a natural and inevitable part of women's aging, involving the loss of the body's reproductive function and significant hormonal changes during the menopausal transition. In turn, women's health-related quality of life changes during this transition, often in relation to the absence or presence of symptoms [1]. Although each woman's experience varies widely, these symptoms include hot flashes and night sweats, urogenital atrophy, sexual dysfunction, mood changes, bone loss, and a predisposition

A. Marcus and W. Wang (Eds.): DUXU 2018, LNCS 10920, pp. 94–109, 2018.
https://doi.org/10.1007/978-3-319-91806-8_8

to diabetes and cardiovascular disease [2]. However, many women ignore such changes and risks, and do not realize the need to improve their health-related behavior and life-style to reduce the negative effects of menopause. Inspired by the increasing prevalence of smartphones across the general population, we think that an adaptive and personalized app that empowers women regarding their menopausal transition would greatly aid in self-care. This is the main rationale behind the ongoing project Vita Nova.

Vita Nova involves the development of a mobile app and service to accompany and coach women regarding menopause, automatically adapting to their wants and needs in order to induce positive health-related behavioral changes. The main goal of the service is to reduce the higher cardiovascular risk inherent in the menopausal transition. A multidisciplinary consortium in the Tuscany Region (Italy) is currently carrying out the project. This consortium is composed of members with different backgrounds and expertise: three private companies (business and ICT services), a public research organ-ization (data modelling and HCI research), a public university (women-related bio-clin-ical and socioeconomics research), and an external consultant (psychology). From the beginning the consortium decided to utilize a user-centered design, in order to overcome many of the aforementioned HCI issues of user adherence in health-related apps. However, we soon realized that research on interaction design of health-related apps for our target users (women in pre-menopause and menopause) was almost non-existent. As a result, we had little information and few guidelines on which to base the persona method in order to better define and communicate certain aspects of the project (e.g., the app's core features and interaction flows). In light of this, we decided to take advantage of the research we were already doing regarding women's health status and behavior, health-related persuasion, and self-care through mobile technology, in order to create such personas, as detailed in the following sections.

2   Background

2.1   Self-Care Through Mobile Health Solutions

By self-care, we refer to the activities people perform in order to prevent their own disease, limit their own illness, and promote and restore their own health, without professional aid but relying on skills and knowledge derived from both lay and profes-sional experience [3]. Health promotion has traditionally been the domain of healthcare professionals, but recent advances in ICT, the ever-increasing burden of healthcare systems, and the ideology of patient empowerment have led to a shift toward personal self-care. In particular, the spread of pervasive and ubiquitous computing (e.g., smart-phones, wearable devices, domestic sensors) has spurred the development of mobile health technology and solutions (also known as m-Health) for self-care. Nonetheless, the availability of m-Health self-care solutions specifically targeting women in meno-pause, as well as the respective scientific literature, are very limited. Moreover, most of these solutions only offer tracking of diet and symptoms, and general information about menopause, or they are used in very narrow clinical contexts. Among the few available apps present in the scientific literature we find MenoPro, conceived and designed for iOS and Android by the North American Menopause Society [4]. MenoPro has the goal of helping gynecology clinicians decide whether patients should undertake pharmaco-logical treatment for menopausal symptoms. MenoPro is intended to be used not only by clinicians, but also by women, as it offers a patient mode. However, this mode has very limited features, as it does not offer self-monitoring over time, is restricted to women aged over 45 years, and does not take into consideration behavioral changes. Furthermore, the available research related to this app does not seem to take into account design aspects of human-computer interaction.

In fact, we found only one study that specifically focuses on the HCI aspect of designing apps for women in menopause [5]. This study investigated the needs of middle-aged Korean women for a menopause-related app, using focus group interviews. The main features of the app envisioned were menstrual tracking and social network support. Given that this study was on the early stages of the app's development cycle, there is no information regarding interaction mechanisms and workflow, nor references to a particular behavior change theory. The study concluded that such an app should be simple and validated by healthcare professionals, and it should provide personalized suggestions, means for social support (family and friends), and comprehensible tracking and data visualization tools. These results are in line with a study on the quality of health and fitness apps in general [6], which identified the fundamental features that such apps should have: user-friendly interfaces, low learning curve, reliable, real-time personal-ized feed-back, user customization, incorporation of evidence-based behavior change techniques, involvement of health professionals, and social networking support. Inci-dentally, all of these characteristics are closely related to the more general design of effective persuasive technology.

2.2 Persuasive Systems

Since time immemorial people have tried to learn how to persuade other people to do or believe something. For instance, already in ancient Greece Aristotle identified three fundamental kinds of persuasive appeal: *ethos*, appeal to ethics, based on the credibility of the persuader; *pathos*, appeal to emotion, based on creating an emotional response; and *logos*, an appeal to logic, based on reason. Interestingly, these and other principles of rhetoric described by Aristotle and later scholars can also be applied to computer systems that act as persuaders, as stated by Fogg [7], the pioneer of persuasive systems. Fogg proposed the use of *computers as persuasive technologies*, a field of study that he called *captology*, based on the acronym of the subject matter [8]. Although the term captology has fallen into disuse [9], Fogg's work paved the way to more recent and detailed conceptual models for persuasive technology, such as the Persuasive Systems Design (PSD) model. PSD was developed by Oinas-Kukkonen and Harjumaa to design and evaluate persuasive systems, as well as to describe their content and software func-tionality [10]. In the context of PSD, the authors build upon their prior definition of persuasive systems as "computerized software or information systems designed to rein-force, change or shape attitudes or behaviors or both without using coercion or decep-tion" [11]. Accordingly, PSD derives its principles from psychology and rhetoric, adapting them to the intersection of four key computer-based fields: human-computer interaction, computer-mediated communication, information systems, and affective computing [12]. The PSD conceptual model (see Fig. 1) is divided into two main aspects: *persuasion context* and *design principles.* The *persuasion context* is composed of three elements that influence whether persuasion can take place or not: intent, event, and strategy. The *design principles* of the PSD model focus on the system's operational level of persuasion and are divided into four dimensions: primary task support, dialogue support, system credibility support, and social support. For a more detailed description of both aspects see [10].

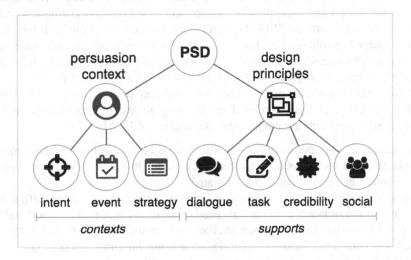

Fig. 1. Overview of the PSD conceptual model

It should be noted that PSD is a general model that can be used across heterogeneous domains such as education and learning [13], ecological consumption [14], marketing and commerce [15], as well as public security and safety [16]. Nonetheless, the health-related domain is the most prevalent area in which PSD is used. For instance, a 2014 review [9] on the efficacy of persuasive technology in 95 studies (in 89 papers), reported that 47.4% of them were related to a health and/or exercise setting, among which several were based on the PSD model. Incidentally, the review's authors concluded that "persuasive technologies indeed seem to persuade people into various behaviors" [9], with one decisive aspect being whether the user is trying to accomplish the target change with or without the system. For health-related initiatives this aspect is less of a problem, as people usually want to improve their own health status regardless of the use technology. Furthermore, the use of PSD has been shown to have positive effects on adherence to health-related persuasive systems that are remotely accessible, such as web-based interventions [17]. For these reasons, we deem PSD particularly apt as the underlying model for persuasive self-care applications, but we think that it is not specific enough to deliver health-related behavior interventions via mobile technology.

2.3   Just-in-Time Adaptive Interventions

Health-related behavior interventions (henceforth *interventions*) are efforts that promote behavioral changes to improve a person's health status and reduce potential risk factors. Therefore, an intervention can be seen as a specialized kind of persuasion regarding health behavior. An *adaptive intervention* is "a sequence of decision rules that specify how intervention options should be adapted to an individual's characteristics and changing needs, with the general aim to optimize the long-term effectiveness of the intervention" [18]. Expanding on this concept and based on the existing research on mobile health apps, around 2014 the framework *just-in-time adaptive interventions* (JITAI) emerged. A solution based on JITAI aims to "provide information, nudges, and interventions when needed or appropriate, tailored to the individual's needs and context, via mobile technologies" [19]. The JITAI framework is composed of four key components common to any adaptive intervention: decision points, intervention options, tailoring variables, and decision rules. The following are descriptions adapted from [20] of how these components are employed in the context of JITAI.

- *Decision points* are points in time at which decisions regarding treatment must be made. In JITAI their selection and frequency are flexible, and they can be classified as scientist-specified or participant-initiated.
- *Intervention options* include the types of support (instrumental, emotional), sources of support (automated, professional, peer group), and modes of support delivery (support provision and/or support availability). In the continuum of health *proximal-distal outcomes*, intervention options that target proximal outcomes are crucial, especially in the case of heightened user vulnerability.
- *Tailoring variables* are specific pieces of information concerning the user that are used to make treatment decisions. These variables can be gathered through active assessments, passive assessments, or both.
- *Decision rules* operationalize individualization by specifying which intervention option to offer, to whom, and when (Fig. 2), according to the values of tailoring variables. They systematically connect tailoring variables (along with their levels, thresholds and ranges) with intervention options, in the form of *if-then* statements.

The JITAI framework is a promising reference methodology for developing not only smartphone health and fitness apps, but also solutions for other ubiquitous and pervasive computing technologies. Despite being relatively new, JITAI has already been proposed or used to develop solutions for depression and anxiety [21], to reduce sedentariness [22], and, in particular, to treat addictive behavior [23], including quitting smoking [24]. However, there are some open questions regarding best practices for design and implementation of JITAI, such as the use of micro-randomized trials [25]. Nonetheless, we think that JITAI, together with PSD, could also be used to improve the interaction design process of a persuasive and adaptive mobile health app, particularly in the definition of personas.

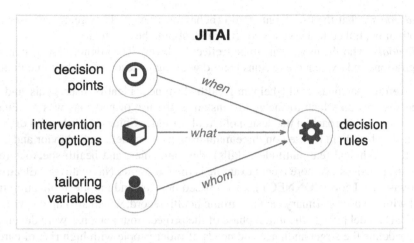

Fig. 2. Main components of the JITAI framework

2.4 Persona Use in Product Design

Personas, or user models, "are detailed, composite user archetypes that represent distinct groupings of behaviors, attitudes, aptitudes, goals, and motivations" [26]. They were introduced in 1998 by Alan Cooper as a support method for interaction design [27]. The key idea behind the method is that "the best way to successfully accommodate a variety of users is to design for specific types of individuals with specific needs" [26], and that personas represent those users with the larger set of key characteristics. Thus, personas help designers determine what a product is and its behavior, communicate with project's stakeholders, build consensus and commitment around the product design, measure the design's effectiveness, and contribute to other project efforts (e.g., marketing and sales).

Personas mainly describe the context of people's behavior regarding a certain product—behavior that is primarily motivated by people's goals. Thus, goals should guide the design of a product's functions and the tasks with which people attain them. To better characterize people's goals in product design, we can refer to the three-leveled theory of cognitive and emotional processing, introduced by Norman [28]. Its design levels, in increasing order, are: (1) *visceral*, the intuitive reaction to a product's sensory aspects (e.g., visual, touch, aural) that are perceived prior to significant interaction; (2) *behavioral* (simple daily behaviors), which can enhance or inhibit both visceral reactions and reflective responses and has been the main focus of traditional design; (3) *reflective*, which involves reflection and careful thought on past experiences, and can enhance or inhibit behavioral processing, yet does not affect visceral reactions. Each level has a different timeframe (the shorter the more immediate) and degree of consciousness (the higher the more conscious), and implies different design considerations. Based this theory, in interaction design and to better define personas, we could delineate three types of user goals [26]:

- *Experience goals:* how the user wants to feel (visceral level). They provide focus for a product's sensorial characteristics: visual design, physical design, interactive feel (latency, transitions, etc.).

- *End goals:* what the user wants to do (behavioral level). They represent user task motivation, linked to a given product, which should be satisfied.
- *Life goals:* who the user wants to be (reflective level). They denote users' personal aspirations and explain the reasons behind wanting to accomplish their end goals.

Therefore, personas could help m-Health designers identify user goals and the desired features on which to focus. For instance, the use of personas was a valuable methodological approach in the design of a tool for older Chinese people with diabetes [29], in which authors focused on three main aspects to model user behavior and characteristics: technical (e.g., attitudes, skills), demographics, and health specifics (e.g., diagnosis, practices). A more recent example is the Consumer Navigation of Electronic Cardiovascular Tools (CONNECT), a web-based desktop and mobile application integrated with the user's primary care electronic health record, which also made great use of the PSD model [30]. In the initial phase of the project, four personas were developed to better define the target audience and needs of older people with high risk of cardiovascular disease. The personas' definition included information such as cardiovascular risk, occupation, household composition, ethnicity, as well as the persona's story, needs, health motivations, influencers, opportunities, frustrations, and relationship with healthcare providers and to technology. Then, the designers specified the persuasion context and design principles of CONNECT according to the PSD model.

For this reason, our persona design process expands this approach by taking into consideration not only the PSD model but also the JITAI framework, to better define user goals and attributes in the context of m-Health for self-care.

3 Persona Design Process

In order to define the personas for Vita Nova, we first conducted initial participatory user research, with both consortium stakeholders and a sample of target users; later we defined the features and principles that the service should have based on the PSD model; and finally, we conducted an expert consultation and demographic analysis to define the initial set of tailoring variables for JITAI. These steps are detailed below.

3.1 Initial Participatory User Research

Although there are several approaches to persona design, prior to their description there should always be extensive user research and analysis, typically carried out by gathering data obtained from a combination of user interviews, internal discussions, and direct observation [31]. It should be noted that Cooper's original interaction design process does not consider personas as part of a participatory approach. In PD, actual (or potential) users are involved along the design process, whereas personas are models intentionally built based on aggregated data collected from actual (or potential) users. Nonetheless, the use of personas in PD has been proven useful for scenario design and product development in general [32], since they share common data gathering techniques. Accordingly, we used a set of PD practices for moderate group sizes (up to 40 participants) and in the phases of the project, midway between the design activities and the user world, based on the taxonomy of Muller and Kuhn for PD practices [33]. In our case, we had already started with a participatory design (PD) approach, involving both the project consortium members and potential end users of the app, to better define the consortium's vision according to their comments [34].

First, we held semi-structured workshops with members of the consortium to consolidate a common vision of the app and a set of expected core functionalities. We then conducted focus group interviews (FGI) with 26 potential users, all women aged 48 to 69 years, to understand their wants and needs, and to gather qualitative feedback on the consortium's vision of the app. Based on this feedback the consortium decided to use storyboard prototyping and conduct a questionnaire to refine the app's core features with an available subset of the FGI participants (18 this time). The storyboards depicted five main use case scenarios to describe how a user would interact with the app and vice versa. As the storyboards' protagonist we used a *provisional persona* called *Laura,* a persona not based upon detailed qualitative data [26], which acted as a rhetorical tool to communicate the consortium's assumptions about the target users and the initial vision of app's main features. Laura is a 50-year-old woman; she is a low-rate daily smoker, performs moderate physical activity, frequently eats unhealthy food, has a moderate body mass index (BMI), and works in an office environment. Laura would like to achieve and maintain a healthier weight, which is why she bought a wearable fitness tracker to monitor her progress while walking briskly. However, she has already begun the menopause transition and is suffering its effects, especially frequent hot flashes. For these reasons, she is interested in an app to better manage her symptoms during menopause and attain a better health-related quality of life.

As a result of this initial approach, we gathered valuable data from the participants regarding smartphone and wearable device use, personal health behavior and tracking habits, interest in the app, and desired functionalities, content, and interaction flows, as well as disposition of and concerns about personal information. These data in turn allowed us to narrow the experience, end, and life goals of our personas. In our case, the primary life goal of users is to attain and maintain a good health-related quality of life during and after menopause. To achieve this, participants wanted the flexibility to focus on as few or many end goals as desired, such as symptom monitoring, diet improvement, physical activity increase, etc. And because of the utmost importance given to their health, participants' experience goals primarily focus on understandable content, professional-looking but friendly appearance, app's credibility and validity, responsive interface, and reassurance in terms of security and privacy. Accordingly, we decided to focus on six user aspects, which we grouped into two sets (see Fig. 3). The first set, health status and behavior (bio-clinical condition, vital statistics and lifestyle, and psychological traits and condition), is the basis of the persuasion context. The second set, user interaction features (skills and knowledge, service expectations, and health goals), is the basis of the interaction design principles.

Fig. 3. Main aspects of Vita Nova's personas

3.2 Selection of PSD Features and Principles

Based on the outcomes of our participatory user research and on the PSD model heuristic described in [12], we outlined the persuasion context and the design principles for our system as follows.

Persuasion Context

- *Intent.* The system aims to persuade Italian women to adopt and maintain good health-related behaviors before, during, and after the menopausal transition, as well as to inform them about menopause (i.e., both behavior and attitude changes). The *persuader* is a multidisciplinary consortium of private and public organizations (detailed in the Introduction), which aims to improve the health-related quality of life of women in menopause, opening as a result new research and commercial opportunities.
- *Event.* The *use context* is about personalized, adaptive and automatic self-care for women in menopause, with the menopausal transition usually starting around ages 45–60 years, although we also target women in early menopause. We revised the age of target users compared to our initial FGI based on the feedback of our health experts, taking into account the preventative scope of Vita Nova. The *user context* of the system regards women who are interested and willing to reduce menopausal effects

and improve their health in a simple and independent manner via innovative mobile technologies. The use of the latter is the basis of the *technology context*: an online mobile application that is primarily single-user, but with a few multi-user features (e.g., to allow peer support).

- *Strategy.* The message will be primarily in the form of a tracking and assistive health tool. The type of content will be informational (general tips, personalized suggestions) and stimulant (alarms, reminders, action prompts). The kind of appeal will be a mix between *logos, pathos,* and *ethos,* which will be adapted to the user based on the principles of the JITAI framework. The *route* will be indirect, with the several available arguments being tailored to the user.

Design Principles

- *Primary task support.* We will use reduction (simplifying the information available to users, with the possibility of more detailed information if needed), tailoring and personalization (based on JITAI), self-monitoring (e.g., diet, symptoms, physical activity, humor), and simulation.
- *Dialogue support.* We will use praise, reminders, suggestions (both general and personalized), similarity and liking (necessary to appeal to users' visceral level of cognitive functioning and satisfy their experience goals).
- *System credibility support.* Besides aiming at a professional and simple look-and-feel (surface credibility) based Google's Material Design guidelines, we will provide validated suggestions and information, based on the experience and knowledge of our health-related experts (trustworthiness, expertise, authority, verifiability), as well as providing the necessary contact means for the consortium's representatives (real-world feel).
- *Social support.* At the moment, we will focus primarily on the use of recognition, cooperation, and competition as a means of interacting with other persons.

3.3 Tailoring Variables for Women's Health Status and Behavior

Regarding the JITAI framework, we had already started to work on tailoring variables to model women's health status and behavior in pre-menopause and menopause, before realizing that such variables could be influenced by the persona definition, and at the same time these variables could influence the personas. Therefore, we had also adjusted the persona design, and will continue to do so if necessary, taking into account the tailoring variables and vice versa, as well as the project's persuasion context and design principles. To define these variables, the user modelling team, together with the health-related experts, made use of their experience and knowledge of the domain, as well as the state-of-the-art literature. In many variable definitions, we also have made use of data analyses and reports on women's health and socio-economics from the Italian National Institute for Statistics (ISTAT).

At the moment of writing, an initial set of 75 tailoring variables have already been defined. Most of these variables (49) come from the bio-clinical domain (e.g., menopause age onset, smoking, physical activity level, weekly salt consumption, frequency of menopausal symptoms); 16 from the socio-economic domain (e.g., marital status, income level, employment status); and 10 from the psychological domain (e.g., willingness to change, locus of control, appeals). To verify the applicability of these variables and their related wording (e.g., clarity, willingness to respond), we also carried out a questionnaire among potential users. This questionnaire was filled out by 43 participants recruited in the Tuscany region, on a voluntary basis, among a population of women in menopause and pre-menopause who were free of chronic diseases. However, given the sensitive nature of the collected data and based on the aforementioned preventative scope of Vita Nova, once we had the participants' answers we further excluded nine women with a BMI less than 18.5 (underweight) or more than 30 (obesity), or not aged 40–60 years, leaving 34 participants who corresponded to our target users.

Thanks to this questionnaire we were able to refine our JITAI tailoring variables where needed, and we also gathered valuable information for the definition of our personas. For instance, of the aforementioned 34 participants, 15 declared themselves to be in menopause, and one was unsure about it. The average BMI of these participants was 22.1 (s = 2.8). Regarding smoking, eight of them are smokers, with an average of 8.8 cigarettes a day (s = 3.1), and two of them were former smokers. All of those who were smokers declared being rather insecure regarding their control over smoking. With regard to physical activity, the average minutes a week of moderate physical activity were 158.5 (s = 197), and 34.2 min a week (s = 74) of intense physical activity. Concerning the perceived inconvenience of symptoms related to menopause, the five most important symptoms (ordered from more to less inconvenient) were tiredness, mood changes, lack of energy, musculoskeletal pain, and loss of concentration.

As our JITAI components' definition continues to evolve we also expect to update our persona description in order to maintain a dynamic yet consistent user representation. In particular, once Vita Nova has attained a reliable user base, these data could also be complemented with historic data on users' behavior or demographics.

3.4 Vita Nova's Personas

Based on the qualitative and quantitative data of the participatory user research and our variable questionnaire, we proceeded to map participants' behavioral variables to identify eventual patterns. For this, we used a relative linear mapping approach, as suggested by Cooper [26], in which we could visually identify clusters of participants along a behavioral axis, as illustrated in Fig. 4. Then, on the basis of the previously identified PSD principles and features, and taking into account the tailoring variables of JITAI, we selected the personas' main attributes that cover our six aspects of interest (Fig. 3). Finally, based on these attributes and behavior patterns, we created four personas: *Anna*, a 52-year-old housewife in perimenopause; *Elena*, a 48-year-old office worker in menopause; *Beatrice*, a 58-year-old retiree approaching post-menopause; and *Carla*, a 44-year-old bank clerk in early menopause. Anna is the primary persona, i.e., she is the main target of our design. Elena, Beatrice, and Carla are secondary personas. In addition, in order to better communicate with the project stakeholders, we created an overview format in which each persona could be succinctly described. For instance, Fig. 5 represents the overview of Anna.

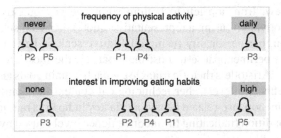

Fig. 4. Example of participants' behavioral mapping

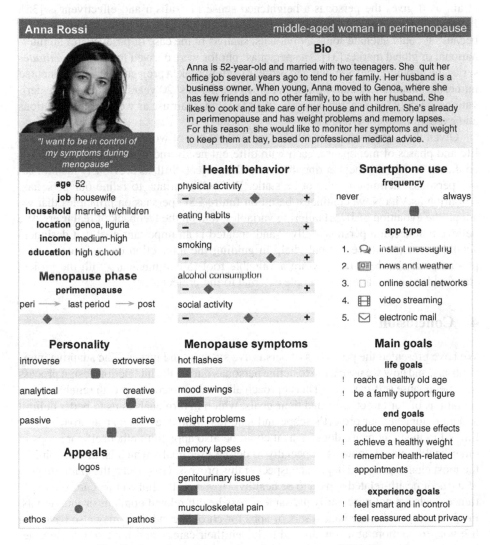

Fig. 5. Overview of *Anna*, the primary persona of Vita Nova

In this overview, from top left to bottom right, we can quickly understand the persona's main motivation (using a representative quote), her vital statistics and socio-economic situation, her personality (using qualitative scales), her current menopause phase status (from perimenopause to post-menopause), the most effective appeals to persuade her (using Aristotle's rhetoric triangle), what her main goals are (at the visceral, behavioral, and reflective levels), her technological context in regards to smartphone use, as well as her menopause-related behavior (via key indicators ranging from negative to positive) and condition (indicating the inconvenience level caused by the main menopause symptoms).

To depict our personas, we decided to use photos instead of drawings or no picture at all, as it gives the personas a heightened sense of realism and effectiveness [35]. However, it should be noted that in some instances the use of photos may not be desirable because it could alienate some individuals, such as in the case of products for an international or global market [31]. The personas' photos were derived from the *Exactitudes* series, by photographer Versluis and profiler Uyttenbroek, a project that has documented numerous identities in major European cities for the past 20 years. Because these derivations are only for research purposes, they fall under fair use as well as the limitations and exceptions to copyright.

Given that our personas are reliable representations of women in different stages of life and phases of menopause, each with different needs and wants, the consortium is confident in utilizing them during the rest of the project. Still, as previously mentioned, our personas' definition will not be static. We will continue to refine our personas' definition as Vita Nova continues, based on future PSD persuasion principles that we adopt, the evolution of JITAI tailoring variables, and on the feedback of real users. We believe that keeping personas "alive" and updated is an important goal that designers should pursue, as these not only help in guiding the interaction design process of a product, but also because they are a valuable tool to communicate with the project stakeholders, users, and other people external to the project.

4   Conclusion

We have presented the principles of persuasive systems and just-in-time adaptive interventions, and how we used them to define personas during the interaction design process of a menopause self-care app. This approach allowed us to come up with reliable representations of our target users and their goals, which in turn enables us to better delimit and communicate our project's scope and features. Moreover, such an approach is not limited to the menopause domain, as it could be also applied to other self-care apps in other health-related domains, especially to define user goals, which is, in our opinion, the most challenging and important aspect of this process. Obviously, the main life goal of users of health-related apps is to be healthy. However, the linked life, end, and experience goals are not necessarily the same across health-related domains or individuals. For instance, on the one hand, users of apps for chronic conditions may also have as a life goal to be more autonomous and to lessen their caregivers' burden. On the other hand, users of fitness apps may also have as a life goal to be more attractive and popular, as staying fit is a status symbol. By the same token, a chronic patient may prefer a simple and reliable device regardless of its aesthetics (experience goal) to ensure daily pill intake (end goal); while a fitness user may desire a stylish and elegant wearable device (experience goal) to monitor and improve workout performance (end goal). Finally, we hope that our research inspires future studies regarding mobile self-care solutions focused on women's health.

Acknowledgements. This work was supported by the Vita Nova project (CUP CIPE D18C15000130008), funded by the Tuscany Region and the Italian Ministry of Education, Universities and Research (MIUR), as part of the PAR FAS (now FSC) and FAR programs. We would also like to express our gratitude to Giulia Mascagni and Andrea Giannini of the University of Pisa for their contribution in the definition of the tailoring variables, as well as for their help in organizing and recruiting participants for our focus group interviews and questionnaires.

 Regione Toscana   **FAS Fondo Aree Sottoutilizzate 2007-2013**   REPUBBLICA ITALIANA

References

1. Avis, N.E., et al.: Change in health-related quality of life over the menopausal transition in a multiethnic cohort of middle-aged women. In: Study of Women's Health Across the Nation (SWAN), Menopause (New York, NY), vol. 16, no. 5, p. 860 (2009)
2. Davis, S.R., et al.: Menopause. Nat. Rev. Disease Prim. **1**, 15054 (2015)
3. Levin, L.S., Idler, E.L.: Self-care in health. Annu. Rev. Publ. Health **4**(1), 181–201 (1983)
4. Manson, J.E., et al.: Algorithm and mobile app for menopausal symptom management and hormonal/non-hormonal therapy decision making: a clinical decision-support tool from The North American Menopause Society. Menopause **22**(3), 247–253 (2015)
5. Lee, M., et al.: Understanding women's needs in menopause for development of mHealth. In: Proceedings of 2015 Workshop on Pervasive Wireless Healthcare. ACM (2015)
6. Higgins, J.P.: Smartphone applications for patients' health and fitness. Am. J. Med. **129**(1), 11–19 (2016)
7. Fogg, B.J.: Persuasive computers: perspectives and research directions. In: Proceedings of SIGCHI Conference on Human Factors in Computing Systems. ACM Press/Addison-Wesley Publishing Co. (1998)
8. Fogg, B.: Captology: the study of computers as persuasive technologies. In: CHI 1997 Extended Abstracts on Human Factors in Computing Systems. ACM (1997)
9. Hamari, J., Koivisto, J., Pakkanen, T.: Do persuasive technologies persuade? - a review of empirical studies. In: Spagnolli, A., Chittaro, L., Gamberini, L. (eds.) PERSUASIVE 2014. LNCS, vol. 8462, pp. 118–136. Springer, Cham (2014). https://doi.org/10.1007/978-3-319-07127-5_11
10. Oinas-Kukkonen, H., Harjumaa, M.: Persuasive systems design: key issues, process model, and system features. Commun. Assoc. Inf. Syst. **24**(1), 28 (2009)

11. Oinas-Kukkonen, H., Harjumaa, M.: Towards deeper understanding of persuasion in software and information systems. In: First International Conference on Advances in Computer-Human Interaction. IEEE (2008)
12. Torning, K., Oinas-Kukkonen, H.: Persuasive system design: state of the art and future directions. In: Proceedings of 4th International Conference on Persuasive Technology. ACM (2009)
13. Ashaikh, R.A., Wilson, S., Jones, S.: A persuasive social actor for activity awareness in learning groups. In: Proceedings of 30th International BCS Human Computer Interaction Conference: Fusion! BCS Learning & Development Ltd. (2016)
14. Shevchuk, N., Oinas-Kukkonen, H.: Exploring green information systems and technologies as persuasive systems: a systematic review of applications in published research (2016)
15. Alhammad, M.M., Gulliver, S.R.: Online persuasion for e-commerce websites. In: Proceedings of 28th International BCS Human Computer Interaction Conference on HCI 2014-Sand, Sea and Sky-Holiday HCI. BCS (2014)
16. Kotthaus, C., Ludwig, T., Pipek, V.: Persuasive system design analysis of mobile warning apps for citizens (2011)
17. Kelders, S.M., et al.: Persuasive system design does matter: a systematic review of adherence to web-based interventions. J. Med. Internet Res. 14(6), 2–25 (2012)
18. Nahum-Shani, I., et al.: Experimental design and primary data analysis methods for comparing adaptive interventions. Psychol. Methods 17(4), 457 (2012)
19. Spruijt-Metz, D., Nilsen, W.: Dynamic models of behavior for just-in-time adaptive interventions. IEEE Pervasive Comput. 13(3), 13–17 (2014)
20. Nahum-Shani, I., et al.: Just in time adaptive interventions (JITAIs): an organizing framework for ongoing health behavior support. Methodology Center Technical report (14-126) (2014)
21. Schueller, S.M., Aguilera, A., Mohr, D.C.: Ecological momentary interventions for depression and anxiety. Depress. Anxiety 34, 540–545 (2017)
22. Thomas, J.G., Bond, D.S.: Behavioral response to a just-in-time adaptive intervention (JITAI) to reduce sedentary behavior in obese adults: implications for JITAI optimization. Health Psychol. 34(S), 1261 (2015)
23. Goldstein, S.P., et al.: Return of the JITAI: applying a just-in-time adaptive intervention framework to the development of m-Health solutions for addictive behaviors. Int. J. Behav. Med. 24, 673–682 (2017)
24. Naughton, F.: Delivering "Just-In-Time" smoking cessation support via mobile phones: current knowledge and future directions. Nicotine Tob. Res. 19(3), 379–383 (2017)
25. Klasnja, P., et al.: Microrandomized trials: an experimental design for developing just-in-time adaptive interventions. Health Psychol. 34(1), 1220 (2015)
26. Cooper, A., Reimann, R., Cronin, D.: About Face 3: The Essentials of Interaction Design. Wiley, New York (2007)
27. Cooper, A.: The Inmates are Running the Asylum-Why High-Tech Products Drive Us Crazy and How 2 to Restore the Sanity. SAMS, Carmel (1999). ISBN 0-67231-649-8
28. Norman, D.: Emotional Design. Basic Books, New York (2005)
29. LeRouge, C., et al.: User profiles and personas in the design and development of consumer health technologies. Int. J. Med. Inform. 82(11), e251–e268 (2013)
30. Neubeck, L., et al.: Development of an integrated e-health tool for people with, or at high risk of, cardiovascular disease: The Consumer Navigation of Electronic Cardiovascular Tools (CONNECT) web application. Int. J. Med. Inform. 96, 24–37 (2016)
31. Nielsen, L., et al.: A template for design personas: analysis of 47 persona descriptions from danish industries and organizations. Int. J. Sociotechnol. Knowl. Dev. (IJSKD) 7(1), 45–61 (2015)

32. Grudin, J., Pruitt, J.: Personas, participatory design and product development: an infrastructure for engagement. In: PDC (2002)
33. Muller, M.J., Kuhn, S.: Participatory design. Commun. ACM **36**(6), 24–28 (1993)
34. Trujillo, A., Buzzi, M.C.: Participatory user requirements elicitation for personal menopause app. In: Proceedings of 9th Nordic Conference on Human-Computer Interaction. ACM (2016)
35. Giboin, A.: From individual to collective personas modeling realistic groups and communities of users (and not only realistic individual users). In: Fourth International Conference on Advances in Computer-Human Interaction (ACHI 2011) (2011)

Comparing User Experience in Interactions with Different Types of Digital Products

Lemeng Xu, Dede Ma, and Pengyi Zhang[✉]

Department of Information Management, Peking University, Beijing 100871, China
{bbc.lmeng,dedema,pengyi}@pku.edu.cn

Abstract. User experience varies when using different types of digital products. Previous research has studied the relationship between product properties, user behaviors, and emotional experiences. In this research, we conducted a diary study of 29 students over two weeks to examine users' emotional experiences of mobile apps, PC software, and terminal devices in relation to product features, interaction results, and users' feedback. Results show that: (1) Users were less "disappointed" when they interact with mobile apps. (2) Users were often "surprised" when using a terminal device. (3) Users mentioned "aesthetics" more with mobile devices than with terminal devices. (4) Users cared more about task complexity and chose to overcome the problem they have met when using a personal computer. These results provide an exploratory understanding of the relationships between product types and other factors and could be useful to cross-platform designers. The results also suggest that user expectation might have an impact when measuring user experience, and this needs further investigation.

Keywords: Emotional experience · Digital products · Diary study

1 Introduction

We are living in a world that is increasingly pervaded by technology. The digital products we interact with on a daily basis are becoming more and more diversified. For example, we use our smartphones to post first decorated selfies on Instagram, computers to make keynotes for presentations, and terminal devices to buy subway tickets. What users experience is a result of a user's internal states such as expectations and motivations, the properties of the product such as complexity and functionality, and the context such as setting and task [1]. Users' experiences differ when they interact with different types of products [2]. Previous research has studied the relationship between factors of product properties, user behaviors and emotional experiences [3]. Jordan and Persson suggested that approaches to affective design need to consider different types of the product [4]. However, relatively less research has examined and compared the different emotional experiences users undergo when interacting with different types of digital products. In this research, we aim to examine users' emotional experiences of different types of digital products in relation to product features, interaction results, and users' feedback.

The rest of the paper is organized as follows: we first give a review of related research, describe the study design, present the results, and conclude with a summary and discussions of the findings.

© Springer International Publishing AG, part of Springer Nature 2018
A. Marcus and W. Wang (Eds.): DUXU 2018, LNCS 10920, pp. 110–123, 2018.
https://doi.org/10.1007/978-3-319-91806-8_9

2   Literature Review

The term "User Experience" (UX) is widely used in many HCI-related fields ranging from psychology to design and business. For example, Alben defined "experience" as all the aspects of how people use an interactive product, "how well they understand how it works, how they feel about it while they're using it, how well it serves their purpose" [5]. Law and others drew the conclusion that UX is dynamic, context-dependent, and subjective [6].

UX is constituted of several elements [7], such as usability, user interface, interaction design, emotional experience and so on [8]. Previous research also discussed how these elements affect the quality of user experience over time [9]. For example, learnability and novelty may be crucial at first, but product's usefulness and social capital will motivate prolonged use. In this paper, we adopt Kuniavsky's definition that the user experience is "the sum of users' perception as they interact with a product" [10]. These perceptions include effectiveness, efficiency, emotional satisfaction, and the quality of the relationship with the entity that created the product.

We refer to emotional experiences as those typically considered in everyday language about emotions, such as happy, excited, worried, and disappointed. Reeves and Nass suggested that on-screen products evoke emotions, both negative and positive [11]. These emotions have different impacts on action readiness: whereas negative emotions stimulate individuals to withdraw from the object, positive emotions inspire individuals to approach the object [12]. The field of engineering took consumer's feeling into account when designing the products [13]. Relationships between product experience and product properties were used to design more attractive products [14]. Previous research has found that positive emotions are considered to be profitable during product usage. For example, the fact that what is considered beautiful is usable in users' opinion highlights the tight relationships between users' positive emotional experience and system's usability [15]. Products that evoke positive emotions are purchased more often and used more often [16].

Users' responses differed markedly when they interact with different types of the product [4]. Obviously, different types of product bring different features, functions, and aesthetic experiences. There has been a large body of research focusing on these differences. For example, the assessment of a product's novelty affects users' preference [17]. Venkatesh and Davis found that system-specific perceived ease of use will adjust to reflect objective usability and subjective enjoyment [18]. But few research has investigated how basic features such as size, weight, speed, and sound affect user experience.

Previous research also discussed users' feedback when interacting with mobile devices and computers. For example, consumers hold positive attitudes for mobile learning, allowing them to view mobile learning as an efficient tool [19]. Park et al. suggested that domain knowledge and accessibility as external variables had a direct effect on experience in computer use [20]. But how the users' feedback different from interaction with different types of product is still need further exploration.

3 Methods

3.1 Data Collection

Twenty-nine undergraduate students were recruited from two sessions of an information management curriculum. Over a two-week period, the participants were asked to record their interaction process with any kinds of digital products (mobile phones, desktops or terminal devices) in a semi-structured text form.

We received 136 records in total: 41 of mobile apps, 50 of PC software, and 45 of terminal devices. Table 1 shows some example records of the three types of digital products.

Table 1. Example records.

Record ID	Digital product	Record
3805	Camera APP (mobile app)	I used my cell phone camera to take selfies with my friends and captured some beautiful sceneries at Peking University. There were 2 cameras build on my cellphone: the front camera (with lower resolution) and back camera (with higher resolution). Sometimes I felt frustrated to use the front camera because I could not stable my hand when I took selfies and the images got blurred. To completely avoid this problem, I need to use a traditional digital camera or the back camera of my cell phone that have optical image stabilization function when taking selfies. But it will be relatively inconvenient. Therefore, the best solution will be to practice more
2903	PKU course registration (PC software)	As an exchange student, I was required to enroll courses through the course registration portal. However, I had an awful experience towards the Portal System. The biggest problem I encountered was that the webpage did not include a guideline for the first-time user. I did not know what tasks I should do at the current stage and I needed to spend extra time contacting the exchange officers to figure out ways to use the system
209	Carrefour storage machine (terminal device)	I used this machine to save package and take package. There was only one white button on the stocker with the word "save" in the middle, a bar code in the middle, the following was the scanning code to take place, and the screen display position was full and the bar code corresponding to the number of boxes. The machine was simple to meet user needs, the downside was that the "save" button was white, not very noticeable

3.2 Data Analysis

We used ground theory approach to analyze the diary data. After open coding, we further refined our coding scheme based on the emotional categorization provided by Cowie et al.'s typology [21]. Figure 1 shows our final coding scheme. We used Nvivo 11 to conduct the analysis. To ensure the coding stability, two coders coded 50 randomly selected records (30% of all data) independently. The overall Kappa coefficient was 0.62. We then asked the third person to join the discussion and resolved the disagreement in coding, updated the coding scheme, and completed the rest of the coding.

A Emotion			
A1 Engage	A101 Interested	A102 Excited	A103 Pleased	A104 Confident
	A105 Amused	A106 Proud	A107 Calm	A108 Content
A2 Unpredictable	A201 Worried	A202 Surprised	A203 Relived	
A3 Withdraw	A301 Anxious	A302 Bored	A303 Disappointed	A304 Guilty
	A305 Despairing	A306 Hurt	A307 Sad	A308 Ashamed
	A309 Disgust	A310 Annoyed	A311 Embarrased	A312 Afraid
	A313 Frustrated	A314 Miserable	A315 Tired	
B Feature			
B1 Category	B11 Mobile App	B12 PC Software	B13 Terminal Devices	
B2 Attribute	B21 Capacity	B22 Size	B23 Weight	B24 Aesthetic
	B25 Speed	B26 Strength	B27 Complexity	B28 Sound
C Result & Feedback			
C1 Result	C11Success	C12 Failed	C13 Stuck	C14 No feedback
	C15 Unclear	C16 Pop-up	C17 Content Erro	C18 Misoperation
	C19 interrupted			
C2 User Feedback	C21 Re-interact	C22 Wait	C23 Ignore	C24 Overcome
	C25 Giveup	C26 Delete & discard		

Fig. 1. Coding scheme.

We then looked for patterns in the codes across different product categories (B1), for example, whether users experienced different emotions (A) or whether different product attributes were mentioned (B2) when interacting with different product types. In general, we explored whether different types of products have significant differences across other factors. We also examined the contexts of use collected through a questionnaire which will be described in Sect. 3.3.

3.3   Questionnaire Design

In addition to the diary entries, we collected additional information about the context of use, the user proficiency of the product, frequency and motivation of use through a questionnaire. Participants filled in a questionnaire for each diary entry they submitted.

The questionnaire results show that 75% of participants defined themselves as a skilled user (score 4–5) of the mobile apps and PC software, and the other 25% defined themselves as novice users (score 1–3). 64% of participants used their product once a day or once a week, 13% used once a month, and the rest were used much less frequently.

As for contexts of use, 31.6% cases were for studying and 31.6% percent were for entertainments. The other contexts included shopping (11, 8%), social (3, 2.2%), transportation (7, 5.1%), finance (3, 2.2%), dining (7, 5.1%), and others (19, 13.9%). When we asked about the product attributes that they were more concerned about on mobile apps and PC software, the top three attributes were: speed, complexity, and aesthetics. As to terminal devices, participants considered complexity more important than speed, followed by aesthetics.

4   Findings

4.1   Emotional Experience

60% of emotions the participants experienced were "withdraw" emotions such as annoyed, disappointed and frustrated. 30% were "engage" emotions such as pleased, relaxed, and excited. 10% were "unpredictable" such as worried and surprised. It seems that participants were more likely to record a bad experience than a pleasant one. The top 10 most frequently mentioned emotions are shown in Fig. 2.

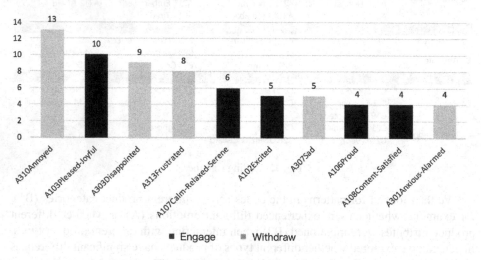

Fig. 2.   10 most frequent emotions.

As Fig. 2 shows, the top three most mentioned "withdraw" emotions are "annoyed" (13, 14.7%), disappointed (9, 10.2%), and frustrated (8, 9%). The top three most mentioned "engage" emotions are "pleased" (10, 11.3%), calm (6, 6.8%), and excited (5, 5.6%).

"Withdraw" emotions were often caused by unsuccessful and interrupted interaction, such as being disrupted by pop-up windows, waiting for the device to respond, or having to repeat the interaction process again. For examples, participants mentioned in the following records:

"I felt annoyed, because a lot of pop-up windows come out when using the bike-sharing app and I must manually close all of them." (Record-27)

"For an electronic device interactive system, the most basic requirement was to run smoothly and do not often crash. This did not meet the most basic requirements. I feel disappointed when system crashed a lot." (Record-2201)

"For this product, If I was a non-paying user, which means the basic functions of the product were not able to use, then the user would feel treated differently, not respected, even resulting in frustration." (Record-3301)

For "engage" emotions, participants could feel good about several things, such as winning a game, a thoughtful tip from a mobile app or even a certain color theme could make them happy. For examples, participants mentioned in the following records:

"It provided Chinese and English subtitles at the same time, I was very happy about it." (Record-4108)

"When using Google Chrome, I felt that it gave me a very comfortable experience compared to other browsers, but I didn't know why." (Record-802)

"I felt a little nervous when using the subway ticket machine for the first time. I think it's from the environment, my heart is full of curiosity and excitement." (Record-806)

4.2 Mobile Apps

Mobile apps are commonly used interactive products in everyday activities. From the questionnaire, we learned that the participants used mobile apps mostly for studying and entertainment. During the interaction with a mobile app, participants reported 13 different emotions in 43 records. The frequency distribution is shown in Fig. 3.

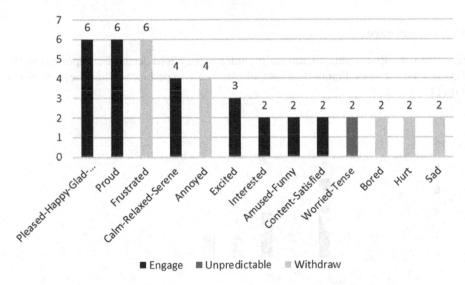

Fig. 3. Emotions mentioned during interaction with mobile apps.

Users often felt pleased when using mobile apps with quick feedback. For example, Participant P33 reported, *"I felt very pleased with this mobile app showing changes of scores when I was playing games."* (Record-3303).

Users were proud of being praised by a mobile app. For example, Participant P33 mentioned, *"I felt proud when the application generates an interface with an MVP cup, saying I was doing well."* (Record-3303)

When interacting with mobile apps, participants also experienced negative emotions such as annoyed and hurt. Participant P8 recorded: *"I am annoyed when something goes wrong with the mobile phone, for example when the camera was difficult to focus. At this point, I would be dissatisfied and annoyed.*" (Record-805)

As to product features, users mentioned about aesthetics, speed, and complexity when they interact with mobile apps. The enjoyment of simple and beautiful interface was mentioned. For example, Participant P2 said, "*I like the application whose interface design is simple and attractive.*" (Record-202) Participant P27 preferred the quick response speed and fast feedback of mobile apps. "*Mobile applications collect information instantly and give response quickly.*" (Record-2704) Easy to use was also considered as an important factor: "*Mobile apps were easy to learn and use with useful functions.*" (Record-2708)

Regarding the results of interaction with mobile apps, participants felt confused and frustrated when they got wrong results or no response during their interaction process. "*When I used the OFO app, its GPS positioning was always inaccurate.*" (Record 2702)

It seems that users got used to the quick feedback on mobile apps, and they expected clear instruction when interruptions occurred. Users often chose to re-interact with the mobile app when they failed in the previous try: "*Because Internet connection failed, I had to re-interact with the applications.*" (Record-2702)

4.3 PC Software

Since the participants were all university students, they used personal computers mostly for studying purposes. Figure 4 shows their emotional experiences when they interacted with PC Software.

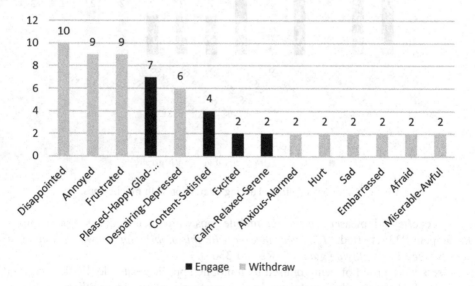

Fig. 4. Emotions mentioned during interaction with PC software.

As Fig. 4 shows, participants felt more negative emotions when they used computer software as opposed to mobile apps. Participants experienced frustration with the slow speed or interruptions of interaction. For examples: *"When the speed is low using Mac Air, I felt devastated and angry."* (Record-3802) *"Too many pop-up windows made me frustrated."* (Record-3904)

Participants felt content with good visual experience on computers. *"My eyes felt relatively comfortable because the screen light was auto-adjusted based on environment."* (Record-3802)

When interacting with PC software, participants also focused on features such as aesthetics, speed, and complexity. For example, when Participant P22 used a code editor application, the color used for highlighting was very helpful. *"The computer always shows a red background to highlight your mistake."* (Record-801) Particularly, participants mentioned the sound that evokes negative emotions during the interaction. *"When I made some mistakes, the computer sounded an awful system beep, which made me really embarrassed in public."* (Record-1103)

As for the results of interaction with computers, "pop-up" windows and "interruptions" were mentioned a lot together. The pop-up windows including ads and help interrupted participants when they were working. *"There were so many pop-up windows when I used a download tool which disturbed me."* (Record-205) Computer software often didn't give any response or instruction when participants did not know how to operate. *"After clicking the 'YES' button, the system had no response and no indication of error."* (Record-205) Faced with these results of interaction, participants often chose to overcome the difficulties when using computers. For example, Participant P35 mentioned he googled the online documentation to find a solution. *"I don't know how to import the music files to my Mac iTunes, so I googled the solution online."* (Record-3506)

4.4 Terminal Devices

The emotions participants experienced when using terminal devices seem to be different with the former two types of digital products. It is possibly because terminal devices were less frequently used and participants were unfamiliar with the operations on terminal devices. The most frequently mentioned emotions during interaction with terminal devices is shown in Fig. 5.

Participants felt disappointed most during interaction when the terminal devices did not work properly as expected. *"I felt very disappointed and frustrated when the vending machine did not dispense goods."* (Record-2210) Participants experienced surprise with terminal devices' unexpected operations. For example, terminal devices can automatically identify user location to save user input. *"When I used the 'intelligent' washing machines, it was a pleasant surprise when it identified my location automatically so I did not need to input my location manually."* (Record-3304)

Regarding product features, participants also mentioned aesthetics, speed, and complexity a lot. At the aesthetic level, besides simple and attractive interface design, participants focused on good typesetting and clear information display. *"The screen shows the information of my prescription that clear and easy to understand."* (Record-2701) As for complexity, the voice prompt and flowchart were helpful to use the terminal devices for the novice users. *"The vending machine has simple but enough*

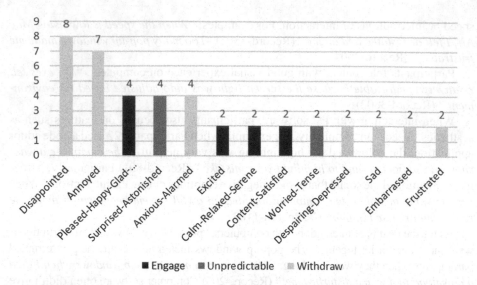

Fig. 5. Emotions mentioned during interaction with terminal devices.

introduction and flowchart that guide people interact with it, which helps me a lot." (Record-2703)

As to the results of interaction with terminal devices, "no feedback" and "content error" was mentioned mostly. Because participants were less familiar with the terminal devices, they felt more confused when there was no response. *"I pushed the button, but nothing happened, and I waited for a while, but still no response. I felt annoyed because I'm not sure if I should push the button again."* (Record-3604) Participants also seemed to experience more Internet connection failure when interacting with terminal devices. *"The vending machine failed to load the QR Code."* (Record-2703) Participants usually re-interact with the devices, either solved the problems or just gave up in the end. *"When the interruption happened, if I couldn't find the solution and I didn't want to wait any longer, I would give up right away."* (Record-701)

4.5 Comparison

Emotions. There is a significant difference in the frequencies of emotions across mobile apps, PC software, and terminal devices ($\chi^2 = 74.30$, $p < 0.05$). Figure 6 shows the comparison. Participants felt more positive emotions when they interacted with mobile apps while felt more negative emotions when they interact with PC software. Specifically, the emotion "proud" and "relaxed" were mentioned much more when participants interacted with mobile apps, and the emotion "disappointed" appeared much more when users interacted with computers. Participants were more often "surprised" when using a terminal device.

Product Features. The participants mentioned different features of the product when they interacted with different types of product. For example, "aesthetics" were

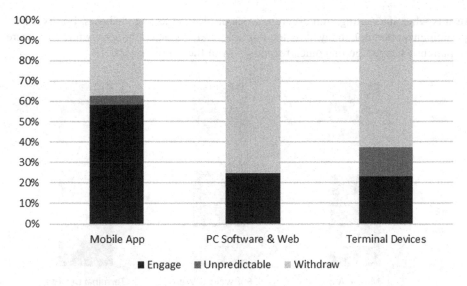

Fig. 6. Users' different emotional experience with different types of product.

mentioned more often with mobile apps than PC software and terminal devices. "Speed" seemed more important when using mobile phones while "complexity" was more relevant when using PC software and terminal devices. It is probably because mobile apps were used more frequently than the other two types of products. Users are used to the quick speed of mobile devices' feedback and they expect easy-to-learn features from unfamiliar devices. The results are shown in Fig. 7.

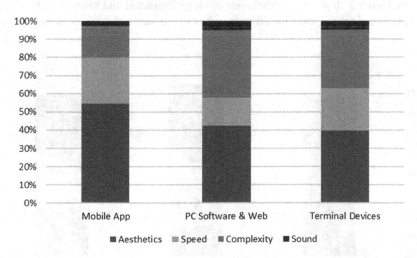

Fig. 7. Product features mentioned when using different types of product.

Interaction Results. Although there is no significant difference between these interaction results across different types of product, participants paid attention to different results when interacting with different types of product as Fig. 8 shows. For example, participants often got annoyed by the pop-up windows on computers, while they were impatient when not getting quick responses from their mobile apps.

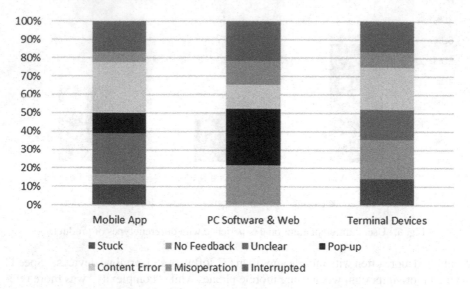

Fig. 8. Different results mentioned when interacting with a different product.

Users' Feedback. With different results of interaction, participants chose different ways to go on. Figure 9 shows that participants often re-interacted and overcome the difficulties. Participants waited and ignored more when using terminal devices as they were not

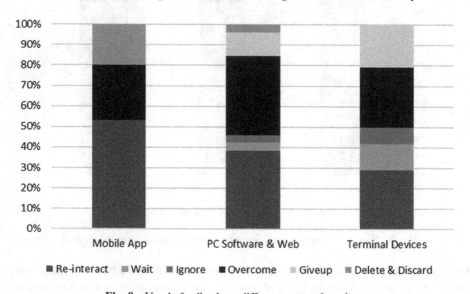

Fig. 9. User's feedback on different types of product.

familiar with them. When the interaction failed, participants often deleted the mobile applications while giving up on terminal devices. It seems that participants had less patience on mobile devices. Meanwhile, there were fewer ways for participants to find help to solve their problems on terminal devices, so giving up seemed to be the only choice.

4.6 User Expectations

After open coding, quantitative analysis, and data display, we found that users tend to have very different emotional tendencies when using mobile phones and computers. Participants seemed to be more "tolerant" to mobile phones, but the use of computers can easily trigger negative emotions. We speculate that this might be caused by user's expectations. In daily life, mobile phones are used more frequently than computers, so participants are more familiar with the possible interaction results on mobile phones, which might trigger less negative emotions, and vice versa.

We found that users are more prone to emotional volatility when they mentioned, "stability" and "predictability". For example, Participant 15 mentioned, *"The interaction process was very painful, mainly due to poor stability, the site collapsed constantly."* (Record-1505) When system behavior was unpredictable, the expectation of the user was difficult to satisfy. We further categorized user expectations into the following three categories (Table 2).

Table 2. Three different types of user expectation.

Record ID	Type	Record
3303	Desire	(Describing a popular game on mobile phone…) After the purchase, the game showed that this was the 10th hero I own, generating a relatively cool interface for sharing with my friends. Then I got the best of the best (MVP) with a new hero in the game and the game immediately gave me an MVP trophy interface and praised me so much that I felt very fulfilled
1808	Previous experience	(Talking about a new change on Samsung's mobile phone…) I did not know when they started in this way. I found Samsung's mobile phone's confirmation button moved from the left to the right. As the confirmation key was on the left, when the small window with "confirm" and "cancel" button popped up, my finger unconsciously presses the left button to confirm. I'm happy about it, because I think such kind of design is in line with my formal experience
3302	Basic needs	(Describing a system bug…) After the system did not respond, I clicked the confirm button. There was no prompt of the error, so I thought the network connection had a problem. I had been waiting and then tried several times with no responses. Finally, after sending the transaction code four more times, I entered the correct transaction code to complete the transaction

There seemed to be a close connection between user expectation and their emotional experiences. This needs further investigation.

5   Conclusion

In this paper, we report differences in users' emotions, product features, interaction results, and users' feedbacks when users interact with different types of digital products. These results provide an exploratory understanding of the relationships between product types and other factors and could make a contribution to cross-platform designers. Furthermore, using a general guideline to interaction design for the different type of products might not be a good idea. This study also suggests that another factor, users' expectation, might have a strong impact when we were measuring user experience in different types of interaction process, and this needs further investigation.

From the results, we confirm that digital products evoke both negative and positive emotions. We find that different types of digital product stimulate different emotional experience. Users were less "disappointed" when they interact with mobile apps. Users were often "surprised" when using a terminal device. We also find users' different experience on product features. Users mentioned "aesthetics" more with mobile devices than with terminal devices. Users cared more about task complexity and chose to overcome the problem they have met when using a personal computer. Results also show that users' feedback differed markedly when they interact with different types of product which confirms previous research. Moreover, users tend to take different actions to interaction results. For example, users were more likely to quit their task on terminal devices than on mobile devices. We speculate that the differences in emotional experiences may have something to do with users' expectations with the products. Olsson's framework [22] that contextualizes layers of expectations into desires, experience-based assumptions, social and societal norms, and must-be expectations may help to understand the connection. This needs further investigation.

Limitations of this research lie in the homogeneity of our participants since they were recruited from the same curriculum with a similar background. In the future, we could expand the span of participants' backgrounds. Future research could also examine the relationship between user behavior, expected/anticipated result of the behavior, and users' emotional experiences.

Acknowledgment. This research is supported partially by the NSFC Grant #71603012. We thank the participants for their time and valuable inputs to this study.

References

1. Hassenzahl, M., Tractinsky, N.: User experience - a research agenda. Behav. Inf. Technol. **2**, 91–97 (2006)
2. Desmet, P., Hekkert, P.: Framework of product experience. Int. J. Des. **1**(1) (2007)
3. Creusen, M.E., Schoormans, J.P.: Product appearance and consumer choice. J. Prod. Innov. Manag. **22**(1), 63–81 (2005)
4. Jordan, P.W., Persson, S.: Exploring users' product constructs: how people think about different types of product. CoDesign **3**(Suppl. 1), 97–106 (2007)
5. Alben, L.: Quality of experience: defining the criteria for effective interaction design. Interactions **3**(3), 11–15 (1996)

6. Law, E.L.C., Roto, V., Hassenzahl, M., Vermeeren, A.P., Kort, J.: Understanding, scoping and defining user experience: a survey approach. In: Proceedings of SIGCHI Conference on Human Factors in Computing Systems. ACM (2009)
7. Deaton, M.: The elements of user experience: user-centered design for the web. Interactions 10(5), 49–51 (2003)
8. Roto, V., Law, E., Vermeeren, A.P.O.S., Hoonhout, J.: User experience white paper - bringing clarity to the concept of user experience. In: Result from Dagstuhl Seminar on Demarcating User Experience, 15–18 September 2010
9. Karapanos, E., Zimmerman, J., Forlizzi, J., Martens, J.B.: User experience over time: an initial framework. In: SIGCHI Conference on Human Factors in Computing Systems, pp. 729–738. ACM (2009)
10. Kuniavsky, M.: Smart Things: Ubiquitous Computing User Experience Design. Morgan Kaufmann Publishers Inc., Burlington (2010)
11. Reeves, B., Nass, C.I.: The Media Equation: How People Treat Computers, Television, and New Media Like Real People and Places. Cambridge University Press, Cambridge (1996)
12. Frijda, N.H., Kuipers, P., Ter Schure, E.: Relations among emotion, appraisal, and emotional action readiness. J. Person. Soc. Psychol. 57(2), 212 (1989)
13. Nagamachi, M.: Kansei engineering as a powerful consumer-oriented technology for product development. Appl. Ergon. 33(3), 289–294 (2002)
14. Schütte, S.: Engineering emotional values in product design: Kansei engineering in development. Institute of Technology (2005)
15. Tractinsky, N., Katz, A.S., Ikar, D.: What is beautiful is usable. Interact. Comput. 13(2), 127–145 (2000)
16. Pham, M.T.: Representativeness, relevance, and the use of feelings in decision making. J. Consum. Res. 25(2), 144–159 (1998)
17. Hekkert, P., Snelders, D., van Wieringen, P.C.: Most advanced, yet acceptable: typicality and novelty as joint predictors of aesthetic preference in industrial design. Br. J. Psychol. (London, England: 1953) 94(1), 111–124 (2003)
18. Venkatesh, V., Davis, F.D.: A theoretical extension of the technology acceptance model: four longitudinal field studies. Manag. Sci. 46(2), 186–204 (2000)
19. Huang, J.H., Lin, Y.R., Chuang, S.T.: Elucidating user behavior of mobile learning: a perspective of the extended technology acceptance model. Electron. Libr. 25(25), 586–599 (2007)
20. Park, N., Roman, R., Lee, S., Chung, J.E.: User acceptance of a digital library system in developing countries: an application of the technology acceptance model. Int. J. Inf. Manag. 29(3), 196–209 (2009)
21. Cowie, R., Douglas-Cowie, E., Tsapatsoulis, N., Votsis, G., Kollias, S., Fellenz, W., Taylor, J.G.: Emotion recognition in human-computer interaction. IEEE Sig. Process. Mag. 18, 32–80 (2001)
22. Olsson, T.: Layers of user expectations of future technologies: an early framework. In: CHI 2014 Extended Abstracts on Human Factors in Computing Systems. ACM (2014)

Conceptual Framework for Affective and Cognitive Product Design

Sol Hee Yoon, Young Woo Kim, and Yong Gu Ji[✉]

Department of Industrial Engineering, Yonsei University, Seoul, South Korea
{yoonsolhee,yongguji}@yonsei.ac.kr, gugstar254@gmail.com

Abstract. In this study, we proposed a conceptual framework of affective and cognitive design based on human-product interaction. Then a systematic approach based on the proposed conceptual framework is presented for the development of an assistive system for designers to gather information and data on how to design new affective and cognitive products. This research can be considered particularly important as it can be extendable to a broad variety of industry and concentrate in aspects of the product from the individual element level.

Keywords: Affective design · Cognitive design · Human-product interaction

1 Introduction

At a start of a new product development, aspiration and intention to generate affective and cognitive successful design are key goals in the design process. Establishing requirements from consumer needs is the most commonly used method to approach when developing a new product. Ideally, previous researches of affective product design emphasized on the needs as well as hedonic aspects of the product as design requirements [8, 11]. However, when we focus on affective aspects of the product, we need to analyze and understand more deeply what aspects of the product influence on the affective experience of users.

Previous researches mostly focus on the impact of affective design on the user and customer value. Khalid and Helander [10] proposed a systematic framework that enables to identify and organize customers' needs in product design. Holistic attributes, styling and functional design were taken into consideration for the framework. Including affective factors on the design of product is a challenging task. Affective and cognitive system are highly correlated with positive user experience from the product [6]. Affects refers to the emotions, sentiment and attitudes that are raised as response from the interaction with the product while the cognitive system deals with the interpretation of the knowledge, meaning and beliefs from the product [7].

During the development stages of the product, designers easily face frustration as not knowing how or what aspects should be considered to get a new affective and cognitive product. Therefore, providing a systematic approach to enable and facilitate the design of cognitive and affective design is of importance.

© Springer International Publishing AG, part of Springer Nature 2018
A. Marcus and W. Wang (Eds.): DUXU 2018, LNCS 10920, pp. 124–132, 2018.
https://doi.org/10.1007/978-3-319-91806-8_10

The objective of the present study is to suggest a systematic and conceptual framework that can assist designer to include affective aspects demanded by the user, based on human-product interaction models, design space of products, and affective attributes. Human-information processing model and perception of product was evaluated to identify elements of the product that can be considered as affective factors related on to design of affective and cognitive product. Thus, suggesting a systematic approach for the development of system with data that can assist designer with their activities.

2 Theoretical Background

Since Desmet and Hekkert [5] when users interact with a product, their emotional experience is related to aesthetic experience of the product and experience of meaning of the product. Aesthetic experience refers to the previous knowledge and perception of the look and feel of the product, whereas the experience of meaning is more related to the memory, meaning and metaphor that the product has [5]. Carliner [2], proposed a framework for the design of information consisting of three aspects. Physical level design which can be linked with surface, texture, and sound design; cognitive level design, which consists on the logic that the product has, how understandable and memorable are; and lastly the affective level design which consisted on the emotion and feeling of the user through the product. Jordan [9] defined the pleasure that users expect when interacting with a product as a benefit that user feel from the perspective of user in 4 categories, ideo-pleasure, socio-pleasure, physio-pleasure, and psycho-pleasure.

Therefore, the present study presents a framework, taking into consideration three different area: (1) Human-product interaction model, (2) Design space, (3) Affective design attribute. The human-product interaction is based on the information processing model where the human perceives information by sensory organs and processes it in their cognitive system to then finally provide an outcome of that information [2]. In this research, therefore we developed the conceptual framework based on three categories: perception design, cognitive design, and affective-response design. The perception design refers to the visual, tactile, and auditory elements of the product that influence on the perception of the product by the user. The cognitive design deals with understandability, memory, and attentional elements from the product. The affective-response design includes elements such as cultural aspects, social aspects and aesthetic aspects of the product. The design space consists of the components that a product has and are considered in the design process, for instance the color or shape of the product [3]. Finally, the affective design attributes refer to the attributes that the product has that influence on the positive affective experience of user in their interaction process and response [5].

2.1 Human-Product Interaction

Carliner [1] introduced a three-part framework for information design based on physical, cognitive, and affective aspects of the human-information processing model. Research of Carliner [1, 2] proposed a model for information design on three levels: (1) physical, cognitive, and affective based on theories of education and instructional design. The physical level is related to design of documentation that assists users to find the required and desired information. The cognitive level design refers to the process where the information is analyzed and understood by the user to achieve their goals. The final, affective design level is the one that motivates the user to perform a task.

Helander [7] proposed a conceptual framework for hedonomics, which refers to the design of pleasurable product and tasks. These model was based on human-information processing which includes the human sensorial perception of the physical object, the cognitive processing of information that finally influences on the response of users.

Since the result of the analysis of previous researches, it is possible to note that it is important to take consideration of aspects of the information processing model for the design of product. Thus, we considered physical level, cognitive level and affective response level of design for the development of the affective and cognitive design framework.

2.2 Affective Product Design

Beyond the importance of the usability of product, emotional and affective aspects of the product are considered relevant for the improvement of user experience when interacting with a product. Norman [12] presented three levels of emotional design: (1) visceral design, (2) behavioral design, and (3) reflective design. Visceral design refers to the initial emotional reaction from the user toward a product by the perception of sensory signals, for instance the "look and feel" of a product. The behavioral design level is related to emotional feedback from the use and performance of the product. Thus, it takes into consideration the function of the product, understandability, usability and physical feel aspects. The reflective design level deals with aspects of the message, culture and meaning that the product transmit to the users.

Desmet [5] presented three types of product experience in the interaction process of users with a product. The aesthetic experience from the beauty and "look and feel" of a product and experience of meaning which refers the memory, meaning and metaphor that the product has. Both aspects merge together will influence on the emotional experience of the user for a product. Further research from Desmet [4], proposed a typology of user emotions when interacting with products. The study presents 9 categories of positives emotions: empathy, affection, aspiration, enjoyment, optimism, animation, assurance, interest, and gratification.

Most of the previous studies focus on physical level design as hedonic and aesthetics aspects of the design. Although those aspect of the product plays a key role in the affective experience of the user, we should also consider a wider perspective of what is affective design.

3   Proposed Conceptual Design Framework

In the present study we present a conceptual framework of affective and cognitive design based on human-product interaction model, product design dimension, and affective design attribute. In this research, we categorized de human-product interaction in perception design, cognitive design, and affective-response design. The perception design focus on visual, tactile, and auditory elements of the product that influence on the perception of the product by the user. The cognitive design deals with understandability, memory, and attentional elements from the product. Finally, the affective-response design includes elements such as cultural aspects, social aspects and aesthetic aspects of the product. Product design dimension refers to the component that compose a product. For instance, color, material, shape, sound architecture. These components of the product were divided so as to facilitate the users with information based on the different attributes. Finally, the affective design attributes refer to the product, human, and interaction attributes that are classified to influence on the affective and cognitive experience of the user.

3.1   Affective Design Framework from the Human-Product Interaction Model

From the review of previous studies, we explain the interaction between human and product as following (see Fig. 1).

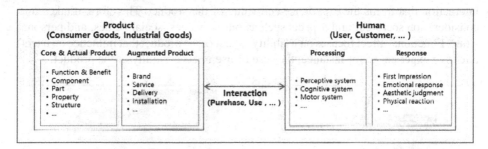

Fig. 1. Aspects of the product and human that influence in the process of human-product interaction.

The product, consumer goods and industrial goods, can be analyzed in two aspects: the core or actual product, and the augmented product. The core or actual product refers to the components that the product has, the functionalities, specifications of the hardware and software, the structural shape, and so on. On the other hand, the augmented product refers to aspects of the products that are presented from the brand, the service the company provides, how it is delivered to the consumers and installation process.

The human, users and consumers, is divided in two aspects in the human-product interaction: processing and response attributes. The processing aspects of human refers to how users perceived the product, how it is addressed in the cognitive system, and how the motor system react to the product input. Hence, the aspects of the user are derived from the human-information processing model. For the response perspective of the human, the model considers the emotional response, aesthetic judgment, physical reaction, and first impression attributes as a result of the interaction of the user with the product. The interaction process includes not only the real use of the product but also, steps such as the decision making process when purchasing a product.

Considering the different aspects of the phenomenon when a human interacts with a product, we can conclude that the affective and cognitive experience is significantly important to be taken into account when developing a new product. As a result, from the three level of design (physical design level, cognitive design level, and affective design level) 12 modules based on the results of the studies.

As shown in Fig. 2, the perception category explains visual, auditory, and tactile sensorial role for the affective human-product interaction. Therefore, assistive information for designers will be based on physical design of the product. The cognitive category refers to how information is processed when interaction with a product. Therefore, aspects of the product that influence to the human attention, thinking strategy and memory will be considered. The perceptual affective response category mostly deals with aesthetic experience that are results of the product physical design. On the other hand, the cognitive affective response level is related to the experience of meaning provided by the product. For instance, the metaphor of that product transmit. The perceptual and cognitive affective response categories represent the relationship between affective response from the human and the physical and cognitive design attributes of the product. That is, it mostly focuses on the result obtained by the interaction with the product. Finally, the affective response category is the result of the product user interaction that forms the experience and value of the product. Therefore, it takes into consideration socio-cultural aspects such as public values, social values, and personal value. Functional affect focuses on usability aspect of the product that influence on users' affective experience. For instance, the ease of use or accessibility of the product.

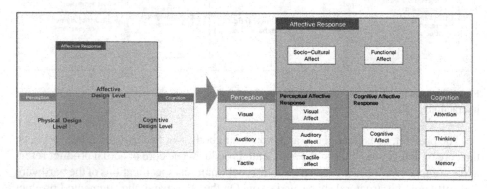

Fig. 2. Proposed framework to explain affective and cognitive aspects of the product from the product-human interaction model.

3.2 Product Design Dimension

The design space enables to divide the product into component. The product design dimensions selected for the proposed framework are the traditional aspect of the product that are associated in the decision making process. These component include:

- *Material* refers to the substances that make up a product. Physical properties of a product can be determined by the type of material. In fact, inner materials can determine the properties such as the weight of the product, and materials used for the surface of a product determine properties such as the texture of the product. In addition, some materials, such as metal and wood, imply their distinct properties to the users themselves.

- *Color* refers to the wavelength of light received by visual perception processes of a user and can be automatically perceived first by the user in the process of perceiving product appearance. Each color can convey particular emotions to the user, and combinations of colors can also create moods. Color is also generally dependent on cultural contexts.
- *Shape* refers to the external form of the product that can be tangible by the user. The space of the products plays an important role in the design of the product as it defines and influence in the first impression of the product and provides knowledge of "what" type of product it.
- *Function and Application* refer to activities that the product can provide to users. A product is generally developed to perform one or more activities which help users make their tasks easier. The user gives utilitarian values of a product depending on how well the product performs its defined tasks, which can be described as performance of a product.

Aspects of the design space are considered of relevant important in the overall process of product development and design. It important to take into consideration all aspects of the design space provide an affective and cognitive successful design to the user.

3.3 Affective Design Attributes

We gathered affective and emotional adjectives related to product affect and affective experience with product and service. A total of 832 words were extracted from previous researches, commercials, review of products, and trend reports. A filtering of repeated words and similar were was conducted and end up with 165 words. We divided and categorized each word in each of the 12 categories of the previously presented conceptual framework. In this research, we only focused on developing two of the twelve categories: socio-cultural affect and functional affect.

Table 1 shows the affective attributes obtained from the categorization of affective words. For this research, we only presented the results of the two categories based on the affective response from the proposed affective design framework.

Table 1. Affective attributes for socio-cultural affect and functional affect category

Socio-cultural Affect	Functional affect
• Eco-friendly • Public interest • Cultural difference • Generation Gap • Popularity • Belongingness • Connectedness • Identity	• Ease of Control • Responsiveness • Comfortability • Intuitiveness • Controllability • Flexibility • Accessibility • Durability • Maintainability • Safety

4 Affective and Cognitive Assistive Design System Development

Based on the proposed conceptual framework for affective and cognitive design, we present a systematic method to implement the developed framework in the development of an assistive system with affective and cognitive information. Figure 3 shows a summary of the system architecture. The human product interaction model includes the 12 categories each with their affective design attributes. Then, an interclass correlation coefficient (ICC) analysis is conducted to see the relationship between the affective

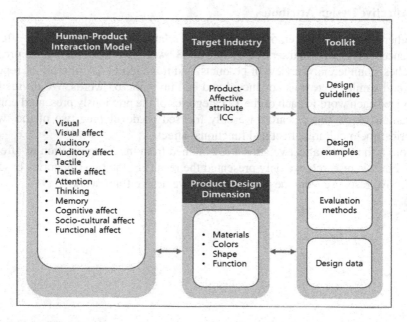

Fig. 3. Systematic development of assistive design system based on the proposed conceptual framework for affective and cognitive designing.

design attribute and product from the target industry. The rating is done by experts of the field with a 5 points likert scale to evaluate the correlation.

Data gathered for the system, are organized based on the affective design attributes from the proposed framework on affective design and the product design dimension. The organized data can be presented in the form of toolkit. For instance, design guidelines, design sample examples, evaluation methodologies, and design specific data. These toolkits can vary depending on the target industry as the affective design attribute changes depending on the target product. Since, the systematic system development process presented in these research, it enables to be used as basis for system development for other industries to assist in the design process of new product.

5   Discussion and Conclusion

Based on the presented framework, we propose a system that can assist designers to include affective and cognitive aspects to the design of product. Not only for one specific industry, but also with the structure of the system, it enables to be extendable to other industries. On the other hand, this study the inter correlation analysis between the affective design attribute and product design dimensions were conducted from the designers' perfective. Thus, further research from the user perfective is needed so as to understand the gap between both perspectives. Further research to analyzed and develop specific and affective attributes each of the 12 categories of the proposed framework should be done.

Also, a common problem for designer is when they a required to develop new affective products. It is easy to end up focusing on aesthetic aspects of the physical design of the product, forgetting all the others attributes, such as functionality, of the product. Good examples are products that are beautiful but has no usable function, that ends up to be unsuccessful in the market. That is, because there was a lack of understanding of what is required to make an affective design. To solve the cognitive and affective design issues presented to designers in the product development process, the current study suggests a conceptual framework for affective and cognitive design, and based on that framework, it suggest a system with human-product information that can assist designer.

Researches on affective design, mostly focus on affective aspects of a product and attributes linked with one product. However, in this study, we emphasis on the extendibility of framework for different industry and products. The framework presented in this study enables designers to be uses as basis for any product development process. Based on the proposed framework, we proposed a system that can provide designer with data to assist them in the process of affective design. Each data was gathered based on elements of each category. Then, they were arranged to provide a more accessibility system as a tool. The system consists of four main information that provides design guidelines, empirical design data, successful design cases, and finally methodology to assist the evaluation of design. We expect that this study can contribute to better develop affective and cognitive product design for developers. Mostly for small industry and start-ups with low resource for expert designers.

References

1. Carliner, S.: Physical, cognitive, and affective: a three-part framework for information design. Techn. Commun. **47**(4), 561–576 (2000)
2. Carliner, S.: Designing better documents. Inf. Manag. **36**(5), 42 (2002)
3. Creusen, M.E., Schoormans, J.P.: The different roles of product appearance in consumer choice. J. Prod. Innov. Manag. **22**(1), 63–81 (2005)
4. Desmet, P.M.: Faces of product pleasure: 25 positive emotions in human-product interactions. Int. J. Des. **6**(2), 1–29 (2012)
5. Desmet, P., Hekkert, P.: Framework of product experience. Int. J. Des. **1**(1), 57–66 (2007)
6. Füller, K., Böhm, M., Krcmar, H.: Designing for positive user experience in product design: a qualitative analysis of toolkit design elements and their implications on emotional reactions and perceptions. In: 2016 49th Hawaii International Conference on System Sciences (HICSS), pp. 1810–1819. IEEE, January 2016
7. Helander, M.G.: Hedonomics-affective human factors design. In: Proceedings of Human Factors and Ergonomics Society Annual Meeting, vol. 46, no. 12, pp. 978–982. SAGE Publications, Los Angeles, September 2002
8. Huang, Y., Chen, C.H., Khoo, L.P.: Kansei clustering for emotional design using a combined design structure matrix. Int. J. Ind. Ergon. **42**(5), 416–427 (2012)
9. Jordan, P.W.: Putting the pleasure into products. IEE Rev. **43**(6), 249–252 (1997)
10. Khalid, H.M., Helander, M.G.: A framework for affective customer needs in product design. Theoret. Issues Ergon. Sci. **5**(1), 27–42 (2004)
11. Lee, S., Harada, A., Stappers, P.J.: Pleasure with products: design based on Kansei, pp. 219–229. Beyond Usabil., Pleasure with products (2002)
12. Norman, D.: Emotion & design: attractive things work better. Interactions **9**(4), 36–42 (2002)

Research on Information Recommendation Optimization Mechanism Based on Emotional Expression and Cognition

Ke Zhong, Liqun Zhang[✉], and Xiaolei Guan

Institute of Design Management, Shanghai Jiao Tong University, Shanghai, China
zhanglliqun@gmail.com

Abstract. The information revolution brought by the rapid spread of the Internet has made people be more dependent on the Internet to obtain information. The internet products based on information are increasing the construction of the information recommendation system. But at present, the information recommendation systems are all limited to the content of information itself, ignoring the differences in the emotional expression of information. This research tried to purpose an approach for the information emotional semantic classification and recommendation based on emotional cognitive model. This research used news Internet product as an example to construct a quantitative coordinates of emotional cognition system through variable control, samples association analysis and statistical data analysis to improve the present information recommendation system. The results of verification experiment indicated that it is practical and effective for information classify and recommend. It is foreseeable that the theory of this research can be applied to other internet products about business, social communication and so on. Meanwhile, the research methods and results can be applied to psychology, sociology research and other specific areas, playing a guiding and testing role.

Keywords: Quantitative coordinates of emotional cognition system
Recommendation system · Emotional cognitive · Emotional expression

1 Introduction

The rapid development of the Internet has led to the emergence of Web2.0, which has the main feature of advocating individualization, and UGC is coming with the development of Web2.0. In the context of this era, the data on the Internet are growing exponentially, and users are more dependent on the Internet to obtain information. And personalized recommendation system was born to solve the above problems. However, the information recommendation systems are all limited to the content of information itself, ignoring the differences in the emotional expression of information.

This research aims to purpose an approach for the information emotional semantic classification and recommendation based on emotional cognitive model. This research put news Internet product as an example, and used variable control to explore the differences between different emotional expressions of information under the same content.

© Springer International Publishing AG, part of Springer Nature 2018
A. Marcus and W. Wang (Eds.): DUXU 2018, LNCS 10920, pp. 133–146, 2018.
https://doi.org/10.1007/978-3-319-91806-8_11

In view of the differences found, professional researchers have proposed a quantitative coordinates of emotional cognition system.

The quantitative coordinates of emotional cognition system constructed in this research innovatively integrates the users' differences in emotion expression and cognition into the information recommendation mechanism, which is quantifiable.

This research creatively proposes the optimization mechanism based on the quantitative coordinates of emotional cognition system. The optimization mechanism has the following advantages,

- Integrating the users' subjective evaluation of information expression into the mechanism, which fills the blank and further enriches the information recommendation mechanism.
- Putting the differences in the emotional expression and cognition of users into the information recommendation system, and the related factors will make recommendation system more comprehensive and diversified, the similarity analysis between users will also be more diversified, eventually making personalized recommendations more precise and effective.
- Adding emotional factors to information recommendation system, which adds more data to the Internet from another dimension, expanding the value of data for the Internet.

The rest of the paper is organized as follows. An overview of emotion, UGC and intelligent recommendation system with current situation is presented in Sect. 2. Section 3 used News Internet Products as an example to explore the differences between different emotional expressions of information under the same content through variable control, samples association analysis and statistical data analysis. The information recommendation optimization mechanism with quantitative coordinates of emotional cognition system are presented in Sect. 4. The verification experiment in order to prove that it is practical and effective for information classify and recommend is presented in Sect. 5. Section 6 is the summary and prospect.

2   Desktop Research

Emotion. Emotion refers to the subjective feelings or experiences of the individual [1]. Emotional experience refers to the individual subjective experience of emotion [2]. Emotion is a part of attitude. It is in harmony with the introverted feelings and intentions in attitude. It is a more complex and stable physiological evaluation and experience of physiology [3, 4]. And for the same thing, each person always has a different emotional feedback and experience [2].

UGC. With the development of the Internet, the interaction of Internet users is embodied. The user is not only the browser of the content of the network, but also the creator of the content of the network [5].

UGC (User Generated Content) is arisen with the concept of Web2.0, which is the main feature of advocating personalization. It is not a specific business, but a new way for users to use the Internet, from the original downloading to downloading and uploading [6, 7].

Recommendation System. Recommendation system is a subclass of information filtering system that seeks to predict the "rating" or "preference" that a user would give to an item [8, 9]. Recommendation system is the product of the development of Internet and e-commerce. It is a high-level business intelligence platform based on massive data mining, providing personalized information services and decision support to customers [10]. In recent years, many successful examples of large-scale recommender systems have emerged. For example, MovieLens recommends movies for users [11], Amazon recommends books, audio-visual resources and other products for users [12], and VERSIFI and TOUTIAO recommend news for users [13]. Meanwhile, personalized recommendation system has gradually become one of the research hotspots in academic circles [14–17] (Fig. 1).

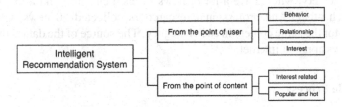

Fig. 1. Intelligent recommendation system

The current research of personalized intelligent recommendation system is limited to the research of user's objective data and subjective behavior data, and the topic classification of content itself [18].

- From the point of users, personalized recommendation is made on the basis of user behavior (praise, comment and so on), user relationship (common friends, etc.), user interest, etc.
- From the point of content, personalized intelligent recommendation for users based on relevant content (keyword association, the same topic), popular content (hot content recommendation) and so on.

However, the research on user's emotion cognition is still blank. Therefore, the main purpose of this study is to explore the relationship between the different expressions of the content and the different emotional cognition of the users.

3   Exploratory Research

There are many scenarios for the application of the intelligent recommendation system, such as the e-commerce industry: Amazon, Taobao, multimedia software: MovieLens, news app: Versifi, Toutiao and so on.

This paper aims to study the relationship between the content and the user's emotional cognition, so we choose the news app as the research object, the reasons are:

- Personalized intelligent recommendation system is widely used in the news app. And news app takes text content as the main part, which is very representative.
- The main product of news app is based on text content, which facilitates the research of the relationship between the content and the user's emotional cognition.
- News app is now widely used in daily life, and the results are highly practical and extensible.
- Data in news app is rich, and easy to obtain.

3.1 Data Collection

The classification of news in news app can be divided into: sports, society, technology, military, health, education, women, estate, culture, automobile, finance and economics, international, entertainment, food, tourism, etc.

Professional researchers chose three categories in the above categories: sports, technology and society, which have a lot of news in each category and a low correlation between each other. And professional researchers collected 20 news with different expressions for the same content in each category. The source of the data is the common Chinese News app and internet.

3.2 Sample Process

Professional researchers processed the collected 60 news, extracting their text content (including the title), using a unified font size, word spacing, fonts to print them on the same white paper. And then researchers numbered them on the back of each white paper, A1 to A20 (Technology), B1 to B20 (Sports), C1 to C20 (Society), took them as the experimental samples of follow-up. Photo of the processed samples is shown in Fig. 2.

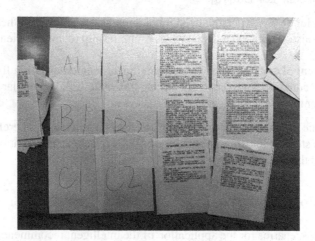

Fig. 2. Photo of the processed samples

3.3   Correlation Analysis

Subsequently, professional researchers respectively did correlation analysis to different kinds of news (20 samples of each kind of news), and observed their correlation results in the derived Euclidean distance model, trying to find out the key factors affecting the user cognitive and emotional differences on it.

Correlation Score
Under the hypothesis that samples in each kind of news search is extensive and representative, the experiment invited three professionals to grade the correlation between any two indicators of 20 samples in each kind of news. The score is on a 9-point scale ranging from 'significant negative correlation' to 'significant positive correlation' [19]. The scoring criteria are based on the professionals' understanding and cognition of each news content. The relevant portion of the score result is shown in Fig. 3.

	A1	A2	A3	A4	A5	A6
A1	1	3	6	4	9	6
A2	3	1	7	2	9	4
A3	6	7	1	6	3	5
A4	4	2	6	1	9	3
A5	9	9	3	9	1	7
A6	6	4	5	3	7	1
A7	2	2	6	2	9	4
A8	3	2	8	3	9	5
A9	2	2	6	2	9	4

Fig. 3. Part screen shot of sample correlation score

Multidimensional Scaling Analysis
The correlation in 3 groups was scored by 3 professionals, and we got the results of 9 sets of correlation scores. Professional researchers then respectively numbered the data results to Group1-A, Group1-B, Group1-C, Group2-A, Group2-B, Group2-C, Group3-A, Group3-B, Group3-C.

SPSS software is used to analyze the samples correlation matrix through multidimensional scale analysis, and factor analysis. The reliability analysis results are as follows (Fig. 4).

According to the results of three sets of correlation scores for each sample, professional researchers selected two of the highest reliability as the follow-up experiment subjects: Group1-B, Group2-A, Group2-B, Group2-C, Group3-A, Group3-C. Meanwhile, we found that the 6 selected groups' reliabilities were all above 0.7. According to the majority of scholars' point of view on the SPSS reliability analysis, the reliability coefficient above 0.7 or more, means that the data needs to be modified, but it still has its value [20, 21]. On the basis that the test data is still valuable, researchers continue to analyze the data by multidimensional scaling analysis.

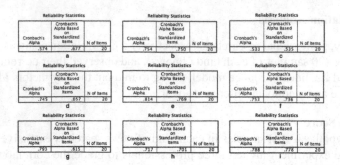

Fig. 4. (a) Reliability statistics of professional Group1-A; (b) reliability statistics of professional Group1-B; (c) reliability statistics of professional Group1-C; (d) reliability statistics of professional Group2-A; (e) reliability statistics of professional Group2-B; (f) reliability statistics of professional Group2-C; (g) reliability statistics of professional Group3-A; (h) Reliability statistics of profession- al Group3-B; (i) reliability statistics of professional Group3-C.

Based on the relevance coefficient in the matrix to build N-dimensional space, the Euclidean distance formula (1) can be used to calculate the spatial distance of two samples. The closer, the more similar samples can be considered.

$$Euclid(1,2) = \sqrt[2]{\left(x_1 - x_2\right)^2 + \left(y_1 - y_2\right)^2 + \left(z_1 - z_2\right)^2} \tag{1}$$

Multidimensional scaling analysis can visually see the spatial distribution of all samples. The results of multidimensional scaling analysis are as follows (Fig. 5).

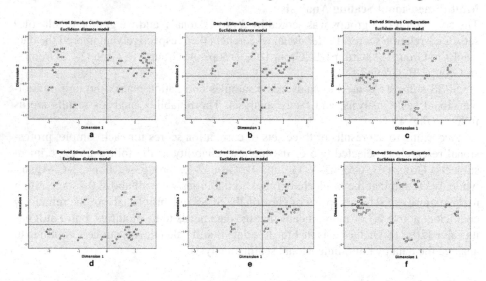

Fig. 5. (a) Multidimensional scaling analysis of Group2-A; (b) multidimensional scaling analysis of Group1-B; (c) multidimensional scaling analysis of Group2-C; (d) multidimensional scaling analysis of Group3-A; (e) multidimensional scaling analysis of Group2-B; (f) multidimensional scaling analysis of Group3-C;

Because the selected samples' difference is the expression of the news, combining the multidimensional scaling analysis results, professional researchers suspected that the main factors that affect the user's cognitive differences are following two dimensions: emotional (more popular and entertainment in expression) and rational (more rigorous and official in expression); simple and rich (the latter will use more relevant content to support expressing the same content).

4 Quantitative Coordinates of Emotional Cognition System

The current personalized recommendation system in news app is based on user's objective data and subjective behavioral data to judge and recommend the topics and columns that users interest in.

However, through the above exploratory experiments, professional researchers found that different expression of news content can cause great emotional and cognitive differences to users.

At the same time, after a certain text analysis, professional researchers suspected that the main factors that affect the user's cognitive differences are following two dimensions: emotional (more popular and entertainment in expression) and rational (more rigorous and official in expression); simple and rich (the latter will use more relevant content to support expressing the same content).

Therefore, quantitative coordinates of emotional cognition system is put forward to optimize personalized recommendation system in news app, make personalized recommendation system more targeted and accurate, to improve user's cognitive efficiency and experience when using the products. Quantitative coordinates of emotional cognition system is shown in Fig. 6.

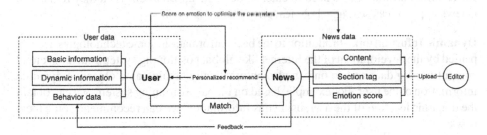

Fig. 6. Quantitative coordinates of emotional cognition system

4.1 News Data

Editor's Upload. When editor is uploading a news, he was traditionally uploading the content and choosing the section of the news. However, in this system, editor needs to score the emotional and rational, simple and rich of the news to get the coordinates of emotional cognition. Then, a news has three main parameters: Content, Section tag, Coordinates of emotional cognition. Given initial coordinates of emotional cognition of news C_{i0}.

User's Feedback to Optimize.   After users read the news, some of them are randomly selected to score the emotional and rational, simple and rich of the news, coordinates of emotional cognition set $C = \{C_{i1}, C_{i2}, ..., C_{in}\}$ can be gotten. The results of the score will be processed according to the relevance between the users' behavior and the news, as follows (Fig. 7).

BEHAVIOR	RELEVANCE
click the news to view when browsing	1
click the news to view after retrieval	1
stay on the news page longer than the average	1
put the news in the favorites after reading	1
comment the news after reading	0.5
forward the news to others after reading	0.5
like the news after reading	0.5
follow the editor of the news after reading	0.5
screenshot on the news page	0.25

Fig. 7.   Relevance of users' behavior and the news

Then the processed results of the score will be attached to the original coordinates of emotional cognition.

As the users continue to read news and score, the coordinates of emotional cognition of the news will be constantly adjusted and optimized.

4.2   User Data

Basic Information.   Users need to enter some basic information when they register in a news app, such as sex, age, hobbies, etc.

Dynamic Information.   In addition to the basic information, some technologies accompanied by the development of the Internet like global positioning system, caching, cloud computing, big data and so on can also automatically obtain some objective dynamic information of the user. For example, based on global positioning system, we can obtain the dynamic location of the user, using this information, we can recommend some local news.

Behavior Data.   When users use news app, they produce a lot of behavior data, which have a certain correlation with the news. It can be seen in Fig. 7.

According to the relevance between the users and the news, we can get the news users are interested in, which based on the three main parameters of the news mentioned above.

In addition, we can also get more information based on the user's behavior data. For example, based on user behavior data, we can get whether a user will be interested in different kinds of news in different periods of time and other details.

4.3   Personalized Recommend

User Similarity Computing.   User similarity computing plays a very important role in collaborative filtering systems, user recommendation systems as well as social network services [22].

The input is a m user's score matrix for n news. We can find neighbor users who are similar to the current interest through user ratings. We can also recommend new news resources to the users according to the neighboring users. The method of finding neighbor users is the user similarity computing. The common methods of similarity measure are Pearson correlation coefficient, cosine similarity, etc.

Pearson correlation coefficient. If user a and u jointly evaluate excessive item set as I_{au}, Pearson correlation coefficient can be used to measure similarity between user a and u. User a and u similarity computation can be expressed as follows:

$$\text{sim}(a, u) = \frac{\sum_{i \in I_{au}} (r_{a,i} - \overline{r_a})(r_{u,i} - \overline{r_u})}{\sqrt{\sum_{i \in I_{au}} (r_{a,i} - \overline{r_a})^2 \sum_{i \in I_{au}} (r_{u,i} - \overline{r_u})^2}} \tag{2}$$

Among it, $r_{a,i}$ and $r_{u,i}$ respectively express user a and u's evaluation of item i. $\overline{r_a}$ and $\overline{r_u}$ respectively represent the average score for the items.

Cosine similarity. The user's score of n items are regarded as the scoring vectors on the n-dimensional projects. $\vec{a}$ and $\vec{u}$ denote the user a and u's scoring vectors respectively. Then the similarity between users can be measured by calculating the angle between different users' scoring vectors.

$$\text{sim}(a, u) = \cos(\vec{a}, \vec{u}) \frac{\vec{a} * \vec{u}}{\|\vec{a}\|/\|\vec{u}\|} \tag{3}$$

Computing user similarity can not only be helpful for recommending new news resources to the users, but also optimize user data and news data to enrich the data of the whole recommendation mechanism.

The Match Between the News Data and the User Data.   Personalized recommend the news to the user based on the match of user data and news data, which is the most commonly recommendation system. But we can see that the recommendation system will be more accurate in the above recommendation mechanism, based on the section tag and emotion score.

5   Experimental Verification

5.1   Experiment Setting

Professional researchers had suspected that the main factors that affect the user's cognitive differences are following two dimensions: emotional (more popular and entertainment in expression) and rational (more rigorous and official in expression);

simple and rich (the latter will use more relevant content to support expressing the same content).

In this chapter, the same professionals used Likert scale to quantify the emotional coordinates of the samples, then the emotional coordinates of the samples would be gotten. Professional researchers classified the samples by the sample correlation score above. The classification results would be compared with emotional coordinates of the samples to see if there is a high degree of consistency to verify the conjecture described in the previous section.

5.2 Experiment Process

Likert Scale. Likert scale is a psychometric scale commonly involved in research that employs questionnaires. It is the most widely used approach to scaling responses in survey research, such that the term (or more accurately the Likert-type scale) is often used interchangeably with rating scale [23].

To verify the conjecture described in the previous section, the professional researchers designed the following 7 point Likert scale (Fig. 8).

<table>
<tr><td></td><td>-3</td><td>-2</td><td>-1</td><td>0</td><td>1</td><td>2</td><td>3</td><td></td></tr>
<tr><td>Emotional</td><td>O</td><td>O</td><td>O</td><td>O</td><td>O</td><td>O</td><td>O</td><td>Rational</td></tr>
<tr><td>Simple</td><td>O</td><td>O</td><td>O</td><td>O</td><td>O</td><td>O</td><td>O</td><td>Rich</td></tr>
</table>

Fig. 8. 7 point Likert scale

Then the professionals scored the same samples in the Likert scale.

According to the scoring results of professionals, professional researchers draw the following coordinates of the 6 samples' scoring results (Fig. 9).

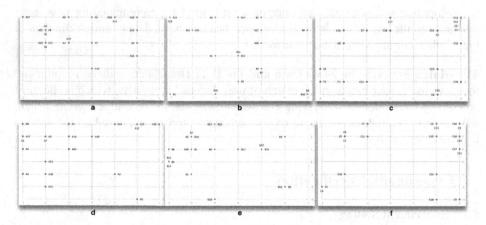

Fig. 9. (a) Emotional coordinates of Group2-A; (b) emotional coordinates of Group1-B; (c) emotional coordinates of Group2-C; (d) emotional coordinates of Group3-A; (e) emotional coordinates of Group2-B; (f) emotional coordinates of Group3-C;

With the dendrograms based on the sample correlation score, professional researchers clustered the samples, as follows (Fig. 10).

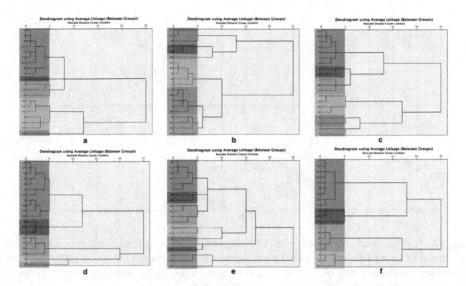

Fig. 10. (a) Dendrogram and sample clustering of Group2-A; (b) dendrogram and sample clustering of Group1-B; (c) dendrogram and sample clustering of Group2-C; (d) dendrogram and sample clustering of Group3-A; (e) dendrogram and sample clustering of Group2-B; (f) dendrogram and sample clustering of Group3-C;

The figure of their multidimensional scaling with clustering is shown in Fig. 11.

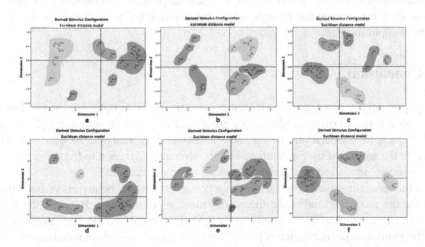

Fig. 11. (a) Multidimensional scaling with clustering of Group2-A; (b) multidimensional scaling with clustering of Group1-B; (c) multidimensional scaling with clustering of Group2-C; (d) multidimensional scaling with clustering of Group3-A; (e) multidimensional scaling with clustering of Group2-B; (f) multidimensional scaling with clustering of Group3-C;

Then the clustering results were put into the emotional coordinates obtained above, we could get the figure as follows (Fig. 12).

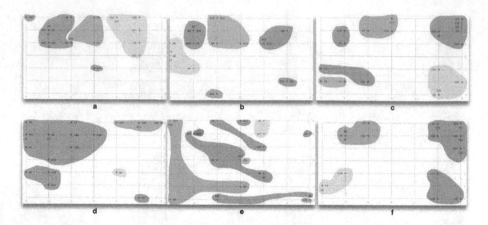

Fig. 12. (a) Emotional coordinates with clustering of Group2-A; (b) emotional coordinates with clustering of Group1-B; (c) emotional coordinates with clustering of Group2-C; (d) emotional coordinates with clustering of Group3-A; (e) emotional coordinates with clustering of Group2-B; (f) Emotional coordinates with clustering of Group3-C;

Professional researchers then compared the emotional coordinates with the clustering results based on the sample correlation score and the figure of multidimensional scaling with clustering.

We can clearly see that there is a high degree of consistency between them, proving that the system mentioned above is very practical and effective in information rank and recommend. It is reasonable to recommend information based on the emotional coordinates as optimization.

6   Conclusion

This paper initially envisages an information recommendation optimization mechanism based on the quantitative coordinates of emotional cognition system through variable control, samples association analysis and statistical data analysis. Its core idea is to integrate the factors of user's emotional expression and cognition to the original information recommendation mechanism to optimize the mechanism.

At the same time, based on behavior psychology, the users' behaviors provide much data for the modeling and make the model more representative. Besides, the users' subjective evaluation of information expression is integrated into the mechanism, which fills the blank and further enriches the information recommendation mechanism.

However, the factors that affect users' cognition and use efficiency should be multidimensional at the level of emotional expression and cognition, not just the two-dimensional displayed in the quantitative coordinates of emotional cognition system. Therefore, we actually need more samples which contain various fields and topics to analysis, and more subjects, including professionals and ordinary users, to get more accurate multidimensional factors.

It is foreseeable that the theory of this research can be applied to other internet products about business, social communication and so on. Meanwhile, the research methods and results can be applied to psychology, sociology research and other specific areas, playing a guiding and testing role.

References

1. Fox, E.: Emotion Science Cognitive and Neuroscientific Approaches to Understanding Human Emotions. Palgrave Macmillan, Basingstoke (2008)
2. Carstensen, L.L., Pasupathi, M., Mayr, U., Nesselroade, J.R.: Emotional experience in everyday life across the adult life span. J. Pers. Soc. Psychol. **79**(4), 644 (2000)
3. Scherer, K.R.: What are emotions? And how can they be measured? Soc. Sci. Inf. **44**(4), 695–729 (2005)
4. Norman, D.A.: Emotional Design: Why We Love (or Hate) Everyday Things (2004)
5. 张淼: 社会化媒体在市场营销中的应用研究. (Doctoral dissertation, 首都经济贸易大学) (2014)
6. 包传颉: 移动视频,领跑 3 g 新应用. 信息通信技术 **3**(2) (2009)
7. Liang, T., Zhang, L., Xie, M.: Research on image emotional semantic retrieval mechanism based on cognitive quantification model. In: Marcus, A., Wang, W. (eds.) DUXU 2017. LNCS, vol. 10290, pp. 115–128. Springer, Cham (2017). https://doi.org/10.1007/978-3-319-58640-3_10
8. Ricci, F., Rokach, L., Shapira, B.: Introduction to Recommender Systems Handbook. ACM (2004)
9. Weaver, A.: Facebook and other pandora's boxes. Access **24**(4), 24 (2010)
10. 任明: 智能信息系统:以关联知识优化数据建模的方法和实践. 浙江大学出版社 (2012)
11. Linden, G., Smith, B., York, J.: Amazon com recommendations: item-to-item collaborative filtering. IEEE Internet Comput. **7**(1), 76–80 (2003)
12. Miller, B.N., Albert, I., Lam, S.K., Konstan, J.A., Riedl, J.: MovieLens unplugged: experiences with an occasionally connected recommender system. In: International Conference on Intelligent User Interfaces, pp. 263–266. ACM (2003)
13. Billsus, D.: Adaptive interfaces for ubiquitous web access. Commun. ACM **45**(5), 34–38 (2002)
14. Hill, W., Stead, L., Rosenstein, M., Furnas, G.: Recommending and evaluating choices in a virtual community of use. In: SIGCHI Conference on Human Factors in Computing Systems, vol. 1, pp. 194–201. ACM Press/Addison-Wesley Publishing Co. (1995)
15. Resnick, P., Iacovou, N., Suchak, M., Bergstrom, P., Riedl, J.: GroupLens: an open architecture for collaborative filtering of netnews. In: ACM Conference on Computer Supported Cooperative Work, pp. 175–186. ACM (1994)
16. Shardanand, U., Maes, P.: Social information filtering: algorithms for automating "word of mouth". In: SIGCHI Conference on Human Factors in Computing Systems, vol. 110, pp. 210–217. ACM Press/Addison-Wesley Publishing Co. (1995)
17. Plume, M.L.: SPSS (statistical package for the social sciences). Encyclopedia Inf. Syst. **38**(4), 187–196 (2003)
18. 邓以克: 基于改进的 SVM-KNN 算法的中文网页层次式分类. (Doctoral dissertation, 浙江大学计算机科学与技术学院 浙江大学) (2010)

19. Xie, M., Zhang, L., Liang, T.: A quantitative study of emotional experience of *Daqi* based on cognitive integration. In: Marcus, A., Wang, W. (eds.) DUXU 2017. LNCS, vol. 10288, pp. 306–323. Springer, Cham (2017). https://doi.org/10.1007/978-3-319-58634-2_24
20. Nie, N.H., Bent, D.H., Hull, C.H.: SPSS: Statistical Package for the Social Sciences. McGraw-Hill, New York (1970)
21. Green, S.B., Salkind, N.J., Jones, T.M.: Using SPSS for Windows; Analyzing and Understanding Data. Prentice Hall PTR, Upper Saddle River (1996)
22. Fang, A., Ya-Zi, L.I.: Computing algorithm of user similarity in virtual medical communities. J. Med. Inform. (2011)
23. Wuensch, K.L.: What is a Likert Scale? And How Do You Pronounce "Likert?". East Carolina University, 4 October 2005. Accessed 30 Apr 2009

DUXU and Children

The Importance of User-Centered Design in Performing Background Checks in Child Care

Fuad Abujarad[1(✉)], Allissa Desloge[1], Kristina Carlson[1], and Sarah J. Swierenga[2]

[1] Yale School of Medicine, New Haven, CT, USA
{fuad.abujarad,allissa.desloge,kristina.carlson}@yale.edu
[2] Usability/Accessibility Research and Consulting, Michigan State University,
East Lansing, MI, USA
sswieren@msu.edu

Abstract. Efficiency, effectiveness, and usability are all essential qualities for a background check process. In child care, these qualities are especially needed to ensure the qualifications of the workforce and the safety of children. With changing child care regulations, Michigan has implemented the Michigan Workforce Background Check (MWBC) system. This study consists of multiple focus groups that were conducted with child daycare providers and consultants to gain feedback on the system and to test its user interface. The goal was to allow the user to have a voice in the development of the system, so changes could be made according to their needs and business process.

Keywords: Criminal background checks · Child care · User-centered design
Government

1 Introduction

According to the National Survey of Children's Exposure to Violence, 15.2% of children experienced maltreatment by a caregiver between 2013 and 2014. Of that group, 5% experienced physical abuse [1]. Child abuse and neglect in child care settings is an issue that the U.S. continues to address. In 1984, a federal screening bill was passed into law as part of the 1985 Fiscal Year Continuing Appropriations Act that required all child care centers to perform a national background check on all staff members [2]. Building on that, in 1998 a public law was passed allowing organizations that provided licensure or certification to individuals caring for children to request federal criminal background checks of potential employees [3]. Though these laws were in place, many facilities found ways around screening potential employees. In 1999, 38 states exempted family child care providers from being regulated, of which only 20 were still conducting background checks and inspections on these exempt providers. In 2003, however, the number of states still conducting background checks increased to 37 out of 38 [4].

Background checking is an expected practice in human resource management in order to detect competency and safety of the potential employee [5]. Utilizing background checks during the hiring process of new employees is essential to avoid negligent hiring. Not only do they protect employers from potential lawsuits, but they protect the people being served. In the case of child care, efficient and effective background checks

© Springer International Publishing AG, part of Springer Nature 2018
A. Marcus and W. Wang (Eds.): DUXU 2018, LNCS 10920, pp. 149–157, 2018.
https://doi.org/10.1007/978-3-319-91806-8_12

are imperative to avoid abuse and neglect [6]. Since children are a vulnerable population, it is essential that the most effective technology be used when determining the fitness of a potential caregiver. Fingerprint-based background checking has been found to be more comprehensive, reduce time, and enhance accuracy; in turn increasing the speed and cost effectiveness of criminal background checks [7].

Though background checks are critical for ensuring child safety, some child care employers see drawbacks to the process. Some believe that the process deters potential candidates from applying; however, a study conducted on the long-term care workforce found that the use of background checks did not reduce the amount of potential job applicants [3]. Other common concerns in the child care industry when it comes to background checks are financial considerations, privacy/confidentiality, and delays in processing [2]. Timing concerns were also observed by researchers that spoke to employers in the long-term care workforce who believe that the current background check system could be improved by reducing the amount of time it takes to receive results [3]. The new and innovative technology incorporated into the Michigan Workforce Background Check–Child Care (MWBC-CC) system addresses these concerns.

In Michigan, child care regulation falls under the jurisdiction of Michigan's Department of Licensing and Regulatory Affairs (LARA) [8]. LARA is responsible for distributing licenses and overseeing facility inspections of over 9,215 child care facilities. LARA segments the different types of child care homes and centers into three groups. The first is Family Child Care Homes, of which Michigan has 3,065, and are defined as "any person who provides care for one to six unrelated children in their home" [9]. The second is Group Child Care Homes, which are defined as "any person who provides care for seven to twelve unrelated children in their home." This type is less common, only accounting for 1,725 of Michigan's facilities [9]. The third, and most common, is Child Care Centers. Michigan has 4,450 Child Care Centers, which are defined as "a facility other than a private residence which receives one or more children for care for periods of less than 24 h a day" [9]. These groupings are important to highlight in order to better understand the child day care businesses in Michigan and how it operates with regards to new legislation and technology, as legislation requires all three facilities to perform background checks through the new MWBC-CC system.

2 Program Background

The 2016 Child Care and Development Fund (CCDF) Final Rule passed by the U.S. federal government requires comprehensive background screening of all child care workers. This screening includes state and national fingerprint checks [10]. Up until recently, Michigan only conducted national fingerprint checks on the program director and the registrant/licensee or licensee designee [11]. In response to federal law, Michigan amended the Child Care Organization Act which passed in 1973. These amendments went into effect in March, 2018. One of the major changes noted in the amendments is that all staff with unsupervised access to children must have a comprehensive background check with national fingerprints, including adult household members, child care staff, and volunteers [8]. Additionally, Michigan did not previously conduct pre-licensure visits or annual inspections for family home providers. The CCDF Final Rule requires that all licensed CCDF providers and license-exempt CCDF providers undergo a pre-licensure and annual unannounced inspection [11]. The new law also mandates that states create a website that describes processes for licensing and monitoring child care providers, processes for conducting criminal background checks, and offenses that prevent individuals from being child care providers [11].

Up until this recent legislation, child care employers were primarily conducting name-based registry checks through the Internet Criminal History Access Tool (ICHAT), which searches criminal history records obtained by the Michigan State Police and the Criminal Justice Information Center, as well as time consuming processing through their local Department of Health and Human Services (DHSS) office for central registry checks. Since the new process was going to be different from the prior name-based checking method, it was necessary to take the new, complex business process requirements and translate them into a new system that includes state and federal fingerprinting. The MWBC system, developed by Drs. Abujarad and Swierenga in collaboration with researchers at Michigan State University, Yale University, and the Michigan Department of Licensing and Regulatory Affairs, originally for long-term care workers [12, 13], incorporated user-centered design methodologies to build and deploy a usable, cost-effective applicant screening process that meets the federal requirements for background checking child care workers. The MWBC system improves the background check process through enhanced communication with the local and national registries, State Police Criminal Justice Information Center, the federal Criminal Justice Information Services (CJIS), and the fingerprinting vendors. This system automates the tasks required when requesting a criminal history record through improved workflow and turnaround time for applicants with no criminal history. This system not only improves the quality background information on the workforce, but by reducing the amount of time it takes to hire a new employee, it also ensures that facilities have an adequate number of staff. A psychological study found a low child to staff ratio led to higher cognitive and social competence in children [14], and this low ratio will be attainable with the MWBC-CC. This system also utilized the state police Rap-back service that allows facilities to receive on-going notification of the criminal history status of employees. If a current employee passed the original background check, but becomes under investigation for a crime during time of employment, the employer is notified [15, 16].

3   User Driven Design Approach: Study

We adapted the User-Centered Design (UCD) approach to develop MWBC-CC, that is, an iterative multi-stage design approach which involves the user's input throughout the development process [17]. UCD gives extensive attention to the user's needs, wants, and limitations at each stage of the design process and allows User Experience (UX) evaluation findings to be incorporated into the design. Implementing UX considerations into design can save time and costs associated with development, maintenance, training, support, documentation, and litigation, and can increase user satisfaction, productivity, task completion, and trust [18]. The expected return on investment for usability efforts is high – over $100 per $1 invested in some cases [19].

Five focus groups were conducted regarding the new MWBC-CC system in order to incorporate a voice of future users. Three focus groups were conducted with child care providers in northern Michigan, southeastern Michigan, and mid-Michigan. The providers in these focus groups discussed their work process and work environment. They also gave feedback on the new system. An additional two focus groups were conducted with child care consultants who work in northern Michigan and mid-Michigan. Consultants are responsible for overseeing the quality of services in licensed child daycares, homes and centers, and for ensuring that the safety of children is maintained through compliance with state laws and regulations. The focus groups with the consultants aimed to inform requirements for the MWBC-CC "Consultant Interface."

4   Providers Focus Groups

4.1   Participants

Participants in all of the focus groups were experienced child care providers from a variety of facility types. The first group included 6 child care providers in the mid-Michigan area (see Table 1), the second focus group included 8 child care providers northern Michigan, while the third group included 9 providers from southeastern Michigan. Across the three groups, 15 of the 23 participants are director/owner positions. The

Table 1. Selected demographics from the first provider focus group.

Pt#	Job role/title	Type of facility	Number of employees	BC frequency	BC performed
1	Owner/Director Childcare Center	Owner/Director Childcare Center (30 children)	12 working for owner	Rarely	ICHAT; registry
2	Program Director	Child Care Center (100+ children)	20 working for Program Director	Less than once/ month	ICHAT
3	Assistant Director	MSU Child Development Lab (2 sites)	8 head teachers working for Director and two Assistant Directors, plus up to 40 student staff and 25 student teachers/semester	Less than once/ month	Good Moral Standards, Mandated Reporter
4	Child Care Provider	Group Home Childcare	2 assistants	Rarely	ICHAT
5	Daycare Provider	Family/Group Home (6 children in home)	No assistants	Rarely	ICHAT
6	Director/Head Teacher	Child Care Center	12 working for Director	Less than once/ month	ICHAT

remaining participants serve in roles as child/daycare providers, licensing and purchasing coordinators, human resource managers, and designees. Only 13 of the 23 providers reported doing background checks "rarely." Three reported conducting checks "less than once per month," and 5 reported doing them "less than once per week." One participant reported completing 1–2 background checks per week, while another has never performed a background check.

4.2   Methods

The focus groups began by having the providers describe their current hiring and background check processes. They also were asked to discuss the process for hiring international applicants and out-of-state applicants. Following that discussion, the MWBC-CC system was described and demonstrated to participants. The research team discussed the new fingerprints-based background check process and how Rap-backs will continue to monitor employees.

4.3   Results from the Three Provider Focus Groups

The providers described their hiring processes, all of which include having a Central Registry check. Some providers indicated that they had the DHSS office conduct the Central Registry check. Others had the employee take care of getting the Central Registry check done at a DHHS facility in their county. Some had the employee then personally pick it up, while others had the information mailed or faxed back to them. Most providers conduct an ICHAT check before the potential employee is hired or has any contact with the children.

Overall reactions to the new system were favorable, as participants want to hire child care workers who have been screened as much as possible. All of the participants understood the flow of the new application process, and the steps to complete it. They had several questions, comments, and suggestions about the facility activation process and the new application process, especially about the new application page (see Fig. 1) and scheduling fingerprint appointments. Participants also suggested providing training for providers who may be less familiar with business processes and technology. Participants were happy about shared fingerprint results, Rap-backs, and flags (for ineligible potential employees). Participants liked the idea that state analysts will take over conducting the checks, but wondered if staffing levels would be sufficient. User interface design recommendations include implementing a "guest access" feature for applicants to be able to fill out the new application form themselves. Participants would also want the team to consider utilizing new technologies to make the fingerprinting process easier. The cost of collecting digital fingerprints was a major topic of the focus group discussion as well. Participants were unclear about how they could best fit the new fingerprint-based check and the ~$50 fee into their current business and workflow processes. They wondered if they will still need to run the ICHAT ahead of time. Creative costs models and applicant-based licensing were requested to deal with the significant increase in the cost of conducting more thorough background checks. Several participants suggested a shared model, where the state would cover part of the cost. Some also recommended establishing a 'professional licensing' model where the background check would stay with the person, rather than the facility.

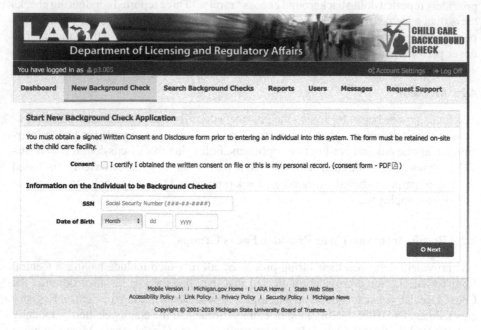

Fig. 1. MWBC-CC new background check application page.

5   Consultants Focus Groups

5.1   Participants

The first consultant's focus group consisted of 10 child care consultants from northern Michigan, and the second group included 9 consultants from mid-Michigan. Most of the consultants have obtained a Master's degree in early childhood or social work or have a BA in early childhood education; several also have CPS experience. These individuals regulate supervision of child care licensees in an effort to maintain ongoing compliance with licensing requirements. The second group of consultants has experience auditing group child care homes, family child care homes, and child care centers. They have been working in their positions anywhere from 1–15 years. Their main responsibilities include conducting facility inspections and writing inspection reports for about 105 faculties each (ranging from 12–125 facilities) across multiple counties.

5.2   Methods

The goals were to get a better understanding of their current processes and to discuss the new background check process. The consultants were then given a demonstration of the new MWBC-CC system that child care providers will be using to conduct fingerprint-based criminal history checks on people who will be working in child care facilities. The research team discussed why the new fingerprints process is needed and the reasons for the increased costs. The new process was described and demonstrated, including how Rap-backs continue to monitor employees. All of the participants understood the flow of the new application process, and the steps to complete it.

5.3 Results from Both Consultant Focus Groups

In regard to workflow, most consultants prepare a weekly schedule for the required unannounced visits (based on a case load report), conduct the site visits, and then go back to their office (DHHS office or home) to complete the paperwork and prepare the reports. The first group expressed concerns around internet connectivity, limited office space to work, and hectic inspection environments and thus preferred doing the majority of their work on paper. The second group of consultants differed in their opinions about technology. They expressed the importance of having an iPhone/iPad interface of the MWBC-CC system since they are mobile employees and are frequently traveling from their office locations to inspection sites.

6 Discussion and Concluding Remarks

The background check approach prevents gaps in the hiring process by providing immediate feedback on the applicant's suitability. This allows qualified child care workers to be hired more efficiently. The user-centered design approach allows for a seamless transition to the new process, which reduces customer support requests and training requests, and avoids gaps in the hiring process that would greatly impact the availability of qualified workers in child care facilities. Employers are now able to immediately determine the fitness of prospective child care workers. Immediate turnaround, improved response times and sharing information through continuous monitoring directly affect the quality of child care and safety. In summary, this project is a great example of how a user-centered design process facilitated the flow of critical information, improved applicant data accuracy, and improved child care safety by eliminating access by known abusers and criminals to children in licensed daycare facilities.

The focus groups revealed that there is significant disparity in technological expertise among child care employers. Staff at corporate-level facilities are very comfortable accessing the web-based application and have dedicated staff conducting large numbers of background checks, i.e., power users, who expect system flexibility, short-cut features, and the most streamlined process possible, while some smaller child care employers have little or no experience using computer-based systems and operate through low bandwidth internet connections. Furthermore, some employers use English as a second language. Thus, the user interface for child care employers has to be easy to learn and use with no or little training and/or need for additional customer support. According to the focus groups and related literature, paying for the background check is a major concern. With this in mind, future research needs to be done on creating a sustainable cost model to ensure long-term success of this program and increase feasibility of replication of the program in other states. In Michigan, LARA was able to work with the legislature and secure $5.5 million dollars to help subsidize 6 fingerprint checks for each family child care home, 8 for each group child care home, and 16 for each child care center. They have also negotiated a reduced cost with the state vendor for these subsidized background checks [8].

Acknowledgment. Funding for this research came from the Michigan Department of Licensing and Regulatory Affairs (MLARA). Specifically, we would like to thank Larry Horvath, Director, Bureau of Community and Health Systems (BCHS), MLARA; Thomas Novak, JD, BA, Manager, BCHS; Mark C. Jansen, Director, Child Care Licensing Division, BCHS; and Cheryl Gandhi, Child Care Program Analyst, Child Care Licensing Division, BCHS, for the support they provided to complete this research.

Any opinions, findings, and recommendations in this article are those of the authors and do not necessarily reflect the view of the Michigan Department of Licensing and Regulatory Affairs.

References

1. Finkelhor, D., et al.: Prevalence of childhood exposure to violence, crime, and abuse: results from the national survey of children's exposure to violence. JAMA Pediatr. **169**(8), 746–754 (2015)
2. Davidson, H.: Protection of children through criminal history record screening: well-meaning promises and legal pitfalls. Dickinson Law Rev. **89**(3), 577–604 (1985)
3. U.S. Department of Health and Human Services, Office of the Assistant Secretary for Planning and Evaluation: Ensuring a Qualified Long-term Care Workforce: From Pre-employment Screens to On-the-job Monitoring. The Lewin Group, Washington, D.C. (2006)
4. Shaul, M.S.: Child Care: State Efforts to Enforce Safety and Health Requirements. Report to the Honorable Sander M. Levin, House of Representatives. GAO-04-786. US Government Accountability Office (2004)
5. Levashina, J., Campion, M.A.: Expected practices in background checking: review of the human resource management literature. Empl. Responsib. Rights J. **21**(3), 231–249 (2009)
6. Connerley, M.L., Arvey, R.D., Bernardy, C.J.: Criminal background checks for prospective and current employees: current practices among municipal agencies. Publ. Pers. Manag. **30**(2), 173–183 (2001)
7. Galantowicz, S., Crisp, S., Karp, N., Accius, J.: Safe at home? Developing Effective Criminal Background Checks and Other Screening Policies for Home Care Workers. AARP Public Policy Institute, September 2010
8. Michigan Department of Licensing and Regulatory Affairs, Bureau of Community and Health Systems Child Care Licensing Division: Special Legislative Edition – Changes to PA 116. Michigan Child Care Matters, Lansing (2018)
9. Michigan Department of Licensing and Regulatory Affairs, Bureau of Community and Health Systems Child Care Licensing Division: A Parent's Guide to Child Care Licensing. Michigan Department of Licensing and Regulatory Affairs, Lansing (n.d.). https://www.michigan.gov/documents/lara/BCAL_PUB_784_9_15_499332_7.pdf
10. Lynch, K.: The Child Care and Development Block Grant - First Five Years Fund. United States, Congress, Congressional Research Service (2014)
11. Michigan Department of Education: Child Care and Development Block Grant (CCDBG) Act of 2014-Summary of Statutory Changes, December 2015

12. Swierenga, S.J., Abujarad, F., Dennis, T.A., Post, L.A.: Improving patient safety through user-centered healthcare background check system design. In: Proceedings of International Symposium of Human Factors and Ergonomics in Healthcare HFES 2013, vol. 2, no. 21, pp. 21–26. Human Factors and Ergonomics Society (2013)

13. Abujarad, F., Swierenga, S.J., Dennis, T.A., Post, L.A.: The impact of usability on patient safety in long-term care. In: Nah, F.F.-H., Tan, C.-H. (eds.) HCIB 2015. LNCS, vol. 9191, pp. 221–231. Springer, Cham (2015). https://doi.org/10.1007/978-3-319-20895-4_21

14. NICHD Early Child Care Research Network: Child-care structure → process → outcome: direct and indirect effects of child-care quality on young children's development. Psychol. Sci. **13**(3), 199–206 (2002)

15. FBI Criminal Justice Information Services: Next Generation Identification (NGI), 06 May 2016. https://www.fbi.gov/services/cjis/fingerprints-and-other-biometrics/ngi

16. Abujarad, F., Swierenga, S.J., Dennis, T.A., Post, L.A.: Rap backs: continuous workforce monitoring to improve patient safety in long-term care. In: Marcus, A. (ed.) DUXU 2013. LNCS, vol. 8014, pp. 3–9. Springer, Heidelberg (2013). https://doi.org/10.1007/978-3-642-39238-2_1

17. International Organization for Standardization: Ergonomic Requirements for Office Work with Visual Display Terminals (VDTs) – Part 11: Guidance on Usability. (ISO Reference No. 9241-11:1998[E]) (1998)

18. Marcus, A.: User interface design's return on investment: Examples and statistics. In: Bias, R.G., Mayhew, D.J. (eds.) Cost-Justifying Usability: An Update for the Internet Age, 2nd edn, pp. 17–39. Elsevier, San Francisco (2005)

19. Karat, C.-M.: A business case approach to usability cost justification for the web. In: Bias, R.G., Mayhew, D.J. (eds.) Cost-justifying Usability: An Update for the Internet Age, 2nd edn, pp. 103–141. Elsevier, San Francisco (2005)

Song of Red Pine Woods - Design and Study of Digital Picture Books for Preschool Children on iPad

Qi Cao[1], Jing-Hua Han[1(✉)], Yu-Yi Ding[1], Shi Huang[2], and Chao Liu[3]

[1] Department of Digital Art, Beijing Forestry University, Beijing, China
hanjing013@126.com
[2] Animation and Digital Arts Academy, Communication University of China, Dingfuzhuang East St., Chaoyang, Beijing, China
bit.stone@163.com
[3] User Interaction Design Academy, Baidu University, Xierqi Road 1002, Haidian, Beijing, China
Liuchao05@baidu.com

Abstract. The cultivation of children's early reading ability is of vital importance in their entire life. As preschool education attracts more and more attention, the primary challenge for many designers of children's books is how to better guide children to read with higher quality. This paper takes the design of *Song of Red Pine Woods* as an example, discusses the actual effects and realization way of interactive design in preschool children's picture books. Based on the author's experiment results in preschool, the paper proves that digital picture books have unique advantages compared to traditional paper picture books, and also proposes new ideas on how to improve children's reading interest and reading experience.

Keywords: Preschool children · Digital picture book · Cognitive features
Interactive design

1 Introduction

The cultivation of early reading ability plays a very important role in preschool children's growth stage and will influence their lifelong learning and thinking ability. During preschool stage, children are experiencing rapid physical growth and gradually mature visual sense, auditory sense, smell sense and so on. Therefore, the design of preschool reading should meet children's special cognitive features and behavioral habits. At present, the quality of picture books in China is patchy. Those with relatively high quality and better popularity are mostly translated works from foreign countries [1].

With continuous development of computer and multi-media technology, the carrier of children's picture books has gradually transformed from traditional paper books into multi-media devices such as iPad. Children's reading mode also changes from manually leafing through the books to touching the screen, so does the route of information transmission which has changed from simple image-text forms into diverse and

© Springer International Publishing AG, part of Springer Nature 2018
A. Marcus and W. Wang (Eds.): DUXU 2018, LNCS 10920, pp. 158–169, 2018.
https://doi.org/10.1007/978-3-319-91806-8_13

compound forms including image-text, videos, audios and so on [2]. The new forms of artistic expression have exceeded storybooks and traditional picture books, and developed into multi-media art that integrates words, images, music and audio [2]. Though there are still many controversies over the use of multi-media products such as iPad, it is undoubted that proper design and use of new interactive multi-media technologies will surely bring benefits for educating children and cultivating their reading ability. In recent years, quite a few excellent design schemes have broadened the way for designing digital picture books for preschool children.

The interactive picture book Little Star that won Apple Design Award 2012 has integrated sensing devices such as gravity sensor, gyroscope and microphone, with touch control and gesture recognition technology (see Fig. 1). Many interactive modes are designed during the reading process. For example, if you drag the sun, the red sun will bounce like a football; if you slide the meadow, the scene will also move; if you click the black-and-white photos, they will turn full colors; if you shake the screen, the small ball will bounce in the screen and the feather duster will also flap up and down. These different interactive modes have brought more surprises and fun to children.

Fig. 1. *Little Star* (Color figure online)

Good Night is a most popular bedtime story in Children Interaction of App Store in 2015 (see Fig. 2). In this picture book, the story is ingeniously integrated with interactive design. Through a repetitive interactive operation of clicking, children can turn off the lights for different animals and help them fall asleep in the scene. The background music creates a quiet and peaceful atmosphere, which also exposes children to the core content of the whole story, that is, it is late, and you should turn off the lights and go to sleep.

According to the cognition features of preschool children and current situation in relevant fields, this paper designs an interactive digital picture book for 3–6-year-old preschool children on iPad-*Song of Red Pine Woods*. Themed on popularization of forest ecology, it helps children know various interesting animals and plants as well as relevant ecological knowledge while reading the story on iPad by designing amusing interactive reading methods and beautiful graphic effects. More details about the interactive design, realization process of the system and experiment in preschool will be introduced in the following.

Fig. 2. *Good Night*

2   Interactive Design for *Song of Red Pine Woods*

2.1   Interactive Process Design

Interactive design is the core content of this digital picture book. Good interactive experience should be based on the cognitive and psychological features of preschool children and follow simple and vivid interactive principle so as to involve children in interactive reading, increase their reading interest and improve reading experience [3]. Relevant experiments will have to be conducted to test and evaluate whether children's reading experience has been improved.

Guided interactive reading method enables children to get involved in the story context of the picture book, increase their confidence and relieve their sense of failure [4]. The whole interactive process of *Song of Red Pine Woods* is realized through designing two task modules, namely, unlock module and reading module. In unlock module, the dynamic prompts on the screen guide children to unlock the role cards at the bottom. Every time when the children click a role correctly, the corresponding profile in the card will be enabled. There will be a pop-up message introducing the role with background dubbing. The role cards will roll out downward after all of them are unlocked, and meanwhile there will be 7 number buttons from 1 to 7. The prompt tone of victory indicates that the task is successfully completed and the play button in the bottom right indicator sign will be enabled.

In this task module, children have to discover prompt information through careful observation. The role introduction after the role cards are unlocked enables the children to know the forest in a more visualized way. The repetitive unlocking operation is designed according to the behavioural habits of children at this age group. Besides, the pictures and audio effects after the role cards are unlocked also bring visual and auditory excitement to children and also increase their sense of pleasure and accomplishment, thus improving their reading interest and encouraging them to acquire knowledge more actively [5].

Only after successfully completing the unlock tasks, users can enter reading module. In this way, children will get a glimpse of main forest species involved in the story before they start reading, which will help them better understand the story.

According to the story, *Song of Red Pine Woods* includes 7 chapters. In reading module, children have two reading modes to choose, including linear and non-linear reading modes. When children click the play button at the bottom right, the story will be played automatically from chapter 1 (linear reading). If children click one of the number buttons, the story will enter corresponding chapter (non-linear reading). The non-linear reading design enables children to choose reading order independently and get back to the home page at any time to choose another chapter (Fig. 3).

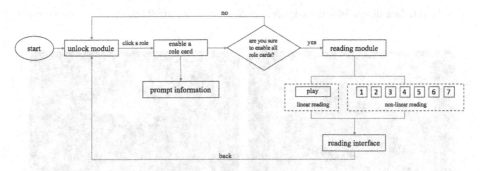

Fig. 3. Interactive process of *Song of Red Pine Woods*

2.2   Interactive Interface Design

Interface is the most direct platform to exchange information with users. Preschool children feature some typical psychological traits such as strong curiosity, unstable attention, active personality, imitation, expectation for recognition and emotional tendency [6]. The interface design of the unlock module adopts a forest style (see Fig. 4), which allows children to get immersive experience in the story once they enter the interface. The animals in the scenarios all adopt cute and cartoon appearance design with simple and smooth lines. The icon design features vines and wood grain elements, echoing the forest theme and satisfying children's curiosity in exploring a forest. In addition, the deep and light color contrast strengthens the yellow background effects and creates stronger visual shock to attract children's attention. The task cards are designed in wooden structure with a concave-convex feeling, matching with the story context. After locked, the roles cards will turn into colourful ones. The yellow stroke effectively distinguishes the locked cards from the unlocked ones to help children better complete the tasks.

In reading module, there are four interactive button icons at four corners of the screen (see Fig. 5). Users can click the top left audio button to turn on/off the story dubbing. The top right home button enables users to get back to the home page, review introduction information of each role or re-select a chapter to read. The bottom buttons can be used to turn the pages, such as backing to the former page or skipping to the next page.

Fig. 4. Interface design of unlock module in *Song of Red Pine Woods* (Color figure online)

Fig. 5. Reading interface Design of *Song of Red Pine Woods*

2.3 Interactive Plot Point Design

Amusement is a necessary element in digital picture books for children. By extracting the story plots from *Song of Red Pine Woods* and integrating human-machine interactions and story plots through ingeniously interactive technologies, the digital picture book allows children to get involved in interactions and enhance their reading interest and experience [7].

In reading module, every single page is a small scene. An array of interesting interaction operations are realized by adding many actions such as clicking, sliding, dragging and shaking the screen in different scenes. For example, in the 5th scene of chapter 1, a big black bear is holding a trunk. The background dubbing is "this big black bear is so impatient that he shake the trunk very violently to enjoy the food in advance". Children can click the bear according to the prompt information on the screen, then the big black bear will start shaking the trunk violently. In this way, an interactive course is completed. Also, at the beginning of chapter 2, there are some yellow leaves on the tree. The background dubbing is "Listen, the winter is coming". Children can shake the screen according to the sliding arrow in the screen, then the yellow leaves on the tree will gradually fall down. Moreover, children can also drag and control the pine cones, click a chipmunk to watch it eating pine cones or cut fruits from the trees by dragging the knives.

These deliberately designed interactive plot points have added more fun to children's reading process, allowing them to transform from merely listening to, reading and watching stories into controlling what happened in the story. This has greatly enhanced children's participation degree and experience, which will dramatically stimulate their reading interest (Fig. 6).

Fig. 6. Interactive interface of *Song of Red Pine Woods*

3 System Realization

During technological realization, many measures were taken at earlier stage to test the effects. Also, the test also used development kits like the three-dimensional game engine Unity. After several tests, Xcode, the official iOS App development kit was finally adopted.

Traditionally, Objective-C is used as the programming language for developing iOS apps. During the development process, we used Swift, issued by Apple in 2014, as the programming language. Swift also supports Functional Programming, Tuple data type and other features which can make the project code more simple and concise, better fit for the rapid iteration development mode and ensure good quality of software project.

This app mainly uses Sprite Kit as its animation engine. As a 2D animation and game engine of Apple, Sprite Kit support Sprite display, animation, audio player, particle effects, physical simulation and other features. Besides, Apple's official development kit Xcode has a built-in scene editor for Sprite Kit. Sprite Kit will greatly save development time and make for rapid iteration. For instance, the code for a series of actions is set for the scene's background as below:

```
background?.runAction(SKAction.sequence([
SKAction.moveBy(CGVectorMake(50,    70),    duration:    4.5),
SKAction.moveBy(CGVectorMake(40,    0),    duration:    3.5),
SKAction.scaleBy(0.8,              duration:              3.5),
SKAction.moveBy(CGVectorMake(0, -100), duration: 6.0)]))
```

With Sprite Kit, an animation sequence such as move upper right, move right, scale down and move upward can be added to the story scenes in this way. It can be seen that the programming code of Sprite Kit is visualized, simple, flexible and convenient.

Through such development method, the subtitles can be added in a simple way and the intervals of each subtitle can also be controlled:

```
let subtitle = SubtitleNode(textAndTime: [    ("We are
wrapped in the hard shell of pine cones,", 3.6),    ("It
won't crash even if falling from a 30-meter-high
tree.",4.5),    ("We won't be able to come up if we fail
to leave this shell.", 6.0)])
```

Therefore, by combining Swift programming language with Sprite Kit animation kit, we are able to realize more flexible interactive effects and guarantee the development efficiency and quality of software project.

4   Experimental Observation

4.1   Experimental Subject

The experiment was conducted in a preschool in Beijing. A total of 72 children were chosen from three levels of classes equally (24 children of P1, P2 and P3 classes of the preschool respectively) and they fell into three groups: Group A/B/C.

4.2   Experimental Method

Experiment 1. Observing the Popularity of Digital Picture Book on iPad and Traditional Paper Picture Book.

Experiment Content: In order to control the influence of irrelevant variable, the author designed a paper picture book of *Song of Red Pine Woods* with the same stories and pictures before the experiment. The teacher gave each child of three groups an iPad with digital picture book *Song of Red Pine Woods* and a paper one. Considering that these children were too young to answer the questionnaire independently, without disturbing children's choice, the teacher recorded their answers through subjective Q&A method.

Table 1. Children questionnaire

No.	Subjective questions	A iPad digital picture book	B Paper picture book
Q1	Which one is more convenient?	A	B
Q2	Which one do you prefer?	A	B

Experiment 2. Test Children's Reading Effects of Digital Picture Book on iPad and Traditional Paper Picture Book.

Experiment Content: 24 members of Group A was divided into Group A1 and Group A2. Each child of Group A1 was given an iPad with digital picture book for reading while each one of Group A2 was given a paper book for reading with the help of the teacher. Children were arranged for reading the story at the same given time. Then the teacher conducted a quantitative test according to the story to check their reading quality. The same experiment was conducted in Group B and Group C.

Table 2. Questionnaire of teacher's evaluation on children's reading quality

No.	Subjective questions	Degree				
Q1	Can you read independently?	1	2	3	4	5
Q2	Can you read without being distracted?	1	2	3	4	5
Q3	How much are you interested in the story?	1	2	3	4	5
Q4	Can you recognise the animals and plants in the story?	1	2	3	4	5
Q5	Can you retell the story?	1	2	3	4	5

*Tick a "√" under corresponding degree: 1 = poor 2 = not bad 3 = just so 4 – good 5 = very good

4.3   Discussion of Experiment Results

Experiment 1. According to the two subjective question in Table 1, the answers of 72 children are presented in pie chart as shown in Fig. 7

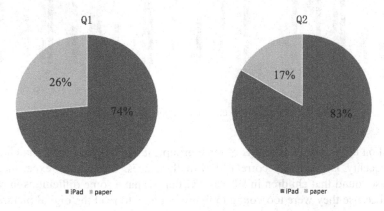

Fig. 7. Pie chart of children questionnaire results

Data analysis and comparison: According to Q1 results, over 70% of children favored that reading on iPad is more convenient. It indicated that digital picture book on iPad has fully considered children's behavioral and reading habits. And the indicative signs and dynamic animations in interface design also bring interesting human-machine interaction experience for children.

According to Q2 results, over 80% of children preferred reading on iPad, which showed children's preference for iPad. Due to strong curiosity and thirst for knowledge, children are inherently inclined to be attracted by interactive screens. Besides, with the popularity of multi-media devices, most children have contacted these interactive electronic devices from a young age.

Experiment 2. Table 2 compares three groups' reading quality of digital picture book on iPad and traditional paper picture book and collects the questionnaire data from Group A, B and C.

According to the experiment results shown in Fig. 8, children reading with iPad generally get higher scores than those reading paper picture books, which indicates that digital picture book on iPad can better improve children's reading quality. In particular, the highest Q3 score in Group A1, B1 and C1 is much higher than that in Group A2, B2 and C2. It can be concluded that iPad has played an effective role in boosting children's reading interest. Children reading with an iPad are more willing to read, which shows that iPad reading is more attractive for children. According to Q2 score in three experiments, it can be seen that children reading with an iPad show obviously better concentration than those reading paper picture books. It proves that interactive reading can immerse children in the story scenes and enhance their reading experience.

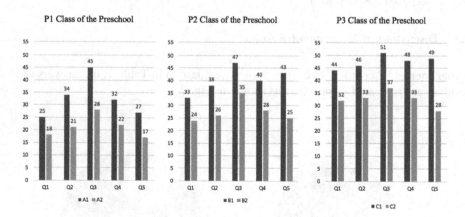

Fig. 8. Bar graph of children's reading quality analysis

Based on the experiment results of three groups, it can be concluded that children's reading quality is positively correlated with their ages. During the experiment, the author also found that children in P1 class (Group A) have some difficulties in reading on iPad because they were too young to figure out how to read the digital picture book on iPad. Also, due to their poorer comprehensive ability and language competence, they are not good at retelling the story. Hence, the reading quality of children in Group A is obviously lower than that in Group B and Group C. During the experiment, children in Group B and C are familiar with reading on iPad. It can be seen from the results in Q4 and Q5 that children reading with an iPad acquire more knowledge than they do in paper picture books.

Based on the experiment results mentioned above, it can be concluded that reading with an iPad can improve children's reading quality. In order to further verify the experiment results, the author conducts a hypothesis test on 72 children's answer data.

Firstly a normal distribution test is conducted to check whether the data of iPad reading and traditional paper reading is of normal distribution. The null hypothesis supports normal distribution and the alternative hypothesis opposed. The test method is shapiro.test.

```
shapiro.test(iPad)#   Normal   distribution   hypothesis
rejected
Shapiro-Wilk normal distribution test
data:  ipad
W = 0.89579, p-value = 0.002623
shapiro.test(paper)#   Normal   distribution   hypothesis
rejected
Shapiro-Wilk normal distribution test
data:  paper
W = 0.79883, p-value = 1.544e-05
```

The p-value is lower than 0.05, so the null hypothesis is rejected.

As the experimental data is not of normal distribution, the author decides to use wilcoxon rank sum test to check the ranked data with no idea about the general distribution. The null hypothesis is that the two sampling scores have no difference. The alternative hypothesis is that the score of the groups reading with iPad higher than that of the groups reading with paper books.

```
wilcox.test(iPad, paper, alternative="greater",exact=F)
Wilcoxon rank sum test with continuity correction
 data:  iPad and paper
W = 1106, p-value = 4.498e-08
```

alternative hypothesis: true location shift is greater than 0

As the p-value is lower than 0.05, so the null hypothesis is rejected and the alternative hypothesis is accepted. That is, the score of the groups reading with iPad higher than that of the groups reading with paper books.

Appendix: R code

```
mydata=read.csv("C:/Users/Yiwei/Documents/Fanyiwei/data.csv")
head(mydata)
ipad=mydata[,1]
paper=mydata[,2]
#Normal distribution test
shapiro.test(ipad)#  Normal  distribution  hypothesis rejected
shapiro.test(paper)#  Normal  distribution  hypothesis rejected
 #Ranked data of non-normal distribution, checked by wilcoxon
```

5 Conclusion

The paper designs a digital picture book *Song of Red Pine Woods* for preschool children based on iPad device. Driven by children's cognitive features and aesthetic demands, the digital picture book enables children to get better reading experience during their interactions with iPad by setting guided reading signs and interesting interactive plot points. During the sampling experiment in a preschool, it can be concluded from the subjective Q&A and questionnaire results that digital picture books are more advantageous than traditional paper picture books to attract children's reading interest and improve their reading quality. With the popularity of more and more multi-media mobile devices, this new reading method has offered a new outlet for improving children's reading ability.

Acknowledgments. This work was supported by the Fundamental Research Funds for the Central Universities (2015ZCQ-YS-02) and Beijing Higher Education Young Elite Teacher Project (YETP0785).

References

1. Jiu, Z., Huang, X.: Difficulties and countermeasures of children's digital picture book publishing. Univ. Publ. **2**, 47–49 (2017)
2. Gao, P.: The integration of picture books and animation. Beijing Institute of Fashion Technology, Beijing (2013)
3. Dai, X.: Children's picture books design based on reading cognition. Packag. Eng. **02**, 150–154 (2016)
4. Luo, H.-T.: The research on the interactive design about children's digital picture books. Jiangnan University, Wuxi (2014)
5. Sheng, X., Hu, X.: Research on interactive book design for children in digital age. Zhuang Shi **8**, 136–137 (2016)
6. Shangguan, D.: 'Children Painting' - the design of digital picture books for young children from cognitive characteristics of young children. Sci.-Technol. Publ. **7**, 79–83 (2015)
7. Kang, K.: Five sensory experience of palm - media kids' picture book. Hundred Sch. Arts **4**, 256–257 (2014)

A Study on Application of AR Three-Dimensional Touch Interaction in Children Education

Yu-Yi Ding[1], Jing-Hua Han[1(✉)], Qi Cao[1], and Chao Liu[2]

[1] Beijing Forestry University, Beijing, China
hanjing013@126.com
[2] Baidu University, Beijing, China
liuchao05@baidu.com

Abstract. This essay presents knowledge that application validity and reasonability of AR technology based on three-dimensional (3-D) touch interaction in children education were investigated. Plants were selected as the theme to design a children education mode dependent on AR 3-D touch interaction; through comparative experiments, impacts of 4 learning styles on knowledge learning effects were respectively compared, book reading, AR visual content display, AR screen multi-touch interaction and AR 3-D touch interaction. This article shows that learning by means of AR 3-D touch interaction is more effective and such a method has the ability to keep users interested in learning and enhance their understanding and memory of advanced knowledge. Although the pure AR visual content display plays a certain promotion role in children education, information content about the knowledge displayed is low accompanied with a single interactive mode. In a word, AR visual content display has certain defects. By contrast, children who adopt AR 3-D touch interaction can achieve a better learning effect, which indicates that such an approach possesses application value.

Keywords: Augmented Reality (AR) · Touch interaction · Children's cognition
Plant education

1 Introduction

Under the general circumstance that information exchange modes and information transmission routes rapidly make progress, people are paying increasingly more attention to and attaching greater importance to knowledge acquisition. Education is aimed at spreading scientific knowledge, research methods, theoretical thoughts and exploring spirit, etc. discovered in the process of research to the society in a proper way, so that they can be cognized and understood by students and even the masses. Resultantly, overall quality of the public is improved. Regarding traditional educational methods, especially children education modes, reading materials in paper are usually used as carriers, for which it has become more and more difficult to satisfy children's actual demands in a new media environment of diversified information content and multi-dimensional spreading forms at present. However, a great variety of digital readings based on personal computer and smart mobile terminals, etc. not only provides novel

© Springer International Publishing AG, part of Springer Nature 2018
A. Marcus and W. Wang (Eds.): DUXU 2018, LNCS 10920, pp. 170–184, 2018.
https://doi.org/10.1007/978-3-319-91806-8_14

and rich learning and entertainment patterns for children, but gives them fresh and interesting interactive experience. Comparing with vivid and interesting digital readings, a combination of characters and pictures in traditional education readings seems to be monotonous. How to design an education mode conforming to children's present demands and develop their interests in knowledge learning is an important subject of the current children education research.

With development and popularization of information technology, forms of children education readings become increasingly varied. Figueiredo and Bidarra [1] propose gamified interactive readings where knowledge is incorporated into games and readers can learn through lively activities. In his opinion, manifestations of AR technology are rich and interesting; therefore, it can be deemed as a preferable carrier of gamified education and dynamic interaction between emerging and heatedly discussed AR technology and children education readings is a beneficial exploration and investigation of children education modes.

AR technology has been applied in the field of children education, such as universe science popularization [2], e-learning [3] and word retention [4], etc. In addition, there exist many outstanding cases.

Chen and Tsai [5] probe into practicality of AR technology in books for children. As demonstrated by relevant results, children hold the positive attitude towards such books and AR can improve their spatial cognitive abilities to a certain degree. According to IRadu [6], AR plays a positive role in book teaching activities, because it is beneficial to enhance knowledge understanding, facilitate long-term memory and elevate children's initiative in learning. Rambli et al. [7] investigate AR based alphabet learning effects of children. Through much experimentation, it has been proven that children are keenly interested in such a learning style. Nevertheless, hardware equipment limitations and a single interactive mode affect their learning effects to a certain extent.

To sum up, previous studies indicate that AR technology plays a certain role in children education field and is conducive to deepening their understanding of cognitive level knowledge. However, existing research on application of AR in children education places emphasis on vision performance in most cases and reveals visual augmented presentation of traditional knowledge information. Besides, interactive modes involved are rather limited.

Specific to above problems, an AR interactive mode based on 3-D touch was proposed. In terms of application, users can perform touch interaction simulation similar to the real 3-D space for AR technology-based models on the screen of a hardware device (e.g., smartphone). If such an approach is applied into children education, more vivid and more interesting interactive experience can be provided to them effectively promoting their cognition and memory of knowledge. Hence, learning effects of them are improved ultimately. To verify application validity and reasonability of AR 3-D touch interaction in children education, a contrast experiment was designed combining characteristics of children's cognition and AR technology with an aim to explore knowledge learning differences subjected to diverse interactive modes and conduct experimental data analysis and conclusion.

In this paper, children's plant education readings independently developed by the author was taken for example to analyze AR technology application status in children education readings at present. Hopefully, shortcomings of its application in children education can be pointed out and an AR based knowledge learning mode in consistency with children's cognitive characteristics be raised. In this way, children are able to learn and memorize knowledge on the premise of remaining highly interesting in them, so as to improve their learning effects in the process of edutainment.

2   Cognitive Characteristics of Children and AR 3-D Touch Interaction

2.1   Cognitive Characteristics of Children

3 to 6 years old children in physiologically and psychologically developmental stages gradually get rid of the way to acquiring information from the outside world by behavior acts and begins to understand and learn the outer world by virtue of their perception. Children are vivacious and restless and love playing. They are good at simulating languages and behaviors surrounding them to establish their own psychological cognition. Moreover, they are also particularly curious about everything in the external world. As they grow up little by little, their sensory functions turn to perfection visually, auditorily and tactilely, etc. Under the dual influence of their exposure to the outer world and their mental and physical maturation, psychological demand patterns with distinctive features take form.

Keen to Simulation. For children in developmental stages, simulation is one of their major learning approaches. At the phase of immature self-cognition, language and behavior contents perceived by simulation are most direct and most effective learning style and their thirst to cognize the outer world makes their simulation psychology more intense.

Strong Curiosity. Children begin to acquaint themselves with outside objects through their own perceptions. In this course, their cognitive competence makes progress and can be built up so as to promote their longing for cognition of new things. Such a promoting effect is directly embodied in the emergence of their curiosity. Meanwhile, their curiosity pushes them to cognize more abundant external information so that their cognitive competence is further fostered. Through such a cyclic and superimposed effect, a psychological demand of intense curiosity is finally generated in children.

Memory Simplification. Memory ability of children is still at a developmental stage. They frequently simplify contents that they have memorized by themselves. In other words, those that they are interested in are maintained, while those nothing special and boring are forgotten. Such psychology of memory simplification leads to children's weak ability to stay dedicated. Consequently, presentation forms should be constantly changed to stimulate their interest points in a manner similar to playing games and extend the time of being engaged.

2.2   AR Technology

According to AR technology, computer graphics and visualization are utilized to make virtual images generated by computer arithmetics superimposed in a real image to combine virtual images and the real image together finally so that scenarios of the actual world can be enhanced or unpacked by virtue of additional information produced by the computer. It is featured with virtual-real synthesis, real-time interaction and 3-D registration. Display equipment based on AR technology presents a visual effect of "virtuality in reality" for users. Not only can dummy objects be displayed in a real 3-D environment, but non-geometrical information about the actual object is presented.

In line with technological features described above, AR technology covers static images, dynamic images and written messages, etc. in terms of visual display. Furthermore, sound effects can be inserted at the time of visual display to further improve its multi-media presentation ability. Interactive mode combining AR technology commonly takes advantage of screen multi-touch, i.e., users conduct single-finger or multi-finger clicks and gesture interaction on equipment screen to move, rotate and zoom 3-D images presented by this technology, etc.

According to preliminary analysis, multi-media presentation ability and virtual-real synthesis effect of AR technology have the capability to meet children's psychological demands and conform to their cognitive characteristics. Regarding children who are observing and reading AR books, virtual information embedded in them cannot be directly perceived by naked eyes; however, if they adopt the camera of a smart mobile device to scan a particular picture in the book, 3-D model hidden can be vividly revealed on the paper. Such sudden senses of freshness and surprise give children rather intense sensory stimuli to simulate their interests in cognitive learning. Meanwhile, behavior acts of using a camera to scan a book and perform screen touch interaction are easy to learn. Children are able to simulate and learn them in a very short time. In this case, their psychological demands are satisfied and their enthusiasm for study retained.

2.3   3-D Touch Interaction

Dependent on IBSE rule [8], objectives of learning investigation, understanding operation, building knowledge framework and changing misunderstanding, etc. should be achieved in the process of reading books for learning. As proposed by Vosniadou [9] in conceptual change theory, psychological model construction consists of three stages, namely, initial model construction, synthetic model construction and scientific model construction. Education mode of AR technology based 3-D touch interaction investigated in this paper is geared to the needs of preschool children 3 to 6 years old. While their most fundamental cognitive competence has been just formed, such children are at a behavioral stage of initial model construction. Therefore, they learn under guidance and education. Considering this, visual, accurate and understandable interactive mode built between knowledge information presentation and contents learnt by children is the core attracting attention.

3-D touch is an interactive mode simulating perspective and occlusion relationship in the real world based on AR technology. Interaction triggered components should be grouped and bound to a 3-D model according to objective circumstances; in addition, grouping cooperation and IK resolving should be carried out for triggering conditions of such components. Interactive components change in consistency with relevant perspective rules and corresponding to variations in scanning and shooting angles and distances of the hardware equipment, so as to guarantee users' interactive experience similar to objective reality. Taking Mimosa pudica as example, its leaves immediately close after it is touched. In a conventional AR interaction solution, the entire plane of a device screen is bound to an interactive trigger. As a result, leaf closure animation of Mimosa pudica can be triggered whenever a user touches the Mimosa pudica model with any part surrounding it on the screen. In line with a 3-D touch based interaction scheme, stems, leaves and flowers of Mimosa pudica are respectively bound to interaction triggers according their biobehavioral characteristics (Fig. 1); besides, effective touch range of a 2-D plane that an interactive component in 3-D space has been projected onto is also figured out. In this way, when the user touches different sections of the Mimosa pudica model on the screen, different behaviors of the model responding to the user's acts can be observed. For example, it the user touches its leaf, the leaf closes; when he/she touches its flower, the flower sways, which share much resemblance with real Mimosa pudica's responding behaviors. In this case, comprehensible and lifelike interactive experience can be incurred in users, not only possessing game enjoyment in terms of interactive mode, but guaranteeing truth-seeking and rigorous requirements for education.

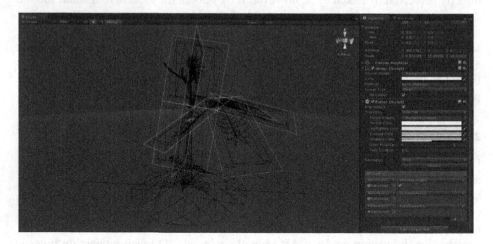

Fig. 1. An interactive trigger in 3-D touch interaction solution.

3 Materials and Methods

3.1 Experimental Design

A knowledge learning style contrast experiment was designed to verify potential defects of AR application in children education and probe into application validity and reasonability of AR 3-D touch interaction proposed in this paper. During the experiment, control variables are testees who have the same educational content, the same learning time and the same learning environment without significant differences, while independent variables are diverse education modes and learning styles.

Educational content adopted by 4 groups of experiments designed is knowledge relevant with Mimosa pudica, Phyllanthus niruri and Aeschynomene indica (Fig. 2), primarily involving their names, flowers biological structural characteristics, stem and leaf structures and habit characteristics. With a similar morphological structure, they are all herbaceous plants featured with alternate growth of plume like compound leaves and are green in terms of the complete stool. Differences of such 3 kinds of plants mainly lie in morphological characteristics of the complete stool, characteristics of flowers and biobehavioral characteristics (petiole of Mimosa pudica's leaf touched becomes pendent and its small lamina closes; but, another two types of plants present no such behaviors). Participants should be questioned after the experiment and the question contained 3 terms with a major aim to investigate their memories about such 3 plants. Then, differences in different learning styles were estimated according to accuracy of their answers. In addition, application validity and reasonability of AR technology based interactive modes in Children's knowledge learning process were thoroughly analyzed.

Mimosa pudica   *Phyllanthus niruri*   *Aeschynomene indica*

Fig. 2. Three kinds of plants learned.

3.2 Questions After Experiment

(1) Which plant foliage closes after being touched? The correct answer is "Mimosa pudica". As biological behavior of leaf closure after being touched is particularly unique among plants, it falls into the category of knowledge of strong features and can be memorized easily. Such a question aims to investigate strongly featured content memorization ability of children tested, effects of different education modes and learning styles during memorization of strong features, and preliminarily explore diverse effects of different AR interaction models on knowledge learning.

(2) Which plant has the largest leaf? The correct answer is "Phyllanthus niruri". Knowledge involved with such a question is poorly featured. As Mimosa pudica, Phyllanthus niruri and Aeschynomene indica share long leaves of pinniform alternate growth; although sizes of individual leaves are different from each other, such

differences are insignificant. Consequently, it is much likely for people to get confused. This question aims to investigate tested children's abilities to memorize details with slight differences, explore detail memorization promoting degrees of different education modes and learning styles, analyze potential problems incurred by application of AR interaction modes in knowledge learning, and compare validity of diverse interaction modes utilized in knowledge learning.

(3) Photos of Mimosa pudica, Phyllanthus niruri and Aeschynomene indica each were presented to children tested (plant display angles in these photos are slightly different from those adopted during their study), they are randomly selected by these children twice without replacement. After each selection, children tested are required to name the corresponding plant in the photo. If correct answers have been given for twice selection, it is noted to be correct; otherwise, it should be noted as being wrong. Such a question comprehensively investigates children's mastery of knowledge they have learned. Due to a high difficulty degree, children who have accurately cognized characteristics unique to different plants have the ability to answer it correctly. On this basis, application validity and reasonability of AR 3-D touch interaction in children education and learning are further explored.

3.3 Experiment Participants

The research implemented by Fleck and Simon [10] addresses that no direct correlation exists between children's understanding of AR space and their genders. No significant differences have been found in the process of learning by children of diverse genders. From perspectives of experimental requirements and humanity, children 3 to 5 years old are featured with poor expression logicality and weak physical fitness; for this reason, 40 6-year-old children were selected as experimental objects with a male-female ratio of 1:1. In addition, academic records of these participants are similar to each other. In-depth learning of plant knowledge is absent in all of them and they are interested in natural plant knowledge without exception. All participants without exposure to any content of AR technology have received qualified training of touchscreen phone usage. Moreover, all participants are willing to join the experiment voluntarily.

3.4 Experiment Content

40 participants were equally divided into 4 groups numbered from 1 to 4. Each group consisted of 5 male and 5 female children. According to the serial number of the experiment, 4 groups of experiments were conducted correspondingly. Considering that participants were rather young and their self-learning and cognitive competencies were still immature, a professional kindergarten teacher was assigned to each experimental group to assist children in their learning, guarantee that they could securely and effectively use AR hardware devices, and perform subjective evaluation and recording of their degrees of concentration on learning. Dependent on key points analyzed and investigated, 4 groups of contrast experiments were designed and presented as follows in details.

Experimental Group 1

As a contrast experimental group, participants under the guidance of a laboratory technician read traditional plant books for children to acquire knowledge about 3 kinds of plants without help of AR technology.

Experimental Group 2

Based on book reading, participants of this group under the guidance of a laboratory technician took advantage of 3-D models and corresponding animation effects of such 3 kinds of plants presented by AR technology to assist their learning and memorization without interactive operations; that is, they only observed visual effects displayed by AR technology.

Experimental Group 3

Based on book reading, participants of this group under the guidance of a laboratory technician took advantage of 3-D models established for such 3 kinds of plants and presented by AR technology to assist their learning and memorization; and, they can not only rotate and zoom such models in an interactive mode by virtue of the touchscreen, but trigger animations corresponding to the relevant plants by touching and clicking the animation play button on the screen.

Experimental Group 4

Based on book reading, participants of this group under the guidance of a laboratory technician studied in an AR 3-D touch interactive mode. Participants were allowed to perform touch interaction for all parts of plants. Different structures of their 3-D models gave diverse types of feedback after screen touch signal reception and their feedback behaviors were rather similar to those of real plants. If a participant repeatedly clicked a construction of the plant, special animation also appears accordingly. For example, if he/she clicks a flower over and over again, an animation effect of petals falling down can be incurred.

3.5 Experimental Procedure

Participants in 4 experimental groups accepted the test at the same time in the uniform learning environment. Experimental period of each group was controlled below 20 min and experiments of different groups did not interfere with each other. After experiments, 3 questions mentioned above were raised to participants to make statistics about correct and wrong answers. Moreover, participants were also required to subjectively evaluate their own experimental processes, that is satisfaction measurement of different learning styles.

3.6 Experimental Data

Experimental data collected were constituted by two parts. First is the statistics about participants' answers to above questions after experiment; second is participants' subjective satisfaction rating about their own experimental forms, which has been classified into Very Dislike, Dislike, Prefer, Like and Very Like. Scores corresponding to such 5 ratings are 1, 2, 3, 4 and 5 respectively.

3.7 Interview

Participants who have completed all experimental contents were interviewed. The interviewing mainly centered on their feelings of participation into the experiment and during the experiment; moreover, reasons for their judgments and answers were briefly inquired targeted at concrete situations of these questions for the purpose of analyzing the relationship between AR technology based interactive modes and the knowledge learning and memorizing.

4   Results and Discussion

4.1   Qualitative Analysis

According to interview results, children making use of AR technology were generally surprised and excited. They were willing to utilize AR technology for their studies continuously. Such emotions have not been found among children reading books and even some of them felt bored. Subjective evaluations made by a laboratory technician of each group on children's learning concentration degrees indicated that children reading ordinary books began to have their attention diverted after 15 min of learning and a small number of them hoped to stop learning. In comparison, those who studied by virtue of AR technology based visual presentation were rather excited when they saw 3-D plant models on the screen; after about 10 min of observation and learning, their attention, however, also began to be diverted. In addition, children who learned by means of AR multi-touch interaction were especially interested in such an interactive mode, repeatedly touched buttons on the interactive interface and observed plant animations after clicked the button. Although they maintained high degrees of excitement in the entire process of experiment, those buttons made their attention diverted to a certain extent. As for children utilizing AR 3-D touch interaction, they were also particularly interested in structures of the 3-D plant model and focused on repeated observation and touch interaction of different plant structures during the experiment.

Participants also evaluated their subjective satisfaction about experimental procedures that they accepted (Fig. 3). Considering that participants in each group only went through education mode and learning style of its own group, statistical graphs of satisfaction could not be compared horizontally and they only played a role in elaborating and describing facts. In line with information expressed in these graphs, participants in Group 1 generally dislike book reading so that their satisfaction about such education mode and learning style is low. Regarding Group 4, participants have been highly satisfied with AR 3-D touch interaction and they are fond of this education mode and learning style.

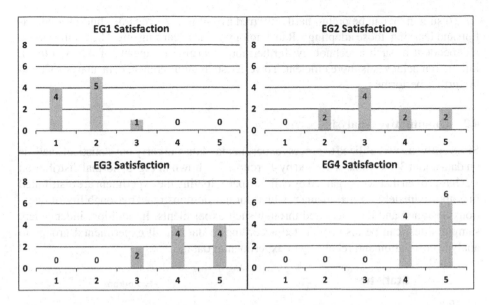

Fig. 3. Satisfaction statistics of experimental groups.

As specified, score assigned to correct answers is 1, while that to wrong answers is 0. Question answering situations of all groups have been presented in Fig. 4. By referring to graphics of each group's statistics, the number of correct answers given by Group 1 is significantly smaller than other groups; and, correct answer counts of Group 4 are higher than those of other groups.

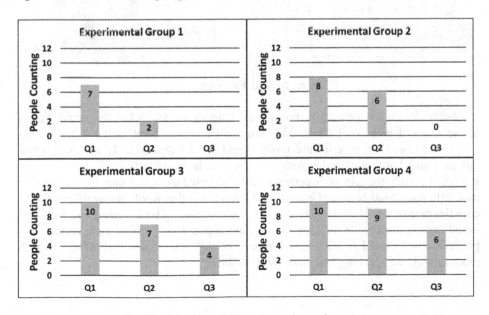

Fig. 4. Answer statistics of experimental groups.

To sum up, it can be preliminarily inferred as follows. As regards children's education and learning, those adopting AR technology gains a learning effect better than those independent of such a technology; furthermore, learning by means of AR 3-D touch interaction achieves is more efficient. To verify such an inference, data analysis should be further performed.

4.2 Quantitative Analysis

SPSS software was utilized to process experimental data and carry out statistical analysis on data about 3 questions answered by 4 groups. As shown in Fig. 5, normal distribution test has proven that scores gained by children participating the experiment are distributed in a approximately normal manner, which further demonstrates reasonability of questions designed and data acquired through such experiments. In addition, independent sample T-test can be also conducted according to data of all experimental groups to analyze correlation and reliability of experimental data.

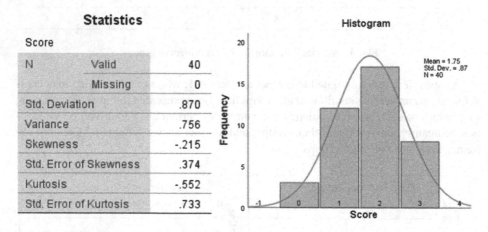

Fig. 5. Normal distribution test.

As for Question 1, answers of groups 3 and 4 are all correct; that is, standard deviation of the data is denoted as 0. Under this circumstance, independent sample T-test is only carried out targeted at experimental groups 1 and 2. As indicated in Table 1, data about groups 1 and 2 are tested and proven to conform to homoscedasticity. Considering that $P = 0.628 > 0.05$, the original hypothesis can be accepted and it is deemed that no significant difference exists between Group 1 and Group 2. In other words, no significant difference lies in strongly featured knowledge learning processes of book reading and AR based visual content display. As all answers of groups 3 and 4 to Question 1 are correct, it is preliminarily believed that interactive modes of AR multi-touch and AR 3-D touch promote children's learning and memorizing abilities.

Table 1. Independent sample T-test results of Question 1 in Groups 1 & 2

Independent Samples Test

		Levene's Test for Equality of Variances		t-test for Equality of Means						
		F	Sig.	t	df	Sig. (2-tailed)	Mean Difference	Std. Error Difference	95% Confidence Interval of the Difference	
									Lower	Upper
Q1 (EG1; EG2)	Equal variances assumed	.987	.334	-.493	18	.628	-.100	.203	-.526	.326
	Equal variances not assumed			-.493	17.677	.628	-.100	.203	-.527	.327

Specific to data obtained from Question 2, independent sample T-tests have been conducted for groups 1 & 2, groups 1 & 3, and groups 1 & 4 respectively (see Table 2). It turns out that all test results conform to homoscedasticity. Among them, $P = 0.074 > 0.05$ in terms of groups 1 & 2, so that the original hypothesis is accepted and such two groups are deemed to be free of significant differences. Regarding groups 1 & 3 where $P = 0.024 < 0.05$, and groups 1 & 4 where $P = 0.001 < 0.05$, the original hypothesis should be rejected and no significant differences exist in groups 1 & 3 and groups 1 & 4. In the process of learning knowledge details, learning effect achieved by AR based visual content display is not significantly different from that obtained by book reading; however, comparing AR multi-touch and AR 3-D touch interactions, differences are rather significant. Under the circumstance that the number of children who correctly answered Question 2 is compared, data of groups 3 & 4 were apparently higher than those of Group 1, which verifies preliminary conclusion drawn during analysis on data obtained by Question 1.

Table 2. Independent sample T-test results of Question 2 in all Groups.

Independent Samples Test

		Levene's Test for Equality of Variances		t-test for Equality of Means						
		F	Sig.	t	df	Sig. (2-tailed)	Mean Difference	Std. Error Difference	95% Confidence Interval of the Difference	
									Lower	Upper
Q2 (EG1; EG2)	Equal variances assumed	3.429	.081	-1.897	18	.074	-.400	.211	-.843	.043
	Equal variances not assumed			-1.897	17.308	.075	-.400	.211	-.844	.044

		Levene's Test for Equality of Variances		t-test for Equality of Means						
		F	Sig.	t	df	Sig. (2-tailed)	Mean Difference	Std. Error Difference	95% Confidence Interval of the Difference	
									Lower	Upper
Q2 (EG1; EG3)	Equal variances assumed	.987	.334	-2.466	18	.024	-.500	.203	-.926	-.074
	Equal variances not assumed			-2.466	17.677	.024	-.500	.203	-.927	-.073

		Levene's Test for Equality of Variances		t-test for Equality of Means						
		F	Sig.	t	df	Sig. (2-tailed)	Mean Difference	Std. Error Difference	95% Confidence Interval of the Difference	
									Lower	Upper
Q2 (EG1; EG4)	Equal variances assumed	1.531	.232	-4.200	18	.001	-.700	.167	-1.050	-.350
	Equal variances not assumed			-4.200	16.691	.001	-.700	.167	-1.052	-.348

Data acquired from Question 2 answered by groups 3 & 4 are further analyzed accompanied with independent sample T-tests. As for relevant results, they have been given in Table 3 and confirmed to be in consistency with homoscedasticity. As $P = 0.288 > 0.05$, the original hypothesis can be accepted and groups 3 & 4 are deemed to have no significant difference. It signifies that AR multi-touch interaction and AR 3-D touch interaction are not significantly different from each other as far as detailed knowledge learning is concerned.

Table 3. Independent sample T-test results of Question 2 in Groups 3 & 4.

		Levene's Test for Equality of Variances		t-test for Equality of Means						
									95% Confidence Interval of the Difference	
		F	Sig.	t	df	Sig. (2-tailed)	Mean Difference	Std. Error Difference	Lower	Upper
Q2 (EG3; EG4)	Equal variances assumed	5.684	.028	-1.095	18	.288	-.200	.183	-.584	.184
	Equal variances not assumed			-1.095	15.517	.290	-.200	.183	-.588	.188

Question 3 is designed to comprehensively investigate children's mastery of knowledge that they have learnt. In this case, children who have accurately perceived the plant learned have the ability to answer it correctly, which is rather difficult. Practical knowledge learning puts more emphases on cognition and memorization of integrated knowledge. Therefore, data obtained through Question 3 are of practical meaning. According to preliminary analysis on related data, it turns out that no correct answers have been achieved from groups 1 & 2. Considering this, independent sample T-test should be conducted for groups 3 & 4 (see Table 4). Test results obtained are in conformity with homoscedasticity, in which case, $P = 0.018 < 0.05$. As a result, the original hypothesis should be rejected and groups 3 & 4 are deemed to significantly differ from each other. As indicated by graphical data above, the number of people giving correct answers in Group 4 is greater than Group 3. It demonstrates that AR 3-D touch interaction is superior to multi-touch interaction in terms of integrated knowledge learning. The possible cause to such an outcome is that buttons on the interactive interface adopted by multi-touch interaction in Group 3 play a role in making children distracted, which further results in learning effect reduction.

Table 4. Independent sample T-test results of Question 3 in Groups 3 & 4.

		Levene's Test for Equality of Variances		t-test for Equality of Means						
									95% Confidence Interval of the Difference	
		F	Sig.	t	df	Sig. (2-tailed)	Mean Difference	Std. Error Difference	Lower	Upper
Q3 (EG3; EG4)	Equal variances assumed	12.054	.003	-2.611	18	.018	-.500	.191	-.902	-.098
	Equal variances not assumed			-2.611	14.918	.020	-.500	.191	-.908	-.092

To sum up, learning efficiency and learning effects acquired by AR based visual presentation and book reading are similar, while AR multi-touch interaction is superior to AR based visual presentation despite that buttons on the interactive interface of the former can distract children from learning; however, AR 3-D touch interaction gives rise to higher learning efficiency and better learning effects. It has the capacity to facilitate children's learning and memorization abilities.

5 Conclusion

Dependent on laboratory findings, children participating the experiment show excitement and surprise of different degrees when they get in touch with AR technology for the first time. Nevertheless, pure AR based visual presentation fails to effectively make children concentrated continuously so that the purpose of learning and memorization ability promoting cannot be achieved in the real sense. When AR multi-touch interaction is adopted, children are able to rapidly learn and simulate touch operations and their interests in learning be stimulated; in this case, excitatory state can be maintained during learning. Nonetheless, conventional buttons on its interactive screen lead to decline of their concentration degrees, reduction of learning efficiency and adverse influence on learning effects. In the case that AR 3-D touch interaction has been utilized by children, they can be excited and engaged in the entire learning process. Thanks to the fact that interaction triggered components of such an interactive mode are integrated into THE plant's 3-D model, only a few buttons are required to guarantee that children concentrate more on cognitive learning and memorization.

Combining children's cognitive characteristics described above, learning and memorization by virtue of watching photos and characters have many defects. Not only does flat image information fail to bring a full range of visual presentation to children, but complicated written messages may incur understanding difficulties in them. Consequently, these children may lose their interests in further cognition and exploration. AR technology can be used to achieve an effect of visual experience enhancement. But, it cannot ensure that children are able to stay focused for a long time in the entire learning process and reasonable interactive modes should be set up to attract children. Although multi-touch interaction has the ability to improve children's learning and memorization concentration degree to a certain extent, they need to rotate and zoom the relevant plant's 3-D model, which is insignificantly correlated to biological characteristics of plants. As a consequence, it is much likely for it to incur memory omission of detailed knowledge. Comparatively, AR 3-D touch interaction makes learning more efficient. Children are able to touch all parts of the plant's 3-D model and observe corresponding interactive feedback animations. With a high skeuomorphism degree and a strong surprised feeling, such an interactive mode guarantees that children can keep interested in learning for a long time and their understanding and memorization of integrated knowledge be effectively strengthened.

In this paper, it has been demonstrated through experiments that AR based visual presentation and multi-touch interaction have certain shortcomings in the course of children education and learning; and, children who adopt AR 3-D touch interaction acquire higher learning efficiency and better learning effects. Children participating the experiment positively respond to gamified interactive mode based on AR and they are especially and strongly interested in 3-D touch interaction featured with skeuomorphism and attractiveness. 3-D touch interaction is a new attempt of AR based interactive modes. In this paper, only its application in children education was discussed. It is believed that such an interactive mode also has certain application values in other domains, which requires further exploring and investigating.

Acknowledgments. This work is supported by the Fundamental Research Funds for the Central Universities (2015ZCQ-YS-02) and Beijing Higher Education Young Elite Teacher Project (YETP0785).

References

1. Figueiredo, M., Bidarra, J.: The development of a gamebook for education. Procedia Comput. Sci. **67**, 322–331 (2015)
2. Sin, A.K., Zaman, H.B.: Live solar system (LSS): evaluation of an augmented reality book based educational tool. In: IEEE Information Technology (2010)
3. Jawad, S., Habib, A., Ali, B.: Enhanced interactive learning using augmented reality. In: IEEE Multi Topic Conference (2014)
4. Barreira, J., Bessa, M., Pereira, L.C., et al.: MOW: augmented reality game to learn words in different languages: case study: learning english names of animals in elementary school. **52**(11), 1–6 (2012)
5. Cheng, K.H., Tsai, C.: Children and parents' reading of an augmented reality picture book: analyses of behavioral patterns and cognitive attainment. Comput. Educ. **72**, 302–312 (2014)
6. Radu, I.: Why should my students use AR? A comparative review of the educational impacts of augmented reality. In: IEEE International Symposium on Mixed and Augmented Reality (2012)
7. Rambli, D.R.A., Matcha, W., Sulaiman, S.: Fun learning with AR alphabet book for preschool children. Procedia Comput. Sci. **25**(25), 211–219 (2013)
8. Minner, D., Levy, A.J.: Inquiry-based science instruction—what is it and does it matter? Results from a research synthesis years 1984 to 2002. J. Res. Sci. Teach. **47**(4), 474–496 (2010)
9. Vosniadou, S.: Capturing and modeling the process of conceptual change. Learn. Instr. (Special Issue) **4**(1), 45–69 (1994)
10. Fleck, S., Simon, G.: An augmented reality environment for astronomy learning in elementary grades: an exploratory study. In: ACM IEME Conference Francophone on L'interaction Homme Machine (2013)

Bridging the Gulfs: Modifying an Educational Augmented Reality App to Account for Target Users' Age Differences

Hannah Klautke[1,2(✉)], John Bell[1], Daniel Freer[1], Cui Cheng[1], and William Cain[1]

[1] Department of Counseling, Educational Psychology, and Special Education,
Michigan State University, East Lansing, MI 48824, USA
{klautkeh,johnbell,freerdan,chengcui,cainwil1}@msu.edu
[2] Usability/Accessibility Research and Consulting, Michigan State University,
East Lansing, MI 48824, USA

Abstract. This case study describes our process of modifying an augmented reality (AR) application called Spartan SR for spatial reasoning training for a different, younger user group. Originally designed for undergraduate college students, the application was modified for use by middle school students. Our modifications were designed to bridge certain gulfs of execution and evaluation in interactions with the application in ways that accounted for differences between college and middle-school students. Differences in age groups included reduced relevant prior knowledge and developmental differences in concrete versus abstract reasoning and problem solving as well as self-regulation and motivation. Using direct observation and focus group interviews, we identified modifications that seemed effective and others that needed additional refinement. Learned lessons include the need to redesign interface elements to help students navigate the Spartan SR environment; the value of introducing "real world" objects to scaffold the transition to more abstract shapes; the power of introducing elements of gamification; and the effects of various difficulty levels. These lessons led to iterative redesigns that have promise for improved user experiences at various age and learner levels.

Keywords: Augmented reality · STEM education · Gamification
Gulf of evaluation · Gulf of execution

1   Introduction

Spatial skills have been found to play critical roles in students' success in science, technology, engineering, and mathematics (STEM) fields [1–3]. However, training for developing spatial skills is too often overlooked, "because spatial thinking is not a subject, not something in which children are explicitly tested" [4]. In addition, traditional print-based materials have inherent limitations for presenting three-dimensional information for supporting the development of spatial reasoning ability. Existing digital technology allows us to explore the affordances of interactive programs (e.g., animation and simulation, augmented reality (AR), and virtual reality [5]) for spatial reasoning

© Springer International Publishing AG, part of Springer Nature 2018
A. Marcus and W. Wang (Eds.): DUXU 2018, LNCS 10920, pp. 185–195, 2018.
https://doi.org/10.1007/978-3-319-91806-8_15

training. In this study, we chose to modify an existing AR application to explore what benefits AR can provide and what makes an AR app usable in the context of spatial skills training in middle school. This application was originally designed to teach spatial skills to college-aged students entering a school of engineering. However, research suggests that adolescence is a critical period for developing spatial thinking, and adolescents with stronger spatial ability are more likely to choose a career in STEM fields [2]. Therefore, we believe applications such as ours (see Fig. 1) that are designed for practicing and developing spatial skills can be beneficial to younger students if appropriately modified for their abilities and approaches to learning. This study describes our design and implementation steps for modifying the AR application for use by middle school students.

Fig. 1. The augmented reality application on a mobile phone

2 Original Design Considerations

The spatial skills development app we used in this study, called Spartan SR, was designed to use augmented reality for a number of reasons. First, AR was deemed to be an excellent medium for spatial skills training since the environment creates a realistic impression of being able to interact with and manipulate digital objects in one's own physical space, giving embodiment to spatial tasks that would be awkward or difficult in real life (e.g., rotating objects in perfect 90-degree increments and cleanly around any of the three possible axes). In addition, AR allows designers to integrate spatial skills development with familiar gamification elements (e.g., unlocking challenges, leveling up, high-score competition, personal bests, etc.) for added learning and motivational incentives. Finally, while there are different types of augmented reality currently available, the choice to use a mobile phone/tablet version was due to the ubiquitous nature of mobile phones and tablets, ensuring that the majority of participants had their own device capable of running our augmented reality program. (Note that we loaned devices for students who needed them.)

In addition, the Spartan SR tool has several constraint-based affordances that traditional printed materials do not possess. As noted, learners can precisely rotate objects 90-degrees on a single axis at a time, which helps them see clear connections between different object states and abstract spatial expressions. Spartan SR was also designed to allow teachers to create their own lesson modules to better fit their class curriculum, as well as access students' progress data for formative learning assessments.

3   Motivations for Using Spartan SR with Younger Users

We had both theory-based and practical motivations for making the application usable for younger students. First and foremost, longitudinal studies show that spatial ability plays a critical role in developing expertise in STEM fields, and that spatial reasoning skill during adolescence is a salient attribute of individuals who go on to achieve advanced educational credentials and occupations in STEM [3]. Second, students around 11 years of age have been found to start becoming interested in STEM subjects, only to often lose this interest again a few years later, which is particularly true for girls [6]. This makes interventions with interactive and playful opportunities to foster the key skill of spatial reasoning and to maintain interest in STEM particularly relevant for learners during this critical window. From a practical standpoint, we recognized spatial reasoning to be a somewhat neglected area in secondary schools. For example, most standardized tests students take, such as SAT, ACT, and GRE exams, do not typically include spatial measures. This reflects a bias in favor of formal mathematics and verbal skills that may be rooted in teachers' and education advocates' own strengths and backgrounds [7, 8]. It is often not until college or beyond that future architects or engineers encounter the intricacies of spatial reasoning, and future mechanics or machinists have to pick up their needed spatial skills on the job [7]. We were also eager to tap into younger learners' often high appreciation for smartphone apps and games when used in school and in class [9], and their appreciation for gamified approaches to learning, such as unlocking new challenges and levels.

4   Differences Between College and Middle-School Learners

In contrast to college students, the middle school users in this case study reported little to no prior experience with three-dimensional coordinate systems, although they did have some basic knowledge about two-dimensional (X and Y) axes. Similarly, the younger users had no previous exposure to the concept of positive versus negative rotations around axes and the related notation (such as "+X" or "−Z").

According to Piagetian theory of cognitive development, problem solving skills in 10–11-year-olds are in the process of becoming more logical, but still depend to some extent on concrete events and objects rather than abstract and hypothetical ones [10].

Children aged 11–15 are right at the transition point where they move from trial-and-error approaches to systematically solving a problem in a logical and methodical way [11]. Since these developments do not occur at the exact same time in every student, sixth grade classes have a broad range of abilities and maturity levels. Conversations with teachers interested in using Spartan SR in their classes also described this age range as marked by often high energy levels, as well as mixed levels of task persistence and emotional maturity.

5   Guiding Principles for Design Modifications

To modify Spartan SR for younger users, we considered the elements of direct manipulation interfaces that Hutchins, Hollan, and Norman describe as gulfs to be bridged by effective design choices for successful user interface interaction to occur [12, 13]. The gulf of execution describes the cognitive effort required to have the system do what you want it to do, whereas the gulf of evaluation refers to the cognitive effort required to make sense of the output displays. To create a sense of directness in interacting with the system, cognitive effort for both is to be minimized.

In the case of Spartan SR, we wanted users to experience various objects to be rotated and compared to a target as though they were moving them in real physical space. Our objective was to make their learning experience as authentic as possible, and to give them a sense of control over the rotation of the objects, within the intentional constraints provided. While we considered enabling direct swiping of the objects on the phone as a way reduce the gulf of execution, we chose to maintain the use of the six rotation icons (three axes in two directions) to support the deliberate practice of mental rotation between the stages of perceiving the object's state and acting upon it.

6   Design Modifications and User Reactions

Given earlier experiences we had with college-age users [14], we felt we needed to make modifications to the app in order to make it more suitable for younger users. Our modifications were related to both evaluation and execution processes in order to maximize practice and feedback with the crucial mental rotation step in between the two. In what follows, we describe the designed changes along with student feedback regarding the efficacy of these changes.

To gather this feedback, we introduced the modified app in three six-grade classrooms over the course of three days. Across the three 50-min class periods, students were asked to work through a series of increasingly challenging games, involving the rotation of objects of varying complexity around the three axes of the coordinate system. For example, during early rounds, users had to match the rotated position of an object to that of a smaller identical target object. A more advanced game asked them to achieve a certain rotation by clicking one or two rotation buttons before the object would be responding. On the fourth day, thirty-three of the participating students (18 males, 15 females; 11–13 years old) took part in one of eight 4–5 person, 50-min focus groups.

Questions centered on their experience using the app overall; on specific features, levels and games within it; and on any suggestions they had for future iterations of the design.

6.1   New Bridges Across the Gulf of Evaluation: UI Practice Opportunities with Familiar Objects

In order to use the application effectively for practicing mental rotation, a user must first perceive the initial orientation of a presented object in space. To meet the younger users' preference for more concreteness, we redesigned the initial practice rounds to include familiar objects such as a simple house, a pickup truck, or a bench (see Fig. 2). User comments indicate that this approach was helpful in building up to more abstract, "engineering-like" random shapes:

"I think the everyday objects (helped) because they're just objects that you know and they're easier to predict what the other sides would look like. Because if you've just got a square face on one of your shapes, there could be like a weird jagged curve on the other side of it."

"The everyday shapes did help you out a lot because you see them every day, everywhere and but the harder ones, like the box ones and stuff, those really made you think, like think ahead, two steps ahead about what they look like in a different form, different angle."

"Well, when you did the beginner (everyday objects), it was easier than intermediate and expert, so it got harder, but you're already kind of ready. All the other lessons built you up."

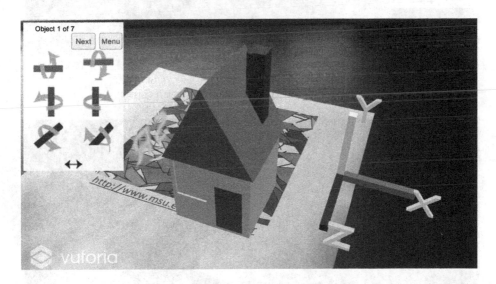

Fig. 2. Everyday objects (e.g., a house as shown in the above figure) were used in our redesign to meet younger users' need for more relatable and concrete objects.

6.2   New Bridges Across the Gulf of Execution: Intuitive Button Design

For the younger users, we wished to scaffold a growing understanding of what rotations around the three different axes looked like. Since learning formal notation was not the goal for this age group, we replaced the original user interface buttons (see the upper-left corner of Fig. 3 for the original rotation notation) with icons of curved arrows going around small segments of the axes, color-coded to correspond with the provided coordinate system model (see the upper-left corner of Fig. 4 for the redesigned icons that correspond with the color-coded axes). Overall, these more intuitive icons used as button labels worked well for the middle school students:

"The arrows helped a lot because otherwise, I wouldn't have no… I would have no idea which way it would go…. Instead of like trying to memorize which buttons do what."

"I used the buttons because it would say like, oh, it's going around a red pole or over the blue bar. And I thought that was really useful."

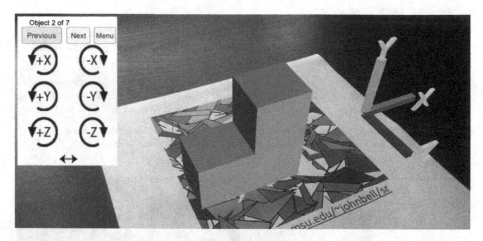

Fig. 3. The original rotation notation (upper-left corner).

Fig. 4. The redesigned rotation icons (upper-left corner).

However, perhaps because they lacked previous exposure to the third dimension (Z-axis) of the coordinate system, some confusion remained regarding the axes over the course of four sessions:

"The Y axis was easy to figure out but I'm like I know what to do but I couldn't figure out which one to click."

6.3   Combining System Cues with Embodied Cognition Guidance

Anticipating we would need to explain the axis system in terms the students could relate to, we redesigned the in-class orientation to the app to connect movement in Spartan SR to movement in the real world. We did this by comparing the axis to physical, full body movements such as somersaults, cartwheels, and pirouettes (see Fig. 5). Some students found this full body embodiment explanation helpful: *"Since I'm a gymnast, I really get that, so (for) the one that you are supposed to turn it like this, I would think of it as like a cartwheel or like a full turn or like a front or backward flip."* However, not all students showed equal enthusiasm for this approach.

Fig. 5. One of our researchers introducing the AR application to one of three sixth grade classes

We also offered an alternative hand-only embodiment explanation, asking students to imagine picking up objects and rotating them by hand following the indicated rotation direction. In our case, there was a bit more appreciation of this approach: *"If somebody put their hand along with the arrow and just tipped it, that's the way it would go. So I used it, I used the buttons because it would say like, oh, it's going around a red pole or over the blue bar. And I thought that was really useful."*

6.4 Providing Additional Strategies for Mental Rotation Practice

We anticipated additional challenges when working with sixth graders as compared to college students. In particular, we expected greater variety in maturity and self-regulation, and weaker problem solving strategies. To help with these challenges, one of our strategies was to include drawing activities with concrete objects. Doing so provided a buffer in terms of time (when some students completed lessons much faster than others), gave more concrete activities than just manipulating a phone interface, and different ways to engage when the phone app was too challenging. In addition, we provided more direct support for students when intervention seemed to be needed.

Direct observation led us to believe that these strategies were very important for this population of students. Some of them needed more support when encountering difficult tasks as well as guidance for how to handle times of significant frustration by particularly challenging task conditions (see Sect. 7.1).

7   Lessons Learned for App Modifications Across Age Groups

Our goal was to make the Spartan SR app more suitable for use with younger learners. We feel this goal of the modification was met, as evidenced by the positive experience and high engagement that the younger users exhibited. Focus group participants frequently mentioned appreciating the "real" appearance of objects in space and one's ability to explore their position and control their movements.

> "I liked that if you moved around the paper … you could see the different sides of the object which made it really cool."

> "It was really fun because it's like you're not actually like touching it in real life but you can move it and it's like real life even though it's not real life."

The younger users also responded positively to the gamification elements of the app, more explicitly so than the original target group of college students. For example, one student described her response to the application's stepwise unlocking of and check-marks for progressively more challenging objects and tasks:

> "It was addicting… Because like every time you get, beat a level, it's like, yes, it's going to the next one and if you mess up, you have to be like, no, I have to redo that, I have to redo and you just keep going."

7.1   A Challenge for Design: Setting an Ideal Challenge Level

Apart from such positive feedback overall, students gave mixed responses to a particular version of a prediction game within the app. In the standard version of this game students had to decide all the moves to make prior to the object's moving. In the advanced version, if a single part was wrong, they would have to start from the beginning. While students generally recognized the prediction game as an activity that really got them to mentally rotate objects rather than using a trial and error approach, the advanced level requiring perfect execution tested the students' persistence and would have lowered feelings of self-efficacy without encouragement and buffering statements on the part of the research team/instructors. Practical suggestions made included allowing the user to choose a desired level of challenge (such as unlocking higher levels even if the current level was completed with errors).

"It was frustrating when I got super far and then I had to restart but whenever I messed up."

"You had to be patient with it. You had to (…) calm yourself down or else you'd get too frustrated. Yeah. It made me frustrated a little bit but I actually, it gave me a challenge and I like challenges."

Importantly, regarding the question of whether one can improve one's mental rotation skills through practice, some students indicated that frustrating moments within the games and errors made throughout were useful in getting better.

"I mean, I think all of us sort of did (improve their skills) in a way, so I think if we did, then anyone could."

"Your brain hurts, (but in) a good way."

These responses suggest that the use of the app was supporting the constructive mindset of the targeted skill as amenable to growth through practice rather than as fixed [15], particularly with this group, which was not something we had expected.

7.2 Additional Takeaways for Future Design Modifications

For the future developments of this kind of AR application for use with middle school students, we took insights both directly from the user feedback and indirectly from overlaying relevant theory and user interface design principles with our experience in the new use context. One category of user feedback was the desire for competition:

"I liked the leader board idea... where you would compete against your classmates if you sign in on the same account and you can like, there'd be a leader board and you could try and compete for first place and you'd know who's in first place."

"I liked the time thing. I think what you could also do because a lot of kids our age and even older kids, they like competition, try to be like the best at something. So maybe in the corner, you could have a leader board or something."

Another category of feedback was regarding object design. That is, the adjustment to add practice objects that users would be familiar with was not only well received, but also encouraged further in a common suggestion for what would make the application better for this age group: *"If they added more realistic shapes that you'd see in real life."*

Based on theory and user interface principles in connection with our observations, we took away additional ideas: First, to provide a brief video tutorial up front that is easily accessible initially and as a reference after getting started. In Norman's (1986) terms, "Visual presence can aid the various stages of activity. Thus, we give support to the generation of intentions by reminding the user of what is possible. We support action selection because the visible items act as a direct translation into possible actions." Second, an application such as ours could provide a replay function that supports a learner's self-correction, aiding "evaluation by making it possible to provide visual reminders of what was done" [13] Third, since a competitive spirit was mentioned as typical of 6th graders by many, but not all participants, we consider options based on motivation research indicating benefits of an alternative to the leader board element of gamification: Providing the goal and feedback on beating one's own time over the course of repeated use of the application, or having leaderboards for different "leagues" to avoid constant direct comparisons between students of widely differing ability instead [16, 17].

8   Summary

We found that in general our design modification of the application was a success for the audience of sixth grade students. Particularly, we encountered benefits from the use of intuitively understandable objects, as well as from scaffolding initial evaluation processes as users needed to focus on getting oriented within the application, with the three axes and directions of possible rotation, and the act of doing so in one's mind. However, based on feedback from the students some aspects of the application require additional changes, such as allowing for errors in completion of game levels and making interface buttons for the rotation of objects more intuitive. Overall, students reported and demonstrated that the majority of this application was motivating even in the face of the challenges the students encountered while practicing this skill that is so valuable for STEM learning. Based on our experience described here, we plan on building on the successful elements of gamification and address the problematic areas so as to improve the user experience of this kind of application for various levels of age and preexisting experience with the application's content.

References

1. Hsi, S., Linn, M.C., Bell, J.E.: The role of spatial reasoning in engineering and the design of spatial instruction. J. Eng. Educ. **86**(2), 151–158 (1997)
2. Uttal, D.H., Cohen, C.A.: Spatial thinking in STEM education: when, why, and how? In: Ross, B. (ed.) Psychology of Learning and Motivation, vol. 57, pp. 147–182. Academic Press, San Diego (2012)
3. Wai, J., Lubinski, D., Benbow, C.P.: Spatial ability for STEM domains: aligning over 50 years of cumulative psychological knowledge solidifies its importance. J. Educ. Psychol. **101**(4), 817 (2009)
4. Shea, D.L., Lubinski, D., Benbow, C.P.: Importance of assessing spatial ability in intellectually talented young adolescents: a 20-year longitudinal study. J. Educ. Psychol. **93**(3), 604–614 (2001)
5. Papastergiou, M.: Digital game-based learning in high school computer science education: impact on educational effectiveness and student motivation. Comput. Educ. **52**(1), 1–12 (2009)
6. Microsoft Corporation: Why Europe's girls aren't studying STEM (2017)
7. Knapp, A.: Why schools don't value spatial reasoning (2012). https://www.forbes.com/sites/alexknapp/2011/12/27/why-dont-schools-value-spatial-reasoning/#4c683cd967b5. Accessed 20 Jan 2018

8. Wai, J.: Three reasons why schools neglect spatial intelligence (2012). https://www.psychologytoday.com/blog/finding-the-next-einstein/201208/three-reasons-why-schools-neglect-spatial-intelligence
9. Newcombe, N.E.: Picture this: increasing math and science learning by improving spatial thinking. Am. Educ. **34**(2), 29 (2010)
10. Ginsburg, H., Opper, S.: Piaget's Theory of Intellectual Development. Prentice Hall, Upper Saddle River (1979)
11. Piaget, J.: The Psychology of Intelligence. Littlefield, Totowa (1972)
12. Hutchins, E.L., Hollan, J.D., Norman, D.A.: Direct manipulation interfaces. Hum.-Comput. Interact. **10**(4), 311–338 (1985)
13. Norman, D.A.: Cognitive engineering. In: User Centered System Design, vol. 31, pp. 32–61 (1986)
14. Bell, J.E., Cheng, C., Freer, D.J., Cain, C.J., Klautke, H., Hinds, T.J., Walton, S.P., Cugini, C.: Work in progress: a study of augmented reality for the development of spatial reasoning ability. In: 2017 ASEE Annual Conference & Exposition (2017)
15. Dweck, C.S.: Motivational processes affecting learning. Am. Psychol. **41**(10), 1040 (1986)
16. DiMenichi, B.C., Tricomi, E.: The power of competition: effects of social motivation on attention, sustained physical effort, and learning. Front. Psychol. **6**, 1282 (2015)
17. Barata, G., Gama, S., Jorge, J., Gonçalves, D.: So fun it hurts–gamifying an engineering course. In: Schmorrow, D.D., Fidopiastis, C.M. (eds.) AC 2013. LNCS, vol. 8027, pp. 639–648. Springer, Heidelberg (2013). https://doi.org/10.1007/978-3-642-39454-6_68

How Animation Improve Children's Cognition in User Interface: A Study of the Kids VOD Application

Wei Li[1,2(✉)], Xuan Zhang[2], and Yi Shen Zhang[2]

[1] Tsinghua University, Beijing 100084, China
stephen82226@foxmail.com
[2] IQIYI, Inc., No. 2 Haidian North 1st Street, Beijing 100080, China
sharonwlw.2017@gmail.com,
zhangys08@mails.tsinghua.edu.cn

Abstract. There have been many studies of cognitive and affective benefits from incorporating the animation in user interfaces, thus, only a few have investigated that how animation in user interface affects children's cognition while they interact with interfaces in their different growing stage. In this paper, we want to figure out if the animation in user interface can benefit the cognition, interaction, and emotion of children at different age range. A study was carried out by comparing a series user interface demos with and without animation based on typical tasks in the Kids VOD APP among two groups of children ages 4–6 years and 7–12 years. The result of this study shows that the two groups of children have differences on the task completion rate, task completion efficiency, and emotion preference. This suggest that applying animation to user interface for children needs consideration of children's age and animation usage scenarios.

Keywords: Animation · User interface · Cognition · Video on demand
Usage scenario

1 Introduction

Nowadays, animation is broadly used in user interface to increase adaptation and understanding of users. It can draw user attention, explain visual changes and put a sense of positive emotion in the user experience [2]. Although there is a growing body of research on animated user interface, less is known about the impact of animated user interface on children. It's still not clear that how animation contributes to children's cognition and performance when they interact with user interface. There are also some limitation in the research on animated user interface. Firstly, author mainly test users from effect of task completion related to adopting animation, but emotional preference in different usage scenario is not fully considered. Secondly, the main purpose of the 12 basic principles of Disney is to produce an illusion of characters adhering to the basic laws of physics and also deal with more abstract issues, such as emotional timing and character appeal [3]. However, it was not created for improving user interfaces at the beginning [4]. There are several new animation design principles which adapt especially for user interface design, such as iOS User Interface Design Guideline [5], Google material design guideline [6], and UMP guideline [7]. Novick [8] discussed how some types of animation can be used for different purpose by connecting types of animation with different communicative functions, which could help to figure out how certain types of animation can be used for different purpose [2]. Last but not least, how usage scenario effects children's cognition to animation should be considered, evaluation should be employed in the specific user task and then we can evaluate the animation in the usage scenario.

This paper aims to investigate the relationships between animation and children's cognition, so as to give suggestions to the design of user interface for children. In this study, we chose the Kid VOD[1], a video on demand application for children in China, because of the increasing demands of children in online video viewing. According to the studies of cognitive development of children, we carried out the usability and interview with two groups of children, ages between 4–6 years and 7–12 years. 3 groups of demos with and without animation were made based on the Kids VOD. The animation we used in the demos were a combination of the most frequently-used types which were based on the types of animation constructed by Novick [8]. We evaluated children's cognition from 5 aspects with the tasks: the completion rate, the efficiency, the memory of content, the understanding of application structure, and emotional preference.

From our study, we concluded that animation has different effects on comprehension and interaction of children among these two age ranges. When children interact with user interface, animation has a positive effect on comprehension, memory, task completion rates and efficiency, preference among children of 7–12 years old, whereas, no significant effect on task completion rates, comprehension and preference among children aged 4–6. Our findings suggested that the use of animation needs to be carefully considered according to the characteristics of the crowd and the usage scenario.

2 Literature Review

When we discuss the topic about the relationship of animated interface and children cognition in the Kids VOD, four parts of literature should be studied: the development of children's cognition in their growth process, the present studies of user interface for children, the present studies of animation in user interface, and the background of VOD service for children.

2.1 The Development of Children's Cognition in Their Growth Process

From the study of cognitive development of children, children obtain different ability of cognition in their different ages, which might lead to different understanding and

---

[1] The Kids VOD is a popular video on demand mobile application for children in China. "VOD" is the abbreviation of "Video on Demand".

preference to animation in user interface. In order to perform successful user study, it is better to know much of children's cognitive abilities [9]. According to Piaget's study, the childhood cognitive development could be divided into four stages: Sensorimotor Stage (Birth through about 2 years), Preoperational Stage (2 to 7 years), Concrete Operational Stage (7 to 11 years), and Formal Operational Stage (11 years and older) [10]. Meanwhile, Nielsen [11], a user experience specialist, claimed researchers should make distinction between young (3 to 5 years), mid-range (6 to 8 years), and older (9 to 12 years) children. In another study, children could be sorted into three age ranges: preschool-aged children (2 to 5 years), elementary-school-aged children (6–10), and middle-school-aged children (11 to 14 years) [12]. Since children's growing stage is an important factor which would influences the ability of cognition and comprehension of children, participants should be grouped as their age range.

According to theories of human cognitive development, children of group ages 7 to 12 are in stage where they learn to reason logically and have difficulties with thinking abstractly. Children as young as 7–8 were able to distinguish between concepts such as usability, fun, and potential for learning [13]. Erickson's theory of psychosocial development claimed that children require emotional support and a feeling of success [14]. According Erickson's theory, whether animation used in user interface can influence children's emotion preference should be investigated.

2.2   The Present Studies of User Interface for Children

Children's cognition differences also reflected on their preference for user interfaces. Taslim [15] found that there were significant differences in children's preferences for interface type and background color. It reported a preliminary analysis of gestures elicited from children ages 5 to 10. They found that there were clear differences in the way older and younger children make gestures, even between the ages of 5 to 10 years. But his research didn't involve preference of animation.

There are also some related researches investigate relationship between children's cognition and user interface. Lorna and Read [16] did a research of designing meaningful icon based on children's understanding for a music application. They explore proper iconic representations for a "record music" function on a mobile device which could be used for reference in VOD interface design of children. It's a general problem to understand the meaning of icon for children in user interface. Their study was carried out with children aged 8 to 10, and they found that graphical user interface could contribute to the users with reading or language problems such as preschoolers. They suggested that the design of icons should be attractive, clear to children. Since users will vary greatly in their abilities and their understanding of functions (especially for children). One of important suggestion is that animations may help to convey the function represented by unfamiliar icons. Azzopardi et al. [17] investigated relationship between VOD service and the everyday patterns and lives of children. They found that children preferred to browse through content rather than natural language. From the studies of how children use user interface, we can conclude that the differences of preference to user interface between children and adults should be fully considered in interface design for children.

2.3   The Present Studies of Animation in User Interface

From the study of current research on animation in user interface, less is known about the study for children, and also, the usability evaluation. A research about the effects of animation on usability and appeal of educational software user interface was conducted by Dyer and Villani [18], which compared 3 interfaces: a static interface, an interface with highlighting/sound feedback, and an interface that incorporated five Disney animation principles. The result of the study did not show significant effects of animation on user task performance, which was measured by activity completion times and number of errors while performing the activities. However, task completion times using the animated interface were consistently lower than that using the static interfaces. Therefore, interface with the animated interface rated more likeable than the other two, because of the smooth transitions between different states, this might suggest that applying animation to user interface can only benefit user's emotion in their interaction with user interface. However, the main purpose of the 12 basic principles of Disney is to produce an illusion of characters adhering to the basic laws of physics and also deal with more abstract issues, such as emotional timing and character appeal [3]. It was not created for improving user interfaces at the beginning. Since there are significant differences between cartoons and interfaces [4], the test materials should follow the design guideline especially for user interface, and should be evaluated in real usage scenarios.

In the past years, iOS, Android have published their design guidelines, and all of these guidelines emphasized the importance of animation in user interface. The Human Interface Guidelines published by iOS platform indicate that animation builds a visual sense of connection between people and content on screen [5], while the Material Design Guidelines published by Android platform consider animation as a more functional elements which can convey status, provide feedback, enhance the sense of direct manipulation, and help users visualize the results of their actions [6]. Novick [8] has constructed an model of animation connecting types of animation with different communicative functions, this model indicates how some types of animation can be used for different purpose in user interface, which means it is constructed with the consideration of the usage scenario of animation.

2.4   The Background of VOD Service for Children

In the recent years, video on demand (VOD) service becomes one of the most popular service around the world. People enjoy all kind of video content across different platform that provide massive online video service such as PC, Pad, Phone, TV. Not only can adults use these service, but also children. Children watch a great deal of online videos, and the amount of time that they spend on watching video continues to increase [20]. Mobile media companies, including the telecom industry and hardware manufacturers, have never considered infants as a part of their target users historically. It is only with the popularity of mobile phone and the emergency of touch screen interfaces that infants can access to mobile technology [21]. Touch screen tablets, for example, are increasingly used in the home as a source of literacy skills as a result of the simplistic tactile operation. This study also claimed that smartphones and the Internet are the most frequently used tools to watch videos by children under the age of 4 years [22].

In China, according to the Research about the Use of Internet of Chinese Teenager and Children in May of 2015 from iResearch[2] [23], over 50 percent of children have access to the Internet in preschool, which indicated the tendency that children might access to the Internet in a lower age. The main devices for children accessing the Internet in China are mobile phones, more than 70% of children use them at any age. Watching video and playing games are the primary online needs for children, followed by learning and doing homework. Comparing the requirements of children in different ages, we can concluded that watching videos and playing games are the common demands of children aged from 3 to 8 years, and the proportion of users who watch video is higher than 70%. Furthermore, we can conclude that the proportion of users who watch video at age 9–11 also reached 63%. By December of 2017, the Kids VOD our test based on had got more than 20 million accumulated users, of which 97% users are under 13 years old. The average time they watching videos is around 60 min per day. The number of users still increases with the quarterly speed of 13%.

Several key factors affecting user experience in using VOD service [24]. Krefetz proposed that the entire viewing experience must be pleasurable from discovery to content selection to the player controls. And thus be as important as content in online video service. Otherwise, viewers will not stick around long enough to figure out if they like the content [25]. He listed four important user interface features that provided good user experience to viewers such as personalizing interfaces, recommendation system, chat feature that viewers chatted while watching videos, and contextualized content. The purposes of providing animation in user interface is to make the system more friendly and likely, achieving good user experience.

3   Research Design

3.1   Context

Researchers have done a lot of studies on the research methods used to find how children use applications, such as experiments and measurement. Scales are normally used as the main methods in these studies. When assessing the animation effect design, researchers would like to design some experimental tasks to examine children's ability of memory and comprehension. Bederson employed the concept of "mental map" and apply the animation transition to help children understand the construction of the application [26]. Thomas and Victor [27] conducted a "recall-recognition" paradigm to explore the effectiveness of different animation effects in improving user's ability to remember the content of applications. During the "recall" process, in order to test how effective these animation was in improving memory, subjects were shown graphical objects with different animation in movement. Moreover, scholars asked children to use an interactive application designed for teaching math and to complete certain

---

[2] iResearch is a provider of online audience measurement and consumer insights in China. http://www.iresearchchina.com/.

experimental tasks. The task completion times and number of mistake were used to indicate children's performance in using the application. Ognjanovic and Ralls [28] considered that children in the usability test might give responses to comfort the examiners rather than express their real ideas. To prevent this kind of experimental error, they advocate using "Peer Tutoring" in the test, in which a child will be assigned a tutor to supervise them to complete the test. As children have difficulty in understanding text, Lorna and Read [16] uses smiley face and photos in the measurement scales to help children express their attitudes and preference, which increased the reliability and validity of the evaluation. Furthermore, young children's responses might be influenced by the examiner or they cannot express their ideas accurately. Therefore, observing young children's expression and manner of speaking will be helpful for understanding children's assessment on products and assignments [28].

In this paper, to examine the effectiveness of the animation design in children's cognitive ability, our research was conducted by 4 methods: experimental task, observation, interview and measurement scale. According to the characteristics of subjects, the methods of observation and interview are used to get more direct information from the subjects. The advantage of observation is to help examiner discover the true feelings of subjects from their expression and behavior, which can prevent subjects from unclear or inaccurate expression, and catering to the examiner's pleasure. Since the subjects of this study were children aged 4–12 guided by the adult examiner in the test process, it would be easily for them to behave to satisfy the examiner and social desirability. Therefore, it was necessary to use the observation in the study.

Moreover, children's click operation was observed in the memory task, because of the limitation in verbal expression of very young children. The order and times of the click could reflect subjects' thinking process when recording. The interview started after the main experimental task, which focused on the doubts in the operation process for the purpose of interpretation of the experimental results. At the same time, in order to know more about users' perception of the animation effect, the subjects were interviewed about their preference of animation usage in other applications they used before. If the subjects failed to express clearly in interview, researcher would change the way of communication, for example, let children drawing as assistance.

3.2   Participants

The age division of this experiment referenced Cognitive-Developmental Theory propounded by Piaget and Inhelder [10] and Erikson's stages of psychosocial development [29]. In Cognitive-Developmental Theory, children of Preoperational Stage and Concrete Operations Stage differ in their thinking characteristics, which may lead to changes of children's ability on understanding dynamic comprehension. In Erikson's stages of psychosocial development, children in Stage 3 (Purpose) start to have autonomy and gradually improve their learning ability in Stage 4 (Competence), which may lead to the difference of task performance. Considering that children need to have adequate communication skills and cognitive abilities to ensure that the experiment is completed independently, the division is determined as the ages of 4–6 and 7–12.

Totally 120 users of Kid VOD application participated in this test, and they were selected by age range and usage experience. Participants were groups by age, the 4–6 years group and 7–12 years group. Each group had 60 participants, and 30 of them didn't have used the "history" function while the other 30 had used that before. The calculation method which was came up by Sauro and Lewis [30] and Jin et al. [31] to calculate the number of required subjects was used in the study. The required samples as a whole would be influenced by some factors: 1. Confidence level α (in this study, when α = 0.9, t = 1.64); 2. The accepted sample bias d (the maximum deviation between the estimated value and the true value; the smaller the deviation, the higher the accuracy, the more required samples. In this study, d = 15%); 3. Quantity N (was regarded as an infinite value in this study). According to the calculation formula of sample size using Eq. (1)

$$n = n\_0/(1 + (n\_0 - 1)/N), n\_0 = (t^2 PQ)/d^2 \tag{1}$$

We could draw that on the assumption α = 0.9 and d = 15%, the overall quantity n = 30, meaning that every test needed 30 subjects. This experiment divided participants into two age groups (4–6 years old and 7–12 years old) and each group used two different demos (with animation effect or without animation effect). Therefore, there were 4 test groups (2 × 2), 30 participants in each group and in this experiment, the history and the encyclopedia function in the Kid VOD were selected for the reason that history is one of the most high utilization rate functions (shown as Fig. 1). An equal numbers of users who had or had not the experience of using history function were distributed in each experimental group on average.

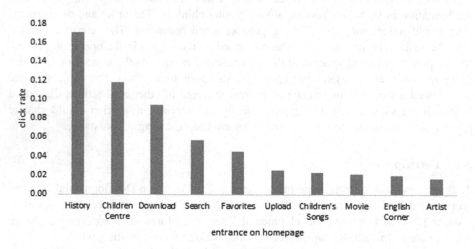

Fig. 1. Distribution of entrance click on homepage functions (monthly value)

3.3   Instruments

Equipment. The experiment was operated in an iPhone with 4.7 inches' screen. According to the 2017 Q2 Summer Report of the Internet from Questmobile [32], the proportion of 4.7 inches' mobile screen used by iOS users is 46%, which is higher than other screen size. The experiments are carried out in a quiet meeting rooms with colorful decoration, to provide the participants a proper and relaxing environment. In order to prevent children from distraction during the experimental process, some animation posters instead of toys were put up in the room. Moreover, voice recorder and camera were prepared to record the experiments. Before the experiment, examiners helped children and their parents to get familiar with the experimental environment, introduced the experiment purpose, the equipment, the privacy protection, and then asked them to sign the informed consents.

Demo Designed for Tasks. This experiment included 3 tasks, all the participants were required to complete these tasks in sequence under the examiners' guidance. The demo used in each tasks were designed based on the Kids VOD. Some of the animation in the demos were developed especially for the study. In the experimental tasks, researchers paid a lot of attention to the information from the subjects' expression and operation through the observation. The types of animation we used in our user test were based on types and functions of animation as discussed in Novick [8]. The types we used in our animation demo are as Table 1. Since the type of gesture in the original table is not clearly defined [2], it seems as an action that users take by hand, not a transition effect in user interface, we moved it out of the table and did not use it in animation design of demos. The types of animation we used was shown as Table 1.

Table 1. Types of animation used in test demo.

Animation types	Used in test demo
A change of place	Yes
A change of size	Yes
Rotation	Yes
A change of color	None
Blur	Yes

Product Series 1

Product series 1 used in task 1 included 3 demo: slow animation effect, quick animation effect and no animation effect (labelled as 1A, 1B, 1C). In task 1, subjects were asked to find and click icons–"History" and "Encyclopedia" to see whether they could learn how to go back to the upper level page from transfer animation effect when entered into this page. The task completion rate was measured by the number of wrong operation and observation of the examiner. The efficiency of completing task was measured through the completion time.

The homepage of the product is shown in Fig. 2. The design of the transfer animation effect and transition animation effect are based on the function of "History" and "Encyclopedia". The unfolding interface of the "History" is shown as in Fig. 3. Following is the description about the animation effects used in the test (take Demo 1A for example):

Fig. 2. The homepage of the Kids VOD application, with the history icon like "clock" in the left column.

Fig. 3. The page of history of the Kids VOD application.

- Transition effect: In the non-playing state, a non-magnified module will expand into the main module if it is clicked. The transition effect will be active in the process of change, and the duration of the page transition is 1.5 s [33].
- Transition animation effect of the icon "History": in the home page, the icon "History" gives a hint by zooming (dynamic hints have more significant impression on children' vision).
- The background texture of the modules and the transition effect adopt the metaphor of jelly.

Product Series 2

Product series 2 used in task 2. There are two sessions of the task 2: "Memorization" and "Representation". Subjects were asked to remember 8 pictures of different cartoons, all the pictures entered with an animation effect or without animation effect, and these two demos are labelled as 2A and 2B. Then subjects were asked to put these pictures in corresponding positions in the paperboard, making a reappearance of what they remembered. This task mainly examined the effectiveness of animation effect in children's memory, which was measured by the memory time, representation time and the accuracy of representation.

The "Memorization" section was as follow:

- There were 8 pictures with light color and deer image shown on the screen, and every picture was the same.
- After clicking each picture, a cartoon in the corresponding position appeared. There were total 8 different cartoons appeared on the screen.
- Demo 2A: cartoons entered from different directions (e.g. the cartoon in the upper left position slide from the upper left)
- Demo 2B: cartoons appeared from the same site directly (without animation effect). The screen showed as Fig. 4, after all the pictures appeared.

Fig. 4. The page with 8 different cartoons.

The "Representation" section was: we made a paperboard of the page as Fig. 4, with light color and placeholder image, showing the corresponding positions. Also, we printed 8 cartoon cards which were the same as the demo showed. Subjects were required to place the 8 cartoon cards in the corresponding positions in their memory. The paperboard and 8 cartoon cards shows in Fig. 5.

Fig. 5. The paperboard of the page with 8 cartoon cards in Task 2

Product Series 3

Product series 3 used in task 3. There were 2 sessions of the task 3: "Memorization" and "Representation". Task 3 ask children to learn the logical construction which combines a series of product pages (the transition with an animation effect or B without animation effect). The two demos are labelled as 3A and 3B. After that, examiner asked children to put the cards in corresponding positions in the paperboard accurately according to the logical construction they learnt from the application. The understanding of the product structure was measured by learning time, representation time and the accuracy of representation.

The "Memorization" section was as follow:

- Demo has 6 screenshots of the Kids VOD application. The logic of page transition is shown as Fig. 6. Only one screenshot and arrows in the corresponding directions appear after each click. Users can redirect the pages in the corresponding direction through clicking arrows or sliding pages.
- Initially, there are the screenshot of homepage and three arrows pointing in different directions. These 3 arrows point to lower left, lower right and right, which separately direct to "Encyclopedia", "History" and sideslip of the homepage (shown as Fig. 7).
- Demo 3A: Transition with animation effect (fade in or fade out).
- Demo 3B: Transition without animation effect (neither fade in nor fade out).

The "Representation" section was as follow: we made a paperboard with 6 wireframes which showed the spatial relationship among screenshots. We printed 6 screenshot cards which were the same as the demo shows. Subjects were asked to put these cards in the corresponding positions depending in their memory, shown as Fig. 8.

Measurement Scale. This study used the measurement scale to measure subject's emotion changes and preference. In order to avoid the individual difference in emotion, we tested the subjects' mood before and after the experiment to capture their mood

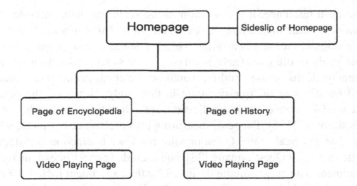

Fig. 6. The construction of pages in Task 3.

Fig. 7. The homepage with arrows in Task 3.

Fig. 8. The paperboards of 6 pages in Task 3.

change. The main reference of the emotion rating scale was from Angold et al. [34], which developed a scale to measure children's emotion. This study made some changes on Messer's original measurement scale, deleting some improper questions (such as whether feel lonely or often cry) and modifying some statements without changing the original intention. Considering children would be impatient of the questionnaire, there were only 3 questions in the questionnaire in this study. However, the certain retest reliability $\alpha = 0.64$ is above 0.5 (it is believed that the questionnaire can be trusted if the reliability is above 0.5) [35]. The scale measuring user preference of products integrated the System Usability Scale [36], Questionnaire for User Interaction Satisfaction V7.0 [37] and After-Scenario Questionnaire [38], and included proper questions that suitable for the experiment. The questionnaire designed for the experiment includes 7 questions, which had good reliability coefficient $\alpha = 0.76$. Besides, the questionnaire used the pictures from Wong and Baker's [39] emotion rating scale. It is believed that using pictures with different expressions is good for helping children understand the content of scale. Finally, researchers focused on the doubts appearing in the operation process and subjects' feelings, including users' preference for animation effect.

3.4 Data Analysis

One-Way Analysis of Variance. For the study of continuous variables by the impact of changes in the classification of the situation, the statistical results are usually expressed by F value.

Paired-Samples t Test. To examine the same body before and after two measurements of the same variable differences, the statistical results are usually expressed with t value.

Independent-Sample t Test. For the study of continuous variables by the dichotomous variable (this experiment is low age, high age) changes in the situation, the statistical results are usually expressed with t value.

Pearson Correlation Analysis. To examine the correlation of two consecutive variables. The statistical results are usually expressed by r value.

4   Findings

Children of different ages have different performance. From a viewpoint of developmental psychology, children in different age groups obviously have different performance in the development of perception, cognition, thinking and emotion. It is also confirmed by the data results. Children aged 7–12 have higher completion rate of the transition task than children aged 4–6, which indicates that children in these two age groups have difference in perception, cognition and thinking. Children aged 7–12 have higher product preference than children aged 4–6, which shows the difference in the development of emotion. All of these show that it is necessary to do more research about the children in different age groups: 4–6 years old and 7–12 years old. The detailed data is shown in Table 2.

Table 2. Different performance of children in different age groups (Time: second).

Tasks		4–6 years	7–12 years	t	Significant difference
Task 1	Number of tips	1.41	0.51	4.42	Yes
	Number of false click	2.07	1.59	1.41	No
	Time of completion	88.02	53.70	4.54	Yes
Task 2	Time of memorization	76.80	67.91	0.75	No
	Time of placement	84.13	52.21	2.42	Yes
	Correct number	6.34	6.75	1.09	No
Task 3	Time of memorization	160.24	126.97	1.45	No
	Time of placement	79.73	68.18	1.02	No
	Correct number	4.18	4.62	1.25	No
General preference	Product preference	4.16	4.41	2.21	Yes
	Mood change[a]	−0.13	0.16	2.00	Yes

[a]Negative value means bad mood.

There is no obvious difference in the task completion rate, understanding of product structure and preference for products when children aged 4–6 use the product with or without animation effect. Besides, from the interview, we found that children from this age group cannot understand the function of animation effect, which might cause distraction and confusion for them. Therefore, applying animation into the application aged 4–6 years old needs careful consideration.

Children aged 4–6 were asked to complete 3 tasks, then, researchers compared the data collected from these 3 tasks. In Task 1, subjects were asked to find certain icons and return to the page of the upper level. By comparison of the number of false click and the number of tips given by examiners, we found that there was no difference in completion rate for 4–6 year-old children when they used the 2 demos with or without animation effect. By comparing the completion time, we found that the completion efficiency is higher when subjects used the demo with animation effect than without animation effect. In the Task 2, subjects were asked to remember the product with or without the assistance of entrance animation. Through comparing the time of memorization, time of placement and the correct number of pictures situated, we found that subjects who used the demo with animation effect spend less time on remembering and putting cards, and have higher accuracy of putting cards in corresponding positions than those used the demo without animation effect. Therefore, we can conclude that animation can improve 4–6 year-old children's memory of product content. In the Task 3, subjects were asked to remember the product structure with or without the assistance of transition animation effect. Through comparing the time of memorization, time of placement and the correct number of pictures situated, we found that children who used the demo with animation effect spend less time on learning and remembering product structure than those who used the demo without animation effect. However, there is no significant difference in time spent on putting cards and the accuracy of pictures situated. Moreover, there is also no significant difference in product preference and mood change between these subjects, which indicates that animation cannot obviously improve subjects' preference for products. The detailed data is shown in Table 3.

Table 3. Different performance of children aged 4–6 when using product with animation effect or without animation effect (Time: second)

Tasks		With animation effect	Without animation effect	t	Significant difference
Task 1	Number of tips	1.16	1.68	1.42	No
	Number of false click	1.80	2.21	0.76	No
	Time of completion	68.92	110.11	3.25	Yes
Task 2	Time of memorization	51.67	97.36	2.62	Yes
	Time of placement	50.39	111.73	3.16	Yes
	Correct number	7.17	5.77	2.91	Yes
Task 3	Time of memorization	114.21	200.00	2.52	Yes
	Time of placement	67.68	90.14	1.44	No
	Correct number	4.65	3.80	1.79	No
General preference	Product preference	4.29	4.06	1.45	No
	Mood change	0.04	−0.31	1.67	No

Children aged 7–12 have better performance in task completion rate, completion efficiency, remembering product content and understanding product structure when they used the VOD products with animation effect than those used the VOD product without animation effect. Therefore, we suggest to develop animation for the products used by children aged 7–12.

Children aged 7–12 were asked to complete 3 tasks, in which the subjects were required to use the product with animation effect or without animation effect. Then, researchers compared the data collected from these three tasks. In the Task 1, subjects were asked to find certain icons and return to the page of the upper level. Through the comparison of the number of false click, the number of tips given by examiners and the completion time, we found that children aged 7–12 who used demo with animation effect showed higher completion efficiency than those used demo without animation effect. Therefore, animation can improve children's task completion rate and completion efficiency. In the Task 2, subjects were asked to remember the position of 8 cartoons with or without the assistance of entrance animation. By comparing the time of memorization, time of placement and the correct number of pictures situated, we found that subjects who used the demo with animation effect spend less time on recall and putting the cards back in place with a higher accuracy than those used the demo without animation effect. Therefore, we can conclude that animation can improve 7–12 year-old children's memory of product content. In the Task 3, subjects were asked to understand and remember the product structure with or without the assistance of transition animation effect. By comparing the time of memorization, time of placement and the correct number of pictures situated, we found that children aged 7–12 who used demo with animation effect perform better than those use demo without animation effect. Therefore, we can conclude that dynamic design can improve 7–12 year-old children's understanding of product structure. Moreover, there is a significant difference in mood change and no significant difference in product preference between these two groups of subjects, which indicates that animation cannot obviously improve subjects' preference for products. The detailed data is shown in Table 4.

Table 4. Different performance of children aged 7–12 when using product with animation effect or without animation effect (Time: second)

		With animation effect	Without animation effect	t	Significant difference
Task 1	Number of tips	0.25	0.76	2.35	Yes
	Number of false click	0.79	2.36	3.60	Yes
	Time of completion	43.32	63.88	2.39	Yes
Task 2	Time of memorization	50.05	92.14	3.80	Yes
	Time of placement	36.42	73.64	3.30	Yes
	Correct number	7.43	5.80	3.32	Yes
Task 3	Time of memorization	101.00	162.21	2.71	Yes
	Time of placement	53.63	86.60	2.17	Yes
	Correct number	5.11	4.11	2.18	Yes
General Preference	Product preference	4.44	4.30	1.27	No
	Mood change	0.22	−0.24	2.27	Yes

In order to explore more deeply about the effect of product preference on children's cognition, we separately analyzed the data collected from 4–6 year-old group and 7–12 year-old group to find the association between product preference and other test items respectively in these 3 tasks. For children aged 4–6, their product preference only has significant association with the understanding of product structure, and the association between these 2 variables is positive. For children aged 7–12, product preference has significant association with task completion rate, completion efficiency and the understanding of product structure. Product preference is positively correlated with task completion rate, completion efficiency and the understanding of product respectively. The detailed data is shown in Table 5.

Table 5. The association between product preference and task completion rate/efficiency. Correlation is significant at the 0.1 level (2-tailed)

Correlation coefficient		4–6 Years		7–12 Years	
		Product preference	Mood change	Product preference	Mood change
Task 1	Number of tips	0.03	−0.09	−0.09	−0.35*
	Number of false click	0.12	0.11	−0.07	−0.10
	Time of completion	0.01	−0.05	−0.33*	−0.51**
Task 2	Time of memorization	−0.24	0.01	−0.33	−0.24
	Time of placement	−0.28	0.12	−0.19	−0.03
	Correct number	−0.02	0.19	0.18	−0.01
Task 3	Time of memorization	−0.06	−0.19	−0.15	0.03
	Time of placement	−0.01	0.23	−0.15	−0.19
	Correct number	0.18	0.30*	0.40*	0.10

We can illustrate from the table that children aged 4–6 and 7–12 have different performance when using demo with different animation effect. By analyzing the association between product preference and several indicators for task completion, we can conclude that: the association between age 4–6 children's product preference and the status of task is relatively independent; whereas, age 7–12 children pay more attention to the design which is reflected by their preference for product. Besides, there are many differences in the psychological development between children aged 4–6 and 7–12, which causes their different needs for animation effect. We will explore more in next stage.

5 Discussion

The value of this study is to find the effect of the animation design on children's cognition by analyzing the situation in which children use the application as usual. Researcher examined the concept of cognition from aspects memory, learning and emotion, and designs 3 experimental tasks to measure these indicators. The operation designed for these tasks is as similar as possible to the original condition when children use VOD application in daily life. Therefore, the effect of the animation on task completion rate and completion efficiency found in this study can reflect children's use of application in normal times.

This study finds that animation design can improve age 7–12 children's task completion rate, confirming that animation design can improve children's experience of using applications in daily life. The memory of product content and understanding of product structure are contained in the usual process of using applications. For instance, whether children can find a certain function smoothly will depend on their memory of the location and icon of the function. Whether children can successfully find the page they want to go will depend on their understanding of the product structure. The tasks in this study detach these elements, exclude the impact of unrelated elements and explore the effect of animation design on memory and understanding of products. Moreover, this study explored the subjects' preference for product and mood change before and after these tasks, while there are few previous studies referring to the effect of emotion. After doing correlation analysis about these relative variables and performance in tasks, we found that children aged 7–12 have more preference for products with animation effect than without animation effect, whereas children aged 4–6 do not have any difference in product preference.

From the viewpoint of the cognitive development of children, the attention spans[3] of children aged 4–6 normally are no more than 4 [40]. When watching the interface of the product, children initially put their attention to the cover of the cartoon, ignoring the prompt animation. However, children aged 7–12 have larger attention spans, which means that they can focus on more details and perform better in the perception of animation effect. From the interview, we also found that children aged 7–12 have better perception of the animation design, while age 4–6 children focus more on using the application (watching cartoons). In general, the study about the preference supports the finding that animation design impacts children's cognitive development.

By analyzing the data collected from the experiment and interview, we found that children of different ages have different performance when they use the product with or without animation effect. When children aged 7–12 use the product with animation effect, they perform better in all aspects than those use the product without animation effect. However, children aged 4–6 only perform better in memory and completion efficiency when they use the product with animation effect. This conclusion can be explored further from the aspects of thinking development and institutional development. From the aspect of thinking development, the main characteristic of thought of children aged 4–6 is concrete image [10], which makes difficult for them to understand

---

[3] The attention spans means the amount of content a person can be aware of at the same time.

the assistance of transition animation. After completing the task, examiners directed age 4–6 children's attention to the animation and asked them to repeat what they saw and feelings. We find that these children do not understand the meaning of transition animation even though they have noticed it under examiners' guidance. Children said "I notice a block turns blue and bigger, but I do not know what it means", "I see a small button flash, but I do not know what to do". It indicates that animation effect causes distraction for age 4–6 children when they learning about the product. However, the characteristic of thought of children aged 7–12 is abstract-logic thinking. They not only feel the animation effect clearly but also understand the meaning of "guiding click" of prompt animation and the support role of "expend and return to the original condition" of transition animation. It makes age 7–12 children complete tasks more quickly with the assistance of animation effect and have better preference for products, whereas age 4–6 children do not have these performances.

Another explanation for "age 4–6 children do not have different performance in task completion rate" is that they are not familiar with searching through clicking. The content is presented in the form of function points in the homepage, which lacks of intuition for children aged 4–6. In the additional test, even though subjects were informed shortcuts, they still chose to sideslip to find content. In the task of understanding product structure, age 4–6 children did not show any difference when using 2 different application, which means it is difficult for them to understand complex structure of the product. As children aged 4–6 do not have the ability of structural thinking, they cannot realize the supporting role of animation effect which designed for helping them to understand. Therefore, we suggest to develop animation design for the products for children aged 7–12, and be more cautious about adding animation into the products for children aged 4–6. In what kind of status children aged 4–6 need more intuitive design is also a problem worthy of further study.

Moreover, researchers explore the effect of speed in transition animation to figure out if animation influences user experience through children's understanding or through sub-consciousness. According to the previous perception research by Jin [33], children can barely notice the existence of animation when it lasts less than 0.5 s, but they can recognize sub-consciously. The result shows that fast animation can't enhance the efficiency of completing tasks for children (Number of tips: $t = 0.83$, $p = 0.41$; Number of false click: $t = 0.83$, $p = 0.41$; Time of completion: $t = 1.57$, $p = 0.12$). Therefore, animation improves user experience through children's understanding and a reasonable speed is expected.

The present research indicates that the best design varies for children of different age group. Moreover, with the different level of children's psychological development, children of 4–6 and 7–12 perform differently over animation products. As for the animation, this research base on Novick's conclusion of animation types [8] to design the test demos, which includes change of position and size. These two animation modes work differently under different circumstances. For example, under content searching circumstance, children memorize better when animation appear from different positions. While under different interface transition circumstance, the transfer animation can improve children's understanding of product structure, and help them remember the position of these pages. However, the impact of animation is different in different age groups, which indicates the need of field study towards children of different age

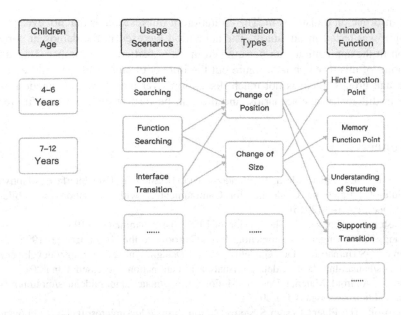

Fig. 9. The role of animation in different ages and scenes.

when setting application scenarios and designing styles. Future study may build up a more complete children development design system through similar research on interface structure design, sound design and visual design (Fig. 9).

6 Conclusion

Animation Design has different impact on children's product application and cognition of diverse age group. From the perspective of Developmental Psychology, there is a significant difference in the attention span, memory mode, thinking mode and emotional development between children aged 4–6 and 7–12. Children aged 4–6 have a relatively small attention span, and rely mainly on mechanical memory and imagery thinking. While 7–12 aged children have a bigger attention span and are capable of abstract logical thinking, also, they tend to develop partnership according to their emotional development. These differences show the distinction of information processing complexity among these two age-range groups. This research finds that animation can provide different impact on children' comprehension and interaction with user interface. When interacting with user interface, animation has a positive effect on comprehension, memory, task completion rates and efficiency, preference among children of 7–12 years old, however, there is no significant effect on task completion rates, comprehension and preference among children aged 4–6. According to the result of tasks and interview, 4–6 year-old children are not able to understand the meaning of animation in application products. In consideration of their attention span and thinking model, animated user interface might have adverse effect on their interaction with user interface. From another aspect, this indicates that children aged 4–6 prefer a more direct way of information transmission. The limitation of our research is that not every type of animation was tested in our study. The animation we used in the demos, if sorted by function in the application, can be summed up as transition and entrance. Because the main point of this research is to figure out the impact of animation on children among diverse age groups, there is not much discussion over the types and function of animation in different usage scenarios, and this can be further studied in the future.

References

1. Dessart, C.-E., Genaro Motti, V., Vanderdonckt, J.: Showing User Interface Adaptivity
2. Liddle, D.: Emerging Guidelines for Communicating with Animation in Mobile User Interfaces, pp. 1–9 (2016)
3. Johnston, O., Thomas, F.: The Illusion of Life: Disney Animation (1981)
4. Chang, B.-W., Ungar, D.: Animation: From Cartoons to the User Interface (1995)
5. Apple: iOS Human Interface Guideline. Visual Design: Animation. https://developer.apple.com/ios/human-interface-guidelines/visual-design/animation. Accessed 4 Jan 2018
6. Google: Android Material Design: Motion. https://material.io/guidelines/motion/material-motion.html. Accessed 4 Jan 2018
7. Microsoft: The Fluent Design System: Motion. https://docs.microsoft.com/zh-cn/windows/uwp/design/fluent-design-system/index#motion. Accessed 4 Jan 2018
8. Novick, D., Rhodes, J., Wert, W.: The communicative functions of animation in user interface. In: Proceedings of the 29th ACM International Conference on Design of Communication (SIGDOC 2011). ACM, New York (2011). https://doi.org/10.1145/2038476.2038478
9. Idler, S.: 5 Key Difference between Kids and Adults (2013)
10. Piaget, J., Inhelder, B.: The psychology of the child. Br. Med. J. 1753–1755 (1913)
11. Nielson, J.: Children's Websites: Usability Issues in Designing for Young People (2010)
12. Hanna, L., Risden, K., Alexander, K.: Guidelines for Usability Testing with Children (1997)
13. Sim, G., MacFarlane, S., Read, J.: All work and no play: measuring fun, usability, and learning in software for children. Comput. Educ. 235–248 (2006)
14. Crain, W.: Theories of Development: Concepts and Applications, 6th edn. Pearson Education, Inc., Upper Saddle River (2011). ISBN 978-0-205-81046-8
15. Taslim, J., Wan Adnan, W.A., Abu Bakar, N.A.: Investigating children preferences of a user interface design. In: Jacko, J.A. (ed.) HCI 2009. LNCS, vol. 5610, pp. 510–513. Springer, Heidelberg (2009). https://doi.org/10.1007/978-3-642-02574-7_57
16. McKnight, L., Read, J.C.: Designing the record button: using children's understanding of icons to inform the design of a musical interface. In: Proceedings of the 8th International Conference on Interaction Design and Children. ACM (2009)
17. Leif Azzopardi, D.D., Marshall, K.A.: YooSee: a Video Browsing Application for Young Children (2012)
18. Dyer, S., Adamo-Villani, N.: Animated Versus Static User Interfaces: A Study of MathsignerTM (2008)
19. Jin, Q.C.: Experimental study on threshold of moto perception. Acta Psychol. Sinica (1957)
20. Burroughs, B.: YouTube Kids: the App Economy and Mobile Parenting (2017)
21. Livingstone, S., Haddon, L., Görzig, A., Ólafsson, K.: Risks and safety on the internet: the perspective of European children (2013)
22. Neumann, M.M., Neumann, D.L.: Touch screen tablets and emergent literacy. Early Childhood Educ. J. **42**, 231–239 (2013)

23. iResearch: Research about the Use of Internet of Chinese teenager and children in 2015. http://www.iresearch.com.cn/report/2383.html#chart. Accessed 4 Jan 2018
24. Bradwell, J.: Does User Experience Match User Expectation in VOD Services? (2015)
25. Krefetz, N.: User experience: to keep viewers, online video must be a joy (2015)
26. Bederson, B.B., Angela, B.: Does animation help users build mental maps of spatial information? In: Proceedings of 1999 IEEE Symposium on Information Visualization, Info Vis 1999 (1999)
27. Thomas, B.H., Victor, D.: Evaluation of animation effects to improve indirect manipulation. In: First Australasian User Interface Conference, AUIC 2000. IEEE (2000)
28. Ognjanovic, S., Jason, R.: Don't talk to strangers! peer tutoring versus active intervention methodologies in interviewing children. In: Extended Abstracts on Human Factors in Computing Systems, CHI 2013. ACM (2013)
29. Erikson, E.: The problem of ego identity. J. Am. Psychoanal. Assoc. **4**, 56–121 (1956). https://doi.org/10.1177/000306515600400104. Accessed 28 Jan 2012
30. Sauro, J., Lewis, J.R.: Quantifying the User Experience: Practical Statistics for User Research. Morgan Kaufmann, Burlington (2015)
31. Jin, Y.J., Du, Z.F., Jiang, Y.: Sampling Techniques, pp. 29–30. China Renmin University Press, Beijing (2015)
32. Questmobile 2017: Q2 Summer Report of the Internet. http://www.questmobile.com.cn/blog/blog_98.html. Accessed 4 Jan 2018
33. Jin, Q.C.: Experimental study on threshold of moto perception. Acta Psychol. Sinica (1957)
34. Angold, A., et al.: Development of a short questionnaire for use in epidemiological studies of depression in children and adolescents. Int. J. Methods Psychiatr. Res. (1995)
35. Reliability: http://myweb.fcu.edu.tw/~mhsung/Research/Research_Methods/DOE/Reliability.htm. Accessed 4 Jan 2018
36. Lewis, J.R., Sauro, J.: The factor structure of the system usability scale. Paper Presented at the First International Conference on Human Centered Design (2009)
37. QUIS: Questionnaire for User Interaction Satisfaction. About the QUIS, version 7.0. http://lap.umd.edu/quis/. Accessed 4 Jan 2018
38. Lewis, J.R.: IBM computer usability satisfaction questionnaires: psychometric evaluation and instructions for use. Int. J. Hum.-Comput. Interact. (1995)
39. Wong, D.L., Baker, C.M.: Pain in children: comparison of assessment scales. Pediatr. Nurs. **14**(1), 9–17 (1988)
40. Huifang, C., Huashan, C.: Experimental study on the development of attention span between 4 and 14 years old. Psychol. Sci. **1**, 47–49 (1989)

An Interactive Digital Storytelling to Identify Emotions and Consequences in the Elementary School Child

Erick López-Ornelas[✉] and Rocío Abascal-Mena

Information Technology Department,
Universidad Autónoma Metropolitana – Cuajimalpa, Cuajimalpa, Mexico
{elopez,mabascal}@correo.cua.uam.mx

Abstract. In this article we focus on children of fifth grade of primary school and how they manage their emotions and feelings in order to improve their social relationships. We conducted a contextual study in order to identify how children interact and discover their social relationships problems. We identify the user profile and propose an interactive storytelling to improve emotional competences and feelings in children. We show a role play story using first-person interaction, and a well-adapted narrative to our users.

Keywords: Digital storytelling · Empathy · Emotions · Interactivity
Moral dilemmas · Conflict resolution

1 Introduction

In recent years, the use of Technological tools has become a social phenomenon. It is common to find a large number of applications and computer programs that facilitate work in all areas. In educational aspects, the applications and resources that we can find are also very remarkable. In this area, the use of technological tools is vital to try to face high rates of school failure and dropout, as well as to respond to the progressive multiculturalism of today's society. Technological tool allows to develop possibilities of methodological innovation that result in the achievement of a more effective and inclusive education.

On the other hand, the need to develop skills to prevent violence and improve school coexistence has led educational institutions to implement national and international programs. Knowing how to solve a conflict, at any educational level, is very important in promoting the development of these skills.

In Mexico some programs are being developed, such as the "Project for School Conviviality" (PACE in Spanish) implemented in primary education since 2015, as well as the attitudinal contents that are addressed in the curriculum of Civic and Ethical content. In this case, the Free Public Text Book and some digital content are supported.

In this study we focus on children at the elementary level, specifically 5th grade. We start from the idea that the forms of interactivity that arise among children of this age can be mediated by a computer agent, educator, family member or other partner, which makes possible the generation of knowledge [1]: they are Forms of learning that

© Springer International Publishing AG, part of Springer Nature 2018
A. Marcus and W. Wang (Eds.): DUXU 2018, LNCS 10920, pp. 218–230, 2018.
https://doi.org/10.1007/978-3-319-91806-8_17

are not necessarily carried out in the classroom and can be presented in settings such as the home or playground where children socialize.

By doing an exploratory and a contextual study, we identified some problems in digital educational materials to strengthen the contents of the subject of Civic and Ethical content, as well as the difficulty of teachers to integrate the existing ones, to the classes.

The objective is, then, to propose an interactive digital story, adapted to the needs of 5th grade students, where they can identify a set of emotions in order to deal with feelings and specially with their consequences in a particular situation. We start from the premise that this will help solve the various common conflicts experienced by children of these ages.

According to this, the second section of this article presents the central concepts on which research is based, relating with emotional competences and empathy. Section 3 the case of study is described; In Sect. 4 we show all the elements of empathy and the storytelling. Then in Sects. 5 and 6 we show the result of the interactive digital storytelling. Finally, a conclusion on the research is carried out in Sect. 7.

2 Emotional Competence and Empathy

Emotional competence, is central to children's ability to interact and form relationships with others [2, 3]. These abilities develop through the lifespan. Preschool and school aged children are becoming adept at several components: (a) awareness of emotional experience, (b) discernment of emotional states; (c) emotion language usage; (d) empathic involvement in others' emotions and (e) awareness that social relationships are in part defined by communication of emotions.

Although often considered from the perspective of individual experience, skills of emotional competence are vividly played out in interaction and within relationships with others; [4, 5].

In the other hand, the ability to care about others and to put oneself in their place is called empathy. Empathy is a learned process and can be successfully modeled in the elementary classroom. Although there are various methods available for improving empathy and other aspects of moral development, one recommended strategy is the use of stories that use moral dilemmas and role-play. This strategy involves (a) the use of formal and informal observations, (b) informal interviews, (c) the choosing of appropriate stories, and (d) large and small group discussions.

When strengthened and acted on, empathy leads to kindness and a caring attitude. When you feel empathy for others, your actions toward them often boomerang back to you. You feel good if you are good to them and, conversely, bad if something hurts them. Adults can support children's empathetic inclinations by letting them know that they are pleased with their sensitivity to others and by assisting and guiding their efforts to give aid [6].

In this article we focus on this empathic involvement and how children live with it. Also we argue that empathy is a very important component in order to improve social relationships among children.

3 Case of Study: Vini-Cubi Elementary School

3.1 Contextual Study

The first step was the identification of the digital content and its relation with the contents of the Free Public Text Book in Ethical content on children attending fifth grade in a public primary in Mexico City. The characteristics of the school that represents the case study are described below.

According to the research objective, we chose a primary school as a case study in the Cuajimalpa area during the period from October 2015 to July 2016. This area was chosen because it is one of the three delegations in Mexico City having the highest percentage of children.

Also, the primary school named "Vini Cubi" (Fig. 1) was chosen for being part of the "Safe School" program, which has as a priority to the Mexico City because is a school that participates in the Digital Inclusion and Literacy Program.

Fig. 1. Vini Cubi elementary school

The following characteristics describe the child population attending the primary school.

- The economic level of families is low; The majority of the children are children of workers' parents.
- The majority of the children are from the suburban area of Mexico City (Napula, Acopilco, Cujimalpa, among others).
- 70% of children are children of single mothers.
- Five children were diagnosed with Asperger's, autism, hemiplegia, having a ADHD (attention-deficit hyperactivity disorder) in the fifth grade group.

In order to draw conclusions about the socio-cultural status and emotional competence of the children, other techniques were applied, which are mentioned below.

3.2   Qualitative Study

Qualitative observation was divided into two steps: non-participant and participant. The first was limited to the process of observation and recording of group dynamics. Subsequently, participant observation was carried out, which consisted in integrating us with the dynamics of learning and socialization of children.

As an example of this, during some classes the teacher indicated to carry out certain activities by groups, to which one of us was integrated by a direct invitation of the children. This integration allowed us to be part of the students' conversations. Also, this integration was extended outside the classroom, since at different times we socialize during break time.

3.3   Non-structured Interviews and Focus Groups

In cases where specific information was needed, non-structured interviews were conducted. In this type of interview, question guides were made with the aim of keeping track of the important information. However, the interviewer was free to improvise issues that might not have been seen at first and that would be enriching for the information they provided. On the other hand, the focus groups had as main objective, to obtain information of the children in a team context.

The focus groups were initiated by dynamics specially designed to work with children, which were applied as an alternative to the questionnaires.

3.4   User Profile Definition

The user profile was defined with the context of children in different aspects. According to information provided by teachers, the academic performance of children is closely related to their family and social environment. In this context we found cases of abandon, and some cases related to drug addiction.

In the academic field the children show a level corresponding to the third grade of primary with a very low academic competence. Regarding their cultural preferences, children listen to "band music", "reggaeton" and "pop and hip hop music". For literary interests, girls prefer proposals like Twilight novels, meanwhile boys prefer some fantasy books.

We also analyses tv shows, "Dragon ball Z" is preferred by boys, and "Monster High" by girls, while "SpongeBob" is a common reference for both genders. Also both, girls and boys, like to play video games and love to download music and be connected on social social networks (Facebook and Snapchat).

In the Fig. 2 we show an infographic that summarizes all this user information. In our case Vini Cubi children.

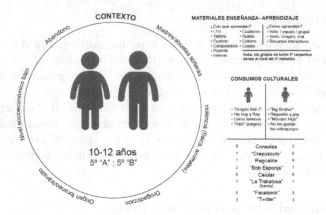

Fig. 2. Infographics showing Vini-Cubi children profile

4 Empathy and Digital Storytelling

Digital storytelling is the art of combining narrative with digital media such as images, sound, and video to create a short story [7]. More than just a simple slideshow of photos set to music, digital stories interweave different media to support the art of telling a tale. In [8] Digital Storytelling Cookbook, the author identifies seven elements that are critical components of effective digital stories. Those elements are:

- Point of view: Outlines the point of the story and the perspective from which the story is told.
- A dramatic question: Sets the tension of the story by identifying issues to be resolved.
- Emotional content: Engages the audience through common emotions and themes (love, pain, humor).
- The gift of your voice: Helps the audience make meaning of images.
- The power of the soundtrack: Sets the mood of the story.
- Economy: Balances the auditory and visual tracks of meaning.
- Pacing: Sustains the attention of the audience by establishing and modifying the rhythm of the story.

While these elements outline the nature of effective digital stories, the process of creating a digital story involves leveraging a wide variety of skills, including researching topics, writing scripts, storyboarding, and assembling the final product using a software [9]. Digital storytelling offers tremendous opportunities for teachers to engage and motivate students. By integrating visual images with written text, digital stories can be used to enhance and accelerate student comprehension, in our case emotional competence [7, 10].

In the other hand, empathy plays a role in order to develop a prosocial behavior in children, and allows a better understanding of social relationships. Empathy is a process which are attributed functions for educational development and the child's learning with respect to others, discovering some moral actions that improve their ability to solve interpersonal conflicts [11].

According to this, some educational institution considers empathy as a fundamental formative procedure in order to develop social skills in the school, as well as a key element for their civic education. We believe this ability could be used widely to improve Civic and Ethical content in the primary school level.

In order to implement the storytelling, we have used the model of empathy proposed by [12]. This model is composed of three main components incapable of being separated: the cognitive, the affective and the psychomotor (Fig. 3).

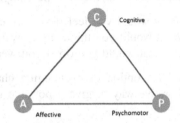

Fig. 3. Model of empath proposed

This model manages the attitude of change and movement of these three components through a learning strategy. Also this model allows to identify the attitude elements in a schematic way, which makes it possible to define some indicators of each components. These indicators are translated in form of verbs that will act in each category. In Fig. 4 we show these components.

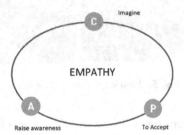

Fig. 4. Empathy model with attitude elements

5 Storyboards and Participative Workshops

For the construction of the prototype, we applied focus groups (4–6 participants) based on the results of qualitative observation. With this approach we obtained important feedback of the prototypes.

5.1   Little Red Riding Hood and Component Exploration

We made a first rapid prototype on paper, where a traditional story the "Little Red Riding Hood" was adapted. We observe that the use of fables in children was very attractive and were very useful to explore some attitude characteristics. Also this story was already used in class to explore some narrative aspects in the class.

The activity included a generic story in whose end the main character accused the wolf of eating her granny. Subsequently, four different stories were narrated from the perspective of one of the characters: the wolf, the Little Red Riding Hood, the granny and the hunter. Each of the participants could choose a character. After reading one of the four stories, three questions were asked about the components of empathy:

- Emotional component: What would you feel if you were (character)?
- Cognitive component: What would you think if you were (character)?
- Psychomotor component: What would you do if you were (character)?

Finally, the children had the option of exchanging characters, as well as constructing an end in a collaborative way to give a possible solution to the conflict in history (Fig. 5).

Fig. 5. First exploratory prototype

In general, after this interaction with the children, it was found that the children did not arrive to manage the conflict in a collaborative way. They do not feel conformable using a character with their opposite sex and it was difficult to appropriate the character.

One of the most relevant findings was that the fiction narrative did not allow us to approach the daily situations of the children, nor to the way in which they could respond and act. In the Fig. 6 we show children interaction facing this paper prototype.

Fig. 6. Children interaction

6 Storytelling Proposal

Taking into account all these findings from previous prototypes, we decided to build the final storytelling. For this story we take into account some characteristics like the use of a digital narrative, the use of first person description. These concepts are explained below.

6.1 Digital Narrative

The starting point was a narrative because during qualitative observation it was detected that this type of practice was used by teachers to teach dilemmas or examples of values and civic practices. So the children were accustomed to these tasks.

By placing the facts in a narrative sequence, every story becomes a sort of allegory with moral significance. And the act of telling a story is "linked to the impulse to moralize reality, that is, to identify it with the social system that is the source of any moral concept that we can imagine" [13].

In addition, interacting with a narrative fiction allows us to learn about our social world and as a result we improve our emphatic behavior [13]. That is why the narrative is taken as a symbolic and immersive value.

6.2 First-Person Interaction

For the final storytelling, we integrated the element of interaction in first person, this concept was taken from the world of video games. In this story, the user has the sensation of being part of the presented story and being able to decide the course of story, thus the user is not a passive observer [14].

According to [14], in this type of interaction the user is seen as a character immersed in the environment, with the ability to respond. The procedure has brought encouraging results in the teaching environment.

We propose that the user have the possibility to make decisions in the course of their interaction with the story, in this way, user experience represents an effective way for the children to be part of the solution created [14].

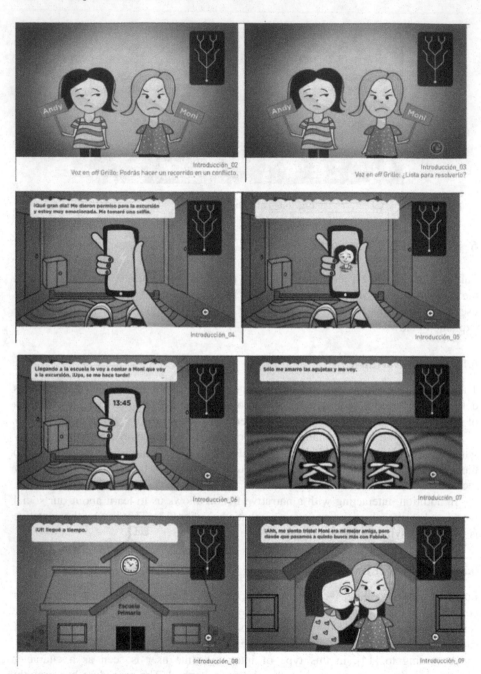

Fig. 7. Final storytelling

Fig. 7. (*continued*)

Fig. 7. (*continued*)

6.3   The Final Story

The story focuses on a conflict so that the students identify and choose an emotion, which allows them to decide the next action and thus the course of history. The different consequences of their choice are experimented by children. Finally, some questions are made in order to encourage some reflection on children.

At this point we designed some different options and paths that the story should have. Since history has several possible paths according to the decision making, it was necessary to establish a navigation map and possible routes according to the choice of an emotion. The navigation map has an introduction, a set of events and actions and the consequences associated with each possible exit of the story (Fig. 7).

7   Conclusions

One of the questions that has been formulated throughout this research has been regarding the relevance and functionality of a digital tool to address issues such as the identification of emotions and empathy. These subjects of an attitudinal nature, it seems that it implicitly poses the condition of working through a face-to-face relationship (in this case, between children and teacher) in which corporal expression play's a special roll.

This storytelling recovers the dynamics used in video games and the interaction in first person. These dynamics present children with a situation of conflict in the way of story, in which the participation of children is required to decide the course of events, linking emotion with decision making.

The case study of a public primary school in Mexico City, allowed us to observe the difficulties in incorporating mobile digital devices into classroom. The use of digital and interactive contents, referring to the subject of Civic and Ethical content, allow to identify the needs of children of the use of different tools in order to get specifics curricula elements.

The study of attitudinal content like empathy emotions is crucial in order to prevent school violence. Although the Ministry of Public Education proposes to these attitudinal content as essential elements for coexistence, in the fifth year of primary education these elements are not available. Regarding the relevance of the digital material in this area, we conclude that is not well explored field. The use of simulation games, which come from the culture of video games and allow situations to be created that are close to reality, which in the case of attitudinal contents are important for test some social practices.

Finally, we consider that a digital storytelling, is only one piece in the learning process. Above all, in the type of attitudinal contents that require a progressive advance in order to observe significate changes.

References

1. Peñalosa, E.: Estrategias docentes con tecnologías: Guía práctica. Pearson, México (2013). Primera ed
2. Parke, R.D.: Progress, paradigms, and unresolved problems: a commentary on recent advances in our understanding of children's emotions. Merrill-Palmer Q. **40**, 157–169 (1994)
3. Saarni, C.: Children's Emotional Competence. Guilford Press, New York (1999)
4. Campos, J.J., Barrett, K.C.: Toward a new understanding of emotions and their development. In: Emotions, Cognition, & Behavior, pp. 229–263. Cambridge University Press, New York (1984)
5. Denham, S.A.: Emotional Development in Young Children. Guilford, New York (1998)
6. Smith, M.: Social and emotional competencies: contributions to young African- American children's peer acceptance. Early Educ. Dev. **12**(1), 49–72 (2001)
7. Robin, B.: Digital storytelling: a powerful technology tool for the 21st century classroom. Theory Practice **47**(3), 220–228 (2008)
8. Lambert, J.: Digital Storytelling: Capturing Lives, Creating Community. Digital Diner Press, Berkeley (2006)
9. Ohler, J.: The world of digital storytelling. Educ. Leadersh. **63**(4), 44–47 (2006)
10. Burmark, L.: Visual presentations that prompt, flash & transform. Media Methods **40**(d), 4–5 (2004)
11. Garaigordobil, M., Maganto, C.: Empatía y resolución de conflictos durante la infancia y la adolescencia. In: Revista Latinoamericana de Psicología, pp. 255–266 (2011)

12. Kamradt, E.J., Kamradt, T.F.: Diseño educativo estructurado para la enseñanza de actitudes. In: Diseño de la instrucción: teorías y modelos: un nuevo paradigma de la teoría de la instrucción, pp. 113–138. Santillana (2000)
13. Mc Ewan, H., Egan, K.: La narrativa en la enseñanza, el aprendizaje y la investigación. Amorrortu Editores, Buenos Aires (1995)
14. Gamboa, F.: Desarrollo de software educativo centrado en el usuario. In: Diseño centrado en el usuario: métodos e interacciones, pp. 105–119. Insignio, Ciudad de México (2014)

Lessons Learned in Designing a Digital Therapeutic Game to Support the Treatment and Well-Being of Children with Cancer

Kamila R. H. Rodrigues[1](✉), Daniel B. F. Conrado[2], and Vânia P. A. Neris[1]

[1] Department of Computer Science, Federal University of São Carlos – UFSCar,
São Carlos, SP, Brazil
kamila.rios@gmail.com, vania@dc.ufscar.br
[2] Federal Institute of Education, Science and Technology of Minas Gerais – IFMG,
Campus Sabará, Sabará, MG, Brazil
daniel.conrado@ifmg.edu.br

Abstract. Therapeutic games not only entertain but also support rehabilitation treatments and help patients and caregivers to understand the therapeutic practices. This kind of game requires careful and responsible development. To the best of our knowledge, there is no variety of methodologies in the literature specifically tailored to develop them. It essentially requires collaborative creation between different domain specialists. Moreover, it is necessary to avoid ad-hoc design processes and favor the structured ones, which can effectively involve and guide stakeholders. Thus, we have adopted a methodology based on Participatory Design and Organizational Semiotics artifacts to guide the design of a therapeutic game that could entertain and inform children who were diagnosed with cancer, as well as their caregivers. The methodology includes the enrichment of Personas, aiming to characterize the intended audience of the therapeutic application. This paper presents an instantiation of such methodology and also describes how the information obtained during that process can aid on therapeutic games design aiming to support the rehabilitation of children under treatment for cancer. We also report some lessons learned from that instantiation, regarding both the methodology application and the specificities of the target audience that should be carefully considered when developing games to support chronic pathologies, especially those involving children.

Keywords: Digital therapeutic games · Childhood cancer
Design process · Personas · Participatory Design · Lessons learned

1 Introduction

Digital games are interactive software systems used for leisure, entertainment and, increasingly, as a tool for education and health [1]. Therapeutic games, in

© Springer International Publishing AG, part of Springer Nature 2018
A. Marcus and W. Wang (Eds.): DUXU 2018, LNCS 10920, pp. 231–243, 2018.
https://doi.org/10.1007/978-3-319-91806-8_18

turn, are games used as tools to support healthcare professionals on their practice [2]. The use of these games can promote the social and cognitive development of the user through activities that allow their evaluation by healthcare professionals [3]. As they serve therapeutic purposes, these games should be carefully managed and design should be well evaluated to ensure their contribution to the intended therapeutic goals [4].

To the best of our knowledge, there is no variety of methodologies in the literature specifically tailored to develop them. This application essentially requires collaborative creation between different domain specialists. Moreover, it is necessary to avoid ad-hoc design activities and favor the structured ones, which can effectively involve and guide stakeholders, as cooperation between healthcare and computer professionals is critical to the game adhesion.

Stakeholders are composed of a multidisciplinary and heterogeneous group of individuals. Conditions, treatments, patients and technical processes, in turn, may vary. Rodrigues et al. [4] point out that given the multiple variables involved to ensure success and quality, a structured process could assist in the design, implementation, evaluation and adoption of digital therapeutic games. These researchers proposed a methodology which requires a multidisciplinary team, with a comprehensive view of the development of this kind of computational system [4]. The methodology employs Participatory Design (PD) [5,6], Organizational Semiotics (OS) artifacts [7] and Personas [8] techniques, enabling stakeholders to participate more actively in the game development process.

In our research, we are developing a game to be used with children who were diagnosed with cancer and are currently admitted into specialized hospitals. Our aim is to transform the treatment in something lighter somehow, by providing to the patient and caregivers an entertainment and information resource, that can also be used by therapists as a work tool. To identify stakeholders and the game's requirements, we have used the methodology proposed by Rodrigues et al. [4]. Thus, we describe in this paper an instantiation of this methodology with the creation of three Personas who represent patients with childhood cancer.

Cooper [8] defines a Persona as a concrete and realistic representation of a system user. This technique is indirectly applied by Rodrigues et al. [4] to collect and summarize information such as gender, age, interests, abilities, etc., about potential users. Rodrigues and her research group have identified that, when dealing with the health domain, it may be necessary to add therapeutic information to the Personas, e.g. the clinical profile and required treatment. They called this modification as Personas Enrichment Process [4]. The enrichment is carried out in a participatory way: hospital professionals contribute in proposing, improving, and evaluating the created personas.

The instantiation of the methodology was conducted in three meetings with therapists from the hospital who were specialized in treating childhood cancer. Peculiar aspects were identified during the Personas enrichment process and should be considered in the game design to support the treatment of childhood cancer. These aspects relate to the target audience, the genre of the game, its mode of interaction and the intended stimuli. The methodology instantiation has also revealed other game features, requirements for the hospital scenario, and characteristics about the children's caregivers that should be considered in the design and development of the game in question. We observed that some characteristics and requirements differ from those identified by Rodrigues et al. in the context of games developed to support mental health treatments. In this paper, we describe some of these differences, in addition to discuss about the instantiation, how the Personas were used to guide the design process of the therapeutic game for children with cancer and some lessons learned during the process.

This paper is organized as follows: Sect. 2 comments about the childhood cancer; Sect. 3 describes some digital games in this context; Sect. 4 describes the Personas Enrichment Process: a methodology to created Personas aimed to support the development of therapeutic applications; Sect. 5 illustrates the creation of Personas using this methodology instantiation for childhood cancer; Sect. 6 describes lessons learned in designing of this digital therapeutic game; and Sect. 7 presents conclusions and future work.

2   Childhood Cancer

Childhood cancer epidemiology data has shown that scientific advances in pediatric oncology have considerably increased the likelihood of cure. According to Brazil's National Institute of Cancer (INCA) [9], there is a 70% chance of remission when cancer is early diagnosed and specialized treatment is provided. These advances have also brought the need for a patient care that addresses quality of life and emotional well-being. That is, the treatment should go beyond prolonging the lives of children with cancer and give support regarding emotional and socialization issues of children and their caregivers [10, 11].

Over the course of the treatment, the child patient is submitted to painfully invasive medical procedures such as chemotherapy, a resource commonly used to treat cancer and the most effective against leukemia (which is the most common cancer in children) [9]. The common side effects of chemotherapy includes fatigue, fever, vomiting, diarrhea, mouth sores, hair loss, among others. The conditions imposed by the treatment require considerable hospitalization time that some children actually live in hospitals. Frequent and long hospital stays are characterized by a period of physical and emotional stress for both, the child and her/his family. The child needs to adapt to that new situation, often apart from friends and family, and it requires strategies to deal with adverse circumstances [10].

To deal with those stressful experiences and invasive medical procedures, a child can play, which is a resource both her/his and caregivers use in hospitals. Healthcare professionals have indicated their application as part of therapy, as it provides stimulating and fun activities to help children feel relaxed and safe [10, 12].

The hospital's multidisciplinary team reported us that the way like patients and caregivers deal with the disease can affect the child's recovery both, positively and negatively. Considering these information, especially about the positive aspects brought about by playing in a hospitalization situation, it is possible to think about the development of therapeutic games aimed at this purpose, which not only entertain patients and caregivers, but which can support therapists during the treatment of these children. The following section describes some initiatives in this regard.

3   Digital Games and Cancer Treatment

We have found some digital games specifically related to cancer treatment. However, these games were developed to explain the disease to patients and elucidate the human body reactions. Most of them are fighting games which simulate the "good soldiers" against the "mutant cells". Such unilateral approach to the subject does not address other important aspects like positive thinking and collaboration with the family, and it also conveys violent mechanics. Those games includes: Re-Mission[1], Bens's Game[2] and Alpha Beat Cancer[3].

Re-Mission is modeled like an interactive fantasy where players are nanorobots living inside a human body. They have to eliminate cancer byproducts along the game. Also, players have to monitor the patients' health and notify any symptoms to the doctor. Each one of the 20 game levels is designed to inform the patient about different kinds of treatment, how they work, and the importance of receiving them. Ben's Game focuses on destroying cancerous cells and collecting shields in order to protect the patient against side effects of chemotherapy. In a very ludic way, the game signifies that scenario with snow monsters (cold), vampires (bleeding) and balls (hair loss). The Alpha Beat Cancer, in turn, is a "point and click" game that works as an adventure guide. The player pass through 21 levels where cancer and the treatment are demystified and oncological terms are introduced in an objective, fun and optimistic way. Parents and family can benefit from those information as well.

Those aforementioned games have generally violent dynamics, focus on fighting mutant cells and informing about cancer. The game we are developing in this work aims to entertain but also to stimulate positive and important aspects in the child's therapeutic process. It is designed to support healthcare professionals on collecting feedback data and to perform interventions along the treatment.

The following section describes the methodology proposed by Rodrigues et al., which was adopted in this work to characterize the design problem and identify the main interested parties to support the treatment of children with cancer.

4   Personas Enrichment Process: A Methodology to Support the Design of Therapeutic Applications

During the Personas Enrichment Process different interested parties are expected to be involved. For therapeutic applications, one reckons on engaging healthcare and computing professionals in a joint effort, where everyone applies design

---

[1] http://www.re-mission2.org.

[2] https://www.giantbomb.com/bens-game/3030-19916/.

[3] http://www.sickkids.ca/index.html.

practices and actively participates in the application construction, attempting to improve the chances of its adoption to ease treatment acceptance.

Since the therapeutic application domain is complex, the development of such computational systems demands a multidisciplinary team with a comprehensive view. It requires a research approach based on a theoretical background that holds an interpersonal, social and cultural perspective [13,14]. Since computing professionals have usually little knowledge about that subject, they should be constantly in touch with other interested parties, bringing about a cycle: "do together - assess - formalize lessons learned" [15].

We have used the methodology proposed by Rodrigues et al. [4], with a comprehensive view of the development of this kind of computational system, to identify stakeholders and the game's requirements. The methodology employs Participatory Design (PD) [6], Organizational Semiotics (OS) [7] and Personas [8] techniques, enabling stakeholders to participate more actively in the game development process.

PD is a practice, or methodology, of information systems development that aims to collect, analyze and design a system with the participation of users, employees, customers, developers and other stakeholders [5]. OS [7,13], in turn, is a discipline that has roots in semiotics applied to organizational processes. It studies the nature, characteristics, functions and effects of information and communication in organizational contexts. OS provides a knowledge basis for promoting reflection and supporting collaboration between people with different backgrounds involved in the interaction design. The Stakeholder Analysis Chart is an OS artifact that provides a comprehensive view of the stakeholders in different points of interest [4,13]. The Evaluation Frame, in turn, is another artifact used by designers where they insert stakeholders' interests, problems to solve and possible solutions raised at discussions with all participants [4,13].

The original technique of Personas, proposed by Cooper [8], defines Persona as a concrete and realistic representation of a system user. Optionally, it may include fictional user details like physical, psychological, and biological characteristics, her/his personality, profession and daily life. Rodrigues et al. [4] decided to add further information to their Personas created according to Cooper's technique. Throughout the activities, the research group have identified that – on the health domain – it would be necessary to add therapeutic information to the Personas, such as the clinical profile and required treatment. They called this modification as Personas Enrichment Process [4]. The enrichment is carried out in a participatory way: hospital professionals contribute to propose, improve, and evaluate the created personas.

The Personas Enrichment Process for therapeutic applications has four steps: (1) it starts with the identification of the stakeholders interested on the development of the therapeutic application. (2) The design team identifies the application end-users, problems to solve, and possible solutions. (3) The design team creates the Personas with the gathered information during the participatory practices and also based in data from the literature. (4) Finally, the design team presents and validates the Personas with the stakeholders.

In step one, a multidisciplinary team instantiates the Stakeholder Analysis Chart [4,13] to identify the main stakeholders of the application development. OS describes Stakeholder Analysis Chart as "an artifact to help the design team on understanding the real situation of the problem and the requirements for the solution" [4]. To use it, the design team discusses and identifies the parts that directly or indirectly influence the solution.

In step two, the design team's goal is to identify the system end-users (possibly patients), the problems the application should address, and discuss possible solutions for those problems. The Evaluation Frame should be used on this step. It allows to identify clinical profiles of patients, medical procedures, patients' relationship with other interested parties, problems involved in creating the application as well as possible solutions [4,13].

In step three, the fictional characters pictured by healthcare professionals become Personas representing real people. The computer team should aggregate information from the literature (public health data) to detail the individuals with relevant information. Afterwards, healthcare professionals should evaluate the correctness of the Personas, approving them provided they are suitable (step four).

The following section presents a collaborative process for the enrichment of Personas that characterize target users of therapeutic applications for support cancer treatment.

5   Creating Personas to Represent Children with Cancer

We explored a participatory approach [4] to the requirement analysis and design. To instantiate the process, a group of professionals from the Brazilian State University of Minas Gerais carried out an extension project in partnership with healthcare professionals of a hospital specialized in treating childhood cancer (Hospital de Câncer de Barretos), currently named to as "Love Hospital".

The project aimed to design a digital therapeutic game for children undergoing cancer treatment. Hospital therapists often employ strategies to help patients face the stressful conditions of the hospitalization process. Some of these strategies include play sessions (with board and digital games) and playing with toys [10]. As playing provides benefits for hospitalized patients, it reinforces the viability of developing digital games with therapeutic purposes.

Three meetings were conducted with a healthcare professional from the aforementioned hospital. In two of those meetings, we have followed the process and conducted participatory practices. The practices sought to discover the domain and target audience in order to clarify the game requirements and identify its desirable genre and other interaction characteristics.

Before the first meeting at the hospital, we did a brainstorming session with the computer team to discuss what we would need to understand about the scenario and how our strategy would be at that moment. A presentation and a list of issues were then drew up for the meeting.

At the hospital, we have also conducted a brainstorming session with an Occupational Therapist (a professional who accompanies patients through their daily routines), in which we introduced the computer team and our project proposal, and were informed about her practices, hospital facilities, context characteristics, age groups and cancer treatment stages. As we were talking about how a game could be used as therapeutic support, we were trying to identify how much experience the child patients have with technology, what playful activities they have at the hospital involving both patients and caregivers, what should be encouraged in those patients, as well as aspects of the hospital infrastructure and whether mobile devices and Wi-Fi network were available.

We were also interested in knowing what draws the attention of those children, what they like to do to entertain themselves, what are their hobbies, what environments they miss, whether there are any physical (prescribed or not) limitations, content limitations (e.g. ethical and religious aspects), whether the family was always around, and the average time spent on therapy.

It was discovered that the hospital admits from newborns to people with 35 years old who have childhood cancer. There are at least three stages of cancer treatment: discovery and clarification, treatment and palliative care. Children are encouraged to play games. For instance, a mobile device may be given to a child when she is undergoing a procedure. The hospital also provides specialized rooms for playing and gaming. We also realize that a variety of stimuli can be provided by games but, for this context, the main ones are positive thinking and hope. We have also found out that children miss their home and school environments, that games can't have the "Game Over" concept, religious issues should be avoided, the game must have informative and ludic nature, and since children often feel nauseous due to treatment, 3D animations should be avoided and audio narratives is prefered, among other characteristics.

According to the occupational therapist, a multidisciplinary team of healthcare professionals works with both the child and her family to provide care. Pediatric cancer centers, like Love Hospital, often have extra support services for children and their families, such as child life specialists, dietitians, physical and occupational therapists, social workers, and counselors.

This first meeting in which teams discuss and clarify design problems is not formally considered in the Rodrigues et al.'s process. We find it essential to understand the dynamics of the hospital and to know the healthcare professionals, as well as to provide a better planning of the next stages of conducting participatory practices for Personas' creation.

In the second meeting, we initialized the Personas enrichment process. The team attempted to understand the context and stakeholders and then create stereotypes of children undergoing cancer treatment. At this stage, the Stakeholder Analysis Chart [4,13] was filled out by the multidisciplinary team.

Figure 1(a) illustrates the final result of the artifact generated in step 1 of the enrichment process.

By using the Stakeholder Analysis Chart, we identified the family, the patients and healthcare professionals as the main stakeholders in the game development. Other actors were mentioned during the practice and were put into the artifact, including: researchers, private and philanthropic companies, the hospital and its agencies, and the government with its diverse representations (ministries and secretariats) [4,13].

Step 2 of the enrichment process characterizes the users by applying the Evaluation Frame [4,13]. Figure 1(b) illustrates the final result of the artifact generated in this step.

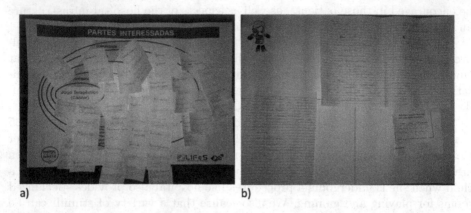

a)   b)

Fig. 1. (a) Instantiation of the Stakeholder Analysis Chart. (b) Instantiation of the Evaluation Frame.

With that artifact, we identified new aspects of the scenario and target audience, and refined those aspects pointed out in the brainstorming session previously mentioned, such as: the children's clinical profile – most were in the age range of 0–35 years and the main kinds of cancer were Leukemia, Osteosarcoma and Central Nervous System (CNS) tumor –, the medical procedures they take (e.g. chemotherapy, radiation therapy and bone marrow transplantation), the patient's relationship with other interested parties (including healthcare professionals and caregivers considered very protective), problems involved in creating and using the game (e.g. side effects of using a 3D style - like nausea -, reading difficulties after some procedures, mobile device hygiene, etc.), and possible solutions to those problems (e.g. choosing 2D formats, audio interactions and protecting devices with a casing). From those first participatory practices, three main Personas' skeletons were identified. The artifact generated by the team has pointed to preliminary images and names for the fictitious patients in creation; they were called Luiza, Caio and Lucas.

Luiza is 12 years old, diagnosed with leukemia and in cancer's discovery stage. Caio is also 12 years old, diagnosed with osteosarcoma (bone cancer), in the treatment phase and had his legs amputated below the knee, because there was disease recurrence and it returned more aggressive. Lucas is 6 years old, diagnosed with CNS tumor and also in the treatment phase. At the time, the computer and healthcare professionals judged that developing a game targeting at patients in palliative stage would be a task that requires more experience, especially from the computer team. The therapeutic goals and stimuli to be considered for such a game would demand a more careful touch and greater sensitivity, since the child is more vulnerable. Therefore, no Persona was designed to represent such patients.

The collected data was enriched with information from the Literature regarding childhood cancer, including INCA Institute, as well as data and reports from scientific papers on the psychosocial aspects of pediatric cancer in Brazil [10] and aspects of life that are affected by the activity of "caregivers" [11]. The computer team added the new information to enrich the previously defined skeletons. They have gathered and organized data from different sources and categorized them to define each Persona's characteristics. Literature data not only confirmed the healthcare professionals statements but also provided complementary characteristics about the individuals. At the end of this step, the computer team have created and enriched the three Personas mentioned above.

Luiza is illustrated in Fig. 2. The excerpts written in italics represent data identified through the practices with professionals combined with data from the literature. The excerpts in bold represent data collected only through the practices. The underlined data, in turn, comprises the summarized literature data.

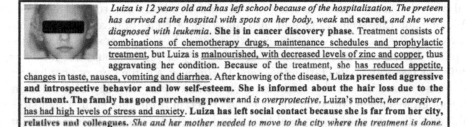

Luiza is 12 years old and has left school because of the hospitalization. The preteen has arrived at the hospital with spots on her body, weak and **scared**, and she were diagnosed with leukemia. **She is in cancer discovery phase.** Treatment consists of combinations of chemotherapy drugs, maintenance schedules and prophylactic treatment, but Luiza is malnourished, with decreased levels of zinc and copper, thus aggravating her condition. Because of the treatment, she has reduced appetite, changes in taste, nausea, vomiting and diarrhea. After knowing of the disease, Luiza **presented aggressive and introspective behavior and low self-esteem. She is informed about the hair loss due to the treatment. The family has good purchasing power** and is overprotective. Luiza's mother, her caregiver, has had high levels of stress and anxiety. **Luiza has left social contact because she is far from her city,** relatives and colleagues. She and her mother needed to move to the city where the treatment is done. **Luiza likes to paint and to use the smartphone, but she is always doing these activities on her own.**

Fig. 2. Luiza's persona resulting from the Process.

After the team completed the set of Personas, they presented and validated them with an occupational therapist of the specialized hospital, which is step 4 of the enrichment process. The professional answered the questions from the evaluation form provided by the Rodrigues et al.'s process asking about the profiles' photos, the family history profile and context, and the clinical profiles of each persona. For example, the therapist suggested changing Luiza's image since she would still be in the discovery stage and, therefore, she would still have hair.

As a result of the step for Design Problem Clarification, provided by the approach, peculiar aspects were identified and should be considered in the game development to support the treatment of childhood cancer. These aspects concern the gender, the form of interaction and the stimuli of the game. Each of the three personas created has different needs. These needs imply on the flexibility of the game regarding pretended stimuli for each profile, and in the flexibility of the game to consider different ways a patient may react to the treatment. Chemotherapy and radiation treatments, for example, make children nauseous. So, a game with 3D interactions or using gyroscope would not be adequate. Another aspect raised in this stage is that, as children have different ages, some patients pre-teens. Pre-teens are in an age of discovering their body; due to treatment – in special due to hair loss (Luiza's case) or limb amputation (Caio's case) – their self-esteem is affected. The required stimuli for these cases are distinct from the average ones, ranging from improving self-esteem and promoting positive thinking, to clarifying the treatment and entertaining children and caregivers.

During the practices in the hospital, the team pointed out the difficulty of the caregivers to deal with children illness. They also pointed that more positive and less protective parents influence their child positively; consequently, their children respond in more positive ways to the treatment. However, some caregivers do not know the treatment and are frightened by the illness and fear of losing their children. In this sense, professionals emphasize the importance of creating games that can clarify children and caregivers, in a playful way, about the treatment and stages of it. So, Personas representing the caregivers were idealized. The professionals also report the importance of illustrating, in a playful way, the changes that occurred in the children's body due to the treatment. A game for this scenario should also allow for a collaborative entertainment between patients, caregivers and even therapists. In this context, the multidisciplinary team understood, at the time, that only one game could not meet the different needs and expectations of users. In this way, a game library - configured and customized by the therapists for each patient - was the suggested solution. Although we have followed all the steps described in Rodrigues et al., other steps and guidelines might be proposed to design therapeutic games; they could especially focus on cases in which the role played by the caregiver is decisive and different profiles for the same pathology are identified.

The next section presents what we have learned when instantiating that process and how we dealt with different requirements. We also discuss how each personas requirements have guided towards a conception of games tailored to this scenario.

6   Lessons Learned in Designing of this Digital Therapeutic Game

As mentioned, different specificities, for the same pathology, did not arise in the context of the hospital that the Rodrigues' group supported and the pathologies that the hospital attended (depression and chemical dependency). The aforementioned specificities emerged in the context of the Love Hospital and to support the cancer treatment. These are features that make the game with more points of flexibility.

The main lessons learned shall be presented as well as some advices for researchers looking forward to instantiating Rodrigues et al.'s approach, which might have specificities that weren't take into account in the Personas enrichment process described earlier.

Brainstormings - Before participatory practices and personas enrichment process, it was needed to introduce the teams, therefore they could know each other, align and elucidate thoughts and plan better the next steps. Our advice: formalize a brainstoming session prior to starting the process.

Overprotective Caregivers - the healthcare professional have emphasized that caregivers play an important role during cancer treatment. On the other hand, there are some pathologies which they aren't so demanded. When caregivers, as well as their health, directly affect the patient's clinical evolution, the design team, while having identified their importance, must study their impact and analyze how is their relationship with the patient, the disease, the treatment and the health professionals. Our advices: when identifying the caregiver importance and possible pathologies that could appear because of her role: (a) elaborate specific Personas to represent caregivers; (b) design games in which patients, caregivers and therapists can collaborate; (c) identify therapeutic stimuli to them that could be addressed by the game; (d) provide resources with information about the disease and treatment in an entertaining way.

Diversity and Flexibility Aspects - we have aimed at alleviating the negative aspects of hospital stays by means of a therapeutic game tailored to children with cancer, but the participatory practices we followed has unveiled that there are different types of infantile cancer, different treatments, and a variety of profiles of children and caregivers, which we didn't foresee. Therefore, we have noticed that it is not possible to develop just one game that could address all the patients. Such diversity for a single context was not predicted in the Rodrigues et al.'s approach. We then decided to design various game modules to fit such diversity. Our advices: when facing such a scenario, design a game that has flexible points and offers a set of possibilities which health professionals can configure according to desired therapeutic aspects. The game may allow customizations for different health professionals such as doctors, psychologists, dietitians etc. That is an important characteristic when a multidisciplinary team is involved (as it is at the Love Hospital).

Following in this direction, a first therapeutic game module idealized met the requirements of the Luiza's persona. Playful and colorful, the game should promote clarifying the treatment of leukemia, stimulating the child's self-esteem and positive thinking, as promoting collaborative interaction with the caregiver. The game would be characterized by characters with human traits and customizable depending on the type of clarification. Positive reinforcements should also be provided to stimulate the child's positive thinking and self-esteem, as well as of the respective caregiver.

7   Conclusions and Future Work

By following the steps proposed by the Rodrigues et al. [4] design process, it was possible to involve healthcare professionals in the creation of a game that also supports their activities as therapists. In addition to involving them in the process, the collection of requirements, containing possible actions; stimuli and therapeutic objectives of the game, is more reliable to the domain under study and may allow more adhesion to the proposed therapeutic application.

While instantiating the process, we could identify additional aspects that can be incorporated into Rodrigues et al.'s approach, by considering the same pathology, such as dealing with the diversity of profiles and treatments in the early stages of game design. It is also important to consider the caregiver and identify her role during treatment.

Studies from computer professionals have also stated that when developing games for children it is essential to follow some guidelines. Most children are curious and interact with objects to find out how they work. They also like movement and fun. Those aspects must be taken into account while designing the gameplay. Colors and visual references to things they enjoy, such as candies, animals, places etc. should be considered as well.

After clarifying the design and identifying the interested parties, our team adopted the Interaction Modeling Language [17] to model scenarios and interactions of the therapeutic game to treatment cancer support. The purpose of the modeling is to verify if the different stakeholders understand the language and the scenario modeled in it, for the later development. This step is not provided by the Rodrigues et al.'s approach, but can be incorporated into the process as stage of a structured and complete methodology for the design of therapeutic solutions.

In this sense, as future work, we advocate an extension of the approach to provide this structured and a well-defined process for a complete creating therapeutic games, with stages of modeling, design materialization and evaluation.

Acknowledgments. The authors would like to thank the healthcare professionals of the Hospital do Câncer de Barretos on the effective participation and contributions to this research project. We would like to thank the UEMG's Dean of Extension for the financial support and also to scientific initiation students involved.

References

1. Grammenos, D., Savidis, A., Stephanidis, C.: Designing universally accessible games. Mag. Comput. Entertainment (CIE) - Spec. Issue: Media Arts Games **7**, 29 (2009)
2. Cheung, M.: Therapeutic Games and Guided Imagery: Tools for Mental Health and School Professionals Working with Children, Adolescents, and Their Families. Lyceum Books, Chicago (2006)
3. Merry, S.N., Stasiak, K., Shepherd, M., Frampton, C., Fleming, T., Lucassen, M.F.G.: The effectiveness of SPARX, a computerised self help intervention for adolescents seeking help for depression: randomised controlled non-inferiority trial. BMJ **344**, e2598 (2012). https://doi.org/10.1136/bmj.e2598

4. Rodrigues, K.R.H., Garcia, F.E., Bocanegra, L., Gonçalves, V., Carvalho, V., Neris, V.P.A.: Personas-driven design for mental health therapeutic applications. SBC J. Interact. Syst. **6**(1), 18–34 (2015). http://seer.ufrgs.br/index.php/jis/article/view/55384
5. Schuler, D., Namioka, A.: Participatory Design: Principles and Practices. Lawrence Erlbaum Associates, Mahwah (1993)
6. Muller, M.J., Haslwanter, J.H., Dayton, T.: Participatory practices in the software lifecycle. In: Helander, M., Landauer, T.K., Prabhu, P. (eds.) Handbook of Human-Computer Interaction, 2nd edn, pp. 255–297. Elsevier Science Inc., Amsterdam (1997)
7. Liu, K.: Semiotics in Information Systems Engineering. Cambridge University Press, Cambridge (2000)
8. Cooper, A.: The Inmates are Running the Asylum: Why High-Tech Products Drive Us Crazy and How to Restore the Sanity, 2nd edn. Pearson Higher Education, London (2004)
9. INCA - National Cancer Institute (Brazil). Coordination of Cancer Prevention and Surveillance. Cancer in Children and Adolescents in Brazil, Rio de Janeiro (2008). http://www.inca.gov.br/tumores_infantis
10. Motta, A.B., Enumo, S.R.F.: Playing in hospital: childhood cancer and evaluation of hospitalization coping (in Portuguese). Psicologia, Saúde Doenças **3**(1), 23–41 (2002). http://www.scielo.mec.pt/scielo.php?script=sci_abstract&pid=S1645-00862002000100003&lng=pt&nrm=iso&tlng=pt
11. Beck, A.R.M., Lopes, M.H.B.M.: Caregivers of children with cancer: aspects of life affected by caregiver activity (in Portuguese). Revista Brasileira de Enfermagem **60**(6), 670–675 (2007). https://doi.org/10.1590/S0034-71672007000600010
12. Lindquist, I.: The Child at the Hospital: Toy Therapy (R.Z. Altman) (in Portuguese). Scritta, São Paulo (1993)
13. Stamper, R.K.: Analysing the cultural impact of a system. Int. J. Inf. Manag. **8**, 107–122 (1988)
14. Schaefer, C.E., Reid, S.E. (eds.): Game Play: Therapeutic Use of Childhood Games, 2 edn. Wiley, Hoboken (2008)
15. Neris, V.P.A., Rodrigues, K.R.H.: Design of therapeutic information systems as indicating through signs. In: Baranauskas, M.C.C., Liu, K., Sun, L., Neris, V.P.A., Bonacin, R., Nakata, K. (eds.) ICISO 2016. IAICT, vol. 477, pp. 203–208. Springer, Cham (2016). https://doi.org/10.1007/978-3-319-42102-5_23
16. Kohlsdorf, M.: Psychosocial aspects in pediatric cancer: study on Brazilian literature published between 2000 and 2009 (in Portuguese). Psicologia em Revista **16**(2), 271–294 (2010)
17. Garcia, F.E., Rodrigues, K.R.H., Neris, V.P.A.: Uma Linguagem de Modelagem de Interação Para Aplicações Terapêuticas. In: Simpósio Brasileiro Sobre Fatores Humanos Em Sistemas Computacionais, São Paulo (2016)

DUXU in Automotive and Transport

Investigating the Effect of Different Autonomy Levels on User Acceptance and User Experience in Self-driving Cars with a VR Driving Simulator

Jana Helgath, Philip Braun, Andreas Pritschet, Maximilian Schubert, Patricia Böhm, and Daniel Isemann[✉]

Universität Regensburg, Universitätsstraße 31, 93053 Regensburg, Germany
daniel.isemann@ur.de

Abstract. The possible transition to fully autonomous cars represents a paradigm shift, which is likely to have a profound impact on driving experience and automobile technology acceptance. Using an online questionnaire, Rödel et al. [7] have found that measures for User Acceptance (UA) and User Experience (UX) decline with increasing autonomy level. In this study, we investigate the differences in UA and UX for vehicles with different levels of automation in a more immersive context. We used a simple driving simulator setup in a virtual reality environment (using an Oculus Rift headset). We designed three tasks which each represented a different level of automation and asked participants (N = 17) to fill out the Car Technology Acceptance Model (CTAM) questionnaire after using each autonomy level. The immersion of the simulator setup was assessed with a standardized questionnaire. In contrast to Rödel et al. [7] results do not show a general decline in UA and UX with increasing autonomy, but suggest that Performance Expectancy, Perceived Safety and Social Influence are significantly higher for the fully automated condition than for no automation. The scores for immersion ranging about the average of benchmark evaluations indicate that the users felt quite immersed, but that there is still room for improving the VR setup.

Keywords: Driving automation levels
Car technology acceptance model (CTAM) · User Acceptance · User Experience
VR driving simulator

1 Introduction

As vehicles are equipped with an ever-increasing amount of Advanced Driver Assistance Systems (ADAS) and tend to act more and more autonomously, the importance of investigating the User Acceptance (UA) and User Experience (UX) in this context is increasing. Currently, there is a trend towards cars, which can drive parts of a route or even the entire route fully autonomously. Some functional prototypes are already available like the Google-Car[1] or the transportation network company Uber Technologies is currently testing multiple autonomous cars in city traffic [2].

---

[1] https://waymo.com/ (last accessed 2/3/2018).

© Springer International Publishing AG, part of Springer Nature 2018
A. Marcus and W. Wang (Eds.): DUXU 2018, LNCS 10920, pp. 247–256, 2018.
https://doi.org/10.1007/978-3-319-91806-8_19

When discussing autonomous cars one has to distinguish between different levels of autonomy. The National Highway Traffic Safety Administration (NHTSA) [4] defines five different levels (0 to 4) of autonomy, ranging from no automation at all to fully self-driving cars.[2] However, cars at Level 0, which means no automation, are not very common anymore. Level 1 provides function-specific automation with the purpose to aid the driver who still has to control the car at all time. Level 2 adds at least two more advanced automated control functions such as adaptive cruise control or lane centering. At Level 3 the car is able to drive fully autonomously in predefined situations for a limited time span, e.g., on highways. And finally, at Level 4, the vehicle is able to act fully autonomously for the entirety of a trip. These changes are likely to have a big influence on how the driver interacts with the car and therefore User Experience probably changes as well. Rödel et al. [7] have conducted a study to examine how different levels of autonomy affect User Acceptance and User Experience. For this purpose, an online-questionnaire was created and answered by 336 study participants. The results indicate that User Acceptance and User Experience are highest at levels of autonomy that have already been deployed in modern cars (i.e. levels 1 and 2 as defined by the NHTSA).

In our study we explore the effects of increased autonomy on UA and UX measures in a more immersive setup. For this we look at three different levels of autonomy (NHTSA levels 1, 3 and 4) using a Virtual Reality driving simulator.

2   Related Work

Our study design is based on the previously mentioned work of Rödel et al. [7] 336 participants with different levels of driving experience and experience with ADAS (automatic driving assistance systems) were asked to imagine five driving scenarios with different levels of autonomy. After each scenario, UA and UX factors were measured using standardized questionnaires. To determine user acceptance the authors used a variation of the Technology Acceptance Model (TAM) by Davis [1]. To determine UA in our study we used an alternative instrument the CTAM introduced by Osswald et al. [5] which will be described in greater detail below. The findings of Rödel et al. [7] suggest that the attitude towards driving systems decreases significantly with the level of autonomy. In addition, the perceived behavioral control is highest at the lowest level of autonomy. The authors conclude that people experience a higher UA and better UX if they are more familiar with the system.

The CTAM was originally developed to research drivers' acceptance of in-car technology but it has also been used for research on autonomous vehicles, e.g. by Robertson et al. [6]. The model is based on the Unified Theory of Acceptance and User of Technology (UTAUT) but extends this model by adding dimensions like safety and anxiety. In contrast to the Technology Acceptance Model (TAM), which focusses on desktop-based systems, the CTAM takes car-related factors such as limited mental resources into consideration as well as the assistance the user gets while performing a driving task. The

---

[2] The NHTSA has discontinued their classification system in 2016 in favor of a similar classification issued by the Society of Automotive Engineers (SAE), but we decided to use NHTSA levels, because this allows for better comparison to previous work.

resulting determinants for the CTAM are performance expectancy, effort expectancy, attitude towards using technology, social influence, facilitating conditions, self-efficacy, anxiety, behavioral intention to use the system, and perceived safety. The questionnaire comprises 39 items that build up these eight dimensions.

Another paper we based our experiment on was published by Helldin et al. [3] that discusses the use of an interface to display uncertainty levels of an autonomous car system. What we found interesting in this study was the setup of the test to determine the users' trust in the autonomous system in general. Therefore, they used a simulator setup where participants could interact with a fully functional cockpit while the environment was displayed on a big projector canvas surrounding them. The authors allowed the participants to get used to the simulator in a 3–5-min test session and presented them with tasks to follow a predefined route and instructions of how to interact with the system afterwards. After each task, the users answered the questionnaire assessing their trust in the system during the task. We followed this setup in our own experiment but added some free text questions and an immersion questionnaire to gain further information.

3   Methods

3.1   Participants

The study was conducted with 17 participants (6 male, 11 female) aged between 20 and 29 years. Most of them were university students and were in possession of a driver's license (15 out of 17). None of the subjects had previous experience with vehicle automation systems but three had used driver assistance systems before.

3.2   Setup

The study was conducted in the Future Interaction Laboratory at the University of Regensburg using an Oculus Rift CV1, a Logitech G27 Steering Wheel, and a self-developed Simulator Application. We designed three tasks in which the participants had to navigate to a destination using the simulator system.

In each task, the participants drove the simulator car through a city landscape with either no automation, semi-automation or full automation. In the semi-automated scenario, the participant had to drive by himself until the car takes over control on the highway. In the fully automated scenario the car drives completely autonomously allowing no interaction from the driver.

Using a within-subjects design each participant had to complete each task in a counter balanced Latin square order to eliminate learning effects (Fig. 1).

Fig. 1. Top: The test setup with the Oculus and the racing chair. Bottom: Screenshot of our simulator from the tester's perspective.

3.3   VR Driving Simulator

We considered using OpenDS[3] as driving simulator for our study, as it comprises various features and is open source and can be extended with additional features like a multi-media panel and autonomous driving. However, after evaluating OpenDS, we found that it was not well suited for our purpose for several reasons. First, it is built for performance-specific tasks, like measuring reaction times. The design of the environment is very basic and just consists of a green plan with some roads on it and some square blocks as houses. This is not very suitable when trying to create an immersive experience. Second, OpenDS does not yet support the consumer version of Oculus Rift (Oculus Rift CV1), which we decided to use. For these reasons, we decided to implement our own driving simulator. We used Unity[4] as game engine for our simulator and the Unity Asset Store[5] to get most of the assets. There is also an Oculus-SDK5 provided for Unity that can be integrated quickly.

We implemented basic vehicle physics and made the car controllable with a steering wheel controller. We added an infotainment system into the car, which can be controlled with buttons on the steering wheel. The infotainment system includes a media-player to playback music and videos and a dummy address book and a dummy hands-free tele-phone. The driving simulator guided the user towards navigation points with an arrow that is displayed on the front shield.

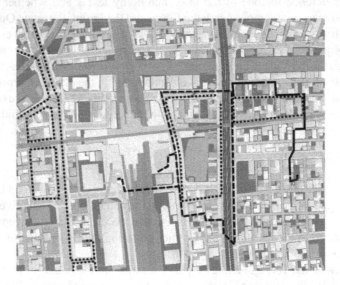

Fig. 2. Top view of the city the participants had to navigate through. The dotted lines show the three different routes participant cars and AI controlled traffic followed in randomized order.

---

[3] https://www.opends.eu/ (last accessed 2/3/2018).

[4] https://unity3d.com/de/ (last accessed 2/3/2018).

[5] https://www.assetstore.unity3d.com/en/ (last accessed 2/3/2018).

There was no need for complex traffic AI, because the user only drives each route once, which allowed for a very simple AI. The traffic just follows certain waypoints repeatedly and also reacts to other traffic and stops if someone else is in front of them. This AI concept had also the benefit that it could be reused for the autonomy functions of the user car. It either is triggered at a certain point on the route (NHTSA level 3) or controls the user car on the entire route (NHTSA level 4). There are audio hints for the user to inform him when the car will switch to autonomous driving or back to manual driving and some feedback when the user has reached his destination (Fig. 2).

3.4   After Task Questionnaire

After a brief introduction to the study setup, the participants provided basic demographic data on themselves and then executed three simulator tasks in a counter balanced Latin square order. All participants had to fill out the CTAM questionnaire after each task.

3.5   Final Interview

After filling out the CTAM for the last task a final interview was conducted with the participants consisting of two qualitative questions asking the participants about their subjective preference for one of the three autonomy levels and whether they could imagine driving an autonomous car in the future and the igroup Presence Questionnaire (IPQ)[6] which was designed for measuring the sense of presence in a virtual environment. The sense of presence is a variable of the user's experience describing how immersed the user feels in the virtual environment. The IPQ consists of 14 items that include questions about the "General feeling of immersion", the "Spatial Presence", the "Involvement" and the "Experienced Realism". These items are answered using a seven-point Likert scale. We used the IPQ to evaluate the immersion of our simulator.

4   Results

In this section, we present the quantitative results of the study followed up by a presentation of the qualitative data and a corresponding interpretation. We will give a thorough description of the evaluation of User Experience (UX) and User Acceptance (UA) factors described in the previous chapter after outlining the IPQ results on the immersiveness of our simulator environment.

We followed the IPQ guidelines for the questionnaire evaluation to arrive at the following results: the values of "Realism" (REAL) – so in how far the virtual experience feels like the reality – and "Involvement" (INV), which describes how much participants feel like being part of the experience, are almost identical to the values offered by the IPQ consortium as average values across several studies. Only the "Spacial Presence" (SP) value that describes how much the virtual surroundings feel like a real world, was slightly lower (our SP: 3.15; average IPQ SP: 3.75). These values suggest that the

---

[6] http://www.igroup.org/pq/ipq/index.php (last accessed 2/3/2018).

immersion generated by our driving simulator environment compares reasonably well against the collected data of evaluations contributed to the IPQ consortium (Fig. 3).

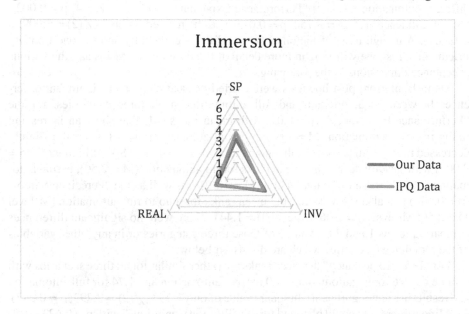

Fig. 3. Our IPQ results in comparison to the whole collection of IPQ answers.

UA and UX for the various conditions were measured with a total of 120 items – 40 items repeated for each autonomy level – in the user experience and user acceptance questionnaires (CTAM) for each participant. Each question consists of a seven-point Likert scale. As suggested in the paper of Osswald et al. [5] each question item was labelled from the most positive rating as number one to the most negative rating as number seven (Table 1).

Table 1. Measured user acceptance and user experience factors.

Abbreviation	Factor
PE	Performance expectancy
EE	Effort expectancy
ATT	Attitude towards using technology
SI	Social influence
FC	Facilitating conditions
SE	Self-efficacy
A	Anxiety
BIS	Behavioral intention to use the system
PS	Perceived safety

Looking at the individual user experience and user acceptance scores measured by the questionnaire we found that some factors are significantly affected by the level of automation provided in the different scenarios of the study. With a significance level of alpha = 0.05 Friedman's Chi Square Test suggested a significant difference between the different automation levels of "Performance Expectancy" ($\chi^2(2) = 12.644$; p = 0.002), "Social Influence" ($\chi^2(2) = 8.758$; p = 0.013) and "Perceived Safety" ($\chi^2(2) = 9.909$; p = 0.007). Although none of the other factors differ significantly across conditions by Friedman's Test, we will look in more detail at the different scenarios and the various acceptance dimensions in the following.

Dunn-Bonferroni post hoc tests were carried out and there were significant differences between no automation and full automation in all three categories: for the "Performance Expectancy" (p = 0.01) with mean ranks (M) that show an increasing rating from no automation (M = 2.62) to partial automation (M = 1.88) and a slightly decreased rating from partial to full automation (M = 1.50); the "Social Influence" (p = 0.004) with steadily decreasing mean ranks for no automation (M = 2.50), partial automation (M = 2.00) and full automation (M = 1.50) – as well as the "Perceived Safety" (p = 0.002) that also show decreasing mean ranks from no to full automation (M(level 1) = 2.50; M(level 2) = 2.06; M(level 3) = 1.44). There were no significant differences comparing levels 1 and 2 or 2 and 3 of those three categories or in any other variables of the remaining categories which are discussed below.

For "Effort Expectancy" the mean ranks are rather similar for all three scenarios with a value of 2.26 for no automation, 2.00 for part automation and 1.74 for full automation and results in a non-significant Chi square value of only 2.793 ($\chi^2(2) = 2.793$; p = 0.247).

Minor differences could be found for "Facilitating Conditions" with p = 0.627 ($\chi^2(2) = 0.933$) and "Behavioural Intention to use the System" ($\chi^2(2) = 1.418$; p = 0.492).

"Self-efficacy" shows the biggest differences of mean ranks between no automation (M = 2.38) and full automation (M = 1.71) which is not significant though ($\chi^2(2) = 5.055$; p = 0.080).

"Anxiety" does not show any significant differences between any of the three levels of automation. The mean ranks show similar differences between no automation (M = 1.65) and partial automation (M = 2.06) and partial and full automation (M = 2.29). But even the difference between no and full automation is not significant ($\chi^2(2) = 3.875$; p = 0.144).

Lastly the "Attitude towards using Technology" mean ranks are also rather similar but differ from the other values in so far as the biggest difference exists between partial (M = 2.15) and full automation values (M = 1.79) which again is not significant ($\chi^2(2) = 1.279$; p = 0.528).

Rödel et al. [7] could distinguish significant differences in all their factors measured by their questionnaire. In contrast to that, this study led only to significant difference in a few of the measured factors. Rödel et al. [7] using an online questionnaire were able to include more participants and had therefor less factors measured per participant.

In our simulator setting only a small sample size including rather young participants could be tested. These factors may in part explain our different result compared to Rödel et al. [7].

Furthermore our new approach to use virtual reality instead of just detailed scenarios as stimulus is also likely to have influenced the outcome. Perhaps our participants could immerse themselves more in using self-driving cars through VR than the participants of Rödel et al. [7] by reading texts.

As mentioned above we also asked the participants two qualitative questions about their personal impression of semi-autonomous and autonomous driving. The results of these give a rather positive impression as nine of the 17 participants named the autonomous scenario as the most pleasant one, five named the partially autonomous scenario and only three the fully manual scenario. This positive attitude was also confirmed by replies to the second question about whether test subjects could imagine driving an autonomous car in the future as 15 participants replied with "yes" and only two mentioned safety issues that made them unsure about their willingness to use this system. These qualitative findings indicate a high acceptance of autonomous driving in our study with a rather young group of participants.

5 Conclusion

Rödel et al. [7] found that UA and UX values are highest for non-autonomous scenarios and concluded that users felt more comfortable in situations they are already familiar with. In contrast our results indicate that Performance Expectancy, Perceived Safety and Social Influence are significantly higher for the fully automated condition than for no automation. The monotonically but insignificantly increasing value for "Anxiety" along the rising levels of autonomy may suggest that people do not experience markedly greater anxiety about future autonomous cars than about the manual driving mode. The insignificant differences in the dimension "Attitude towards using technology" are harder to interpret. Perhaps the autonomous driving scenarios and the interior design of the simulated levels of autonomy were too similar and therefore un-realistic, and did not quite match the user's expectations, so that their attitude towards using the new technology in autonomous cars was adversely affected. The factor "Self-efficacy" shows, that users tend to think, that they could handle fully autonomous cars better in comparison to manual and partially autonomous cars. In this regard, autonomous driving is also perceived as more efficient than partially automated driving or manually driving.

In conclusion, investigating user acceptance of different autonomy levels in an immersive approach with a VR driving simulator delivered different results compared to previous research. Future work has to examine autonomous driving in VR with a more elaborated and perhaps more futuristic and at the same time more realistic driving simulator design as well as an increased sample size including participants of more varying age.

References

1. Davis, F.D.: Perceived usefulness, perceived ease of use, and user acceptance of information technology. MIS Q. **13**(3), 319–340 (1989)
2. Hawkins, A.J.: Uber's self-driving cars are now picking up passengers in Arizona - The Verge (2017). http://www.theverge.com/2017/2/21/14687346/uber-self-driving-car-arizona-pilot-ducey-california. Accessed 31 Mar 2017

3. Helldin, T., Falkman, G., Riveiro, M., Davidsson, S.: Presenting system uncertainty in automotive UIs for supporting trust calibration in autonomous driving. In: Proceedings of the International Conference on Automotive User Interfaces and Interactive Vehicular Applications - AutomotiveUI 2013, vol. 5, pp. 210–217 (2013). https://doi.org/10.1145/2516540.2516554
4. NHTSA: National Highway Traffic Safety Administration. Preliminary Statement of Policy Concerning Automated Vehicles (2013)
5. Osswald, S., Wurhofer, D., Trösterer, S., Beck, E., Tscheligi, M.: Predicting information technology usage in the car: towards a car technology acceptance model. In: Proceedings of the 4th International Conference on Automotive User Interfaces and Interactive Vehicular Applications, pp. 51–58 (2012). https://doi.org/10.1145/2390256.2390264
6. Robertson, R.D., Meister, S.R., Vanlaar, W.G.M.: Automated Vehicles: Driver Knowledge, Attitudes, & Practices. Traffic Injury Research Foundation, Ontario (2016). https://search.informit.com.au/documentSummary;dn=365036984144993;res=IELENG
7. Rödel, C., Stadler, S., Meschtscherjakov, A., Tscheligi, M.: Towards autonomous cars: the effect of autonomy levels on acceptance and user experience. In: Proceedings of the 6th International Conference on Automotive User Interfaces and Interactive Vehicular Applications, pp. 1–8 (2014). https://doi.org/10.1145/2667317.2667330

Improving Deaf Driver Experience Through Innovative Vehicle Interactive Design

Jingpeng Jia$^{(\boxtimes)}$, Xueyan Dong, Yanjuan Lu, Yingjie Qian,
and Dai Tang

Beijing Union University, Beijing, China
tjtjingpeng@buu.edu.cn

Abstract. This study aims to explore the application of storyboard and combination of storyboard and the technology of Internet of things (IoT) into the vehicle interactive design to improve deaf drivers' experience. To achieve the aim, we introduced the storyboard approach into user need study and product prototype design, and practiced in the course of user experience at Beijing Union University. Our results show that the method has two benefits for students: 1. They can utilize storyboard to quickly understand the usage context of products without knowing the whole producing processes in real setting. 2. They can form future insights on the introduction of IoT into the vehicle interactive design, the deaf driving system, which has not been developed yet. This paper presents the approach in detail.

Keywords: Vehicle interaction system · Interaction design · Deaf driving
User experience · Internet of things

1 Introduction

The special education college at Beijing Union University is a unique high education institution in Beijing, which offers the entrance to university for deaf students. It has an undergraduate major called visual communication especially provided for students with hearing disability and its education aim is to provide universal knowledge on visual interaction design. It specializes in offering services for hearing disabled students on interactive design and service design. It has accumulated research and design experience on vehicle interaction design for deaf drivers for many years. The journey map method using storyboard plays an increasingly important role in the educational curriculum in recent years. In order to let students better understand the method and effectively apply it to user study and design practice, we organize the interactive user experience curriculum which aims to enable students to master the journey map method [1, 5, 9] based on the storyboard and encourage them to think about the application of internet of things (IoT) technique to vehicle interaction design for improving the deaf driving experience.

In the course, key challenges for students are: 1. How to apply the journey map to find challenges the deaf driver might have. 2. What is the cognity of driving behaviors? 3. How to get insights on introducing technology into the improvement of the deaf drivers' experience. 4. to examine whether the designed scheme can effectively solve pain points problems, and whether it suits on the deaf driving habits and can be applied

© Springer International Publishing AG, part of Springer Nature 2018
A. Marcus and W. Wang (Eds.): DUXU 2018, LNCS 10920, pp. 257–269, 2018.
https://doi.org/10.1007/978-3-319-91806-8_20

to the social context where users are [2]? Traditional product design processes and supermarket study methods are insufficient to find latent needs of users [12]. To address the issue, we provide a journey map approach based on storyboard. This method can assist designers in three ways. First, it can help designers build the potential contexts of using the product. Second, it can enable designers to empathize effectively such that they can have insight into hidden needs of users. Last, it can be used as tools to verify to what extent the adaptability of design scheme can reach.

In addition, it is worth noting that the development of autonomous driving technology has brought new opportunities for vehicle-mounted interaction design. There are many problems in the driving process, which may be solved based on the interactive design of the automatic driving technology. Therefore, it is necessary to stress the importance of autonomous driving technology in this course. However, for classroom teaching, in order to allow students to fully understand the characteristics of autopilot technology and design innovative interactive functions based on this technology, teachers need to solve the following three questions: First, introduce the basic knowledge of philosophy of technology to students. In this way, students are aware of the important role that technology plays in social development. At the same time, they also cultivate students' philosophical thinking ability and historical mission. On this basis, students are allowed to consider the value of technological progress from the perspective of social ethics. Second, to provide effective and streamlined automated driving technology learning materials, so that students can quickly understand the basic characteristics of automatic driving technology. Third, students are encouraged to think about the possibilities of future development with a mindset of development so that students can continuously cultivate their own creative thinking and creative design awareness.

2 Related Work

Recently, there are many IT companies such as Google and Baidu, and some car producing corporations including Volkswagen and Volve, and Tesla, devoting to the study of autonomous vehicle technologies [3, 4, 6]. It is possible that the increasing improvement of technology can help disabled people to get around in a safe and effective way. However, autonomous technique still has limits. First, the objective of pilotless automobile is to reduce the involvement of human drivers into driving so as to prevent accidents [7]. But this deprives the rights of drivers with enjoyment. Second, the fully automatic driving mode has strict requirements on driving environment. Under some complex road conditions and most of country roads, autonomous driving is difficult to implement. Therefore, how to provide deaf people with enjoyment and consider their safety during driving still need to be addressed.

Moreover, in recent 1–2 years, many car-producing companies, such as Audi, begin to focus on the study of advanced self-piloting techniques. Nowadays, various types of products developed by these companies are increasingly developed and put into the consumption market. The problems that consumers have in the use of these products effectively reflect the real consumer demand for autonomous driving technology. For students' learning activities, it is necessary to understand as much as possible the application cases of these automatic driving technologies and their related experiences and lessons. For example, almost all autopilot product developers have encountered the following problems in product development activities: Between different countries and even different cities, there are usually significant differences in pedestrian behavior, traffic complexity, and driver driving habits. Based on the above experience, it is necessary to provide basic learning materials for students in ethnographic research methods, anthropology and sociology. And urge students to learn the above knowledge after school hours. On this basis, teachers should guide students to consciously conduct corresponding in-car interaction design according to different cultural environments.

3 Settings

The interactive experience course aims to equip students with design theory while gaining practical experience in the development of interactive prototypes, and enrich their ability to study user behaviors to propose solutions based on storyboard. In the course, how to design and draw the cartoon storyboard is introduced in detail. In contrast to video show, the application of storyboard can save the cost and help students quickly form the context of using products in mind [7, 8, 11]. It can also help students find out the real paint points that users have so as to think of solutions of how to utilize the technology of Internet of things [14, 15].

Fifteen deaf students participated in this course and were equally divided into 3 groups. Each group was asked to first learn and understand the basic principles and features of the Internet of things. Then, based on the desk research and field research, they were requested to draw the storyboard of driving process for deaf people and analyze the problems that deaf drivers may have during driving. In the end, students were supposed to use storyboard to think, design and show a new vehicle interactive solution to address the problems.

For the teachers' team, three instructors were assigned to the course, one was responsible for instructing innovation strategy, one has the background of information technology and one was supervise the design methodology. The innovation teacher provided students with instruction on business model, user study, and demand analysis. The IT teacher took charge in helping student accurately understanding the features and theories of self-piloting technique. The design method instructor was responsible for giving guidance to student's design practice during the design solution and storyboard drawing phase. The three instructors explained the meaning and methods of interdisciplinary research for students from different perspectives based on their own knowledge background and practical experience. Particularly, students were introduced to user needs research methods, innovative product strategies, computer functional boundaries, Stanford creative design methods and storyboard drawing techniques.

4 Approach

Our research objective is to explore the use of storyboard to the use experience study and to investigate how Internet of things can assist in designing vehicle interactive system for improving deaf driver experience. This is an interesting challenge that presents itself to designers, developers, and researchers. The course lasted for a total of eight calendar weeks. It ran in parallel with others and was scheduled to take up one day per week. We developed a design brief together with the brief holder who contributed some money to purchase partial drawing materials and expenses. While the course does not provide any training on painting, we made sure that each team had at least one student who is a drawing expertise in drawing various contexts and human actions.

The course consists of five iterations with varying lengths, each iteration produces a storyboard with a different focus. The iterations can be summarized as the form of assignments given to the students. We envisage using customer-centered [12, 13] as the design guidance. Students need to stick to the guidance throughout the whole process starting from thinking of solutions to conducting user study and testing designed schemes. In addition, when students try to utilize technology to solve pain points, they also need to consider the sustainable development of human beings as a principle. On the complement of the course, students are required to show a storyboard, which can clearly explain their interactive design. One important judgment is to check whether the presented design scheme is effective for improving driving experience for the deaf.

5   Interactive Behavior Design

Throughout the whole research, students utilized the field study based on storyboard to investigate user needs and design solutions. To ensure an accurate flow of thoughts, a research through design approach is taken, in which the generation of knowledge and the development of applications go hand in hand. Research through design is used as a form of research to contribute to a design activity [16, 17]. The leading principle in the course is customer-centered and it was used in each design step. However, in fact, to strictly stick to this principle is quite difficult. Students often put their own thoughts to users. During the practice, this problem was revised many times. Additionally, it is even more difficult for students to take consideration of human sustainable development since this requires students to have a broad background on humanity, philosophy and society science. The use of storyboard offers a platform for exploring user needs and find solutions to new design, therefore filed research based on storyboard lay foundation for the whole research. During the building of storyboard, relying on the direct experience of user field and technology principle, students gain better understand on driving behaviors of deaf people and the features of Internet of things. This is vital for forming the final solution. Below are brief descriptions of three interactive design concepts concerning what problems students find out for deaf drivers.

5.1   Dealing with Traffic Accident

Especially in large cities in China, complex road conditions lead to frequent traffic accidents. Once the accidents happen, drivers have many troubles to deal with, such as traffic responsibility confirmation, submitting the accident report to their insurance company and booking the repairmen for their vehicle. Due to the communication difficulties between deaf and normal people, deaf drivers may have more challenges than the normal. In future, with the expansion and applications of the Internet of things, solving such problems becomes possible. First, the laser and x-ray recognition system can be installed on vehicles such that vehicles can identify the responsibility according to road condition and vehicle self-condition. Second, the computer system of insurance company can send the insurance report to drivers' car or phone in a second and it can also give suggestions on where to find repairing points. Thus, it makes the accident more convenient for deaf drivers to deal with. The details of the design process can be found in Fig. 1.

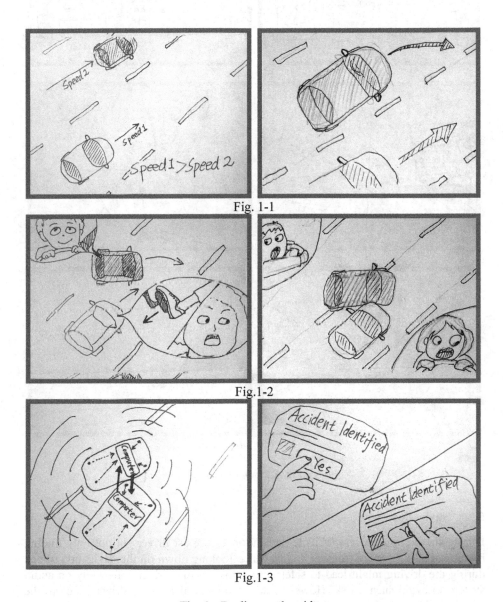

Fig. 1-1

Fig.1-2

Fig.1-3

Fig. 1. Dealing road accident

Fig.1-4

Fig.1-5

Fig.1-6

Fig. 1. (*continued*)

5.2   Navigation

During the driving process, vehicle navigation can assist drivers in not only finding routes but also escaping from the traffic. Since looking down on the navigation screen during the driving might lead to safety problems, normal drivers often rely on audio system to avoid such a risk. However, this is unhelpful for deaf drivers. Due to the hearing problems, deaf people have to receive the navigation information via visual signals. Relying on the Internet-of-things, the problems mentioned above can be addressed. Once the deaf driver types into his destination, the navigation can synchronize his needs to the cloud so that the cloud system can automatically query the same needs that normal drivers have. Once the query is done, the cloud can send back the information about normal drivers to the deaf' computer. At this time, the deaf driver can see a car in front, which is indicated on their front window through augment reality. Thus, he just needs to follow the indicated car to find the correct route. The details of the process can be seen in Fig. 2.

Fig.2-1

Fig.2-2

Fig.2-3

Fig. 2. Navigation

Fig.2-4

Fig.2-5

Fig.2-6

Fig. 2. (*continued*)

5.3   Advance Warning System

During driving, due to the visual range limitation of the vehicle reflector, drivers cannot find the coming car from rear side. This brings a safety risk when drivers try to change lanes. Since deaf drivers cannot hear the alarming made by the rear car. This situation is even more dangerous for them. In the setting of Internet of things, this problem can be addressed as follow. First, the laser radar can detect the car from rear side and the vehicle can remind the deaf driver through shaking his steering wheel or showing the indicator. Second, each car was issued an identification number so that the driving behavior features can be uploaded to the cloud. If the car from rear has bad driving behavior, the deaf' car automatically will turn on special lights or shake the steering wheel to warn him. The details of designing process is shown in Fig. 3.

Fig.3-1

Fig.3-2

Fig.3-3

Fig. 3. Advance warning system

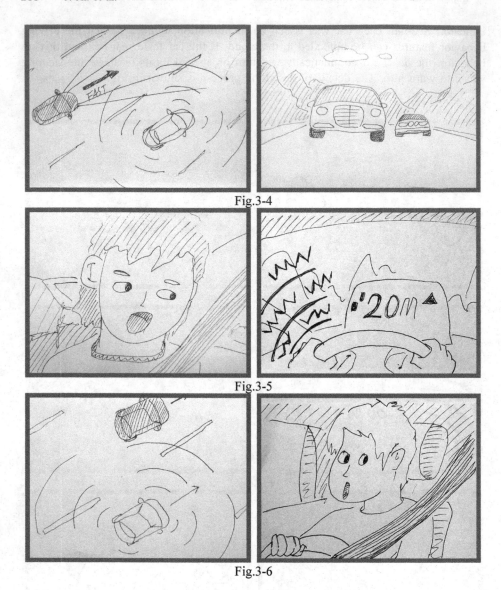

Fig.3-4

Fig.3-5

Fig.3-6

Fig. 3. (*continued*)

6   Discussion

All designed storyboards provide a platform for exploring the customers' pain points and play a vital important role in the practice of the course. Throughout the course, students conducted a comprehensive study on the deaf drivers' physical and behavior features. This lays great foundations for subsequent design. Using the storyboard, students designed various services that function in vehicle interactive design for deaf drivers. This greatly assists students in understanding the approach of drawing storyboard.

As required by the teaching program, the objective of the course is to require students to master the way of making storyboard and learn how to conduct the study of user needs and design interactive functional methods. The course in this study was conducted in a group form, thus it can collect various ideas. On the other hand, each group member can contribute his/her knowledge to his or her group. But such a form also has limitations. First, personal talents are hardly to be shown. Second, for those who have basic background of drawing storyboard, this course does not provide any advanced programs. This may hinder their ability to explore better design. Last, students who are responsible for drawing the storyboard may lack of sufficient training on the study of user needs and interactive design as drawing the storyboard takes a lot of time. To solve the problems, there is more to do on how to improve existing teaching program.

The course was done in an educational setting but not in a practice setting of commercial product development, because in the educational setting teachers can take control in every important step, which does not provide student chances to experience the real productive setting, a more complicated and varied setting. Thus, how to introduce practical business needs to high educational courses remains a problem. The limitations of this course include the short amount of time, insufficient knowledge and lack of comprehensive user tests. Therefore, students lack of training on user tests.

In addition, it is particularly noteworthy that in this course, although students showed a good sense of innovation and good creative design capabilities, it is still difficult to effectively implement the three factors of business operation mode, brand development strategy and marketing model. Comprehensive considerations. This is highly linked to the fact that students rarely have contact with actual business projects. Therefore, it is necessary to introduce more practical projects for students and to conduct high-quality business thinking teaching. After all, the effective formulation of business strategies is a prerequisite for the development of high-quality user experience research and design.

7   Conclusion

We discussed the application of storyboard to interactive design by applying it to a university course. The teaching results show that in the course the storyboard approach can stimulate students' creativity and encourage them to apply design thinking to exploration of user needs. Our contribution to the existing education system is improve the vehicle interactive design for the deaf so that autonomous vehicles can bring deaf drivers with indeed benefits. We have two main findings. First, storyboard is a direct way for deaf students to conduct user needs study and propose solutions, and it requires a low cost. Second, the application of storyboard makes the introduction of advanced technology into interactive design feasible. At least, students can easily for see how Internet of things (IoT) can be applied to the solution of designing a deaf driving system in the future.

8 Future Work

First, we will cooperate with companies that can provide prototype production services to build high-fidelity prototype for the design solutions presented in this course. Then, the deaf driver will be recruited to try each interactive function of the prototype product. During this process, students will observe problems in the existing solution. On this basis, students will make improvements to the design plan and create new prototype products. This allows continuous iteration of the design.

Moreover, in order to improve the teaching quality of innovative product design, a toolkit is required for new projects using the storyboard method so as to make user study and design process clear and make existing methodology more practical for students to understand and apply. Also, it requires students to fully understand the context about users. Thus, user study and product design using storyboard can be more effective. In the future, we will work on these tasks.

Last, students will be required to continue to pay attention to the latest developments in IoT technology and autonomous driving technology. Teachers will use new technologies to guide students to provide new solutions to problems encountered by deaf people during driving. The solutions should also be tested whether they are effective.

Acknowledgements. We thank all participated students for their enthusiasm and hard work. We also thank Dr. Xueyan Dong for providing technology support on Internet of things. We would like to send our great thanks to professor Yanjuan Lu for contributions on the design method. We also want to thank the support from the company, Volkswagen in China for providing practicing opportunities.

Funding. The publication of this research project was supported by the BUU Scholar Scheme Funds for researchers at Beijing Union University (No. 12210611609-039).

References

1. Alexander, K., Fenker, M., Granath, J.Å., Haugen, T., Nissinen, K.: Usable workplaces: action research. In: Proceedings of CIB 2005, Combining Forces – Advancing Facilities Management & Construction through Innovation Series, pp. 389–399 (2005)
2. Bitner, M.J., Booms, B.H., Tetreault, M.S.: The service encounter: diagnosing favorable and unfavorable incidents. J. Mark. **54**(1), 71–84 (1990)
3. Gummesson, E., Kingman-Brundage, J.: Service design and quality: applying service blueprinting and service mapping to railroad services. In: Kunst, P., Lemmink, J. (eds.) Quality Management in Services, pp. 101–114. Van Gorcum, Maastricht (1992)
4. Nenonen, S., Nissinen, K.: Usability walkthrough usability walkthrough in workplaces – what, how, why and when. In: Proceedings of CIB 2005, Combining Forces – Advancing Facilities Management & Construction through Innovation Series, vol. IV, pp. 413–422 (2005)
5. Jarvenpaa, S.L., Lang, K.R.: Managing the paradoxes of mobile technology. Inf. Syst. Manag. **22**, 7–23 (2005)

6. Jumisko, S.H., Ilvonen, V.P., Väänänen-Vainio-Mattila, K.A.: Effect of TV content in subjective assessment of video quality on mobile devices. In: Proceedings of SPIE — The International Society for Optical Engineering, pp. 243–254 (2005)

7. Venkatesh, V., Brown, S.A.: A longitudinal investigation of personal computers in homes: adoption determinants and emerging challenges. MIS Q. **25**, 71–80 (2001)

8. Xu, X., Ma, W., See-To, E.W.K.: Will mobile video become the killer application for 3G? — an empirical model for media convergence. Inf. Syst. Front. **12**, 311–322 (2010)

9. Zhang, D., Adipat, B.: Challenges, methodologies, and issues in the usability testing of mobile applications. Int. J. Hum.-Comput. Interact. **18**(3), 293–308 (2005)

10. Hoeben, A., Stappers, P.J.: Taking clues from the world outside: navigating interactive panoramas. J. Pers. Ubiquit. Comput. **10**(2–3), 122–127 (2006)

11. Nardi, B.A., Whittaker, S., Bradner, E.: Interaction and outeraction: instant messaging in action. In: Proceedings of the 2000 ACM Conference on Computer Supported Cooperative Work, pp. 79–88. ACM Press, New York (2000)

12. Cleaveland, M.C., Larkins, E.R.: Web-based practice and feedback improve tax students' written communication skills. J. Account. Educ. **22**, 211–228 (2004)

13. Mohrweis, L.C.: The impact of writing assignments on accounting students' writing skills. J. Account. Educ. **9**, 309–325 (1991)

14. Wixon, D.R.: Measuring fun, trust, confidence, and other ethereal constructs: it isn't that hard. Interactions **18**(6), 74–77 (2011)

15. Thüring, M., Mahlke, S.: Usability, aesthetics and emotions in human–technology interaction. Int. J. Psychol. **42**(4), 253–264 (2007)

16. Archer, B.: The nature of research. J. Codesign **2**, 6–13 (1995)

17. Avison, D.E., Lau, F., Myers, M.D., Nielsen, P.A.: Action research. Commun. ACM **42**(1), 94–97 (1999)

Interactive Car Parking Simulation Based on On-line Trajectory Optimization

Jungsub Lim, Hyejin Kim, and Daseong Han[⊠]

School of Global Entrepreneurship and ICT, Handong Global University,
Pohang, Republic of Korea
jsrimr@naver.com, gobetty20@gmail.com,
dshan@handong.edu

Abstract. This paper presents an on-line trajectory optimization method to simulate the autonomous parking of a car-like vehicle in an environment with static or dynamic obstacles. We employ a stochastic and derivative-free optimization technique called Covariance Matrix Adaptation (CMA) to seamlessly integrate collision events between the car and the environment into the formulation of our autonomous parking problem without resorting to any preprocessing steps to make the problem differentiable. Given the current and target car states, our system repeatedly predicts a sequence of control inputs for a short time window to move the car to the target while shifting the window along the time axis, which facilitates on-line performance. We also present a simple and effective scheme to make our optimization robust to environmental changes by adjusting its parameters in an on-line manner. We show the effectiveness of our method through simulation results for garage parking, parallel parking, and interactive parking based on on-line user input.

Keywords: Autonomous car parking · On-line trajectory optimization
Simulation · Motion planning · Stochastic optimization

1 Introduction

Over the last few years, autonomous driving has been one of the most important topics in many research areas due to the ever-growing demands and market scale for autonomous vehicles. Many technical innovations have been presented to effectively address the topic and commercial autonomous cars have already been being in market in several countries. However, it is still very challenging to robustly control an autonomous vehicle in urban environments, where it must recognize and obey traffic lights and also needs to avoid colliding with other moving vehicles and pedestrians whose motions are not fully predictable in general while moving to the destination. Instead of dealing with the topic as a whole, we focus on how to autonomously park a

Electronic supplementary material The online version of this chapter (https://doi.org/10.1007/978-3-319-91806-8_21) contains supplementary material, which is available to authorized users.

© Springer International Publishing AG, part of Springer Nature 2018
A. Marcus and W. Wang (Eds.): DUXU 2018, LNCS 10920, pp. 270–284, 2018.
https://doi.org/10.1007/978-3-319-91806-8_21

vehicle while avoiding obstacles in a computer simulation through numerical optimization with simple and intuitive objectives given on-line user input such as a desired parking location and orientation. Although the car parking is much simplified version of the autonomous driving problem, it can be very useful not only for attaining the goal of the latter but also for equipping conventional vehicles with an intelligent parking system.

In this paper, we present an on-line trajectory optimization method for autonomously moving a car to a desired parking slot based on a stochastic and derivative-free optimization method called covariance matrix adaptation (CMA) [1]. CMA repeatedly alternates evaluating a given objective function at possible solutions populated by a multivariate normal distribution and updating the distribution with the evaluation results until a certain termination condition is satisfied. Since the method does not rely on any derivative information of the objective function, an objective for collision avoidance from environmental obstacles, which introduces discontinuity into optimization in general, can be seamlessly integrated into a problem formulation together with the other objectives. It effectively removes precomputation steps to enforce the differentiability of objectives unlike existing derivative-based frameworks.

In order to facilitate on-line performance, we also employ a model predictive control (MPC) scheme, which repeatedly solves a finite-horizon trajectory optimization problem for a relatively short time window while shifting the window along the time axis. Since our MPC framework continuously re-computes the optimal trajectory in run time, environmental changes can be more effectively dealt with on the fly. The result of MPC is a sequence of optimal control vectors for the time window, each of which is composed of the front wheel angle and acceleration of the car. In turn, these control vectors are provided to the simulator to update the current car state.

The contributions of this paper are two-fold. In the systematic point of view, we present an on-line control framework which can produce realistic parking movements in an environment with static or dynamic obstacles according to a desired location and orientation interactively given by the user. In the technical point of view, we formulate an autonomous car-parking problem with simple and intuitive high-level objectives based on a stochastic and derivative-free optimization technique. Our method does not rely on any complicated system analysis or control law design. We also introduce an MPC scheme to effectively support on-line performance and to enhance time efficiency. This is due to the fact that MPC does not compute the whole trajectory to reach a final destination at once but repeatedly optimizes a trajectory for a short time window while moving it along the time axis. Our method is effective to generate convincing parking movements for challenging scenarios such as moving a car into a narrow parking slot while avoiding a moving obstacle without any reference trajectory or preprocessing.

2   Related Work

For the autonomous parking problem, various approaches have been proposed over the last decades. Control design and analysis for wheeled mobile robots have been actively done by transforming their kinematic equations to so-called chained form [2]. Reeds and Shepp simplified car movements to a combination of circular and linear motions, and then calculated the minimum-length path [3], which has also been adopted by many other researchers [4, 5]. However, this approach works only in an obstacle-free environment.

Laumond et al. proposed a motion planner for mobile vehicles based on a two-step approach [6]. In the first step, the planner computes a collision-free holonomic path, which is relatively easy to derive. The path is then transformed into the corresponding non-holonomic one by integrating non-holonomic constraints. Muller et al. also employed this approach using the clothoid curve [7]. However, it is difficult to derive the non-holonomic path corresponding to a holonomic in general, which often results in a lot of maneuvering efforts. In order to avoid this complexity, our problem formulation relies on simple high-level objectives supported by derivative-free optimization.

Kim et al. derived collision-free reachable areas for every movement of a vehicle, and then connected points in these areas to generate multiple path candidates [8]. This method is effective to deal with environmental changes, such as the change of an obstacle position or parking space. But it cannot deal with moving obstacles. Unlike this, our method can avoid moving obstacles as well as static.

Barraquand and Latombe discretized a configuration space into a grid map and then planned a path on the map by exhaustive search equipped with heuristic rules [9]. The scheme provides practical solutions in many cases. However, the method's accuracy for generating a collision-free path is not guaranteed and it requires high computing power.

Sampling-based approaches have successfully applied to path planning. LaValle and Kuffner proposed Rapidly-exploring Random Trees (RRT) [10], which generates a tree structure by connecting the randomly sampled nodes satisfying certain constraints and conditions until the tree includes a target position. Its effectiveness was also demonstrated in the 2007 DARPA Urban Challenge [11, 12]. Probabilistic roadmap (PRM) was proposed by Kavraki et al. to plan a path in high-dimensional configuration spaces [13]. PRM planners allocate samples in a configuration space and construct a path graph connecting these sample points.

A two-phase path planning approach was proposed for autonomous vehicles by Dolgov et al. [14], which was also experimentally validated in the same competition mentioned above [12]. In the first phase, A* algorithm is used to search a kinematically feasible trajectory. Then, a derivative-based optimization is employed to improve the trajectory in the second phase. In order to keep the objective function differentiable in this phase, nearest obstacles at each time step must be precomputed and fixed in the previous phase. Unlike this approach, we propose a single-phase path planning framework that seamlessly integrates an obstacle avoidance objective into optimization without any precomputation steps.

There have been also efforts to apply artificial intelligence techniques such as fuzzy controllers [15] or neural networks [16] to motion planning problems with wheeled mobile robots. These are relatively easy to implement but the performance is highly dependent on their training data set.

Zips et al. suggested a fast motion planning algorithm for a wheeled vehicle based on heuristic rules, where the next move is determined by taking into account only a resulting state of the vehicle followed by the move but not the total path [17]. However, since the algorithm is rule-based, it is hard to be generalized. For example, an algorithm for parallel parking on the left side cannot be applied to that for the right side. Also, it does not work in a dynamic environment.

Tassa et al. proposed a variant of differential dynamic programming (DDP) to support bound constraints on control variables [18] unlike the original version which can deal with only unconstrained variables. The method was effectively applied to the car parking problem in an obstacle-free environment so as to constrain the wheel angle and acceleration to their respective valid ranges. In more complicated environments with obstacles, however, it would be difficult to integrate the constraints for collision avoidance into an objective function because these are generally not differentiable while DDP requires a differentiable objective function. In order to address this issue, we employ a sampling-based optimization method called CMA [1]. It does not require any derivative information, which allows us to enforce collision avoidance constraints to an objective function in an intuitive manner.

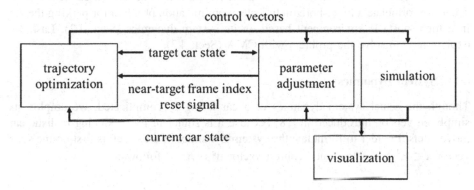

Fig. 1. System overview.

3 System Overview

Our system consists of three main components: trajectory optimization, parameter adjustment, and simulation (Fig. 1). Provided with the current and target car states and optimization parameters such as the near-target frame index and reset signal, the first component repeatedly solves a finite-horizon trajectory optimization problem for a short time window with CMA while shifting it along the time axis. It then produces a sequence of control vectors to make the car closer to its target state composed of the car position, speed, and orientation. In order to save computational time, the optimization starts with all the context data of the last optimization including the mean and covariance of a normal distribution maintained by CMA.

The second component computes the near-target frame index and reset signal to make trajectory optimization produce a better result and performance given the current and target car states together with the control vectors. The former represents an index to the first of the frames at which the car state is close enough to the target state while it is also true at all the following frames. It is used to make an objective function encourage optimization to quickly converge to the target car state once the car comes near it. If the latter is on, the trajectory optimization is completely restarted without relying on any context data of the last optimization. It is often needed because CMA may have got stuck at a local optimum depending on the sampling data populated from its last normal distribution.

When the resulting control vectors are given to the last component, they are used to update the current car state. In the remaining sections, we do not deal with the simulation component in details but focuses on the first two components because the third component can be implemented by the system dynamics of the car introduced in trajectory optimization (Scct. 4.1).

4 Trajectory Optimization

In this section, we first discuss the simplified system dynamics of a car (Sect. 4.1). Then, we formulate a finite-horizon trajectory optimization problem for parking the car in a multi-obstacle environment based on its system dynamics (Sect. 4.2). Last, we explain how to solve the problem with CMA (Sect. 4.3).

4.1 System Dynamics

Though the actual system dynamics of a car is highly complicated, we employ its simplified version introduced in [18] because it is sufficient for producing realistic car movements. In order to formulate the system dynamics of a car, let us first define state vector $\mathbf{x} \in \mathbb{R}^4$ and constrained control vector $\mathbf{u}^c \in \mathbb{R}^2$ as follows:

$$\mathbf{x} = \begin{bmatrix} x \\ y \\ \theta \\ v \end{bmatrix} \text{ and } \mathbf{u}^c = \begin{bmatrix} \omega \\ \alpha \end{bmatrix}. \tag{1}$$

$$\omega^{lo} \leq \omega \leq \omega^{hi}, \tag{2}$$

$$\alpha^{lo} \leq \alpha \leq \alpha^{hi}. \tag{3}$$

Here, (x, y) is the midpoint between the back wheels. θ is the angle of the car with respect to the x-axis and v is the speed of the front wheels. ω and α are the angle and acceleration of the front wheels whose valid ranges are constrained by Eqs. (2) and (3), respectively. In all our experiments, we set $\omega^{lo} = -50°$, $\omega^{lo} = 50°$, $\alpha^{lo} = -15 \,\mathrm{m/s}^2$, and $\alpha^{hi} = 15 \,\mathrm{m/s}^2$. Then, system dynamics $\mathbf{x}' = \mathbf{f}^c(\mathbf{x}, \mathbf{u}^c)$, which returns next-step state $\mathbf{x}'$ given current state $\mathbf{x}$ and control $\mathbf{u}^c$, is formulated as follows:

$$\mathbf{f}^c(\mathbf{x}, \mathbf{u}^c) = \begin{bmatrix} x + b \cdot \cos(\theta) \\ y + b \cdot \sin(\theta) \\ \theta + \sin^{-1}\left(\sin(\omega)\frac{f}{d}\right) \\ v + h \cdot \alpha \end{bmatrix}, \tag{4}$$

where d is the distance between the front and back axles and h is the integration step size. f and b are the rolling distance of the front and back wheels, respectively, as shown below:

$$f = h \cdot v, \tag{5}$$

$$b = f \cdot \cos(\omega) + d - \sqrt{d^2 - f^2 \sin^2(\omega)}. \tag{6}$$

We refer readers to [18] for more details on the above car dynamics.

Since CMA is an unconstrained optimization method, we introduce new control vector $\mathbf{u} = [u_1 \quad u_2]^{\mathrm{T}}$ which is used to express ω and θ as functions of unconstrained variables u_1 and u_2, respectively:

$$\omega(u_1) = \omega^{lo} + \frac{(\omega^{hi} - \omega^{lo})}{2}\left(1 - \cos\left(\pi\frac{u_1 - \omega^{lo}}{\omega^{hi} - \omega^{lo}}\right)\right), \tag{7}$$

$$\alpha(u_2) = \alpha^{lo} + \frac{\alpha^{hi} - \alpha^{lo}}{2}\left(1 - \cos\left(\pi\frac{u_2 - \alpha^{lo}}{\alpha^{hi} - \alpha^{lo}}\right)\right). \tag{8}$$

Here, bound constraints $\omega(u_1) \in [\omega^{lo}, \omega^{hi}]$ and $\alpha(u_2) \in [\alpha^{lo}, \alpha^{hi}]$ are always satisfied no matter what values control variables u_1 and u_2 have. With the new control vector $\mathbf{u}$, we define the unconstrained version of system dynamics $\mathbf{x}' = \mathbf{f}(\mathbf{x}, \mathbf{u})$ as follows:

$$\mathbf{f}(\mathbf{x}, \mathbf{u}) = \begin{bmatrix} x + b \cdot \cos(\theta) \\ y + b \cdot \sin(\theta) \\ \theta + \sin^{-1}\left(\sin(\omega(u_1))\frac{f}{d}\right) \\ v + h \cdot \alpha(u_2) \end{bmatrix}, \quad \text{where} \tag{9}$$

$$f = h \cdot v, \tag{10}$$

$$b = f \cdot \cos(\omega(u_1)) + d - \sqrt{d^2 - f^2 \sin^2(\omega(u_1))}. \tag{11}$$

4.2   Problem Formulation

Based on the system dynamics in Eq. (9), our system optimizes state trajectory $X = \{\mathbf{x}^1, \mathbf{x}^2, \ldots, \mathbf{x}^N\}$ for a short time window of N frames to drive the autonomous car to reach target state $\bar{\mathbf{x}} = \begin{bmatrix} \bar{x} & \bar{y} & \bar{\theta} & \bar{v} \end{bmatrix}^{\mathrm{T}}$ composed of target position $(\bar{x}, \bar{y})$, target orientation $\bar{\theta}$, and target speed $\bar{v}$. In order to do so, we formulate a finite-horizon trajectory optimization problem to find control vector sequence $U = \{\mathbf{u}^1, \mathbf{u}^2, \ldots, \mathbf{u}^{N-1}\}$ given current car state $\mathbf{x}$ and target car state $\bar{\mathbf{x}}$ together with near-target frame index k and reset signal η:

$$\min_U J(X, U) \tag{12}$$

$$\text{subject to} \quad \mathbf{x}^1 = \mathbf{x}, \tag{13}$$

$$\mathbf{x}^{i+1} = \mathbf{f}(\mathbf{x}^i, \mathbf{u}^i), \tag{14}$$

$$i = 1, 2, \ldots, N - 1.$$

Here, $\mathbf{x}^i$ and $\mathbf{u}^i$ are the state and control vectors of the car at frame i, respectively. $J(X, U)$ is the objective function that specifies high-level objectives to perform car-parking tasks using state trajectory X and control vector sequence U. The first two constraints in Eqs. (13) and (14) represent that state trajectory X starts from the current state and the state transition in the trajectory can be made only by the system dynamics.

Objective function $J(X, U)$ is formulated as the sum of the following cost terms:

$$J(X, U) = c^{dir} + c^{tgt} + c^{col} + c^{eng} + c^{len}. \tag{15}$$

The first cost term c^{dir} is used to drive the car to have the same orientation with the target orientation before it gets close to the target state by taking into account differences between target orientation $\bar{\theta}$ and orientation θ^i at frame $i \in [1, k-1]$:

$$c^{dir} = h \cdot w^{dir} \cdot \sum_{i=1}^{k-1} \mathrm{sabs}(\bar{\theta} - \theta^i). \tag{16}$$

Here, w^{dir} is the weight constant and $\mathrm{sabs}(x)$ is the smoothed version of absolute function $|x|$ as follows [20]:

$$\mathrm{sabs}(x) = \sqrt{x^2 + \gamma^2} - \gamma. \tag{17}$$

In Eq. (17), γ is the coefficient used to adjust the smoothness around at $x = 0$. As γ becomes larger, the function is more smoothed. We set $\gamma = 1.0$ in all our experiments. As pointed out in [20], we adopt $\mathrm{sabs}(x)$ instead of a commonly-used quadratic cost term because the former increases almost linearly as x gets farther from zero. It prevents the optimization from chasing after the target too hard when the car state is currently quite far from the target, which results in more natural car movements. Cost term c^{dir} plays an important role especially when the car's initial orientation is opposite to its corresponding target so as to align them before moving to the target position.

The second cost term c^{tgt} is defined as a weighted sum of differences between target car state $\bar{\mathbf{x}}$ and car state $\mathbf{x}^i$ at each frame $i \in [k, N]$ to reach the target car state after aligning the car orientation with its target as shown below:

$$c^{tgt} = h \cdot (w^{tgt})^{\mathrm{T}} \sum\nolimits_{i=k}^{N} \begin{bmatrix} \mathrm{sabs}(\bar{x} - x^i) \\ \mathrm{sabs}(\bar{y} - y^i) \\ \mathrm{sabs}(\bar{\theta} - \theta^i) \\ \mathrm{sabs}(\bar{v} - v^i) \end{bmatrix}, \tag{18}$$

where $w^{tgt} \in \mathbb{R}^4$ is the weight vector. Cost term c^{tgt} encourages the optimization to converge to the target car state as quickly as possible starting from frame k once the car has come near the target car state at frame k.

The third cost term c^{col} is used to avoid collisions between the car and any of environmental objects:

$$c^{col} = h \cdot w^{col} \cdot \sum\nolimits_{i=1}^{N} \sum\nolimits_{j=1}^{n_c^i} \phi(i, j, \mathbf{x}^i). \tag{19}$$

In the above equation, w^{col} is the weight constant. n_c^i is the number of contact points between the car and the environment at frame i and $\phi(i, j, \mathbf{x}^i) \geq 0$ is the function that returns the penetration depth at contact point j at frame i. Our system computes the penetration depth by simply executing a conventional collision detection algorithm during the evaluation of the cost term in an on-line manner without any precomputation. This is possible because our system employs a sampling-based optimization method, which allows us to deal with a non-differentiable objective like collision avoidance in the same way with differentiable ones.

The fourth cost term is to make the synthesized path smoothed by minimizing the front wheel's acceleration and the change of its angle at each frame $i \in [1, N-1]$ with weight vector $w^{eng} \in \mathbb{R}^2$ as follows:

$$c^{eng} = h \cdot (w^{eng})^{\mathrm{T}} \sum\nolimits_{i=1}^{N-1} \begin{bmatrix} (\omega^i(u_1) - \omega^{i-1}(u_1))^2 \\ \alpha^i(u_2)^2 \end{bmatrix}. \tag{20}$$

Here, $\omega^0(u_1)$ is the front wheel angle that has been applied in the last simulation time step. The last cost term c^{len} is used to minimize the length of the synthesized path to the target position, that is, the sum of the Euclidean distances between a pair of consecutive points on the state trajectory as follows:

$$c^{len} = w^{len} \cdot \sum\nolimits_{i=1}^{N-1} \left\| \begin{bmatrix} x^{i+1} \\ y^{i+1} \end{bmatrix} - \begin{bmatrix} x^i \\ y^i \end{bmatrix} \right\|. \tag{21}$$

Here, w^{len} is the weight constant.

We solve the above trajectory optimization problem with CMA. The details of how to use CMA and the role of reset signal η are explained in Sect. 4.3.

4.3   Optimization

Given current car state $\mathbf{x}$ and target car state $\bar{\mathbf{x}}$ together with near-target frame index k and reset signal η, our system repeatedly solves a trajectory optimization problem explained in Sect. 4.2 at each simulation time step using CMA, which facilitates on-line performance. CMA maintains multivariate normal distribution $\mathbf{y} \sim N(\boldsymbol{\mu}, \boldsymbol{\Sigma})$, iteratively updated based on the evaluation results of a given objective function at the samples populated by the distribution until a certain condition is met. In our problem, multivariate random variable $\mathbf{y}$ is regarded as the concatenation of control vectors $U = \{\mathbf{u}^1, \mathbf{u}^2, \ldots, \mathbf{u}^{N-1}\}$ as

$$
\mathbf{y} = \begin{bmatrix} \mathbf{u}^1 \\ \mathbf{u}^2 \\ \vdots \\ \mathbf{u}^{N-1} \end{bmatrix} \in \mathbb{R}^{2(N-1)}. \tag{22}
$$

If reset signal η is on, our system purely restarts CMA with $\boldsymbol{\mu} = 0$ and $\boldsymbol{\Sigma} = \sigma^2 I_{2(N-1)}$, where σ is a coefficient (standard deviation for each individual random variable of $\mathbf{y}$) and I_m is an $m \times m$ identity matrix (we set $\sigma = 0.6$ in all our experiments). Otherwise, all the context data of the previous optimization including $\boldsymbol{\mu}$ and $\boldsymbol{\Sigma}$ is reused to enhance time efficiency under the assumption that a solution to the current optimization will be similar to that of the previous one. In the cases when the assumption does not meet, e.g., in the case when the user has changed the target position, reset signal η is turned on by the parameter adjustment component (Sect. 5) before executing CMA.

At each optimization, the update of the normal distribution of CMA is done in a different way depending on the value of η. If η is off, it is iterated a specific number of times (300 times in all our experiments). Otherwise, CMA is completely reinitialized as mentioned above and the update is iterated more times (500 times in all our experiments).

After finishing the update, mean $\boldsymbol{\mu}$ is used as the current solution to our autonomous parking problem. We provide the first control vector in $\boldsymbol{\mu}$ to the simulation component to update the current state of the car.

5   Parameter Adjustment

Given current car state $\mathbf{x}$, target car state $\bar{\mathbf{x}}$, and current control sequence $U = \{\mathbf{u}^1, \mathbf{u}^2, \ldots, \mathbf{u}^{N-1}\}$, the parameter adjustment component (Fig. 1) computes near-target frame index k and reset signal η. The former represents an index to the frame at which the car is close enough to the target state, and the latter is used to completely reinitialize CMA. We first explain how to compute near-target frame index k in Sect. 5.1. We then discuss how to determine reset signal η in Sect. 5.2.

5.1   Near-Target Frame Index Computation

In order to compute near-target frame index k, our system first produces state trajectory $X = \{\mathbf{x}^1, \ldots, \mathbf{x}^N\}$, where $\mathbf{x}^1 = \mathbf{x}$ and $\mathbf{x}^{i+1} = \mathbf{f}(\mathbf{x}^i, \mathbf{u}^i)$ for $\mathbf{u}^i \in U$, $i = 1, 2, \ldots, N-1$, and then measures how close the car state is to target car state $\bar{\mathbf{x}}$ at each frame using the following function derived from cost term c^{tgt} in Eq. (18):

$$\varphi(\mathbf{x}^i) = h \cdot (\mathbf{w}^{tgt})^{\mathrm{T}} \begin{bmatrix} \mathrm{sabs}(\bar{x} - x^i) \\ \mathrm{sabs}(\bar{y} - y^i) \\ \mathrm{sabs}(\bar{\theta} - \theta^i) \\ \mathrm{sabs}(\bar{v} - v^i) \end{bmatrix}. \tag{23}$$

Based on the measurement results, the system searches the frames satisfying $\varphi(\mathbf{x}^i) \leq \epsilon_1$ and $\left\| \begin{bmatrix} \bar{x} \\ \bar{y} \end{bmatrix} - \begin{bmatrix} x^i \\ y^i \end{bmatrix} \right\| \leq \epsilon_2$ in reverse order staring from the last frame, where ϵ is a small constant (we set $\epsilon_1 = 0.1$ and $\epsilon_2 = 0.5$ in all our experiments) and sets k to the index to the first of these. The former condition represents the car state must be close enough to the target car state and the latter one the car position must be near the target car position. The computed k is passed to the trajectory optimization component to determine how many frames are involved to align the car orientation with the target one before moving the car to the target position (See the formulation of c^{dir} and c^{tgt} in Sect. 4.2).

5.2 Reset Signal Computation

Whenever the optimization finishes, our system updates the near-target frame index using the new control sequence from the optimization. Let us denote the updated index by k' and the previous one by k. If $k' < k$, it means that the car becomes closer to the target state and otherwise it gets farther from the target or there is no improvement. Our system keeps track of the number of times when $k' \geq k$ denoted by T, while resetting $T = 0$ otherwise. Then, if $T > T_{max}$, where T_{max} is the maximum number of trials that have failed to find more improvement (we set $T_{max} = 5$ in all our experiments), our system turns reset signal η on to completely restart the optimization as explained in Sect. 4.3 in order to encourage CMA to find a better solution with a new normal distribution. However, we do not use this scheme when k' is less than small threshold k_{min} (we set $k_{min} = 10$ in all our experiments), because it means that the car is already quite near the target state and any more improvement is hard to be made. Our system also activates reset signal η when the user has changed the target state to restart the optimization with the new target.

6 Experimental Results

We show results for garage parking (Sect. 6.2), parallel parking (Sect. 6.1), and interactive parking (Sect. 6.3) based on on-line user inputs. The proposed framework was implemented in C/C++ programming languages. We adopted the C implementation of CMA [19] to solve our trajectory optimization problems. All experiments were conducted on a desktop computer with Intel Core TM i7 processor (3.5 GHz, 6 cores) and 32 GB memory. We set $h = 0.05$ s and used the time window of 3.5 s ($N = 70$). All the weight values used for all experiments are provided in Table 1.

Table 1. Weight values.

w^{dir}	w^{tgt}	w^{col}	w^{eng}	w^{len}
10^{-1}	$(5,5,3,1)$	10^5	$(10^{-1}, 10^{-5})$	10^{-3}

6.1   Garage Parking

In this experiment, we applied our method to park the car driving into a garage without and with a dynamic obstacle moving near it when the car's initial orientation was different from the target one by 90 degrees (See the supplementary video). In the former (Fig. 2), the car first changed its orientation in front of the entrance to be aligned with the target orientation and then immediately moved into the garage. In the latter (Fig. 3), the car first moved to a side wall of the garage to avoid collision with the moving obstacle (red car) unlike the former case, while the obstacle was passing by the entrance of the garage, and then moved backwards until fully entering the garage.

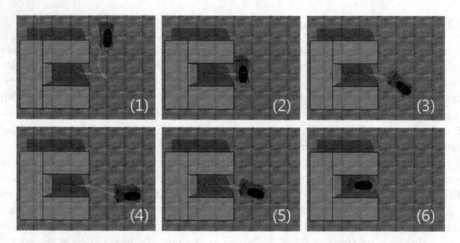

Fig. 2. Garage parking without a moving obstacle.

6.2   Parallel Parking

We conducted experiments on parallel parking without and with a moving obstacle (See the supplementary video). In the former (Fig. 4), the car first headed left-forward in preparation for getting into the parking space and then moved backward handling to the left near the wall behind. It steered to the right toward the side wall to adjust its orientation more accurately. In the latter (Fig. 5), we observed that the car moved much more forward than the former case to avoid collision with the moving obstacle. After this, the car showed a similar sequence of moves to the former.

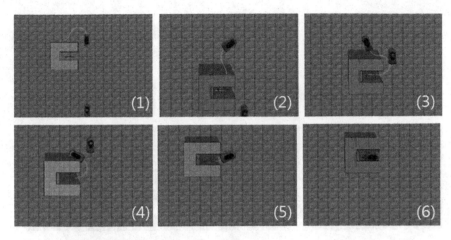

Fig. 3. Garage parking with a moving obstacle. (Color figure online)

Fig. 4. Parallel parking without a moving obstacle.

6.3 Interactive Parking

In this experiment, our method allowed the user to interactively change the environment by moving the position of the walls and introducing a moving obstacle (red car) at any time point as well as the target position and orientation (See the supplementary video). Whenever the environment changed, our method restarted the trajectory optimization to find a new path that reflects the current environmental changes while rejecting the previous path (Fig. 6). As the moving obstacle appeared at a certain time point and approached, the car moved backward to avoid collision with it. After this, however, it moved back to the target position while satisfying the target orientation as well.

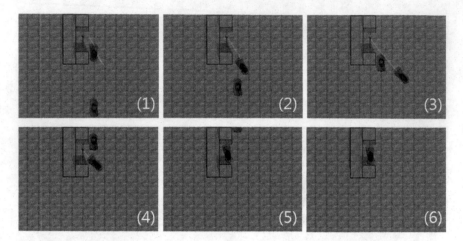

Fig. 5. Parallel parking with a moving obstacle.

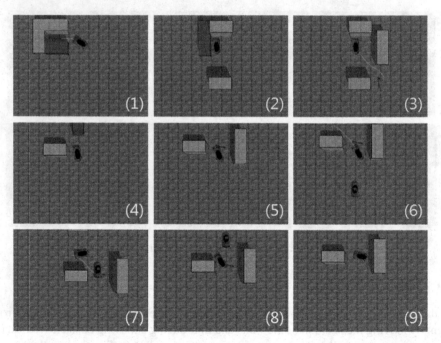

Fig. 6. Interactive parking with on-line user intervention. (Color figure online)

7   Conclusions

In this paper, we presented an on-line trajectory optimization framework for generating the parking movements of a car in a multi-obstacle environment. The proposed system repeatedly generates an optimal control sequence to drive the car toward the target state by solving a finite-horizon trajectory optimization problem for a short time window while moving it along the time axis. As an optimization solver, we employed a sampling-based optimization technique called CMA, which requires no derivative information for an objective function. It facilitates formulating a car-parking problem with high-level objectives and dealing with collision events between the car and environment without any precomputation. We also proposed a simple and effective scheme to adjust optimization parameters such as near-target frame index and reset signal so that it may converge into the target state quickly and keep improving its solution. Our method can produce convincing parking maneuvers for garage parking, parallel parking, and interactive parking with on-line user inputs.

Though our framework can effectively avoid collision with a moving object as well as static obstacles, there is no theoretical guarantee on this constraint. We also assumed that the environmental state is fully known to perform collision detection, but it is not available to actual autonomous vehicles in general. This issue could be addressed by introducing a more realistic problem setup based on sensor inputs for environmental information. Our framework is somewhat slower than real time due to a large number of optimization variables (138 variables). It would be an interesting future research direction to implement the evaluation of an objective functions on GPU to improve the performance.

References

1. Hansen, N., Müller, S.D., Koumoutsakos, P.: Reducing the time complexity of the derandomized evolution strategy with covariance matrix adaptation (CMA-ES). Evol. Comput. **11**(1), 1–18 (2003)
2. Sekhavat, S., Laumond, J.P.: Topological property for collision-free nonholonomic motion planning: the case of sinusoidal inputs for chained form systems. IEEE Trans. Robot. Autom. **14**(5), 671–680 (1998)
3. Reeds, J., Shepp, L.: Optimal paths for a car that goes both forwards and backwards. Pac. J. Math. **145**(2), 367–393 (1990)
4. Hsieh, M.F., Ozguner, U.: A parking algorithm for an autonomous vehicle. In: 2008 IEEE Intelligent Vehicles Symposium, pp. 1155–1160. IEEE, June 2008
5. Lee, K., Kim, D., Chung, W., Chang, H.W., Yoon, P.: Car parking control using a trajectory tracking controller. In: International Joint Conference on SICE-ICASE 2006, pp. 2058–2063. IEEE, October 2006
6. Laumond, J.P., Jacobs, P.E., Taix, M., Murray, R.M.: A motion planner for nonholonomic mobile robots. IEEE Trans. Robot. Autom. **10**(5), 577–593 (1994)
7. Muller, B., Deutscher, J., Grodde, S.: Continuous curvature trajectory design and feedforward control for parking a car. IEEE Trans. Control Syst. Technol. **15**(3), 541–553 (2007)
8. Kim, D., Chung, W., Park, S.: Practical motion planning for car-parking control in narrow environment. IET Control Theor. Appl. **4**(1), 129–139 (2010)
9. Barraquand, J., Latombe, J.C.: Nonholonomic multibody mobile robots: controllability and motion planning in the presence of obstacles. Algorithmica **10**(2–4), 121 (1993)
10. LaValle, S.M., Kuffner Jr., J.J.: Randomized kinodynamic planning. Int. J. Robot. Res. **20**(5), 378–400 (2001)

11. Kuwata, Y., Fiore, G.A., Teo, J., Frazzoli, E., How, J.P.: Motion planning for urban driving using RRT. In: IEEE/RSJ International Conference on Intelligent Robots and Systems, IROS 2008, pp. 1681–1686. IEEE, September 2008

12. Buehler, M., Iagnemma, K., Singh, S. (eds.): The DARPA Urban Challenge: Autonomous Vehicles in City Traffic, vol. 56. Springer, Heidelberg (2009). https://doi.org/10.1007/978-3-642-03991-1

13. Kavraki, L.E., Svestka, P., Latombe, J.C., Overmars, M.H.: Probabilistic roadmaps for path planning in high-dimensional configuration spaces. IEEE Trans. Robot. Autom. $12(4)$, 566–580 (1996)

14. Dolgov, D., Thrun, S., Montemerlo, M., Diebel, J.: Path planning for autonomous vehicles in unknown semi-structured environments. Int. J. Robot. Res. $29(5)$, 485–501 (2010)

15. Zhao, Y., Collins Jr., E.G.: Robust automatic parallel parking in tight spaces via fuzzy logic. Robot. Auton. Syst. $51(2–3)$, 111–127 (2005)

16. Gorinevsky, D., Kapitanovsky, A., Goldenberg, A.: Neural network architecture for trajectory generation and control of automated car parking. IEEE Trans. Control Syst. Technol. $4(1)$, 50–56 (1996)

17. Zips, P., Bock, M., Kugi, A.: A fast motion planning algorithm for car parking based on static optimization. In: 2013 IEEE/RSJ International Conference on Intelligent Robots and Systems (IROS), pp. 2392–2397. IEEE, November 2013

18. Tassa, Y., Mansard, N., Todorov, E.: Control-limited differential dynamic programming. In: 2014 IEEE International Conference on Robotics and Automation (ICRA), pp. 1168–1175. IEEE, May 2014

19. https://www.lri.fr/~hansen/cmaes_inmatlab.html

20. Tassa, Y., Erez, T., Todorov, E.: Synthesis and stabilization of complex behaviors through online trajectory optimization. In: 2012 IEEE/RSJ International Conference on Intelligent Robots and Systems (IROS), pp. 4906–4913. IEEE, October 2012

Exploring Potential User Experience Design for Traditional Chinese Service Station: A Case Study in Guangzhou, China

Zhen Liu[1], Yifan Meng[1], Di Xu[2], Jun-en He[3(✉)], Xiusheng Gu[3], Lijun Jiang[1], Xiaohua Li[1], Shaoxin Wu[1], and Zhengquan Li[1]

[1] School of Design, South China University of Technology, Guangzhou 510060, People's Republic of China
[2] Total Sinochem Oil Co., Ltd., Shanghai 200122, People's Republic of China
[3] Sinochem Oil Guangdong Co., Ltd., Guangzhou 510627, People's Republic of China
hejunen@sinochem.com

Abstract. At present, a number of countries including China announced the future will ban the sale of gasoline and diesel vehicles to achieve the full motorization of the car. Traditional Chinese service station is now facing a historical critical moment of 'business transformation'. The After Market (AM) is a key within the transformation, which refers to all kinds of markets after the sale of the whole vehicle, including oil. The elements of AM can be selling products of a service station. However, the satisfaction level of user experience is the key to the AM and company strategies to service station. The aim of this paper is to investigate potential recommendations for the potential best practices of service station based on user experience design. However, the potential best practice guide has the limitation that it examines what is already existing, rather than delving into the problem areas to identify new reference frames that can then provide information on the future of service station design. The case study methodology has been adopted to investigate the problem which included desktop secondary research and 5 site visits. The context then has been examined in which illustrate the factors, such as service station onsite factors (i.e. visual display, architectural layout and structure, onsite refueling service journey including service store shopping journey), and offsite factors (i.e. internet+ operation factors, and customer management factors), which contribute to the better user experience design. This leads into a potential framework that examines the measures that exist to improve user experience.

Keywords: Service station · User experience · Oil after market · Service journey
Internet+ · Case study

1 Introduction

At present, the world economy is recovering moderately. China's economy is still maintaining a steady and favorable trend, with Gross Domestic Product (GDP) growing by 6.9% year-on-year [1]. There is an abundant supply and fierce competition in the domestic oil-related product market. According to statistics, the apparent consumption of domestic refined oil products increased by 5.5% over the same period of last year [2], and the demand for gasoline and kerosene remained strong. Diesel oil reversed its declining trend and achieved a year-on-year increase. Domestic refined oil sales market, with companies such as PetroChina and Sinopec's large-scale petrochemical production and sales, are still dominant. With the gradual opening up of some domestic oil and petrochemical markets, foreign large petrochemical companies have gradually entered some regions and fields. As a result, competition in the domestic refined oil sales market has been aggravating.

On the other hand, a number of countries announced the future will ban the sale of gasoline and diesel vehicles to achieve the full motorization of the car. The Zero Emissions Coalition (ZEC) will stop selling fuel cars by 2050 at the UN Climate Conference in 2015 [3], and will only allow new-generation zero-emission vehicles to go public. The coalition is sponsored by California and is now rapidly expanding to 13 members, including several U.S. states, as well as Germany, the Netherlands, Norway and the United Kingdom. Recently, several major emission countries have already made specific deadlines. At present, many European countries have announced plans to ban the sale of fuel cars. At the media exchange meeting on 2015 Annual Report on the Development of Fuel Consumption in China's Passenger Vehicles [4], Jiang Kejun, a researcher at the Energy Research Institute of the National Development and Reform Commission, predicted that after 10 years, China will not have any internal combustion engine powered traditional cars among the incremental new cars it sells. Instead, pure electric-powered new energy vehicles. This means that by 2030 China will realize a comprehensive new energy vehicle.

Under above complicated and pressured situation, traditional Chinese service station is now facing a historical critical moment of "business transformation". The After Market (AM) is a key within the transformation, which refers to all kinds of markets after the sale of the whole vehicle, including oil, the expenses incurred in the course of using the automobile, maintenance, spare parts, beauty and modification, leasing, insurance, advertising, decoration and so on [5]. It also covers driving school, parking lot, car fan club, rescue system, traffic information service and used car in a broad sense. The elements of AM can be selling products of a service station. From the profit point of view, according to the '2013–2017 China Automotive Aftermarket Blue Book' [6] statistics, in the developed countries market, AM services accounted for about 60% of all types of services, while the market service margin is also higher than the gross profit margin of new car sales.

By fully exerting the advantages of integration and marketing network, the service station companies actively cope with excess resources and the highly competitive market situation; co-ordinate the optimization of internal and external resources and fully expands the market; flexibly adjust marketing strategies, launch brand gasoline and raise the retail share of high-grade gasoline; optimize the layout of gas stations; speed up the optimization and reformation of refined oil storage and transportation facilities and further improve the marketing network; vigorously develop the automotive natural gas business and promote the construction and operation of gas station; and use information technology to explore and establish the 'Internet + Sales + Service' new business model, to accelerate the development of new business.

However, the satisfaction level of user experience is the key to the abovementioned AM and company strategies to service station. Currently, inadequate effort has been made to explore potential user experience design for traditional Chinese service station to provide better service towards new future of service station, which is the focus of this paper.

2   Research Method

The aim of this paper is to investigate potential recommendations for the potential best practices of service station based on user experience design. However, the potential best practice guide has the limitation that it examines what is already existing, rather than delving into the problem areas to identify new reference frames that can then provide information on the future of service station design. The case study methodology has been adopted to investigate the problem which includes visiting five of service station sites and desktop secondary research. The context then has been examined in which illustrate the factors, such as service station onsite factors (i.e. visual display, architectural layout and structure, onsite refueling service journey including service store shopping journey), and offsite factors (i.e. internet+ operation factors, and customer management factors), which contribute to the better user experience design. This leads into a potential best practice guideline that examines the measures that exist to improve user experience.

3   Service Station Case Study

3.1   Service Station Site Survey

Five service station in Guangdong, China have been surveyed, which are owned by major refined oil companies such as Sinochem, Sinopec, Petrochina, Caltex, and Shell. Service station onsite factors to user experience design have been explored, which are visual display, architectural layout and structure, onsite refueling service journey, and service store shopping journey.

Onsite Visual Display. Visual display of the service station is acting as a key role to visual identity of the company, which assists the customer to identify the service station from long distance. The design of visual display can help with improving customer experience on site. Most of the surveyed service stations use main colors from their companies' logo, which is a safe strategy for company visual identity purpose.

Architectural Layout and Structure. Architectural layout is designed to perform a function and meets most customers' needs when they stop for service, can be exciting and unique. The approach taken in designing the architectural layout and structures is generally more about creating spatial facility for staff, pumping bays, repetitive metal canopies and bathrooms that all comply with regulations, which can help with creating brand recognition for the service station and company, which is a key factor in business growth. Most of the surveyed service stations adopt the architectural structure of rectangular top and the four square pillars, where the onsite convenience stores are located behind the atrium of the pumping bays. One of the service stations is divided by the convenience store, where the store is in the middle of the station atrium with one refueling area on the left side, which is covered by rectangular steel structural roof and supported by six square pillars; and another refueling area on the right side, which is a white umbrella canopy roof and structure.

Onsite Refueling Service Journey. A customer/service journey map is a widely used tool to represent user experience with a service. Onsite refueling service journey map can help with identify opportunities for improving user experience. As shown in Fig. 1, the surveyed service stations currently employ mechanism among customer, store person, and service person, by which the refueling service journey end up with either the customer handing over a receipt copy or not for discharging.

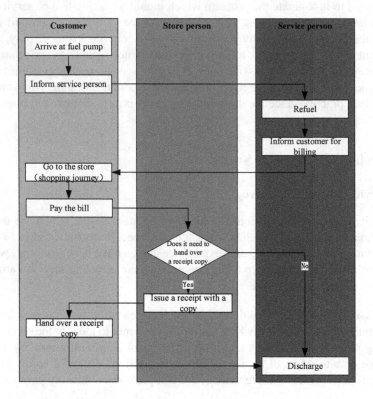

Fig. 1. Service station onsite refueling service journey map.

Service Store Shopping Journey. The service store shopping journey is a part of abovementioned service journey in terms of payment action of refueling, which helps with creating more on-shop selling opportunities, and plays a main role in onsite customer experience. As such, the layout design for the stores is essential to attain above aims, which should consider methods for designing journey routes for refueling and shopping, whilst laying down certain products on the routes to increase and improve value and efficiency of the journey to the both of the customers and service station. For example, the customers can see the 'promotion zone' directly in the both of 'shopping' and 'refueling payment' routes.

The shopping journey design is influenced by the architectural layout and structure of the service station, such as the location of pumping bays to the store, and the number of doors for entering the stores. Shopping journeys for the five cases of the surveyed stores are illustrated in following sections.

Store Shopping Journey (Case A). As shown in Fig. 2, the most profitable beverage and snacks are placed in conspicuous places. Convenience stores use the same checkout aisle as the supermarket, in line with the user's general behavior. Cooked food area is relatively simple, only equipped with hot water bottle and instant noodles.

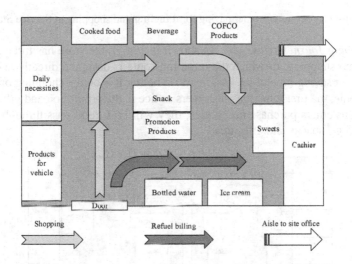

Fig. 2. Store layout for customer paying for refueling and shopping at Service Station A.

Store Shopping Journey (Case B). As shown in Fig. 3 of the floor plan, the promotional items are displayed opposite to the front door, where no matter on which route, the customers will notice the promotion products first. Shopping route is designed for the customer from the door to cashier, where the payment route needs to be set to go through the high-profit beverage and snacks areas. When the customers buy snacks, they can see the liquor cabinet behind the promotional items. The magazine rack is set up close to the ice cream area, where when the customers buys a magazine, children may take the ice cream straight out of the fridge.

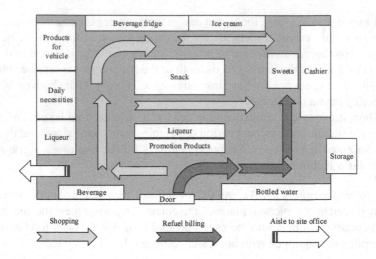

Fig. 3. Store layout for customer paying for refueling and shopping at Service Station B.

Store Shopping Journey (Case C). As shown in Fig. 4, the store has three routes for refueling and shopping, of which the refueling route is designed directly and short to the cashier for saving time of the customers. Whether it is on the shopping or refueling payment route, the first thing that customers notice is the promotion and gift products. When the customers purchase necessities, they will be sure to pass through the high-profit beverage, snacks and gifts area.

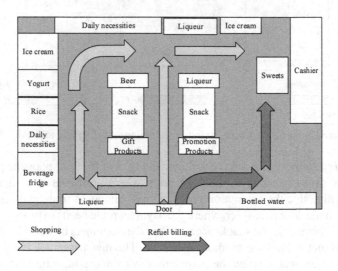

Fig. 4. Store layout for customer paying for refueling and shopping at Service Station C.

Store Shopping Journey (Case D). The shopping space is large, and there are a number of products available for purchase, where there are several circular routes designed for shopping. As shown in Fig. 5, the layout is designed that after customers' purchase of the beverage, they will pass through the cooked food area, which will help with stimulating the consumers to spend more and also they will pass through areas such as snack, wine and other products with higher profit margins. The stores also have counters selling souvenirs and coffee.

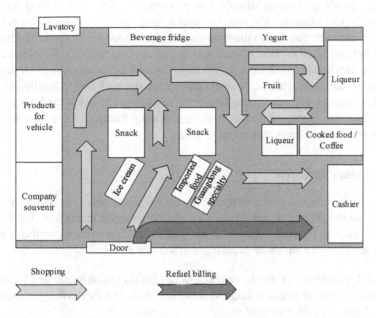

Fig. 5. Store layout for customer paying for refueling and shopping at Service Station D.

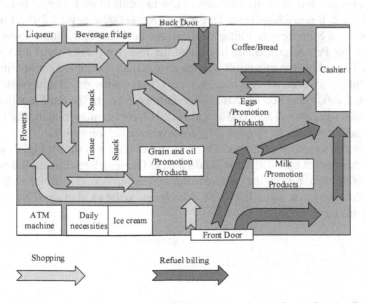

Fig. 6. Store layout for customer paying for refueling and shopping at Service Station E.

Store Shopping Journey (Case E). As shown in Fig. 6, if the customers enter the store from front door to the cashier without shopping, they need to go through the grain and oil, milk and eggs promotion area, whilst customers with the same purpose entered from the back door to the cashier also need to go through promotion of cooked food area. As such, these goods are easy to stimulate more spending. The cooked food (coffee and bread) area is very conspicuous, and distinguish from other areas with dark color.

When consumers enter from the front door and go shopping along the left hand side, they will initially see the grain, oil and milk for promotion and then the moon cake gift area. When they go for cold drinks, they will go through a promotion area for high-profit snacks and tissue, meanwhile, consumers enter from the back door for daily necessities, they will go through the same promotion area for high-profit snacks and tissue. The lay out setting for two entrances creates circular shopping routes to force the customers to meet certain products for potential purchasing.

3.2   Secondary Research

In the age of the new internet information technology and new 'fan economy', mother companies of the service stations have used the information technology for their daily operations, such as internet+ operation, and customer management, aiming for contributing to better onsite customer experience at service stations.

Internet+ Operation. Methods, such as China's Baidu search results and Baidu Index, official website, social media official account, and mobile APP, have been used for the purpose of internet+ operation of the service stations.

Search Engine Results and Index. The China's Baidu search results and Baidu Index can be treated as a mirror of the user experience in terms of user interest to the service.

For Sinopec, Baidu related results are about 18,800,000 at Sep 17, 2017, ranked first was a result of Sinopec gas filling card online business hall (http://www.sinopec-sales.com). For PetroChina, Baidu has found the relevant results about 16,100,000, at Sep 17, 2017, ranking the first result was the PetroChina Kunlun oil card online service platform (http://www.card.petrochina.com.cn/). For Caltex oil, Baidu related results were about 2,700,000 at Sep 17, 2017 (https://chevron.cn.chi??). For Sinochem, Baidu related results were about 1,050,000 at Sep 17, 2017, for example, ranking the first result was Sinochem's website homepage (http://www.sinochemoil.com/).

The comparison among Sinopec, Petrochina and Caltex is shown Fig. 7, where the Sinochem has not yet included in the Baidu index. The search results and Index indicate the trend of the search from the customer during certain period of time, such as seven days, 30 days, 90 days, and a half year, which can assist to plan strategic actions for improving user experience.

Fig. 7. Comparison of Baidu index for service station companies (Sep 17, 2017).

Official Website. Official website of a company has the most authority for its products and services, which is crucial for user experience aligning products and services of the service stations. Sinochem petroleum oil retail business does not have own official sales site. But under the company's official website of the oil sales department and station promotion section mention the product sales, and product promotion program information are found on a page that was last update time of December 5, 2014. In addition to its official website, Petrochina and Sinopec also set up special oil sales websites. Petrochina has set up an online service platform for Chinese petroleum Kunlun gas filling card, and Sinopec has set up a special online business hall. Their website built a complete online service system related to the oil retail business for the onsite service.

Social Media Official Account. WeChat index and WeChat official account can be used for operation to achieve better customer experience. The WeChat indexs for Sinochem, Petrochina, Sinopec and caltex are shown in Fig. 8, in which Petrochina gained the highest index at Sep 17, 2017 and the leading top index during the last 90-days period.

Fig. 8. Comparison of WeChat index for service station companies (Sep 17, 2017).

Sinochem, sinopec and PetroChina have established their own official WeChat accounts, as shown in Table 1, which contain an account interface for the main account information and interactive interface for service function areas, such as refueling cards, promotions, and customer experience.

The official account of the three companies are complicated, including the company's account and the provincial companies account, such as official account 'Sinochem oil sales' and other accounts for different provincial companies. In addition, the provinces have their own internal account, and external account, such as 'Sinochem Guangdong Oil' and 'Sinochem Guangdong Co., Ltd', which are mainly used for corporate culture propaganda. In order to unify the sales entrances of refined oil products, Petro-China has set up a special official account, the 'PetroChina e Station', for the promotion of refined oil products and convenience stores. It also provides information on the site of service stations, and the inquiry of account of fuel card, card recharge and other products from customer service. Sinopec relies on the official account of each province to provide information for refueling services, refined oil market, and named 'easyjoy' convenience stores.

Mobile APP. Both of PetroChina and Sinopec have developed APP mobile clients, whereas Sinochem has not. PetroChina's 'PetroChina Hospitality e Station' APP is a client software for all self-service customers. With mobile payment and refueling card services as its core, the APP focuses on 'people, vehicles and life' to provide customers

Table 1. Social media WeChat official accounts interfaces for service station companies (Sep 17, 2017).

Company	Account interface for main account information	Account interface for service functions
Sinochem	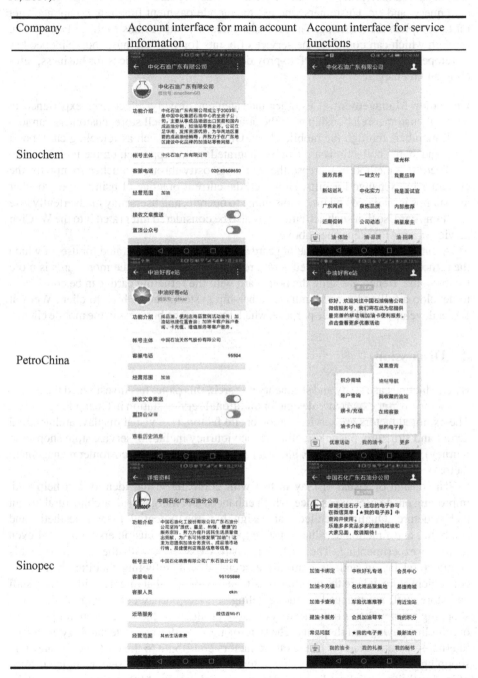	
PetroChina		
Sinopec		

with an efficient, convenient and smart service platform. Core functions include service station navigation, refueling mobile payment, refueling card online recharge, gas filling card query, and etc. Customers who use the mobile payment function, do not need get off to complete the refueling. The APP also integrates the 'Points Mall' of PetroChina, through which can complete the service of points for exchanging goods. Sinopec has developed a business office APP to provide customers with services for business, refueling and recharge.

Customer Management. Customer management directly affect user experience in terms of customer relationship with the products. In the Shell store, customers can join Shell members through the mobile client. Other services such as refueling card, point card, and stamp collection card can be integrated in this approach on the mobile.

There is a method to increase the user's viscosity through voucher stamps for the customer in exchange for gifts. However, the current practice of using paper voucher and stamps is outdated and time-consuming to operate, and users may inadvertently lose the stamp card, so that such activities may also be considered integrated into the WeChat service or an APP mentioned above.

At present, Sinochem's refueling card and point card are separated for use, of which the refueling card cannot be used across regions. For the users, the more cards is more troublesome. Hence, merging the point card with the refueling card, can be considered to develop a full and user friendly membership system, and to bind to client WeChat IDs or develop an APP for the purpose, which integrate the business to the mobile clients.

4   Discussion

By conducting case study and secondary research, this paper has investigated the potential factors to user experience design for traditional service station in Guangdong, China. The explored factors are service station onsite factors (i.e. visual display, architectural layout and structure, onsite refueling service journey including service store shop-ping journey), and offsite factors (i.e. internet+ operation factors, and customer management factors).

The design of visual display in line with company visual identity can help with improving onsite user experience, which enhances and merges with architectural layout and structure. Quality architectural design has the potential to add aesthetic and symbolic, and functional value to user experience for the customers who could even return to experimenting. The customer onsite experience with the service station's architectural layout and structure are associated with refueling facilities and onsite convenient store, where the customer onsite behaviors [7] that interact with service staff and store staff, are mapped on the refueling service journey containing service store shopping journey that is influenced by on-store products on the store layout for purposes of refueling paying and shopping. The state-of-the-art information technology enhanced internet+ operation factors of the offsite factors contribute to the customer onsite store shopping journey, which include four integrated factors, such as search engine results, official website, social media official account, and mobile APP. Another set of offsite factors, i.e. customer management factors, can be improved through development and the use of social media official account and mobile APP. The membership system is the core factor among the customer management factors, which associates with refueling card system and is enriched by voucher stamp system. Therefore, as shown in Fig. 9, the above discussed factors have been illustrated in a proposed framework of potential user experience design to China's service station.

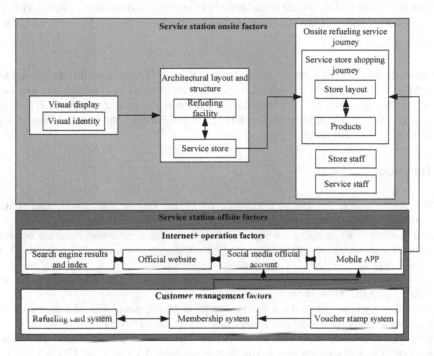

Fig. 9. A framework of potential user experience design to China's service station based on the identified factors.

5 Conclusion

Service station is a symbolic facility of its mother fuel company. The user experience onsite the service station influences customer interest, royalty and long term relationship to the company, which includes following potential onsite factors: visual display (i.e. visual identity), architectural layout and structure (i.e. refueling facility, and service store), onsite refueling service journey including service store shopping journey (i.e. service staff, store staff, store layout, and products). Whilst, onsite service can be enhanced by potential offsite service methods provided by the fuel company, such as internet+ operation factors (i.e. search engine results, official website, social media official account, and mobile APP), and customer management factors (i.e. membership system, refueling card system, and voucher stamp system). This paper explored the above potential factors to user experience design for traditional service station in Guangdong, China, via case study and secondary research, which opens up a new way for research on service station. Additionally, based on the identified factors, a framework of potential user experience design to service station has been proposed for the future use for improving services of service station in China in welcoming the incoming new era of internet+ information technology and sustainable energy. This paper provides methods and insights of the potential factors to user experience design for traditional service station in China, which could benefit to service stations across the world. The future research will be implementing and validating the proposed Framework with its factors.

Acknowledgements. The authors wish to thank all the people from Sinochem Oil Guangdong Co., Ltd, who provided their time and efforts for site investigation. This research is supported by Sinochem Oil Guangdong Co., Ltd and South China University of Technology (SCUT) project funding x2sj-D5170570, SCUT grant j2rs/K5172210, and Fundamental Research Funds for the Central Universities 2017ZX013.

References

1. The State Council the People's Republic of China. http://english.gov.cn/state_council/ministries/2017/10/19/content_281475913362978.htm. Accessed 30 Jan 2018
2. Hydrocarbon Engineering. https://www.hydrocarbonengineering.com/petrochemicals/29082017/sinopec-shares-1h17-refining-and-chemicals-segment-update/. Accessed 30 Jan 2018
3. UN Climate Change Conference Paris 2015. http://www.un.org/sustainabledevelopment/cop21/. Accessed 30 Jan 2018
4. Jiang, K.: China passenger vehicle fuel consumption. Development Annual Report 2015. The Innovation Center for Energy and Transportation, P.R. China (2015)
5. Ramesh, S., Donald, H., Ratna, B.C.: Remanufacturing for the automotive aftermarket-strategic factors: literature review and future research needs. J. Clean. Prod. **17**(13), 1163–1174 (2009)
6. 2013–2017 China Automotive Aftermarket Blue Book. http://www.xinhuanet.com/auto/2017-05/11/c_1120953127.htm. Accessed 30 Jan 2018
7. Kitamura, R., Sperling, D.: Refueling behavior of automobile drivers. Transp. Res. Part A: Gen. **21**(3), 235–245 (1987)

Extraction of Key Factors and Its Interrelationship Critical to Determining the Satisfaction Degree of User Experience in Taxi Passenger Service Using DEMATEL

Chunrong Liu[✉], Yi Jin, and Xu Zhu

Shanghai Jiao Tong University, Shanghai 200240, China
cheeronliu@sjtu.edu.cn

Abstract. The user experience of consumers as passengers in taxicab is an important determinant of the satisfaction degree of taxi passenger service. In this study, twelve main factors influential to user experience in taxicab are selected based on twenty-one preliminary factors collected by questionnaire survey and depth interview. The face-to-face surveys are deployed with Decision-Making Trial and Evaluation Laboratory (DEMATEL) questionnaires to evaluate by subjects the directions and the degrees of the interactions between any two main factors. The scores of the Prominence and the Relation of main factors are calculated in DEMATEL tool with thirty-two effective pieces of data as input, and the causal diagram is drawn. The findings show that three factors including 'the driver's familiarity with the local roads', 'long detours and intentional slowly driving' and 'driver's chatting to passenger(s) when driving', are key factors influencing the satisfaction degree of the passenger's user experience, while other three factors such as 'weather conditions' and 'driver's talking on the cell phone when driving', have great impact on other main factors, respectively. It can be summarized that the degree of satisfaction of taxi passenger is highly relevant to taxi driver side in the following ways: (1) due to the negative economy and timeliness, the driver's unfamiliarity with the local roads and behaviors of long detours and intentional slowly driving will heavily decrease the satisfaction degree of user experience; and (2) due to the unsafety, the same is true for driver's chatting to passenger(s) and talking on the cell phone when driving.

Keywords: Taxi passenger service · The satisfaction degree of user experience
Decision-Making Trial and Evaluation Laboratory (DEMATEL)
Consumer research

1 Introduction

As one of flexible and convenient means of public transportation in cities, taxicab has been one of the important vehicles for people's daily personal mobility [1]. The quality of taxi service and the satisfaction degree of user experience of passengers reflect from a certain side the city's integral civilization image and overall service quality [2].

© Springer International Publishing AG, part of Springer Nature 2018
A. Marcus and W. Wang (Eds.): DUXU 2018, LNCS 10920, pp. 299–313, 2018.
https://doi.org/10.1007/978-3-319-91806-8_23

Therefore, having impact on a city's civilization image and the quality of service supply, it is an important subject that the key influencing factors critical to deter-mining the satisfaction degree of user experience and its interrelationship are explored and discovered so as to take tailored measures to overcome the potential problems in taxi industry, to elevate taxi service quality, and as a result, to finally raise the levels of user experience and the satisfaction degree of taxi passengers as consumers.

2 Literature Review

In the field of taxi service and taxi industry, numerous studies have been conducted by researchers. Many theories and methods in management science and economics are employed to explore pricing, management mode, business model, competition and service in taxi industry. Curry et al. [3] studied the advantages and disadvantages of taxis and modes of public transport by establishing a queuing model for passengers to take a taxi at an airport. Cairns and Liston-Heyes [4] studied the competition and regulation issues in the taxi industry, considering that price and access controls are necessary. Xiong [5] put forth the proposal of getting rid of the single mode of taxi market operation by breaking up the administrative monopoly. Yang et al. [6] studied the non-linear pricing of taxi service. Gu and Zheng [7] explored the rationality of taxi pricing system. Anderson [8] and Rayle et al. [9] compared two for-profit models with traditional taxis and the new share rides, and its impact. Zhang et al. [10] probed into the relationship between taxi service strategy and income. Hai et al. [11] and Shi and Lian [12] studied the demand-supply equilibrium between passengers and taxis. Leng et al. [13] studied the impact of the appearance of taxi app and the apps' commercial competition on the taxi market pattern and service mode.

Meanwhile, some principles in computer science and mathematics are used in solving the taxi-related technical problems. Osswald et al. [14] carried out optimal design of HMI for electric taxis. Moreira-Matias et al. [15, 16] studied the time and spatial distribution regularity of taxi passenger. Yan et al. [17] proposed a method for the most efficient taxi scheduling. Hu [2] ranked passengers' needs according to their importance in optimizing taxi service quality by quantifying these needs with QFD method.

In addition, some studies focus on the behavioral and psychological aspects of taxi driver and/or passenger groups. Zhang and Wang [18], Brandenburg et al. [19] and Tang et al. [20] studied why taxi drivers refuse to take passengers, what factors arouse a taxi driver's anger when driving, and how taxi drivers perceive the routes. Shen [21] evaluated single taxi and its affiliated company with multiple indicators by introducing Customer Satisfaction Index and developed recommendations about service improve-ment. Li [22] studied the effective mechanism for dealing with customer complaints in taxi service to integrate passengers' feedback into the taxicab management by Cus-tomer Relationship Management. Zhou [23] targeted to solve problems in user expe-rience by using Customer Experience Management methodology in taxi service research.

In the field of research on passenger's user experience involving in the mental feelings and physical sensations [24] in the whole process of travel, researchers' interests mainly focus on exploring the space design, emotional experience, service design, experience design and efficiency improvement in public places such as trains, buses, airplanes or airports and platforms, and on planning the public transport system from the perspective of management to optimize passenger's user experience. Hensher et al. [25] investigated the role of service quality in enhancing user experience of bus passengers in deregulated markets with Generalized Ordered Choice preference model. Stradling et al. [26] put forth an approach to improve people's experience in mobility by city bus after surveying and analyzing the factors that result in people's dislike for taking a bus. Acevesgonzález et al. [27] compared the behavioral differences between young passengers and elderly passengers in keeping a stable stance while traveling by bus, and suggested improving the experience of older passengers by strengthening the regulation of bus drivers. Ahmadpour et al. [28] studied interior design of airplane cabins from the perspective of passengers' physical and psychological comfort, and developed design recommendations and an evaluation model. Bogicevic et al. [29] and Ahmadpour et al. [30] explored the factors affecting passenger's experience and comfort in airplane trips. Harrison et al. [31] discussed the framework for adaptive terminal design from the perspective of passenger-orientation based on a concept model of user experience in the airline industry. Chou and Kim [32] employed Structural Equation Model method in analyzing the influential factors to the degree of satisfaction and royalty of passengers of high-speed trains, and in making recommendations from the aspects of marketing strategy and corporate image. Foth and Schroeter [33] probed into how real-time passenger information systems can make a difference in improving the passenger experience. Li and Li [24] put forward user experience-oriented solution by planning optimization so as to enhance the passenger's experience of bus service. Fu et al. [34] discussed interior space design of trains in terms of space experience, spatial scale, the behavior of passengers. Dai [35] analyzed the passengers' perception of interior design of underground carriages, and developed recommendations about function design optimization to improve passengers' visual and emotional experiences [36]. Zheng [37] and Zhou [38] explored, with methods of service design and passenger behavior research, how to improve terminal transfer efficiency for passengers to enhance passengers' degree of satisfaction.

Generally speaking, there are less studies on user experience and its degree of satisfaction in taxi passenger service. The purposes of the existing researches mainly lies in (1) instead of more targeted and detailed studies on user experience of taxi passenger, taxi passenger's user experience is usually used to analyze other problems, for example, to improve taxi management mode and operation mode; (2) There are few researches focusing on influential factors critical to determine the degree of satisfaction of taxi passenger while currently focusing on the overall feeling of taxi passenger in a general way, for example, feeling of taxi's inner environment experience or service process in temporal dimension. In this study, by employing Decision-Making Trial and Evaluation Laboratory (DEMATEL) method, the interrelationship between main influencing factors to user experience in taxi passenger service is explored to extract the key factors critical to determining the satisfaction degree of user experience and to discover the structural elements in the satisfaction of user experience in taxi passenger service.

3 Method

3.1 DEMATEL Procedure

Decision-Making Trial and Evaluation Laboratory method was originally developed by the Science and Human Affairs Program of the Battelle Memorial Institute of Geneva for exploring and solving complicated and intertwined problems by understanding the structure and the cluster of intertwined problem, and identification of workable solutions by a hierarchical structure [39–44].

As an effective methodology for analyzing systematic elements of complicated and difficult problems using graph theory and matrix tools [45], DEMATEL method has been successfully applied in many fields involving in social security reliability [46], market strategy [47–49], research and development in manufacturing and management [50–52], suppliers and supply chain [53–56], logistics industry [57], business partner selection [58], performance evaluation [59], investment strategy, construction projects [60, 61], project risks [62], whole vehicle and auto component design and manufacture [50, 63–65], disaster response education [66, 67], 68 gender equality [69], data transmission technology [70, 71], e-tailer credit evaluation [72], sustainable development and environment protection [73–77], and agricultural field [78].

DEMATEL method is used in this study as a tool to extract the critical influencing factors by defining main influencing factors and exploring the interrelationship between them, aiming at unveiling the specific structure of taxi passenger's satisfaction of user experience for taxi service quality improvement.

The DEMATEL procedure in this study comprises the steps of (1) defining the main influencing factors that impact upon the satisfaction degree of taxi passenger's user experience in the taxi service; (2) inviting subjects to estimate the direction of influence and the degree of priority when each of the main factors is compared with each of other main factors in DEMATEL questionnaires with one of four level values; (3) generating the direct relation matrix Z; (4) calculating with developed DEMATEL tool the λ value, the normalized direct relation matrix and the direct/indirect relation matrix T, and the corresponding Prominence value, i.e., (D+R), and Relation value, i.e., (D−R), of each main factor; (5) drawing a causal diagram in which the directions and degrees of the impact factors can be directly observed to help build the problem structure; and (6) extracting the key influencing factors from the main factors to identify the relationship between the main factors.

3.2 Twelve Main Influencing Factors

In order to mine the information on both user experience of passengers in the taxicab and what factors have impact upon their perception of the satisfaction with taxi service, a large number of consumers who often take taxi and a number of taxi drivers are investigated by combined user research methods such as brain-storming, observation, self-report and in-depth interview. Meanwhile, the problems taxi passengers face in taxi rides are collected as supplementary information to be analyzed by reviewing related literatures and online forums.

After a large quantity of descriptive statements and sentences gathered by channels motioned above are processed and analyzed, the following twenty-one factors are summarized and defined as the preliminary influencing factors concerning taxi passenger's user experience. According to temporal dimension, they are organized into the following factor categories: (1) four factors occurred before getting in the taxi-cab, including 'time to wait for pick-up', 'rising in price during peak times', 'unmatched vehicle information', and 'canceling order'; (2) twelve factors during taxi ride, including 'driver's talking on the cell phone when driving', 'the driver's familiarity with the local roads', 'driver's chatting to passenger(s) when driving', 'long detours and intentional slowly driving', 'information on the destination', 'weather conditions', 'designated location for pick-up', 'picking others up during taxi ride', 'pettish driving mood', 'buckling up seat belts when driving', 'driver's smoking when driving', and 'time-phased pricing'; and (3) five factors occurred after taxi ride, including 'driver's using counterfeit money', 'driver's using fake invoices', 'driver's returning articles left on taxicab by passengers', 'an additional charge', and 'evaluation on driver's service'.

At last twelve main influencing factors are sorted out and given serial number Factor 1 to Factor 12 as the following: (1) Factor 1 - 'driver's talking on the cell phone when driving'; (2) Factor 2 - 'the driver's familiarity with the local roads'; (3) Factor 3 - 'driver's chatting to passenger(s) when driving'; (4) Factor 4 - 'long detours and intentional slowly driving'; (5) Factor 5 - 'information on the destination'; (6) Factor 6 - 'weather conditions'; (7) Factor 7 - 'designated location for pick-up'; (8) Factor 8 - 'picking others up during taxi ride'; (9) Factor 9 - 'pettish driving mood'; (10) Factor 10 - 'buckling up seat belts when driving'; (11) Factor 11 - 'driver's smoking when driving'; and (12) Factor 12 - 'time-phased pricing'.

3.3   DEMATEL Questionnaire

The DEMATEL questionnaire (Table 1) is used for users as consumers and passengers to estimate the direction of interaction and the degree of relative priority of each factor listed in first column to each factor listed in first row in Table 1. The priority degrees of factors in first column over factors in first row are defined in four levels, i.e., value '0' means 'do not affect', value '1' means 'slightly affect', value '2' means 'fairly affect', and value '3' means 'strongly affect'. Totally, thirty-two pieces of effective data are collected from DEMATEL questionnaires.

3.4   DEMATEL Operations

Direct Relation Matrix. By processing and averaging the thirty-two pieces of effective data, the elements in direct relation matrix Z of the interactions between twelve main factors are obtained as listed in Table 2.

The degrees of interactions between main factors are then calculated with a DEMATEL operation tool developed, as shown in the figure in Appendix. And the λ value of 0.0653168, the elements in the normalized direct relation matrix, the elements in the direct/indirect relation matrix T, and the values of Prominence and Relation of every factor among twelve main factors are derived.

Table 1. The DEMATEL questionnaire

	Factor 1	Factor 2	Factor 3	Factor 4	Factor 5	Factor 6	Factor 7	Factor 8	Factor 9	Factor 10	Factor 11	Factor 12
Factor 1	0											
Factor 2		0										
Factor 3			0									
Factor 4				0								
Factor 5					0							
Factor 6						0						
Factor 7							0					
Factor 8								0				
Factor 9									0			
Factor 10										0		
Factor 11											0	
Factor 12												0

Table 2. The elements in direct relation matrix Z

	1	2	3	4	5	6	7	8	9	10	11	12
1	0.00	0.90	0.21	1.59	1.21	0.31	1.03	1.52	1.66	0.66	1.00	0.66
2	1.00	0.00	1.76	2.07	2.35	0.21	2.52	2.07	1.38	0.62	0.48	0.86
3	1.40	0.83	0.00	0.97	1.03	0.17	1.00	1.24	1.59	0.28	0.69	0.28
4	0.72	0.97	0.76	0.00	0.86	0.07	1.59	1.35	1.10	0.31	0.38	1.07
5	0.52	1.44	1.38	1.28	0.00	0.14	1.69	1.24	0.93	0.21	0.38	0.52
6	0.76	0.72	0.76	1.45	0.69	0.00	0.79	1.00	1.62	0.45	0.45	0.55
7	0.76	0.93	0.62	1.03	0.62	0.07	0.00	1.00	0.52	0.24	0.21	0.52
8	1.07	0.69	0.90	1.62	0.69	0.07	1.17	0.00	0.86	0.38	0.28	0.86
9	1.14	0.69	1.55	0.83	0.55	0.14	0.62	0.52	0.00	0.79	1.07	0.45
10	0.41	0.17	0.31	0.35	0.14	0.03	0.28	0.28	0.59	0.00	0.21	0.14
11	0.86	0.48	1.55	0.48	0.41	0.07	0.38	0.31	0.13	0.41	0.00	0.17
12	0.21	0.59	0.52	1.03	0.52	0.10	0.48	0.59	0.66	0.17	0.17	0.00

Direct/Indirect Relation Matrix. The elements in direct/indirect relation matrix T are as listed in Table 3. By listing all elements in matrix T in a sequence of number, the quartile deviation, i.e., 0.084, of this sequence is calculated as the threshold to measure the strength of interactions between factors. If all values in the row and the column that correspond to an element in the matrix T are below this threshold value at the same time, the corresponding row and column will be removed.

Prominence and Relation. The Prominence value, i.e., (D+R), and Relation value, i.e., (D−R), of each of twelve main factors are calculated and listed in Table 4. The Prominence indicates the relative weighting (percentage) of one factor's influencing strength in total influencing strength of all factors, while the Relation indicates to what extent one factor has influence on or is influenced by other factors and the absolute

Table 3. The elements in direct/indirect relation matrix T

	1	2	3	4	5	6	7	8	9	10	11	12
1	**1.00**	**0.15**	**0.26**	**0.23**	**0.18**	0.04	**0.20**	**0.22**	**0.23**	**0.09**	**0.12**	**0.11**
2	**0.18**	**0.12**	**0.26**	**0.29**	**0.26**	0.03	**0.31**	**0.28**	**0.23**	**0.10**	**0.10**	**0.15**
3	**0.14**	**0.13**	**0.10**	**0.16**	**0.14**	0.03	**0.16**	**0.17**	**0.19**	0.06	**0.09**	**0.12**
4	**0.12**	**0.13**	**0.15**	**0.10**	**0.13**	0.02	**0.20**	**0.17**	**0.16**	0.06	0.07	**0.12**
5	**0.11**	**0.17**	**0.19**	**0.19**	**0.09**	0.02	**0.22**	**0.18**	**0.16**	0.05	0.07	**0.09**
6	**0.12**	**0.12**	**0.15**	**0.19**	**0.12**	0.01	**0.15**	**0.16**	**0.19**	0.07	0.08	**0.09**
7	**0.10**	**0.11**	**0.11**	**0.14**	**0.10**	0.01	0.08	**0.13**	**0.10**	0.04	0.05	0.08
8	**0.13**	**0.11**	**0.15**	**0.19**	**0.12**	0.02	**0.17**	**0.90**	**0.14**	0.06	0.06	0.11
9	**0.14**	**0.11**	**0.19**	**0.14**	**0.10**	0.02	**0.13**	**0.12**	**0.09**	0.08	**0.11**	0.07
10	0.05	0.03	0.05	0.05	0.03	0.01	0.05	0.05	0.07	0.01	0.03	0.03
11	**0.10**	0.08	**0.17**	**0.10**	**0.08**	0.01	**0.09**	**0.09**	**0.15**	0.05	0.04	0.05
12	0.06	0.08	**0.09**	**0.12**	0.08	0.01	**0.09**	**0.09**	**0.09**	0.03	0.04	0.03

Note: The elements in bold type indicate those with values above the
threshold of 0.084.

value of the Relation value (D−R) represents the influencing strength. The positive
Relation value of one factor means it has an impact upon other factors while a negative
Relation value means it is influenced by other factors. It can be observed in Table 4 that
Factor 2, i.e., 'the driver's familiarity with the local roads', has the maximum value of
Prominence, and Factor 10, i.e., 'buckling up seat belts when driving', has the minimum value of Prominence. This indicates that the degree of driver's familiarity with the
local roads is the most important influencing factor related to passenger's user experience in taxicab while the drivers' buckling up seat belts when driving is the least
significant influencing factor.

On the one hand, all factors' values of Prominence in Table 4 can be averaged as
mean value, 2.400. Eight factors with Prominence value above 2.400 can be lined in
order from larger Prominence value to smaller Prominence value as follows: Factor 2
('the driver's familiarity with the local roads'), Factor 4 ('long detours and intentional
slowly driving'), Factor 3 ('driver's chatting to passenger(s) when driving'), Factor 1
('driver's talking on the cell phone when driving'), Factor 8 ('picking others up during
taxi ride'), Factor 9 ('pettish driving mood'), Factor 5 ('information on the destination'), and Factor 7 ('designated location for pick-up').

On the other hand, as for Relation value, it can be observed in Table 4 that five
factors have positive Relation values, indicating that they have impact upon other
factors. More specifically, Factor 6 ('weather conditions') has the strongest impact
upon other factors, and both Factor 2 ('the driver's familiarity with the local roads')
and Factor 1 ('driver's talking on the cell phone when driving') have great impacts
upon other factors, respectively, while Factor 11 ('driver's smoking when driving') and
Factor 5 ('information on the destination') have minimal positive influence on other
factors.

Table 4. Prominence and Relation values

Prominence (D+R)		Relation (D−R)	
Factor 2	**3.653**	Factor 6	1.211
Factor 4	**3.335**	Factor 2	0.961
Factor 3	**3.305**	Factor 1	0.574
Factor 1	**3.264**	Factor 11	0.173
Factor 8	**3.101**	Factor 5	0.123
Factor 9	**3.079**	Factor 12	−0.177
Factor 5	**2.978**	Factor 10	−0.247
Factor 7	**2.892**	Factor 8	−0.401
Factor 11	1.874	Factor 3	−0.425
Factor 12	1.792	Factor 4	−0.511
Factor 6	1.657	Factor 9	−0.519
Factor 10	1.165	Factor 7	−0.764
Mean value: 2.400			

Note: Items in bold type indicate Prominence values above the mean value, 2.400.

On the contrary, seven factors left have negative Relation values indicating that they are influenced by the five factors with positive Relation values mentioned above. To be specific, Factor 7 ('designated location for pick-up') is influenced strongly by other factors while Factor 9 ('pettish driving mood'), Factor 4 ('long detours and intentional slowly driving'), Factor 3 ('driver's chatting to passenger(s) when driving') and Factor 8 ('picking others up during taxi ride') are also influenced clearly by other factors.

3.5   DEMATEL Causal Diagram

The causal diagram for twelve main factors influencing taxi passenger's user experience is built and drawn as shown in Fig. 1, where the horizontal axis stands for the Prominence value (D+R) while the vertical axis for the Relation value (D−R).

In the causal diagram, a vector line indicates the direction of influence of one factor to another factor pointed to, and solid lines indicate stronger influencing degree while dotted lines weaker one. As illustrated in Fig. 1, Factor 2 ('the driver's familiarity with the local roads') has stronger influence simultaneously on five factors, i.e., Factor 3 ('driver's chatting to passenger(s) when driving'), Factor 4 ('long detours and intentional slowly driving'), Factor 5 ('information on the destination'), Factor 7 ('designated location for pick-up') and Factor 8 ('picking others up during taxi ride'). This indicates that whether or not a taxi driver is familiar with local road networks and, as a result, with the corresponding route to the designated destination, plays a pivotal role in determining the satisfaction degree of taxi passenger's user experience because of its direct influence on driver's related behaviors, including talking with and inquiring to passengers while driving, detouring and driving slowly, knowing basic information on the destination, and picking passengers up timely at the designated location.

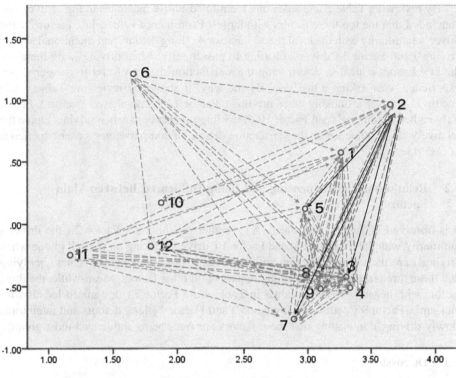

Fig. 1. The causal diagram

4   Conclusion and Discussion

4.1   Key Factors Influencing the Satisfaction Degree of Taxi Passenger's User Experience

The top three factors with the largest Prominence values including Factor 2, Factor 4 and Factor 3, and the top three factors with the largest Relation values including Factor 6, Factor 2 and Factor 1, are fetched from Table 4 and reorganized in order as listed in Table 5.

Table 5. The top three factors in Prominence and the top three factors in Relation

The top three factors in Prominence	The top three factors in Relation
Factor 2 - 'the driver's familiarity with the local roads'	Factor 6 - 'weather conditions'
Factor 4 - 'long detours and intentional slowly driving'	Factor 2 - 'the driver's familiarity with the local roads'
Factor 3 - 'driver's chatting to passenger(s) when driving'	Factor 1 - 'driver's talking on the cell phone when driving'

By reviewing Table 5 and analyzing mentioned-above messages in Fig. 1, it can be concluded that the top three factors with largest Prominence values, i.e., Factor 2 ('the driver's familiarity with the local roads'), Factor 4 ('long detours and intentional slowly driving') and Factor 3 ('driver's chatting to passenger(s) when driving'), are therefore the key factors critical to determining the satisfaction degree of taxi passenger's user experience when taking a taxi ride. By the way, it shows by reviewing Table 4 that Factor 11 ('driver's smoking when driving'), Factor 12 ('time-phased Pricing'), Factor 6 ('weather conditions') and Factor 10 ('buckling up seat belts when driving') have the relatively slight influence on the satisfaction degree of taxi passenger's user experience in taxi ride.

4.2   Relationships of Influencing and Being Influenced Between Main Factors

It is observed in Table 5 that Factor 6 ('weather conditions'), Factor 2 ('the driver's familiarity with the local roads') and Factor 1 ('driver's talking on the cell phone when driving') are the top three factors with the largest positive Relation values, implying that these three factors have the strong impact upon other factors. Mean-while, the three factors with negative Relation values in Table 4 are Factor 7 ('designated location for pick-up'), Factor 9 ('pettish driving mood') and Factor 4 ('long detours and intentional slowly driving'), indicating that these factors are ones being influenced most greatly.

4.3   Discussion

In this study, twelve main influencing factors are obtained and defined by analyzing twenty-one preliminary factors collected by means of brainstorming, questionnaire and in-depth interview and so on. And by using DEMATEL method and operation tool, three key factors critical to determining the satisfaction degree of user experience in taxi passenger service are extracted out of these main factors, including (1) the driver's unfamiliarity with the local roads; (2) long detours and intentional slowly driving; and (3) driver's chatting to passenger(s) when driving. And furthermore, three factors influencing greatly on other factors are discovered, i.e., (1) weather conditions; (2) the degree of familiarity with the local roads; and (3) whether or not a taxi driver talks on the cell phone when driving.

Among five different factors listed above, it is found that four factors except the non-human factor 'weather conditions', are related to the taxi driver side. The findings in this study show that user experience and its degree of satisfaction of taxi passenger during taking taxi ride are related to and influenced by comprehensive factors.

On the one hand, two key factors, 'the driver's familiarity with the local roads' and 'long detours and intentional slowly driving', are directly related to the amount of passengers' payment. This implies that the passenger's feeling that a taxi driver is unfamiliar with the road networks, has heavily negative effect to the degree of satisfaction of the passenger's user experience.

On the other hand, the driver's behaviors stated by one key factor, 'driver's chatting to passenger(s) when driving', and one influencing factor, 'driver's talking on the cell phone when driving', have direct impact upon and are related to driving safety and the passenger's safety during taxi ride. This indicates that the satisfaction degree of the passenger's user experience will be also greatly reduced if a taxi driver frequently acts in behaviors such as chatting to passenger(s) or talking on the cell phone while driving.

In addition, it can be elicited from interpreting the causal diagram that whether or not a taxi driver is familiar with the corresponding routes to the passenger's destination, has also direct impact upon the passenger's user experience and their evaluation on the degree of satisfaction with taxi passenger service.

Appendix

See Fig. 2.

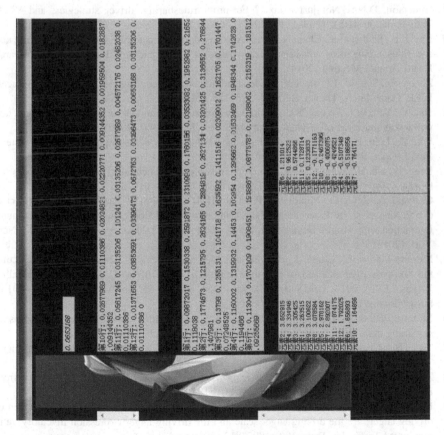

Fig. 2. The output listed in the interface of DEMATEL operation tool

References

1. Liu, L., Chen, Y., Zhang, W.: Passenger demand forecast model for Beijing taxis. Transp. Res. **13**, 89–92 (2010). (in Chinese)
2. Hu, S.: Study on the evaluation index system of taxi service to passengers demand oriented. Logist. Eng. Manag. **37**, 129–130 (2015). (in Chinese)
3. Curry, G.L., Vany, A.D., Feldman, R.M.: A queueing model of airport passenger departures by taxi: competition with a public transportation mode. Transp. Res. **12**, 115–120 (1978)
4. Cairns, R.D., Liston-Heyes, C.: Competition and regulation in the taxi industry. J. Public Econ. **59**, 1–15 (1996)
5. Xiong, Z.: Beijing taxi market legal regulations. Master's thesis, Capital University of Economics and Business, Beijing (2013). (in Chinese)
6. Yang, H., Fung, C.S., Wong, K.I., et al.: Nonlinear pricing of taxi services. Transp. Res. Part A **44**, 337–348 (2010)
7. Gu, H., Zheng, J.: Economic analysis of taxi price system - taking Beijing as an example. Price Theor. Pract. **04**, 16–18 (2002). (in Chinese)
8. Anderson, D.N.: "Not just a taxi"? For-profit ridesharing, driver strategies, and VMT. Transportation **41**(5), 1099–1117 (2014)
9. Rayle, L., Shaheen, S., Chan, N., et al.: App-based, on-demand ride services: comparing taxi and ridesourcing trips and user characteristics in San Francisco. Transportation Research Board Annual Meeting (2014)
10. Zhang, D., Sun, L., Li, B., et al.: Understanding taxi service strategies from taxi GPS traces. IEEE Trans. Intell. Transp. Syst. **16**, 123–135 (2015)
11. Hai, Y., Yan, W.L., Wong, S.C., et al.: A macroscopic taxi model for passenger demand, taxi utilization and level of services. Transportation **27**, 317–340 (2000)
12. Shi, Y., Lian, Z.: Optimization and strategic behavior in a passenger-taxi service system. Eur. J. Oper. Res. **249**, 1024–1032 (2016)
13. Leng, B., Du, H., Wang, J., et al.: Analysis of taxi drivers' behaviors within a battle between two taxi Apps. IEEE Trans. Intell. Transp. Syst. **17**, 296–300 (2015)
14. Osswald, S., Zehe, D., Mundhenk, P., et al.: HMI development for a purpose-built electric taxi in Singapore. In: Proceedings of the 15th International Conference on Human-Computer Interaction with Mobile Devices and Services, MobileHCI 2013, pp. 434–439. ACM, New York (2013)
15. Moreira-Matias, L., Gama, J., Ferreira, M., Mendes-Moreira, J., Damas, L.: On predicting the taxi-passenger demand: a real-time approach. In: Correia, L., Reis, L.P., Cascalho, J. (eds.) EPIA 2013. LNCS (LNAI), vol. 8154, pp. 54–65. Springer, Heidelberg (2013). https://doi.org/10.1007/978-3-642-40669-0_6
16. Moreira-Matias, L., Gama, J., Ferreira, M., et al.: Predicting taxi–passenger demand using streaming data. IEEE Trans. Intell. Transp. Syst. **14**(3), 1393–1402 (2013)
17. Yan, S., Chen, C.Y., Wu, C.C.: Solution methods for the taxi pooling problem. Transportation **39**, 723–748 (2012)
18. Zhang, S., Wang, Z.: Correction: inferring passenger denial behavior of taxi drivers from large-scale taxi traces. PLoS ONE **12**(2), e0171876 (2017)
19. Brandenburg, S., Oehl, M., Seigies, K.: German taxi drivers' experience and expression of driving anger: are the driving anger scale and the driving anger expression inventory valid measures? Traffic Inj. Prev. **18**(8), 807–812 (2017)
20. Tang, L.L., Li, Q.Q., Chang, X.M., et al.: Modeling of taxi drivers' experience for routing applications. Sci. China: Technol. Sci. **53**, 44–51 (2010)

21. Shen, H.: Method of calculating satisfaction index of passengers on taxi services. Jiangsu Commun. **11**, 31–32 (2003). (in Chinese)
22. Li, D.: Passenger experience-oriented Beijing taxi complaints effective mechanism. Decis. Inf. **5**, 96–97 (2015). (in Chinese)
23. Zhou, G.: From customer experience to passenger experience: the value of experiential management in taxi services. China Mark. **19**, 27–28 (2015). (in Chinese)
24. Li, D., Li, L.: Discussion on passenger experience-oriented optimum design of conventional bus. In: Proceedings of China Urban Transportation Planning Annual Meeting and the 27th Symposium, pp. 1–12. China Architecture & Building Press, Beijing (2014). (in Chinese)
25. Hensher, D.A., Mulley, C., Yahya, N.: Passenger experience with quality-enhanced bus service: the tyne and wear 'superoute' services. Transportation **37**, 239–256 (2010)
26. Stradling, S., Carreno, M., Rye, T., et al.: Passenger perceptions and the ideal urban bus journey experience. Transp. Policy **14**, 283–292 (2007)
27. Acevesgonzález, C., May, A., Cook, S.: An observational comparison of the older and younger bus passenger experience in a developing world city. Ergonomics **59**, 840–850 (2016)
28. Ahmadpour, N., Lindgaard, G., Robert, J.M., et al.: The thematic structure of passenger comfort experience and its relationship to the context features in the aircraft cabin. Ergonomics **57**, 801–815 (2014)
29. Bogicevic, V., Yang, W., Bilgihan, A., et al.: Airport service quality drivers of passenger satisfaction. Tourism Rev. **68**, 3–18 (2013)
30. Ahmadpour, N., Robert, J.M., Lindgaard, G.: Aircraft passenger comfort experience: un-derlying factors and differentiation from discomfort. Appl. Ergon. **52**, 301–308 (2016)
31. Harrison, A., Popovic, V., Kraal, B.J., et al.: Challenges in passenger terminal design: a conceptual model of passenger experience. In: Proceedings of the Design Research Society (DRS) 2012 Conference, pp. 344–356. Chulalongkorn University, Bangkok (2012)
32. Chou, J.S., Kim, C.: A structural equation analysis of the QSL relationship with passenger riding experience on high speed rail: an empirical study of Taiwan and Korea. Expert Syst. Appl. **36**, 6945–6955 (2009)
33. Foth, M., Schroeter, R.: Enhancing the experience of public transport users with urban screens and mobile applications. In: International Academic Mindtrek Conference: Envisioning Future Media Environments, pp. 33–40. ACM, New York (2010)
34. Fu, Z., Zhang, L., Wu, Q.: About inner space design for trains. Art Des. **4**, 34–37 (2008). (in Chinese)
35. Bai, W.: Analysis of interior decoration of subway carriages in the view of ride experience. Mod. Decor. (Theory) **9**, 17 (2016). (in Chinese)
36. Xu, J., Zhang, B., Wang, Y.: Emotional design of metro interior facilities. Packag. Eng. **16**, 168–172 (2017). (in Chinese)
37. Zheng, Z.: Service design of urban transfer guidance system with 'unity of knowledge and practice'. Packag. Eng. **38**, 19–23 (2017). (in Chinese)
38. Zhou, K.: Analysis of transfer behavior and research on transfer facility configuration in high-speed railway passenger transport hub. Doctoral dissertation, Harbin Institute of Technology (2013). (in Chinese)
39. Wu, H., Chang, S.: A case study of using DEMTEL method to identify critical factors in green supply chain management. Appl. Math. Comput. **256**, 394–403 (2015)
40. Lin, T., Yang, Y.H., Kang, J.S., Yu, H.C.: Using DEMATEL method to explore the core competences and causal effect of the IC design service company: an empirical case study. Expert Syst. Appl. **38**, 6262–6268 (2011)
41. Shieh, J.I., Wu, H.H., Huang, K.K.: DEMATEL method in identifying key success factors of hospital service quality. Knowl.-Based Syst. **23**, 277–282 (2010)

42. Wang, W.C., Lin, Y.H., Lin, C.L., Chung, C.H., Lee, M.T.: DEMATEL-based model to improve the performance in a matrix organization. Expert Syst. Appl. **39**, 4978–4986 (2012)
43. Wu, H.H., Chen, H.K., Shieh, J.I.: Evaluating performance criteria of employment service outreach program personnel by DEMATEL method. Expert Syst. Appl. **37**, 5219–5223 (2010)
44. Wu, W.W.: Segmenting critical factors for successful knowledge management implementation using the fuzzy DEMATEL method. Appl. Soft Comput. **12**, 527–535 (2012)
45. Bianchi, C., Montemaggiore, G.B.: Building 'dynamic' balanced scorecards to enhance strategy design and planning in public utilities: key-findings from a project in a city water company. Revista de Dinámica de Sistemas **2**(2), 3–35 (2006)
46. Li, Y., Hu, Y., Zhang, X., et al.: An evidential DEMATEL method to identify critical success factors in emergency management. Appl. Soft Comput. **22**, 504–510 (2014)
47. Altuntas, S., Dereli, T.: A novel approach based on DEMATEL method and patent citation analysis for prioritizing a portfolio of investment projects. Expert Syst. Appl. **42**, 1003–1012 (2015)
48. Lu, X., Wang, K., Hu, J., et al.: A fuzzy-DEMATEL-based analysis of the factors that influence users' participation behaviors under the crowdsourcing model. Manag. Rev. **29**, 101–109 (2017). (in Chinese)
49. Zhang, C., Wu, B.: Measurement of credit risk on China's peer-to-peer online lending. Stat. Inf. Forum **32**, 110–115 (2017). (in Chinese)
50. Vinodh, S., Balagi, T.S.S., Patil, A.: A hybrid MCDM approach for agile concept selection using fuzzy DEMATEL, fuzzy ANP and fuzzy TOPSIS. Int. J. Adv. Manuf. Technol. **83**(9–12), 1979–1987 (2016)
51. Shi, R., Yang, J.: Analysis and research on influencing factors of civil aviation air traffic controllers' performance based on DEMATEL. J. Civil Aviat. Univ. China **34**, 31–35 (2016). (in Chinese)
52. Wu, W.W., Lee, Y.T.: Developing global managers' competencies using the fuzzy DEMATEL method. Expert Syst. Appl. **31**, 499–507 (2007)
53. Su, C.M., Horng, D.J., Tseng. M.L., et al.: Improving sustainable supply chain management using a novel hierarchical grey-DEMATEL approach. J. Clean. Prod. **134**, 469–481 (2016)
54. Mirmousa, S., Dehnavi, H.D.: Development of criteria of selecting the supplier by using the fuzzy DEMATEL method. Procedia - Soc. Behav. Sci. **230**, 281–289 (2016)
55. Khompatraporn, C., Somboonwiwat, T.: Causal factor relations of supply chain competitiveness via fuzzy DEMATEL method for Thai automotive industry. Prod. Plan. Control **28**, 538–551 (2017)
56. Lan, S., Zhong, R.Y.: An evaluation model for financial reporting supply chain using DEMATEL-ANP. Procedia Cirp. **56**, 516–519 (2016)
57. Li, Y., Huang, J., Chen, M.: The analysis of factors influencing on the collaborative development of manufacturing industry and logistics industry based on DEMATEL. J. Wuhan Univ. Technol. (Inf. Manag. Eng.) **39**, 550–555 (2017). (in Chinese)
58. Büyüközkan, G., Güleryüz, S., Karpak, B.: A new combined IF-DEMATEL and IF-ANP approach for CRM partner evaluation. Int. J. Prod. Econ. **191**, 194–206 (2017)
59. Ranjan, R., Chatterjee, P., Chakraborty, S.: Evaluating performance of engineering departments in an Indian University using DEMATEL and compromise ranking methods. Opsearch **52**(2), 307–328 (2015)
60. Nilashi, M., Zakaria, R., Ibrahim, O., et al.: MCPCM: a DEMATEL-ANP-based multi-criteria decision-making approach to evaluate the critical success factors in construction projects. Arab. J. Sci. Eng. **40**, 343–361 (2015)
61. Liu, C.: Analysis of influencing factors of lean construction capability: based on DEMATEL method. Eng. Econ. **27**, 33–37 (2017). (in Chinese)

62. Luo, R., Yang, C.: Analysis of risk factors of PPP project based on DEMATEL method - a case study of Qingdao metro Line 3. Contemp. Econ. **15**, 136–137 (2017). (in Chinese)
63. Li, Y., Mathiyazhagan, K.: Application of DEMATEL approach to identify the influential indicators towards sustainable supply chain adoption in the auto components manufacturing sector. J. Clean. Prod. **172**, 2931–2941 (2018)
64. Liu, G., Huang, D., Liu, C.: Preference of car form feature based on DEMATEL method. China Packag. Ind. **24**, 34–36 (2014). (in Chinese)
65. Yang, F.: Study on influence of passenger car's form on consumers' purchase decision. Master's thesis, Shanghai Jiao Tong University, Shanghai (2016). (in Chinese)
66. Zhou, X., Shi, Y., Deng, X., et al.: D-DEMATEL: a new method to identify critical success factors in emergency management. Saf. Sci. **91**, 93–104 (2017)
67. Muhammad, M.N., Cavus, N.: Fuzzy DEMATEL method for identifying LMS evaluation criteria. Procedia Comput. Sci. **120**, 742–749 (2017)
68. Li, H., Ren, Y., Tao, M.: Research on the key influencing factors analysis of the graduate education quality in China based on DEMATEL method. Sci. Technol. Innov. Herald **14**, 209–212 (2017). (in Chinese)
69. Raghuvanshi, J., Agrawal, R., Ghosh, P.K., et al.: Analysis of barriers to women entre-preneurship: the DEMATEL approach. J. Entrep. **26**, 220–238 (2017)
70. Sharma, V., Kumar, R., Kumar, R.: QUAT-DEM: quaternion-DEMATEL based neural model for mutual coordination between UAVs. Inf. Sci. **418**, 74–90 (2017)
71. Li, X., Lu, P., Li, C.: Analysis on the influencing factors of disruptive innovations in the state grid and the comprehensive ranking based on Delphi and DEMATEL method. Sci. Technol. Manag. Res. **37**(6), 127–133 (2017). (in Chinese)
72. Li, R., Wang, X.: Application of GRA-DEMATEL in influence factors of e-tailers credit evaluation. J. Commer. Econ. **22**, 89–91 (2017). (in Chinese)
73. Büyüközkan, G., Güleryüz, S.: An integrated DEMATEL-ANP approach for renewable energy resources selection in Turkey. Int. J. Prod. Econ. **182**, 435–448 (2016)
74. George-Ufot, G., Qu, Y., Orji, I.J.: Sustainable lifestyle factors influencing industries' electric consumption patterns using fuzzy logic and DEMATEL: the Nigerian perspective. J. Clean. Prod. **162**, 624–634 (2017)
75. Liang, H., Ren, J., Gao, Z., et al.: Identification of critical success factors for sustainable development of biofuel industry in China based on grey decision-making trial and evaluation laboratory (DEMATEL). J. Clean. Prod. **131**, 500–508 (2016)
76. Chen, Y., Liu, J., Li, Y., et al.: RM-DEMATEL: a new methodology to identify the key factors in PM2.5. Environ. Sci. Pollut. Res. Int. **22**, 6372–6380 (2015)
77. Tyagi, M., Kumar, P., Kumar, D.: Assessment of critical enablers for flexible supply chain performance measurement system using fuzzy DEMATEL approach. Global J. Flex. Syst. Manag. **16**, 115–132 (2015)
78. Niu, L., Jiang, Y.: Study on farmers' willingness and its influencing factors towards small-scale irrigation based on DEMATEL methods. China Rural Water Hydropower **10**, 194–200 (2017). (in Chinese)

What Sensory Desires Make Young Chinese Users Prefer One Instrumental Panel Form of Passenger Car to Another?

Chunrong Liu[✉], Yang Xie, and Yi Jin

Shanghai Jiao Tong University, Shanghai 200240, China
cheeronliu@sjtu.edu.cn

Abstract. To investigate into what and how sensory desires affect young Chinese users' perceiving and liking instrumental panel (IP) form, young users as consumers with age of 25 to 35 are invited to estimate on both similarity of ninety-seven IP samples of passenger car in fifty-five main auto brands in Chinese market, and similarity of meanings of fifty-six image words. The cluster analysis is conducted and ten representative image words, i.e., 'Layered', 'Prospective', 'Rough', 'Graceful', 'Economical', 'Exciting', 'Delicate', 'Dynamic', 'Favorite' and 'Solemn', are extracted as representative images. With multidimensional scaling the perceptual map is plotted for qualitative morphological analysis, and sixteen IP forms are generated by orthogonal design and evaluated by users from the perspective of each of ten representative images in turn with semantic differential method. A multivariate linear regression analysis is then completed to examine the relationship between image 'Favorite' and other nine representative images. It is found that four sensory images including 'Exciting', 'Graceful', 'Delicate' and 'Solemn', in bigger to smaller coefficient order, play significant ($P < 0.001$) and positive roles in determining the feeling of 'Favorite' image, making young Chinese users prefer one IP form of passenger car to another.

Keywords: User research · Instrumental panel form of passenger car
The perceptual map · Multivariate regression analysis

1 Introduction

Body mass, shape and graphics are the basic cognitive elements of form features, corresponding to different aesthetic images and semantics [1]. Form is the carrier of communication between designers and users. The designers embody the design intent in the form, and the user interprets it as an objective of cognition. In different emotional environment, the users' perception concerns of car form will change [2]. At the same time, designers and consumers have different concerns about cars. Car designers need to integrate emotional design elements into the design practice [3].

The automotive interior design is an important part of car form design and an effective vehicle that designers meet users' need to emotional design elements as means to improve the competitiveness of automobile product. The automotive interior is not only the carrier for functional operation space of driving tasks, but one for the emotional experience and psychological appeal of consumers [4], while being under the

© Springer International Publishing AG, part of Springer Nature 2018
A. Marcus and W. Wang (Eds.): DUXU 2018, LNCS 10920, pp. 314–328, 2018.
https://doi.org/10.1007/978-3-319-91806-8_24

premise to conform to the overall design style and to meet both the requirements in automotive ergonomics and the physiological and psychological needs of consumers.

Various studies in the field of the interior design have been carried out, involving mainly in human-machine interaction, user experience, emotional design through cognitive exploration, and design trends. Based on principal component analysis, Wu et al. [5] found that the main factors influencing user's emotion in the interaction design of car navigation interface are stylization cognition factor, emotional cognitive factor and the decorative cognitive factor. With the method of case analysis and theoretical framework construction, Zeng et al. [6] proposed a storyboard tool integrating 'software' and 'hardware' human-machine interface design, and verified the effectiveness and feasibility of this method. Liu and Zhu [7] reviewed the art-of-the-state of world-wide studies on in-vehicle information system shared between the occupants including driver and passengers. Mao [8] systematically analyzed design concept, process and method of user experience in automotive interior, and suggested a new way for innovative automotive interior design. Wu [9] identified that interior form is one of the important factors in construction of the security in automotive interior design process. Liu et al. [10] found that the overall contour-based shape of the center console is one of the main factors influencing consumers' 'delicate' imagery demand on the interior form. Leder and Carbon [11] found that curvature and innovativeness have great influence on the aesthetics of automotive interior form. Karlsson et al. [12] found that personality and aesthetic form design should be more emphasized during the automotive interior design.

These studies present the importance of the automotive interior in car styling and design field. As the most important part in the automotive interior, the instrumental panel (IP) form of passenger car, has both function of technology and function of aesthetics, presenting the difference in the interior form style and brand identification.

In China's passenger car market, Chinese consumers with age of 30 to 39 has become the main force in passenger car owners, and those with age of 20 to 29 have greatest potential to be the first-time passenger car buyers in 2016 [13], while the percentage of Chinese consumers with age of 25 to 34 has grown to 16.77% according to the demographic data of China Statistical Yearbook 2017 [14]. Thus, in this study, with young Chinese consumers with age of 25 to 35 as subjects, their perceptual characteristics of similarity of IP forms of passenger car and psychological characteristics of imagery needs on IP form are investigated and analyzed to help uncover and understand the key images that make young Chinese users prefer one IP form of passenger car to another.

2 Method

2.1 Similarity Judgment on IP Form

According to the sales statistics of passenger cars in 2017 in the Chinese market [15], passenger cars with engine displacement 1.0L to 2.0L contribute to the high sales volume for the ordinary passenger car market while those with engine displacement 2.0L to 3.0L to the sales volume for the high-end passenger car market. Thus, in this study the pictures of IP forms of mass-production passenger cars with engine displacement between 1.0L and 3.0L are searched and collected from the Internet, and ninety-seven IP forms are selected after preliminary screening, covering fifty-six auto brands (sub-brands) as listed in Table 1 in China's passenger car market.

To avoid the possibility that color aspect distracts the subject from IP forms presented in the pictures, every picture is converted into black-and-white color mode, and IP form in each picture is presented centrally on the white background with outlines of seats and windshield while brand logo on the steering wheel in each picture is removed. A processed picture is as shown in Fig. 1.

Table 1. The brand list of IP form samples

Audi	BYD	Lincoln	BMW	Beijing Benz	Chang'an-Mazda	Dongfeng-Honda	Dongfeng-Nissan
Skoda	Chery	FAW Hongqi	HAWTAI	Dongfeng Aeolus	Brilliance Zhonghua	Tianjin FAW	Dongfeng-Peugeot
Lifan	Acura	FAW-Mazda	Haima	SSANG YONG	SAIC-VW	FAW-Toyota	Dongfeng Venucia
OPEL	Volvo	FAW Besturn	Lexus	Chang'an Ford	SAIC-GM Chevrolet	SGMW Bao Jun	SAIC Roewe
SAIC MG	JAC	Infiniti	GAC-FIAT	Soueast Motor	GAC Trumpchi	GAC Ji' ao	SAIC-GM Buick
FAW-VW	Tesla	Renault	Great Wall	Hyundai	Dongfeng-Yulong Luxgen	Dongfeng-Citroën	BAIC MOTOR
Jaguar	KIA	Chang'an	GEELY	GAC-Honda	BAIC SENDUA	Chang'an-Suzuki	GAC-Toyota

Fig. 1. An example of processed picture of IP form

The subjects are invited to evaluate the similarity between IP forms. A piece of similarity matrix data is generated after a subject completed the similarity judgment task with a customized grouping task tool developed by the first author's team for the experiment on similarity judgment of IP form. Totally, 60 effective pieces of similarity matrix data are gathered from sixty subjects including thirty-three male subjects and twenty-seven female subjects from different discipline backgrounds. With these similarity matrices an averaged similarity matrix is calculated and used for a cluster analysis and a dissimilarity matrix is derived from this averaged similarity matrix for use in the later phase.

2.2 Similarity Judgment on Image Words' Meaning

The preliminary image words in this study, being related to form description and evaluation of the overall automotive interior and the whole instrument panel and its parts, are collected mainly by web searches from comments and articles or descriptive news on car websites, car advertising, car review magazines and relevant literatures. Totally, one hundred and thirty-seven preliminary image words are obtained.

These image words are then judged and analyzed to evaluate the similarity and/or inclusion relation in meanings. The image words with less correlation to describing and evaluating the overall automotive interior and whole instrument panel and its parts, with very similar meaning to another image word, or with meaning included in meaning of other image words, are removed out of the image words set. Finally, fifty-six image words for describing the interior IP form are obtained as listed in Table 2.

Table 2. The image words selected for describing IP form

Individualized	Sporty	Delicate	Intelligent	Commercial	Smooth	Stretched	Feminine
Audacious	Modern	Speedy	Lightsome	Perfect	Strong	Popular	Rational
Practical	Slim	Concise	Forceful	Swanking	Clear	Advanced	Safe
High-quality	Supernormal	Sharp	Accurate	Hard	Capacious	Classic	High-tech
Ebullient	Innovative	Unaffected	Solemn	Wieldy	Elegant	Cosy	Exciting
Favorite	Casual	Economical	Graceful	Sturdy	Luxurious	Prospective	Distinguished
Layered	Dynamic	Rough	Harmonious	Decorative	Off-road	Young	Surprising

Fifty-six pictures are then made, each of which presents an image word (in Chinese character) at the center with white background, and used as input into a customized grouping task tool for the experiment on similarity judgment of meanings of image words, in which process young subjects with age of 25 to 35 from different discipline backgrounds are invited to estimate the similarity of meaning between fifty-six image words.

As the result of one subject's estimate on the similarity between image words' meanings, a piece of similarity matrix data is generated by grouping task tool after he/she completed the similarity judgment task. Totally, 40 effective pieces of similarity matrix data are obtained, among which twenty pieces are from twenty subjects with age of 25 to 29 including eleven male subjects and nine female subjects while another twenty pieces from twenty subjects with age of 30 to 35 including ten male subjects and ten female subjects.

2.3 Representative Image Words

Based on above forty pieces of similarity matrix data on image words' meaning, an averaged similarity matrix is calculated and used to carry out a hierarchical cluster analysis. The dendrogram resulted from the hierarchical cluster analysis is plotted as shown in Fig. 2.

After analysis of the sectioning ways in the dendrogram, it is appropriate that all fifty-six image words are classified into nine categories or six categories. When all image words are classified into nine categories, each category include 6, 9, 6, 8, 1, 2, 5, 5, and 14 image words, respectively, while when classified into six categories, each category include 6, 9, 14, 1, 7, and 19 cases, respectively. According to the related cluster analysis principle [16] that, in cluster analysis process, it is ideal for all samples to be classified as 'evenly' as possible into categories (although it is usually difficult), it is reasonable to classify all image words into nine categories, i.e. nine clusters as illustrated in Fig. 2 with blue sectioning line on the left.

To select the specific representative image words from each of nine categories, a cluster analysis in K-Means method is carried out and each sample's distance to the center of the category which this sample belongs to is obtained. The sample(s) with the minimum distance value among samples in a category can be chosen as the representative image word(s) for the category. The representative image words for all nine categories are preliminarily obtained, including image words 'Layered', 'Prospective', 'Rough', 'Graceful', 'Economical' and 'Sturdy', 'Exciting', 'Distinguished', 'Dynamic', and 'Solemn' that stand for representative(s) for each category, respectively.

By comparing meanings in Chinese of image words in the fifth category and in the seventh category, respectively, it is balanced to define 'Economical' as representative image word for the fifth category and 'Delicate' for the seventh category. In addition, image word 'Favorite' is added to measure the degree of the subjects' preference of IP form. As a result, ten image words, i.e., 'Layered', 'Prospective', 'Rough', 'Graceful', 'Economical', 'Exciting', 'Delicate', 'Dynamic', 'Favorite' and 'Solemn', are extracted from total fifty-six image words from nine categories and selected as final representative image words as listed in Table 3.

2.4 Samples' Distribution and Form Change in the Perceptual Map

With the dissimilarity matrix generated in previous similarity judgment on IP form, the multidimensional scaling is carried out, and as result, the two-dimensional perceptual map of users' perception of ninety-seven IP forms is plotted as shown in Fig. 3. In this figure, the circle marks for the samples in the same category are filled with the same color, and coordinate system is added. The perceptual map reflects the spatial position and form change clues in the cognitive space of users [17].

Furthermore, ninety-seven pictures of IP form samples are printed and placed on a physical plate in the corresponding locations as presented in the perceptual map, and

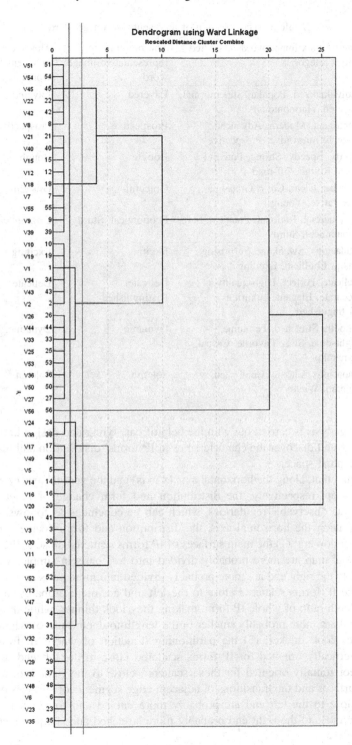

Fig. 2. Dendrogram resulted in cluster analysis for selecting representative image words (Color figure online)

Table 3. The selection of representative image words

Cluster	The fifty-six image words classified into 9 categories	The preliminary representative image words	The selected representative image words
1	Individualized, Popular, Supernormal, Layered, Harmonious	Layered	Layered
2	Intelligent, Modern, Advanced, Hi-tech, Innovative, Prospective	Prospective	Prospective
3	Sporty, Speedy, Strong, Forceful, Hard, Rough, Off-road	Rough	Rough
4	Concise, Clear, Cosy, Graceful, Decorative, Young	Graceful	Graceful
5	Commercial, Rational, Practical, Safe, Economical, Sturdy	Economical, Sturdy	Economical
6	Audacious, Swanking, Surprising, Sharp, Ebullient, Exciting	Exciting	Exciting
7	Delicate, Perfect, High-quality, Accurate, Elegant, Luxurious, Distinguished	Delicate, Distinguished	Delicate
8	Smooth, Stretched, Feminine, Lightsome, Slim, Favorite, Casual, Dynamic	Dynamic	Dynamic, Favorite
9	Capacious, Classic, Unaffected, Solemn, Wieldy	Solemn	Solemn

qualitative analysis is carried out with the help of car styling and design knowledge so as to analyze and discover the characteristics in IP forms' distribution and form shift in users' perceptual space.

It is found that, along the horizontal axis (x axis) and the vertical axis (y axis) in the perceptual map, respectively, the distribution and form change of ninety-seven IP forms indicate observable regularities, which can be concluded as follows.

Firstly, along the horizontal axis, the distribution and form change can be summarized as following: (1) the main surfaces of IP forms scattered close to the left end in the perceptual map are more probably divided into less parts in simpler ways, while those close to the right end are more probably divided into more parts in more complex way; (2) the IP forms scattered close to the left end are more probably larger in the length-to-depth ratio of whole IP form, making they look thinner, while those close to the right end are more probably smaller in the length-to-depth ratio of whole IP form, making they look thicker; (3) the partitioning direction of whole IP form is more probably vertically oriented for IP forms scattered close to the left end, while more probably horizontally oriented for those scattered close to the right end; and (4) the edges of surfaces and the transitions of adjacent edge segments of surfaces of IP forms scattered close to the left end are probably more curved and rounded, respectively, while those close to the right end probably more stretched and sharper, respectively.

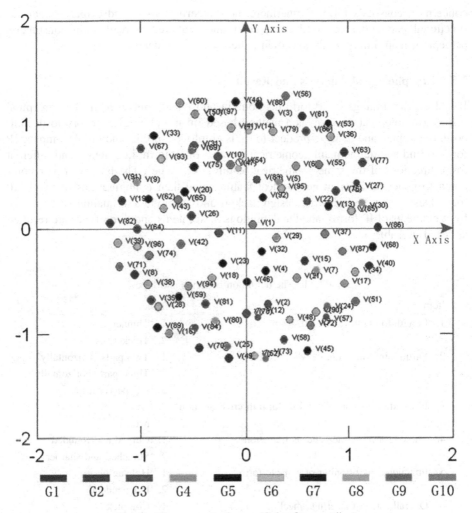

Fig. 3. The perceptual map (Color figure online)

Secondly, along the vertical axis, the distribution and form change can be summarized as following: (1) the central console in IP forms scattered close to the top end bulge more probably out relative to the surfaces of IP forms, while those close to the bottom end are more probably integrated into the IP form; and (2) the central consoles and the IP forms scattered close to the top end are more probably layered and fluctuating in Y0 section, while those close to the bottom end are more probably flattened and smooth in Y0 section.

In summary, two dimensions can be figured clearly in consumers' perceptual space on IP forms of passenger car, which are related to overall feature and functional feature of IP forms, respectively. The former is embodied in partitioning and length-to-depth ratio of whole IP surface, curved or stretched edges of IP surfaces, and round or sharp transitions between the edges of surfaces, while the latter is presented by the difference concerning console's form. Furthermore, both steering wheel and display screen, as functional part and area in IP form, are found scattered at random in consumers' perceptual map, implying its uncertain pattern of form changes.

2.5 Morphological Analysis and Result

Based on the findings in IP form distribution and change unveiled in the perceptual map, morphological analysis as a method based on morphological theory to decompose, recombine and analyze product form, is employed in this study to decompose IP form to find and define main geometrical features of IP form, i.e., 'item', and different form directions of the same geometrical feature, i.e., 'type'. The latter can be recombined to generate different geometrical features and then configurations of whole IP form. Designers with industrial design background are invited to qualitatively analyze form elements of IP forms, and the definitions of six items and thirty types are resulted as listed in Table 4.

Table 4. The definition of items and types

Items	Types
1. 'Length-to-depth ratio of IP form'	1. 'Thinner'
	2. 'Thicker'
2. 'Partitioning direction of whole IP form'	1. 'Two parts horizontally'
	2. 'Three parts horizontally'
	3. 'I-Type vertically'[*]
3. 'Fluctuation of console and IP form in cross section'	1. 'Less'
	2. 'More'
4. 'The edges of surface and its transition'	1. 'Curved and rounded'
	2. 'Stretched and sharper'
5. 'Functional partitioning of console form'	1. 'Holistic'
	2. 'Independent'
6. 'Overall form of steering wheel'	1. 'Complex'
	2. 'Simple'

*Note: 'I-Type' indicates the IP form is partitioned vertically by the relatively independent form of central console extending to the top surface of IP form.

The first four items, i.e., 'Length-to-depth ratio of IP form', 'Partitioning direction of whole IP form', 'Fluctuation of console and IP form in cross section', and 'The edges of surface and its transition', present the overall form feature dimension; the last two items, i.e., 'Functional partitioning of console form' and 'Overall form of steering wheel', present the functional partitioning form feature dimension. For more comprehensively overviewing the form feature of the overall IP component in the interior, the item 'overall form of steering wheel' is taken into consideration and defined as one item because the steering wheel is an important component element occupying a very large fraction of the picture of IP form as viewed from the rear of the interior.

2.6   Orthogonal Experiment Design Plans

Orthogonal experiment design is an effective way to reduce experimental runs and be widely employed in engineering fields. For IP form composition, six items, i.e., 'Length-to-depth ratio of IP form', 'Partitioning direction of whole IP form', 'Fluctuation of console and IP form in cross section', 'The edges of surface and its transition', 'Functional partitioning of console form' and 'Overall form of steering wheel' which are summarized from the morphological analysis, and thirty types are imported to generate sixteen orthogonal experiment design plans, being named Card ID 1 to Card ID 16 as listed in Table 5, respectively.

Table 5. The sixteen orthogonal experiment design plans

Sample ID	Card ID	Item 1	Item 2	Item 3	Item 4	Item 5	Item 6
51	1	Type 2	Type 1	Type 1	Type 1	Type 2	Type 2
28	2	Type 1	Type 1	Type 2	Type 2	Type 2	Type 1
17	3	Type 1	Type 3	Type 2	Type 1	Type 1	Type 2
21	4	Type 1	Type 1	Type 2	Type 2	Type 1	Type 2
94	5	Type 2	Type 2	Type 2	Type 1	Type 1	Type 2
85	6	Type 2	Type 1	Type 1	Type 1	Type 1	Type 1
48	7	Type 2	Type 2	Type 2	Type 1	Type 2	Type 1
56	8	Type 1	Type 1	Type 1	Type 1	Type 1	Type 1
33	9	Type 1	Type 1	Type 1	Type 1	Type 2	Type 2
90	10	Type 2	Type 1	Type 2	Type 2	Type 1	Type 2
24	11	Type 2	Type 3	Type 1	Type 2	Type 2	Type 2
18	12	Type 1	Type 3	Type 2	Type 1	Type 2	Type 1
44	13	Type 1	Type 2	Type 1	Type 2	Type 2	Type 2
64	14	Type 2	Type 3	Type 1	Type 2	Type 1	Type 1
27	15	Type 2	Type 1	Type 2	Type 2	Type 2	Type 1
50	16	Type 1	Type 2	Type 1	Type 2	Type 1	Type 1

According to the form composition of items and types of sixteen orthogonal experiment design plans listed in Table 5, the form compositions of the existing ninety-seven IP form samples are analyzed by morphological analysis to match sixteen orthogonal experiment design plans. It is found that there exist ten IP form samples with corresponding serial number 17, 21, 24, 28, 44, 48, 51, 64, 85 and 94 among all ninety-seven samples, which properly match ten out of sixteen orthogonal experiment design plans, respectively. In addition, other six IP form samples with corresponding serial number 18, 27, 33, 50, 56 and 90 are chosen as left six orthogonal experiment design plans after form direction in a specific type is modified manually, more specifically, transforming form direction under Item 1 for samples No. 18, No. 27 and No. 50 while under Item 2 for samples No. 56 and No. 33, to match corresponding orthogonal experiment design plans.

Fig. 4. Sixteen IP forms corresponding to orthogonal experiment design plans in Card ID order

The IP forms corresponding to final sixteen orthogonal experiment design plans are as shown in Fig. 4. Compared with the results of previous cluster analysis with the averaged similarity on IP forms, it can be observed that these sixteen form plans are relatively evenly distributed in ten categories of IP form, presenting good representative for all IP form samples.

2.7 Semantic Differential Evaluation

The Semantic Differential (SD) method is used in semantic evaluation experiment in this study. The users are invited to fulfil semantic evaluation on IP forms corresponding to final orthogonal experiment design plans from the prospective of each of ten selected representative images, respectively. The subjects complete the evaluation task in a relatively quiet environment, and sixteen pictures of IP forms are printed in appropriate size to ensure that the subjects be able to scan and compare the IP form and its features clearly.

The rating data of subjects' semantic evaluation on sixteen IP forms by each image are recorded. And totally 61 effective pieces of rating data from semantic evaluation experiment are collected, among which 30 pieces are from male subjects and 31 from female subjects both with age of 25 to 35.

2.8 Regression Analysis and Results

With above sixty-one effective pieces of rating data, a multivariate linear regression analysis is carried out to estimate if the image 'Favorite' has dependency on other nine representative images, i.e., 'Layered', 'Prospective', 'Rough', 'Graceful', 'Economical', 'Exciting', 'Delicate', 'Dynamic', and 'Solemn'.

In regression analysis, whether all partial regression coefficients are zero is tested, outputting the ANOVA result as shown in Fig. 5 and indicating that there exists at least one image variable with no-zero partial regression coefficient and the fitted model is statistically significant ($P < 0.001$).

ANOVA[b]

Model		Sum of Squares	df	Mean Square	F	Sig.
1	Regression	6648.746	9	738.750	50.644	.000[a]
	Residual	14091.254	966	14.587		
	Total	20740.000	975			

a. Predictors: (Constant), Solemn, Economical, Layered, Rough, Exciting, Prospective, Dynamic, Graceful, Delicate

b. Dependent Variable: Favorite

Fig. 5. The result of ANOVA

The estimates on partial regression coefficients of variables, i.e., the image 'Solemn', 'Economical', 'Layered', 'Rough', 'Exciting', 'Prospective', 'Dynamic', 'Graceful', and 'Delicate', are also solved as listed in coefficients result in Fig. 6. It can be observed that in the fitted model, for variables named 'Exciting', 'Graceful',

Coefficients[a]

Model	Unstandardized Coefficients		Standardized Coefficients	t	Sig.	Correlations			Collinearity Statistics	
	B	Std. Error	Beta			Zero-order	Partial	Part	Tolerance	VIF
1 (Constant)	1.226	.478		2.564	.010					
Layered	.075	.027	.075	2.782	.006	.157	.089	.074	.968	1.033
Prospective	.066	.029	.066	2.236	.026	.287	.072	.059	.816	1.226
Rough	-.010	.027	-.010	-.359	.719	-.082	-.012	-.010	.935	1.070
Graceful	.180	.030	.180	5.926	.000	.394	.187	.157	.765	1.307
Economical	-.057	.027	-.057	-2.076	.038	-.105	-.067	-.055	.937	1.067
Exciting	.200	.030	.200	6.641	.000	.395	.209	.176	.772	1.296
Delicate	.160	.032	.160	5.017	.000	.402	.159	.133	.690	1.449
Dynamic	.101	.030	.101	3.340	.001	.338	.107	.089	.762	1.312
Solemn	.121	.029	.121	4.220	.000	.286	.135	.112	.858	1.165

a. Dependent Variable: Favorite

Fig. 6. The result of coefficients and collinearity statistics and so on

'Delicate' and 'Solemn', P value is less than 0.001, and all of them have positive coefficient value of 0.200, 0.180, 0.160, and 0.121 in bigger to smaller coefficient order, respectively, indicating these variables play a significant ($P < 0.001$) and positive roles in determining the dependent variable, i.e., the image 'Favorite'.

3 Conclusion

The purpose of this study is to explore what key images affect young Chinese users' preference of IP form, the most important component in passenger car's interior. Based on the data obtained in similarity judgment experiments, and by means of cluster analysis, multidimensional scaling, morphological analysis, and orthogonal experiment design, ten representative images are selected including 'Solemn', 'Economical', 'Layered', 'Rough', 'Exciting', 'Prospective', 'Dynamic', 'Graceful', 'Delicate', and 'Favorite' in users' perceiving the IP form. With the data obtained in SD evaluation experiment on sixteen IP form plans generated, the linear relationship between young Chinese users' preference for IP form from the point of image 'Favorite' and their perception of other nine representative images is regressed.

The result of regression analysis indicates that images including 'Exciting', 'Graceful', 'Delicate' and 'Solemn' are statistically significant sensory desires with positive impact on IP form evaluation of young Chinese users with age of 25 to 35. And as by-product, it is unveiled that users' perception of IP form can be reduced into two-dimensional space, and the perceived difference and form change in users' perceptual map are embodied both in the overall form features such as partitioning way and length-to-depth ratio of whole IP surface, and local ones such as console form.

The findings in this study imply the probability that conveying and strengthening sensory quality in motioned-above four determinant image dimensions in IP form design of passenger car, will be helpful to make young Chinese users prefer one instrumental panel form of passenger car to another in Chinese passenger car market.

References

1. Catalano, C.E., Giannini, F., Monti, M., Ucelli, G.: A framework for the automatic semantic annotation of car aesthetics. Artif. Intell. Eng. Des. Anal. Manuf. **21**, 73–90 (2007)
2. Schmitt, R., Köhler, M., Durá, J.V., et al.: Objectifying user attention and emotion evoked by relevant perceived product components. J. Sens. Sens. Syst. **3**(2), 315–324 (2014)
3. Helander, M.G., Khalid, H.M., Lim, T.Y., Peng, H., Yang, X.: Emotional needs of car buyers and emotional intent of car designers. Theor. Issues Ergon. Sci. **14**(5), 455–474 (2013)
4. Gu, F., Zhao, D.: Construction of the emotional semantic pool for automotive interior design evaluation. Packag. Eng. **37**(20), 30–34 (2016). (in Chinese)
5. Wu, L., Lei, T., Li, J., Li, B.: Skeuomorphism and flat design: evaluating users' emotion experience in car navigation interface design. In: Marcus, A. (ed.) DUXU 2015. LNCS, vol. 9186, pp. 567–575. Springer, Cham (2015). https://doi.org/10.1007/978-3-319-20886-2_53
6. Zeng, Q., Zhao, J., Tan, H.: Mood board tool and methods in vehicle HMI interaction design. Packag. Eng. **35**(22), 22–26 (2014). (in Chinese)

7. Liu, C., Zhu, X.: A review on in-vehicle information system design based on gesture interaction. Zhuangshi **5**, 100–102 (2016). (in Chinese)
8. Mao, L.: A study on user experience design for automobile's interior. Master's thesis, Nanjing University of Science & Technology, Nanjing (2012). (in Chinese)
9. Wu, Y.: The construction of security on vehicle design. Zhuangshi **4**, 135–136 (2013). (in Chinese)
10. Liu, L., Tang, J., Gao, J.: Research on automobile interior design based on operation process of Kansei Engineering. Modern Manuf. Eng. **11**, 94–98 (2010). (in Chinese)
11. Leder, H., Carbon, C.C.: Dimensions in appreciation of car interior design. Appl. Cogn. Psychol. **19**(5), 603–618 (2005)
12. Karlsson, B.S.A., Aronsson, N., Svensson, K.A.: Using semantic environment description as a tool to evaluate car interiors. Ergonomics **46**(13–14), 1408–1422 (2003)
13. Analysis of the ratio of potential car buyers for the first time to car consumers in different types. http://www.chyxx.com/industry/201711/580329.html. Accessed 15 Jan 2018
14. China Statistical Yearbook. http://www.stats.gov.cn/tjsj/ndsj/2017/indexch.htm. Accessed 15 Jan 2018
15. Car sales ranking list. http://price.pcauto.com.cn/top/k0.html. Accessed 15 Jan 2018
16. Zhang, W.: Advanced Course of Statistical Analysis Using SPSS, pp. 235–260. Higher Education Press, Beijing (2004). (in Chinese)
17. Liu, C., Zhu, X.: Young consumers' perception of form style of passenger cars. Packag. Eng. **37**(24), 6–10 (2016). (in Chinese)

Young Chinese Consumers' Perception of Passenger Car Form in Rear View

Chunrong Liu[✉], Yi Jin, Xiaoguo Ding, and Yang Xie

Shanghai Jiao Tong University, Shanghai 200240, China
cheeronliu@sjtu.edu.cn

Abstract. It aims to explore the perception of passenger car form in rear view of young Chinese consumers as the main force in China's passenger car market. Young Chinese consumers as subjects are invited to estimate the similarity of eighty form samples of triple-compartment passenger car form in rear view selected by engine displacement and brand. Then seven form categories are classified by cluster analysis and consumers' perceptual map is plotted by multidimensional scaling, respectively. The gradual form change related to the distribution of eighty form samples in the perceptual map is further analyzed qualitatively. It is found that (1) in their cognitive process, young Chinese consumers perceive and judge the passenger car form in rear view and its variation by both overall and local form features. The former are features including ratio of height to width, stiff or round style, and richness of details and sense of depth in trail, while the latter are ones such as taillights, the blend between side window and the side of body, and the upper surface of trunk; and (2) the degree of variance in the form in rear view of passenger cars in current Chinese market is limited since the samples in each of seven categories are distributed dispersedly in the perceptual map.

Keywords: Passenger car form in rear view · Consumer research
The perceptual map · Quantitative and qualitative analyses

1 Introduction

People make value judgments mainly by visual information [1]. Consumers' perception of passenger car form also starts from the visual appearance of car body form. In China, passenger car form has been the fourth most important factor among fourteen main factors that affect consumers' purchase decisions [2]. Passenger car form that fulfills the expectations of consumers can not only cause the consumers' attention and the emotion of pleasure, but stimulate consumers' purchase decisions and behaviors.

Numerous studies have been carried out on car form and related consumers' perception and behaviors in the following topics: (1) in the field of sensory engineering, studies focus mainly on consumer preference of passenger car form and its image, evaluation model and quantitative consumer's cognition, involving in the difference of form and image preference between male and female consumers [3–5], form preference analysis of female user groups [6], autobody form evaluation model [7, 8], imagery processing

© Springer International Publishing AG, part of Springer Nature 2018
A. Marcus and W. Wang (Eds.): DUXU 2018, LNCS 10920, pp. 329–341, 2018.
https://doi.org/10.1007/978-3-319-91806-8_25

and aesthetic cognition [9, 10], evaluation on the attractiveness of passenger car form [11, 12], contextual collaboration in car styling [13], car styling development based on consumers' preferences [14], and semantic-oriented car styling [15]; (2) in the field of branding and product identification, studies involve in form genes of specific brands, recognition of consumer's perception, consumer's perception towards car brands [16], car recognition rate and consumer's perception based on the archetype theory [17], design strategy for enhancing brand recognition and consumers' long-term memory [18], aesthetic features' influence on consumer's perception of brands [19], styling DNA design methodologies [20], and semantic feature extraction and visualization of passenger car form genes of specific brands [21] and so on; (3) in the field of form perception, studies involve in consumer's form perception model, form perception differences between designers and consumers [22], side-view form perception [23], perceptual modeling based on fuzzy rules [24], form design reference model [25], consumer's expression mode for describing car form [26], feeling quality of car profiles [27], car form prototype fitting [28], automobile sketch design [29], formative elements of car styling [30], and design language of passenger car form [31]; and (4) in addition, some studies involve in passenger car form design trends [32], evolution in automotive styling design [33], and the relationship between car form design and culture [34, 35].

In general, these studies usually pay attention to consumer's perception of overall car form viewed from specific angles such as front quarter view [36], front view [37], side view [38, 39], while some local forms in car form such as the headlight, the rearview mirror and wheel hub [40, 41] are studied as well.

It has been proven by first author's team that, when taking a close look at and perceiving the passenger car form, Chinese consumers concern most the appearance of passenger car form in front quarter view among the most regular five viewing angles of passenger car form [42], i.e., side view, front view, rear view, and rear quarter view in addition to front quarter view. At the same time, however, it is observed that the difference between the Prominence values of four viewing angle factors, i.e., side view, front view, rear view, and rear quarter view, is small because the Prominence values of these four factors are very close [42]. This implies that it is also necessary to explore the consumers' perception of passenger car form at different viewing angles including rear view. Meanwhile, there exist numerous brands and models of passenger cars in current Chinese domestic market, and the sales volume of passenger cars with engine displacements between 1.6 L to 2.0 L has a rising tendency since 2009 [43]. Meanwhile, passenger car consumers in China tend to be younger obviously [44]. In this context, focusing on passenger car form in rear view with engine displacements between 1.5 L to 2.4 L in Chinese market in 2016, subjects aged 18 to 30 including undergraduate and graduate students, professionals from different industries are invited and investigated to explore the cognitive features of young consumers on passenger car form in rear view.

2   Method

2.1   Preparatory Phase

Eighty pictures of form samples of passenger car form in rear view are collected from websites such as online forums, involving in thirty major brands (or sub-brands) in Chinese passenger car market, including BBAC (Beijing Benz), Beijing-Hyundai, BYD, Changan Ford, Changan-Mazda, Changan, Great Wall, Dongfeng-Honda, Dongfeng-Peugeot, Dongfeng-Nissan, Dongfeng-Citroen, Dongfeng, Dongfeng-Yueda-Kia, GAC-Honda, GAC-Toyota, GAC, Qoros, BMW-Brilliance, Chery, SAIC Volkswagen, SAIC-GM (Buick and Chevrolet included), SAIC MG, SAIC Roewe, FAW Audi, FAW-VW, FAW-Toyota, FAW Hongqi, FAW-Mazda and FAW.

All pictures are selected ensuring that they were photographed visually at as same angle as possible in order to reduce experimental error in the later investigation phase. Furthermore, in order to avoid the possibility that car body color will distract the subjects from passenger car form presented in the pictures, all pictures are converted into black-and-white color mode, and passenger car form in each picture is presented centrally on the white background while the brand logo and license plate in each picture are removed (some examples of processed pictures are as shown in Fig. 1). Finally, all eighty pictures of form samples of passenger car form in rear view are marked randomly with serial numbers of V1, V2, ⋯ , V79, V80.

Fig. 1. An interface of grouping task tool

2.2   Investigation Phase

In this phase, a number of consumers as subjects are invited to take part in the investigation into the similarity between eighty form samples. Every subject is kindly asked to estimate on the similarity between any pair of form samples in eighty pictures and to classify eighty pictures according to his/her own judgment with an interactive tool developed by the first author's team [36, 38] for grouping task as shown in Fig. 1. One piece of similarity matrix data is generated by the tool after a subject completed his/her trial and evaluation. Totally, thirty-nine pieces of effective data are collected, consisting of twenty pieces of data from male subjects and nineteen from female subjects.

3   The Results of Quantitative and Qualitative Analyses

3.1   Cluster Analysis

An averaged similarity matrix is obtained by averaging original similarity matrices acquired in the investigation phase, and it is then analyzed by hierarchical cluster analysis method and a dendrogram as result is plotted.

By observing and analyzing the dendrogram, it is reasonable to classify eighty passenger car forms into seven categories according to the related cluster analysis principle [45] that in cluster analysis process, it is ideal for all samples to be classified as 'evenly' as possible into categories (although it is usually difficult). The seven categories are named G1, G2, G3, G4, G5, G6, and G7, including 11 samples, 13 samples, 9 samples, 12 samples, 12 samples, 10 samples, and 13 samples, respectively.

3.2   Multidimensional Scaling

A dissimilarity matrix can be obtained by transforming the mentioned-above average similarity matrix, and the perceptual map is plotted as shown in Fig. 2 by multidimensional scaling method using this dissimilarity matrix. By perceptual mapping, all subjects' averaged judgment on the dissimilarity, i.e., the distance measurements between samples of passenger car form in rear view, is mapped into a two-dimensional consumers' perceptual space where eighty form samples are distributed. In the perceptual map shown in Fig. 2, all passenger car form samples in each of seven categories are illustrated in a specific color and the samples in the same category are marked by the same color.

In the addition, the distribution range of the samples from each category of G1 to G7 is outlined in the perceptual map, respectively, as shown in Fig. 3. It can be observed that the samples from each of categories are dispersed in the two-dimensional perceptual space.

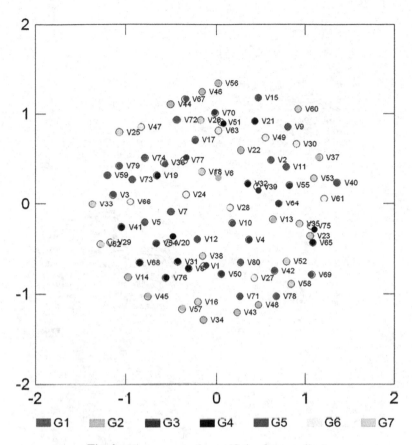

Fig. 2. The perceptual map (Color figure online)

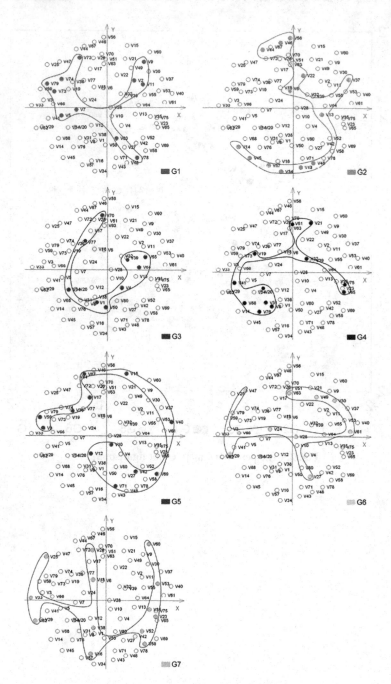

Fig. 3. The distribution of samples in each of seven categories in the perceptual map

3.3 Qualitative Analysis of Form's Distribution and Gradual Change in the Perceptual Map

To probe into the properties in the distribution and transition of passenger car form in rear view in consumers' perceptual space, all eighty form samples' pictures are printed and placed on a physical plate in the corresponding locations as presented in the perceptual map. The qualitative analysis process is completed with the help of knowledge in related car styling and design field.

It is found that in the perceptual map, along the horizontal axis (x axis), the vertical axis (y axis), and the x' axis and y' axis by rotating x axis and y axis 45° counterclockwise, respectively, the distribution and gradual change of passenger car form in rear view indicate certain regularities which are concluded and illustrated as shown in Fig. 4 (the xoy coordinate system and x'oy' coordinate system are outlined in this figure to facilitate the description below) and further discussed in details as follows.

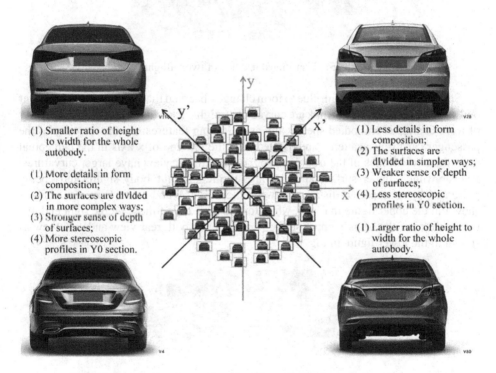

(1) Smaller ratio of height to width for the whole autobody.

(1) More details in form composition;
(2) The surfaces are divided in more complex ways;
(3) Stronger sense of depth of surfaces;
(4) More stereoscopic profiles in Y0 section.

(1) Less details in form composition;
(2) The surfaces are divided in simpler ways;
(3) Weaker sense of depth of surfaces;
(4) Less stereoscopic profiles in Y0 section.

(1) Larger ratio of height to width for the whole autobody.

Fig. 4. Sample locations and gradual form change in the perceptual map

Form Changes Along the X Axis. Firstly, there is a certain clue to form change observed that whether or not there exist continuous transitional edges, i.e., curves and lines as edges' projection in rear view, between the upper outlines of two taillights and the upper decorative part above the license plate area, implying the form feature whether or not there is a morphological link of two taillights. This property of form change is embodied specifically as following features: for the majority of the passenger car forms scattered and located onto the left end of x axis in the perceptual map, there is a continuous transition between taillights' outlines and decorative parts' edges as shown in the upper figure in Fig. 5, while for the majority of those on the right end, there is no continuous transition feature but an apparent discontinuity or positional transition as shown in the lower figure in Fig. 5.

Fig. 5. Transitional features of two taillights

Secondly, there is a certain clue to form change observed that the upper and the lower outlines of upper surface of trunk are curved or straight shape in rear view. This property of form change is embodied specifically as following features: for the majority of the passenger car forms scattered and located onto the left end of x axis in the perceptual map, the two outlines of the trunk's upper surface in rear view have larger curvatures, and the trunk's upper surface slide towards the rear of autobody significantly being presented by an apparent distance between the curve A and curve B in rear view as shown in the upper figure in Fig. 6, while for the majority of those on the right end, the two outlines of the trunk's upper surface are flatter in both rear view and side view as shown in the lower figure in Fig. 6.

Fig. 6. Curved and flat shape features of trunk's upper surface

Thirdly, there is a certain clue to form change observed that the whole outline of the taillight is profiled as a combination of curved or flatter segments in rear view. This property of form change is embodied specifically as following features: for the majority of the passenger car forms scattered and located onto the left end of x axis in the perceptual map, the whole outline of a taillight is mainly composed of curves connecting each other smoothly at intersecting point with less acute angles as shown in the left figure in Fig. 7, while for the majority of those on the right end, the taillight's whole outline is mainly composed of stretched and flatter curves/lines connecting each other with sharp angles as shown in the right figure in Fig. 7. This finding shows that consumers consider a local feature, i.e., the outline shape of taillight form in rear view, as a basis for evaluating the similarity between passenger car forms in rear view.

Fig. 7. Taillight's outline features

Form Changes Along the Y Axis. Firstly, there is a certain regularity in form change observed in the degree of roundness of passenger car form in rear view. This property of form change is embodied specifically as following features: for the majority of the passenger car forms scattered and located onto the upper end of y axis in the perceptual map, the adjacent surfaces intersect at stiffer and flatter edges' profile as viewed from the rear and the angles between adjacent surfaces are smaller with clear transitional edges as shown in the left figure in Fig. 8, while for the majority of those scattered and located onto the lower end of y axis in the perceptual map, the angles between surfaces are larger with smoother transition and more curved profiles as viewed from the rear as shown in the right figure in Fig. 8.

Fig. 8. Stiff and round features in the overall form

Secondly, there is a certain regularity in form change observed in autobody's shoulder area, conveying the relationship between the side window surface and side autobody surface of passenger car form in rear view. This property of form change is embodied specifically as following features: for the majority of the passenger car forms scattered and located onto the upper end of y axis in the perceptual map, the surfaces of side window and the side of autobody in rear view blend smoothly without acute angles as shown in the left figure in Fig. 9, while for the majority of those scattered and located onto the lower end of y axis in the perceptual map, those surfaces intersect with clear or acute transition as shown in the right figure in Fig. 9.

Fig. 9. Relation features of side window and the side of body in rear view

Form Changes Along the X' Axis and the Y' Axis. The certain regularities in form change along the x' axis and y' axis, respectively, in the perceptual map are discovered by qualitative analysis.

Firstly, for the majority of the passenger car forms scattered and located onto the negative end of x' axis in the perceptual map as shown in Fig. 4, they have more stereoscopic profiles in Y0 section due to the more bumped flows and ups and downs of surfaces and its transitions, and the surfaces of rear autobody form are divided in more complex manner resulting in richness of details in trail form composition and stronger sense of depth of surfaces. On the contrary, for the majority of the passenger car forms scattered and located onto the positive end of x' axis in the perceptual map as shown in Fig. 4, they have less bumped profiles in Y0 section due to the less ups and downs of surfaces and its transitions while the surfaces of rear autobody form are divided in simpler ways resulting in less details in form composition.

Secondly, by observing all eighty pictures of passenger car forms along the y' axis, it is observed that there is a significant regular variation of ratio of height to width. This property of form change is embodied specifically as following features: the passenger car forms scattered and located onto the negative end of y' axis in the perceptual map look more probably taller by maintaining a larger ratio of height to width for the whole autobody as shown in Fig. 4, while the majority of those scattered and located onto the positive end of y' axis look shorter due to a smaller ratio of height to width for the whole autobody as shown in Fig. 4.

4   Conclusion

In the fiercely competitive Chinese market of passenger cars with mainstream 1.5 L to 2.4 L engine displacements, it is a make-or-break necessity for automakers and its design studios to understand the perceptual characteristics of passenger car form of young Chinese consumers as the main force in China's passenger car market and form's dissimilarity and variance exposed in their morphological cognition. In this study, their perception of passenger car form in rear view is investigated by quantitatively analyzing data with cluster analysis and by qualitatively examining the clues to morphological shifts in the perceptual map derived from multidimensional scaling.

It is found that there exist observable regularities, i.e., the differential form features and gradual changes, in young consumers' perceptual mapping of passenger car form in rear view when evaluating the similarity between the form samples. On the one hand, it reflects obviously young consumers' cognitive ability of identifying the dissimilarity of passenger car form in rear view. On the other hand, it shows that as viewed from the rear, there is certain difference between the production models in current triple-compartment passenger car market segment in China.

The perceived differential form features and gradual changes are determined by both overall and local form features as shown in Fig. 4 in details, which have influence on young consumers' perception of passenger car form in rear view. In general, however, the dispersed distributions of form samples for all categories in the perceptual map implies probably that this kind of difference is limited among the production models in current Chinese passenger car market segment.

These findings imply that intentional design differentiation for targeted young consumers by means of both the local and overall form features in rear view while considering form coordination, is helpful for an automaker to distinguish its own passenger car form in rear view and product identity from competitors.

References

1. Kantowitz, B.H., Roediger, H.I., Elmes, D.G.: Experimental Psychology. East China Normal University Press, Shanghai (2001). (in Chinese)
2. Yang, F.: A study of the influence of passenger car styling on consumer purchase decision. Master's thesis, Shanghai Jiao Tong University, Shanghai (2016). (in Chinese)
3. Li, M., Lu, Z., Huang, L.: Imagery cognition of automobile form based on eye movement tracking and semantic differential methods. Art Educ. (4), 212–214 (2016). (in Chinese)
4. Yu, D.: A study on the factors of automobile styling with preferences of young people in China. In: Computer-Aided Industrial Design and Conceptual Design, vol. 2, pp. 1022–1027. IEEE, Yiwu (2011)
5. Yoon, H.K., Fu, K., Zhou, J., et al.: Chinese sensitivity analysis for a compact car exterior design. Sens. Sci. **15**(2), 317–327 (2012)
6. Yang, L., Cheng, Z.: Female psychology, consumption preference and automobile form design. Mod. Decor. (Theory Ed.) (3), 136 (2015). (in Chinese)
7. Fu, L., Yu, H., Li, X.: Projection principle and evaluation model of autobody surface modeling cognition-intention. J. Jilin Univ. (Eng. Technol. Ed.) **45**(1), 49–54 (2015). (in Chinese)
8. Jing, C., Zhao, J.: The automobile modeling evaluation from the perspective of product experience. Packag. Eng. **35**(22), 17–21 (2014). (in Chinese)
9. Hu, T., Zhao, J., Zhao, D.: Pattern study of design imagery processing and aesthetic cognition. Zhuangshi (2), 104–105 (2015). (in Chinese)

10. Jagtap, S., Jagtap, S.: Aesthetic design process: descriptive design research and ways forward. In: Chakrabarti, A. (ed.) ICoRD 2015 – Research into Design Across Boundaries Volume 1. SIST, vol. 34, pp. 375–385. Springer, New Delhi (2015). https://doi.org/10.1007/978-81-322-2232-3_33

11. Chang, H.C., Lai, H.H., Chang, Y.M.: A measurement scale for evaluating the attractiveness of a passenger car form aimed at young consumers. Int. J. Ind. Ergon. **37**(1), 21–30 (2007)

12. Chang, H.C., Chen, H.Y.: Optimizing product form attractiveness using Taguchi method and TOPSIS algorithm: a case study involving a passenger car. Concur. Eng. Res. Appl. **22**(2), 135–147 (2014)

13. Yusof, W.Z.M., Hasri, M., Ujang, B.: Innovation in form generation: anthropomorphism for contextual collaboration in car styling. In: Abidin, S.Z., Legino, R., Noor, H.M., Vermol, V.V., Anwar, R., Kamaruzaman, M.F. (eds.) Proceedings of the 2nd International Colloquium of Art and Design Education Research (i-CADER 2015), pp. 189–204. Springer, Singapore (2016). https://doi.org/10.1007/978-981-10-0237-3_20

14. Jiang, C.: Styling and development of heavy truck based on the study of consumers' preferences. Master's thesis, Shanghai Jiao Tong University, Shanghai (2013). (in Chinese)

15. Wang, B., Li, B.J., Hu, P., et al.: Semantic-oriented shape exploration for car styling. In: 2014 5th International Conference on Digital Home, pp. 368–373. IEEE (2014)

16. Pednekar, A.P.: Empirical study of consumer perception towards select car brands. J. Commer. Manag. Thought **4**(4), 837–842 (2013)

17. Zhu, Y., Zhao, J.: Automobile modeling based on archetype theory. Packag. Eng. **35**(6), 24–28 (2014). (in Chinese)

18. Lu, Z., Zhang, Y., Cheng, B., et al.: A study on the cognitive mechanism of car styling based on style feature. Automot. Eng. **38**(3), 280–287 (2016). (in Chinese)

19. Ranscombe, C., Hicks, B., Mullineux, G., et al.: Visually decomposing vehicle images: exploring the influence of different aesthetic features on consumer perception of brand. Des. Stud. **33**(4), 319–341 (2012)

20. Abidin, S.Z., Othman, A., Shamsuddin, Z., et al.: The challenges of developing styling DNA design methodologies for car design. In: 16th International Conference on Engineering and Product Design Education, pp. 738–743, University of Twente, The Netherlands (2014)

21. Hu, W., Chen, L., Liu, S., et al.: Research on the extraction and visualization of vehicle brand form gene. Mach. Des. Res. **27**(2), 65–68, 79 (2011). (in Chinese)

22. Hu, T., Zhao, J., Zhao, D.: Imagery cognition differences between designers and users on automobile modeling. Packag. Eng. **36**(24), 33–36 (2015). (in Chinese)

23. Huang, D.: Research on side-view forms of sedans based on the form dynamic theory of visual perception. Master's thesis, Shanghai Jiao Tong University, Shanghai (2015). (in Chinese)

24. Wan, X.R., Che, J.M., Han, L.: Car styling perceptual modeling based on fuzzy rules. Appl. Mech. Mater. **201–202**, 794–797 (2012)

25. Chuang, M.C., Chang, C.C., Hsu, S.H.: Perceptual factors underlying user preferences toward product form of mobile phones. Int. J. Ind. Ergon. **27**(4), 247–258 (2001)

26. Chang, H.C., Lai, H.H., Chang, Y.M.: Expression modes used by consumers in conveying desire for product form: a case study of a car. Int. J. Ind. Ergon. **36**(1), 3–10 (2006)

27. Lai, H.H., Chang, Y.M., Chang, H.C.: A robust design approach for enhancing the feeling quality of a product: a car profile case study. Int. J. Ind. Ergon. **35**(5), 445–460 (2005)

28. Li, R., Dong, S.: Styling aiding methods based on emotional words and car styling prototype fitting. Packag. Eng. **37**(20), 25–29 (2016). (in Chinese)

29. Huang, Q., Sun, S.: Research on automobile sketch design based on image cognition model. J. Zhejiang Univ. (Eng. Sci.) **40**(4), 553–559 (2006). (in Chinese)

30. Li, Z., Xia, J.: A quantitative method on formative elements optimization of car styling design. Adv. Mater. Res. **118**, 748–752 (2010)
31. Gao, S.: Research on design language of affecting image cognition of automobile form. Packag. Eng. (2), 65–69 (2012). (in Chinese)
32. Zhu, X., Liu, C.: Fashion trend in automobile design. Art Sci. Technol. **27**(3), 254, 266 (2014). (in Chinese)
33. Huang, Z.: Research on evolution of automotive design style. Master's thesis, Shanghai Jiao Tong University, Shanghai (2010). (in Chinese)
34. Huang, Z.: Modern car design and traditional culture. Art Des. (Theory) (1), 184–186 (2010). (in Chinese)
35. Bluntzer, J.B., Ostrosi, E., Sagot, J.C.: Styling of cars: is there a relationship between the style of cars and the culture identity of a specific country? Proc. IMechE Part D: J. Automob. Eng. **229**, 38–51 (2015)
36. Liu, C., Zhu, X.: Young consumers' perception of form style of passenger cars. Packag. Eng. **37**(24), 6–10 (2016). (in Chinese)
37. Zhang, Y., Lu, Z.: A design method of automobile front face for users' cognizance. J. Graph. **34**(5), 93–98 (2013). (in Chinese)
38. Liu, C.: Design Strategy Development for Product Innovation. Shanghai Jiao Tong University Press, Shanghai (2015). (in Chinese)
39. Yao, X., Hu, H.Y., Li, J.: Kansei engineering in automotive body-side styling design. In: 2011 IEEE 18th International Conference on Industrial Engineering and Engineering Management, vol. 1, pp. 143–147. IEEE, Changchun (2011)
40. Luo, S.J., Fu, Y.T., Zhou, Y.X.: Perceptual matching of shape design style between wheel hub and car type. Int. J. Ind. Ergon. **42**, 90–102 (2012)
41. Fan, D., Wang, X., Zhou, M.: Perception of car's wheel hub based on principal component analysis. Sci. Technol. Inf. (10), 119–120 (2010). (in Chinese)
42. Liu, G., Huang, D., Liu, C.: Preference of car form feature based on DEMATEL method. China Packag. Ind. (24), 34–36 (2014). (in Chinese)
43. Comprehensive data analysis of automobile market (2016). http://auto.sohu.com/20160124/n435664393.shtml. Accessed 24 Jan 2016. (in Chinese)
44. The influence of slowing growth of Chinese macroeconomics in 2016 on automobile sales and characteristics, demand and capacity of consumer populations. http://www.chyxx.com/industry/201612/476907.html. Accessed 18 Dec 2017. (in Chinese)
45. Zhang, W.: Advanced Course of Statistical Analysis in SPSS, pp. 235–247. Higher Education Press, Beijing (2004). (in Chinese)

A Method of Car Styling Evaluation
Based on Eye Tracking

Zhaolin Lu[1,2(✉)], Shaobing Xu[2], and Bo Cheng[2]

[1] Department of Art and Design, Hefei University, Hefei 230601, China
luzhaolin9807@gmail.com
[2] Department of Automotive Engineering,
State Key Laboratory of Automotive Safety and Energy,
Tsinghua University, Beijing 100084, China

Abstract. In order to remedy the weakness of traditional subjective evaluation method and acquire the users' objective assessment on automotive form design, a method of Auto form evaluation based on eye tracking is proposed. First, the index system is structured on the basis of heatmap including striping the background, extracting color characters by HSV model and calculating the statistic of grey level histogram. Second, the evaluation on auto form is defined as binary classification, and the function model is built by Fisher discriminate. The reliability and practicality of this method was validated by taking a case. The result showed that overall accuracy of this method was high. So a feasible technical approach for the rapid evaluation of automotive styling is provided.

Keywords: Car styling · Evaluation methods · Eye tracking · Feature extraction · Discriminate function

1 Introduction

2013' Survey of China Association of Automobile Manufacturers showed that more than 75% China users considered the physical appearance as the primary determinant factor when they planed to purchase cars [1]. Whether a car is accepted by the market depends largely on whether the car's styling design can win the praise of consumers. Usually users' ultimate psychological aesthetic evaluation originates from the car appearance recognition through the access of product images. On top of this, in recent years, the studies of car styling design involve two main aspects: design methodology and design evaluation.

Researcher Yadav et al. proposed a fuzzy approach which has been adopted for calculation of the relative importance of different aesthetic attributes; this proposed method has been illustrated using customer survey data and four out of 12 aesthetic attributes were found to be attractive [2]. It is very important for the current automobile industry to establish matching rules between wheel hubs and car types Luo et al., For the purpose of providing guidelines for wheel hubs selection, therefore, a case study on 6 typical types of cars and 20 wheel hubs was presented, examined their shape design styles and accordingly proposed a methodology for evaluating the perceptual matching

© Springer International Publishing AG, part of Springer Nature 2018
A. Marcus and W. Wang (Eds.): DUXU 2018, LNCS 10920, pp. 342–350, 2018.
https://doi.org/10.1007/978-3-319-91806-8_26

quality [3]. In order to examine how companies strategically employ design to create visual recognition of their brands' core values, researchers Karjalainen carried out an explorative in-depth case study concerning the strategic design efforts of Volvo, and it was found that the company fostered design philosophies that lay out which approach to design and which design features are expressive of the core brand values [4].

About car design evaluation, a fuzzy Technique for Order Preference by Similarity to Ideal Solution (TOPSIS) approach which was integrated triangular fuzzy number, linguistic variables and TOPSIS was proposed to generate the overall performance score for each alternative, and the alternative with the highest score was finally chosen Zhang et al. [5]. In industry, design selection and refinement decisions are frequently based on consumers' one-time aesthetic impressions of a proposed design, so researchers Coughlan et al. reports on a study in which the same group of people were asked to evaluate a design prototype on two separate occasions at a 3-month interval, and the results reveal that their perceptions of a design concept appear to change with repeated exposure [6].

In general, the deficiencies exist in the previous study of car styling evaluation as following: ① Car form elements are usually interrelated, and then it is difficult to define them independently. So, the simple evaluation accumulation of the car form elements does not provide a complete result because users' comprehensive cognitive processing is based on overall product image. ② The evaluation to product design is fundamentally a kind of subjective description and perceptual knowledge based on intrinsic and external performance of products, although the previous study shows that the product image can be quantified. So this evaluation is still some kind description to the ambiguity phenomenon with individual differences. And the objective criteria are still lacked.

This paper presents a car styling evaluation method based on eye tracking feature, including: ① The IISV model is used to extract the color features and compute the statistic value of gray histogram. ② The car styling evaluation is defined as a problem of dichotomous, hence the discriminate function is constructed. Accordingly, the overall evaluation of car appearance modeling is realized and the objectivity standard is established.

2   Research Framework

Research shows that 80%–90% external information of human is obtained by visual sense. Since the middle of the 20th century, with the application of camera technology, especially the development of high-precision eye tracker, the research to eye movement in related disciplines is greatly promoted [7]. According to the previous study, the human eye movement mainly includes three ways: ① Fixation; ② Saccade; ③ Follow. The main parameters of eye tracking include: ① number of fixation points; ② fixation time; ③ fixation frequency; ④ fixation time ratio; ⑤ scan path; ⑥ first fixation point. With static forward range reaching 180°, users can quickly scan the features while observing the car shape. At the same time, the information processing of "feature bundling" is performed in the human brain. Therefore, the cognitive process of information can be obtained by eye tracking experiment, and overall evaluation to a car styling can be done.

2.1   Index System Establishment Based on Heatmap

In order to be applied in practice expediently, a large number of eye tracking data needs to be processed in a reasonable visualization manner to intuitively express the spatial and temporal distribution characteristics of eye movement data. At present, the main processing ways include: scanning path method, heatmap method, Area of interest method, three-dimensional space method, Andrienko et al. [8]. For the evaluation of car styling, the key is to measure the attractiveness index of the car features to the visual sense and compare the intensity of the influence of every feature on the image cognition. Heatmap can be used to find the most attractive visual object to the user, easily compare the intensity of product features, and it has the advantage of supporting multi-user data display. Therefore, the indicator system will be built based on heatmap in this paper.

Step 1. Color Feature Extraction.   In order to coincide with human eye characteristics, the heatmap RGB model need to be transferred into HSV color model. In this HSV model, H represents color, $H \in [0, 360]$; S represents saturation, $S \in [0, 1]$; V represents brightness, $V \in [0, 1]$. Since the value of saturation and brightness in heatmaps are set to fixed, the chromaticity value is extracted as the color feature. Furthermore, the mean value of chromaticity, K is used as an indicator, i.e.

$$K = \frac{1}{N} \sum_{m=0}^{N} K_m \tag{1}$$

In formula (1), N is the total number of pixels in the heatmaps, and K_m is the chromaticity value corresponding to the m_{th} pixel.

Step 2. Gray Scale Histogram Feature Extraction.   In order to obtain the further information, in this paper the method of gray histogram feature extraction is adopted to process the heatmaps. The grayscale histogram is essentially a discrete function representing the gray level, i.e.

$$H(i) = \frac{n_i}{N}, i = 0, 1, \ldots \ldots L - 1 \tag{2}$$

In the formula (2), i represents the gray scale, L represents the number of gray levels (0 to 255), n_i represents the number of pixels which have the gray scale i in the heatmap, and N represents the total number of pixels of the heatmaps. Based on above, the index system is established by statistical feature as shown in Table 1:

Table 1. Statistical indicators based on gray histogram

Indicator name	Interpretation	Calculation formula
Mean Value of Gray Scale	The average gray level of the image	$\mu = \sum\limits_{i=0}^{L-1} iH(i)$
Variance	The discrete distribution of image gray value	$\sigma^2 = \sum\limits_{i=0}^{L-1} (i - \mu)^2 H(i)$
Skewness	The asymmetry degree of the image histogram distribution	$\mu_S = \dfrac{1}{\sigma^3} \sum\limits_{i=0}^{L-1} (i - \mu)^3 H(i)$
Peak State	The state of the gray distribution of the image close to the mean	$\mu_K = \dfrac{1}{\sigma^4} \sum\limits_{i=0}^{L-1} (i - \mu)^4 H(i) - 3$
Energy	The uniformity of the squared gray distribution	$\mu_N = \sum\limits_{i=0}^{L-1} H(i)^2$
Entropy	The uniformity of histogram grayscale distribution	$\mu_E = - \sum\limits_{i=0}^{L-1} H(i) \log_2 [H(i)]$

2.2 Sample Classification for Car Styling

The evaluation of car styling can be regarded as a process of samples classification essentially. That is, car styling would be divided into several levels such as not bad, good, very good and so on by the indexes. In the actual application, Two-Classifications which mean Auto forms are divided into two categories of G1 and G2 is implemented easily. For example, Auto form is divided into "high degree of recognition" and "low degree of recognition". Further the two categories of Auto form will be compared in order to sum up the design method of vehicle recognition, and the new vehicle model of the identification will be forecasted. Thus, in this article the definition is as following:

Definition 1. Let the set of vehicle samples be $C = \{C_1, C_2, C_3 \dots C_n\}$, and the index of the color feature and the gray scale histogram feature from the vehicle samples heatmap are regarded as characteristics. So the set of characteristics is $X = \{X_1, X_2, X_3, X_4, X_5, X_6, X_7\}$. In the set, X_1 is Mean Value of Gray Scale (μ); X_2 is Variance (σ^2); X_3 is Skewness (μ_S); X_4 is the Peak State (μ_K); X_5 is the Energy (μ_N); X_6 is Entropy (μ_E); X_7 is mean value of chromaticity (K). The values above form a 7-row, n-column matrix:

$$\begin{bmatrix} X_{11} & X_{21} & X_{31} & \cdots & X_{n1} \\ X_{12} & X_{22} & X_{32} & \cdots & X_{n2} \\ X_{13} & X_{23} & X_{33} & \cdots & X_{n3} \\ X_{14} & X_{24} & X_{34} & \cdots & X_{n4} \\ X_{15} & X_{25} & X_{35} & \cdots & X_{n5} \\ X_{16} & X_{26} & \cdots & \cdots & X_{n6} \\ X_{17} & \cdots & \cdots & \cdots & X_{n7} \end{bmatrix} \qquad (3)$$

For a vehicle model $C_j \in C(1 \leq j \leq n)$, its characteristics set is $\{X_{j1}, X_{j2}, X_{j3}, X_{j4}, X_{j5}, X_{j6}, X_{j7}\}$. So the Eigen-values can be composed of a seven-dimensional eigenvector values:

$$X_j = \left(x_1, x_2, x_3, x_4, x_5, x_6, x_7\right)^{\mathsf{T}} \tag{4}$$

Definition 2. A linear discriminate function is established for vehicle models in the following form:

$$d(x) = w_1 x_1 + w_2 x_2 + w_3 x_3 + \dots + w_7 x_7 + w_8 \tag{5}$$

In the formula (5), $d(x)$ represents the discriminate value; $x_1, x_2 \dots x_7$ represents six Eigen-values based on the heatmaps; $w_1, w_2 \dots w_7$ represents the discriminate coefficient and the w_8 is the constant value. For two classifications of vehicle models, the following decision rules are adopted:

$$d(x) = \begin{cases} <0, & \text{then } S \text{ belong to } G_1 \\ >0, & \text{then } S \text{ belong to } G_2 \\ =0, & \text{then } S \text{ belong to } G_1 \text{ or } G_2 \end{cases} \tag{6}$$

2.3 Linear Function Model Based on Fisher Discriminate

Fisher discriminate is recognized as one of the most effective methods for feature extraction [9], especially for dichotomous analysis. Its basic idea is to reduce the dimension by projection method so as to minimize the difference between similar samples and to expand the differences between different sample types. The projection line of the optimal direction needs to be obtained through sample training. So the linear function is constructed based on Fisher's discriminate.

The overall method flow in this paper is shown in Fig. 1:

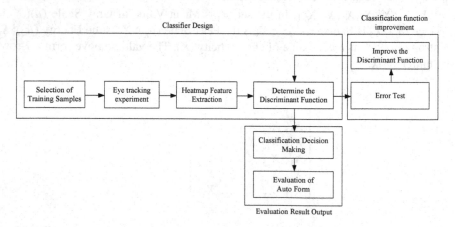

Fig. 1. The method of vehicle model evaluation based on eye tracking

3 Experimentation

In order to verify the above research framework, this paper verifies by experiment. The main experimental steps include: ① Training sample selection; ② Eye tracking tests and feature extraction of training samples; ③ Discriminate function model establishment.

3.1 Training Sample Selection

Car styling is classified as "high degree of preference (G1)" and "low degree of preference (G2)". The front shape is the part which can convey the image and style information mostly. Total of 30 pictures of different brands of car were collected. And the pictures are processed as achromatic color, and the resolution was set to 600 dpi. A total of 17 participants have average more than two years of driving experience. And their average age is 24.8 years old. A questionnaire survey was "Do you like the styling of this car?", using Likert Scale of −3 (No) to 3 (Yes). Statistics show the highest and lowest scores were 1.06 (Cruze) and −1.18 (Citroen C1). Respectively, these two car were chosen as training sample material (Fig. 2).

Fig. 2. Training samples

3.2 Eye Tracking Tests and Feature Extraction of Training Sample Selection

Equipment of the Test. The test equipment was a Dikablis head-mounted eye tracker manufactured by the company, Ergonieers of Germany. It worked in a monocular tracking mode to capture human left eye pupil by infrared camera. Before the test, the equipment was calibrated again by every participant. In experiment, the training sample pictures were presented in full screen on the 19 "monitor. The participants took the

Fig. 3. Experimental scene

sitting posture and remained watching the display screen horizontally at a distance of about 90 cm. (as shown in Fig. 3).

Process of the Test. Atotal of 11 participants included 7 males and 4 females. After introduction about the purpose of test and the equipment, the participants were asked to watch the sample pictures for visual aesthetic for 15 s, and the eye movement result was processed by D-lab software.

3.3 Heatmaps Processing and Feature Extraction

The heatmaps of 11 participants were generated by software. Only one participant's heatmap is shown here in Fig. 4:

(No.1)   ....(No.2)

Fig. 4. Heatmap of training samples

First, the heatmaps of training samples were stripped from the background meanwhile the color information were coded. Then, the color heatmaps were processed as grayscale images to obtain a histogram. The left heat map in Fig. 4 is taken as an example as shown in Figs. 5 and 6 after processing.

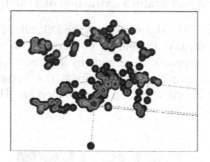

Fig. 5. Heatmap of training samples

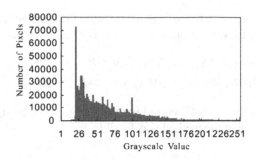

Fig. 6. Histogram of gray

The heatmap features of 11 participants were extracted, and the statistics calculated shown in Tables 2 and 3:

Table 2. Statistics calculated of Sample No. 1

	$X_1 = \mu$	$X_2 = \sigma^2$	$X_3 = \mu_S$	$X_4 = \mu_K$	$X_5 = \mu_N$	$X_6 = \mu_E$	$X_7 = K$
Participant 1	76.346	1788.728	0.716	−0.486	0.008	7.155	208.956
Participant 2	79.026	2129.913	0.810	−0.278	0.008	7.253	204.916
Participant 3	78.364	2043.521	0.881	−0.027	0.008	7.247	204.922
Participant 4	79.672	2119.298	0.653	−0.595	0.008	7.274	201.987
Participant 5	78.162	2061.861	0.648	−0.596	0.008	7.270	204.800
Participant 6	79.783	1946.110	0.703	−0.403	0.008	7.253	204.865
Participant 7	72.196	1734.479	0.747	−0.514	0.009	7.112	211.551
Participant 8	85.691	2230.868	0.444	−0.792	0.007	7.354	195.052
Participant 9	75.153	1853.770	0.731	0.427	0.008	7.168	209.516
Participant10	69.907	1841.278	1.067	0.499	0.009	7.104	208.741
Participant11	67.869	1675.367	0.979	0.238	0.009	7.047	214.489

Table 3. Statistics calculated of Sample No. 2

	$X_1 = \mu$	$X_2 = \sigma^2$	$X_3 = \mu_S$	$X_4 = \mu_K$	$X_5 = \mu_N$	$X_6 = \mu_E$	$X_7 = K$
Participant 1	71.672	1777.848	0.822	−0.147	0.008	7.134	214.830
Participant 2	76.022	2102.735	0.686	−0.328	0.009	7.196	201.925
Participant 3	75.403	1790.197	0.570	−0.523	0.008	7.160	207.962
Participant 4	72.638	1997.063	0.724	−0.391	0.008	7.165	209.644
Participant 5	76.849	1799.905	0.536	−0.554	0.009	7.149	204.490
Participant 6	84.029	2209.908	0.514	−0.664	0.007	7.355	200.821
Participant 7	72.214	1690.260	0.742	−0.194	0.008	7.143	212.836
Participant 8	73.551	2065.443	0.788	−0.256	0.008	7.185	203.025
Participant 9	72.778	1574.610	0.627	−0.456	0.008	7.114	217.732
Participant10	75.336	2266.348	0.767	−0.257	0.008	7.245	201.653
Participant11	73.065	1978.316	0.892	0.130	0.009	7.175	206.489

According to the research framework above, with the statistics in Tables 2 and 3 by Fisher discriminated, the discriminate function was constructed as:

$$d(X) = -0.755X_1 + 0.009X_2 - 36.676X_3 + 9.960$$
$$X_4 + 2707.174X_5 + 39.319X_6 + 0.364X_7 - 310.079 \tag{7}$$

Compared with the results of 7-point Likert scale ($-3\sim+3$), no significant difference existed. So, that indicated the method was feasible.

4   Conclusions

A method of Auto form evaluation based on eye tracking is proposed. The Experiment result showed that overall accuracy of this method was high. So a feasible technical approach for the rapid evaluation of automotive styling is provided.

Acknowledgements. The author would like to thank National Natural Science Foundation of China (No. 51205228), Anhui Natural Science Foundation Project (No. 1508085QG144).

References

1. China Association of Automobile Manufactures, et al.: Annual Report on Automotive Industry in China. Social Science Academic Press, Beijing (2013)
2. Yadav, H.C., Jain, R., Shukla, S., et al.: Prioritization of aesthetic attributes of car profile. Int. J. Ind. Ergon. **43**(2), 296–303 (2013)
3. Luo, S.-J., Fu, Y.-T., Zhou, Y.-X.: Perceptual matching of shape design style between wheel hub and car type. Int. J. Ind. Ergon. **43**(2), 90–102 (2012)
4. Karjalainen, T.-M.: When is a car like a drink? Metaphor as a means to distilling brand identity through product design references. Des. Manag. J. **12**(1), 66–71 (2001)
5. Zhang, F., Yang, M., Liu, W.: Evaluation of automobile form design based on fuzzy TOPSIS. Comput. Integr. Manuf. Syst. **20**(2), 276–281 (2014)
6. Coughlan, P.: Once is not enough: repeated exposure to and aesthetic evaluation of an automobile design prototype. Des. Stud. **20**(6), 553–563 (1999)
7. Hyoenae, J., Radach, R., Deubel, H.: The Mind's Eye: Cognitive and Applied Aspects of Eye Movement Research. Elsevier Science BV, Holland (2003)
8. Andrienko, G., Andrienko, N., Burch, M.: Visual analytics methodology for eye movement studies. IEEE Trans. Vis. Comput. Graph. **18**(12), 2889–2898 (2012)
9. Yang, S.: Pattern Recognition and Intelligent Computing: Publishing House of Electric Industry, Beijing (2011)

The Analysis of Visual Communication Design of Commonweal Information Through Interactive Design Thinking - Public Commonweal Information Design and Communication in Urban Traffic Spatial Environment as an Example

Shi Peng[1(✉)], Chao Liu[2], and Wentao Wang[2]

[1] Beijing Jiaotong University, Shangyuancun 03, Haidian, Beijing, China
751346564@qq.com
[2] User Interaction Design Center, Baidu, Xierqi Road 1002, Haidian, Beijing, China
{Liuchao05,wangwentao}@baidu.com

Abstract. This urban traffic spatial environment design in china step into the age of more focused on meeting the deep psychological needs of passengers. In modern society, the need for information transmission is more accurate and effective. Designer should pay attention to the way of information communications, which should be transmit more faster and topic should be accepted by users directly, generate better feedback, increase user experience. Interaction design at this stage of development trend is mostly stay in the field of development and research of network interface and virtual product. This comprehension of the design field and design thinking is very limited. By learning from the thinking model of interactive design, in the conditions of Internet information design thinking mode and design method for user all over society, which can be also a very effective method and thinking for graphic design, product design, environmental design and other design disciplines as well as effective combination of all this design field to create better public environment, apply it to the future city service of design innovation, in order to design more original, humanism, science and technology and the product all interactive design feature join altogether, meet the demand of experience economy design trend and bring the mature experience economic market product with infinite prospect to public users. In this paper, we study and discuss the communication and design of the commonweal information which is easy to be ignored in the traffic spatial environment. Take advantage of this thinking mode of interactive design to enhance the communications effect of commonweal information and obtain ideal social effect in future.

Keywords: Commonweal information · Traffic environment · Interactive design
Design thinking of interactive design

© Springer International Publishing AG, part of Springer Nature 2018
A. Marcus and W. Wang (Eds.): DUXU 2018, LNCS 10920, pp. 351–362, 2018.
https://doi.org/10.1007/978-3-319-91806-8_27

1   Important Value of Commonweal Information in Modern Society

The main symbol to measure the degree of modernization, attraction and humanization of a city is the information service of a city that not only meet the basic functional needs of people but also the acceptability and emotional experience of information interaction design for user [1].

Commonweal Information is aimed at standardizing people's behavior and promoting social public consciousness, which is educational information in order to conduct public welfare induction and propaganda of behavior norms. Public information propagandizes, educates and disseminates the correct social culture idea for people. Commonweal Information is an important information to disseminate the spirit of the city which Is a comprehensive representation of the degree of urban development. It reflects the civilization and cultural taste of a city in a detail, the more advanced society is, the more creation, dissemination and consumption of spiritual and cultural products [2].

Improving the level of public information design in urban space has become an inevitable trend of the development of user service in public transportation environment. Modern utilitarian values often lead people to pay too much attention to material function and pragmatism, ignoring the important significance of spiritual factors to people and society. The modern humanism design idea requires the designer not only to pay attention to the material medium that carries the traffic function, but also to go deep into people's inner world, and to create the design that can trigger the emotion resonance [3]. Taking urban traffic space environment as an example, this paper discusses the new trends and changes of information design in modern urban spatial environment and how to carry out commonweal information visual communication design through interactive design thinking. Enhance the public thinking consciousness and provide a better travel experience for the daily commuters in the city. The significance of emotional experience to urban traffic space.

Urban traffic space refers as the space environment of indoor and outdoor, vehicles, buildings, roads and public facilities related to urban public transport which carrying the daily commuting of the city. If the city is treated as a living body, people are the blood and the traffic space is the blood vessel to maintain the daily operation of the city. Numerous user emotional experiences of daily trips for users play an important role in the healthy operation and development of the city.

Experience come from Emotion and feeling. Emotional experience in the field of Psychology refer to the positive or negative psychological reflection and attitude when a person to define an objective thing. Emotional experience reflects many aspects relate with people, for example human social relations, living conditions, interaction between people and environment and so on, which permeated into many fields of social life with a distinctive social character [4]. The meaning of emotional experience in is refer that Whether or not the Information received by the user is conforms to one's own physical and psychological needs, and then produce subjective experience and attitude that comes naturally in mind of passages [5].

Although emotion is inspired and came from the characteristics of information transmitted, But unlike Psychological activity of cognition, it is not a direct reflection of things and behavior, Therefore, the emotional experience is based on the thing or objects which as the factor to activate the people's mind. Emotional experience is the subjective experience and attitude produced through thus intermedia that related to people's own human nature needs, which reflects the relationship between human needs and practical effects of satisfying needs [6].

Feeling and Emotional experience is a necessary part of life. It has an important influence on people's cognition and thinking. Without the participation of emotional factors, people's ability to make decisions will be impaired. Especially with the development of science and technology, People pay more attention to their emotions and experiences than ever before. Essentially, emotion is hidden in all perceptual activities, but the degree of exertion is different. Without the maintenance of human value system, human activities will be difficult to sustain. However, memory and thinking activities are measured by emotional value, which makes people's activities more purposeful.

Emotional factor is an important part of human experience and an important factor to be considered in any design. It is also the need of space and environment design and to meet the needs of space spiritual needs. The design needs to get rid of the external appearance, go deep into the inner world of people mind, arouse the emotional resonance, and achieve the inner needs of love, respect and self-realization of audience.

The role of traffic environment in the new era is changing quietly. Public transport space no longer act as independent carriers, but as urban elements. The traffic environment space is no longer a tool to separate travel into different pieces, but an important clue to bridge the relationship between people and the city. The function and form of traffic environment space have been expanded, which is quite different from the space only for traffic, and has become a city scenic spot worthy of being visited.

Designing meaningful space is an effective way to express emotion and create a good experience. The meaning of emotion embodies the intersection of space and user's feeling, emotion and cultural value. Through the interactive experience between the user and the design object, the deep symbolic meaning, culture, social meaning and other design concepts behind the form can be explained. The mature design of space has extended its tentacles to the depths of the human mind. By endowing the design with metaphorical color and aesthetic sentiment, giving the design the profound meaning, let the user understand and feel kind-hearted.

Experience refers to the experience of knowing the things around us through practice. Emotional experience is a kind of unforgettable experience, from the mind, connected with life. Westerners like to make coffee and drink coffee, like Chinese people making tea and tasting tea. Is to create an experience that elevates the mood of coffee drinking. In the process of interaction between people and things, let the little experience and details of the endless aftertaste. Space design has entered an era of experience in which coffee making is as important as coffee drinking. Successful experiences should be able to work through a holistic, all-around sense of vision, hearing, smell, touch. Grasp the "sparks" generated by the collision between Design objects and passengers' thoughts. The value of emotional experience will be far greater than the form itself, which is characterized by continuous, interactive, participative and experiential activities. People all have the experience that passive acceptance alone can't really understand the intrinsic nature of a thing, nor can it feel the emotion that something brings to people. Only the interactive process can give people a deep experience and deep feelings.

2   Commonweal Information Need to Be Interact with the User in a More Emotional Way

American psychologist Maslow defines human needs as five progressive level - 1. physiology, 2. safety, 3. belonging and love, 4. esteem 5. Self-actualization. From the perspective of interactive information design and user experience, the main body of information system in urban traffic space is functional information to help people to complete a series of behavior related to the road finding or public transportation conveniently and quickly which is corresponding to the basic needs of people and it is the necessary information in the travel process. The commonweal information corresponds to the high - level psychological demand such as actualization, esteem which is need to communicate with audience and be understood through emotional cohesion and appeal, achieve the function of transmitting social consciousness and guidance, as shown in Fig. 1. It is not necessary but play the role to improve the healthy, orderly and efficient development of society, to provide better experience and well - being for the daily travel passengers.

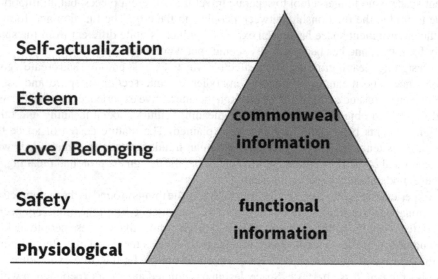

Fig. 1. The commonweal information corresponds to the psychological demand of Maslow

Space environment design from simple to complex, from functional to contain spiritual and cultural factors, the formation and development of this design trend is the reflection of the gradual rise of the demand level of humanism. The injection of affective factor to the product in design process is not the designer's whim, but the inherent requirement of human sensibility. Therefore, designers should pay attention to the needs of people, whether in the traditional or modern society, the fundamental reason why emotional needs are so common lies in its return to human perceptual life, Meet the spiritual needs and development of human beings [7].

The space environment has a huge impact on human behavior and emotions, it can even be said that designers have an important responsibility for the psychological and physical health of users. While significant progress has been made in the aspect of scientific and technological, there are still many deep psychological needs that are deliberately or unintentionally ignored.

When it comes to Prohibition and standardization information design for public, serious performance style and expression may not be proper way to attract the attention of users and wrong expression attitude, On the contrary, will make passengers nervous and alert, it cannot achieve the goal of information design. By contrast, from the perspective of reverse thinking, the humorous and witty style and expression is more acceptable and can achieve the purpose of publicity. Therefore, the designer of the information system needs to make a deep research on the passengers' psychology as far as possible, and pay attention to the detailed feelings and emotional experiences of the passengers in the process of information cognition. This is the basis for passengers' willingness to accept these rules and advice.

At present, the commonweal information design set up in the public transport space in China is generally ignored. The way in which it exists is stiff and rigid. It's hard to resonate with the user, Therefore, it does not play a role in promoting and guiding social culture. At the same time, it cannot be a factor to improve the user's travel experience and psychological satisfaction, even become information rubbish in the space and repelled by people. For example, "No smoking", "respecting the elderly and loving the young" which simple and shabby expression of traditional preaching slogans neglects the emotional experience and loses the place effect of information cognition for audience. Lack of expression that touches the heart of the audience in information interaction, it is difficult to arouse the audience's emotional resonance, as shown in Fig. 2.

Please give up your seat to the elderly,
the sick and the disabled

Please queue up for tickets

pull over for wating, get down first
and then get on the train

Fig. 2. Commonweal information design set up in the public transport space in China

3 Analysis of the Attitude for Commonweal Information Design

The design and expression of commonweal information originates from the attitude between the designer and the users. The purpose and starting point of design public information should not be to limit the behavior of passengers or result in psychological feeling of coercion, threat, and tension against the user's mind [8]. The design attitude should be as a guide to passenger behavior and change the user's way of thinking, not to prevent and limit as rules.

There is an interesting example of this point that completely different design concept between the ticket machines of the Japanese Intercity Railway and other ticket checkers in other countries. The passageway of the ticket check-in machine is completely open without door to prevent ticket evasion behavior and passengers can normally pass through in an orderly manner. When passengers leave the station, they will put the electronic ticket on the card reader to check in, if the ticket is invalid, the check-in machine alerts the management, and the gate closes, blocking passengers trying to escape. In general, most passengers have good consciousness to abide regulations, in the peak period passengers can pass smoothly in a short period of time, as shown in Fig. 3.

The Design of cultivating Social consciousness   Design of preventing ticket evasion

Fig. 3. The contrast between ticket machines of the Japanese Intercity Railway with others

This design concept embodies the humanized management thought which take into account the psychological activities and the social thinking orientation of people when they encounter the management and rule. The design propose of ticket gate should be quick and simple for passengers to enter and leave, instead of restricting, monitoring and guarding passengers who will consciously act according to the rules and abide the law, While showing respect and trust to passengers.

Under the guidance of this design concept, it can improve the quality of passengers and importance for people's self-consciousness and self-esteem. On the contrary most of the design simply to regulate people's behavior as the purpose, to treat passengers with a mind of guarding against them Suppose that, in the absence of regulatory and institutional restrictions, would it lead to selfish that encourages irregularities? By meeting the psychological needs of self-esteem, which can influence people's consciousness, even in the absence of supervision, people can consciously observe order in the interest of the pubic.

4 Analysis of Successful Cases of Commonweal Information Design

The following three successful design cases from information interaction design and user experience perspective, preliminarily discuss the visual communication character-istics and expression techniques of successful commonweal information.

The commonweal Information design in the Japanese subway space is characterized by the use of a slightly humorous Japanese comic story style into the dissemination of information. Through the combination of simple drawing and exaggerated expression, a kind of special clear and simple visual expression is formed. Ideally control the rela-tionship between the amount and readability of information, easy to read and understand. Japanese comics are a cultural industry serving all ages, with a wide audience, fuse comics design style into the commonweal information can bring the subject of topic closer to their audiences, therefor present the matter of the merits, pros and cons is more easily accepted by people, as shown in Fig. 4.

Fig. 4. The commonweal information design in Japanese subway space

Most of the issues involved in commonweal information are trivial matters that do little harm, at the same time, we need to use the effect of public opinion to curb these seemingly ordinary violations. There is a lack of intensive contradiction to produce explosive and inspirational and produce social public opinion effect. The cleverness of the design in France lies in the creation and exaggeration of contradictions, using meta-phors to create contradictions, as far as possible by creating visual impact and thought confrontation points, increasing attention to information, bring visual and psychological strong sense of shock. To the audience. For example, to produce isomorphism from the signifier of ontology with the meaning of the vehicle, the behavior of noisy people who do not observe public order is as annoying and unjustifiable like an animals, so audience will percept a sense of freshness and impact. The humor can really touch people's hearts and create a profound mockery to violator, so that the audience has a profound thinking about the problem, as shown in Fig. 5.

Fig. 5. The commonweal information design in France traffic space

The problems that need to be solved is the information design of the usage specification for the luggage rack above the passenger seat in high-speed railway train in China. The information are include following items: leave Storage space that easier to pick up luggage For short passengers please; reasonably arrange your luggage to allow more luggage to be placed in limited storage space, Try to use the storage space above your seat to reduce encroachment of others storage space. In contrast to the old design thinking, These ways of information expressing that is more acceptable to the audience, Reduce resistance by users, reduce and avoid critical, educational attitudes towards users which resulting in a blocking of information communication. By thinking in a different

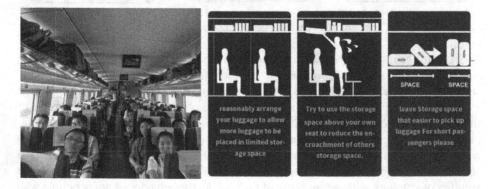

Fig. 6. The commonweal information design in china high speed train

position, enable the audience to stand on the point of view of the disadvantaged, generate compassion to difficulties they suffered, as shown in Fig. 6.

5   Using Interactive Design Thinking to Analyze the Visual Communication Design of Commonweal Information

5.1   The Relationship Between the Environmental Requirements of Modern Design and Interactive Design Thinking

When a large number of socialized Internet products that affect the entire industrial chain or even have the characteristics of ecosphere blending, the business model gradually matures, the design field the designers once serviced for, the product design attributes, design process, evaluation criteria for design results are quite different from the traditional design methods we used to be familiar with. Interaction design, user interface design, experience design thinking, situational design thinking mode, information design, iterative design, user and group focus design research method, perception technology, many various new design ideas, methods and technology [9]. These new innovation are overwhelming for designers and infiltrate into the traditional design field, Affected the traditional design methods and procedures, affect the design process of the relationship between the designer and the user, the designer's attitude towards the user. Interaction design thinking series various new design methods are becoming important clues and traditional design idea, and the correlation with systemic become designers also have to pay attention to and grasp the design concept.

Interactive design thinking served as the important clue to combine various design methods and idea of new and traditional, the relevance and systematization of new and traditional design thinking become the idea that designers have to pay attention to and grasp. In the current design trend. Interaction design at this stage of design development trend is mostly stay in the field of network interface and virtual product development research, this comprehension of the design field and design thinking is very limited. By learning from the thinking model of interactive design, in the conditions of Internet information design thinking mode and design method for user all over society, which can be also a very effective method and thinking for graphic design, product design, environmental design and other design disciplines as well as effective combination of all this design field to create better public environment, apply it to the future city service of design innovation, in order to design more original, humanism, science and technology and the product all interactive design feature join altogether, meet the demand of experience economy design trend and bring the mature experience economic market product with infinite prospect to public users.

Interactive design thinking is the results of the intersection and integration of different design disciplines, which is a systematic mode of thinking. Interactive design thinking is inheriting traditional design methods combined with new design thinking, its ideas and methods have been paid attention to and applied in different design fields related to the Internet industry. Interactive system design thinking and methods are not only the one that can guide design, and it allows designers to look at and evaluate their design behavior method from different perspectives, create new, practical and interesting products for users, design and create new living, working and entertainment behaviors and experiences. There is not obvious boundary for different design field in the future, Rather than the design field is highly integrated, the design method or thinking not precisely targeted in one single industry or field, but develop towards to the direction of combination between broad and professional. The interactive design mode of thinking is an important essence of guiding designers to improve themselves, When jump from one industry to another, they should be able to adapt quickly find and locate their own existence value also. Future trends in design and industry tell us the designer should have these advantage at the same: having knowledge As an expert in a single industry; able to have a wide relevant of understanding in wide different field at the same time, which will be very important ability In order to be better cooperate with a wide range of related areas designers and team to create products with a deep understanding of people's life [10].

5.2 The Analysis of Design Rules for Interactive Thinking

Interactive design thinking is to study and research how people interact with information and define the interaction and association between people and information, its main features is the interaction between users and information, that viewed as a process rather than an independent static one-way transmission. Although most of the commonweal information exists as static visual information, there is a greater need for users to interact with information and produce intimate interactive between them. By considering the idea of interactive design, when its information can be better understood by users and serve the audience, so using interactive design thinking is a shortcut to improve the acceptance of information and enhance the user experience of visual communication design of commonweal information in traffic space. Design rules are summarized as follows:

(1) Enhance Attention of User to Information

In modern society, attention is a very valuable and precious resource. In the process of information exchange and communication, it must be able to ensure that the information in the environment is able to notice and quickly understand by the audience with limited attention. The primary requirements of communication for commonweal information is attracted the interest of the audience, for example, through the simple, direct and narrative visual interaction process of comics painting style, the image expressed not only exaggerated but also more humorous and interesting. At first catch the eye of the audience in an instant, then giving people visual impact and shock power, by the way of purposeful exaggeration and more prominent displays, in order to lead audience to focus on the core and thrust of the problem as well as the characteristics of the point of view, which can enhance the degree of acceptance and persuasion of the corresponding ideas, generate more public opinion value and attention with the theme.

(2) Changing the Role of Users in Process of Information Exchange

The traditional design of commonweal information communication regards the audience as a single external receiver. The commonweal information communication needs to take the audience as a part of the process of information interaction, stimulate the subjective initiative of the audience who can actively feedback and interact with the information. Let the audience participate in the information communication process and create the corresponding emotion. The key to the thinking of information interaction design lies in changing of user's role, who transformed from the passive information receiving object to the main body in the process of information communication. Through this kind of thinking, not only can reduce the audience's resistance to this kind of information, but directly reaching the user's higher level of psychological and emotional experience, therefore we can get good feedback on the content advocated by commonweal information, for example, to express information through personification and metaphor, Stimulate the audience's thinking and imagination, the user is not a passive information audience, Instead, they will unconsciously create associations and reflections on the basis of the information clues provided, to understand what is commonweal information is meant and comprehend the content with deep thinking.

(3) Situational Thinking

The narration of commonweal information need to be described with whole process include cause and effect of the problem and it's hard to go through all the problems and details, because of the limitations of many different conditions. By describing and communicating the key parts of the problem, the user thinks through the context described and the interrelationship between the information which enable take users themselves into the situation with their own logic thinking, create the experience and feeling in the scene and form a responsive behavioral situation in the mind. This narrative is actually based on story and situation, the realization of the whole process of thinking in context is based on the premise that the user brings his own feelings and experiences into the situation. The user is not an outsider any more, but through the interaction of information, Subjectively entering the scene and then get into the story, form their own thinking attitude to looking at problems and try to solve the problem maybe, produce a deeper understanding of the point, for example figurative expression of commonweal information that users can improve their feelings and thinking about things and situations, which will promote and induce users to create appropriate associations and feelings, thus producing a deeper understanding of story and topic.

(4) Empathy Thinking

Empathy thinking arises from the imitating circumstances and experiences of others with disadvantages, creating the same painful feelings in mind of audience. Empathy is the main source of high-level thinking consciousness, for example, psychological satisfaction of self-actualization. The user will be associated with their subjective feelings to the situation of disadvantages, the formation and generation of such thinking and feeling cannot be achieved through education and preaching, so users need to have a relevant understanding of the causes and consequences of the matter as well as the seriousness of the problem, oneself may forms the epiphany and the understanding to the idea express by commonweal information. So this kind of thinking comes into being based on the instinct to bring users into the situation of the disadvantaged, put oneself in a position of the weak, consider and perceive the inconvenience and pain who suffered.

For example Interactive design of commonweal Information for High-speed Railway luggage storage need to change the user's perspective of thinking, which can help the audience to stand in the perspective of the disadvantaged through situational display of information, who will considering the experiences and feelings of the person with a weak body, transposition thinking play an important role in communication function of commonweal information again.

6   Conclusion

The function, mode, effect of information communication should be paid more attention in modern society. And the accuracy of information dissemination, More quickly and directly accepted by users which is foundation for produce good information feedback and interaction, increase user experience are important factors either. Through the analysis of different information and audience characteristics, in the context of the new information communication and interaction mechanism, thinking mode of interactive design redefined the traditional field of visual communication in graphic design which is inevitable.

References

1. Fry, H., Ketteridge, S., Marsall, S.: Student learning. In: Fry, H., Ketteridge, S., Marsall, S. (eds.) A Handbook for Teaching and Learning in Higher Education. Routledge, Abingdon (2015)
2. Joseph, P.B., Gilmore, J.H.: Experience Economy. Mechanical Industry Press, Beijing (2002). Trans. by Xia, Ye-liang
3. Xue, W.: Public Environmental Facilities Design. Liaoning Arts Press, Shenyang (2006)
4. Wang, Y., Wang, J.: Urban Environmental Facilities Design. Shanghai People's Arts Press, Shanghai (2006)
5. Guan, Y.: Reserch on Products Experience Design. Wuhan Technology University, Wuhan (2006)
6. Liu, X.: Analysis of the interactive products design in experience economy era. Art Des. (2010)
7. Zhou, W., An, X.: Interaction design in public facilities. Art Educ. (2010)
8. Banerjee, T.: The future of public space-beyond invented streets and reinvented places. APA J. **67**, 9–24 (2001)
9. Saffer, D.: Designing for Interaction. New Riders Press, Berkeley (2007)
10. Liu, W., Tang, L.: Theoretical Investigation of Furniture Design in the Contemporary Era. China Forestry Press, Beijing (2007)
11. Zhang, F.: Four characteristics of ancient Chinese aesthetics. Theor. Stud. Lit. Art (2013)

Interaction Design of Autonomous Vehicle Based on Human Mobility

Jingyan Qin[✉], Zeyu Hao, and Shujing Zhang

School of Mechanical Engineering, University of Science and Technology Beijing, Beijing, China
qinjingyanking@foxmail.com

Abstract. Autonomous vehicle extends human mobility time and space dimensions under the background of intelligent transportation system big data and artificial intelligence, and drives the three flows which include logistic, financial flow and information flow to expand the new human mobility interaction paradigm. Mobility includes not only space and physics movement, but also information and time transformation, Navigation Design and wayfinding changes. Under the new social network and knowledge map human movements based on three flows (materials flow/logistic, information flow, financial flow) take place in the three time (past, present, future) and spaces (cyberspace, inforsphere, noosphere). Consequently, the interaction model of human and autonomous vehicle based on human mobility has changed. In the model, the person is not only an individual, but also includes people in the sharing mode among the offline and online social networks which support the users identity duality in cyberspace, as well as the third life virtual agent or avatar driven by artificial intelligence in intelligent transportation systems. Human-Mobility Interaction (HMI) model supports the vehicles to complete the independent material flow driven by the information flow. The information structure and paradigm in the HMI transforms with the intelligent information in the digital environment and artificial intelligence algorithm in cyberspace. The information architecture has more interactive features of feedforward and feedback self-driving information. User Generated Contents (UGC), Professional Generated Contents (PGC) in autonomous vehicles, and Occupational-ly-generated Contents (OGC) under Intelligent Transportation System increase dramatically in Human-Mobility Interaction which correspondingly change interaction design, interface design, media and visual design.

Keywords: Autonomous vehicle · Human mobility · Interaction design

1 Introduction

Human Mobility indicates a regular movement of human individuals or groups in time and space [1]. Human factors in the social system implied in human mobility, include not only the rule of spatiotemporal distribution and evolution of human movement, also contains the flowing characteristics in the information space, cyberspace and noosphere synchronization of material transfer, information transformation and financial transaction or energy transit. In the process of human mobility and three flows, the human-human interaction, human-environment interaction, and the human-machine interaction

© Springer International Publishing AG, part of Springer Nature 2018
A. Marcus and W. Wang (Eds.): DUXU 2018, LNCS 10920, pp. 363–374, 2018.
https://doi.org/10.1007/978-3-319-91806-8_28

among the humans, things and the natural or digital environment have come into being. With the rapid development of autonomous vehicle, intelligent transportation system and intelligent mobile telecommunication, Human Mobility increases much more research contents about the crowds movement pattern, material information and financial flows owned by the individual moving line, block chains spaces interaction. The human movements based on three flows (materials flow/logistic, information flow, financial flow) take place in the three time (past, present, future) and three spaces (cyberspace, inforsphere, noosphere). The research on Human Mobility has social and comprehensive significance for urban planning [2], traffic prediction [3], disease monitoring [4], location-based advertising [5] and location-based service system economy, social network system [6]. The existing research methods for Human Mobility focus on data acquisition methods [7–9], data analysis methods [2, 5, 10–15] and data application or influence [1, 6, 16]. As a new vehicle transportation form for human beings, autonomous vehicle can independently collect data, analyze data and apply data through sensors and AI algorithms [17], so as to expand the connotation and denotation of human mobility. Aiming at the human mobility of autonomous vehicle, this paper discusses the interaction design method in content, function and media by analyzing the three elements of interaction design.

The paper mainly use literature survey about human mobility and autonomous vehicles, the field study on potential users of the autonomous vehicle (1 worker and 1 housewife, 1 primary school pupil, 3 undergraduate students, 3 free occupation persons, 1 experts) chose four typical family members and typical users to do the field research which include 1 office worker, 1 housewife, 1 primary school pupil and 1 university student. The research directly observed, collected the video recording, and interviewed in-depth with the typical users (based on unstructured interviews) for one year. The survey on the other 6 subjects conducted in-depth interviews and scenario simulation, and a collection of recordings and interview notes as reference data. At the same time through Participatory Design, four typical users participate in the study. The interaction design results were tested by user evaluation and expert review (using Likert scale) by high fidelity prototype.

2 Human Machine Interaction and Human Mobility Interaction

HMI (Human Machine Interaction) is essentially about developing easy, effective, and pleasing interactive products [18]. The three elements of interaction are closely related to the design of human communication and interactive space [19]. With the popularity of Internet of Things(IoT) and intelligent mobile communication devices, the subject and object of interaction have changed. The main body can interact with information and do not need entities. The behavior of judgement, decision-making and execution of objects is changed from passivity to initiative. Human mobility is integrated into the transfer of information based on information density and information exchange on the basis of physical migration, meanwhile, Human Machine Interaction transforms into Human Mobility Interaction. The new Human Mobility Interaction can be divided into different representations of the subject as presence, telepresence and co-presence. The entity user driver controls the car in the presence style Human Mobility Interaction, and the virtual user driver controls the autonomous vehicle in the telepresence style Human Mobility Interaction (see Fig. 1). In the co-presence style Human Mobility Interaction, the users have the duality identity, normally the real user driver who is driven by human intelligence and the virtual user driver who is driven by artificial intelligence third life joint control the autonomous vehicle. In the HMI interaction, the relationships among the materials, information and financial energy synchronously change with the new paradigm of Human Mobility. In 2018, for example, Beijing city took out the issuance of traffic decrees including "Beijing Road Vehicle Automated Driving Ability Evaluation Test Content and Method (Trial)" and "Beijing autonomous vehicle closed test site technical requirements (Trial)" two documents which was issued by The Beijing Municipal Traffic Commission Joint Municipal Public Security Traffic Management Bureau and Economic Information Commission [20]. Beijing Evaluation of road test ability content is divided into five aspects: cognition and ability to comply with traffic regulations evaluation and execution capability assessment, emergency disposal and artificial intervention ability evaluation, driving ability assessment, internet e-driving ability assessment. In these capabilities, cognition and execution the traffic regulations evaluate HMI presence and telepresence performance. Emergent information processing and human intervention, comprehensive driving ability and internet e-driving abilities require the HMI co-presence performance.

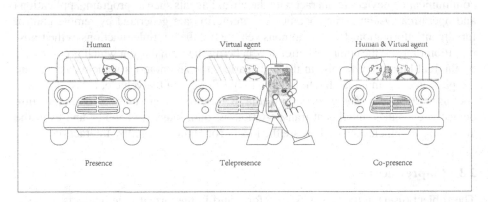

Fig. 1. Three kinds of presence based on human mobility of autonomous vehicle.

2.1 Presence in Human-Mobility Interaction

In the presence style Human-Mobility Interaction, the subject (user) needs to interact with the object in the state of the entity. The identity of the subject is single in the physical space, the driver and passengers, the information disseminator such as information communication users have no ability to identity multiple roles. The interactive behavior occurs mainly between the real person and the entity of the vehicles. As seen the scene 1 of presence (see Fig. 1), mobility refers to the real person or object motion based on physical spatiotemporal movement, the moving path is effected and determined by individual driving concept, life style wisdom, user experience, preferences, environmental factors, material flow, information flow and financial flow by the real time and physical space constraints. Real people produce the driving behavior through physical operation, the main distribution in human cognition lies in the driving behavior in human-computer interaction. And the interactive contents focus on-the-spot handling information. The driver and the passengers have interactive tasks independently, and their identity and function of operation cannot be parallel superimposed. The media of interaction is the vehicle and physical interface as the main information carrier.

2.2 Telepresence in Human-Mobility Interaction

In the telepresence mode of Human-Mobility Interaction, the subject (user) interacts with the objects (autonomous vehicle) through the virtual agent. In the autonomous vehicle, users can achieve the goal of picking up passengers on the autonomous vehicles without staying in the vehicle. The subject (user) takes information as a carrier to control the driverless vehicle through virtual agents or avatars, which enriches the form and contents of human mobility. As seen the scene 2 presents the telepresence mode for interaction (see Fig. 1). The user communicates through mobiles application to remote control the autonomous vehicle. Telepresence means the substance moving in the different spatiotemporal physical environment though the information flow in the info-sphere and forms the new human mobility. The real humans use the intelligent tele-communication devices to interact with the virtual agents such as program, applications and operation systems. The contents for interaction are generated by remote control intelligent information. The autonomous vehicle has the multiple functions as the transportation tool and the communication media being the virtual agent which is controlled by the real humans remotely. In these scenarios, the autonomous vehicle can pick up the passengers summoned by the users without drivers in the vehicle, move from one spot to another spot. The interaction media include intelligent mobile communication devices, telematics, intelligent transportation system, internet of things and even the autonomous vehicles themselves are the media for Human-Mobility Interaction.

2.3 Co-presence

The subject (user) in the real substance form and in the virtual state interacts with the object (autonomous vehicle) in the same space (autonomous vehicle) and time. The virtual agent or avatar subject include the real user at the present time and in the past time, also include the individual user's human intelligence and artificial intelligence from citizen crowds wisdom. The virtual subject includes the dual users and the virtual agent for the real user, as well as the avatar formed by the third life driven by artificial intelligence. The choices for the OD moving path are determined by the joint decision of human intelligence and artificial intelligence. As seen the scene 3 shows the co-presence mode scenario (see Fig. 1). Human mobility has developed together with human intelligence and artificial intelligence. In the autonomous vehicle, the identity of the users transform from the driver to passengers in the most scenarios. The interaction behaviors take the emphasis on the travel experience rather than driving experience, while the interaction contents take the non-driving behavior as the main target tasks in the process of the human mobility. The leading function transform from the driving to mobile entertainment, mobile dating and casual mobile learning. The autonomous vehicle has become the leading media and the main carrier interface of the three flows in human-mobility interaction.

2.4   Three Core Flows for Human-Mobility Interaction

Human mobility include material flow logistics, information flow and financial flow. Information flow as the core movement drives the logistics and financial flow. In the autonomous vehicle, information flow embraces the non-digital information from the real vehicle, also stores digital information from the autonomous vehicle and the intelligent transportation system. The way of obtaining information includes not only the digital information of people, vehicles and environment detected by sensors, but also the digital information in intelligent transportation system, as well as the self-quantified information obtained by the driverless car. Autonomous vehicles can be used as the carrier of information to achieve the fusion flows of material and information in the presence, telepresence and co-presence human mobility.

In the information flow, the affiliation between people and information has changed. The social network formed by the inherent information of users, that is, the birth identity information, the conversion transformation information and emergent impromptu information have formed a new knowledge map. In the material flow, the subordinate relationship between man and autonomous vehicle has changed. Independent human and autonomous vehicle are associated with information flow. In the scenarios of self-driving, autonomous vehicle dominates human mobility and also is controlled by the crowds wisdom based on Artificial Intelligence. Autonomous vehicle with autonomous vehicle or vehicles interaction is also driven by information flow. Even if there is no one in autonomous vehicle, the material flow also forms between autonomous vehicle and autonomous vehicle. The relationship between the autonomous vehicle and humans is equal and self-forming system. The paradigm of human mobility changes from centralization to flat networks concern with individual and group data contents service design. In the capital flow, it reflects the human-vehicle and human-mobility interaction between autonomous vehicle and the online & offline flows environment from IaaS (Infrastructure as a Service), PaaS (Platform-as-a-Service), SaaS (Software as a Service) to DaaS (Data as a Service), AaaS (Algorithm as a Service) and AIaaS (Artificial Intelligence as a Service). The self-driving environment includes not only the natural non-digital environment but also the intelligent transportation system form a mixed environment of human mobility.

Logistics. The principal and subordinate relationship between the human and the vehicles has been changed. As seen the scene 3 (see Fig. 1), the autonomous vehicle is controlled by the virtual agent when the users stay in the vehicle. The autonomous vehicle has the dominant human mobility. When user stays out of the autonomous vehicle, human-machine interaction is made up of the human-vehicle interaction, vehicle-vehicle interaction and vehicle-environment interaction. Humans and vehicles separately interact with the human mobility through information flow. The paradigm of human mobility becomes more and more flat agile networks. Autonomous vehicles and humans can be separated (each of them are materials), emphasizing independence (autonomy), and autonomous vehicles can move independently as we-media itself.

Information Flow. The principal and subordinate relationship between the human and information has been changed. As seen the scene 2 and scene 3 (see Fig. 1), information generates from self-quantified, user-generated contents from the cognitive redundancy, artificial intelligence analyzes the big data for the human-mobility interaction and transforms the non-intelligent information into intelligent information for the autonomous vehicle. Information exists in the virtual agent or avatar independently or flows embedded in the humans in the autonomous vehicle. The identity information, impromptu information and the transformation information construct the new social network system among human-vehicle interaction and human-mobility interaction. The information develops with the big data as the knowledge graph for autonomous vehicle and expands the human mobility which include the individual and crowds service design. Non-digital information and digital information contribute to the data contents service for human mobility. In the scenario of driverless car, users' cognitive focus is liberated from driving behavior. The cognitive redundancy and self-quantified constitute a new information flow, and stimulate the birth and flow of social capital flow through data exchange.

Financial Flow. In the intelligent transportation system big data and self-quantified autonomous vehicle small data exchange process, algorithm and data form the new service [21]. Users and autonomous vehicles receive the crowds wisdom service through data sharing and artificial intelligence. Data as a service and AI algorithm as a service ignite the economic value of data oil. The information flow drives the financial flow from offline to online service system and big data platform. Human-Machine Interaction transforms into Human-Mobility Interaction through IaaS (Infrastructure as a Service) to PaaS (Platform-as-a-Service) and SaaS (Software as a Service).

3   Human Mobility and Three Elements of Interaction Design

3.1   Data Collection Method and Interaction Design Content

The data collection method for Human Mobility corresponds to Interaction Design content-level design. Human Mobility usually considers three aspects: geographic context, distance attenuation, individual spatial behavior characteristics, population density in the region, spatial distribution, individual differences (commuting activities), the factors that influence the forecast are age, population density, number of visiting information towers, external parameters, etc. [8] Previous Human Mobility data acquisition mainly relied on bank notes dispersion and GPS, and later CDR (Call Detail Record) enabled us to capture the dynamic information of individual movement and social interaction, thus predicting what new link will be developed in The Social Network, we can get its regularity on Spatiotemporal by investigating the frequency and duration of contact between users, but CDR has two biggest limitations: sparse time and rough space [9]. With the widespread use of smart mobile phones, our expanded use of Human Mobility data through the widespread use of cellular and GPS [7], and to ensure continuous connectivity, PSNs (Pocket Switched Networks) leverage human mobility and local/global connectivity to transfer data between mobile users' devices, exploiting human mobility to provide occasional Communication opportunities [22], Disruption-Tolerant Networks (DTNs) can store the data they are transmitting or forwarding while disconnected from the network until a contact is made that can be relayed when needed, thus sending the message end to end [23]. Autonomous Vehicle obtains data about the user's personal movement path and the surrounding context of the user during movement through sensors such as LIDAR, Ultrasonic sensor, camera and GPS (Global Position System) [17]. With autonomous Vehicle, we can make up for the problems of low value of human data acquisition, single user information, lack of continuous path data in the individual space and low accuracy (see Fig. 2). With Autonomous Vehicle, we can not only get third-person GPS data, but also first-person viewers' data. Flattening data sources enables interactive content to support Mass Customization's data content services. Autonomous Vehicle enables self-quantified approaches from "Around Me" information through wearable smart devices [24], extends to "Include Me" information in Autonomous Vehicle, Quantified the individual's small data to make it more comprehensive and includes the inherent identity information, impromptu information and transformation information, enable Interaction Design's content design to provide mass customization (MC) data services to individuals, mass computing of big data under mass-based individual data, and mass data usage as a public resource for mass, It is necessary to pay attention to the scope of application of data and the ethical and moral issues of design. Data and design should be people-oriented and can't harm people

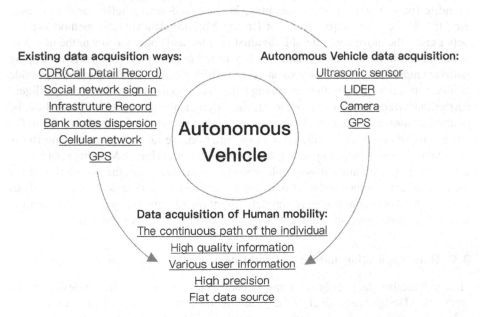

Fig. 2. Autonomous vehicle expanding of human mobility data collection method.

themselves. On the basis of this, the laws, cultures, contexts and social contracts of the applied area should be respected. Therefore, in Autonomous Vehicle interactive content design, users and Autonomous Vehicles require a service agreement and social contract, users accept the premise of data services is the need to share their own data, Autonomous Vehicle also requires the user's authorization to the user's personal data applied to the mass service. Authorization to the user's personal data applied to the mass in service is dramatically. Autonomous Vehicle interactive content needs to be based on hosting logistics, information flow as a driving force to transform and promote logistics and financial flows, supporting Mass Customization's data content services under self-Quantified.

3.2 Data Analysis Method and Interaction Design Function

Human Mobility data analysis method corresponds to Interaction Design functional level design. Through intervening opportunities model [2], Lévy flight model [10], radiation model [11], d-EPR model [12], deep learning models (the deep belief network (DBN) and deep neural network (DNN)) [13], Exploration and Preferential Return (EPR) model [14], gravity model [15], a hybrid Markov-based prediction model [5], triangulation [25] and other model analysis. Human Mobility pays more and more attention to the analysis of an individual's laws of movement in time and space and thus predicts the individual user's movement path, The Social Network, preferences, and the like. For example, E Mucceli et al. Classify PI (people and points of interest) into nine categories by analyzing the frequency and duration of user visits: arts & entertainment (aquariums, casinos, etc.), education (schools, universities, etc.), Food (coffee, restaurant lamp), religion (church, mosque, etc.), outdoor & sports (gymnasium, stadium etc.), nightlife (bars, nightclubs etc.), shopping, Service (self-service teller, dentist, doctor, etc.) [9]. Through the improvement of Human Mobility data analysis method, we can better grasp the movement rule of individual or mass and apply the law to the development of Autonomous Vehicle interaction function. For example, users with overlapping paths are more likely to form new social relationships [6]. Autonomous Vehicles provide similar services to users with overlapping paths. Autonomous Vehicle, as an intelligent carrier that wraps the human movement, can calculate the passenger's PI based on the contextual awareness in a timely manner, achieving the result of being there. So in the design of Autonomous Vehicle interaction function, we need to pay attention to the elements of speed (computing speed, feedback speed, etc.) Human Mobility data collection in the past is dominated by people, need to be analyzed after the completion of the movement, autonomous Vehicles now move with people, data collection and analysis can be carried out simultaneously, through instant mobile context-awareness computing and mobile computing, to achieve where the resulting interactive features.

3.3 Data Application and Impact and Interaction Design Media

Human Mobility data application and impact study corresponds to the design of the Interaction Design media level. Urban planning, traffic forecasting, disease surveillance [1], commercial promotion, and the construction of The Social Network System [6, 16] can be better achieved through the mastery of the human trajectories in human mobility [1, 9]. Autonomous Vehicle as a medium, itself, can take on Human Mobility data applications. It is divided into weapons and containers. The former can exist as a medium carrying single functions, such as work tools and vehicles in dangerous places. The latter may exist as inclusive and adaptable containers, such as mobile self-media, shared space for economic mobility, and the like. Autonomous Vehicle as a carrier of information, the inherent identify information, impromptu information and transformation information of people and vehicles constitute a new The Social Network, Affected by a typology of mechanisms of change in social networks (relational mechanisms, Dynamics of Reciprocity, Dynamics of Repetition, Dynamics of Clustering and Closure, Dynamics of Degree) under Human Mobility [26], In the design of Autonomous Vehicle interactive media, we need to consider how to make the new The Social Network become one-way relationship from one-way interdependence, how to maintain stability, reciprocity, trust and good relations.

4 Autonomous Vehicle Interaction Model and Information Architecture

The Interaction model for the Human Mobility based on Autonomous Vehicle has changed. Users in the model include real physical humans, virtual agent information, individual, mass, users in the online social network and offline social network system, cyberspace identity duality role multiplicity of people, and people who make Collective Intelligence decisions based on the Intelligent Transportation System. The objects in the model also changed. Autonomous Vehicle has independent integrity. It can independently control the flow of logistics driven by information flow. The context in the model also changed. Non-intelligent traffic and intelligent traffic systems formed a hybrid Human Mobility context. In the present study, the Interaction model is modeled after the Flickr User Model (see Fig. 3). There are three key elements in the autonomous Vehicle Interaction model: users, mobile devices, autonomous vehicle. There are three kinds of relationships in mobility: active mobility, passive mobility, and follow-up mobility. Each of the three types of relationships is related to the mobile terminal. Users map to the autonomous vehicle through strong associations with the mobile terminal, and are categorized as three major functions: call, send, share. Three major features have enabled autonomous vehicle to promote the three major streams of "taking you moving": information flow, material flow, extension of financial flow, Three streams in the context of the realization of the function, the sharing of location, the birth of the data, the provision of services to individuals and their families, friends, people in the vicinity linked together to achieve the promotion of activities and financial returns, the exchange, transaction and mutual transit of the three major streams enable the system to achieve a coordinated and continuous operation in the continuous updating and agile development. Artificial Intelligence and Human Intelligence work together in this system.

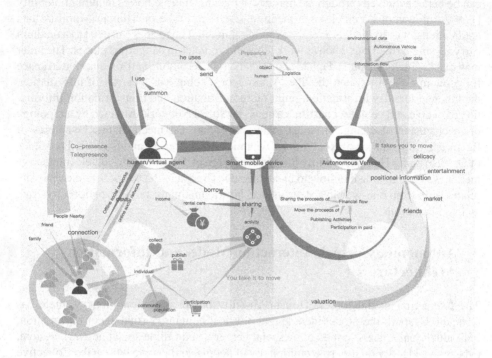

Fig. 3. Autonomous vehicle interaction model.

Information architecture for the Human-Mobility Interaction based on autonomous vehicle and intelligent transportation system has changed, and it contains digital information in cyberspace and intelligent information under the Artificial Intelligence algorithm. Meanwhile, information architecture has more interactive features of feedforward and feedback, content is enriched by UGC (User Generated Contents), PGC (Professional Generated Contents) and OGC (Occupationally-generated Contents). Information architecture under the corresponding interactive design, interface design, media design, visual design has changed.

5   Conclusion

Human Mobility not only reveals the distribution and evolution of spatiotemporal based on human's own movement, but also includes the flow characteristics of material, information and financial energy movement in synchronization with people in information space, cyberspace and noosphere. Autonomous Vehicle extends the connotation and denotation of Human Mobility through data collection, data analysis, data application and impaction. Human Mobility makes Autonomous Vehicle have theoretical support for the content, function and media of Interaction Design. Human Mobility and Autonomous Vehicle transform the Human-Machine Interaction into Human-Mobility Interaction, and the interaction of the new Human Mobility can be divided into presence, telepresence and co-presence mode under different subject representations. In the three major flow streams for Human-Mobility Interaction, people and vehicles are independent and make use of information flow to create the interaction among humans, vehicles and intelligent transportation system. The paradigm of Human Mobility is more flat and diversified. Information can be generated by Self-Quantified initiatively, exist independently in the form of virtual proxy or co-exist in the Autonomous Vehicle, digital information and non-digital information form the data content services design of Human Mobility, which stimulate the birth and flow of financial flows through the use of algorithms and data services.

References

1. Gonzalez, M., Hidalgo, C., Barabasi, A.: Understanding individual human mobility patterns. Nature **453**(7196), 779–782 (2008)
2. Horner, M., O'Kelly, M.: Embedding economies of scale concepts for hub network design. J. Transp. Geogr. **9**(4), 255–265 (2001)
3. Kitamura, R., Chen, C., Pendyala, R., et al.: Micro-simulation of daily activity-travel patterns for travel demand forecasting. Transportation **27**(1), 25–51 (2000)
4. Kleinberg, J.: Computing: the wireless epidemic. Nature **449**(7160), 287–288 (2007)
5. Qiao, Y., Si, Z., Zhang, Y., et al.: A hybrid Markov-based model for human mobility prediction. Neurocomputing **278**, 99–109 (2018)
6. Wang, D., Pedreschi, D., Song, C., et al.: Human mobility, social ties, and link prediction. In: 17th ACM SIGKDD International Conference on Knowledge Discovery and Data Mining, KDD 2001, pp. 1100–1108. ACM, San Diego (2011)
7. De Montjoye, Y., Hidalgo, C., Verleysen, M., et al.: Unique in the crowd: the privacy bounds of human mobility. Sci. Rep. **3**(1) (2013)
8. Song, C., Qu, Z., Blumm, N., et al.: Limits of predictability in human mobility. Science **327**(5968), 1018–1021 (2010)
9. Oliveira, E., Viana, A., Sarraute, C., et al.: On the regularity of human mobility. Pervasive Mob. Comput. **33**, 73–90 (2016)
10. Shin, R., Hong, S., Lee, K., et al.: On the Levy-walk nature of human mobility: do humans walk like monkeys? In: The 27th Conference on Computer Communications, INFOCOM 2008, pp. 924–932. IEEE, Phoenix (2008)
11. Simini, F., González, M., Maritan, A., et al.: A universal model for mobility and migration patterns. Nature **484**(7392), 96–100 (2012)
12. Pappalardo, L., Rinzivillo, S., Simini, F.: Human mobility modelling: exploration and preferential return meet the gravity model. Procedia Comput. Sci. **83**, 934–939 (2016)
13. Kim, D., Song, H.: Method of predicting human mobility patterns using deep learning. Neurocomputing **280**, 56–64 (2018)
14. Song, C., Koren, T., Wang, P., et al.: Modelling the scaling properties of human mobility. Nat. Phys. **6**(10), 818–823 (2010)
15. Jung, W., Wang, F., Stanley, H.: Gravity model in the Korean highway. EPL (Europhys. Lett.) **81**(4), 48005 (2008)
16. Feng, L., Kang, L., Jie, C.: Research on human mobility in big data era. J. Geo-Inf. Sci. **16**(5), 665–672 (2014)
17. Shi, W., Alawieh, M., Li, X., et al.: Algorithm and hardware implementation for visual perception system in autonomous vehicle: a survey. Integr. VLSI J. **59**, 148–156 (2017)

18. Rogers, Y., Sharp, H., Preece, J.: Interaction Design: Beyond Human-Computer Interaction, 2nd edn. Wiley, Hoboken (2011)
19. Winograd, T.: From computing machinery to interaction design. In: Denning, P., Metcalfe, R. (eds.) Beyond Calculation the Next Years of Computing, pp. 149–162. Springer, Berlin (1997)
20. http://www.bjjtw.gov.cn/xxgk/tzgg/201802/t20180202_190649.html,2018/02/09
21. Qin, J.: Impaction of artificial intelligence on interaction design. Packag. Eng. **38**(20), 27–31 (2017)
22. Hui, P., Chaintreau, A., Scott, J., et al.: Pocket switched networks and human mobility in conference environments. In: 2005 ACM SIGCOMM Workshop on Delay-Tolerant Networking, pp. 244–251. ACM, Philadelphia (2005)
23. Silva, A., Burleigh, S., Hirata, C., et al.: Congestion control in disruption-tolerant networks: a comparative study for interplanetary and terrestrial networking applications. Ad Hoc Netw. **44**, 1–18 (2016)
24. Qin, J., Cao, S., Wang, X.: User experience design for green IT products through wearable computing and quantified self. In: Marcus, A. (ed.) DUXU 2016. LNCS, vol. 9747, pp. 507–515. Springer, Cham (2016). https://doi.org/10.1007/978-3-319-40355-7_48
25. Mindell, J., Anciaes, P., Dhanani, A., et al.: Using triangulation to assess a suite of tools to measure community severance. J. Transp. Geogr. **60**, 119–129 (2017)
26. Rivera, M., Soderstrom, S., Uzzi, B.: Dynamics of dyads in social networks: assortative, relational, and proximity mechanisms. Ann. Rev. Sociol. **36**, 91–115 (2010)

Design Process of a Mobile Cloud Public Transport Application for Bus Passengers in Lima City

Juan José Ramírez[✉], Juan Arenas, and Freddy Paz

Pontificia Universidad Católica del Perú, San Miguel, Lima 32, Lima, Peru
{jjramirez, fpaz}@pucp.pe, jjarenas@pucp.edu.pe

Abstract. Deficient public transport affects life quality and the economic progress of modern cities. As it is difficult to improve public transport systems, in this paper we propose an application for bus passengers. The design of this mobile app is part of an ongoing project that aims to improve the public transport experience in Lima city, the capital of Perú. We envision a cloud-based community-driven mobile app that updates passengers with real information about buses. The presented information would be provided by and delivered to both users and public transport companies. With this intention in mind, we conducted a formative test with potential users. As a result, we created personas inspired by the interview participants. In addition, we built an interactive prototype in pursuance of conducting an expert heuristic evaluation and summative tests with real users. Finally, we provide conclusions and future work ideas.

Keywords: Public transport · Mobile passenger application · Design process
User interface design · Experimental case study

1 Introduction

Public transport plays a fundamental role in citizens' life quality and nation's economic progress [1]. Additionally, it has repercussions in job generation, industry strengthening, and social wealth creation [2]. The promotion of sustainable mobility minimizes negative social, economic and environmental externalities. Furthermore, it contributes to the structuring of more compact, clean, safe, active and healthy cities, providing greater and better opportunities to the inhabitants [3].

Lima, the capital of Perú, is the third largest city and the fifth most populous in Latin America [4]. Consequently, it has considerable mobility needs: 68.8% of the Peruvian public transport fleet is located in Lima [5] and more than 70% of trips made there are related to public transport [6]. According to *"Lima Cómo Vamos 2016"* survey, it is estimated that 80% of Lima citizens use public transport regularly [7]. However, the same survey mentions that 54% of Peruvian people consider public transport service as bad or very bad and 46% consider public transport related problems as the second most serious problem facing Lima, right after citizen insecurity.

© Springer International Publishing AG, part of Springer Nature 2018
A. Marcus and W. Wang (Eds.): DUXU 2018, LNCS 10920, pp. 375–388, 2018.
https://doi.org/10.1007/978-3-319-91806-8_29

In order to understand the problems that plague Lima´s public transport, we must acknowledge its course of development and the reasons behind its evolution. From the second half of the 20th century, Lima suffered a demographic explosion due to migration from the countryside to the city [8]. Between 1940 and 2007, the city had a population increase of 1300% [4]. Public transport, managed directly by the State, was not enough [9]. Informal transporters began to proliferate, offering lower prices and new routes without complying with the regulation. Nonetheless, Lima faced a severe shortage of public transport, which affected 90% of the population [9].

In this context, multiple State decrees were approved in 1991 that completely liberalized the service. Regulations on companies, minimum fares, and delimited routes and vehicles restrictions were removed and the importation of second-hand vehicles was allowed. Informality was institutionalized [10]. In this manner, Lima went from having an over demand of transport to an oversupply of obsolete, polluting and unprepared public transport units [4, 10–12].

In 1998, new measures were taken to control the chaos that prevailed. The qualifying title, needed to provide the service, was reintroduced. The title also established a limited number of routes per concessionaire. The concessionaires could only be companies and would have responsibility for the infractions committed in their routes. However, these measures did not specify that the fleet must belong to the concessionaires.

Faced with this legal loophole, so-called "shell companies" were formed. They obtained the concessions of the routes from the Municipality and then they outsourced the fleet. However, the outsourcing company wouldn't provide the service directly, through non-labor relations they agreed with drivers to perform the operational service. In this way, neither the concessionaire company nor the owner company assumed responsibility for the drivers, but the profits.

This situation is what is known as "Cent's War". Bus drivers do not earn a fixed salary or receive work benefits, so they needed to work more than 12 h daily where their profit is proportional to the number of passengers they carry. Quality ceases to be a consideration in this system, since the economic stability of the workers, who are usually low-income people, depends on their daily earnings. This causes the effects presented in Table 1.

As it has been shown, the problem of public transport in Lima city is complex and has its roots in poor government decisions. On one hand, companies have acted reactive to the problems of the city, instead of having a culture of prevention and planning. On the other hand, the citizens of Lima do not receive a quality public transport system that meets their basic needs. This has happened because of the scarcity of reliable information in a timely manner for decision making. The city of Lima does not have a static nature, on the contrary, it is in constant change. The only alternative for transport companies to anticipate the new needs of urban mobility is through the efficient use of information technologies.

Additionally, it has been demonstrated that the information obtained from information technologies contributes to strengthen the relations of the organizations with their clients [13]. The positive results of the information systems and the management of the relationship with customers are diverse and widely documented as client prioritization [14], retention of new clients [15], user satisfaction [16], business efficiency [17], customer loyalty [18], impact on the market and corporate image [19] and business profitability [20].

Table 1. Noxious effects of Lima public transport system.

ID	Proposed name	Explanation
1	Recklessness and lack of respect for traffic rules	Many drivers perform reckless and irresponsible maneuvers. This increases the number of accidents related to public transport. Adding this to a national police prone to corruption, the problem of accidents worsens
2	Rivalry between operators	A concessioner can outsource the routes with multiple owners, who in turn can outsource with multiple drivers. For this reason, they do not see other drivers as co-workers, but as adversaries
3	Units full	This causes discomfort and even endangers human lives. It is common to see passengers and/or bus collectors hanging outside of moving vehicles
4	Selective collection of passengers	Drivers usually avoid picking up passengers who delay (elderly people, pregnant women, people with children in arms, etc.) or pay less (school and university students)
5	Irregular collections	Bus collectors ask for fares under the prices required by the companies, even though this is not guaranteed by the municipal authorities
6	Breach of bus stops	They omit bus stops when they are in a hurry or stop at unauthorized stops to pick up/drop off passengers
7	Disinformation on routes	The constant changes and reforms carried out by the municipality in order to organize public transport, alter routes and bus stops, generating confusion among passengers
8	Inability to communicate complaints	Passenger complaints do not arrive in a timely manner to transport companies or municipal authorities, which prevents improvement of the service
9	Traditional methods for operational control	In the calculation processes of operator remuneration, passenger collection and user transport, controls with high error rates are used
10	Unnecessary pauses	It is common for operators to prefer to stay longer than necessary at strategic stops. This extends the travel time even when there is no traffic congestion in between

To mitigate the public transport problems that afflict Lima city, a new project arises. The mentioned project seeks to empower the decision making of companies, improve the existing relationship with passengers, to meet the information needs of each and to control the effects of the problem that put at risk the opportunities and quality of life of the Lima inhabitants. Although the project is focused on having an impact on Lima, the built solution can be replicated in any other city with similar issues.

The project solution is an ecosystem of applications, each with a target and a set of objectives. The projects includes a mobile application for passengers, an mobile application for company managers, a mobile application for bus drivers, a web application for bus companies and web server. This paper we present exclusively the design process behind the development of the mobile application for passengers.

In this sense, the solution designed must take into consideration the needs of the users, as well as the experience of them while using the product, to increase the chances of real success and impact on a real environment. This is why several techniques will be used to ensure the usability of the product, starting from the user-centered design and refining the solution through various evaluation strategies.

2 Preliminary Research

2.1 Papers and Related Work

Mobile Application with Information of Public Transport Routes in Lima from the User's Location
This project develops an application for mobile phones that can list the routes of urban public transport companies in Lima city taking as input data the user's location information [21].

Bus-Station-Passenger Intelligent Information System
This project develops a GPS information system to monitor the location of public transport buses in the city and deliver this information in a timely manner to passengers through screens at bus stops with an estimated time of arrival of the bus and transport companies [22].

2.2 Software and Related Products

TuRuta
TuRuta is a Peruvian application that seeks to help passengers know the lines to take to get from one place to another in Lima city. The information comes from a passenger community [23] (Fig. 1).

Fig. 1. Screenshots from TuRuta application

Moovit

Moovit is a mobile application that lists the public transport routes of many cities in the world (including Lima) and shows the ways to get from one place to another. Also, estimate the arrival time by consulting public information about the traffic. It obtains its information from its users [24] (Fig. 2).

Fig. 2. Screenshots from Moovit application

3 System Design

3.1 Formative Test

Objective

- Identify what is most important to passengers and focus the solution on delivering value to them.
- Adjust and refine the profile of the target audience, based on information collected in interviews with subjects who comply with the profile defined later.

Recruiting Participants

Young people from 15 to 30 years of age who are mainly mobilized by public transport buses. They have a medium-high-end cell phone and are interested in using technology to solve their daily problems.

Methodology

Following the methodology proposed by Rubin and Chisnell [25], two semi-structured questionnaires were prepared: the first one with 30 questions for passengers, to further segment the target audience and make the solution more personalized.

The questionnaires were sent in advance to the study subjects and later personal interviews were conducted with an average duration between 20 and 40 min. The scope of the interview was 15 passengers, which were chosen due to their similarities with the previously defined profile.

Results

The data plan is totally related to the specifications of the users' devices. As the applications will be used during the public transport routes in the city, they must be constantly connected to the Internet.

Approximately, 80% have Android devices. However, the specifications of these Android devices are varied. If we only consider those devices considered as high-end and that have a broad mobile data plan, the rate Android vs. iOS is 5 for every 3. It is for this reason that we will cover both platforms in the solution.

Among all the interviewees, we see a high level of use of social networks such as Instagram, Facebook and Twitter. The proposed solution must take advantage of this common factor to be able to acquire new users.

In relation to the use of taxi applications such as Uber, EasyTaxi and TaxiBeat, we see that in most cases, it is inversely proportional to the frequency of use of the public transport system. In addition, the degree of use is usually absolute: either they do not use taxi applications or they use them assiduously. We see a great opportunity to replicate this usage in those who use public transport frequently.

Users' appreciation of public transport in the city is similar to that presented in the "*Lima Como Vamos 2016*" survey [7], since many consider the service as bad. Regarding companies, the most repeated qualifier is "informal". They consider that companies care little or nothing about the satisfaction of their passengers. However, none have tried to communicate with the companies to present their complaints.

Of the problems presented, users are identified mainly with "Units full and people hanging". Secondly: "Imprudence in driving" and "Disinformation on routes and stops". In third place "Irregular Collections" and "Rivalry among operators".

3.2 Personas Creation

From these meetings, profiles of potential users benefited by the solution have been drawn up, which will then be presented through the technique of creating people [26]. This technique consists of the creation of imaginary characters that will represent potential users and whose expectations are assumptions based on interviews with real users [27]. Thus, the subsequent design of the solution will be focused on the users, considering their goals, desires and frustrations (Figs. 3, 4 and 5).

Fig. 3. Persona 1

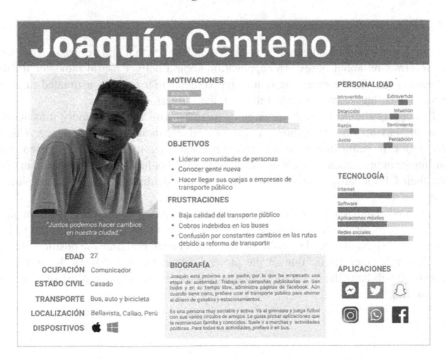

Fig. 4. Persona 2

Fig. 5. Persona 3

3.3   Interactive Prototype

We envision a cloud-based community-driven mobile app that updates passengers with real information about buses. The application should deliver useful indicator for the passengers such as the exact location of the vehicles in a map, an estimated time for arrival to next bus stops, the size of the unit, the fullness, etc.

Passengers should have the possibility to share with the community information about the bus they are travelling on, and to evaluate their travel experience. This is information is really important for transport companies that are compromised with continuous improvement of their service. Passengers should also be able to share in real-time their GPS location during the time they are inside the buses, so users can locate buses in a map.

It is predictable that this behavior, of passengers sharing their current position, may not be precise or reliable. That's the reason the project also includes bus companies. Companies that have agreed with this project will share in real time the position of their vehicles with other application of the project, aimed for bus drivers. In exchange, companies will have the feedback from their passengers in relation to the service they provide (Fig. 6).

Fig. 6. Initial app concept prototypes

4 Design Evaluation

4.1 Expert Heuristic Evaluation

The interfaces received a usability analysis applying the heuristic evaluation method by experts not involved in the project. The experts received the functional prototypes of the solution's interfaces and presented a report with the identified problems, relating each one of these with Nielsen's heuristic that is not met.

The experts identified 15 problems. With this feedback, we redesigned the prototypes, in order to evaluate them again with potential users. The final prototypes are presented in the following image (Fig. 7).

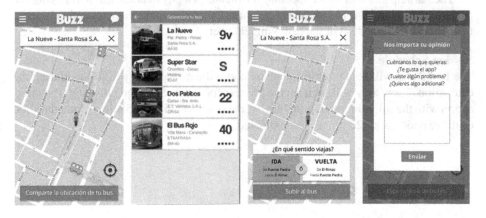

Fig. 7. Final app concept prototype

4.2 Summative Test

Objective

To validate the usability of the developed solution, it was decided to perform a summative study of usability with potential users. The solution will be qualified as valid when it is useful, efficient, effective, satisfactory, understandable and accessible.

Research Questions

1. Do the objectives and motivations obtained in the previous exploratory study case have been efficiently reflected in the solution?
2. How easily do the participants find the information they were looking for?
3. How successful are the participants performing the requested tasks?
4. How long do they take on average to complete the requested tasks?
5. What are the obstacles that users encounter when carrying out the main flow of use of the solution?

Methodology

A case of summative study was prepared and executed, following the methodology proposed by Rubin and Chisnell [25].

In this case study participants are asked to perform specific tasks with the solution, in order to analyze their interaction with the implemented tool. The role of the moderator is to resolve doubts about the tasks to be performed, without influencing the actions of the participants.

In addition, a test was performed before and after the interaction of the participants with the solution in order to obtain quantitative measures of their opinion on the proposed solution in the context of the problem. The oral and written opinions they recorded will serve as qualitative information and will be presented in the analysis section.

The participants will sign a meeting certificate as a physical means of verifying the performance of the test. The identities are not associated with the answers and only serve to confirm the realization of the test with real users.

Session Schedule

The first 3 min will be a brief introduction about the methodology to follow during the evaluation. Then, they will perform the pre-test for 5 min. Subsequently, start the interaction with the solution for 10 min. Finally, the post-test will last 5 min. A total duration of the experiment of 25 min is approximated.

Tasks

The list of tasks that participants will be asked to perform using the solution developed is shown in the following Table 2.

Table 2. Task list

ID	Task name
1	Understand the application concept
2	Create an account in the application
3	Log in to the application
4	Visualize buses of a line
5	Display information of a vehicle
6	Climb a bus and share location
7	Give a report to the community
8	View user profile
9	Sign out

Location And Setup

The test must be conducted in a controlled, closed and silent environment, in which there are no elements that can distract attention or affect the interaction between the participants and the solution developed.

The necessary equipment is mobile devices and computers with internet access for each participant, both elements must connect with internet connection.

Results

The quantifiable results obtained in the evaluation are presented in the following graphs (Fig. 8):

Fig. 8. Study results

Analysis

- In the graph "Problem vs. Solution", we see that almost all the problems presented are considered between serious and very serious.
- Question 2 (traffic rules), 3 (rivalry between operators) and 11 (vehicles in poor condition) are related to transport companies. In the introduction of the study only contextualized on the problems of public transport and the relationship with a possible mobile application.
- Question 6 (irregular collections) is not considered in the final iteration proposed in the present project, so its low rating is foreseen.
- The qualification in questions 4 (excessive number of passengers), 8 (disinformation of routes), 9 (communication with companies) and 12 (indefinite hours) is very positive.
- Question 1, regarding the impact of the solution on the general situation of transport, is that it improves it by 57%.
- Question 13 (possibility of solution) and 14 (interest in solution) are not greatly affected by the influence of the solution.
- Question 15, about the number of participants who want to use the application after the evaluation, was little reduced.
- As there is no prior evaluation, the baseline for the average time per task is estimated at 2 min. On average, no task exceeds the established threshold.
- We see that the tasks that have produced the most conflicts with the users are task 6 ("Upload a bus") and 7 ("Give information").
- Among the suggestions recommended by users, many of these had been considered as functionalities, but due to resource limitations, it was decided to postpone it for future versions. Recommendations are related to "Search engine for lines", "Estimated times", "Travel progress", "Intelligent use of data", "Final report", "External report", "Multiple reports", "Level information".

5 Conclusions and Future Work

A mobile application was designed, with the needs and interests of public transport passengers in Lima city. We conducted a formative test with potential users. As a result, we created personas inspired by the interview participants. In addition, we built an interactive prototype in pursuance of conducting an expert heuristic evaluation and summative tests with real users.

The next challenge proposed by this project is to scale the information technology infrastructure that supports the solution in order to be able to cope smoothly with a larger number of users. If the developed solution really wants to impact the public transport situation in Lima, it is fundamental to perform a refactoring of the server architecture and other components. Stress tests should be done, among other non-functional evaluations, to ensure the continuity of the service when concurrently serving hundreds of passengers and transport companies, and even more, if you want to replicate this solution in other cities, both in Peru and in other cities in Latin America.

On the other hand, once the solution goes into a production environment, there will be an immense amount of passenger location data. These data are the key to understanding the way in which the city is mobilized, the places that require more attention from the authorities or that may be a great business opportunity for companies. It is for this reason that research is also proposed related to computer science that exploits the large amount of data available, effectively and efficiently, to be able to anticipate the needs of the city and make changes proactively, instead of waiting to have an untenable situation to decide to take action.

References

1. Antunes, E.M., Simões, F.A.: Engenharia urbana aplicada: um estudo sobre a qualidade do transporte público em cidades médias. Rev. Bras. Gestão Urbana **5**, 51–62 (2013)
2. Mendes, R., Luiz Wittmann, M., Flores Battistella, L., Richter Skrebsky, A., Santos Da Silva, M.: Inovação em serviços de transporte público. Organ. em Context. **8**, 86 (2012)
3. Poole Fuller, E.: ¿Hacia una movilidad sustentable? Desafíos de las políticas de reordenamiento del transporte público en Latinoamérica . El caso de Lima Towards Sustainable Mobility? Challenges of the public transportation reorganization policies in Latin America. Let. Verdes, Rev. Latinoam. Estud. Socioambientales, 4–31 (2017)
4. Strategia: Transporte Público ¿La luz al final del túnel? Strategia **31**, 41–43 (2014)
5. Borjas Giraldo, G.: Análisis, diseño e implementación de un sistema de información para la administración de horarios y rutas en empresas de transporte público. PUCP - Ingeniería Informática (2013)
6. Japón/JICA A de CI de: Encuesta de Recolección de Información Básica de Transporte Urbano en el Área Metropolitana de Lima y Callao (2014)
7. Vamos, L.C.: Cómo vamos en movilidad. Sexto informe de resultados sobre calidad de vida (2016)
8. Margarito, J.G.: Diseño de una red de comunicaciones para la implementación de un sistema de transporte inteligente en el centro histórico de lima (2006)
9. Poole Fuller, E.: Rectificando las fallas del mercado: balance del proceso de implementación en lima del sistema integrado de transporte (SIT) y propuesta para su perfeccionamiento bajo un régimen de servicio público (2016)
10. Bielich, C.: El transporte Publico Limeño y La guerra del centavo. Argumentos (2009)
11. Barrantes Ríos, W.A., Bejarano Nicho, G.M.: Implementación de un algoritmo recocido simulado para el diseño de rutas de transporte público para lima centro (2015)
12. Vega Centeno, P., Dextre, J.C., Alegre, M.: Inequidad y fragmentación: movilidad y sistemas de transporte en Lima Metropolitana (2011)
13. Harrison, D.E., Hair, J.F., Bellenger, D.: Information quality, customer relationship management, and marketing decision making. AMA Winter Educ. Conf. Proc. **27**, B–13–B–14 (2016)
14. Zablah, A.R., Bellenger, D., Johnston, W.J.: An evaluation of divergent perspectives on customer relationship management: towards a common understanding of an emerging phenomenon. Ind. Mark. Manag. **33**, 475–489 (2004)
15. Hilldebrand, B., Nijholt, J.J., Nijsenn, E.J.: Exploring CRM effectiveness: an institutional theory perspective. J. Acad. Mark. Sci. **39**, 592–608 (2011)
16. Mithas, S., Krishnan, N., Fornell, C.: How information management capability influences firm performance. MIS Q. **35**, 237–256 (2011)

17. Krasnikov, A., Jayacharana, S., Kumar, V.: The impact of customer relationship management implementation on cost and profit efficiencies: evidence from the US commercial banking industry. J. Mark. **73**, 61–76 (2009)
18. Kumar, V., Shah, D.: Building and sustaining, profitable customer loyalty for the 21st century. J. Retail. **80**, 317–329 (2014)
19. Reinman, M., Schilke, O., Thomas, J.K.: Customer relationship management and firm performance: the mediating role of business strategy. J. Acad. Mark. Sci. **38**, 326–346 (2010)
20. Ernst, H., Hoyer, W., Krafft, M., Krieger, K.: Customer relationship management and company performance—the mediating role of new product performance. J. Acad. Mark. Sci. **39**, 290–306 (2011)
21. Añazgo, A., Larios, E.: Implementación de un aplicativo para teléfonos móviles que indique las rutas de transporte público de la ciudad de lima a partir de la ubicación del usuario. Pontificia Univevrsidad Católica del Perú (2010)
22. Sungur, C., Babaoglu, I., Sungur, A.: Smart bus station-passenger information system. In: 2015 2nd International Conference on Information Science and Control Engineering, pp. 921–925 (2015). https://doi.org/10.1109/ICISCE.2015.209
23. Micro T Tu Ruta. http://turuta.pe/. Accessed 5 Jun 2017
24. Company M Moovit Features. https://www.company.moovitapp.com/features?utm_medium=Organic&utm_source=web_app. Accessed 5 Jun 2017
25. Rubin, J., Chisnell, D.: Handbook of Usability Testing: How To Plan, Design, and Conduct Effective Tests (2008)
26. Castro, J.W., Acuña, S.T., Juristo, N.: Integrating the personas technique into the requirements analysis activity. In: Proceedings of the Mexican International Conference on Computer Science, pp. 104–112 (2008). https://doi.org/10.1109/enc.2008.40
27. Baumann, K.: Personas as a user-centred design method for mobility-related services. Inf. Des. J. **18**, 157–167 (2010). https://doi.org/10.1075/idj.18.2.07bau

Factor Model for Passenger Experience in the Aircraft Cabin Design

Siyu Ren, Xinyi Tao, and Ting Han[(✉)]

School of Design, Shanghai Jiao Tong University, Shanghai, China
{Vikey,hanting}@sjtu.edu.cn, 307175338@qq.com

Abstract. As the rapid growth of the economy, people have improved the standard of living and quality of life, paying more attention to how they feel towards the world. Thus, user experience becomes an important consideration in the aircraft cabin design. A systematical understanding of aircraft cabin design from the perspective of user experience is challenging but worth exploring. In this paper, we first modeled relevant influencing factors. Specifically, we studied passenger behaviors and related touch points in the cabin by analyzing the general flight process. After dividing aircraft cabins into several system areas, such as the front service area, seats and passenger service unit, we identified the product components and their attributes in each area to form our model. Based on the factor model, further research was carried out on these influence factors. Relevant investigations and interviews were conducted with aircraft interior designers, user experience researchers and passengers. Finally, we reached to a conclusion and categorized key factors which would impact passenger experience in the aircraft cabin.

Keywords: Passenger experience · Aircraft cabin design · Factor model

1 Introduction

User experience is becoming increasingly important as demand for air travel rises [1]. The riding experience of an aircraft is directly related to the choice of the consumer and becomes a key future economic driver [1]. As a result, mastering knowledge of passenger experience in the aircraft cabin could be a competitive advantage in the airline industry. However, different from ordinary products such as chairs and mobile phones, aircraft cabin contains have complicated structures since they contain various aspects such as product, space and human-machine interaction. Besides, a variety of passenger behaviors could happen in the aircraft such as resting, eating, walking, reading, etc., which would create a lot of user touch points. Each time a touch point is changed, user's overall experience is affected.

A large number of cabin elements need to be considered in the design process in order to achieve a better passenger experience. So far, a number of studies [2, 3] have found some key elements that affect passenger experience in the aircraft cabin, such as legroom and cabin space. But these factors don't create a systematic cognition of the cabin. Other studies [4, 5] provide some basic models on passenger experience, such as the thematic structure of passenger comfort experience, and a new model of key factors which influence aircraft passengers' comfort. These models are difficult to apply to

© Springer International Publishing AG, part of Springer Nature 2018
A. Marcus and W. Wang (Eds.): DUXU 2018, LNCS 10920, pp. 389–405, 2018.
https://doi.org/10.1007/978-3-319-91806-8_30

specific design processes by designers and stakeholders since they are too general and broad. To have a systematic and practical understanding of factors that influence passenger experience in the aircraft cabin, we conducted a study from the aspect of cabin design and constructed a key factor model on passenger experience.

In this paper, we utilized the example of studying passenger experience under the general situation in a single-channel plane cabin. Rather than airline services, this paper focuses on the design of plane cabin. First, we studied on user behavior and product system. A factor model was presented which includes three systems, eight subsystems, several high-level factors and underlying factors. Then, investigations and literature review were conducted, which led to the conclusion of our key influence factors. The research framework is shown below (see Fig. 1). The result of this study can be used to help aircraft cabin designers and other stakeholders in the aviation industry understand the key factors and priorities of aircraft cabin design with regard to passenger experience. Meanwhile, the model provides a new way to quantitatively evaluate the passenger experience in terms of aircraft cabin design and lays a solid foundation in this area.

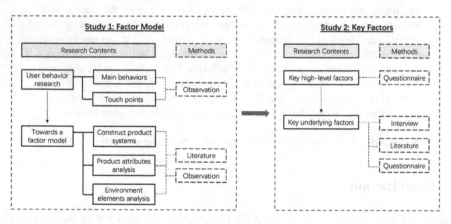

Fig. 1. The research framework.

The rest of this paper is organized as follows. Section 2 focuses on existing related work in academic and industry fields. Sections 3 and 4 contain two research studies. The first study is based on factor model to introduce approaches employed in the user behavior research and modeling of influence factors. The second study includes employed approaches, data collection, analysis and discussion on the influence level of high-level and underlying factors. Section 5 dwells on discussion, limitation and further research. Conclusion is presented in Sect. 6.

2   Related Work

Airlines and aircraft manufacturers have made a lot of effort to provide better passenger experience. For example, a small table that can be folded two times in the United Arab Emirates and large legroom in Cathay Pacific is praised by many people [6]. China

Eastern Airlines began to provide WIFI services on board since January 18, 2018 [7], enabling users to communicate with the outside world rather than spend a boring time. The Airbus divided concept air cabins into different activity zones, such as entertainment, relaxation and working zones, to meet specific needs [8]. In recent years, Commercial Aircraft Corporation of China Ltd (COMAC) has independently developed a large civil aircraft C919. Its industrial design department also attaches great importance to the study of user experience. For example, Ai summed up the evaluation factors of the comfort of the civil aircraft [9], and Lening studied the application of the user experience research in the interior design of civil aircraft [10].

Some academic research has been carried out on influence factors for passenger experience in the aircraft cabin. These studies can be categorized by two types.

The first type of research identified some key factors that have a significant impact on passenger experience. For example, Budd [11] presented airline passengers' perceptions of space, time, distance, and speed of mobility would affect their experience. The study by Vink [2] showed clear relationships between comfort and legroom, hygiene, crew attention and seat/ personal space. Similarly, in separate empirical studies, by analyzing the result of face-to-face questionnaires, Greghi et al. [3] found major discomforts during air travel are related to seat and cabin space. These studies do identify a number of influencing factors, but still lack a systematic understanding of aircraft passenger experience influential elements.

The second type of research built a system of relevant elements affecting passenger experience. A large number of related studies have been carried out by Naseem Ahmadpour. He presented eight themes and outline their particular eliciting features in one of his studies. The eight themes are physical well-being, peace of mind, satisfaction, pleasure, proxemics, aesthetics, association and social [4]. In a later study, researchers verified the eight themes by using Principal Component Analysis with varimax rotation [12]. Ahmadpour et al. [13] also presented a model identified four emotion groups that are closely related to comfort. In addition, Patel and D'Cruz [5] presented a new model of key factors which influence aircraft passengers' comfort. The factors are individual characteristics, personal travel context, the pre-flight and in-flight environments, interaction with others, activities, current state, current needs and adaptive behaviors, perceived control. These studies tried to construct models related to the passenger experience. However, since they carried out studies from the perspective of experience itself or passenger emotion, the meaning of these factors is usually very board.

Besides, there are some other relevant studies. These studies focus on the relationship between one or some specific elements and passenger experience. Brindisi and Concilio [14] modeled passengers' perceptions of aircraft cabin comfort regarding a characterization of an environment considering temperature, relative humidity, and noise level. The study by Kremser et al. [15] showed, there is a maximum overall well-being at a seat pitch of 34 inches to 40 inches, depending on the passengers' anthropometry. Pennig et al. [16] presented aircraft interior noise could be optimised reducing passengers' noise perception as 'bright' and 'shrill' as well as 'irregular' and 'varied'. In his study of *Aircraft Interior Comfort and Design*, Vink and Brauer [17, p. 47] specifically summarized the factors associated with the level of seat comfort, such as the curve of the backrest, adjustable button and so on. Although these studies can't form a comprehensive consideration of the factors in the cabin, they provide an important reference for our research.

In general, research on systematic and practical understanding of factors that influence passenger experience in the aircraft cabin is still limited. We aim to construct a key factor model from the perspective of cabin design to benefit the design processes and experience evaluation.

3 Study 1: Factor Model

This study aims at uncovering the influence factors of aircraft cabin that affect passenger experience and the relation between them. Although an experience is essentially subjective, the passenger behavior and the design content of the aircraft cabin are relatively clear and fixed. Qualitative investigations were conducted based on a real flight and cabin design. By analyzing the content of collected data and related literature, a factor model for passenger experience in the aircraft cabin design was constructed.

3.1   User Behavior and Touch Point Research

Methods. To clear passengers' general behavior, a survey was carried out in a real flight. Six researchers observed and recorded passengers' behavior from entering the cabin to leaving the cabin during a three-hour flight. We recorded activities related to the products provided in the cabin design, regardless of activities related to the products that were carried in by passengers themselves. After the flight, passenger's main behaviors were extracted based on observation record. Then, the corresponding touch points for each behavior were clear.

Results. A flight can be divided into four phases: take-off, cruise, approach, and landing [24]. Accordingly, the passenger behaviors inside the aircraft cabin are divided into five stages. The main behaviors of passengers are shown by stage as follows. Note that a passenger may only have some of these behaviors in a flight.

1. Before Take-off. Passengers enter the cabin through boarding bridge and look around for seats. After finding their seats, they put carry-on baggage in overhead bin and sit in their seats.
2. Take-off. Passengers fasten their seat belts, put their tray table and seat in the upright position, and keep window shade open.
3. Cruise. Passenger behaviors during this stage include two types. The first type is various activities that involve their own arrangements over time, including going to the lavatory, resting, eating, working, and using the entertainment system. The second type is adjustment of surrounding environment, including adjusting their seat, airflow knob, reading light and window shade.
4. Approach and Landing. Passengers fasten their seat belts, put their tray table and seat in the upright position, and keep window shade open.
5. After Landing. Passengers leave their seats, take out their baggage from overhead bin and leave the cabin through aisles.

When the above behaviors occur, passengers touch the product on the plane. As a result, different product components act as touch points that affect passenger experience in the aircraft cabin. Since similar products have different characteristics, the differences between product components are also seen as factors that influence passenger experience. We consulted the relevant product components and their characteristics according to the above behaviors (see Fig. 2).

Stage	Mian Behaviors	Product Components	Product Characteristics
Before Take-off	Enter the cabin through the boarding bridge	Welcoming placard	Color, Slogan content
	Look around for seat	Sign of seat number	Position, Recognition degree
	Put the carry-on baggage in the overhead compartment	Overhead bin cover	Open mode
	Sit in the seat	Backrest, Seat cushion	Width, Firmness
Take-off	Fasten the seat belt	Seat belt	Length, Switch mode
	Lock the tray table in place	Tray table	Storage mode
	Put the seat in the upright position	Adjustment button	Position, Instructions
	Keep window shade open	Window shade	Adjustment mode
Cruise	Go to the lavatory	Toilet, Trash bin, Water tap	Cleanliness, Open mode
	Rest	Backrest, Seat cushion	Width, Firmness
	Eat	Tray table	Dimensions
	Work	Tray table	Dimensions, Position after putting down
	Use the entertainment system	HD display	Size, Fluency
	Adjust the seat	Adjustment button	Position, Instructions
	Adjust the airflow knob	Individual vent	Switch position
	Adjust the reading lamp	Individual reading light	Switch position
	Adjust the window shade	Window shade	Adjustment mode
Approach and Landing	Fasten the seat belt	Seat belt	Length, Switch mode
	Lock the tray table in place	Tray table	Storage mode
	Put the seat in the upright position	Adjustment button	Position, Instructions
	Keep window shade open	Window shade	Adjustment mode
After Landing	Leave the seat	Legroom	Seat pitch
	Take out the baggage from the overhead compartment	Overhead bin cover	Open mode
	Leave the cabin through the aisles	Aisle	Width

Fig. 2. Passengers' general behavior and related touch points.

3.2 Towards a Model of Influence Factors

Though a preliminary analysis of passenger behaviors and experience, we found that the product components in the cabin and their attributes can be considered as passenger experience influential factors. Thus, a factor model was built from the view of cabin products.

An aircraft cabin can be divided into three relatively closed areas from the perspective of space, including the front service area, the main cabin and lavatories (see Fig. 3). The front service area refers to the area between the boarding gate and the bulkhead. Generally, there are welcome slogans and flight attendants. The main cabin is the main activity area for passenger on the plane. It can be divided into seven subsystem areas, including seats, passenger service unit (PSU), overhead bins, portholes, inflight entertainment (IFE) system, interior trim panels. There are a number of product components under each subsystem. In a plane, there are more than one lavatory, which have similar product components inside, such as a toilet, a hand basin and so on.

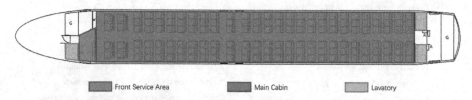

| | Front Service Area | | Main Cabin | | Lavatory |

Fig. 3. An aircraft cabin can be divided into three relatively closed areas.

Then we built the model, in which we identified three systems: front service area, main cabin and lavatory. And the main cabin is divided into service subsystems, including seats, PSU, overhead bins, portholes, IFE system, interior trim panels and signs. Moreover, there are two levels of influence factors in the model. The product components in front service area, lavatory and all subsystems are defined as the high-level factors. And the attributes of these product components are considered as the underlying factors (see Fig. 4).

In order to clarify high-level factors and underlying factors, we conducted literature review and field research. In field research, researchers personally experienced the use of product components in an airplane cabin prototype. Products features were recorded in detail through photos and text. We take the analysis of underlying factors related to individual vent in PSU as an example to show detailed research process.

Literature Review. Xu presented that it's necessary to ensure that passengers corresponding to each PSU can easily use the function buttons of individual vent when design air conditioning personal ventilation module [18]. In other words, the location of function buttons on individual vents has an impact on the passenger experience.

Field Research. The functions of individual vent are air supply, air volume adjustment, air flow direction adjustment. Therefore, the related attributes that affect experience are air flow form, air temperature, wind regulation mode, and whether the wind direction is adjustable. Besides, the shape of individual vent affects the passenger's visual experience and becomes one of underlying factors.

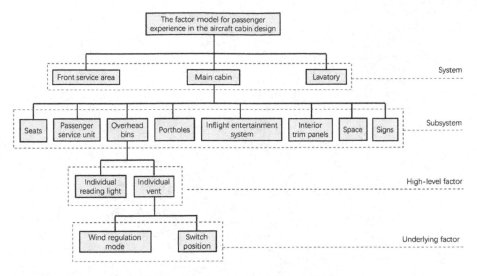

Fig. 4. The framework of factor model.

To sum up, underlying factors related to individual vent include switch position, air flow form, air temperature, wind regulation mode, shape, and whether the wind direction is adjustable.

We clarified most factors in accordance with this idea. But the passenger experience is influenced not only by product components. The pre-flight and in-flight environments are important factors which influence aircraft passengers' comfort [5]. And a lot of studies [16, 19] on the relationship between passenger experience and environment elements such as sound and thermal have been carried out. As a result, environmental impact factors were added to the three systems. For example, "sound" is added as a high-level factor. The related underlying factors are volume, type and the frequency of occurrence.

Afterwards we asked aircraft cabin designers of COMAC for comments on this model. We adjusted the model according to their suggestions and gained their approval in the end. The final model divides the influencing factors into three product systems: front service area, main cabin and lavatory. And the main cabin is divided into eight subsystems: seats, passenger service unit, overhead bins, portholes, inflight entertainment system, interior trim panels, space and signs. There are a number of high-level factors affecting the passenger experience under front service area, lavatory and each subsystem of the main cabin. And there are also several related key underlying factors under each key high-level factor (see Fig. 5).

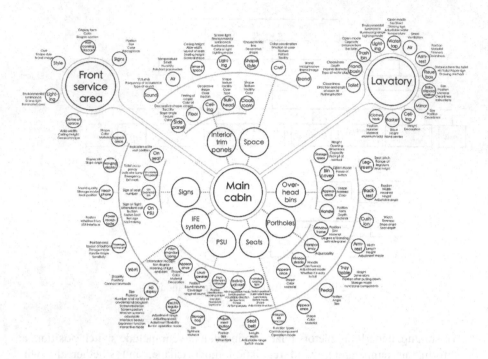

Fig. 5. Factor model for passenger experience in aircraft cabin design.

4   Study 2: Key Factors

As shown above, there are many high-level and underlying factors in aircraft cabin design related to passenger experience. Various surveys were carried out in order to find out the priority indexes.

4.1   Key High-Level Factors

Methods. In order to find out the influence level of each high-level factor on passenger experience, a questionnaire survey was carried out. Total 67 high-level factors in our model were included in the questionnaire, shown as following.

- The front service area: sense of space, lighting, style, welcoming placard, signs.
- The main cabin:
  - Interior trim panels: side pane, floor, ceiling, bulkhead, cloakroom.
  - Space: sound, air, sense of space, lighting, shape style, CMF (color, material and furnish), brand.
  - Overhead bins: storage space, bin cover, appearance, handle.
  - Portholes: window frame, transparency, window shade, appearance.
  - Seats: legroom, backrest, seat cushion, armrest, tray table, pedal, appearance, integrated function, seat belt, adjustment button, storage bag, electric regulation.

- PSU: individual reading light, individual vent, flight attendant call button, loudspeaker, appearance, information lamp.
- IFE system: HD display, Wi-Fi, passenger control unit, power receptacle, headphone, hanging display, appearance.
- Signs: sign on PSU, sign on overhead bin, sign on interior trim panel, sign on seat.
- The lavatory: toilet, hand basin, trash bin, lighting, water tap, air, armrest, tissue box, baby disposal station, mirror, ceiling, basket, clothes hook.

The participants were asked to evaluate the importance of each high-level factor according to their experience. The influence is divided into three levels in the evaluation, including general influence (score = 1), important influence (score = 2), key influence (score = 3).

Participants. Total 16 participants attended the experiment. Their ages ranged from 21 to 45 years old. Their career experiences ranged from 2 to 25 years. Ten of them were aircraft interior design experts from COMAC, the other six were postgraduate students majoring in design from Shanghai Jiao Tong University who have certain knowledge and experience in this research area. The investigation scene is shown in Fig. 6.

Fig. 6. Investigation scene of questionnaire survey.

Data Analysis. After the survey, the mean value, mode and standard deviations were calculated for each factor. In order to judge the influence of high-level factors, a hypothesis about the standard of influence division is put forward. Define the mean of influence as X.

The null standard: When $1 \leq X < 1.67$, the factor is a general factor. When $1.67 \leq X < 2.33$, the factor is an important factor. When $2.33 \leq X3 \leq 3$, the factor is a key factor.

The result of factor influence level based on this standard was contrasted with the result according to the mode. If both results were consistent, the standard will be accepted. A data of 38 randomly selected factors scored by 10 experts were used to test this hypothesis. Results are presented in Table 1. Overall, both outcomes of the 34 items are the same.

Table 1. Mean score, mode score and standard deviation of some high-level factors.

System	Subsystem	High-level factor	Avg	Mode	Std. dev.
Front service area	-	Sense of space	1.89	2.00	0.78
		Lighting	2.11	2.00	0.78
		Style	1.89	2.00	0.78
Main cabin	Space	Sense of space	2.50	3.00	0.85
		Lighting	2.40	3.00	0.70
		Sound	2.70	3.00	0.67
		Air	2.60	3.00	0.52
	PSU	Individual reading light	2.50	3.00	0.85
		Individual vent	2.10	2.00	0.74
		Flight attendant call button	2.10	2.00	0.74
		Information lamp	1.80	1.00, 2.00	0.79
		Loudspeaker	2.00	2.00	0.82
	Overhead bins	Storage space	2.63	3.00	0.52
		Handle	1.50	1.00	0.76
		Appearance	1.75	2.00	0.71
	Portholes	Transparency	2.00	2.00	0.87
		Window shade	2.00	2.00	0.71
	IFE system	HD display	2.88	3.00	0.35
		Wi-Fi	2.11	2.00	0.60
		Power receptacle	2.20	2.00, 3.00	0.79
		Headphone	1.67	2.00	0.50
	Seats	Backrest	2.78	3.00	0.44
		Seat cushion	2.67	3.00	0.71
		Armrest	2.20	2.00, 3.00	0.79
		Tray table	2.10	3.00	0.88
		Adjustment button	1.56	1.00	0.73
		Storage bag	1.44	1.00	0.53
		Seat belt	2.11	2.00	0.78
Lavatory	-	Toilet	2.44	3.00	0.73
		Hand basin	2.00	2.00	0.87
		Trash bin	1.89	2.00	0.78
		Water tap	1.89	2.00	0.78
		Tissue box	1.33	1.00	0.50
		Armrest	1.78	2.00	0.67
		Baby disposal station	1.44	1.00	0.88
		Mirror	1.38	1.00	0.52
		Basket	1.33	1.00	0.50
		Clothes hook	1.11	1.00	0.33

After analyzing the other four factors, we can conclude that both results of the three factors are relatively consistent. The three factors are information lamp, power receptacle and armrest. Scores of these factors have more than one mode. And the result of factor influence level based on our standard was contrasted with the result according to one of the mode. Take power receptacle as an example. The mode of this factor is 2.00 and 3.00, which means the factor is an important factor or a key factor. The mean of this factor is 2.20, which means the factor is an important factor according to our standard. Therefore, the two results can be considered relatively consistent.

On the whole, the consensus rate of both results is as high as 97.37%, which means our standard of influence division can be accepted.

Result. Based on our standard of influence division, the influence level of all high-level factors was identified. There are 27 key factors, 24 important factors and 16 general factors. All key factors are listed below.

- The front service area: sense of space, lighting.
- The main cabin:
  - Interior trim panels: side pane.
  - Space: sound, air, sense of space, lighting.
  - Overhead bins: storage space, bin cover.
  - Portholes: window frame, transparency.
  - Seats: legroom, backrest, seat cushion.
  - PSU: individual reading light, individual vent.
  - IFE system: HD display, Wi-Fi, passenger control unit.
  - Signs: sign on PSU, sign on overhead bin.
- The lavatory: toilet, hand basin, trash bin, lighting, water tap, air.

4.2   Key Underlying Factors

Following the results from Sect. 4.1, all key high-level factors were presented. Three different surveys were conducted to identify key underlying factors related to the 27 key-level factors above.

Methods. Literature review was conducted first to count the number and importance of each underlying factor. We searched with different terms of each key high-level factor name and related terms such as "design", "experience", and "evaluate" with the aid of Google Scholar. Besides, we focused only on English and Chinese articles for comprehension. Next, fact-to-face interviews was carried out to gather aircraft cabin designers' opinion. Six designers (3 male, 25–45 years of age) were asked to assess the importance of underlying factors relevant to their areas of expertise and select the most critical 1–3 factors. The interview scene is shown in Fig. 7. Finally, using a questionnaire, six user researchers (3 male, 22–35 years of age, 3–8 flights a year) were asked to independently indicate the importance of each underlying factor according to their experience. The influence is divided into two levels, including critical influence (score = 1), non-critical influence (score = 0).

Fig. 7. Investigation scene of face-to-face interview survey.

Analysis. By considering the three surveys above, key underlying factors were clarified. We take the analysis of underlying factors related to sound in space as an example to present detailed process. As mentioned in Sect. 3.2, the underlying factors of "sound" include volume, type and frequency of occurrence.

In literature review, a total of 4 related articles were found. Zhang et al. [20] found that noise volume (loudness) is most important, followed by sharpness, pitch, roughness and other parameters. Public transport hygiene requirements standard provides that cabin noise needs to be lower than 80 dB [21]. And Chen and Xia [22] emphasized that efforts should be made to adopt various sound insulation, sound absorption and noise reduction measures to improve the relative layout of aircraft sound sources, reduce cabin noise level and create a good working environment. In addition, Lei and Jiang [23] presented that cabin noise should be as low as possible to ensure the comfort of occupants and passengers.

On the whole, the "volume" factor is mentioned in all of the four studies. Moreover, one article pointed out that the volume of sound is most important. The "frequency of occurrence" factor is mentioned in two papers. The "type of sound" factor is only mentioned in one of them. Therefore, from the perspective of literature review, the "volume" is a key factor and the rest are non-critical.

Interview records show that three designers did assessment on this high-level factor. Their opinions are presented below.

Designer 01: The "volume" and "frequency of occurrence" are important.
Designer 02: The "volume" seriously affects passenger experience.
Designer 03: The "volume" is the most important factor, followed by the "frequency of occurrence".

From the above opinions, the "volume" factor is considered as a key factor by all designers. Some designers think the "frequency of occurrence" is important. The "type of sound" factor was almost never mentioned. Therefore, from the perspective of designers, the "volume" is a key factor, followed by the "frequency of occurrence".

The results of questionnaire survey are presented in Table 2. All six user experience researchers agreed the "volume" is a key factor. People who believe that the "frequency of occurrence" or "type of sound" is critical were respectively no more than half. Therefore, from the perspective of user researchers, the "volume" is a key factor.

Table 2. Underlying factors of "sound" and the numbers of researchers who considered it as a key factor (N = 6).

Underlying factor	Volume	Frequency of occurrence	Type of sound
Number of votes	6	2	0

We come to a conclusion after comprehensively considering the result of literature review and the opinions of designers and researchers. The "volume" is a key factor, and the "frequency of occurrence" and "type of sound" are non-key factors.

Results. All 27 key high-level factors were studied based on the same thought of analysis. As a result, there are 41 relevant underlying factors that have key impact on passenger experience. All key underlying factors are listed below (see Table 3).

Table 3. Key underlying factors of key high-level factors.

System	Subsystem	KEY high-level factor	KEY underlying factor
Front service area	-	Sense of space	Aisle width
		Lighting	Environmental luminance
Main cabin	PSU	Individual vent	Wind regulation mode, Switch position
		Individual reading light	Switch position, illuminated area, Luminance
	Signs	Sign on PSU	Sign of flight attendant call button
		Sign on overhead bin	Sign of seat number
	Overhead bins	Storage space	Height
		Overhead bin cover	Open mode
	Space	Sense of space	Ceiling height, aisle width
		Air	Temperature, smell
		Sound	Volume
		Lighting	Scene light, environmental luminance
	Interior trim panels	Side panel	Decorative shape, tactility
	Portholes	Window frame	Position, size
		Transparency	Adjustability

(continued)

Table 3. (*continued*)

System	Subsystem	KEY high-level factor	KEY underlying factor
	IFE system	Passenger control unit	Position and layout of buttons
		HD display	Size, fluency, number and variety of on-demand program
		Wi-Fi	Stability, fluency
	Seats	Legroom	Seat pitch, range of legroom
		Backrest	Radian (fit to body curve), width
		Seat cushion	Width, firmness
Lavatory	-	Toilet	Cleanliness
		Hand basin	Cleanliness
		Trash bin	Open mode
		Lighting	Environmental luminance
		Water tap	Open mode
		Air	Smell

The results of Study 1 and Study 2 are combined and presented in the following image (see Fig. 8).

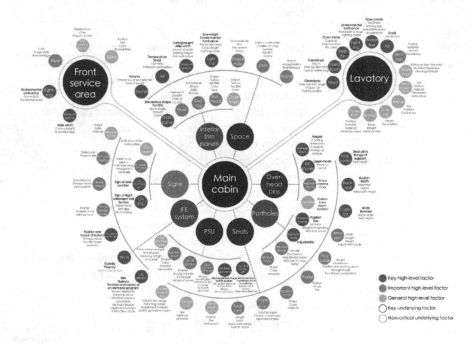

Fig. 8. The factor model with information of factor influence level.

5   Discussion

The aircraft cabin interior design is complicated. It's challenging to systematically understand it from the perspective of user experience. We focused on factors within cabin body and presented a key factor model for passenger experience in the aircraft cabin design.

In our study of the high-level factors' influence level in Sect. 4.2, we used the mean of scores as the indicator. Common statistical value that can reflect the trend of data concentration are the mean and the mode. For a certain set of data, there may be more than one mode value. But they can only have one mean value. If the mode was used as the indicator, the influence level of some factors couldn't be determined. Therefore, we chose the mean value as the indicator of influence level and used the mode to test whether the division standard of influence level is acceptable.

In study 2, the methods we used to find out key underlying factors are different from the methods used in the study of key high-level factors. Only questionnaire survey was conducted when we tried to find out key high-level factors. But when it came to key underlying factors, we also carried out the literature review and face-to-face interviews except for questionnaires. The differences between these methods are mainly due to the limitation of participants and rich language connotation. Most aircraft designers can correctly understand the meaning of each high-level factor and assess their influence level. However, since underlying factors are too detail-oriented, it is difficult for most designers to be familiar with them. Therefore, designers were only required to rate underlying factors in their area of expertise. Additionally, names of underlying factors were determined by us, so others may not be able to accurately understand the meaning. Through face-to-face interviews, we can be aware of whether respondents correctly understand the meaning of the factors. If not, we clarify the meaning of these factors on the spot. So, we used the face-to-fact interview to gather the opinions of expert designers. Meanwhile, literature review and questionnaire survey of user researchers were also conducted to get a more accurate and convincing result.

Limitations. When building the model, we regarded the factors as relatively independent. Thus, interactions between factors are not evaluated in our study. On one hand, each factor is defined based on cabin body and can be considered as a relatively independent entity. On the other hand, it is more convenient for us to clear up the structure of a large number of factors by ignoring the correlation among factors of the same level. But we still have to acknowledge and clarify possible correlations to build a more accurate model.

Also, sample size of our surveys was small in statistical terms. Although the participants were carefully selected to enhance the validity of research results, small sample size may still cause the problem of generality of results. More representative populations could be required to achieve a more convincing conclusion.

Further Research. This paper focuses on factors that affect the passenger experience. However, flight attendants and aircraft maintenance personnel are also users of aircraft cabins. Different users have different behaviors. Factors that affect other users' experience may differ from the factor model in this paper. It is advised to build factor models for other users' experience and compare their similarities and differences.

The model is based on the products in the aircraft cabin interior. An in-depth quantitative study of the relationship between aircraft cabin interior and passenger experience can be carried out based on this model. Future research could address to create a mapping system between passenger experience and these factors by studying the relationship between factors and the relationship between factors and passenger experience.

6   Conclusion

Passenger experience is an important issue in the design and development of civil aircraft. In this paper, we aimed to get a systematic and practical understanding of factors that influence passenger experience in the aircraft cabin. A factor model was built to give an image of all factors and priorities with regard to aircraft cabin design. It includes three systems, eight subsystems, 67 high-level factors and several underlying factors. All high-level factors are divided into key factors (27 factors), important factors (24 factors) and general factors (16 factors). And there are 41 key underlying factors relate to key high-level factors, the rest are non-critical. This research provides a new practical guideline to improve the passenger experience in the aircraft cabin design.

Acknowledgements. This paper is sponsored by MOE (Ministry of Education in China) Liberal arts and Social Sciences Foundation (Project No. 17YJAZH029). Many sincere thanks to Professor Han Ting and the DMI team. Special thanks to Zhang Xinyue, who helped me a lot in English writing.

References

1. Patel, H., D'Cruz, M.: Passenger-centric factors influencing the experience of aircraft comfort. Transp. Rev. **38**(2), 252–269 (2018)
2. Vink, P., Bazley, C., Kamp, I., Blok, M.: Possibilities to improve the aircraft interior comfort experience. Appl. Ergon. **43**(2), 354 (2012)
3. Greghi, M.F., Rossi, T.N., de Souza, J.B., Menegon, N.L.: Brazilian passengers' perceptions of air travel: evidences from a survey. J. Air Transp. Manag. **31**, 27–31 (2013)
4. Ahmadpour, N., Lindgaard, G., Robert, J.M., Pownall, B.: The thematic structure of passenger comfort experience and its relationship to the context features in the aircraft cabin. Ergonomics **57**(6), 801–815 (2014)
5. Patel, H., D'Cruz, M.: Passenger-centric factors influencing the experience of aircraft comfort. Transp. Rev. **38**(2), 252–269 (2018)
6. Zhihu: What kind of good flight experience have you experienced. https://www.zhihu.com/question/19730160. Accessed 21 Jan 2018
7. China News: http://www.chinanews.com/gn/2018/01-20/8429113.shtml. Accessed 18 Jan 2018
8. Airbus: The Airbus Concept Cabin: http://www.airbus.com/innovation/future-by-airbus/the-concept-plane/the-airbus-concept-cabin. Accessed 18 Jan 2018

9. Ai, L.: Comfort evaluation of civil aircraft cabin space. Chin. Sci. Technol. Inf. (13), 97–98 (2016)
10. Wang, L.: User experience research method in civilian aircraft interiors design. Equip. Manuf. Technol. (7), 85–87 (2016)
11. Budd, L.C.: On being aeromobile: airline passengers and the affective experiences of flight. J. Transp. Geogr. **19**(5), 1010–1016 (2011)
12. Ahmadpour, N., Robert, J.M., Lindgaard, G.: Aircraft passenger comfort experience: underlying factors and differentiation from discomfort. Appl. Ergon. **52**, 301–308 (2016)
13. Ahmadpour, N., Robert, J.M., Lindgaard, G.: Exploring the cognitive structure of aircraft passengers' emotions in relation to their comfort experience. In: KEER2014. Proceedings of the 5th Kanesi Engineering and Emotion Research. International Conference; Linköping, Sweden, 11–13 June 2014, no. 100, pp. 387–394. Linköping University Electronic Press (2014)
14. Brindisi, A., Concilio, A.: Passengers' comfort modeling inside aircraft. J. Aircr. **45**(6), 2001–2008 (2008)
15. Kremser, F., Guenzkofer, F., Sedlmeier, C., Sabbah, O., Bengler, K.: Aircraft seating comfort: the influence of seat pitch on passengers' well-being. Work **41**(Suppl. 1), 4936–4942 (2012)
16. Pennig, S., Quehl, J., Rolny, V.: Effects of aircraft cabin noise on passenger comfort. Ergonomics **55**(10), 1252–1265 (2012)
17. Vink, P., Brauer, K.: Aircraft Interior Comfort and Design; Ergonomics Design Management: Theory and Applications. CRC Press, Boca Raton (2011)
18. Xu, J.: Study on layout of passenger service unit (PSU) for civil aircraft. Sci. Technol. Vis. (13), 22–24 (2016)
19. Cui, W., Ouyang, Q., Zhu, Y.: Field study of thermal environment spatial distribution and passenger local thermal comfort in aircraft cabin. Build. Environ. **80**, 213–220 (2014)
20. Zhang, R., Qin, H., Pan, K.: Evaluation and analysis of acoustic quality in aircraft cabin. Mod. Vib. Noise Technol. (8) (2010)
21. Liu, J., Li, B., Pei, J., Wang, C., Xiao, X., Liu, X.: Subjective and objective experimental study of cabin environment in different seasons. J. Tianjin Univ. (Sci. Technol.) (2), 103–110 (2015)
22. Chen L., Xia, Y.: Review of noise standard and control methods for civil aircraft cabin. Sci. Technol. Vis. (27), 130 (2015)
23. Lei, S., Jiang, Z.: Guidelines of aircraft cabin environment acoustics design. Acta Aeronaut. Astronaut. Sin. **15**(6), 716–719 (1994)
24. Lee, Y.H., Liu, B.S.: Inflight workload assessment: comparison of subjective and physiological measurements. Aviat. Sp. Environ. Med. **74**(10), 1078–1084 (2003)

Smart Flashlight: Navigation Support for Cyclists

Bing Jing Wang, Cheng Hung Yang, and Zhen Yu Gu[✉]

Design Department, Shanghai Jiaotong University, Shanghai, China
zygu@sjtu.edu.cn

Abstract. The number of people commuting by bicycle is constantly increasing, while the ways of navigation for riders have potential safety hazards for they tend to separate the rider from physical environment. We note that safety remains a challenge, as interaction with a device in traffic will generally be less safe than passive, stationary use. For navigation using a map while cycling in an urban environment, we studied an solution: An arrow shaped beam would be projected on the ground in front of the rider and the direction the arrow points at shows the turning direction. (Figure 1). In addition to the conceptual description, we did a user testing, and results showed that the system we designed is much safer, helpful and which kept attention on the route. Every participant was able to reach an unknown destination within an unexplored environment easily. Our findings will be a good reference for designing navigation systems for bikes and even for cars, helping cyclists and drivers be more attentive to their environment while navigating.

Keywords: Projection technique · Bicycle traffic safety · Navigation support

1 Introduction

According to a recent report from the American National Highway Traffic Safety Administration (NHTSA) [1], 17% of reported car crashes are caused by some sort of driver distraction. Navigation systems are among the devices that cause these distractions, and one solution is to apply holographic projection technique to its design. And as a result of advocating a healthy lifestyle and reducing automobile exhaust emission, the number of people commuting by bicycle is constantly increasing.

In addition to, the process of riding requiring a certain amount of concentration, the rider also has to pay attention to the environment, making further actions potentially dangerous. Despite this, the ways we acquire navigation information, especially when maneuvering in transportation modes, are not convenient enough. One suggestion in improvement is through a voice guided system, that needs us to hear out a string of information including the name of the up-coming roads, the distance to them, and the directions to turn. However, information delivered like this could be a cognition burden, especially in busy periods or in a noisy environment. A more simpler suggestion was that one could simply check the route information on the phone whilst stopped at a crossroad, however yet again, the method poses potential safety hazards, as they tend to separate the rider from the physical environment. Thus, a third suggestion is proposed,

© Springer International Publishing AG, part of Springer Nature 2018
A. Marcus and W. Wang (Eds.): DUXU 2018, LNCS 10920, pp. 406–414, 2018.
https://doi.org/10.1007/978-3-319-91806-8_31

what if the environment could instead become a responsive part of the information domain?

Fig. 1. Directions shown by smart flashlight

The prototype we will discuss in the following paper is one demonstration of the idea above. This prototype is designed with bicycle riding in the evening in mind. We have only utalized direction arrows from the map instead of the whole map as we could simplify rider's cognition. We then have the arrows projected on to the ground, and would change according to the navigation app. Since we are supposed to wear use lights on our bikes when we are riding in the evening to ensure safety, this prototype should not be deemed as an extra burden for the riders. With our suggestion, we have conducted some user surveys and investigations to testify some parameters refer to the prototype.

2   Related Work

2.1   Bicycle Dynamic

Bicycles and motorcycles are single track vehicles and the stability of them is related to their self-stability and human-bicycle system. This self-stability is generated by a combination of several effects that depend on the geometry, mass distribution and forward speed, and the human-bicycle system refers to remaining upright whilst riding - the rider must lean forward in order to maintain balance. This forward/backwards lean is usually produced by momentary steering in the opposite direction, called counter steering. Counter steering skills are usually acquired by motor learning and executed via procedural memory. [2–4] In brief, cycling is one sport that needs constant concentration, and, since mobile devices are worn and used at almost all times, designing for interaction in motion is necessary.

2.2 Visual Angle

Similar to the research of Kaufmann and Ahlström [3], our study focused on comparing map navigation using a smart-phone versus a portable projector. However, in our study, we evaluated two alternative display types for map navigation during cycling and factors affecting this task. One such visual-spatial factor was eye-to-digital information distance (EI), which can be understood as the radius of a circle whose center is the cyclist's face and ends at the phone view or the projected view. In our study, the navigation information was either visible at an arm's length from the eyes of the cyclist or on the ground in front of the them. Besides EI, another factor is normal-view-to-digital information distance (NVI). There is thus a distance between the normal view and the information displayed by the mobile and by the projection. For the rider, the normal view is ahead, towards the road. The normal view is characterized by the field of view (FOV) and the line of sight directed ahead. If digital information is presented outside of the FOV, the rider's head is required to move towards that information.

2.3 Prior Experiment

For in-vehicle systems such as radios and navigation systems, design recommendations have been made by the American National Highway Traffic Safety Administration (NHTSA 2010) and by the European Human Machine Interface Task Force (Godthelp et al. 1998). According to these guidelines, primary task performance (i.e. driving), should not be impaired by the secondary task. While operating a navigation system, the driver has to be able to steer his car with at least one hand, have the ability to interrupt the navigation task at any time, have clear view of the dis-play, and the driver's main focus should be on the road. As display design and driver's focal point are inherently related, these two recommendations have been tested as a separate entity in automobiles (Broström et al. 2016). A similar system to the one demonstrated here used a bike-mounted projector as an augmented headlight to display speedometer data1. Findings from exploratory bike trips using handlebar-mounted smartphones reported that map navigation is possible while cycling. It was reported that by not offering turn-by-turn navigation, the bike rider could be more aware of the environment, but most cyclists had to stop to read the map anyway, "since they found it too small" [5]. In a stationary indoor study involving memorizing locations on a map, smartphone displays were compared with handheld projectors. For that task and context, spatial memory improved 41% when using projectors [5]. We note that safety remains a challenge, as interaction with a device in traffic will generally be less safe than passive, stationary use.

Automotive ergonomics state humans are comfortable with eye movements of 15° above or below the line of sight, and can easily tilt their heads 30° upward or downward [6]. These fields of view parameters are relevant to the. Research on car driver attention and behaviour revealed how map system configuration (audio, visual, or audio-visual) inside a car influences eye glance frequency [7].

2.4   Similar Products

Actually, the design for riding navigation, has many excellent results to give us some thoughts. For example, this Heilos Bars smart handlebar (Figs. 2, 3). You can see in the picture that the LED lights used for navigation are flashing at the two ends of the handle to indicate the direction, and the colour of the lamp can change with the speed. There is also an LED lamp in the front for lighting the road. This product is not yet on the market, so we are looking forward to its reflection. However, this way to get information is not the way we are familiar with. That's why we would like to use the indication arrows that are consistent with the navigation app.

Fig. 2. Heilos Bars smart handlebar (Color figure online)

Fig. 3. Heilos Bars smart handlebar (Color figure online)

3   Prototype Design

To turn our prototype into a real product, the problem of the openness of map software resources would be encountered, but the good news is that these resources are gradually opening up in recent years. For example, Baidu Android navigation SDK provides a simple and easy-to-use navigation service interface for Android mobile terminal applications. As a result, developers can easily achieve accurate navigation function for applications.

So here, we have designed a simulation experiment. The materials of the experiment are the Arduino uno board, the servo motor, the Bluetooth module, a flashlight, and the shading plate printed by the 3D. We send signals through the Bluetooth to the Arduino board. Through the compiled program, the servo motor will control the shading plate to rotate to the corresponding angle according to the signal, so that the arrow shaped beam emitted by the flashlight through the shading plate will point to the right turning direction at the right time (Fig. 4).

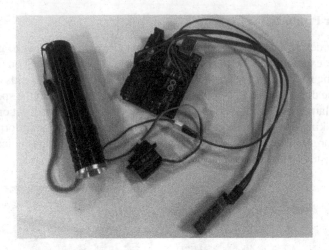

Fig. 4. Prototype

4   Experiment

The international standard ISO 9241 defines product availability as follows: "specific users when use a product for a specific target under the specific use scene feel the effectiveness, efficiency and satisfaction." [8] Effectiveness means that users can reach their target. Efficiency means that users have no need to do idle work to achieve a goal on the shortest path. Satisfaction means that there is no big problem in effectiveness and efficiency. Also, it should be considered from the deeper levels. It doesn't bring the unpleasant experience to users.

Only to conform to the definition of ISO 9241 and satisfy the above-mentioned three elements can it realize the product availability. In measuring problem seriousness, the effectiveness problem should be firstly solved. Then, under the situation of allowable time and costs, efficiency and satisfaction should be solved as much as possible. This time, we tested the product availability and we used the product prototype for design.

Availability testing and in-depth interview are used as our testing method.

4.1   Participators

We recruited 7 participators in the campus (4 men and 3 women). The mean age of 7 participators was between 20 years old and 45 years old. The mean age was 29.1 years old. Three of them are professors and the rest are all college students.

4.2   Props

We select a common bicycle as the experimental bicycle. We put the product prototype on the flashlight support. The experimental route was constructed by Map application program. The flashlight would display the route information on the ground, shown in

Figs. 5, 6. The arrow shaped beam emitted by the flashlight through the shading plate will point to the right turning direction at the right time.

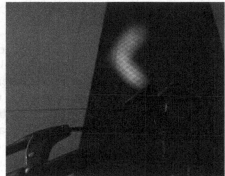

Fig. 5. Forward sign   **Fig. 6.** Left sign

4.3 Assignment

The experimental time was arranged in the evening. Volunteers who were invited were required to arrive in another unknown place that they haven't been there before from a place. Volunteers must arrive at the assigned destination in line with the route direction provided by the product prototype on the bicycle. Before the experiment, we would show the rough position of the destination on the Map app first, but the specific direction and riding route should be pointed out by the product prototype during the riding. In the route selection, we designed a 1.6 km route, which includes 7 corners.

For safety reasons, we selected a route inside the university to do the experiment. Before starting a task, users could adjust the angle of the flashlight. When volunteers rode a bicycle, they received the navigation instruction to arrive at the destination as riding a bicycle, hoping that they will realize their surroundings and use their visual spatial function, instead of blindly following up with orders. Thereafter, they were asked to complete a questionnaire and we subsequently conducted an interview, taking into account their questionnaire answers. We used the collected data for an informal assessment of our prototype to incrementally adjust the system and the experiment.

The experiment also had two recorders. One person should observe the testing task when users operated a product and recorded information on the experimental process (distance, time and speed). Another one is supposed to perform an in-depth interview.

4.4 Measures and Analyses

Effectiveness. Measurement of task completion: we marked operational result of each volunteer as failure, partial completion or all completions. In the route, including 7 corners in 1.6 km, the success rate of volunteers completing the turning operation in each corner was calculated.

Efficiency. Efficiency could be measured by time. We started to time when volunteers took the task card and finished timing when volunteers announced that we have already completed it. As calculating the efficiency of each task, we used users' mean timing divide by times of common users' skillful riding. The larger numerical value is, the lower efficiency will be.

Satisfaction. The satisfaction gets involved in the users' subjective evaluation, thus it should be collected through users' self-evaluation scale. Here, we referred to the single-item seven-point user experience measurement scale used by Jakob Nielsen [11]. [9] The project took eight component scales (shown in Fig. 7), such as "complicated—simple" and "traditional—novel", which belong to 7-score system. Top four projects stand for the practical product quality scale, and the last four projects represent the enjoying quality scale. In the end, volunteers were asked their favorite one in the riding navigation equipment used in the process, as well as whether our product concept could help them a lot.

obstructive	o o o o o o o	supportive
complicated	o o o o o o o	easy
inefficient	o o o o o o o	efficient
confusing	o o o o o o o	clear
boring	o o o o o o o	exiting
not interesting	o o o o o o o	interesting
conventional	o o o o o o o	inventive
usual	o o o o o o o	leading edge

Fig. 7. User experience questionnaire [11]

5 Results

5.1 Effectiveness

Experimental results indicated that 7 volunteers could complete the task, but 2 of them slightly paused in the experimental process at one complex intersection. They stopped a little while because they were not sure of the direction which they need to turn to.

We also tried to use the flashlight under different environments to check the directional readability of display. Only when there are vehicles with high beams passing by, our navigation system would fail to be distinct on the ground.

5.2 Efficiency

We started to time from riding from start to finish of the task for volunteers. Baidu navigation app showed it takes 7 min to finish the task on average. Through the navigation system, 7 respondents completed a task for 5.8 min averagely, which was much faster than the app suggested. The experiment indicated the flashlight projection scheme had the higher efficiency for traditional users who directly used a mobile phone. In interviewing users who used a mobile phone for navigation in the past, majorities of them indicated that they had to stop their bicycle to check the mobile phone map, because they couldn't ride while operating a mobile phone. Stopping to operate a mobile phone could reduce their riding efficiency and is also quite dangerous. The navigation form of the flashlight projection could make them pay more attention to the surroundings, thus they could greatly use their visual spatial function and improve the overall riding efficiency.

5.3 Satisfaction

On a whole, user experience questionnaire and interview results indicated that, comparing to the existing form of navigation, our new scheme was more attractive, stimulating, high-efficient and novel. (Table 1) All volunteers could arrive in the destination in line with the direction projected by flashlight. In addition they also showed that this design could make them pay more attention to surrounding environment. Users had the higher satisfaction for our flashlight navigation system.

Table 1. User experience questionnaire [11]

	Pragmatic quality				Hedonic quality			
	Supportive	Easy	Efficient	Clear	Exiting	Interesting	Inventive	Leading edge
Mean	2.3	1.0	2.3	2.6	2.1	2.0	2.4	2.3
Variance	0.6	2.3	0.2	0.3	0.5	0.7	0.6	0.9

Notes: For the user experience scales average values per scale are shown. All scales have a range from −3 to +3.

5.4 Improvement

Some volunteers suggested that our navigation system could be made as a part of the bicycle, instead of an extra flashlight installed on the bicycle. In this way, it can reduce users' trouble in carrying the flashlight when going out. They also noted that in addition to the direction, more road information should be added, such as danger and the sketch of a complex intersection to show more clearly of the exact road we should turn on.

6   Conclusion and Future Work

In this paper, we have discussed a navigation system that improves the traditional navigation scheme, and have tested it. The prototype might be insufficiently elaborated, however the testing results were unexpectedly satisfactory. All testers indicated that this was a very effective navigation mode. In future research, a larger focus on artificial engineering study will be added, such as the relationship between bright degree and identification of projection lamps, placement angle of projection lamps and projection information contents, and so on. At present, holographic laser projections have already been used for the brand-new navigation mode of automobile design. This might be similar to the prototype that we discussed. It is therefore possible to realize safer navigation modes through the vehicle design like bicycles.

References

1. National Highway Traffic Safety Administration, Visual-Manual NHTSA Driver Distraction Guidelines for In-Vehicle Electronic Devices, Notice of proposed Federal guidelines, 77 FR 11199, pp. 11199–11250 (2012). https://federalregister.gov/a/2012-4017. Accessed 11 Aug 2012
2. Kooijman, J.D.G., Meijaard, J.P., Papadopoulos, J.M., Ruina, A., Schwab, A.L.: A bicycle can be self-stable without gyroscopic or caster effects. Science **332**(6027), 339–342 (2011). https://doi.org/10.1126/science.1201959. Bibcode:2011Sci...332.339 K
3. Meijaard, J.P., Papadopoulos, J.M., Ruina, A., Schwab, A.L.: Linearized dynamics equations for the balance and steer of a bicycle: a benchmark and review. Proc. R. Soc. A **463**(2084), 1955–1982 (2007). https://doi.org/10.1098/rspa.2007.1857. Bibcode:2007RSPSA.463.1955 M
4. Sharp, R.S.: Motorcycle steering control by road preview. J. Dyn. Syst. Meas. Control. ASME. **129**(1), 373–381 (2007). https://doi.org/10.1115/1.2745842
5. Jensen, B.S., Skov, M.B., Thiruravichandran, N.: Studying driver attention and behaviour for three configurations of GPS navigation in real traffic driving. In: Proceedings of the SIGCHI Conference on Human Factors in Computing Systems, CHI 2010, pp. 1271–1280. ACM, New York (2010)
6. Dancu, A., Franjcic, Z., Fjeld, M.: Smart flashlight: map navigation using a bike-mounted projector. In: SIGCHI Conference on Human Factors in Computing Systems, pp. 3627–3630. ACM (2014)
7. Kaufmann, B., Ahlström, D.: Studying spatial memory and map navigation performance on projector phones with peephole interaction. In: Proceedings of the SIGCHI Conference on Human Factors in Computing Systems, CHI 2013, pp. 3173–3176. ACM, New York (2013)
8. Peacock, B., Karwowski, W.: Automotive Ergonomics. Taylor & Francis, London (1993)
9. Jensen, B.S., Skov, M.B., Thiruravichandran, N.: Studying driver attention and behaviour for three configurations of GPS navigation in real traffic driving. In: Proceedings of the SIGCHI Conference on Human Factors in Computing Systems, CHI 2010, pp. 1271–1280. ACM, New York (2010)
10. Gediga, G., Hamborg, K.-C., Düntsch, I.: The IsoMetrics usability inventory: an operationalization of ISO 9241-10 supporting summative and formative evaluation of software systems. Behav. Inf. Technol. **18**(3), 151–164 (1999)
11. Schrepp, M., Hinderks, A., Thomaschewski, J.: Applying the user experience questionnaire (UEQ) in different evaluation scenarios. In: Marcus, A. (ed.) DUXU 2014 Part I. LNCS, vol. 8517, pp. 383–392. Springer, Cham (2014). https://doi.org/10.1007/978-3-319-07668-3_37

Smart Information Service Design Based on Autonomous Vehicles

Qiong Wu[✉], Long Qin, Yin Shuai Zhang, and Jie Chen

Academy of Art and Design, Tsinghua University, Beijing, 100084, China
qiong-wu@tsinghua.edu.cn

Abstract. With the development of information technology, automobile is moving from manually-controlled mechanical products to smarter system-controlled products. The paper talked about the change of the human-machine interaction and the corresponding smart information service design for autonomous vehicles. In particular, the paper analyzed what would happen on driver's disappearance and the changes of the interior space, in particular, how to afford the transferring of multi-functions and sharing. Through the study of the relationships between people, vehicles, information and environment, the paper explored the possible contents of smart information service, interaction ways provided by driverless vehicles and solutions for other public services except for transportation.

Keywords: Information service design · Autonomous vehicle
Interaction design

1 The Background of Autonomous Vehicle

Automobile is a product of technology and many innovations happens in the car industry. Nowadays, with the developments of autonomous vehicles, automobile is moving from manually-controlled mechanical products to smarter system-controlled products. As a result, the functions and usages of automobiles have changed a lot, from purely means of transportation to functional mobile spaces, which afford both mobile and various of services. Autonomous car refers to a new generation of car with partial or full automation by incorporating advanced sensor, control, actuator system and other devices, utilizing new technologies such as information and communication, internet, big data, cloud computing and artificial intelligence. Obviously, we have already lived in a multiple-screen environment visible or invisible, more intelligent in-car life and smart service based on the deep user research need to be discussed, and there should have been many possibilities and innovations.

Autonomous vehicle is the vehicle that is capable of sensing its environment and navigating without human input. (Gehrig and Stein 1999) A well-known autonomy level definition[1] is from the Society of Automotive Engineers, which defines five levels of autonomous vehicles: Drive Assistance, Partial Automation, Conditional Automation, High Automation and Full Automation, whether Automated driving system monitors the driving environment is a watershed, and the last 3 phases is much more closed to "no-driver" cars, Although there are different directions to achieve "no-driver" execution (Fig. 1).

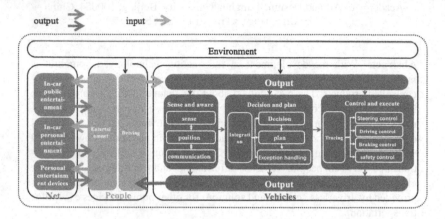

Fig. 1. The technical frame

2 The Interaction Design of the Autonomous Vehicles

Interaction is the way people use machine. Since the birth of the car, the interaction between people and vehicles has been an important topic. In addition to driving, the basic control, most people now have a certain degree of smart interactive experience between people and vehicles: such as easily obtaining vehicle state information (speed, mileage, current location, vehicle maintenance information, etc.), traffic information, cruise control, Bluetooth hands-free settings, air conditioning and sound settings.

---

[1] (1) Drive Assistance: automated system is a driver assistance system, driver and automated system shares control over the vehicle.

(2) Partial Automation: the driving mode-specific execution by one or more driver assistance systems of both steering and acceleration/deceleration using information about the driving environment and with the expectation that the human driver perform all remaining aspects of the dynamic driving task.(3) Conditional Automation: the driving mode-specific performance by an automated driving system of all aspects of the dynamic driving task with the expectation that the human driver will respond appropriately to a request to intervene,(4) High Automation: the driving mode-specific performance by an automated driving system of all aspects of the dynamic driving task, even if a human driver does not respond appropriately to a request to intervene.(5) Full Automation: the full-time performance by an automated driving system of all aspects of the dynamic driving task under all roadway and environmental conditions that can be managed by a human driver.see also at https://en.wikipedia.org/wiki/Autonomous_car.

Human-machine interaction on autonomous cars obtained more attention. The communication and interaction between human and intelligent vehicles through images, sounds, vibrations, etc. is the way to use cars, and people can fully understand the information about vehicle operation and traffic environment, and make autonomous cars fully understand people's intentions and needs only through careful design.

Not only as a transportation vehicle, but as an important living space for people, the interior design of the car has never been reduced to pursuit of entertainment and comfortable life. Nowadays, with the rapid development of internet technology, a variety of connected services flooded, and there are huge increasing needs for in-car interaction. As shown in the Fig. 2, a taxi driver in Beijing use different mobile phones to communicate, receive travel services and entertainment.

Fig. 2. The multiple screens provided by mobile phones in a Beijing Taxi

More and more car manufacturers, including Tesla, Mercedes-Benz have introduced cars with a huge tough screen and many LCD screens. The integration of multiple screens including the LCD instruments, HUD, the control screen and the car information terminal, HMI entertainment screen in the rear seat, inside and outside the rearview mirror and other carriers is a hot topic. Especially when sharing is considered to be a promising direction with the development of autonomous vehicles, the connection between personal equipment and car equipment should be considered seriously.

Liberated from driving, people in-car can take their time freely and with the convenient internet service, more information service and applications will make the car to be a special information "terminal". Cars are no longer simply transportation tools from point A to point B. More human-machine (HMI) interfaces appear on the road, advanced in-car interaction with more intelligent interaction, such as voice control, touch control, gesture recognition, facial expression recognition, VR\MR, and even artificial intelligence was shown in the car. Real-time information services related to transportation greatly affect the transportation experience, which in turn affects the operational efficiency of the entire urban transportation system, at the same time, a large number of cars form a huge network of urban traffic awareness and the collected information will further optimize the quality and efficiency of real-time traffic information. Big data provides the foundation for broader connectivity, greater awareness and deeper intelligence. The change brought about by new information should not only be efficiency, but more innovative ideas, products and services. Therefore, it is particularly important to study and explore the information service from the perspective of design (Fig. 3).

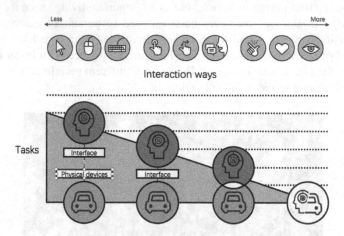

Fig. 3. Development of automobiles HMI

3   Smart Information Design for Driverless Vehicles

With the development of self-driving vehicles and related information technology, the interior space, human-computer interface and interactive process of automobile are undergoing a revolutionary change, and the automobile is gradually completed the change from a delivery machine to an intelligent agent provide mobility, communication and entertainment service, new applications on autonomous vehicles are booming, such as mobility office, digital consuming and online education.

Since the autonomous vehicle will take over all the driving work, the driver of the vehicle will become relatively free within a certain space. The car at this time to the people inside, no longer means the traditional delivery tools, people are not forced to sit in just for mobility, but to have a relatively private space for work, entertainment, and other actions. The car interior design will focus on making people feel free in the future.

In a flexible car interior space, screen visible or invisible can be everywhere in the future. People in car can use a variety of devices for online shopping, watching movies, and even playing VR games. Self-driving vehicles armed with huge screen display, projection, gesture control, voice recognition and AR technology could afford a complete virtual world for passengers.

Some new innovations on material, information technology will enrich the in-car experience. For example, the seat can record passengers' physical information, such as heart rate, weight, so as to change according to different acquirements, and the seat can become a massage seat, offering massage treatments to passengers. Perhaps in the future only serious medical needs such as major surgery will be performed in physical hospitals, some simple treatments can be finished on the car on the way to hospital.

The impact of self driving on vehicles can make most vehicles lose the "privatization", while greatly expanding their "personalization" for individuals. It is said that shared cars would be accepted by most people with the development of autonomous car technology, that is, people do not need to have their own cars, the interior will become detachable and customizable through the Internet platform, people can set and make their own interior settings. The interiors could serve with different appearance in different sceneries even though in sharing, and it is also the best stage for the passengers to show their personality.

In the new space of autonomous cars, people can sit relative to each other due to changes in the layout of the seats, thus increasing the interactivity between passengers and many new possibilities on how to make use of the time in car. It is possible that the overall seating arrangement is like a small conference room or playroom where people can meet and talk, or make more free interactions.

4   The Project on Information Service Design and Interaction Design of Shared Driverless Vehicles

This year, Tsinghua University and UISEE Co., Ltd. plan to launch a project on information service design and interaction design of shared driverless vehicles. In the project, we will mainly explore the design of the autonomous vehicles for short-haul access, which refers to the transportation of people or goods between two fixed locations within a relatively short distance (usually within 10 km), such as the transportation to the aircraft far from airport lounges, transportation between communities and subway, bus and other transport hubs, transportation between different attractions within the scenic areas.

4.1   Key Questions

The key questions are as following:

1. Human-Machine Interaction of shared driverless cars
   In the project, we will discuss the interaction design for the people before, during and after using the shared driverless vehicles, explore how to effectively convey the vehicle's action plans and intentions to the passengers, pedestrians and how to use the vehicles.
2. The resource utilization of driverless vehicles
   To explore how to make use of the mobility and huge information processing capability of driverless vehicles to provide city public services other than transportation.

4.2   Main Tasks

1. User research on taking shared driverless vehicles

To analyze the different driving scenarios and user psychology based on the driver's disappearance and the changes of the interior space, in particular, how to afford the transferring of multi-functions and sharing. Before people really trust a driverless car, people must have confidence in the basic way they interact with the car. The project will focus on the research of operating authority priority and interaction rights settings among passengers.

2. Information and interactive design of shared driverless vehicles

David Benyon argued that people, activity, context and technology are four key factors for designing interactive systems. In the project, we will study the relationships between people, vehicles, information and environment, and discuss the contents of smart information service and interaction ways provided by driverless vehicles. The interactions between people and vehicles involve not only the passengers in the car, but also passengers outside the car and pedestrians. Besides, the interaction between vehicles and environmental facilities also has a significant impact on the use of vehicles. The project will focus on information and interaction design between passengers and vehicles. The interior space of the driverless car could provide many new experiences: windows (including sunroof) as a smooth surface in the vehicles are suitable for touch operations; with voice, gestures and other new interactive ways, multiple users can complete independent or collaborative operations easily. We will study many use scenarios and interactions with the car, such as reservation, controlling, emergency handling, parking, obtaining safety aids, navigating, communication, entertainment, real-time monitoring, redundant alarm, equipment interconnection and other information services (Fig. 4).

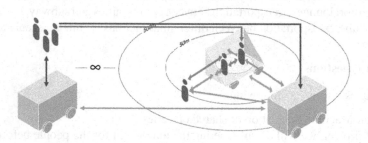

Fig. 4. Interaction model of driverless cars

The city transportation information service is very important for the city trip, which refers to the real-time information to the citizens about road traffic conditions, time interval between transfer stations, best transfer station, cost, weather conditions, destination status and other information through the whole trip. Normally, those information is provided through the mass communication, network, vehicle-mounted devices, road-side screens, etc. for citizens to choose appropriate transportation ways with efficiency. The great computing capability of driverless car could provide information service for the passengers in much more exciting ways, which is definitely worth discussing.

3. Public service design based on driverless vehicles

Operating costs for driverless vehicles are greatly reduced, and with a smart, removable space, driverless vehicles can afford many urban public service functions. The project will fully study the new public service design chance provided by driverless vehicles, such as express delivery, car renting, temporary functional space, etc.

The level of public service design not only reflects the design level of a country or region, but also reflects its design ethical standards. Only by digging out the essential needs from the interaction between people, cars and environment, and solving the problems in a larger ecosystem, can we give full play of public services and achieve the best social benefits. In the project we will study the whole service process by bringing together the needs of service providers and other relevant people for co-creating, emphasizing the involvement of all stakeholders. In the information service design system, the subject of experience is not merely from the passengers in car, but extends to other related people and a larger group. The project will explore new feasible service design by studying the existing context composed by vehicles, pedestrians, non-motor vehicles, signal lights, traffic signs and many other related factors.

4.3 Scheme and Some Concepts

The project will focus on the core interaction between people and driverless vehicles and carry out the research from the theory and method, as well as the design practice. At the theory and method level, the focus is on user psychological analysis, behavior analysis, putting forward the interaction design flow, method and evaluation system.

At the practice level, the focus is innovation design and demonstrating applications design on information service and interactions between people, shared driverless vehicles and the environment. We will explore some use scenarios to find some directions, such as work and entertainment. For example, with smart information service, passengers can easily organize their work, personal schedule, and get the information they need for the destination more conveniently. AR, VR and smart automatic control system (including temperature, light, odor, even the scenery around etc.), the multi-screen system can afford an amazing, unforgettable, and pleasing experience to every passenger by games, movies, online shopping, internet surfing and so on.

Here is an example about working in car, which will be easily to carry out. The screens in car can be used as expansion screens of personal devices. Passengers can log into the cloud platform, and the system would provide the access to download, upload, review, edit, and also guarantee the privacy (Fig. 5).

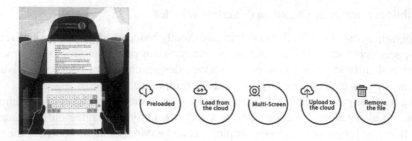

Fig. 5. Expansion screens and cloud service in autonomous cars

Some location-based service would be interesting. For example, passengers could connect to the scenery nearby through AR or VR facilities, or they may also find hidden massages on the way left by people outside the car from the window. If they found something outside they were interested in, like a charity donation massage from the house pass by, they could instantly go-for-it, or be involved (Fig. 6).

Fig. 6. Location based service

4.4 Possible Innovations

1. The change on driverless vehicles will have a significant impact on people's behavior, interaction and cognitive habits. The research is from the perspective of passengers and related people, through the analysis and research on the information and interaction design between people, vehicles, environment and information, combining the development of multi-channel interactive technology. It will present some innovative smart information service designs of driverless vehicles in a more complete human-machine interaction dimensions. These problems are quite different from how people control and use machines for decades, thus the solutions and achievements are very innovative.

2. The project will innovatively try to put forward the interactive performance evaluation standards from the perspective of users for driverless vehicles. As to the new vehicles, data will be the main index of cars instead of horsepower, living will be the main use of the vehicles instead of driving, interactions will be the main content of car evaluation instead of the traditional ones. The new evaluation standards will be presented on the basis of evaluation criteria of traditional cars and smart terminals,

and it will play an important role on the long-term development of driverless vehicles.
3. The project will propose some possible new public services and corresponding service designs based on driverless vehicles except transportation service. Driverless vehicles not only provide new transportation ways, but also have a great deal of potentials with the flexible space, the powerful information processing capabilities and the mobility, which can afford a variety of urban public services and be beneficial to save resources and sustainable developments.

5 Conclusion

In any case, interaction is just the way that the car is used. How to make fully use of the smart mobile agent is still on the way. In the future, autonomous cars will become people's intelligent mobile terminal, and more mobile-based services will be spewing out, bringing new business models and opportunities. The situation is almost the same with smart phones, calling is just one of many services ultimately serving people, and those truly affected peoples' life are the applications.

There are already many changes in the industry. Mercedes-Benz CONNECT was created to rebuild the brand as a lifestyle instead of transportation manufacturer. It supported to connect Mercedes-Benz vehicle at anytime and anywhere, and gave you fast and easy access to help and supports, like emergency call, remote diagnosis, and so on. All these are convenience, infotainment, safety and security, connected by the Mercedes-Benz CONNECT mobile app. Many automotive manufacturers sought cooperation with those companies providing information service, such as DIDI, APPLE with MOBILES, UBER, GOOGLE with TOYOTA, LYFT with GM.

Obviously, technology is always evolving, which make us expect for future smart cars, and innovative design will ultimately meet people's needs and carry people's imagination.

Acknowledgments. This research was supported by 2016 Culture and Arts Research Project, Ministry of Culture, P.R. China, the number is 16DG56;
    Feng zhou from UISEE gave many great comments and shared his thoughts generously.

Reference

1. Intelligent car innovation and development strategy, published by National Development and Reform Commission, Industry Coordination Division. http://www.gov.cn/xinwen/2018-01/07/content_5254108.htm
2. Benyon, D., Turner, P., Turner, S.: Designing Interactive Systems. Pearson Education Limited, Carmel (2005)
3. Gehrig, S.K., Stein, F.J.: Dead reckoning and cartography using stereo vision for an autonomous car. In: IEEE/RSJ International Conference on Intelligent Robots and Systems (1999)

Acceptance and Effectiveness of Collision Avoidance System in Public Transportation

Xiaonan Yang[✉] and Jung Hyup Kim

Department of Industrial and Manufacturing Systems Engineering,
University of Missouri, Columbia, USA
xyr29@mail.missouri.edu, kijung@missouri.edu

Abstract. This study investigated the acceptance and effectiveness of a lane departure warning and forward collision warning in public transportation. Five professional drivers from the Older Adult Transportation Service (OATS) participated in this study. During the experiment, the total number of alarms for each day was collected from the testing vehicles, and survey responses were also gathered from the drivers. Questionnaires were designed to determine whether the collision avoidance system performed as expected and any potential crashes avoided due to the use of the devices. Our results indicated that 75% of drivers showed significant differences in driving behavior after they used the collision avoidance system. 60% of drivers reported positive feedback for the lane departure warning and 40% of drivers felt confident in the forward collision warning.

Keywords: Collision avoidance · Lane departure warning
Forward collision warning · Public transportation system

1 Introduction

Recently, collision avoidance technology (CAT) had emerged as a new way to reduce the number of car accidents. Numerous technologies have been introduced to develop a better solution for crash avoidance [1–3]. Breakthroughs in the development of CAT offer a promising future in vehicle safety and in saving human lives. Those technologies should be thoroughly evaluated in the context of driving to understand how CAT systems may influence driving performance and safety. However, the previous studies related to CAT evaluation were mainly focused on the false-positive warning rate, the lane change test, and the warning prevention test in driving simulators (or the closed-course test tracks). According to our previous study, drivers showed different visual scan paths and driving performance when they received different types of stimulus warning in a real driving condition [4]. For that reason, the need for testing the warnings in on-road environments is growing, and little research has been performed in open-road conditions to investigate the acceptance and the effectiveness of the collision avoidance systems.

There are also several factors that can influence driving behavior, such as personality, emotion, demographics, policy, spatial and temporal elements [5, 6], inadequate mental workload, distractions, stress, anxiety, and time pressure, which can affect driving performance [7, 8]. The combinations of these influential factors can affect the driver's acceptance level and the effectiveness level of CAT systems in a vehicle. Hence, it is important to investigate whether or not implementing CAT could influence these factors negatively while driving an open track.

The frequent false alarms cause driver aversion to the warnings, sometimes high false alarm rate even can cause the increases in mental workload and distraction of driving [9]. According to the previous research did by Maltz and Shinar [10], drivers tend to ignore the false alarm and treat it as noise to avoid any unnecessary reaction. However, most of the previous research was conducted based on the driving simulator, so it is necessary to test the influence of collision warning in real driving, especially from the drivers' perspective. The collision avoidance technologies have shown potential benefit in reducing vehicle accidents. However, their success has heavily relied on driver's acceptance [11]. To measure user acceptance of CAT system, the technology acceptance model (TAM) [12] was used in this study. The model evaluates person's attitude toward using the system (A) and the perceived usefulness (U). The model was applied in other research and tested how age, gender, and environment influence the acceptance and effectiveness of collision warning [13]. Compared to other models, such as AttracDiff, User Experience Questionnaire (UEQ), or meCUE, TAM is a simple and powerful model which focuses on user acceptance behavior on system-related technology.

The purpose of this study was to conduct a usability study of a collision avoidance system in public transportation. The benefits of implementing CAT in a public transportation system were revealed through this study. To conduct the usability study, five professional drivers from OATS tested the device for three weeks. The experiment was designed to monitor how the drivers performed differently in real-world driving environments after the instrument was installed. The tested CAT device sensed vehicles in the forward path and other lanes, as well as generated warnings in response to a collision threat. We hypothesized that the total number of alarms, including lane departure and forward collision warning, should be reduced significantly if there was an impact on driving habits caused by the warnings from CAT. Furthermore, this study was designed to conduct a user perception and opinion survey for the collision avoidance system, as we collected survey responses from the drivers. The survey was designed to gather their perception and feedback on the collision avoidance system. Based on the result from drivers' survey responses and the warning reports, the acceptance and effectiveness of the collision avoidance system were evaluated.

2   Method

2.1   Apparatus

Five Ford E350 buses were used as testing vehicles for the experiment (see Fig. 1). The seating capacity is twelve passengers. These vehicles were operated by Older Adults Transportation Service (OATS) center in Columbia, Missouri. Since the drivers provide transportation service to customers, the driving path was totally based on the clients' needs during the study without any prior design.

Fig. 1. Study vehicle

The collision avoidance device typically consists of multiple sensors and provides the environmental information surrounding the vehicle. In this study, we selected one of the well-known aftermarket advanced driver assistance systems as a collision avoidance device. The device uses a combination of a vision sensor, camera, and an image processing board to detect signals. This combination allows it to better detect where the lines of roads are and to calculate the distance between vehicles. The device includes the forward collision warning (FCW) and the lane departure warning (LDW) features. The details of the collision avoidance device are below:

- FCW (>15 mph): various levels of sound and visual warning. It could cover both high and low speed for the distance between front vehicles. The visual warning is represented by a red car icon on the display.
- LDW (>37 mph): audio (a series of high-pitched beeping sound) and visual (flashing two white lane indication sign on display) alerts
- Connected to a vehicle's turning signal. This function is developed to avoid the LDW with turning signal since drivers intentionally change lanes.

The collision avoidance device was installed in all testing vehicles. A sensor camera was located near the top center of the windshield. The display unit was located at the bottom left corner of the car. Figure 2 shows the location of the device display.

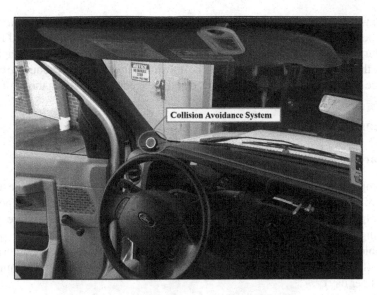

Fig. 2. Collision avoidance system setup

2.2 Participants

Five professional drivers (4 males and 1 female) from OATS participated in the study. All participating subjects in the study had enough driving experience to be considered expert drivers. The mean age of male drivers was 70.25 (SD: 6.495), and the only one female driver is 39 years old. The average driving experience of male driver was 55.5 years (SD: 7.297), and the female driver has 22 years driving experience. All five participants had at least one year of working experience in this current position of OATS. They were all professional drivers and familiar with the driving path of daily working. Each driver had assigned vehicle; they drove the same vehicle every day for work.

2.3 Procedure

The experiment was conducted in three stages: (1) stealth stage, (2) training stage and (3) active stage. For the stealth stage, the collision avoidance device did not provide any audio and visual warnings to drivers. The participants were asked to drive their vehicles as they had in the past without any knowledge of the collision avoidance system. However, the device was turned on and kept working by itself. A black box was also installed to record the number of warnings from CAT device. When the device detected any threats in driving, those events were recorded as alerts in a database without notifying drivers. The stealth stage was set as the baseline of drivers to collect their normal driving data in daily working. The experiment was conducted for three weeks as the stealth stage. After that, the drivers learned how the collision avoidance system works. During the week of the training, the drivers learned how the warning works without hearing any warning from the device while driving. After the training, we checked the driver's awareness regarding the collision warning. Finally, the audio and visual systems were turned on during the driving as the active stage. The data was collected for three weeks during the active stage as well to compare with data from stealth stage. After finishing the all three stages, we provided the questionnaires to drivers about the collision avoidance device based on they experienced and the feedbacks of using the CAT device.

3 Measures

3.1 Warning Report

After completing all three stages: stealth stage, training stage, and active stage, the total number of alarms for each day was gathered as the result of the warning report. This report helped us to see the effect of the collision avoidance system while driving. Comparing the warning data between the stealth stage and the active stage provided measurable outcomes of the effectiveness of the CAT device, such as normalized warning (how many warnings were generated per 100 miles and a total number of warnings per day).

3.2 Questionnaires

We designed and conducted a user perception and opinion survey for the collision avoidance system. This post-experimental survey contained 30 questions, including demographic information, driving experience, and a perceptive measures scale. The questions were reviewed and validated by a subject matter expert in the field of human environmental sciences. We visited the OATS center three times and handed out the questionnaires after the active stage. The drivers answered the questions and provided their feedback separately without any interactions between colleagues. All questions were related to the driver's feelings about the device and experience of using it during the active stage, such as *"How often did you meet heavy traffic with collision avoidance system?"*, *"Do you think the collision avoidance system helps you in reforming your driving habits?"*, and *"How often did you check the collision avoidance system monitoring display when there was a sound warning?"*, to understand drivers' overall driving behavior changes by collision warning and driving conditions. We also asked them to answer the questions about whether the CAT system provided a correct warning or not (e.g., *"Do you think the collision avoidance system provides the accurate forward collision warning?"*). The scale was from 1 to 7 (1 represents to "never", 7 is "always", medium level 4 as "sometimes"). Also, some questions were designed to analyze user's acceptance and willingness of driving with the collision avoidance system (e.g., *"Did you feel safe driving with this collision avoidance warning compared to driving without it?"* and *"Would you desire to drive with the collision avoidance warning?"*). Questions also covered other items like "pleasant" and "annoying". Unpleasant may happen when drivers think the system kept judging them even though the warning was helpful. Annoying is about the drivers' negative feeling about the warning sound and sensitive level if they think the warning is the noise. The measuring scale was from point 1 to 7.

The larger rating score meant a better user experience, like "very safe, very desirable", while rated score 1 corresponded to "very unsafe, very undesirable."

3.3 User Acceptance Model

In the questionnaires, some questions were designed to calculate the user acceptance level of the collision avoidance system. Son et al. [13] studied drivers' acceptance model of the advanced driving assistance system in terms of *'safe,' 'desirable,' 'pleasant'*, and *'comfort.'* In the user acceptance model, *'Safe'* means the level of feeling safe while using the system. *'Desirable'* is defined as the rate of driver's interest to use the system after the test. *'Pleasant'* reflects the driver's preference level of this technology. *'Comfort'* reflects the level of tranquility about the technology. Among these four subjective experiences of feeling, *'safe'* and *'desirable'* represent positive responses, while *'unpleasant'* and *'annoying'* indicate negative feedback. The Technology Acceptance Model (TAM) was also used to quantify the computer-related technology acceptance behavior (A) of the user [12]. It is based on perceived usefulness (U) and perceived ease of use (EOU).

$$A = U + EOU \tag{1}$$

The usefulness (U) is based on 'safe' and 'desirable' rating scale from the participant's response.

$$U = (S_{safe} + S_{desirable})/2 \tag{2}$$

Where S_{safe} is the subjective score of safety rating. $S_{desirable}$ is the subjective score of desirable rating from the survey results.

The ease of use (EOU) term is calculated by using the subjective rating of *'pleasant'* and *'comfort'* in the questionnaires:

$$EOU = (S_{pleasant} + S_{comfort})/2 \tag{3}$$

Where $S_{pleasant}$ is the subjective score of pleasant rating. $S_{comfort}$ is the subjective score of comfort rating.

Finally, the user acceptance of CAT is measured by the mean of the usefulness (U) and the ease of use (EOU).

$$A = \left(\frac{U + EQU}{2 * C_{Ratingscale}} \right) * 100\% \tag{4}$$

Where $C_{Ratingscale}$ is the subjective rating scale (from 1 to 7).

4   Results

4.1   Warning Data Analysis

Table 1 shows the normalized number of weekly warnings. Because of a failure in a data collection device in vehicle #4, the warning data from four testing vehicles (#1, #2, #3, and #5) were used in this analysis. According to the result, we could see the decrease in the number of FCW when the data from stealth stage was compared to the active stage $[F(1,17) = 7.934, P = 0.012]$. It means that FCW from the device significantly influenced the driving behavior related to a forward vehicle collision. As time goes by, drivers tried to adjust their driving behavior to avoid warning after experiencing with CAT warning for a period of time. Also, there was a weak significant difference on LDW $[F(1,17) = 4.78, P = 0.044]$. According to the individual warning report three subjects showed significant difference on FCW between stealth mode and active mode (subject 1 $[F(1,24) = 24.55, P < 0.001]$, subject 2 $[F(1,6) = 10.63, P = 0.004]$, and subject 5 $[F(1,22) = 12.5, P = 0.002]$). For LDW, only one subject showed a significant difference between stealth mode and active mode $(F(1,24) = 16.03, P = 0.001)$.

Table 1. Comparison of normalized weekly warning

Type of warning	LDW		FCW	
	M	SD	M	SD
Stealth stage	45.5	21.4	54.0	34.0
Active stage	27.0	13.7	19.0	15.5
P-value	**0.044**		**0.012**	

4.2   Questionnaires

The survey results (see details in Table 2) showed that the average condition of heavy traffic driving was 5.4 out of 7, with around 50% on the highway while 30% urban driving. The path familiarity rating was 5.4 out of 7. Both results indicated that the drivers had experienced medium-high level of workload during the experiment. Regarding the attention paid to the collision avoidance system, the warnings influenced their visual attention, and the drivers checked the device visual display after they acknowledged alarms. Based on the driver's experience during the experiment, they experienced that both warnings had a similar accuracy level $[F(1,4) = 2.08, P = 0.187]$. The accuracy of FCW and LDW from the user' perspective rating were 4.8 and 5.8 out of 7, respectively.

Table 2. Survey results

Question	Scale	M	SD	Min	Max
Age	–	64	13.8	39	80
General driving experience (year)	–	48.8	14.9	22	65
Working experience of OATS (year)	–	5.5	4.90	1	15
Familiarity with driving path	1 to 7	5.4	1.2	4	7
How often met with heavy traffic	1 to 7	5.4	1.50	3	7
Percentage of highway driving	0 to 100	50	29.2	15	100
Percentage of urban driving	0 to 100	30	19	15	60
Attention on CAT system	1 to 7	4.8	1.6	2	6
Frequency of checking the device display	1 to 7	5.8	1.94	2	7
FCW accuracy from drivers' experience	1 to 7	4.8	1.16	3	6
LDW accuracy from drivers' experience	1 to 7	5.8	0.75	5	7
Improvement in driving behavior	1 to 7	5.4	1.02	4	7
Effectiveness of CAT	1 to 7	5.8	0.75	5	7

4.3 Questionnaires

Table 3 shows the average score of the user acceptance level of the device. According to the five drivers' responses, their acceptance level of the collision avoidance system was about 69.28 out of 100. Also, there was no significant difference on user acceptance level between FCW and LDW [$F(1,4) = 0.05$, $P = 0.824$].

Table 3. Acceptance level (Scale 0–100%)

Item	M	SD	P-Value
Overall user acceptance	**69.28**	24.91	
User acceptance of FCW	**70.71**	24.26	0.824
User acceptance of LDW	**74.28**	19.351	

5   Discussion and Conclusion

This study investigated the acceptance and effectiveness of a collision avoidance device in public transportation. The objective of the study was to estimate the potential benefits of implementing collision avoidance technology (CAT) to public transportation. Five professional drivers from OATS participated and tested the collision avoidance device for several weeks.

The results showed that there was a significant difference in the total number of weekly warnings between the stealth stage and the active stage. It means that the collision avoidance system was accepted by drivers and appeared to have positive effects on their driving behavior. However, the impact of LDW was less significant than that of FCW. Three out of five drivers showed a significant reduction in the number of FCWs. On the contrary, for LDW, only one driver demonstrated a major improvement in his driving behavior. One of the possible explanations for this difference is dissimilar driving behavior regarding forward collision and lane departure. According to the research done by Gasper et al. [14], drivers commonly responded with a combination of braking and steering when they detected threats of forward collision or lane departure. They found that the drivers chose different maneuvers to avoid the potential hazard, depending on their detection time of the threat. In the present study, the detection time of forward collision and lane departure were different, and it was based on the detection algorithms of the device. It means that the sensitivity level of the algorithms could influence the effectiveness of the collision avoidance device.

For the acceptance level, the overall acceptance was about 69%. Compared to the previous study [13], there is no significant difference in the acceptance level between public transportation vehicles and passenger vehicles. However, the user acceptance level for LDW from the driver in a public transportation vehicle was higher than the passenger vehicle (FCW: 71.7%, LDW: 69.5%).

Besides, according to the drivers' feedback, three drivers (subjects 1, 3, and 4) reported positive feedback for the lane departure warning. Also, two drivers (subjects 1 and 3) felt confident about the forward collision warning. Subjects 1 and 3 (one male and one female) recommended using the collision avoidance system with public transportation. They said that the device helped them to maintain lane position and to be aware of measuring the distance from a leading vehicle. Although it took time to become familiar with both LDW and FCW, both drivers had no problems with using the device after they got used to it. Many drivers reported that potentially safer after installing the collision warning device since it can correct driving habits in some degree. Some drivers said they used turn signal more frequent with lane departure warning exist. The user acceptance level of subjects 1 and 3 were 80% and 78%, respectively. However, subjects 2 and 4 showed negative feedback with using the collision avoidance system. Subject 2 said that the warnings distracted and annoyed him due to a lot of false warnings. His user acceptance level was 20%. He stated that he would prefer to use the device in a personal car rather than a public transportation system because passengers get nervous due to the audible alarms. Also, when he drove in a city with heavy traffic congestion, he was often frustrated by the many forward collision warnings generated because of the close distance with front cars, which are hard to avoid in heavy traffic. Subject 4 also had several negative comments about the device. He felt the FCW function should be improved further because the device was not beneficial in larger cities. Subject 5 agreed to keep the collision avoidance system in a vehicle.

This study showed that a CAT system appeared to have positive effects on their driving behavior. The overall effectiveness of a CAT system was about 75%, and the acceptance was about 69%. In short, 75% of drivers (3 out of 4) showed significant differences in driving behavior after they used a CAT device. 60% of drivers reported positive feedback for the lane departure warning. 40% of drivers (2 out of 5) felt confident about the forward collision warning. The OATS drivers reported 69.28% of acceptance level of using the CAT device. All our findings support that there are potential benefits to implementing CAT in a public transportation system. However, it is vital to understand how drivers set their threshold to accept the warning from collision avoidance features. It can be concluded that it is essential to study how a driver uses a CAT device to avoid unexpected negative impacts and provide appropriate safety parameters.

Encouragement should be provided to administrators to install the CAT systems in public transportation vehicles as the results of the current study show satisfactory effectiveness and acceptance levels.

In conclusion, CAT systems are beneficial to prevent vehicle accidents. However, these technologies should be evaluated, in the context of driving, to understand how the CAT devices influence driving performance and safety in real driving conditions.

There are several identified limitations in this study. First, this study considered only a limited age group of drivers. According to the research done by Son et al. [13], an advanced driver assistance system is more efficient for older drivers over age 70. They also reported that the acceptance of collision warning might differ by drivers' age and gender on a wider variety of vehicles. Future research should consider recruiting the entire age group to see if the acceptance and effectiveness changed in different age groups. Second, although we could estimate the benefits of using CAT in a public transportation vehicle, it was impossible to see the reduction rate of vehicle crashes during the experiment. Therefore, future research should study the effectiveness of CAT in a public transportation system for a longer duration (>6 months) to observe the changes in the number of vehicle crashes. Moreover, for this study, we did not include any physiological measures to assess drivers' response to collision warning in a real driving environment. In the future, we plan to introduce some physiological data analysis, such as eye tracking data, electromyography (EMG) data to reflect the collision warning impact on driving behavior.

Acknowledgments. Missouri Employers Mutual supported this research.

References

1. Mukhtar, A., Xia, L., Tang, T.B.: Vehicle detection techniques for collision avoidance systems: a review. IEEE Trans. Intell. Transp. Syst. **16**(5), 2318–2338 (2015)
2. Schwall, M.L., et al.: Testing and analysis of autonomous emergency braking systems using the Euro NCAP vehicle target. In: ASME 2014 International Mechanical Engineering Congress and Exposition. American Society of Mechanical Engineers (2014)
3. Thompson, J., et al.: The transport for new south Wales FleetCAT (fleet collision avoidance technology) trial: drivers attitudes to the technology. In: Australasian Road Safety Conference, 2016. ACT, Canberra (2016)
4. Yang, X., Kim, J.H.: The effect of visual stimulus on advanced driver assistance systems in a real driving. In: IIE Annual Conference, Proceedings of Institute of Industrial and Systems Engineers (IISE) (2017)
5. Ellison, A., Greaves, S., Bliemer, M.: Examining heterogeneity of driver behavior with temporal and spatial factors. Transp. Res. Rec.: J. Transpo. Res. Board **2386**, 158–167 (2013)
6. Mesken, J., et al.: Frequency, determinants, and consequences of different drivers' emotions: an on-the-road study using self-reports, (observed) behaviour, and physiology. Transp. Res. Part F: Traffic Psychol. Behav. **10**(6), 458–475 (2007)
7. Haque, M.M., et al.: Decisions and actions of distracted drivers at the onset of yellow lights. Acc. Anal. Prev. **96**, 290–299 (2015)
8. Palat, B., Delhomme, P.: A simulator study of factors influencing drivers' behavior at traffic lights. Transp. Res. Part F: Traffic Psychol. Behav. **37**, 107–118 (2016)

9. Horowitz, A.D., Dingus, T.A.: Warning signal design: a key human factors issue in an in-vehicle front-to-rear-end collision warning system. In: Proceedings of the Human Factors and Ergonomics Society Annual Meeting. SAGE Publications Sage CA, Los Angeles (1992)
10. Maltz, M., Shinar, D.: Imperfect in-vehicle collision avoidance warning systems can aid drivers. Hum. Fact.: J. Hum. Fact. Ergon. Soc. **46**(2), 357–366 (2004)
11. Eichelberger, A.H., McCartt, A.T.: Toyota Drivers' Experiences with Dynamic Radar Cruise Control, the Pre-Collision System, and Lane-Keeping Assist (2014)
12. Davis, F.D., Bagozzi, R.P., Warshaw, P.R.: User acceptance of computer technology: a comparison of two theoretical models. Manag. Sci. **35**(8), 982–1003 (1989)
13. Son, J., Park, M., Park, B.B.: The effect of age, gender and roadway environment on the acceptance and effectiveness of Advanced Driver assistance systems. Transp. Res. part F: Traffic Psychol. Behav. **31**, 12–24 (2015)
14. Gaspar, J., et al.: Driver behavior in forward collision and lane departure scenarios. SAE Technical paper (2016)

A Design for a Public Transport Information Service in China

DanDan Yu[✉], MuRong Ding[✉], and Cong Wang[✉]

Art and Design Academy, Beijing City University, Beijing, China
diane_yu@139.com

Abstract. This paper presents the initiative design research and projects of developing a public transport information service in China based on big data analysis technology and ubiquitous computing. Follow the blooming of information technology; Artificial Intelligence begins to intervene deeply into people's ordinary life in China. The cities need new design to solve urbanization issue, improve the well being of its citizens. In this paper, we put the emphasis on the introduction of our information model and the information service system. The information service model will create new design thinking and opportunities for solving the complicated urban problem. We design a public transport information service system that includes Tidal-waiting line, Dynamic station board, APP called "TravelMate" and so on. The public transport information service design project based on the information service model is showed as examples, and hope to provide a new framework for the further design research in urban media design.

Keywords: Information service · Public transport
Smart cities and public service design

1 Introduction

China is currently developing at a rapid pace, with social and economic development alongside continuous urban expansion exerting tremendous pressure on urban public transport. As living standards have gradually increased, private car ownership raised year by year. Meanwhile, traffic congestion, air quality has dropped significantly, contributing to environmental degradation, and making travel more difficult for city dwellers. The government has begun attaching great importance to and advocating for low-carbon green living and greater ecological consciousness in society. This has involved encouraging greater use of buses, although bus congestion, inefficiency and long waiting times have seriously hampered the implementation of the national bus priority strategy. Making public transport "more convenient to travel, more comfortable to ride, more convenient to transfer, and safer to operate" is a central theme to new urban society.

Taking Beijing, China as an example: Beijing has 913 public transport lines, including 894 public bus and 19 rail traffic. From January to July 2017, passenger traffic in Beijing reached 4,068,579,400, including 1,908,978,000 public bus. In July alone, passenger traffic reached 607,938,100 passengers, including 272,375,100 public bus. It is evident that public bus are an important component of Beijing's public transport

© Springer International Publishing AG, part of Springer Nature 2018
A. Marcus and W. Wang (Eds.): DUXU 2018, LNCS 10920, pp. 435–444, 2018.
https://doi.org/10.1007/978-3-319-91806-8_34

network, as well as the principal means of transport for most Beijing residents. Therefore, improving the experience of taking public bus will not only improve public bus' environment, but also entice more citizens to use public transportation, hence remedying the issue that arise with public transportation as caused by rapid urbanization.

This project uses large data technology and perception technology to collect and analyze urban public traffic data so as to establish a city information service model. Through this model, the system of the urban public transport service department is designed. The system creates an intelligent bus service system using Tidal waiting lines, dynamic stop signs, data dispatching, platform swipe cards and other service points, so as to enhance the urban public transport experience, while simultaneously optimizing bus resources and reducing urban traffic pressure.

2   Research Context and Concepts

At present, the traditional Chinese urban transportation system is the primary bottleneck restricting sustainable urban development, meanwhile, traffic congestion and the associated environmental pollution and safety problems have become more urgent on the urban planning agenda. According to Brenda Dervin's Sense-Making Theory, there is a vast gap between passengers' application situation and the existing traffic information service. A stakeholder-based information service for cognition and habits is needed to bridge this gap, which in turn will help to balance the demands of passengers, bus companies, government supervision and public security.

In the context of artificial intelligence and the big data era, data mining and information visualization have enabled network resource sharing and real-time data availability, which will change how public transportation is serviced and how people go about their daily lives.

2.1   The Main Problems of Urban Public Transportation

In recent years, the number of motor vehicles and road traffic in China has increased dramatically, especially in big cities. Moreover, increasing levels of public transport vehicles, line extensions and raw vehicle numbers mean that traffic congestion is still a very serious issue, which is worsening in its severity. Using the GAD map in combination with an open data platform, Ali cloud ODPS released "2015Q3 urban traffic analysis report in China". This report's data show that traffic congestion has also resulted in direct economic losses, with the highest opportunity cost being in Beijing, where commuters waste on average 808RMB per month due to congestion. Furthermore, congestion emissions contain a large number of carbon dioxide, oxide, particles and sulfur dioxide, which ultimately worsen the already severe air pollution causing frequent fog and haze.

Declines in bus speed and uneven traffic intervals are common in major cities. Situations such as too many buses arriving at once and large periods with no buses seriously affect the quality of public transport service. Due to the lack of modern managements practices, the operation process of Chinese public transport is lagging, officials are "invisible and unable to listen", often completely oblivious to the shortcomings. Bus waiting times are long and running speeds slow, especially for bus users. Moreover, vehicle operation information and route details are not being provided to passengers in time. For the government, the actual bus company operation cannot be obtained, and effective supervision cannot be realized. For the bus enterprise itself, operating data is inaccurate and the processing cycle long, meaning operational analysis and decision support cannot be provided.

2.2 The Main Problems of Urban Public Transportation

Bus platforms are a critical component of bus service systems, which govern waiting times, rest periods, inquiry management as well as social and other functions. In order to satisfy fundamental human needs as they relate to waiting in accordance with the concept of service design, it is imperative to provide better coordination and balancing of informational and emotional needs.

Most Chinese bus stations are serviced by 3 bus lines or more, but narrow platform space, numerous bus routes and one-way information transmission can cause doubts and worries for passengers, making them take the wrong bus, sit in the wrong direction, stand in overcrowded buses and getting caught in conflict. For example, passengers waiting for different buses are mixed together, but in order to avoid being overlooked, those waiting typically enter the driveway, occupying the bus lane. Given this, most drivers do not drive directly into the station so as to avoid being blocked by the crowd, meaning they instead stop on the main road with no fixed stopping point. Taking buses as an example, passengers wait in the mixed group, with passengers in the driveway taking the lead in obtaining information so as to board the bus more quickly, thus causing riots and cutting off those waiting for the bus engendering further chaos [1]. Information transmission is untimely, uncertain and random. Passengers have to retrieve the stopping information themselves, sometimes running to catch up with the buses, which causes security risks and traffic chaos (Fig. 1).

Fig. 1. The situation of waiting bus

2.3 The Main Problems in Urban Public Transportation Information

Information release procedures for urban public transportation affect urban dweller mobility to a great extent. However, in most Chinese cities, public transport information is too weak to release, the lack of real time dynamic information (such as arrival times and traffic densities) has caused serious information asymmetry, weakening passengers' sense of participation in and the reliability of public transport. According to the survey of the project, the most frequently used, and most trusted method for obtaining information is still asking passers-by.

According to practical experiences at home and abroad, it is clear that the best manner for solving urban traffic problems is the further development of public transport, and the establishment of an Advanced Public Traffic System so as to improve road traffic capacity and the operation and management of public transport. At the same time, this can improve living conditions and promote sustainable urban development.

3   Design Framework and Process

The smart public transportation service system we designed is based on Internet of things technology, and is an innovative service mode transforming intelligent buses through perception, transmission and application [2]. This mode establishes a new interactive service platform for passengers, bus drivers and bus dispatchers. This information service transforms the bus service into a known, visible and controllable service system. Urban residents are hence provided with new means and experiences for travel, thanks to the Internet, radio frequency identification, smart phones and big data analysis platforms. Passengers now have access to different travel modes, travel times, route selection, passenger flow analysis and efficiency analysis (Fig. 2).

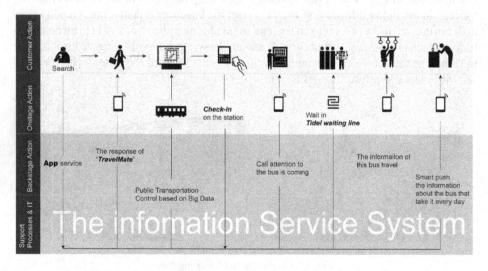

Fig. 2. The Blueprint of the public transportation service system

3.1 The Design Principle for an Urban Public Transport Service System

For a large number of commuters, the public transportation system is their first contact with society on a daily basis. The first place they go every morning is the bus stop. Therefore, an all-round enhancement and promotion of the public transport experience can not only entice more passengers to take the bus, but can also solve problems relating to urban traffic and safety concerns. By improving commuters' travel experience, urban livability and residents' well-being are improved.

The design of the public transport service system in accordance with the service design concept mainly follows the following principles:

1. A human-centric approach, which includes passengers, platform cooperators, public transport drivers, operation and dispatch personnel, as well as government supervisory departments.
2. Using large data and data mining technology to correctly guide stakeholders in the public transport service system.
3. Using artificial intelligence to forecast preferences and behavioral habits, while offering personalized recommendations and guidance.
4. Simplifying the information transfer process using information visualization, hence shortening the information transmission duration, and accurately conveying timely and effective public transport information.
5. Establishing sustainable development for the public transport service system, thus improving the service experience and solving urban problems.

3.2 The Information Service Model

Sense-Making Theory divides the information search into the following three stages: 1. SITUATION, which refers to information query; 2. GAP, which refers to better understanding the gap formed by information discontinuity; 3. HELP, which refers to the meaning of information to the individual, each person's use for information is based on their situational response, while the use of information for everyone is a response to the situation, with the purpose of filling the gap or solving the problem. Passenger demand for information is closely related to the pertinent scenario, and hence a new information service model has been formed for the public transport service system, which is centered around passengers. This model is made up of five rings [3]:

1. "Situation" refers to passenger travel circumstances and the information demand. Passengers inquire with regards to travel routes, arrival time and congestion.
2. "Orientating" refers to information feedback and guides passenger behavior. In response to passenger requests, the system feeds back the answer to users and guides their travels.
3. "Action" refers to passengers being led to form behavioral habits. Passengers arrange travel according to the information available. Passenger information is then stored on the system and analyzed to form a portfolio for each passenger.

4. "Influence" refers to the provision of active assistance to passengers through notifications and tips. Based on passenger data analysis, the system can anticipate user needs and make suggestions for further travel.
5. "Reverberating" refers to passenger feedback on helpful information provided. Passengers provide feedback on system notifications and hints, and offer suggestions to help the system better learn passenger habits, in order to more accurately anticipate individual users' needs (Fig. 3).

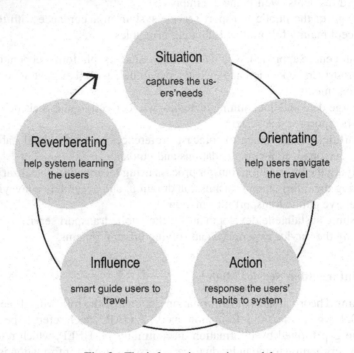

Fig. 3. The information service model

This information service model employs information lookup and an intelligent data platform, transferring urban public information to urban residents through 5 links in order to help people lead easier lives.

3.3   The Design Touch-Point of Urban Transport Service System

Our public transport service system design [4] is centered on passengers and stakeholders. Moreover, the information service, through 5 service contact points, is able to solve practical problems, improve service quality and provide a comprehensive urban public transport experience, which helps urban dwellers have smooth, comfortable and pleasant trips. The service contact points are designed as follows (Fig. 4):

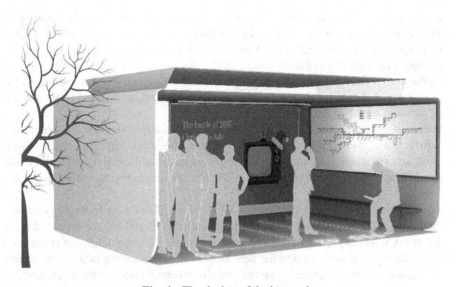

Fig. 4. The design of the bus station

1. Tidal waiting line [5]: Adjust different bus line waiting space on the same platform according to real time circumstances. The data platform uses ground sensors to

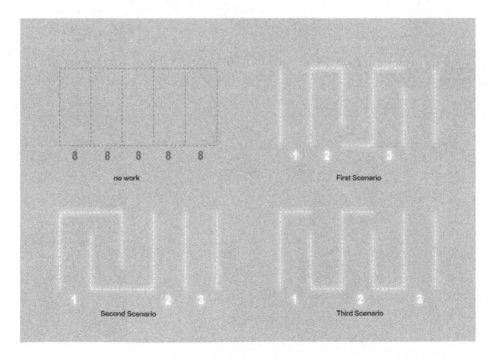

Fig. 5. The design of Tidal waiting line

measure user flow in real time, which is combined with previous data mining to analyze passenger flows at various times on the same platform so as to control ground LED lamps for the waiting lines. Further combining this with traffic volume and waiting time data for different points in the queue can help resolve the issue of inefficient space allocation as caused by early morning and evening peaks. At the same time, this reduces passenger anxiety while waiting, and allows user to adjust their routes based on real time data (Fig. 5).

2. Data-based scheduling: According to real-time information on tide waiting lanes and vehicle traffic, data analysis is conducted to guide bus dispatchers in vehicle adjustment, so as to manage urban public transport resources at the macro level, efficiently dispatching vehicles and personnel, and reducing wasted manpower, space and energy.

3. Dynamic station boarding [6]: Stations which use LED display technology expand the visual range and amount of information available, including stop names, driving direction, fares, expected arrival time, the location of late vehicles, the congestion levels facing said vehicles and the flow of said vehicles among other information. At the same time, passengers scan the two-dimensional code for their selected line using their mobile phone, providing real-time information customized to the user. Passengers can hence sensibly arrange their spare time before the vehicle is expected to arrive, and also choose the most suitable line. Through the transmission of key information, the bridge is formed, and the informational gap plugged, thereby reducing passenger anxiety, enabling them to make an informed decision (Fig. 6).

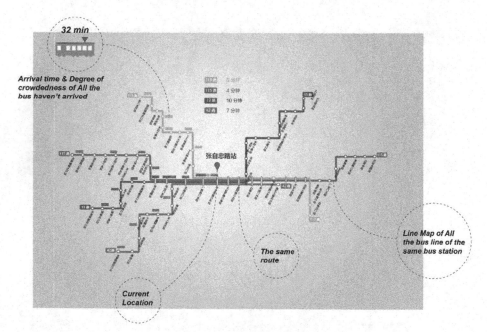

Fig. 6. The design of dynamic station boarding

4. Station check-in: Instead of swiping their card on the bus, passengers can swipe at the station, using either their mobile phone or bus card to check-in. This will helped reduce passenger crowding at the doors because of card search and swipe times, thus reducing vehicle waiting time and congestion near stations.

5. Public Transportation App: The integrated development of the public transport information app, TravelMate., in addition to current bus app query lines and other functions, will allow passengers to collect real-time information. Users are alerted to real-time changes in route plans through TravelMate anytime and anywhere, and can query related information. For example, when passengers are getting ready for work in the morning, they receive a system notification: "there is a traffic jam this morning, please leave 20 min early or consider an alternative route". Moreover, when passengers are waiting for a bus on the platform, TravelMate can prompt users. Based on the time analysis, passengers know whether they have time to buy a drink at the supermarket, and can then get a vehicle entry warning when the vehicle is arriving. When getting to the station, the user knows the arrival time and whether there have been any traffic jams through TravelMate. In congestion, TravelMate can provide passengers with information related to estimated arrival time, so that passengers can optimize their journey.

4   Conclusion and Future Work

In our proposed work, we sought to establish a framework, which adequately represents information flow, different elements and their relationships, in a manner accessible to various audiences. The Information Service Framework is a result of this vision.

Furthermore, we shortly introduced the Public transport information service system based on the information service model we designed in order to improve the travel experience in smart cities and to satisfy passengers, variety, and dynamic requirements. Then, we presented our real-time public transport information service based on tidal waiting lines, resulting in the front-end Android application, TravelMate, which provides more personalized, rich and clear information.

For future work, we plan to further develop the information service model, while enhancing the different services of all app features. Moreover, we intend to accrue a noticeable user base and carry out field experiments with these real users. Their feedback is important to identify future improvements for the service.

Acknowledgments. Many thanks to my students Wang Cong, Ding Mu Rong, Fu Sheng Wu, Jang Yu Shan, Zhang Zi Qi, Sun Hao Yue, members of the project. Their works are very essential for the paper.

References

1. Ran, Z.F.: Service Design Research of Information Service Interface in Public Transportation. 1994–2017 China Academic Journal Electronic Publishing House
2. Fei, H.F.: The Research on Application of Experience Design for City Bus Station. 1994–2017 China Academic Journal Electronic Publishing House
3. Nan, S.: Research on humanized design of modern bus platform. J. Nanyang Normal Univ. **16**(9), 51–53 (2017)
4. Bin, Q.L., Feng, H.C., Yu, D.: The cloud platform of smart bus travel based on big data. New Technology and New Products of China, no. 12, p. 25 (2016)
5. Sen, L.H., Bei, Y., Zi, C.X.: On design of innovation structure of bus station of guanggu square in Wuhan. Idea and Design, pp. 48–52
6. Farkas, K., Fehér, G., Benczúr, A., Sidló, C.: Crowdsensing based public transport information service in smart cities. Infocommun. J. **VI**, 13–20 (2014)
7. Lin, S.-Y., Chao, K.-M., Lo, C.-C.: Service-oriented dynamic data driven application systems to urban traffic management in resource-bounded environment. SIGAPP Appl. Comput. Rev. **12**, 35–49 (2012)
8. Tang, F., Li, M., Guo, M.: Shanghai grid and intelligent urban traffic applications. In: Asian Technology Information Program (ATIP) 3rd China HPC Workshop SC07 Conference, Reno, Nevada, 11 November 2007
9. Graells, E., Saez, D.: A day of your days: estimating individual daily journeys using mobile data to understand urban flow. In: Proceedings of the Second International Conference on IoT in Urban Space, Urb-IoT 2016, pp. 1–7 (2016)
10. Wang, S.-M., Huang, C.-J.: User experience analysis on urban interaction and information service in smart city nodes. In: Chinese CHI 2014, pp. 103–109, April 2014

Research on User Needs of Digital Consumption Services in Communicating Vehicles Context

Di Zhu[✉]

Beijing Normal University, Beijing, China
di.zhu@mail.bnu.edu.cn

Abstract. In trend of communicating vehicles, user needs become a central issue for automobile companies. Vehicles as digital mobile devices, users will not only have more comfortable driving experience, but also more efficient life. This paper main concern is about user needs, touch points and potential scenarios based on digital consumption services in communicating vehicle context. Several practical and innovative UX research and design methods and techniques were applied. We found 22 user needs clustered under 4 main themes. These findings suggest that in general vehicles satisfy possessive, create a sense of belonging and security. Vehicles create an independent space, can vent users' emotions, also can drive far away from an unpleasant situation, or experience a new world. In the future, we should design more directly and efficiently way to interact with users, and consider the long-term problems of users.

Keywords: User needs · Digital consumption · Communicating vehicles

1 Background

From the Internet to Internet of Things, world connected by different approaches. China holds the world's second-largest vehicle holdings. As Fig. 1 shows concept of connected vehicles, at the end of 2017, there are over 200 million vehicles in China having yet to be connected to the Internet. At the same time, technologies to build Internet of vehicles have matured to a point in which mass deployment is both possible and feasible (Barros 2014). Mobile Internet is evolving towards Internet of Things through enabling technologies (Vermesan et al. 2013). This allows vehicle to share Internet access with other devices both inside as well as outside the vehicle.

Many automobile companies noticed that a growing trend and a significant business opportunity for connecting their cars. And China is globally pioneering a new wave of digital lifestyles through its hyper-connectivity, rapid smart phone adoption, centralized service ecosystems by BAT and most importantly, people's openness to adopt new technologies and social behaviors. As such, using context of China today to explore user needs can give us insights of what the rest of the world might require in the future. China is particularly noticeable in e-commerce, the proportion of Unicorn Enterprises and the

© Springer International Publishing AG, part of Springer Nature 2018
A. Marcus and W. Wang (Eds.): DUXU 2018, LNCS 10920, pp. 445–456, 2018.
https://doi.org/10.1007/978-3-319-91806-8_35

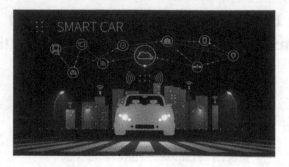

Fig. 1. Concept of connected vehicles

speed of the development of the industry, especially in mobile payment popularity as showed in Fig. 2. Chinese payment transaction scale is 11 times than American.

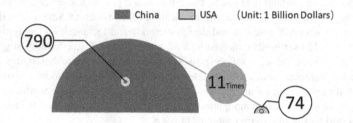

Fig. 2. China and US mobile payment transaction scale in 2016

Users tend to be individualize and diversify their consumption. Digital Economy Companies are more user-oriented than traditional. On the one hand, enterprises collect users' information through digital mobile platform to estimate their preferences, so as to accurately advertise and encourage users to buy more things for electronic payment such as Alipay and WeChat pay. On the other hand, diversification and individualization of new products and services provide more possibilities for digital consumption in the context of

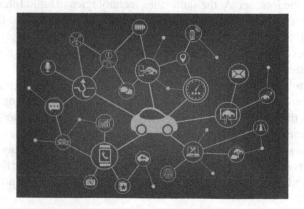

Fig. 3. Services in communicating vehicles

communicating vehicles (Xu Xu 2017). With the development of technologies, more and more things users can do on vehicle services (Romano 2017). As Fig. 3 shows, it will be more different kinds of services and stakeholders participated in the Internet.

User can buy material goods also tangible services such as car washing and rescuing services. And more recently digital virtual space such as websites, virtual worlds and video games has emerged that may allow for an actualization of consumer fantasy beyond what material goods and experience can offer (Denegri-Knott and Molesworth 2010). At present user can buy digital virtual consumption, for instance, a game character, new skin, piece of music and so on. Figure 4 gives some examples of current consumption of the Internet.

Fig. 4. Examples of current consumptions through the Internet

In the trend of communicating vehicles, user needs have grown up to be a crucial issue for automobile companies. Vehicles as digital mobile devices, users will not have more comfortable driving experience, but also more efficient life. Until now, many researches already got user needs from smart phones, tablets and smart TVs, etc., but companies cannot directly apply those in the context of communicating vehicles. Users will prefer different interactions in different context. More than 54 percent of Chinese drivers prefer customized Internet services—higher than that of any other country as showed in Fig. 5. With far more big cities than in Western countries, China is currently under a rich variety of Internet services and a large number of active Internet users. Besides, an average Chinese works longer hours a day than his or her Western counterpart. This among others, explains the Chinese desire to stay connected with their families and friends by using technology (Väänänen-Vainio-Mattila 2011). China has more mobile phones and social media users than any other country. The combined active WeChat accounts crossed 468 million in September 2014, with a monthly increase of 39 percent over the same period last year. The aim of this paper is to determine present user needs, touch points and potential scenarios based on communicating vehicle for digital consumption services (Tencent 2014).

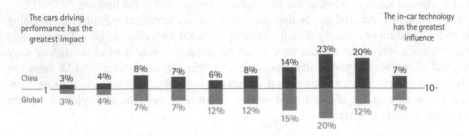

Fig. 5. On a scale from 1 to 10 (10 meaning that in-car technology has the greatest influence over the car purchase decision and 1 meaning that the vehicle's driving performance has the greatest impact on the car purchase decision), what score would you assign for your view?

2   Settings

This paper is based on Communicating Vehicle Project of PSA and BNU. As a first collaboration between OpenLab Design at PSA Groupe and UX Master Program (BNUX) at Faculty of Psychology at Beijing Normal University (BNU). The UX design project will be conducted to equip students with UX theory while gaining practical experience in a real project setting, and to provide designers, researcher, and developers at PSA with first-hand data, insights, and mockups on new ways of interacting with future communicating vehicles in a Chinese Context. This project belongs to the Open Innovation network between PSA Groupe and a number of great schools of design and engineering worldwide, and it is intended to compare the results and specificities between Europe, America, and China. This project will last from September 2017 to June 2018 (Zhou 2015).

As Fig. 6 demonstrates that the core research team is consisted of 3 PSA OpenLab experts, 2 BNU faculty members, and ca. 10 BNUX master students. After the kick-off meeting held with ca. 69 master students at BNU in Beijing. They were split into 12 groups to explore the topic for 2 months. From the beginning of November 2017, as the second-year students, we take knowledge from the exploration and carried on our own work as graduation projects. This paper main concern is a question of user needs, touch points and potential scenarios based on digital consumption services.

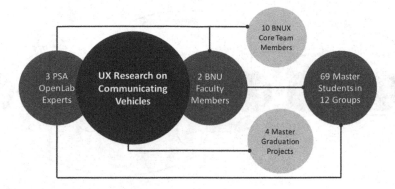

Fig. 6. Settings of communicating vehicles project

Several practical and innovative UX research and design methods and techniques will be applied as shown in Fig. 7, such as context-mapping, collage, mind-map, interviews, sketching, data analysis, etc.

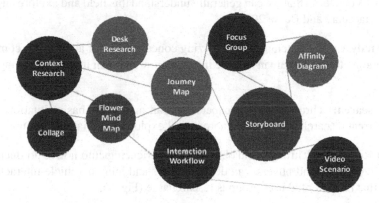

Fig. 7. Methods in project

3   Research Process

This paper takes iterated process to explore and define user needs of digital consuming in communicating vehicles context as showed in Fig. 8. It is composed with quantity and quality research methods.

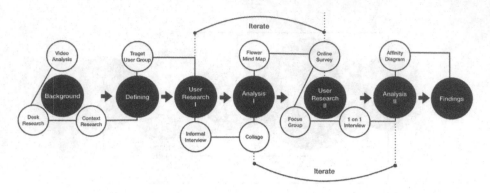

Fig. 8. Fully process research step

3.1 Background

In order to understand development status and trends of the automobile industry and the Internet of Vehicle, so that we can generally understand this field and explore target user groups (Macaulay and Busse 2009).

Video Analysis: By watching and analyzing concept video of automobile companies, understanding trends of human-vehicle interaction, which can inspire following design work.

Desk Research: Through reading papers, we can master the basic situation of IOV, know Current research in China and abroad and explore potential user groups.

Context Research: Through field observing, experiencing automotive products, interviewing with staffs and buyers, can deeply understand human-vehicle interaction and verified that the potential user group is researchable (Fig. 9).

Fig. 9. Interview target user group

3.2 User Research I

Then we did informal interviews to understand users' lifestyle and attitude towards digital consumption, etc. It is a time effectively method to know about users.

Informal Interview: We had several informal interviews with target user group and preliminary understood target user groups' daily life, hobbies, interpersonal communicating and so on.

3.3 Analysis I

Further discussed and analyzed target user groups' concerns based on previous research, and clarified scope of further research.

Collage: As Fig. 10 shows, it can help you to define for whom and for what problem or challenge you plan to design (Delft et al. 2013). Through previous understanding of target user group, divergent thinking and summarizing several key points of target user group (Cross 2008).

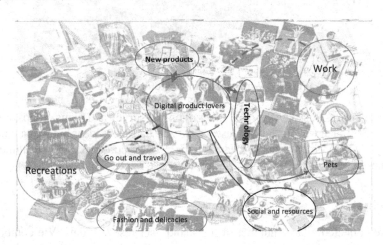

Fig. 10. A collage of target user group

Flower Mind Map: Based on keywords from collage, continuing divergent thinking and making points specifically.

So, we can define target user group, built basic demographic and psychological information of target user groups.

3.4 User Research II

In this phase, based on the result of former research, further digging out target user's pain points and needs of communicating, mobility, consumption, and target user's respective concerns.

452   D. Zhu

Online Survey: Through clusters from collages and flower mind maps to set up an outline of the questionnaire and sending it to target user groups. Then we did cross-analysis and correlation analysis to explore target user group's behaviors and connection between behaviors and demographic factors.

Focus Group Interview: According to results of online survey, conduct group interviews to further identify causes and significance of these behaviors. In order to understand users' deep behavior preferences and motivations better as well as quickly shorten the distance between interviewers and participants, we set many toolkits to trigger users' memory. Focus groups were required to discuss and present the result of discussion with toolkits. As Fig. 11 shows of toolkits to help users to think about what is their work environment preference (Sanders and Jan Stappers 2013).

Fig. 11. Work environment preference toolkits

1 on 1 Interview: Based on the overcomes of online survey and focus groups, the semi-structured approach was chosen because we already had some ideas but we cannot figure out everything. In order to dig out valuable points, we conducted in-depth interviews within these points to clarify target user group's real needs.

3.5 Analysis II

When we collected a large number of first-hand user research data. We combined all kinds of results together to analyze user needs of digital consumption services in the context of communicating vehicles. Analysis follows steps as Fig. 12 shown.

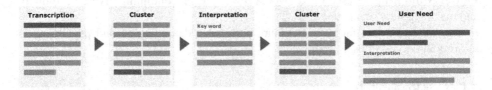

Fig. 12. Analysis interviews' results steps

Transcription: It is the process of transcribing the recording of the interviews and focus group is also a process of familiarizing and rethinking the interviews.

Affinity diagrams I: Clustered what participants said (Fig. 13).

Fig. 13. Affinity diagram I

Interpretation: It is the process of finding benefits and understanding motivation.

Affinity diagrams: Clustered by participants' benefits to find the original benefits.

Going down this, we got 22 users' needs from 4 benefit themes.

Finally, we visited 48 4S shops in different district in Beijing to define target user group, interviewed 251 participants to explore motivations, needs and frustration of them, read 327 papers to understand market and technologies, collected 2487 online surveys, finally got 567,592 words transcription.

4 User Needs of Digital Consumption Services

This section presents our main findings about user needs of digital consumption services. The findings are clustered under 4 main themes: the third space, purpose, design guidelines and satisfy desire. As a starting point, Sect. 4.1 provides an overview of users' attitude identified in the previous work.

4.1 User Attitudes

The attitudes of the users towards digital consumption services in their daily life were quite positive both in focus group interviews and 1 on 1 interviews. They mentioned that they are connected to a careless world, because they can use Alipay and WeChat pay almost everywhere. As the name suggests, they are ways to pay for goods and services online, and majority of transactions processed are conducted on mobile devices. At the same time, more and more merchants across China and around the world are accepting cash less, it will be more convenient. At present, they are enjoying life that connected to the digital world. Besides, they are more rely on digital consumption not only downloading digital media, using digital facilities, downloading digital applications and buying digital devices, but also buying membership, downloading online resources, asking experts to answer questions.

However, criticism of digital consumption was brought up in many interviews. Most information of digital consumption relies on digital information services, they communicate, search details, etc. on the Internet. In the face of the situation of Internet information explosion, the lack of trust, and the promotion of knowledge blocked, reliability has become a serious problem of digital consumption. Many participants said that they were afraid to buy products services online especially expensive product. When they buy products and services online often refer to comments below, but numerical records are easy to forge. So, users will spend more time to considerate which one to purchase. Some questions about the conventional wisdom that the Internet creates a "level playing field" for large and small retailers and for retailers with and without an established reputation. Users recognized differences in size and fame among Internet stores, and those differences influenced their assessments of store trustworthiness and their perception of risk, as well as their willingness to patronize the store.

As they said digital consumption world is convenient but it lacks of trust. Participants mainly wanted solutions to ease their life in certain functions.

4.2 The Third Space

Vehicles as the third space of users, besides home (the first space), company (the second space), give more opportunities to development of digital consumption in context of communicating vehicles. Users need an independent space where users can take a rest and think, and this space is also can protect their privacy. Vehicle is a secluded place, and one of the participants mentioned that he hopes to have a rest when he feels tired during self-driving trip with his friend. Sometimes users want to escape from an unpleasant environment for a while. Some users choose to travel, and some users choose to do something they like. During an interview, a user mentioned that he arranges tourism regularly. It slows him down enough not only to draw attention to where he is in his body, but also to his breath. Some days, it's just what he needs. Users need to vent their emotions. When they are driving, it is a closed and safe environment, and there are many users who choose to talk to their friends or family members about their work and life troubles and pressure. Some users will ease their stress by shopping online.

4.3 Purpose

In order to engage better in the future, there are many participants can choose the way of combining exertion and rest, take a nap, play games, watch variety shows, etc. In this approach, different brain regions can be activated, long-term excited can have a rest. To experience a new environment, many participants choose to reward themselves by traveling. They want to experience a brand-new environment and find out details that they cannot perceive in the previous environment.

4.4 Design Guideline

After the user interviews, we summarized two design guidelines that are required to pay more attention.

Precise and efficient. Under the development of the digital age, users expect more direct and efficient way to display information. Information bombing doesn't have the function of the interference user judgment as before. From the perspective of participants, they like to read more precise information, save their time, which allows users to trust in the product or service more.

Save for a rainy day. Users already have the basic cognition to a lot of information, according to the situation related to prepare in advance, but because of too much information at the same time, in context of vehicle network, need to use the advantage of network interconnection, under the right circumstances in an appropriate way to remind the user needs.

4.5 Satisfy Desire

As a subordinate of the user, the vehicle satisfies the owner's possessiveness of the item, and also gives the user a sense of belonging. The user feels accepted and accepted by others or the group. When user driving vehicle, there has the feeling of control, the user can control the direction as he wants.

5 Discussion

These findings enhance our understanding of users' authentic needs of digital consumption in communicating vehicle context. The main weakness of this study was the paucity of real experience in communicating vehicle context. Future research should therefore concentrate on the investigation of what kinds of information they need and when they need. It helps us to explore more opportunities in context of communicating. It would be interesting to do user test of individuals within target user group.

6 Conclusion

In the study of quantitative and qualitative researches found 22 user needs of 4 themes in communicating vehicle context. These findings suggest that in general vehicles satisfy possessive, create a sense of belonging and security. Vehicles create an independent space, can vent users' emotions, also can drive far away from an unpleasant situation, or experience a new world. In the future, we should design more directly and efficiently way to communicate with users, and consider the long-term problems of users.

Acknowledgements. The author wishes to thank the mentors of Communicating Vehicle Project for their valued co-operation: Professor Wei Liu, Lecture Yancong Zhu, also wish to thank team members: Meng Zhang, Tianyu Gao, Yuwei Fan, and all first-year master students of BNUX.

Funding. The publication of this research project was supported by the Fundamental Research Funds for the Central Universities (No. 01900-310422110).

References

Barros, J.: How to build vehicular networks in the real world. In: ACM (2014)

Vermesan, O., Blystad, L.C., et al.: Smart, connected and mobile: architecting future electric mobility ecosystems. In: Design, Automation & Test in Europe Conference & Exhibition, pp. 1740–1744. IEEE (2013)

Xu Xu, J.: The development of the digital economy in China, new trends, new models and new path. Chinese Economic and Trade (THEORY EDITION) (2017)

Denegri-Knott, J., Molesworth, M.: Concepts and practices of digital virtual consumption. Consum. Mark. Cult. **13**(2), 109–132 (2010)

Tencent.: Tencent's Operations in Third Quarter (2014). http://www.askci.com/finance/2014/11/13/105756upl_all.shtml

Sanders, E.B.N., Jan Stappers, P.: Convivial toolbox. Generative Research For the Front End of Design, vol. 31, no. 10 Suppl., pp. 14–21. Auk (2013)

Delft, T.H., Boeijen, A.V., Daalhuizen, J.: Delft Design Guide. BIS Publishers, Amsterdam (2013)

Cross, N.: Engineering design methods. Wiley, Hoboken (2008)

Zhou, Q.: Strategy first, execution second: teaching design strategy in technical communication. Commun. Des. Q. Rev. **3**(3), 53–55 (2015)

Romano, B.: Managing the internet of things. In: ACM Sigcse Technical Symposium, pp. 777–778. ACM (2017)

Macaulay, C., Busse, D.: Using user research in creativity: informing systems, service and product experience design. In: ACM Conference on Creativity and Cognition, pp. 495–496. ACM (2009)

Väänänen-Vainio-Mattila, K.: Towards user-centered mashups: exploring user needs for composite web services. In: CHI 2011 Extended Abstracts on Human Factors in Computing Systems, pp. 1327–1332. ACM (2011)

DUXU, Culture and Art

Study on Display Space Design of Off-line Experience Stores of Traditional Handicraft Derivative Product of ICH Based on Multi-sensory Integration

Bingmei Bie, Ye Zhang, and Rongrong Fu[✉]

East China University of Science and Technology, No. 130 Meilong Rd, Shanghai 200237, China
Muxin789@126.com, Missccchina@yeah.net

Abstract. With the increasing of Intangible cultural status, as the main transmission medium, the off-line experience store is the most common way for the public to contact with the traditional handcrafts of Intangible cultural heritage, it not only continues the emotional experience of the audience, but also plays an essential role of the Intangible Cultural Heritage even after the exhibition.

However, the visit to some off-line experience stores of traditional handicraft derivative product and museums shows that the existing off-line experience stores have a monotonous, homogeneous, low-end and cannot cause the public to pay attention to the traditional handcrafts effectively. After the exhibition of most people, they are not only stay on the superficial memory level of the traditional handcrafts, the off-line experience stores which extended from the traditional handcrafts cannot better disseminate cultural values also.

Based on this problem, this paper makes a design study from the perspective of multiple senses, and puts forward the design criteria of Multi-sensory experience design principles combining with digital multimedia technology, which concluded VR, CyberGrasp Data glove, Beyond Tactile Experience and so on. This paper analyzes the psychology of customers' timely feedback in digitalized situation, and creates immersive experience atmosphere, realizes the digital situation display and the interactive experience of the off-line experience stores of traditional handicraft derivative.

Keywords: Interaction design · Multi-sensory experience
Intangible Cultural Heritage (ICH) · Traditional handcrafts
Off-line experience store
Off-line experience stores of traditional handicraft derivative product

1 Introduction

Multi-sensory fusion immersion experience design can make the audience fully participate in such good experience, arouse people's pleasure and comfort, but at present, there is not much relevant research in this field, mainly focused on: (a) The introduction of the concept of multi sensory integration, and the introduction of some sensory fusion methods, and the corresponding application and technical support [1]. (b) The

© Springer International Publishing AG, part of Springer Nature 2018
A. Marcus and W. Wang (Eds.): DUXU 2018, LNCS 10920, pp. 459–470, 2018.
https://doi.org/10.1007/978-3-319-91806-8_36

development trend of multi-sensory experience which main manifestation is the use of visual, auditory, and olfactory senses to restore the real scene, but it lacks the interactive experience between the senses [2, 3]. (c) Off-line experience stores which dominated by vision at past should be more designed in the direction of the multi-sense atmosphere [4]. (d) The characteristics of tactile experience and olfactory experience in multi-sensory are attracting more and more attention. It can stimulate the development of human's emotional value and enable people to deeply remember the information they reflect, so as to achieve the purpose of knowledge popularization and consumption [5, 6].

Nowadays, as the main transmission medium of the Intangible Cultural Heritage, the off-line experience stores are the most common way for the public to contact the Intangible Cultural Heritage. From many practices, we know that the multi-sensory design method can significantly improve the audience's experience in the given environment, because of the characteristics of Intangible Cultural Heritage crafts, it can only rely on its handicraft derivative product for mass communication. Therefore, the focus of this paper is using design method of multi-sensory fusion to promote the space design of intangible cultural heritage off-line experience stores of traditional handicraft derivative product, enhance the communication effect of the intangible cultural heritage.

The concrete structure of the article is divided into the following parts: the first part is the analysis of the existing problems on the substantive marketing of the traditional handicraft products. The second part is that through the research and interview analysis we found that the existing mode of off-line experience stores of ICH of traditional handicraft derivative product is difficult to effectively stimulate public concern, it is difficult for audience and traditional handcrafts to have a interactive communication, and the homogenization of products, the same phenomenon is obvious. In the third part we will set the example as "Shanghai style jade carving" to elaborate on which technologies can be used to play a more better role in the multi-sensory experience store, and to allow users to experience ICH.

The fourth part expounds the prospect and value of the off-line experience stores of ICH of traditional handicraft derivative product on multi-sensory integration.

2   The Integration of Intangible Cultural Heritage and the Design Techniques of Multi-sensory Integration

Intangible Cultural Heritage is the invisible and generation-by-generation cultural heritage of mankind. It embodies the development characteristics and cultural connotation of a nation, and it is the cultural gene of different nationalities' historical evolution. The cultural feature of a country has become the pillar of its cultural survival, and it is the mission of every country to protect and inherit its outstanding cultural heritage. It is the important source that awakens the national cultural memory and makes the nation develop and grow. Since the 50's, from Japan to many countries around the world, the protection and inheritance of intangible cultural heritage has been carried out as a national key work. The protection and inheritance of Intangible cultural heritage in China has also been on the right way in the last few decades. (the following Intangible Cultural Heritage is replaced by the "ICH")

2.1 The Existing Problems of Integration of Intangible Cultural Heritage

However, although the protection and inheritance of ICH have been dominated by the government and supported by the state funds for a long time, as the following reasons: (1) The way of protection leading by government is simple. (2) Most traditional hand-crafts of ICH is difficult to keep up with the trend of the times because of its complex process, time and effort, high price and lack of creativity. The protection and inheritance of traditional handcrafts of ICH still faces a severe test. If "no remains" can not be closely combined with contemporary cultural value and the life of contemporary people, it will inevitably be forgotten by the society. Traditional handicraft derivative products is the most common ways of public access to ICH, while the off-line experience store is the main transmission medium. Its inheritance and dissemination of ICH, the continuation of the experience of the audience after the exhibition can also play a good role.

2.2 The Design Techniques of Multi Sensory Integration

Through the research of first-tier cities of Shanghai (Shanghai Natural History Museum, Shanghai Museum, Fosun Foundation) and Nanjing (Nanjing Museum), second-tier cities Zhengzhou (Henan Museum) and Ningbo (Ningbo Museum, Ningbo Museum of Art, Southern Song Dynasty stone Museum), We found that the current off-line experience stores of traditional handicraft derivative product have the following problems: (a) Most of the off-line experience store are often arranged in places unnoticed, such as the edge of the exit corner. (b) The basic layout of the experience stores are the same, lack of characteristic, no more than the shelfs after the glass counter, it make the customers lack of desire to buy. (c) The layout of the products is rather messy, and there is not special region for different kind products. (d) Most of the off-line experience store use a single visual design, lack of the scene of interactive experience and new technology to guide customers to buy products.

Taking the Republic of China Venue in Nanjing Museum as an example, the Republic of China Venue simulates the historical environment, set up the above century decoration style of the rickshaw, the old Post office, barber shop, pharmacy, restaurant and other small scenes to foil the grand view of the Republic. Each of these scenes can not only be seen, but also can be visited. On the basis of retaining the original core of the Republic of China's culture, the Republic of China Venue simulated the performance of the scenes, forms and ways of communication, and moved the culture of the Republic of China from the historical books to the real life of visitors, breaking the boring and telling process of the museum. With a real visit to deepen the multi-sensory experience and the better interaction experience, it has built a famous scene experience Museum.

After interviews with tourists visited by the Nanjing Museum, we find that this multi-scene fusion mode brings visitors a very vivid sense of interactive experience. From the moment of walking into the venue, tourists are naturally brought into the era of the Republic of China Atmosphere. Visitors in the shops are full of interest of the products instead of conflict of emotion. It solves the problem that the existing "non-legacy" product line experience Shop is uniform, the product layout is messy and the lack of scene interaction.

Multi-sensory integration refers to the user experience of instant feedback through visual, auditory, tactile, smell, taste, and digitized situations through multiple channels and multi-media. To realize the art direction of relative concentration of users in the relatively closed display space of the experience store, Use more natural and harmonious way of media convergence, more novel art form of expression, use of digital media technology and new variety of communication channels, the use of display space of multi-sensory integration design, realize the fusion of the traditional handicraft and the digital media art and the design of exhibition space, realize the active interaction between traditional handcrafts and visitors which is more positive than traditional display methods.

From the case of Republic of China Venue in Nanjing Museum, we found that the use of interactive multi-sensory integration experience mode and digital technology as well as new art forms, it can solve the problems in off-line experience stores of off-line experience stores of ICH of traditional handicraft derivative product. Therefore, in the following sections, we will elaborate on which technologies can be used to play a more better role in the multi-sensory experience store, and to allow users to experience ICH.

3   The Use of the Design Techniques of Multi-sensory Integration

According to our research, visual and auditory integration is the most common in museum shops and off-line experience stores of ICH of traditional handicraft derivative product. For example, the Ningbo Museum provides visitors with a restored sugar cake making scene, according to the dialectal cartoon figures on the screen, the coin tossed in the box around will get a box of sugar cake, which simulates the scene of selling sugar cake in the Song Dynasty engage visitors in the interactive experience. In the South Song Dynasty stone carving Museum, the museum uses a large display infrared sensor and an XBOX to allow visitors to experience the virtual makeover.

However, although the visual and auditory interaction as means of technology has been developed, but research shows that touch, taste and smell will be added to the ICH exhibition and off-line experience store which can increase the richness of the visitor experience, even memory. We believe that the combination of sense of touch and sense with smell and visual and hearing can significantly improve the sensibility of the visitors. It highlight the design theme of derivative products of ICH, it will help visitors better understand the ICH, understand the cultural value of derivative products of ICH, and bring more profound interactive experience to visitors.

Now we will take the technology of "Shanghai style jade carving" as an example, and elaborate on the technical means to achieve this traditional handcrafts and the experience of its derivative product.

3.1   Shanghai Style Jade Carving

Shanghai style culture is based on the Wu Yue culture in modern China. It combines the classical and elegant of Wu Yue culture. After the opening of the port of Shanghai, the modern industrial civilization in Europe and the United States, which has a profound impact on Shanghai, has gradually formed a unique cultural phenomenon in Shanghai, which is different from other cultures in China. The most representative of traditional handcrafts of ICH of Shanghai is the "Shanghai style jade carving", however, because of the difficulty of exploitation of jade and the complex of jade carving, in the visit of jade carving, visitors can not have a deep understanding of the formation of jade carving process, can not really touch the jade carving crafts also. So in the off-line experience store of "Shanghai style jade carving", we will let the visitors have a multi-sensory experience from four parts which named "Jade mining experience area", "Jade carving experience area", "Jade carving crafts experience area" and "Production of exclusive souvenir area" (Fig. 1).

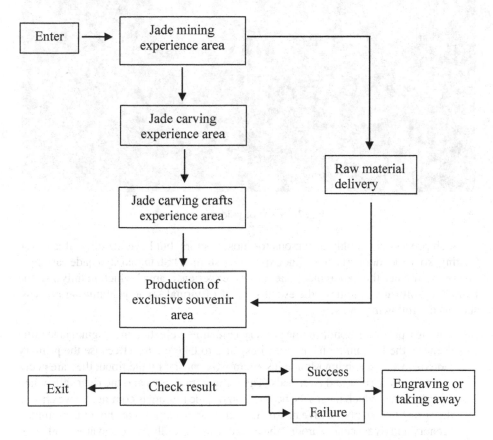

Fig. 1. Off-line experience store of Shanghai style jade carving.

3.1.1 Jade Mining Experience Area

As we all know, the exploitation of jade has been over five thousand years, and it is still in the ascendant. Taking jadeite jade as an example, for most of the floodplain deposits are basically depleted, the miners have no more mining except for the highly difficult gravel layer. The workers first use dynamite to fry the hard place, then use the excavator bucket to lift the rock away to other sides. The experienced Jade Pickers will wait in the place where the stones are poured, pick and choose the stones which maybe the jade during their experience. The stones which are not selected after first choose will be transported to the place not far away for the second picking. Picking will not be finished until the whole mountain is dug (Fig. 2).

Fig. 2. Scene of jade mining 1.

Such process is not only dangerous for most visitors, but have the low value of the visiting, so in the four parts of off-line experience store of "Shanghai style jade carving", visitors will enter the panorama "Jade mining experience area" which mainly use the Pano2VR software to achieve the establishment of virtual scene jade mining process, such as the following show:

(a) Taking a panoramic photo of the primary jade mine: selecting the original jade mine scene in the Kunlun mountain area in spring to take photos (Because the primary jade deposits on Kunlun Mountains are mostly carried by the flood, they are accumulated in the river and river beds. The temperature rises and the river falls when spring comes, which means the best season of jade mining is coming. So we choose the spring to take photos. We mainly use panoramic cameras to shoot the mountain scenery and river scenery around the collection. Secondly, the excavators and other tools used to collect jade are taken to take a view. Finally, the stones which are chosen will be shooting detailed.

(b) Correction of panoramic photos and classification: classify the photos and build a material library. In order to ensure the authenticity and completeness of the photos, they will be are colored and corrected.

(c) Sort the photos and set up interactive hot spots: open the Pano2VR5.0.1 X64 version software and import the processed photos in the Tour Browser in order. In order to achieve barrier free switching between adjacent scenes, interactive hot spots are set up in each panoramic photo, and the effect of scene switching is configured.

(d) Make a new skin, add navigational map: because the skin is equivalent to the control center in the panoramic roaming system, the 360 degree full screen function can be realized. On the basis of the skin of the software, the realization of the virtual scene system of the "Jade mining experience area" also needs to replace the original hot icon and realize the navigation thumbnail. First, select the "add hotspot template" tool through the skin editing window, create a new hot icon by double clicking on the skin display window, integrate the hotspot ID and the hotspot ID in panoramic scene, that is, achieve the new hot binding. Second, select the new hot spot icon from the material library to add to the skin display window, and take the icon under the hot directory to finish the replacement of the hot new icon. After that, in order to realize one key span switching in different scenes, we need to add a navigation map. We will add the mountain view, the river view, the excavator structure diagram, the coordinate map and the view diagram to the skin display window from the material library. Select the "addnode marker" and create nodes in the skin display, add the prepared material to the node directory, then connect the node with the scene to complete the navigation map production.

(e) Add audio material: select "images" or "videos" in the panorama display window to simulate the sound of the jade collection.

(f) Generating a complete panoramic system: in the Pano2VR software, the editing area should be selected everywhere. (the system chooses HTML5 format). Select the "Generate output" tool to export the system and complete the system production.

(g) Simulation of temperature: humidity and odor: by setting the temperature sensor and humidity sensor in the "Jade mining experience area", we simulate the weather conditions and geographical environment in the real scene, and regularly release the smell of stone and soil mixed when mining.

In this area, with the help of Pano2VR software and the temperature and humidity sensor and the release of odors, we achieve three sensory integration of vision, hearing and smell, and solve the practical problems of visitors' "invisible, unable to feel and experience". After the visiting of "Jade mining experience area", visitors will have a gamble whether the stone is emerald or not according to hints on the display screen. The selected stone will be sent to the fourth part of the off-line experience store which named "Production of exclusive souvenir zone" to make the souvenir (Fig. 3).

Fig. 3. Scene of jade mining 2.

3.1.2 Jade Carving Experience Area

Jade carving process takes a long time and does not have the conditions of viewing experience, but its carving process is exactly the essence of "Shanghai style jade carving", and it is also the key for visitors to experience the traditional handcrafts of "Shanghai style jade carving". In the "Jade carving experience area", we will combine the sense of touch and vision to make the visitors experience the process of jade carving (Fig. 4).

Fig. 4. Scene of jade mining 3.

First of all, we will make a video to record the whole process of jade crafts from stone to finished, and make the 3D modeling of the jade handcrafts and carving tool (include of cutting machine, electronic pen, polishing tools) to model 3D production, and the carving stage is divided into the process such as the bottle mouth, a bottle body and a hanging ear. Next, the visitor will select the engraving phase according to the hint on the screen, and choose the corresponding carving tool. After that, visitors will take the CyberGrasp data glove to the first touch of the 3D Modeling arts and crafts. The induction signal will produce real contact through special mechanical device of Cyber-Grasp data glove during the visitors touch the 3D virtual object (Fig. 5).

Fig. 5. Scheme of the visitors 1.

The induction lines in the glove are designed especially for fine pressure and friction, and the motor on the 5 fingers is a high quality DC motor, in this way, the user's hands will not destroy the real sense of virtual reality by penetrating the virtual objects. When the visitor's hand is exerting force, the force will be transmitted through the exoskeleton to the tendons connected to the fingertips. The five drivers of the CyberGrasp data glove are set individually, each finger can be set individually, or visitors can not touch the virtual objects. Through CyberGrasp's force feedback system to touch the rendered 3D virtual image, it feels like touches the real thing, and experience the vibration touch that the tool engraving brings (Fig. 6).

Fig. 6. Scheme of the visitors 2.

3.1.3 Jade Carving Crafts Experience Area

Generally, the exquisite jade carving crafts are placed in the showcase. Because of its high value and high preservation conditions, it does not have the condition of touching. We will use the hyper tactile experience [7] to project the 3D virtual image in "Jade carving crafts experience area". When the visitor touches the virtual image, it will block the sensor, so that the sensor can transfers the signal to the sonic projector. Through the Ultrasonic transducer array which is placed under the Sonic transmission monitor, the focused ultrasound is transmitted through an interactive surface. It affects visitors' hands directly and forms multiple feedback points to give them different tactile attributes. Visitors can receive local feedback related to their touching behavior.

In this area, we will divide the "Jade carving crafts experience area" into several parts during different jade materials, such as Hetian jade, Suet jade, Emerald and Mo jade. When the visitor touches the 3D virtual jade carving product in this part, it will pass the sensor signal of the super tactile experience to the central processor, and then the signal will be transmitted to the controller port fragrance to release the fragrance of this part. When the stream of people increases in this part, the concentration of fragrance will increase through infrared sensor. When the smell sensors have monitoring the increase of fragrance concentration, it will send signals to the central processor, the central processor will send signals to prompt visitors to go to the area with less traffic. Through the combination of olfactory senses, tactile senses and visual senses, it not only helps visitors to experience jade carving crafts better, but also limits the flow of people in the area by smell.

3.1.4 Production of Exclusive Souvenir Area

After the experience of the past three area, visitors will come to the "Production of exclusive souvenir area" and choose whether to make it become the exclusive jade products.

When visitors gambling fails, they can also carved in stone and take it away. When visitors gambling success and hope that it is made into exclusive souvenirs, the system will provide the pattern or style uploaded by visitors, and send the stone and pattern to Shanghai Jade professional engraver, they will make the exclusive souvenir of you.

This will not only promote the inheritance of "Shanghai style jade carving" handcrafts, but also combine skills, experience and commercialization to avoid the disappearance of ICH.

4　Prospect and Value

Through the investigation of several museums, art galleries and art centers, this paper summarizes the existing problems of the traditional handicraft inheritance of ICH.We put forward the design techniques of multi-sensory integration(Mainly with vision and touch, smell as a supplement). Combine the traditional handcrafts with the digital media art and the design of display space design harmoniously, realize the active interaction between the product and the visitor. Put the off-line experience store of Shanghai style jade carving as a example, elaborate on how can we use VR technology, CyberGrasp data glove and odor sensor technology etc. to make vision and tactile sensation and smell fusing in the off-line experience store. It provides a specific and feasible way from handcrafts demonstration and experience to the derivative product selling. Realize the concept of living protection of ICH (Fig. 7).

Fig. 7. Scheme of the visitors 3.

Here, visitors can experience and learn the ICH in person, and no longer just watch it. Through the comprehensive multi-sensory experience, The visitors grasp more abundant cultural connotation in the intangible cultural heritage, have a deeply understanding of the unique charm of derivative product, so as to enhance the emotional identity of ICH, enhance the interest of traditional handcrafts of Intangible Cultural Heritage, and guide more people to join the inheritance and protection of Intangible Cultural Heritage. It can be seen that the application of multi sensory integration design concept to the space design of off-line experience stores of ICH of traditional handicraft derivative product is not only the trend of off-line experience store, but also the effective way to spread Intangible Cultural Heritage (Fig. 8).

Fig. 8. Scheme of transporting stones.

References

1. Wang, S.: Discussion on the cognition and dissemination effect of multi senses in museum exhibition. Sci. Pop. **068**(3), 064–073 (2017)
2. Helmefalk, M., Hulten, B.: Multi-sensory congruent cues in designing retail store atmosphere: effects on shoppers' emotions and purchase behavior. J. Retail. Consum. Serv. **38**, 1–11 (2017)
3. Vi, C.T., Ablart, D., Gatti, E., Velasco, C., Obrist, M.: Not just seeing, but also feeling art: mid-air haptic experiences integrated in a multisensory art exhibition. Int. J. Hum Comput Stud. **108**, 1–14 (2017)
4. Kang, H.: On the display design of the museum's creative shop. Study on the Cultural Industry of the Chinese Museum, pp. 236–242 (2016)
5. Hashim, A.F., Taib, M.Z.M., Alias, A.: The integration of interactive display method and heritage exhibition at museum. Soc. Behav. Sci. **153**, 308–316 (2014)
6. Levent, N., Pascual-Leone, A.: The Multisensory Museum: Gross-Disciplinary Perspectives On Touch, Sound, Smell, Memory, and Space. Rowman & Littlefield Publishers, Lanham (2014)
7. Long, B., Seah, S.A., Garter, T., Subramanian, S.: Rendering volumetric haptic shapes in mid-air using ultrasound.AGM Trans. ACM Trans. Graph. **33**, 1–10 (2014)

Artelligent: A Framework for Developing Interactive Computer Artwork Using Artificial Intelligent Agents

Francisco de Paula Barretto[1](✉) and Suzete Venturelli[2]

[1] Laboratory of Research, Creation and Innovation, Federal University of Bahia,
Salvador, Bahia, Brazil
kikobarretto@gmail.com
[2] Computer Art Research Lab, University of Brasilia,
Brasilia, Federal District, Brazil
suzeteventurelli@gmail.com

Abstract. This theoretical and practical research adopts a transdisciplinary point of view and proposes a new concept and framework described as Artelligent aimed to facilitate the development of autonomous artwork based on AI techniques that are able to demonstrate creative/adaptative behavior. The word Artelligent has its origin at the junction of Latin words ars/artis and intelligere. The word ars, corresponding to the Greek term tékne, basically describe a practical skill to produce artifacts and, at the same time, indicate knowledge, science or methodology related to some art-scientific theory. In this case, we consider that it involves the expression or an imaginative skill represented in its broader aspects such as painting, music and literature associated with some emotional or aesthetic potential. The word intelligere, also derived from Latin, is at the root of the word intelligent and is a composition of the word inter, that is, between, and legere, which means choose, collect, harvest, gather. Together, inter and legere mean perceive, recognize, understand, understand and perform. An Artelligent system can be defined as an autopoietic system, which through the use of specific techniques of artificial intelligence, represents knowledge in an extensible way and considering the principles that describe the human creative process, is able to demonstrate recognizably emergent results in a given environment. It is also presented a framework in order to clearly define the techniques, concepts and principles that should be applied or considered in order to create such Artelligent systems, especially considering the concepts of autopoiesis, created by Maturana and Varela (1970) and emergence as a heuristic for creativity or novelty creation.

Keywords: Artelligent · Artificial intelligence · Computer art
Computer creativity · Interaction

A. Marcus and W. Wang (Eds.): DUXU 2018, LNCS 10920, pp. 471–489, 2018.
https://doi.org/10.1007/978-3-319-91806-8_37

1   Introduction

Artificial Intelligent researchers aim, through the improvement of specific models and techniques, to achieve the best solutions for specific problems such as machine learning, computer vision and computer creativity. The discussion we intend to bring on with this paper is about the possible applications of AI that underlie the development of artificial agents able to demonstrate creative behavior in an artistic environment, based on the concepts of emergence and autopoiesis. The first has roots on Latin "emergere" that means 'bring to light' and is defined by Cariani [1] as the emergence of new entities that in one sense or another, could not have been predicted based on what preceded them, while autopoiesis (from the Greek "auto" which means "itself" and "poiesis" which means "creation") describes the autonomous systems, able to self-reproduce and self-regulate, while iterate with the environment. This environment iteration might unroll, only in an indirect way, changes on the autopoietic system's internal processes and structures [2] that might lead to a deterministic-emergent transition.

According to Wilson [3], the development of algorithms and heuristics that allow computers to perform complex and sophisticated analysis or demonstrate complex behavior, as create artworks, represents some of the greatest challenges of modern scientific research. This challenge derives not only from the development of new technologies able to support the computational requirements of such algorithms, but also the need to understand the phenomenon of intelligence and creativity through new perspectives and approaches, raising new questions on this philosophical issue.

We do not intend to engage in such a subjective discussion about intelligence or creativity but rather present a framework to help artificial agent designing focused on achieving computer creativity artwork. In this approach, the system's intelligent behavior, as described by Smith [4], requires knowledge representation and some kind of machine learning or a certain degree of autonomous adaptation to the environment. Therefore, we might ask how to design Smith's knowledge representation in an autopoietic system and how emergence can be seen as creativity.

On the other hand, we are deeply interested in investigating if computer creativity can be simulated using a series of algorithms, mostly from AI techniques such as Artificial Neural Networks (ANN), Genetic Algorithms (GA) and Multi-Agent Systems (MAS). One possible approach might be the identification of creative behavior in intelligent systems which main goal was not necessarily creativity simulation. The identification of such creative systems might be attained through the detection of emergent results, since (as will be discussed in this paper) one of the main characteristics of creativity, as in emergence, is the occurrence of new information, forms or expressions that didn't exist before or wasn't programmed or expected to arise. These intelligent systems which demonstrate emergent characteristics might as well be identified as autopoietic since usually the might be able to self-regulate, like Artificial Neural Networks.

Many researches might unroll in the junction of these mentioned areas, mainly involving the concepts of creativity, consciousness, emergence and autopoiesis aiming to create or simulate through AI techniques some capabilities that are inherent to human existence. These simulations might unroll through the development of artistic-intelligent systems that are able to express themselves autonomously in artistic terms such as music or visual arts. Therefore, some artworks that approach those above-mentioned concepts will be presented in order to illustrate the presented framework.

Finally, this paper presents a brief definition of what is an artistic-intelligent system, defined here as an Artelligent System, as well as defines a list of principles that should help the development of such systems, based previous works [5–7].

2 Emergence and Creativity

One can also define emergence as the appearance of macro patterns due to micro processes, so we can find in nature several examples of emergence. According to Cariani [1], the main emergent events of the universe includes particles, atoms and molecules creation, in a microscale, and stars, galaxies and black holes formations in a macroscale. One may even question if the laws of physics and even time itself are emergent aspects from the evolution of the universe.

However, emergence is something broader than the mere appearance of new structures and new patterns. It also includes fundamentally new organizations of matter and information processes along with a new world cognitive point of view. In a natural context, it is clear that the emergent transitions may involve one or more of these fundamentally new formations but it does not ordinarily apply to computer models given the different context and environment in which relationships are built: cyberspace. In a binary context, the establishment of new connections and the creation of new entities demand a new approach on the subject because one might question if the emergent transitions are possible in a virtual environment, which is a deterministic system.

Kujawski [8] affirms that it is possible for something new, unpredictable, emerge from a Turing machine once we understand the difference between rules and laws. The first is a set of well-defined formal procedures while the latter represents universal conditions. There are algorithms or a set of rules behind any emergent phenomenon, regardless their nature. A good example of emergence in a simple rules system is the Game of Life, created by John Conway in the 1950s and described in [9].

In general, emergence designates a behavior that has not been explicitly programmed in a system or agent. Pfeifer and Bongard [10] point out three kinds of emergence: (i) a global phenomenon arising from a collective behavior, (ii) individual behavior as the result of an interaction between the agent and the environment and (iii) emergence behavioral from a time scale to another.

The ant-trail formation is an example of the first emergence kind. The ants, themselves, are unaware of the fact that they are forming a trail that will determine the shortest path to food. So, when observing a population (even if it's artificial) we might focus on the dynamic emergent characteristics of this population.

A nice example of the individual behavior as the result of an interaction with the environment is the artistic installation named La Funambule Virtuelle [11], from Marie-Hélene Tramus and Michel Bret, where a virtual acrobat evolves to keep up on a tightrope, reacting to the movements of the public. The character tries to reproduce the position of the iterator while trying to stay on the rope. In this installation, through an ANN, the balancer is able to learn to remain on the rope during the user interaction. From the learned gesture, a new behavior emerges through movements that were not taught, endowing the character of what the artist calls "the ability to improvise".

Finally, the third kind of emergence concerns time scales. They must be incorporated from three perspectives: (i) short-term, which regards current state of the mechanism, (ii) learning and development from the ontogenetic point of view and (iii) evolutionary, phylogenetic perspective. Therefore, the three time scales - short-term, ontogenetic and phylogenetic - should be considered in order to determine whether the system is able to demonstrate emergent behavior in any of these scales.

A deeper level of emergence called "epistemic emergence" involves, of course, the emergence of new perspectives intrinsically linked to the sensorial changes. The improvement or development of new sensorial organs allows an organism to evolve into another lineage, along with new world perspectives. This kind of development also occurs in our technological evolution as we build artifacts such as thermometers, clocks, telescopes, and that extend our senses or reactions as an extension of our natural biological functions.

The installation Bacterial Orchestra (2006) by Lübke and Cornéer [12] is a good example of a creative emergence not declared by artists, expressed through autonomous objects/artifacts where an emergent phenomena emerges from a collective behavior. It consists of an orchestra formed by several autonomous cells able to hear and reproduce the sounds of the environment. The sound material comes from the ambient sound where the cells are immerse, such as people talking, sound of steps or sounds that other cells reproduce. Thus, together, they behave as a more complex organism working on an weak-defined and open domain.

Each unit of this ecology is a simple system with a microphone and a speaker. The cell is initialized randomly with a set of parameters encoded in its chromosome that will determine how it will respond to sound stimuli. The simple interaction between the cells results in a kind of microphone effect that enables new sound evolutions. These evolutions are capable of generating sound patterns that were not predicted, creating a more complex sonic space over time as the sounds reverberate through each of the cells in a kind of feedback, making it difficult to limit the scope of possibilities presented by the installation.

2.1   Creativity Identification and Classification

According to previous works [5–7,13] it is possible to consider emergence as a heuristic to creativity but since there are several levels of emergence it is necessary to use some grade scale in order to classify from a lower-level emergence to a higher-level emergence. From psychology point of view creativity might not be defined as something that can be seen in a binary way - creative or not creative - but rather presents itself as a result of several variables and could be categorized according to their "creativeness".

As for Artificial Intelligence, there is also no consensus as to the definition of creativity to this day (and there might never be). However, there are some definitions that converge in the sense that there is in the creative process some emerging function of re-signifying or creating something new, implying in the reconstruction of the past or reinterpretation of the present [14–16].

Although it is clear that there are several levels of creativity, there is a categorization in two main creativity levels: little-C and Big-C [17]. This type of categorization allows us to evaluate the different algorithms according to the potential generation of emergent and creative results. When comparing theoretical conceptions this quantitative distinction between little and Big-C is necessary. Big-C refers to unambiguous examples of creative expression, such as the Miles Davis Jazz or Picasso's paintings. In contrast, little-C focuses on daily everyday creativity, for example when a person develops a new way to cook a recipe when there is a necessary ingredient missing and later receives compliments for the new recipe.

Like most dichotomies, however, this approach lacks a certain degree of softness for cases at intermediate levels. Paradoxically this approach may seem overly inclusive in some cases and non-inclusive to others. For example, if we compare three people: (i) a non-eminent artist who works professionally with the teaching and selling of watercolors, (ii) an amateur watercolor painter who uses his free time to paint, and (iii) a high school student who likes to paint sporadically. Each case qualitatively exhibits different levels of creativity, although none of them can be characterized as Big-C (if we compare with Cézanne or Kandinsky, for example).

In this sense, should the three cases mentioned above be included in the same category? By grouping we can obscure potential differences between subcategories. One way to address this kind of limitation is to create more restrictive categories with more precise cuts following "clear" examples of creativity. However, in making sharper cuts there is the risk, already mentioned, of excluding potential creative manifestations of a more subjective nature.

In order to mitigate this limitation in the traditional dichotomy, we can consider two new categories: mini-C and Pro-C [18]. The mini-C category helps differentiate subjective and objective forms of creativity that would fit into the little-C category, opening space for more subjective, personal, internal, mental or emotional forms of creativity [16]. The Pro-C category helps distinguish the fuzzy area between little-C and Big-C. Pro-C makes room for "professional" creators (such as professional artists) who have not yet attained (and might never attain) eminent status, but are still far beyond little-C creators (such as hobbyists, for example).

So, using the four-C categories proposed by Kaufman and Beghetto [18] we can classify creativity from a low-level to a higher level: mini-C representing changes in our understanding that cause impact on individuals, little-C for everyday creative thoughts and actions in any aspect of our lives which impact on individuals and their influence zone, Pro-C for creative acts of experts and experienced agents within a community or domain which impacts in a community or system and Big-C to represent eminent exceptional creativity which impact on culture, society and the world. Although there are still gaps and the number of categories is not sufficient to describe all possible levels of creativity, the four categories will be used in this research to help describe the creative potential of the algorithms.

Furthermore, Rhodes [19] developed a research that aimed to identify the multifaceted creative construction as approached in this paper. According to Rhodes, there are four Ps: Person, Process, Product and Press/Place. These Ps as used to describe the main factors that are involved in novelty creation and each component describe a fundamental aspect of a creative process. Person component includes the cognitive abilities, biological and personality bias of the creative agent which operate to a Process to create ideas, which include the stages of preparation, incubation, illumination and verification. Product represents ideas expressed in form of language, object or any other creative final outcome of the creative process. The environment and its relationship and co-evolution with the creative agent is described in Press/Place.

Together these aspects of creative creation help to describe the creative context in which a given creative outcome. This is quite important when using algorithms because it can help to describe not only how the system behave in a holistic way but also understand which are the main factors, agents and components involved. In this sense, creative outcomes are a result of creative processes engaged by creative agents which are then supported by a creative environment. More recently an extended version of this framework has been presented adding two more Ps: Persuasion and Potential [16].

3   Autopoiesis and Knowledge Representation

The concept of autopoiesis, as the organization of the living, originated in the work of Chilean biologists Maturana and Varela in the 1970s [2]. This idea was developed in the context of theoretical biology and was early associated with the artificial life simulation long before the term "artificial life" have been introduced in the late 1980s in [20].

Today the concept of autopoiesis continues to have a significant impact in the field of artificial life computing. Luisi presents a good review in [21]. Furthermore, there was also an effort to integrate the notion of autopoiesis to the field of cognitive sciences.

To be more precise, an autopoietic system is organized as a production processes network of components (synthesis and destruction) which: (i) continuously regenerate themselves in order to form a network able to reproduce components and (ii) this network constitutes the system as a distinct unit in the domain in which it exists. In addition to these two explicit criteria for autopoiesis, we can add another important point: that identity self- constitution implies on the creation of a relational domain between the system and its environment. Froese and Ziemke describe this relational domain in [22]. This emergent domain is not predetermined but possibly co-determined by the system and environment's organization, Fig. 1. Any system that meets the criteria for autopoiesis also generates its own domain of interactions while its identity emerges.

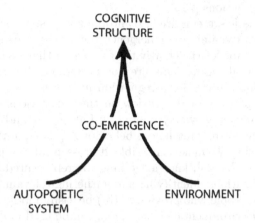

Fig. 1. Graphic representation of an autopoietic system cognitive co-emergence, simplified from [22]

A single cell organism, Fig. 2, is a perfect example of a paradigmatic autopoietic system and illustrates the circular production network that is inherent to the autopoietic self-production system. In the unicellular case, this circular relationship is expressed by the co-dependence between the limits determined by the membrane (external) and the metabolic network (internal). This metabolic network builds itself and distinguishes from the environment as a unified system. This bounded system formation is only possible due to the external system (membrane), which prevents components from dispersing in the environment. On the other hand, this external system is only constituted because there is an internal functional metabolic network. This whole system might be artificially reproduced by AI techniques such as ANN and GA.

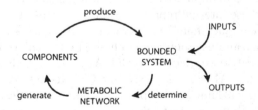

Fig. 2. Single cell organism self-regulation cycle, adapted from [21]

The concept of self-organization can be interpreted in many different ways, but in terms of autopoietic is worthy of being presented by two aspects: (i) determining local-to-global, so that the process has its emerging identity global constituted and constrained as a result of local interactions and (ii) determining global-to-local and global identity where its ongoing contextual interaction constrain local interactions [23].

Finally, autopoietic systems are also autonomous systems since they are characterized by such a dynamic co- emergence but are specified within a specific domain. It is important for the creativity of a system that its changes and adaptations of the internal mechanisms are not performed directly by an external agent, but through an internal self-regulation mechanism.

We do not intent to present a review on the foundations of knowledge representation. Such review is widely offered by Lakemeyer and Nebel in [24]. We will assume that the agent's intelligent behavior requires knowledge acquisition, storage and processing. To make it possible, it is essential to represent it. According to Rich and Knight [25], knowledge must be represented in such way that: (i) capture generalizations, identifying and gathering relevant properties, (ii) be understandable for people who provide it, (iii) be easily modifiable to allow error correction, reflect environmental changes, (iv) can be used in different situations even if incomplete or inaccurate, (v) help to overcome their own data volume, helping to limit the number of possibilities that should be considered.

To the machine, this symbolic pattern should be consistent enough to generate an abstraction of the domain where it is embedded. This abstraction allows it to perform operations on these patterns in order to achieve problems potential solutions. This set of symbolic patterns, in turn, may alter its collection of patterns, which consist in the agents knowledge base, through internal processes, in an autopoietic way. It means that its internal processes, self-contained in the autopoietic machine, can only change the internal organization of this set of symbolic patterns. We might say, relying on Maturana and Varela, that the autopoietic machine is a self-homeostatic system that has its own organization as a variable that remains constant. The autopoietic organization means that processes concatenated in a particular manner such that these processes produce the components of the system and specify it as a unit.

Craik [26] specified three fundamental steps for defining an agent-based knowledge: (i) the stimulus must be translated into an internal representation; (ii) cognitive processes manipulate the representation to derive new internal representations; (iii) these internal representations are translated into stimulus.

Most of the techniques found in literature represents knowledge explicitly through abstractions and use some kind of heuristic to achieve intelligent behavior. However, alternative approaches to GOFAI (Good Old Fashioned Artificial Intelligence) or classic AI, such as ANN and GA, are interesting because they bring other non-explicit knowledge representation possibilities. We should highlight that even though non-explicit knowledge is used, disregarding the need for logic, syntactic or semantic knowledge structuring, it also needs to be structured in some way. We might, therefore, consider how the agent will be able to make its own infers, alter its owns perceptions and iterate with the environment, as a circular production network.

4   Creativity Models and Computer Algorithms

In addition to the categorization of levels of creativity, Kozbelt [17] proposes a categorization of creativity theories, organized in 10 categories, which stand out for their convergence with the concepts presented in the development of this research: Developmental, Stage and Componential Processes, Evolutionary and System.

4.1   Developmental Approach

The theories related to the developmental approach are interesting to this research because they facilitate the understanding of how to plan favorable environments so the creative potential is reached. In this sense, this approach emphasizes the creative aspects of Person, Place and Potential and their results can range from mini-C to Pro-C. Although the Products do not occupy a prominent place in this approach, they play an important but tacit role. This implicit participation of the Product happens because this theory considers that there is a temporal trajectory that begins with more subjective forms of creativity (mini-C) and evolves to more tangible and mature forms of creative expression [17].

This temporal relationship is of significant importance in the context of this research because if we analyze an initial generation of random genetic algorithms, we cannot say (yet) that any creative process is expressed. However, after a few generations we can begin to see some progress regarding emergent creative processes. Another relevant aspect is the interaction between the agent and the environment where this interaction is responsible for the evolution of the creative process itself. Through this interaction the creative agent is cognitively evolved and therefore creativity could be considered as a co-evolutionary outcome of this environment-agent interaction.

4.2   Stages and Componential Processes

The theories that are fit in this approach are based on the four-stage process described by Wallas [27]. The initial stage is preparation (i) where the individual gathers information about the environment and defines a problem or objective that must be solved. Subsequently, there is the incubation process (ii) which involves a certain temporal dedication to distance oneself from the problem and dedicate itself to the cognitive process of understanding it. If the second stage is effective, then we have what Wallas considers illumination (iii). In this third stage a solution or idea presents itself to the individual (or is discovered by him). Finally, we proceed to the verification (iv) stage where the individual actually applies the solution, executes the idea and verifies the possible implications.

However, the model proposed by Wallas suggests a linearity that can hardly be verified but proposes a model of processes that if applied recursively in iterative and incremental cycles executed several times can help to refine a potential idea in order to make it increasingly adapted.

It is important to highlight that the four stages described from the human cognitive point of view find perfect equivalence in the stages found in simple reflex agents [28], Fig. 3. For an agent, the first stage (i) is the acquisition of knowledge, where it must perceive the environment through its sensors, for example. In the second stage (ii), the agent uses this representation of the world to develop some kind of reasoning. In the third stage (iii), the agent decides which is the "best" response/action. Finally, the agent performs this action (iv) through its actuators and returns to the first stage to iteratively start the process all over again.

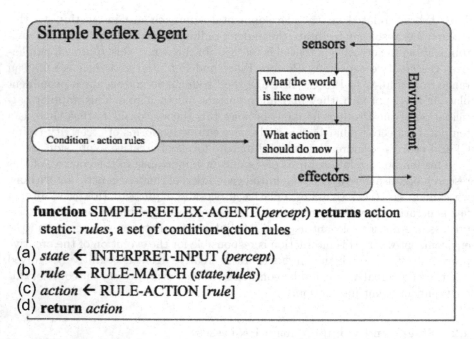

Fig. 3. Model and simple reflective agent algorithm highlighted the processes of (a) preparation, (b) incubation, (c) illumination and (d) verification adapted from [28]

4.3   Evolutionary

According to Kozbelt et al. [17], several researches like Lumsden, Simonton and Johnson-Laird have proposed several theories of creativity based on Charles Darwin or Jean-Baptiste Lamarck biological evolution ideas. Among these theories, the Dean Simonton research [29–34] stands out as strong candidate for the most comprehensive, generally speaking, Darwinist model from a psychological point of view.

The basis of the Simonton model is, in fact, the two-stage process described by Campbell in [16], involving the "blind" generation of a set of ideas/hypotheses and the retention and selective elaboration on this set. From this point of view, ideas are randomly combined [34], below the level of consciousness. The most interesting combinations are then consciously elaborated in order to produce creative products which in turn are judged by other individuals.

Campbell's argument for a sophisticated quantitative model of how creative productivity develops during an agent's ontogenetic process resembles the algorithms described in evolutionary computing, such as GA, and has an important impact on understanding the eminent nature of creative processes and environments. This model assumes that there are initial differences in the creative potential between different individuals. In this sense, over time, a certain agent is able to expand his creative potential through, mainly, the exercise of the process of creation and learning from this process [32]. This theory, in a way, is consistent with described in the developmental approach.

4.4 Systems

A broader and more ambitious way of approaching creativity is to characterize it as an emergent result of a complex system that contains several subcomponents interacting with each other. Each of these subcomponents should be considered in order to propose a richer and more meaningful understanding of creative processes and results. The systemic approach proposes a more qualitative and contextualized view of creativity, almost counteracting the evolutionary quantitative view [17].

This approach emphasizes a more collaborative creativity, which is highly dependent on social conditions, rather than a vision of intrapsychic processes and individual contributions. In this sense of collaborative creativity, we can consider that systems and populations of agents with "lower" cognitive power may also demonstrate a creative characteristic that emerges from the interaction that happens inside this population. Therefore, if we consider a Multi-Agent System able to develop cognitive processes as well as act autonomously on the environment, it is also possible to model algorithms that in some way demonstrate an emergent creative behavior.

5 Developing Creative Agents

There is some effort within the AI field, especially in the cognitive AI area in order to turn the agent design principles more explicit. The discussion about these principles initially proposed by Rolf Pfeifer in the 1990s has been addressed in [10, 23, 35, 36], culminating on a thorough review by Froese and Ziemke in [22], Table 1.

These principles are divides into two main groups: (i) design procedure principles (P-X) and (ii) agent design principles (A-X). While the first group deals with the general philosophy linked to the chosen approach, the second deals

Table 1. Agent design principles, apdapted from [36]

#	Name	Description
P-1	Synthetic methodology	Understanding by building
P-2	Emergence	Systems designed for emergence are more adaptive
P-3	Diversity-compliance	Trade-off between exploiting the givens and generating diversity solved in interesting ways
P-4	Time perspectives	Three perspectives required: 'here and now', ontogenetic, phylogenetic
P-5	Frame of reference	Three aspects must be distinguished: perspective, behavior vs. mechanisms, complexity
A-1	Three constituents	Ecological niche (environment), tasks, and agent must always be taken into account
A-2	Complete agent	Embodied, autonomous, self-sufficient, situated agents are of interest
A-3	Parallel, loosely coupled processes	Parallel, asynchronous, partly autonomous processes; largely coupled through interaction with the environment
A-4	Sensorimotor coordination	Behavior sensory-motor coordinated with respect to target; self-generated sensory stimulation
A-5	Cheap design	Exploitation of niche and interaction; parsimony
A-6	Redundancy	Partial overlap of functionality based on different physical processes
A-7	Ecological balance	Balance in complexity of sensory, motor, and neural systems: task distribution between morphology, materials, and control

more specifically with the methodology used for the development of autonomous agents [36]. Pfeifer and Bongard [10] present how these basic principles might be extended in order to include specific insights for each area and problem related to adaptive systems, artificial evolution and distributed systems.

The emergence design principle (P-2), as defined by Pfeifer et al. [36], is extremely relevant in this research because it demonstrates the convergence of the discussed theories towards the application of emergence as heuristics for the development of intelligent systems that demonstrate "natural" behavior. This principle is shared by many AI computational approaches in the minimal sense that the agent behavior must always emerge from the interactions with its environment.

This principle states that if we intend to develop adaptive systems, we must aim for emergence. The term emergence itself is somewhat controversial but here we use it in a pragmatic sense: something not planned or predictable. By aiming to develop an emergent agent, its cognitive structure will be the result of the history of its interactions with the environment.

To Pfeifer and Gomez [23], the relationship between behavior and emergence goes far beyond simple interactions between agent and environment. Thus, in a strict manner, the behavior is always emergent since it cannot be reduced to a simplified internal mechanism: it is always the result of the interaction system-environment. In this sense, Pfeifer et al. [36] indicate that emergence ceases to be a phenomenon with discrete characteristics (that is emergent or not emergent) and becomes as a matter of "emergence level": the less influence the designer's choices has on the current behavior of the agent, the higher is the emergence level. The systems developed to demonstrate an emergent behavior are usually more robust and adaptive. A system, such as genetic algorithms, that specifies the initial conditions and mechanisms for development (learning) will automatically explore the environment in order to shape its cognitive structure.

Another interesting design principle A-1, named "three constituents", highlights the importance that any autonomous system should never be designed in isolation. Froese and Ziemke [22] point out that we must consider three components of the system that are correlated: (i) the activity field or environment, (ii) the purpose and desired behavior, and (iii) the agent itself. These three components lead us to a clear intersection with the autopoietic approach. Furthermore, Froese and Ziemke also propose that in order to better understand the intelligence phenomenon we must think the agent as a holistic system rather than study its internal components in isolation. Of course, it does not invalidate the development of the components individually, but to Froese and Ziemke, if we want to achieve a greater scientific understanding of intelligence we must investigate how the adaptive behavior emerges holistically from the dynamic brain-body-world.

As a complement to A-1, the A-2 principle is also important in this research because it denotes a clear intersection with the concept of autopoiesis. A-2 proposes that in order to better understand the phenomenon of intelligence we must search for complete agents rather than the study of the internal components of the agent in isolation. Of course, it does not invalidate the development of the components alone, but if we want to better understand intelligence we must investigate how adaptive behavior emerges from the holistic brain-body-world dynamics. Still on A-2, Pfeifer and Gomez [23] point out that agents of interest must be autonomous, self-sufficient, embodied and situated in a given context.

6   Artelligent Framework

After presenting all the main concepts and principles that guided this research, we could define an Artelligent system as an autopoietic system that through the use of artificial intelligence techniques, represents knowledge in an extensive way and considering the principles that guide the human creative process is able to demonstrate results that are acknowledged as emergent in a given environment. However it is necessary to clarify each of the component parts that were discussed in this paper since it certainly won't group any artistic system that just involves art and artificial intelligence.

From a more objective point of view we can say that an Artelligent system should comply with the following principles, that were defined during this research and are now presented in a summarized form:

- Use an intelligent agent or a set/system of intelligent agents, considering it's task environment;
- Use an AI technique, to describe an implement the previous point, that facilitates the exhibition of an emergent behavior (such as GA, ANN and MAS);
- Represents knowledge in a extensible or emergent way (explicitly or not);
- Apply the agent design principles, minimizing the designer role in the knowledge construction of the agent as well as maximizing the role of agent's adaptation and learning;
- Consider at leadt two Ps: Person, Process, Product or Press/Place;
- Be able to generate Products that could be classified, at least, as mini-C;
- Consider at least one of the psychological approaches to creativity: developmental, stages and componential processes, evolutionary or systemic;
- Demonstrate an autopoietic agent behavior concerning the management of its internal knowledge and cognitive structures;
- Be able to exhibit emergent behavior (combinatory or epistemic) or demonstrate some kind of dynamic co-emergence with the environment.

To an Artelligent system it is obvious the huge AI field influence since without those techniques it would be extremely hard to propose such a framework or a system able to represent knowledge, learn, evolve and adapt. In an Artelligent system, knowledge representation plays a fundamental role since on top of this ability cognitive and evolutive processes unroll. In this sense, the role of the designer must be to provide a platform where the agent or system might be able to create through an interactive processing of it's own knowledge.

Among the available AI techniques, we tend to highlight in this research those which are closer to biological models such as Genetic Algorithms, Artificial Neural Networks and Multi-Agent Systems. These three approaches naturally exhibit an intrinsic emergent behavior due to their biological inspiration. In GA, even though we can determinate the main evolutionary goal through a fitness function, the evolutionary process that occurs in successive generations of individual is emergent.

This emergent behavior that can be seen in the GA is similar to what we can observe in ANN, where knowledge representation is made through the regulation of the synaptic weights for each neural connection. If we create two ANN with similar topologies, with the same number of neurons and layers, and we present them with the same stimulus in the same environment we can't state that the knowledge will be identically represented in both ANNs.

When considering this cognitive structures, able to store and process knowledge, we should consider that knowledge representation is not determinant to the achievement of emergent results but should be seriously considered according to the chosen approach. When dealing with a MAS approach we can verify that main focus is shifted from individual cognitive behavior to collective behavior construction. In order to allow emergent behavior to rise from the interaction of a set of agents it is necessary to provide some kind of explicit or non-explicit communication protocol. In this sense, we could consider that communication and it's protocol and form are an important part of this knowledge representation to this agents.

Multi-Agent Systems are able to demonstrate some emergent self-organization and are based in the fact that each agent is autonomous and can define it's own goals and objectives in order to determine which actions it should do. In this kind of approach, we can develop artificial agents with a very low cognitive structure (such as ants) since the emergent characteristic is in the interaction between agents of a given population, society or ecosystem.

When thinking of an agent that will be part of an Artelligent system, we must consider it autopoietic in the sense that it must be self-sufficient and autonomous to manage its own internal mechanisms, as described earlier in this paper. We must also consider the agent design principles and consider not only the internal representation of the agent but also take into account the environment and the relationships that he will establish with it. From this point of view, the designer plays a key role in correctly choosing how to represent the environment accordingly so that the agent can interact with it but at the same time the designer must be aware that there must be enough room to cognitive construction or social self-organization of agents happen in an emergent way through an autopoietic process.

In order to illustrate those principles, we would like to briefly present Zer0[1], a gameart that invites the player to enjoy a drift in a universe ruled by geometric shapes, which is described in [7]. In this multi-agent system where each agent is visually represented by a pulsating geometric shape. Each shape has an internal clock that regulates its pulses. Every time a pulse intersects with another a sound event is generated, creating the game emergent soundtrack.

There are basically two kinds of similar agents: user-controlled and autonomous. The second is highlighted in this paper, while the first is a slightly modified version of the autonomous one in order to allow the user control its movement. The characteristics of our autonomous agents are:

- Perception
  - Position
  - Other agents (through pulses)
  - Lifespan
- Actions
  - Pulse
  - Move
  - Stand
- Goals
  - Increase lifespan
  - Move

---

[1] An video recording of the interaction can be seen at https://vimeo.com/84191758.

– Interact
– Environment
  – Infinite 2D Space
  – Multi-agent

Each agent has an internal lifespan that is initialized randomly. Since the lifespan decreases, the individuals aim to expend their lifespan though the interaction with other shapes. Every time their pulses collide, both agents increase lifespan and earn points. The larger the amount of points, more geometrical "sides" the agent has. The user agent starts with one side (a single line), than evolves side by side: triangle, rectangle, pentagon and so on.

As we can see at Fig. 4, the agent perception is based on the perception component. This component informs the agent how is the world right now, including other agents that are nearby, its actual position and lifespan (internally represented). Based on this set of information it updates his internal world representation and then the inference machine reasons which action might be suitable.

The inference machine is based rule-based agent architecture. For example, if it is not time to generate a pulse (according to its internal clock) and there are no agents nearby, move.

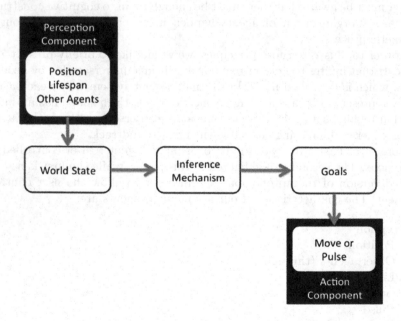

Fig. 4. Internal autonomous agent generic architecture.

As stated before, the agents are able to establish communication through pulses and each one of those pulses is a signal. Each time they interact, they increase their lifespan. These interactions trigger sound events, thus generating the game soundtrack. Those interactions are briefly represented in Fig. 5.

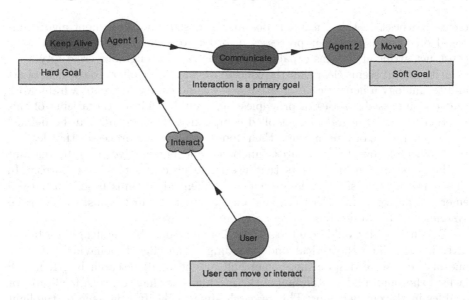

Fig. 5. Two autonomous and one human agent represented in TROPOS [37] early requirements initial diagram.

This environment might be described as partially observable, since it has a finite range of environment perception. Since the world's next stage depends on other factors than the agent's actions, it is stochastic. Also, this environment is constantly evolving while the agent is deliberating and there is no time interval. These two last characteristics impose some time constraints since the agent must answer quickly.

In this experiment the visual representation and the game soundtrack emerge from a complex environment defined with simple rules. The agents evolve along with the environment, creating some kind of self-identity, required in order to reach an autopoietic level.

7   Conclusion

In this paper we've tried to show evidences that may help to clarify why the autopoiesis concept can be quite interesting for artists and scientists. Computer artists, especially, may find in this concept several technological challenges that might inspire them to produce artwork. AI theorists may find fascinating and inspiring the ontology behind what was presented. The papers that deal with interactivity, autonomy and creativity can be enriched when consider all aspects of autopoiesis and emergence.

The concept of emergence offer to the art and technology fields a heuristic for creativity. If emergence can be defined as pure novelty, then understanding the processes that lead to these events, structures, functions and emerging perspectives may be relevant to the construction of artifacts that use these processes to create newness. In this sense it is possible to design and implement algorithms based on natural emergent processes in order to expand human creativity or construct artificial systems capable of demonstrate autonomous creativity.

Although it seems clear that the concept of emergency offers to the field of art and technology a heuristic for creativity, it was necessary to create a framework that encompassed a series of principles that could facilitate the arising of this emergence with a degree of controlled complexity. If emergence can be defined as the emergence of pure novelty, then understanding the processes that lead to these emergent events, structures, functions, and perspectives may be relevant to the construction of artifacts that use these processes to create novelty. In this sense, it is possible to design and implement algorithms based on natural emergent processes in order to expand human creativity or to construct artificial systems capable of demonstrating autonomous creativity.

To conclude, it would be interesting to list some possible challenges for future investigation. The theoretical understanding of intelligent behavior would be one of them since despite more than half a century of research in AI, it still lacks a thorough under- standing of the mechanisms that controls, facilitates or enables intelligent behavior. This research aims to clarify this issue by the light of autopoiesis and emergence as foundations for cognition and intelligence.

References

1. Cariani, P.: Emergence and creativity. Itau Cultural, pp. 22–41 (2009)
2. Maturana, H., Varela, F.: Autopoiesis and cognition: the realization of the living. In: Boston Studies in the Philosophy of Science, vol. 42, 1st edn. D. Reidel Publishing Company (1980)
3. Wilson, S.: Information Arts. The MIT Press, Cambridge (2002)
4. Smith, B.: Prologue. In: Reflection and Semantics in a Procedural Language, pp. 31–39. MIT (1985)
5. Barretto, F.: Emergência enquanto heurística para criatividade em agentes de inteligência artificial aplicados à composição algorítmica. Seminário Música Ciência Tecnologia 1(4), 143–150 (2012)
6. de Paula Barretto, F., Venturelli, S., do Rego, G.G.: Towards an emergent and autopoietic approach to adaptative chord generation through human interaction. In: Stephanidis, C. (ed.) HCI 2013. CCIS, vol. 373, pp. 579–583. Springer, Heidelberg (2013). https://doi.org/10.1007/978-3-642-39473-7_115
7. Barretto, F.: Zer0: An emergent and autopoietic multi-agent system for novelty creation in game art through gesture interaction. In: Procedia Manufacturing, 6th International Conference on Applied Human Factors and Ergonomics (AHFE 2015) and the Affiliated Conferences, AHFE 2015, vol. 2, pp. 850–857. Elsevier (2015)
8. Kujawski, G.: Emergence: the expression of the unexpected. Itau Cultural, pp. 22–41 (2009)
9. Gardner, M.: The fantastic combinations of john conway's new solitary game "life". Sci. Am. 223, 120–123 (1970)
10. Pfeifer, R., Bongard, J.: How The Body Shapes The Way We Think: A New View on Intelligence. The MIT Press, Cambridge (2007)

11. Tramus, M.H., Chen, C.Y.: La funambule virtuelle et quorum sensing, deux installations interactives s'inspirant du connexionnisme et de l'évolutionnisme. La création artistique face aux nouvelles technologies (2005)
12. Cornéer, O., Lübcke, M.: Bacterial orchestra. Cornéer & Lubcke Website (2006)
13. Barretto, F.: Artelligent: arte, inteligência artificial e criatividade computacional. Ph.D. thesis, University of Brasilia (2016)
14. Hennessey, B., Amabile, T.: Creativity. Ann. Rev. Psychol. **61**, 569–598 (2010)
15. Runco, M.A., Albert, R.S.: Creativity research: a historical review. In: The Cambridge Handbook of Creativity, pp. 3–19 (2010)
16. Kozbelt, A., Beghetto, R.A., Runco, M.A.: Creativity research: a historical review. In: The Cambridge Handbook of Creativity (2010)
17. Kozbelt, A., Beghetto, R.A., Runco, M.A.: Theories of Creativity. The Cambridge Handbook of Creativity (2010)
18. Kaufman, J.C., Beghetto, R.A.: Beyond big and little: the four C model of creativity. Rev. Gen. Psychol. **13**, 1–12 (2009)
19. Rhodes, M.: An analysis of creativity. Phi Delta Kappan **42**, 305–310 (1961)
20. Langton, C.: Artificial life. In: Artificial Life: Proceedings of an Interdisciplinary Workshop on Synthesis and Simulation of Living Systems, vol. 4, pp. 1–47 (1989)
21. Luisi, P.: Autopoiesis: a review and a reappraisal. Naturwissenschaften **2**(90), 49–59 (2003)
22. Froese, T., Ziemke, T.: Enactive artificial intelligence: investigating the systemic organization of life and mind. Artif. Intell. **4–3**(173), 446–500 (2009)
23. Pfeifer, R., Gomez, G.: Interaction with the real world - design principles for intelligent systems. Artif. Life Robot. **1**(9), 1–6 (2005)
24. Lakemeyer, G., Nebel, B. (eds.): Review on the Foundations of Knowledge Representation and Reasoning. LNCS, vol. 810. Springer, Heidelberg (1994). https://doi.org/10.1007/3-540-58107-3
25. Rich, E., Knight, K.: Artificial Intelligence. McGrawHill, New York City (1993)
26. Craik, K.: The Nature of Explanation. Cambridge University, Cambridge (1943)
27. Wallas, G.: The Art of Thought. Hartcourt Brace and World, San Diego (1926)
28. Russel, S., Norvig, P.: Artificial Intelligence: A Modern Approach. Prentice Hall, Upper Saddle River (2003)
29. Simonton, D.K.: Genius, Creativity and Leadership. Harvard University Press, Cambridge (1984)
30. Simonton, D.K.: Scientific Genius. Cambridge University Press, Cambridge (1988)
31. Simonton, D.K.: Emergence and realization of genius: the lives and works of 120 classical composers. J. Pers. Soc. Psychol. **61**, 829–840 (1991)
32. Simonton, D.K.: Creative productivity: a predictive and explanatory model of career landmaks and trajectories. Psychol. Rev. **104**, 66–89 (1997)
33. Simonton, D.K.: Scientific creativity as constrained stochastic behaviour: the integration of product, person and process perspectives. Psychol. Bull. **129**, 475–494 (2003)
34. Simonton, D.K.: Creativity in Science: Chance, Logic, Genius and Zeitgeist. Cambridge University Press, Cambridge (2004)
35. Pfeifer, R.: Building 'fungus eaters': design principles of autonomous agents. In: Proceedings of the 4th International Conference on Simulation of Adaptative Behavior, pp. 3–12 (1996)
36. Pfeifer, R., Iida, F., Bongard, J.: New robotics: design principles for intelligent systems. Artif. Life **1–2**(11), 99–120 (2005)
37. Bresciani, P., Perini, A., Giorgini, P., Giunchiglia, F., Mylopoulos, J.: Tropos: an agent-oriented software development methodology. Auton. Agents Multi-Agent Syst. **8**(3), 203–236 (2004)

Conceptual Framework for Supporting the Creation of Virtual Museums with Focus on Natural User Interfaces

Guilherme Corredato Guerino[1(✉)], Breno Augusto Guerra Zancan[1],
Tatiany Xavier de Godoi[2], Daniela de Freitas Guilhermino Trindade[1],
José Reinaldo Merlin[1], Ederson Marcos Sgarbi[1], Carlos Eduardo Ribeiro[1],
and Tércio Weslley Sant'Anna de Paula Lima[1]

[1] Center of Technological Sciences, State University of Paraná, Bandeirantes, Paraná, Brazil
guilherme.guerinosi@gmail.com, brenozancan@gmail.com,
{danielaf,merlin,sgarbi,biluka}@uenp.edu.br,
terciowspl@gmail.com
[2] Computer Department, Federal Technological University of Paraná,
Cornélio Procópio, Paraná, Brazil
tatigodoi_11@hotmail.com

Abstract. The Virtual Museum is an important instrument that allows people access to works that are often inaccessible due to the physical location of traditional museums. However, oftentimes developed Virtual Museums present problems that directly affect its usability. Thus, in this article the conceptual framework VWNUI (Virtual Museum with Natural User Interfaces) is proposed, which provides a conceptual model and guidelines related to the Natural User Interfaces to support the developers of Virtual Museums. The conceptual model is composed of elements and sub-elements that a Virtual Museum must contain, while the guidelines propose recommendations that the Virtual Museum should follow. To verify its applicability, the framework is supporting the development of a Virtual Museum to safeguard the history of a city. The Museum is still in the development phase, however, from the experiences reported by some users, it can be observed that the proposed framework can help and stimulate the creation of Virtual Museums that promote better experiences to their visitors.

Keywords: Virtual Museum · Conceptual framework · Natural User Interfaces
Usability · Communicability · Interactivity

1 Introduction

The Virtual Museum is an important means of communication that allows preserving historical information that is often lost. It constitutes an environment that breaks the barrier of space and time and can, according to [14], facilitate the informative, pedagogical and aesthetic reception provided by conventional museums. The virtual museum takes little time to be built (compared to physical museums), is independent of geographical location, and is an alternative for many individuals who do not know of the existence of physical museums or are not motivated to visit it, because of different reasons that can difficult access.

[11] analyzed 36 Virtual Museums and found several usability gaps that directly affect the public accessing these museums, discouraging them from exploring the content they offer. In this context, the Natural User Interfaces can be a solution to usability problems, since, according to [1], the user can interact with digital content using gestures, sounds, and ringtones, which are more intuitive than the use of artificial control devices. According to [18], many users do not have much intimacy with computer systems, allowing the Natural User Interfaces to assist these user profiles.

Thus, it is possible for users to take advantage of the skills acquired during their daily practices, and this, in turn, contributes to the learning time for using the Natural User Interfaces to be less than that required for learning a traditional interface.

Considering this scenario, it is important to propose models that support designers of virtual environments in the creation of spaces that provide good interactivity, intuitiveness and usability. According to [12], the framework is described as a model that can be reused several times to create new software. Connecting this concept with the Natural User Interfaces techniques is possible to have guidelines for creating Virtual Museums that provide good experiences to users.

Thus, in the work is proposed a conceptual framework to support the creation of Virtual Museums with focus on Natural User Interfaces. The methodological steps involved 4 stages: (i) Diagnosis of the elements that should compose a virtual museum; (ii) Diagnosis of the characteristics of Natural User Interfaces; (iii) Proposing a conceptual framework to support the creation of Virtual Museums; (iv) Validation of the framework in the creation of a Virtual Museum to safeguard part of the patrimony of a city.

2 Natural User Interfaces

[21], show that natural expression is directly linked to the way users use and how they feel during the use of those applications. Therefore, the Natural User Interfaces (NUI) are defined as a completely invisible interface, which, even so, allows the user to use it in a practical and increasingly better way.

According to [3], NUI's arises with the goal of using daily user skills for interaction with content. In this way, it is possible for users to take advantage of the skills acquired in their daily lives and this, in turn, contributes to the learning time for using the Natural User Interfaces is less than that required for learning a traditional interface.

[9] defines the seven main characteristics of the Natural User Interfaces, which are listed in Table 1.

Table 1. Characteristics of Natural User Interfaces.

Characteristics	Definition
User-centered	Attend the needs of different user profiles
Multi-channel interface	Use sensory and motor channels to gain additional attributes of users' intentions and thereby increase the naturalness of the interaction
Inexact	Understand the demands of users and correct possible mistakes made by them due to the inaccuracy of the users' thinking
High bandwidth	Consume high bandwidth to process the large amount of input information, such as voice and image
Voice-based interaction	Study how users use the system by voice, whether natural or synthesized
Image-based interaction	Use human behavior, to understand the picture and then make some decision
Behavior-based interaction	Use user behavior through the position, movement, and characteristics of expression of parts of the human body to understand action and make decision

Various types of devices can aid in capturing motion and sound and contribute directly to the Natural User Interfaces, such as 3D sensors, microphones, cameras and touch sensitive devices. Thus, any type of movement or human activity can serve as input for systems that interact with Natural User Interfaces, such as gestures, manipulation of physical and virtual objects, body movements, facial expressions, voice input and sign language [6].

It is possible to understand that the presentation of the interface and interaction is directly linked to the mode of reaction of the user when using the technology, be it positive or negative. Interaction interfaces, according to [10], influence positively when using different sources, well combined colors, graphic elements and the disposition of all these attributes to create a good interface.

According to [20] these types of interfaces help to reassure the user, and, more patients, they can wait for a longer time to load the site, for example. However, according to [15], when the interface is confusing or does not work right, users may feel offended, and most often become annoyed with the application. These difficulties encompass the entire computational scope, including the Virtual Museums, technological environment which is discussed in this work.

3   Virtual Museums

According to [17], a virtual environment can be defined as a graphical environment that simulates the presence of the user in this environment, through a computer and the elements that compose this virtualization.

According to [13], a virtual museum can be defined as a collection of digital content that is made available on the web. One of the advantages of this type of technology, for [5], is the possibility of check works that are present in physical locations that are often inaccessible to their users. Already for [4], the main advantage is the enrichment of the virtual environment through virtual multimedia such as texts, graphics, animations, videos, among others.

It is also emphasized that in a virtual museum, it is possible for each visitor to create their own route of interest, according to their experience, personal tastes and cultural level. In this scenario, it is important that the environment is accessible enough to include inexperienced or somewhat disabled users who limit them to using environments that are not accessible.

The Virtual Museums are classified into three groups by [7]:

- Group 1: collections existing only in the virtual environment, without referents in the physical world;
- Group 2: collections with referring in the physical world, the virtual museum being a digital presentation of what already exists; and
- Group 3: there is no physical reference, but the collection exists physically and has been digitized and made available in a virtual environment.

Another classification concerns the types of Virtual Museums, which can be: two-dimensional, three-dimensional and digitally modeleds. The two-dimensional presents only texts and photographs, in which the user can select some information that needs to be seen and to obtain more details through the presentation of a figure coming from the collection. The three-dimensional present a real environment (through a photo or film) providing the user a rich interaction, given that he can navigate as if he were walking in a physical museum. The digital models are widely developed with digital forms, not having photos or movies that exist in the real world.

Independent of the group to which it belongs or of its type, [11], developed a study on the usability in Virtual Museums in which they highlighted the main problems:

- Virtual museums have large amounts of content: too much content can irritate users, who will spend less time in the website. In addition, users can make selections without considering all options. Therefore, many explanations about the same content may confuse users who want information about a specific topic.
- Virtual museums use artistically designed graphical user interfaces: this type of layout can cause disorientation and distraction for users who wish to take some action. In addition, the elements of this type of interface can be confusing and meaningless to users.
- Virtual museums have interfaces that encourage exploration: this type of interface encourages navigation, as well as requiring users to make choices without understanding its consequences.
- Virtual museums are designed by museum professionals: when Virtual Museums are developed by people who work with museums, specifics vocabularies and organizational schemes are used that are unfamiliar to people who are not in this context.
- Virtual Museums are often intended to complement physical museums: in this case, users have access to information they want both before and after the physical visit. The virtual visit is a complement to the physical visit.

Considering all these factors, and based on the characteristics of the Natural User Interfaces, a conceptual framework is proposed that intends to support the construction of three-dimensional museums that provide good usability and a friendly, intuitive and interactive interface.

4   VMNUI: Conceptual Framework for Supporting the Creation of Virtual Museums with Focus on Natural User Interfaces

Commonly, in software development, it is realized that developers use the same resources to develop new programs. In this sense, framework is understood as a model that can be reused several times for the creation of new software [12]. [19] shows that in addition to being a standard model, a framework has characteristics that are adaptable to the needs of the developers, so that their classes are customized when there is a need.

A conceptual framework, which is the proposal of this work, is an abstract representation that forms real world patterns, so to relate this abstraction to the software in development [16]. For [8], a conceptual framework means that the product generated from the use of the framework is not executable software, its main objective being to propose a conceptual schema of the data that will be used later to make explicit the specific data of the application. This conceptual scheme represents an interconnected system, or a relation of suppositions, expectations and/or beliefs, resulting in a provisional theory guiding research.

Based on the diagnoses made and based on the main factors of the interactive systems design proposed by [2], and also, mainly, by the work of [17], is proposed the conceptual framework VMNUI (Virtual Museums with Natural User Interfaces). The framework is composed by the conceptual model and the proposed guidelines, with emphasis on the Natural User Interfaces, seeking to support the creation of three-dimensional Virtual Museums.

The conceptual model proposed here is a work of the group of IHC, which develops two complementary researches, this with a focus on Natural User Interfaces and the principles of usability, interactivity and communicability, and the other focusing on the accessibility aspects of Virtual Museums.

4.1   Conceptual Model

The conceptual model, which considers the inherent aspects of a virtual museum, presents three elements, following the organization proposed by [2]: (i) People, who have their roles in the use of the virtual museum, and their specificities, as specific languages and physical or psychological differences; (ii) Components, that are the ways in which the contents will be arranged in the virtual museum and (iii) Activities, which are linked to the functions that each role plays. The conceptual model is shown in Fig. 1.

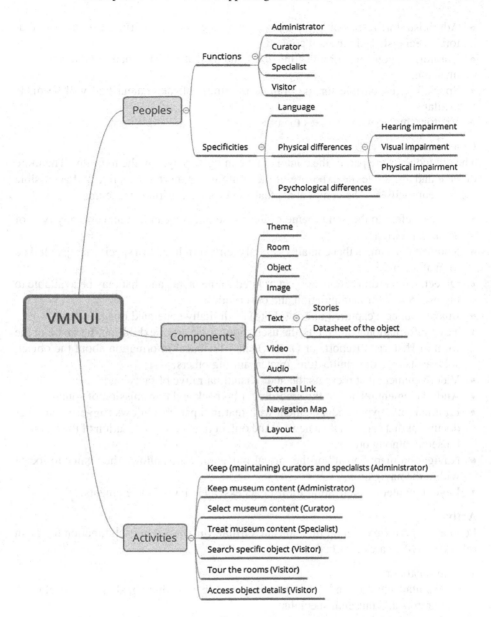

Fig. 1. Conceptual model of VMNUI (Virtual Museum with Natural User Interface)

Peoples

It can be said that it is impossible the existencia of a virtual museum without the collaboration of people who contribute to the growth of this museum. Thus, in the model are presented the different roles that people can assume in the Virtual Museum.

- Administrator: responsible for maintaining (registering, altering, excluding) curators, specialists and museum content.
- Curator: responsible for selecting the content that will be made available in the museum.
- Specialist: responsible for the graphic treatment of the content that will be made available.
- Visitor: anyone who accesses the museum.

Components

The components are part of the content that can be displayed in the museum. The more diverse and attractive the exposure of the content, the more interactive and accessible the museum will be. The components that can contain a Virtual Museum:

- Theme: refers to the main theme of the Museum, and can be related to any type of art or exhibition.
- Room: environment that contains several elements related to a specific subject linked to main theme.
- Object: a three-dimensional object, related to the theme and that may be available to the user touch for manipulation and observation.
- Image: can be a captured image (photo) or digitally generated image.
- Text: information available to the user about some art or exhibition. It can be in the form of Historical Reports or Object Data - technical information about the object, such as its date of manufacture, owner, among others.
- Video: element that presents the audiovisual narrative of facts
- Audio: element related to the recording, playback and transmission of sound.
- External link: hypermedia element with featured part that allows triggering another document that can contain a news of the object or exhibition, location of the physical museum, among others.
- Navigation map: "plant" of the virtual museum, which allows the visitor to locate within the navigation.
- Layout: content organization for user access, and view of the elements.

Activities

People can perform different functions in Virtual Museums. For each function the main related activities are described:

- Administrator
  - Maintain curators and specialists: responsible for including, altering or excluding curators and museum specialists.
  - Keep content of the museum: responsible for, keep the content sent by the curator.
- Curator
  - Select the contents of the museum: person with extensive knowledge about the theme of the museum. It selects the content, arts and important exhibits that the virtual museum will have.
- Specialist
  - Treat the contents of the museum: responsible for dealing with the contents of the museum, providing images, videos and audios with good resolution.

- Visitor
  - Search and access a specific object: directly search for an object of your personal interest, without browsing other rooms and accessing objects that are not in your interest.
  - Take a tour of the rooms: make a visit as if you were in a physical museum, accessing different objects and browsing the rooms.
  - Access object details: access information from different objects, such as date of manufacture, owner, place that has been rescued, etc.

We can observe that the conceptual model provides a base of elements and sub-elements for developers of Virtual Museums. It is not necessary that the virtual environment has all the elements and sub-elements proposed in the model, but the more diverse the display of the content, the more interactive and enjoyable the Museum will be.

4.2 Guidelines for Creating Virtual Museums

As previously mentioned, the conceptual framework is also composed by some guidelines that have the function of assisting virtual museum developers in constructing more intuitive and pleasant environments.

Considering that because it is independent of geographical location, Virtual Museums can reach a wider range, it is necessary stay tuned for some important aspects related to the diversity of **People** that can access the Virtual Museum, they are:

- **Languages**: The virtual museum must have a multilingual translation option, covering the widest possible audience, regardless of the language spoken by the visitor.
- **Physical differences**: attention must be paid to the different types of deficiencies (auditory, visual, physical, psychological, among others) and the limitations they can impose on access to a virtual environment. Some important project decisions can minimize these limitations, such as interaction through the use of voice commands, in the case of the visually impaired, and the use of more intuitive and good signaling paths in the case of cognitive limitations. As previously mentioned, a complementary study to this research thoroughly discusses issues related to accessibility in Virtual Museums.

In the **Components** axis, the elements that are contained in a Virtual Museum are described, therefore, for this axis are listed the main guidelines proposed in this research, linked to the use of the Natural User Interfaces.

- **Use 360° images for better navigation in the virtual room, where the user can rotate in all possible angles and walk through the museum, as if visiting a physical museum:** linked to the ROOM sub-element, this guideline concerns the user's browsing mode during their virtual visit. The development of Virtual Museums can have different paths that depend on the choice of museum dimension. Virtual museums can be two-dimensional, three-dimensional or digitally modeled. For this guideline to be covered in development, it is necessary for the museum to be three-dimensional. Thus, through the 360° room, made by means of equirectangular photos it is possible for the user to rotate horizontally 360° and vertically 180°, having the impression of actually being inside the room.

- **Use 3D function so that the works can be rotated horizontally, exploring every detail of the exhibition:** this guideline aims to increase the interaction of the user with the museum, so that the information sought by the user is passed in the most natural way possible. Therefore, it is necessary to make the works available in 3D format, so that users can rotate them and from various angles observe all the details of the object. Linked to the OBJECT sub-element, this guideline provides an interaction with optimal usability to the user.

- **Use the touchscreen interaction of the user, providing better usability and interaction of the same with the software:** the touchscreen interaction is an example of a Natural User Interface, which according to [3] aims to use daily user skills to facilitate interaction. In this case, the touchscreen will be used in the manipulation of the 360° room and 3D objects. Linked to the LAYOUT sub-element, this guideline provides the possibility that just with the touch the user can navigate through the Virtual Museum and have experiences as if in a real environment.

- **Allow the voice command to perform some action, so that the museum becomes more accessible:** linked to the SPECIFICITIES sub-element, this guideline fits into issues of disability and accessibility. Voice recognition is also a mechanism that is embedded in the Natural User Interfaces. Therefore, it is necessary that the Virtual Museum has forms of voice capture for the execution of an action. If user has a physical disability that prevents you from navigating in a simple way through the touchscreen, voice recognition will do the job and the user can navigate in the same way.

- **Give attention to the questions of physiology and kinesthesia, avoiding difficult movements and very repetitive actions:** according to [11], Virtual Museums must contain interfaces that stimulate user exploration. However, care must be taken with the difficulty and repetition of actions. Linked to the LAYOUT sub-element, this guideline refers to the user-friendly interface, which needs to be exploratory, making users feel at ease both to search for specific content and to navigate without direction. In addition, users need to clearly understand the consequences of their choices and locate quickly if they are looking for a specific item.

- **Give attention to quantity of information and your exhibition, seeking to promote good visibility of all elements of the interface:** yet according to [11], Virtual Museums must possess a correct amount of information and content. Linked to the LAYOUT sub-element, this guideline seeks to guide the care of not inserting in the virtual environment excessive information that suffocates the user. Too much content can irritate users, who will feel unmotivated and leave the Virtual Museum. In addition, the excess content can make the user not know what is accessing and focus only on one area, without knowing the existence of others. Also, for those looking for specific content, a lot of information about this content can confuse users who perform a simple search.

These guidelines are intended to support the development of Virtual Museums with good usability and interactivity in order to please their end user regardless of the theme of the content displayed in the museum. These guidelines were applied in the development of a Virtual Museum that sought to contribute to the historical rescue of a small city in the interior of Paraná - Brazil.

4.3   Application of the Framework in the Creation of a Virtual Museum

In order to verify the applicability of the framework proposed in this work, it began the process of developing a Virtual Museum to safeguard the history of the city of Bandeirantes - Paraná/Brazil. The Museum is under development, following the proposed elements and guidelines.

In this way, as it is possible to be observed in the Fig. 2, were created 360° rooms related to the relevant collections of the museum, in which the user can rotate for all the angles. This guideline presented by the framework increases the user's ability to interact, giving him the impression of visiting a real environment.

Fig. 2. Example of a 360° room developed in the Virtual Museum.

In Fig. 3, one can observe the use of a 3D object. When the user clicks on an object, the object is displayed in 3D format. Then, the user can rotate it horizontally, observing all the details of the work.

Also, the Virtual Museum under development follows the guideline related to kinesthesia and physiology, providing easier and intuitive navigation to the user. The amount of content and elements made available in the museum was also selected in order to follow the last guideline provided, and with this, the Museum presents a cleaner interface to provide better visibility to the user, who has easy access to all available information.

As the Museum is under development, not all elements and sub-elements have yet been created, nor have all the proposed guidelines in the conceptual model been applied. Sub-elements such as video, audio, and external link are being prepared to be inserted

Fig. 3. Example of using a 3D object available in the Virtual Museum

into the environment. The guidelines that refer to the use of voice recognition and aspects of accessibility are being addressed, as already mentioned, in a parallel work by this research group, considering the complexity and breadth of its implications.

Thus, based on the findings of [11], and considering the use of the guidelines proposed by the framework VMNUI already made so far, it is possible to observe that the Virtual Museum presents: a quantity of non-excessive content; a real environment (which was not created artistically) seeking to bring more meaning to the user and a clean interface in order to facilitate and encourage its exploitation.

A first version of the museum was made available to a group of users (8 people) who used the virtual environment and provided feedback on their experience. From the reports, it was observed that, following the elements and guidelines proposed by the VMNUI, it was possible to create a virtual museum that would provide, in general, a good navigation experience. Some issues were pointed out, among them, the difficulty of people with disabilities in the hands of executing commands that require greater intervention, such as the rotation of an object for example. Thus, although the Natural User Interfaces contribute positively to the accessibility of the environment, it is very important to add the accessibility guidelines (already under development in parallel work) to the VMNUI framework.

5   Final Considerations

The museum, being an important means of communication, needs to take advantage of all the technological and communication development available, in order to improve the process of interaction with its public. There are several Virtual Museums available on the web, however, the vast majority have a limitation in relation to navigation, not taking advantage in a significant way of the functions that virtuality offers.

In this sense, the Natural User Interfaces can be presented as a good alternative to make navigation in a virtual museum more attractive and intuitive, in which the senses are better stimulated and provide a greater sense of being in a real environment.

Thus, this research presented a conceptual framework - VMNUI to support the creation of Virtual Museums as a focus on the use of Natural User Interfaces.

For the development of the conceptual model were listed and analyzed the main elements that should compose a virtual museum. Based on the composition of the elements, guidelines based on the use of Natural User Interfaces were proposed.

The application of VMNUI was started in the development of a Virtual Museum that rescues and makes available the historical data of a municipality. The museum has contents of the rural area of the city, as well as pieces about inactive railroad that passes through the city and objects of Japanese culture. The whole museum was arranged in three rooms 360°, in which it is possible to rotate the 3D objects that the room has. The elements were arranged so as not to overlap and in a way that facilitated the handling action.

A group of people, had access to the first version of the Museum, and could relate their experience in the environment. From the experiences reported it can be observed that the proposed framework can support and stimulate the creation of new Virtual Museums, which enhance interactivity, communicability and intuitiveness.

References

1. Arrais, M., Grossi, M.G.R., Martins, A.R.G.: Interface Natural do Usuário: Aplicações para a Inovação do Ensino a Distância com o Uso do Microsoft Kinect®. In: 18° Congresso Internacional de Educação a Distância (ABED), vol. 18, São Paulo (2012)
2. Barbosa, S.D.J., Silva, B.S.: Interação Humano-Computador, 1st edn. Campus, Rio de Janeiro (2010)
3. Blake, J.: Natural User Interfaces in .Net. 1st edn. New York (2011)
4. Chengwei, Y., Chengle, Y., Shijun, L., Xiangxu, M., Rui, W.: An approach of personalized 3d scene customization based on multimedia resource. In: International Conference on Multimedia and Signal Processing (CMSP), pp. 131–135 (2011)
5. Guidi, G., Trocchianesi, R., Pils, G., Morlando, G., Seassaro, A.: A virtual museum for design: new forms of interactive fruition. In: 16th International Conference on Virtual Systems and Multimedia (VSMM), pp. 242–249 (2010)
6. Jain, J., Lund, A., Wixon, D.: The future of natural user interfaces. In: Proceedings of the 2011 Annual Conference Extended Abstracts on Human Factors in Computing Systems, pp. 211–214. ACM, New York (2011)
7. Lima, D.F.C.: O que se pode denominar como Museu Virtual segundo os museus que assim se apresentam. In: Encontro Nacional de Pesquisa em Ciência da Informação, pp. 2451–2468, João Pessoa (2009)
8. Lisboa, J.F.: Projeto Conceitual de Banco de Dados Geográficos através da Reutilização de Esquemas, utilizando Padrões de Análise e um Framework Conceitual, Porto Alegre (2000)
9. Liu, W.: Natural user interface - next mainstream product user interface. In: IEEE 11th International Conference on Computer-Aided Industrial Design and Conceptual Design, Yiwu, vol. 1, pp. 203–205 (2010)

502   G. C. Guerino et al.

10. Lopes, L.A., Guilhermino, D.F., Coleti, T.A., Elero, R., Sgarbi, E.M., Guerino, G.C., Anastacio, P.R., Ribeiro, C.E.: An analysis of a heuristic to assist sociability evaluation in online communities. In: Kurosu, M. (ed.) HCI 2016. LNCS, vol. 9731, pp. 257–267. Springer, Cham (2016). https://doi.org/10.1007/978-3-319-39510-4_24
11. Marty, P.F., Twidale, M.B.: Lost in gallery space: a conceptual framework for analyzing the usability flaws of museum web sites, vol. 9, no. 9. First Monday (2004)
12. Mattsson, M.: Object-oriented frameworks: a survey of methodological issues. Licentiate thesis. Department of Computer Science, Lund University, Sweden (1996)
13. Moura, I.B.G., Mendes Neto, F.M., Sousa, P.S.M.: Utilização do Framework Jade no Desenvolvimento de um Museu Virtual 3D com Recomendação Personalizada de Conteúdo. Exacta, Belo Horizonte, vol. 5, pp. 83–97 (2012)
14. Muchacho, R.: Museus virtuais: a importância da usabilidade na mediação entre o público e o objecto museológico. In: Livro de actas do 4° Congresso da Associação Portuguesa de Ciências da Comunicação, Portugal, pp. 1540–1547 (2005)
15. Preece, J., Sharp, H., Rogers, Y.: Interaction Design: Beyond Human-Computer Interaction. 4th edn, New York (2002)
16. Rocha, L.V., Edelweiss, N.: GeoFrame-T: a temporal conceptual framework for data modeling. In: Proceedings of the 9th ACM International Symposium on Advances in Geographical Information Systems, ACM-GIS, Atlanta (2001)
17. Schneider, E.I.: Uma contribuição aos Ambientes Virtuais de Aprendizagem (AVAs) suportados pela Teoria da Cognição Situada (TCS) para pessoas com deficiência auditiva. Santa Catarina (2012)
18. Silveira, M.S., Prates, R.O.: Uma Proposta da Comunidade para o Ensino de IHC no Brasil. In: XIV Workshop Sobre Educação em Computação, WEI 2007, vol. 1. pp. 76–84, Rio de Janeiro (2007)
19. Taligent Incorporation: Building object-oriented frameworks. http://lhcb-comp.web.cern.ch/lhcb-comp/Components/postscript/buildingoo.pdf. Accessed 6 Feb 2018
20. Tractinsky, N., Shoval-katz, A., Ikar, D.: What is beautiful is usable. Interact. Comput. **13**, 127–145 (2000)
21. Wigdor, D., Wixon, D.: Brave NUI World: Designing Natural User Interfaces for Touch and Gesture, 1st edn. Elsevier, New York City (2011)

Rethink of Urban Arts: AR Technology with Participatory Experience of New Urban Arts

Ziyang Li[1(✉)], Hao He[2], and Xiandong Cheng[1]

[1] Beijing City University, No. 269 Bei Si Huan Zhong Lu, Haidian District, Beijing, China
li.ziyang@bcu.edu.cn
[2] China Central Academy of Fine Arts, No. 8 Hua Jia Di Nan St.,
Chaoyang District, Beijing, China

Abstract. This paper primarily discusses the interactions between citizens and the urban arts. It uses the augmented reality (hereinafter referred to as AR) application of paintings on bridges in the Yantai Economic Development Area (hereinafter referred to as YEDA) as an example to expound the use of an AR application in urban arts and the relationship between citizens and urban arts. As long as tourists download our AR application on their smart-phones and scan the paintings on the nine bridges of the YEDA, virtual creatures related to the paintings will appear on their screens. The users will then be able to interact and play games with the virtual animals. Through such interactions, we can discover that urban arts installations are neither sole artworks nor information carriers placed in cities with the purpose of conveying certain information. In fact, they are brand-new facilities that can interact and communicate with people. They allow tourists to transfer from appreciators of turban arts to participants and creators of urban arts, formulating the fascinating interactions between human beings and urban arts.

Keywords: Design thinking · Urban art · Augmented reality · Interactive design
User Centred Design

1 Introduction

The Yantai Urban Art Project was commissioned by the YEDA. When we talk about Urban Art we will mention sculpture, graffiti and installation. *the definition of "Urban Art", is either based on the mission of art work to improve the quality of urban landscape or on a variety of art works in the city; however the interesting point here is that the Urban Art is not clearly determined in the previous studies. How can it affect the quality of urban landscape? And whether all works of art in the city are caused such qualities? With the distribution of artworks all over the cities and failure to reach their maximum determined targets, it seems that Urban Art has been backed away from its original essence and subdued by some styles attenuating its values as much as decorations and ornaments of city[1].* Because the urban arts are characterized by existing in the public space, they are often viewed as vandalism and destruction of private property. But Yantai Urban Art Project's goal is not only to create an art landscape for public to enjoy but also to use interactive methodes to engage visitors to play with the art work and influence their behavior.

2   Objectives

- This project will study public's experience of Urban Arts and find a way to encourage public participating into it. We will study the background context of engagement and participating.
- We will research the reasons restricting public to participate into Arts. How can we encourage public get involved into Urban Art or to create a participatory experience for public.
- Research the HCI design field and User Centred Design methology.
- Gamified methodology to encourage public participating.
- Study public's emotion especially Achievement Emotions.
- The technologies behined New Urban Art.

The study of public's experience of Urban Arts. Urban Art is a general idea about visual art forms in urban areas. What we have often seen in city are graffiti, sculptures, and installations. Most of these art forms are viewed by public by a passive way which means the art will be there and public will give it a glance when people pass through it. *Definition of art is a specific form and shape of social consciousness and its aim is to reflect the reality correctly and multilaterally for the purpose of reaching the aim and loftiness which has passed a very tortuous and difficult way. What has caused evolution of urban arts is creating the pictures which have full resemblance to the reality, because they have public addresses and are seen in the paths of the city and daily passing of life. General art are meaningful activities that can be recalled as art. This art has been*

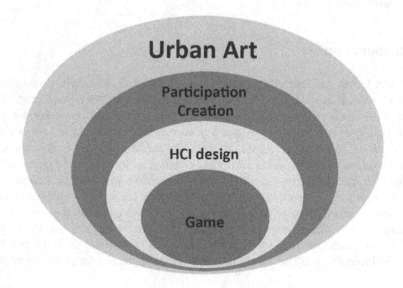

Fig. 1.   Participatory urban arts diagram

shaped in the city space with public investment or by persons and is paid attention by the public and it is appeared with a clear aim and in the form of general activities of the city[2]. It means that art is not only related with author's ideas to express but also involved with audience's perception and participation (Fig. 1).

Participation is not only a set of techniques. It is more of a state of mind (psychology) or an attitude towards others. A good technique is more like a belief that will encourage everyone to participate and enjoy the process. If we can provide people with the right tools to help them to participate, they will be able to invest in activities and feel happy to enjoy in them.

2.1   Participatory Experience

When we design for uses and audiences to participate that we need to pay attention for a problem. That is our users and audiences are made up of different age groups and they have different knowledge backgrounds, which lead to a different cognitive development levels. The congnitive development theory can provide us a very good foundation and be a effective guideline to help us design. The theories we have researched related to these below:

We explore the world and observe law of nature and make summaries just like what scientists do. Piaget has recognized two fundamental congnitive processed that they work somewhat in a way of supporting each other. Piaget called the first one "Assimilation", which is a process involved to incorporate new information into an existing cognitive structure. The second one is called "Accommodation", which is to form a new cognitive structure that can incorporate new information. As summed up by Piaget that "Assimilation" and "Accommodation" these two simultaneous processes represent a balanced system. Piaget emphasizes the repetition of experience of individual and subjective, which can help human being to develop an understanding of the world and move from one stage to another. Piaget hoped to be able to use his theory to involved into the educational system so that can have new thinkings on the cognitive sciences. The related documents involves Vygotsky's theory which supports the idea that the cognitive development is highly intrinsic.

There are so many researches emphasise that design should take care of user's experience and the cognitive theory is a very important study field for it. Through the better understanding of cognitive theory we can do better design for users and have a effective guideline for design methodology. The result would be perfect to bring a better participatory experience to users.

Besides audiences' personal knowledge background and structures there are a lot of other factors will affect their experience in cognitive process which are including individual needs, motivation, and degree of participation. If we can encourage our users from different dimensions by using multiple measures their degree of participation can become higher. If a user has more knowledge or experience in some aspects of his/her own, the higher amount of information he/she will get. Different forms of participation can bring different degrees of cognitive behavior and influence to users, stimulate users' different senses, interests and behaviors, all of which can affect users' degree of information acquired in cognitive process.

In the book "Emotional Design – Why We Love or Hate Everyday Thing", Donald A. Norman mentioned Three Levels of Processing. They are Visceral, Behavioral, and Reflective. The visceral level is fast: it makes rapid judgments of what is good or bad, safe or dangerous, and sends appropriate signals to the muscles (the motor system) and alerts the rest of the brain. This is the start of affective processing. These are biologically determined and can be inhibited or enhanced through control signals from above. The behavioral level is the site of most human behavior. Its actions can be enhanced or inhibited by the reflective layer and, in turn, it can enhance or inhibit the visceral layer. The highest layer is that of reflective thought. Note that it does not have direct access either to sensory input or to the control of behavior. Instead it watches over, reflects upon, and tries to bias the behavioral level[3].

Donald mentioned the actual product can be not only the present of functions and problems but also can solve the problem for our feelings and needs, and more importantly it can help user to create his or her personal identity and social status. Therefor, understand users' cognitive style and level will help designers to learn users' basic needs and encourage them to participate into designated experience.

It is very important for us to create a sound participation environment for users. In our daily basis circumstances to create a direct access for users is a very hard challenge. We have to study these challenges when we do the design to understand users' needs in new era. How people perceive things in urban and use new technologies to help them explore the art world.

It is full of challenge to encourage different kind of people happily to dedicate into a event in the ordinary environment. A good design will reach the goal successfully but the bad design will tear people away from urban art.

2.2 Games Are Better Participatory Experience

Games can represent the most effective participation. By playing games the participation will be greatly improved. Many of our current studies and theories, especially HCI are related to Malone's idea back to the 80s of last century which is based on the fun of games. Those information can provide us the theoretical ideas and explanation for design a interesting user experience. We did some research about how game can encourage the participation and what benefit it could bring to us.

Salen and Zimmerman did many researches to define "Game" at 2003. They found that most of the definitions are about rules, objectives and descriptions of how to play. In 2013 Adams had a definition of game: "a type of play activity, conducted in the context of a pretended reality, in which the participant(s) try to achieve at least one arbitrary, nontrivial goal by acting in accordance with rules.[4]"

According to the definition a game is an activity including one or more players. This activity will involve players to reach certain objectives or give players a set of rules to tell them what can do or can not do. The goal of game is to have fun or pleasure but it can also provide training, education or simulation opportunities.

Game has become a part of our daily life since long time ago. Nowadays new technologies have involved into the game and featured it digitalized and virtualized which makes it more easily to play at anytime and anywhere.

Many researches explored the positive impact of the game in general or particular. A large number experts and scholars studied how game will have benefit on cognition for participants in our life. When people play games it can help to improve their cognitive skills especially for space. It could be very helpful for users to get involved into urban art as participants but not only visitors. Game is a very effective means to encourage and stimulate positive emotions and it can promote the development of social skills. Jan McGonigal mentioned in his book "Super Better" that traditional games are complicated and hard to master, so when players are in the process of play they will be pushed to learn more general and challenging skills and abilities[5].

Design and develop a game is a very complicated work and process. This is not simply a task that can be done by playing. It requires not only creativity but also many cognitive skills. Designing a game is a tough and complex task. It can provide participants a strong learning environment. Game can offer a varity of opportunities to exercise many different skills.

Game is one of the most participatory activities. The process of design a game is very participatory too. The definition of design a game is: "It is a process of creating and designing content and rules for a game.[6]" Game should be as simple as possible at the beginning because simple is easy to participate. Game should be fun and attractive so players can reach a high active state. Fun will stick players and enhance their desire to participate, then allow them to reach a flow state. Moreover it is very important to have a good structure with rules of the game, and a attractive way to elicit players' emotion. For example, The ability to provide feedback to players to encourage them to continue to participate and learn. To make players feel satisfied and constantly stimulate their adrenaline. To motivating the participants' creativity through different measures.

2.3   The Process of Design a Game (Project)

There are so many methods to design a game. Some like to design it based on personal experience and imagination which is called "My Way". But we believe that the method of human centered design is one of the best to adopt. Because in this way, we can put players at the center of design, so we can have better understanding of players' needs and behavior. By following a user centered design approach, designers should focus on the most important two functions of games during the design process. First, it needs to be able to make the players happy, and second it needs to be able to fell empathy with players. There are 3 main steps to design a game in our project:

1 Analysis goals and game design concepts.
2 The development of game concept.
3 Prototyping development.

For our project, it's very important to analyze our goals first and then to get ideas to conceptualize them. They are foundations. We will think what do we need and what to do for a game as a participatory urban art project. It is very important to think about the core mechanism for the project. Core mechanism can represent the core of participation.

It can create participatory methods and processes. It can define the challenges of participation and provide participants with the rules to be completed in the challenge. It also determines the impact of the actor's behavior on the project (Fig. 2).

Fig. 2.   Yantai Economic Development Area bridge pier 122.

3   YEDA AR Procedure Design

The AR Project in Yantai is initiated by YEDA to provide interactive experience in art between people and the city. By means of Augmented Reality (AR), tourists can use their smartphones to look for 9 AR targets in the paintings of the bridge piers, and to interact with the virtual objects they find. Tourists are encouraged to combine the virtual objects with the real painting and to experience the joy within.

The YEDA Bridge is 5 km in length with paintings reflecting four seasons on its piers. Based on the design drawings of the paintings, 9 piers that are appropriate for interaction are selected. The following factors are considered: Location, Light and shadow, Recognition degree of the paintings.

3.1   Location

Considering the fact that the pier paintings are 30 m^2 in area and the equivalent focal length of cameras in iPhone 4s and other following iPhone devices is 28 mm–35 mm, the best distance for interactive experience is 15 m from the pier. We follow the tourist route in person to measure the distance between the road and the pier to find the piers best for interaction (Fig. 3).

Fig. 3. Yantai Economic Development Area bridge pier 122.

3.2 Light and Shadow

The AR Project in YEDA is an outdoor AR experience. As a result, the change in natural light and shadow can have an influence on recognition of the pier paintings. Thus, we choose those paintings influenced as little as possible by the natural light and shadow, i.e., the paintings facing north or without direct exposure to natural light (Figs. 4 and 5).

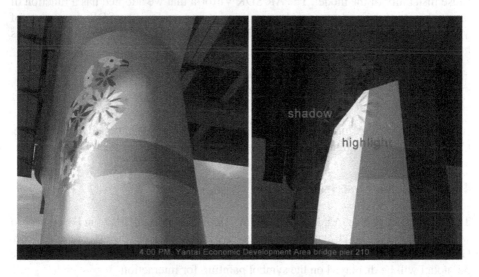

Fig. 4. Yantai Economic Development Area bridge pier 206.

9:00 AM   4:00 PM

Yantai Economic Development Area bridge pier 160

Fig. 5. Yantai Economic Development Area bridge pier 132.

3.3   Recognition Degree of the Paintings

The recognition degree of the paintings can influence tourists' experience, so paintings with high degree of recognition are our first choice. Recognition degree of AR symbols shows whether the symbols can be properly recognized under various conditions and the speed of their recognition. Besides, symbols with low degree of recognition can cause instability of the model. The AR SDK Vuforia that we adopted has a function of rating the recognition degree of the paintings. After reading the SDK documents of Vuforia and some tests, we find that paintings satisfying the following three conditions have higher degrees of recognition:

– The paintings have numerous corner angles;
– The corner angles are evenly distributed;
– Single elements in the paints are small.

After filtering, we have 15 piers that are suitable for AR interactive experience. Combining the tourist route and storytelling together, finally we select 9 of them.

4   YEDA AR System Design

The AR Project in YEDA adopts the gaming engine of unity3d 2017, and is combined with Vuforial. First of all, symbol paintings are detected using the AR camera. Then, GPS location detection is carried out[7]. If the two detections match with each other, the 3d model will be displayed on the symbol painting for interaction.

The AR Project in YEDA aims at providing interactive experience in art between tourists and the city. We do not want that kind of interaction where tourists turn on their smartphone cameras to recognize a fixed card. Instead, in the interaction experience, tourists are required to place themselves in the real artistic scenes of the city. Thus, proper interaction ways should be that, the tourists are in YEDA Liuzihe Park, and he or she turns on the smartphone camera to recognize the paintings on the piers and interacts with the virtual images generated. Therefore, the proper procedure should be that, GPS location of the tourist should be recognized immediately after he or she recognizes the symbol, and if the tourist is in the correct location, the model and animation should be displayed for interaction (Fig. 6).

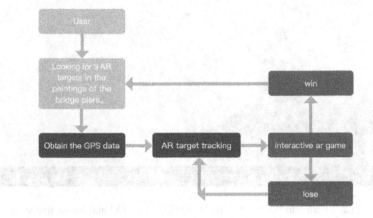

Fig. 6. Yantai Economic Development Area AR project flow diagram.

4.1 Obtain the GPS Location Data of Users

GPS location of the tourist should be obtained immediately after the tourist recognizes the symbol, and compare the data with target zones (in unity3d, Input.location.lastData.latitude and Input.location.lastData.longitude can be used to obtain users' current longitude and latitude information). If the tourist happens to be around a painting, the model and animation should be displayed for interaction.

4.2 Time Limit on Interaction Games

Because the AR Project in YEDA is an outdoor project, tourists' maximum interaction time with the virtual images should be limited to 60s in order not to cause traffic jam (Fig. 7).

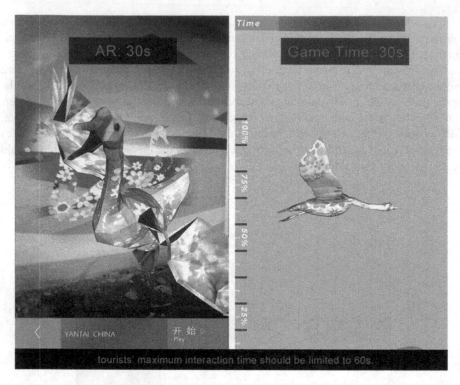

Fig. 7.   Yantai Economic Development Area bridge pier 132 and interactive ar game.

5   The Technologies Behind New Urban

The number of Internet users transmitting bandwidth through radio wave for exceeded that through cable. Nowadays, online chatting, messaging and posting through mobile data has become an incredibly important thing in our daily lives. However, the "internet of things" has brought about far more than just interpersonal relationship maintaining. For example, we can check the location of our car through smart phones, check the traffic congestion condition using map applications, obtain weather information using weather applications, and communicate with the sensors all around the city through smart phones. Even so, our interaction with public urban art has been insufficient. Sculptures on streets and wall pictures can only beautify cities. It would be a great experience for people to interact with urban art through some technical methods while appreciating them.

Augmented Reality (AR) is the main technique we adopted to realize YEDA. Although the people-art interaction goal has been achieved, there are still two remaining problems. First, most urban art works are three-dimensional like sculptures, except two-dimensional paintings, companies' logos and graphic advertisements. However, most AR image recognition is based on two-dimensional characteristics recognition, and three-dimensional logo recognition is not stable; besides, most AR is realized through smart phones at present, where users download applications through Google Play or App Store to recognize logos and display virtual objects. The process of waiting for downloading relevant applications decreases users' experience. In March 2017, Jerome Etienne developed a solution to realized AR on web browsers[8]. It enables instantaneous video stream through webrtc, and renders three-dimensional virtual objects. Therefore, we may not necessarily have to rely on any application in the future; by opening safari browser on phones to automatically activate cameras, we can scan any urban art work to display the virtual object and enable interaction with it, creating a pleasant and convenient interaction experience (Fig. 8).

Fig. 8. Realized AR on web browsers (Safari).

6   Summary

This paper discusses the process of people-art interaction and the existing problems, and rethinks the relationship between urban art and people. This paper proposes that people's participation in and interaction with urban art works in the future should be strengthened. In YEDA, we used Augmented Reality for viewers to scan the art paintings on piers and then to interact with the generated three-dimensional models. In the future, the interaction experience can be even better with the development of digital technology. More items can be displayed also, to fully convert viewers into participants and creators.

References

1. Adelvand, P., Mousavilar, A.S., Mansouri, S.A.: "Urban art" as a landscape phenomenon in today's society. Bagh-I-Nazar **13**, 43–50 (2016)
2. Mokhles, F.: Urban art typology in the urban view of India. Bagh-I-Nazar **11**, 27–36 (2014)
3. Norman, D.A.: Emotional Design: Why We Love (or Hate) Everyday Things, p. 22. Basic Books, New York (2005)

4. Adams, E.: Fundamentals of Game Design, 3rd edn. Pearson, Allyn and Bacon, London/Boston (2013)
5. McGonigal, J.: SuperBetter: A Revolutionary Approach to Getting Stronger, Happier, Braver and More Resilient - Powered by the Science of Games. Penguin, London (2015)
6. Schell, J.: The Art of Game Design: A Book of Lenses. Morgan Kaufmann Publishers Inc., San Francisco (2008)
7. Broschart, D., Zeile, P.: Architecture: augmented reality in architecture and urban planning. In: Buhmann, E. (ed.) Peer Reviewed Proceedings of Digital Landscape Architecture 2015 at Anhalt University of Applied Sciences, pp. 111–118. Wichmann, Berlin (2015)
8. Etienne, J.: ar.js. (2017). https://github.com/jeromeetienne/AR.js

Study on Introducing Digitalization in Folk Art

Taking Beautiful! Chinese New Year Paintings as an Example

Song Lu[✉]

Shandong University of Art and Design, No. 1255, University Road, University Science Park, Changqing District, Jinan, Shandong, People's Republic of China
slu009@qq.com

Abstract. The rich and colorful folk arts are varied in categories, but its inheritance and protection are experiencing a period of stagnation with the social development due to the traditional recovery and protection approaches. Digitalization of folk arts is an effective approach to protect folk arts forming with the development of computers. Taking *Beautiful!Chinese New Year Paintings* as an example, this paper analyzes the necessity of introducing digitalization into the protection of folk arts, with the mutual relationship between folk arts and digitalization as main clue and combining the technology application in animation production.

Keywords: Folk arts · Digital animation · Spring Festival paintings of Yangjiabu
Animation based on Spring Festival paintings

1 Rich and Colorful Folk Arts Provide Materials for Digitalization

Folk arts, as the public culture existing in the daily life, are the visual and graphic arts created by the folk populations to meet their demands on social life. Folk arts have a long history, as well as deep roots that they rely on for existence and development. Digitalization means the process that voices, texts, graphs, images, animations, motion pictures and other multi-media information are subject to digital processing on computers through the modern multi-media technologies. Folk arts are converted into digital arts that can display folk arts more visually. Specifically, digital animation is a method that can realize the perfect combination of multi-media technologies and folk arts. Rich and colorful folk arts provide abundant materials for the creation of digital animation.

Folk arts have a long-standing relationship with animation. The animations, ranging from the first animation *Princess Iron Fan* produced by WansBrother to the first puppetoon *Dream of being Emperor* of China, reflect the styles and characteristics of folk arts. The forms and colors of Spring Festival paintings were embodies in the animations such as *The Monkey King*, *Prince Nezha's Triumph against Dragon King*, *Pride General*, *A Small Carp's Adventures*, etc., produced by Shanghai Animation Film Studios. Folk toys made of different raw materials have different effect, and they were perfectly integrated into the animations such as *Princess Peacock*, *A Daoist from Lao Mountain*, *Inscription of Dragons*, *Watermelon Gun*, *Fake or Real Li Kui*, etc. The folk drawing techniques on ceramics and porcelains were fully displayed on Fish Dish and Conflict. The styling features of folk paper-cut were skillfully used in *Fishing Child*, *Pigsy Eats Watermelon*, *Ginseng Baby*, *Red Army Bridge*, *A Mouse Marriage*, *Eight Immortals with Flea*, etc. The styles, colors, materials, themes, etc. of folk arts are indirectly or directly employed in the creations of Chinese animations. Paper-cut animated cartoon *Fishing Child*. An animated cartoon using styles and colors of Chinese New Year paintings (Fig. 1).

Fig. 1. Paper-cut animated cartoon *Fishing Child* (Color figure online)

Simple, exaggerate, generalized and concise styling features of folk arts such as shadow puppet, puppet, Spring Festival paintings, paper-cut, folk toys, etc., fit exactly with the motion ways and rules of animation, and match perfectly with the styling requirements of animation. The beautiful, pure and intense colors of folk arts are accord with the art language and the pattern of manifestation of animation. Therefore, in the history of Chinese animation, the puppet animation, paper folding animation, paper-cut animation, clay sculpture animation, etc. corresponding to folk arts. In 1970s, the creation of Chinese animation won the good reputation of "Chinese School of Animation" in the international animation circle. Traditional folk art was well referenced and explored in animations, becoming the source and basic material of animation creation (Fig. 2).

Fig. 2. An animated cartoon using styles and colors of Chinese New Year paintings (Color figure online)

2 Necessity of Digitalizing the Spring Festival Paintings of Yangjiabu

Yangjiabu is located at the south bank of Laizhou Bay, Bohai Sea, and 10 km in the northeast of downtown of Weifang City. Yangjiabu makes Spring Festival paintings seasonally, from the end of busy season in autumn to the December 23 of lunar calendar. The themes of Spring Festival paintings include exorcising evil spirits, auspicious sign, folk customs, tales of legend, historical stories, fiction and opera, current event and humor, acrobatics and entertainment, scenery and flower, auspicious birds and beasts, etc. Farmers post gate paintings, door paintings, paintings with a character of "fu (fortune)", beauty paintings, paintings with standing children, moonlight paintings according to their demands in daily life, which are full of rich folk and local flavors (Fig. 3).

Fig. 3. Spring Festival paintings of Yangjiabu: *Men Busy at Ten Farming Activities*

Yangjiabu Spring Festival paintings have passed over 500 years from Ming Dynasty to now. Since Jiajing Period of Ming Dynasty, Yangjiabu has begun to make Spring Festival paintings, and over 30 stores such as Jixing, Tongshunde, Yongsheng, etc. were opened in Qianlong Period of Qing Dynasty and over 80 stores were reached in Daoguang Period of Qing Dynasty. The situations with "over thousands of painting varieties and hundreds of workshops" and "painting skills was popularized every house-hold" appeared. In Xianfeng Period of Qing Dynasty, Yangjiabu integrated the local styles with the styles of Yangliuqing Spring Festival paintings in Tianjin, which not only carried forward the "half-printing, half-drawing" technique of Yangliuqing and expanded the contents, but also enriched the varieties. Afterwards, Yangjiabu Spring Festival paintings developed towards an unprecedented prosperous period, and some paintings were even exported to foreign countries. In the period of "Culture Revolution", the layout designs of Yangjiabu Spring Festival paintings were damaged because they were one of "four olds", but in recent years relevant departments and the artists of Yangjiabu Spring Festival paintings began the systematic arrangements and collections of traditional Spring Festival wood-block prints. Through efforts in all directions, Yang-jiabu Spring Festival wood-block print was listed into the first batch of National Intan-gible Cultural Heritage on May 20, 2006 as approved by the State Council (Fig. 4).

Fig. 4. Yanjiabu Spring Festival painting: number one scholar got married (Color figure online)

Although Yangjiabu Spring Festival paintings are properly protected, the values, believes, ways of thinking and aesthetic ideas of the public and the relationship between traditional lifestyle, culture and natural ecology change with times, which is a significant impact on the existence of Yangjiabu Festival Paintings. "We have no reasons to force the publics to post those paintings of immortals in loud colors in their chic rooms."[1] The functions of Spring Festival paintings have been faded out in the modern society, and its markets narrow down largely with the reduction of sales volume. In addition, Yangjiabu Spring Festival paintings, like other intangible cultural heritages, are also at the embarrassing situation of "lacking the inheritors". How to review Yangjiabu Spring Festival paintings in a better way is urgent for its protection and inheritance. The traditional collection and sorting of Spring Festival paintings are just a passive protection, and deeper exploration is required by other approaches such as digital animation. Digital animation restores the characteristics of Spring Festival paintings by its technologies, which makes it easy to be accepted by the publics, and also conforms to the visual appreciation habits nowadays. Thus, digital animation ushers a new approach for protecting the intangible cultural heritage. Feng Jicai, in his interview about *The Protection of Chinese Folk Culture*, noticed that "what we pass down to our descendant is not just the written record, but also those visible, audible and dynamic".

In 1990s, Chinese government actively applied for the "World Cultural and Natural Heritages", and put more efforts in restoring and protecting the folk culture and art. Specifically, the protection on folk cultural and artistic heritages is mainly implemented

[1] Pan Lusheng Digitalized Folk Art [C]: Theory Committee of China Artist Association. Collected Works of Chinese Art Chengdu Forum, Current Meaning of National Traditional Art. Chengdu: Sichuan Art Publishing House, 2007.263.

from three aspects: investigation and recording of folk handicrafts and cultural ecological protection, collection and sorting of folk artworks, tourism regeneration and development of folk artworks. However, the above three approaches have their limitations due to their particularities. First, folk art spreads widely, almost covering most regions throughout the country; second, folk art has a variety of forms. Therefore, it is complex cause to protect the folk art.

Facing the conflicts between the reasonable development and utilization and the effective protection of ethnic and folk art culture heritage, "it is necessary to keep consistent with the country's modernization, and utilize the modern digital information acquiring and processing technology to the protection of ethnic and folk handicrafts and its ways of cultural existence."[2] It is necessary to establish a comprehensive, digitalized and virtual basic framework for the protection, inheritance and development of ethnic and folk art heritage.

From the theory level, the digitalization of folk art provides theories and models for the digitalized digging, storage, propagation and development of intangible cultural heritage, as well as provides education methods and basis for the future protection of intangible cultural heritage. From the content level, a comprehensive, digitalized and virtual basic framework for the protection, inheritance and development of ethnic and folk art heritage based on computers needs to be established, and a symbolic library for ethnic and folk art that can be applied to modern design, covering the basic element base of folk Spring Festival painting art, symbolic library of common Spring Festival paintings and Spring Festival painting library needs to be constructed. From the technology level, it is required to explore and embrace the multi-media virtual scene modeling technology of intangible cultural heritage, the coordinated display technology with multi-media virtual scene and the computer-based innovative design technology of Spring Festival painting.

3   Trial of Digitalized Spring Festival Painting –*Beautiful!Chinese New Year Paintings*

The animation *Beautiful!Chinese New Year Paintings* was produced by a production team of Shandong University of Art and Design after more than 40 days hardworking by the end of December 2010. The animation takes Yangjiabu Spring Festival paintings, including *Men Busy at Ten Farming Activities*, *Women Busy at Ten Domestic and Weaving Activities*, *Number One Scholar Got Married*, *Celebration of the Lantern Festival*, etc., as the creative materials, uses the theme music of the feature film *Celebration of Spring Festival* as the background music with a large amount of sound effects. The animation keeps the original styles of Weifang Spring Festival paintings, and repaints the figures and scenes by digital technology to display the traditional and two-dimensional Spring Festival paintings in a new form of digital animation. The animation

---

[2] Tang Jialu. Cultural Ecology of Folk Art [M].Beijing: Tsinghua University Press, 2006.

displays the actual joyful scenes from farm work, needle work to family life and celebration of Spring Festival, and is filled with the rich local flavors as well as the simple
and distinct artistic style (Fig. 5).

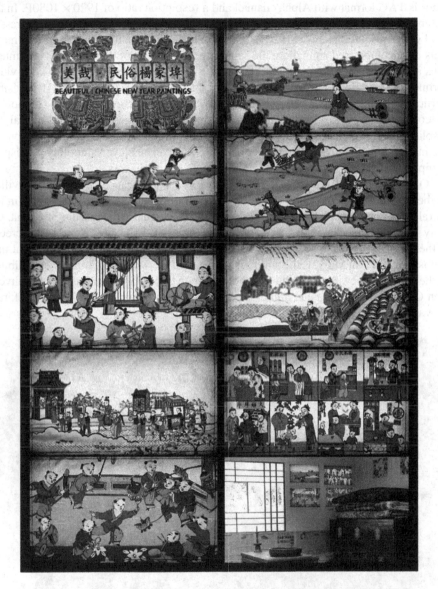

Fig. 5. Animation *Beautiful! Chinese New Year Paintings* (Color figure online)

To vividly show the true Yangjiabu Spring Festival paintings and better convert
image information to digital signals, many international standards were adopted during
the design and production of this animation. First of all, for the key performance indicators of image resolution and sharpness, the resolution ratio was determined as 800 PPI

(Pixels PerInch), scanning gray level 256, number of color 24bit that are internationally universal. The storage file is the PSD hierarchical file with a resolution ratio of 3508 × 2480. While producing the output sequence frame animation, the image technical indicator is TAG format with Alpha channel and a resolution ratio of 1920 × 1080P. In the composition stage of character animation and scenes, the output format is uncompressed AVI with a resolution ratio of 1920 × 1080P. In the stage of editing the composite materials of uncompressed animation, the sampling frequencies of dubbing files and music files are high quality 320Kbps MP3 audio files. The final output format is MP4 video format with a resolution ratio of 1920 × 1080P, 1125 vertical scanning lines, 1080 visible vertical scanning lines, an aspect ratio of 16:9 and H.264 code. The final technology video format of the displaying and demonstrating systems is the standard digital TV display model, which is the most high-end high definition format in the world, supports the internationally universal computer platform and can be played smoothly on display equipment such as back protection, plasma, LCD and projectors.

On January 10, 2011, the animation made its first appearance on Weifang Pavilion in the "Handicraft in the Countryside: Exhibition of Cultural Industry Research in the Rural Areas of Shandong Province" organized by National Art Museum of China. On May 13, 2011, the animation was displayed on spherical LED device and LED screens at the entrance of Shandong Pavilion on the 7th China (Shenzhen) International Cultural Industries Fair. On May 21, the animation, as one of the works of China, was exhibited in the New Age New Media Exhibition held in Jinan Expo Garden International Convention Center. *CCTV News* and *Shandong News* and also obtained a very high click rate on various web portals (Fig. 6).

Fig. 6. Displaying on the 7th China (Shenzhen) International Cultural Industries Fair

This animation allows the publics to understand and view the national intangible cultural heritage –Yangjiabu Spring Festival paintings. It is especially important that the production team of Shandong University of Art & Design begins to systematically research and explore new thoughts to protect more intangible cultural heritage by multimedia digital art approaches. These approaches make Spring Festival paintings advance with the times and adapt to the modern aesthetic idea while showing a more real appearance of heritage, and the intangible cultural heritage can be inherited, developed and utilized in wider and more comprehensive ways.

4   Conclusions

In view of the specialty of current existing environment of folk arts and the transformation of in Chinese society, economy, culture and lifestyle, devoting to the research and development of digitalized protection technology is a reasonable and effective solution for the restoration and protection of ethnic and folk arts. The research and development of digital key technology of ethnic and folk arts will provide technical possibility for the conservation of ethnic and folk arts, the academic research and industrialization, etc.

References

1. Hui, Y., Yabin, S.: History of Chinese Animated Movies. China Film Press, Beijing (2005)
2. Xiaolu: Traditional Aesthetic Features of Domestic Animated Movies and its Cultural Source. Shanghai People's Publishing House, Shanghai (2008)

The Integration of New Media Art and Chinese Traditional Culture

Yunqiao Su[✉]

Shandong College of Arts and Design, No. 1255, College Road,
Changqing District, Jinan, People's Republic of China
630492407@qq.com

Abstract. New media art integrates artistic creation, media dissemination and real-time interaction together, which is both an art carrier and a media for dissemination. It is different from the traits of traditional art and provides new opportunities for extending the inheritance and continuation of traditional Chinese culture. In the era of the information age and globalization, it is necessary to guide the students to create new media art combining Chinese traditional culture factors and promote the collision and integration of Eastern and Western cultures for the development of new media art in China in the future.

Keywords: New media art · China · Tradition · Culture

1 Introduction

Art is a miracle blooming in human civilization. Works of art concocts various cultural and historical features of different time and space. In the course of history, continuity and innovation have never stopped. New media art combines artistic creation, media dissemination and real-time interaction together. It is both an art carrier and a media for communication. Apart from the traditional forms of expression, interactive works of art with the utilization of digital technology can simultaneously stimulate people's senses of vision, hearing and touch as well as other feelings, which significantly enhance people's aesthetic experience. This new media art, with this dramatic distinction from traditional art, offers new opportunities for expanding the inheritance and continuation of traditional Chinese culture.

2 Art Features of New Media

New media art usually refers to all works of art created using media and technical means [1]. In the 1960s, contributed by the rapid development of technology and media, new media art came into being. Today, under the background of global information technology, the new media art presents new features in terms of creation methods, communication carrier, exchange display, etc.

2.1   Highly Convenient Reproduction of Art Works

The uniqueness of a work of art determines the difficulty of its reproduction. The early human reproduction can hardly ever present the artistic value of the original work. The advent of photographic techniques has greatly increased the convenience of reproduction … moreover, more and more works of art are precisely designed for being duplicated. And digital technology is a powerful assist in the promotion of works of art. For example, the reproduction of video is pretty convenient, which can be played in the medias such as cinema, television and the Internet, greatly enhancing the visibility and influence of the work and obtaining more business value. Another example is the 3D printing technology, with which the high-precision reproduction of three-dimensional works of art is realized.

2.2   The Wide Range of Art Media Material

New media art has broadened the scope of art media, of which any material can be used for art creation. Combine different media materials to create and express concept, thereby generating new connotation. As early as 1996, the CAVE, a work of new media interaction, is created by Jeffrey Shaw, a professor of media art from the City University of Hong Kong, of which the artist manipulated wood figures and images as mediums to control the interaction between the projection of the surroundings images and the virtual world.

2.3   The Improved Aesthetic Appreciation of the Public

Traditional works of art are often caviar to the general. Viewers tend to keep a certain distance, which is inconvenient for close contact and feeling the art. The new media art are different, which eliminates the gully between viewers and creators. In direct and real-time communication, the interaction between viewers and works of art has even become an integral part of the artwork.

3   The Integration of New Media Art and Chinese Traditional Culture

We are in an era of rapid information dissemination. The key to integrate the new media art into the cultural perspective and aesthetic thinking of Chinese people lies in the artistic creators' interpretation of Chinese traditional culture. As one of the four ancient civilizations passed down from ancient times, the traditional Chinese concepts, symbols, languages, art styles and performances are all precious sources of creativity. The core of the creation of new media art integrating modern science, technology and communication features sources from the author's creativity; media and technology are considered as the carrier and means of realizing new media art work. In the course of college new media art teaching in recent years, the author has been trying to guide students to pay attention to Chinese traditional culture and help students explore and establish art language independently. Instruct students to follow the creative process of "creativity - media - expression - feedback" step by step. The source of creativity can be directly derived from all aspects of Chinese traditional culture. However, the creation in real sense is not to apply or copy mechanically, but to think independently on the basis of proper interpretation. For example, the reflection on the spirit of Confucianism, Buddhism and Taoism in China; and the comparison study of certain characteristics of Chinese and Western culture and so forth are by no means isolated cases. After the initial formation of the concept of creativity, the carrier of the work of the media can be determined; encourage students to diversify their perception of the media, and to repeatedly compare the related similarities and differences. Such as the sense of vision, sound, smell, touch and so on. The perception of expression is the key to artistic creation. With regard to the integration of new media art and traditional Chinese cultural factors, there are several creative angles to consider:

3.1 Fusion of Chinese Traditional Culture

Confucianism, Taoism, and the Buddhism introduced during the Han Dynasty into China these three schools of traditional Chinese culture formed a unique ideological system of ethics and morality in Chinese religions, which interprets the relationship between Chinese and nature, and embodies the uniqueness of Chinese philosophy and world view. One of the most remarkable is the philosophical thought of "harmony between man and nature".

The concept of "harmony between man and nature" stems from the religious belief totem of ancient human beings and wishes to be blessed by gods. At the same time, as a country dominated by farming civilization, the forerunners of China are full of admiration and gratitude for nature. This psychological expectation has been tempered in the precipitation of a long history and developed into a unique psychological and cultural characteristic of Chinese nation. As stated in Chuang Tzu's Qi Wu Lun (Equality of All Substances): "Heaven, earth and I exist together,everything and me are in unity.". This is the concept of integration of man and heaven. The idea of "harmony between man and nature" holds that man is a part of nature and that man and nature should maintain a harmonious and unified state. For thousands of years, this kind of appeal has being running through Chines' blood and has penetrated into the essence of traditional Chinese culture and various fields.

Among the student graduation works in 2016, some students applied digital techniques to create a series of quite interesting interactive works in the form of Chinese ink paintings, which is called "Meditation" (Fig. 1). The viewer, sitting on the particular futon, contemplates his life from the different ink figures produced in the flow of thought through a few minutes of meditation, which embodies the author's reflection on the unity of heaven and man under the idea of "harmonious relationship between man and nature".

3.2 Fusion of Aesthetic Taste of Chinese Art

China's artistic field has a wide range, whose aesthetic core is the expression of artistic conception. Artistic conception is a category of aesthetics combining "meaning" and "state". It is a kind of art form with meaning and state exceeding the original objects

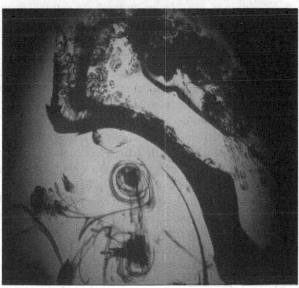

Fig. 1. Meditation

Fig. 1. (*continued*)

that is achieved through the external image in art work. "Meaning" is the artist's subjective creation, and "state t" is an objective reflection of life; the harmonization of the two aspects achieves artistic conception. "When there is a scene, there is mood state". This opinion points out the two basic elements that constitute the artistic conception: mood and scene, of which the mood is subjective, and the scene is objective. When mood and scene blend together, the two are united and inseparable. From the perspective of aesthetic activities, "artistic conception" is a spiritual sphere obtained by transcending the limitation, concretes, and environment, from which certain philosophical enlightenment can be perceived. In terms of the creation of artistic conception, Zong Baihua once said: "It is an important area for understanding the aesthetic characteristics of Chinese nation." How to express the far-reaching artistic conception through the use of technical means and media at the moment is the point that we should think about. In addition to displaying unique oriental aesthetic and taste from the aspects of traditional Chinese art forms such as paintings, calligraphy, music, dance, ancient gardens, arts and crafts, it is also possible to implant modern concepts and thereby creating new media art works with artistic conception. Such as the student work "Sound Polaroid" (Fig. 2) under my guide, it is a sound visualization interaction device combining physical device with computer programming. The experimenter presses the button to activate the device, which will collect sound through the "lens" to interact, therefrom visualizing the abstract sound. And then, in accordance with the sound fluctuations from experience, corresponding Chinese radical will be generated and scattered on paper, which will be printed out as souvenirs for those who participated the experience. This interactive device expressed two aspects of meanings: First, "spread is misreading"; Second, "all things are numbers." The final presentation of the

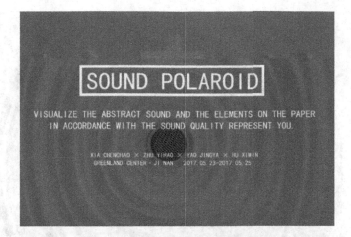

Fig. 2. Sound polaroid

Fig. 2. (*continued*)

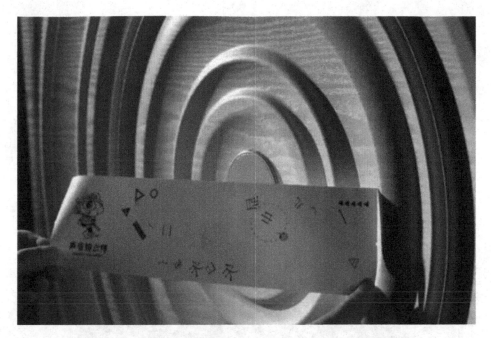

Fig. 2. (*continued*)

work breaks down people's perception of normal things and delivers them unexpected experience.

There is another student work called "The City in Eyes," which collects various types of wastes of urban life as a creative element, and then put them together into a physical model. At first glance, it is rather like a bunch of chaotic waste in ballistic shape. However, when people enter the interactive area, the light media will be activated. Under the illumination of light, a silhouette image of a classic woman of ancient time looking up to the Air City is casted on the wall, showing the different aspects of article from different perspective and under minor changes (Fig. 3).

This art work, with the utilization of "butterfly effect", attempts to explore the harm and beauty brought about by the development to the earth and human beings, thereby pondering about the sentimental relationship between humans and cities, so as to seek commonalities that have been passed through thousands of years in the unique aesthetic of Chinese.

3.3 Collision Between Eastern and Western Cultures Under the Context of Globalization

In the trend of the gradual convergence of global economy and cultures, as well as information globalization, traditional cultures and art creations in every country are inevitably affected by foreign cultures. How to promote the innovation of new media arts positively is a topic worth to be discussed. Some art creators, on the one hand, neglect, negate or even destroy their own traditional artistic heritage. On the other hand, they go all out to worship and imitate the external art forms, thus reflecting the "lack of proper self-confidence." In fact, both the passionate and straightforward western expression, and the subtle and euphemistic Eastern metaphor are indispensable in artistic creation. Sometimes the collision between the two will create new and exciting sparks. For example, a student uses digital technology to create a series of graphic works, whose contents are westerners who arrange funeral in Chinese style, which have

Fig. 3. The city in eyes

Fig. 3. (*continued*)

given rise to the thinking on various issues encountered by Chinese traditional customs in the course of globalization. Among the installations works created by students, the visual elements of Chinese, European, American, and African cultures are all fit into a square dark box; the audience can see the contents of the dark box through a square hole, showing the phenomenon of cultural integration in the context of globalization. In another piece of student installation art, the roles of Chinese shadow play are introduced in a Gothic-style European building; through the windows of the building, looming shadow-play figures can be seen. The thought-provoking work led the audience to concern about the demise of Chinese tradition culture.

4   Conclusion

President Xi Jinping, during his visit to Europe, emphasized: "We must maintain our confidence, endurance, and determination to our own culture." "Cultural confidence" can be considered as "cultural consciousness." The well-known sociologist Fei Xiaotong holds that: cultural confidence refers to a person's perception to his cultural the specific source, development process and future under specific environment; it is self-awakening and self-creation of culture."

China's cultural confidence stems from the splendid history of civilization created by the Chinese nation in 5,000 years, and its cultural elements have deeply rooted in the soul of the nation. So when talk about the ancient Great Wall, the Terracotta Warriors, the Silk Road or the new "Four Great Inventions" (HSR, Alipay, bike sharing and online shopping), people are full of confidence in their own country's culture. This is the proudness generated spontaneity. It also determines that on the basis of "cultural confidence," under the background of globalization, the collision and integration of Eastern and Western cultures will be an inevitable path for the development of Chinese new media art in the future.

References

1. Ling, C.: An Outline of New Media Art. Tsinghua University Press, Beijing (2007)
2. Benjamin, W.: Greet the era of Aura Demise. Guangxi Normal University Press, Guilin (2008). (Translated by Xu Qiling and Lin Zhiming)
3. Wu, L.: A discussion on the research of Chinese architectural culture and the historical mission created. Urban Plann. (01), 27 (2003)

The "Living State" Research of China Non-material Cultural Heritage on Digital Age

Taking the Nanjing Jinling Sutra Office as an Example

Xiaoxian Wang[✉] and Hao Liu

School of Design Arts and Media, Nanjing University of Science and Technology,
200, Xiaolingwei Street, Nanjing 210094, Jiangsu, China
11048456@qq.com

Abstract. Intangible cultural heritage is considered as the basic identification mark of the nation for many nationalities. With the changes of the times and the development of science and technology, intangible cultural heritage programs of the traditional art and skill types with technique as the core have faded out of people's lives even gradually demised because of the changes of social demand, the lacking of inheritors and inadequate protection. So how to protect and inherit the intangible cultural heritage and how to provide a driving force for its survival and development by design innovation under modern conditions?

Nanjing Jinling Sutra Printing House, established in the fifth year of the Tongzhi Period (1866) and engaging in the gathering, collection, research and publishing of sutra, it has collected lots of precious sutra and statue engravings. Till now, the Printing House has collected 125,318 pieces of Buddhist classical engravings, completely protected and inherited traditional woodblock printing skill of China originated from over 1,300 years ago and formed a unique artistic style of books. The "Chinese woodblock printing technique", represented by Nanjing Jinling Sutra Printing House, etc., was inscribed on the World Representative List of the Intangible Cultural Heritage of Humanity by the UNESCO in 2009. Its book art has profoundly embodied the art symbol of traditional Chinese culture in the aspects of text and image, layout and binding, material and technology, etc., with unique aesthetic features of ancient Chinese art. Its master-to-apprentice mechanism of book art is even one of the representative methods and approaches of Chinese cultural and artistic inheritance.

The woodblock printing of Jinling Sutra Printing House includes four manual procedures of sample writing, engraving, painting and binding. Wherein, writing and engraving have a high request on professional skills of the operators, which need a long-term training and cultivating mechanism of apprentice learning from master and oral teaching that inspires true understanding within. The aesthetic value embodied by manual engraving is the precious aspect of artistic style of books but also a shortage for the passing on of the woodblock printing art. For instance, the difficulty in cultivating professional talents, the accurate requests on one-time molding of engraving skills, the labor and time-consuming in product output efficiency, increasing space requirements on storage of woodblocks, technical requirements on long-term preservation of woodblocks (anti-damping, anti-moth, fire proofing) etc. Besides, there are only four masters and apprentices of

© Springer International Publishing AG, part of Springer Nature 2018
A. Marcus and W. Wang (Eds.): DUXU 2018, LNCS 10920, pp. 535–549, 2018.
https://doi.org/10.1007/978-3-319-91806-8_42

three generations in Jinling Sutra Printing House at present, and two of whom are the only apprentices of their masters, talent training and technology inheritance are confronted with a great risk of uncertainty. Although woodblock printing plays an important role in the development and inheritance of China's traditional culture and artistry, it still has equally prominent technical limitations. Therefore, how to conduct effective and living research on such intangible cultural heritage and use digital technology for its comprehensive protection and inheritance in the digital times has become a particularly necessary proposition.

After preliminary research, the writer believes that the current protection and inheritance for intangible cultural heritage programs have the following patterns: first of all, inheriting the project originally; secondly, on the basis of original inheritance, thinking about how to combine the traditional skills with modern life, and how to integrate the intangible cultural heritage with times elements in innovative approaches, so that it can be inherited lively. The writer believes that, nowadays, living state is an important characteristic of China's intangible cultural heritage. So, the development of contemporary intangible cultural heritage shall be effectively put into the market as a circulation commodity with higher added value and cultural value and interact and promote with the market to become a driving power and motive power for the development of social culture.

Keywords: Jinling Sutra Printing House · Living state · Design drive Innovation

1 Introduction

Intangible cultural heritage is considered as the basic identification mark of the nation for many nationalities. With the changes of the times and the development of science and technology, traditional intangible cultural heritage programs of the art and skill types have faded out of people's lives even gradually demised because of the changes of social demand, the lacking of inheritors and inadequate protection. It is the original intention of this subject to protect and inherit the intangible cultural heritage, seek the motive power for innovation, provide a driving force for its survival and development with design innovation so that it can be integrated into modern living methods and realize diverse cultural innovation methods, construct a sustainable development ecological system of "inheritor – intangible culture - environment", and embody more cultural value, social value and economic value in this digital era.

2 Jinling Sutra Printing House and Jinling Sutra Printing Technique

2.1 Jinling Sutra Printing House

As one of the "Four Great Inventions" in human history, "woodblock printing technique" is called "living fossil" in the printing history. It has played a great role in the civilization process of China, even the world. The woodblock printing technique of Jinling Sutra Printing House is the continuation of this ancient craft. As the engraving, printing, publishing and circulating center for Chinese woodblock Buddhist sutras in modern China, Jinling Sutra Printing House has won a great reputation at home and abroad since its foundation in 1866 by the Lay Buddhist YANG Renshan. The sutras engraved and published by the Sutra Printing House are famous for its accurately and strictly selected works, pure contents, prudent emendation, the good-looking large characters and exquisite paper stock. In 2009, the "Chinese Woodblock Printing Technique" inherited by Jinling Sutra Printing House, Yangzhou Guangling Ancient Book Printing Press and Sichuan Dege Sutra Printing Institute is inscribed on the *List of the Intangible Cultural Heritage of Humanity* of the UNESCO simultaneously.

Nanjing Jinling Sutra Printing House is the first privately-founded sutra publishing institute in modern times, which has integrated the functions of sutra collecting, engraving, printing, circulating and Buddhist study. It is not only the first sutra printing house founded in the late Qing Dynasty, but also the only sutra printing house existed in China. It not only completely preserves the ancient woodblock water print technique, but also collects large number of valuable Buddhist sutra blocks, such as 1,600 pieces of blocks for Huayan Sutra engraved in the 43rd–59th year of the Kangxi Period in the Qing Dynasty (1704–1720), which is an important physical materials for researching the status of sutra engraving in the southern Jiangsu in the early Qing Dynasty.

2.2   Jinling Woodblock Sutra Printing Technique

Jinling Woodblock Sutra Printing Skill is composed of three basic contents, such as cutting blocks, printing and binding (Fig. 1). There are over 20 procedures from writing sutra to engraving, including loading sample, engraving characters, brushing ink, scraping printing, paging, folding, aligning, classification, penetrating spill, line folding, etc.

Fig. 1. Basic Contents of Jinling Woodblock Sutra Printing Skill

Block cutting can be divided into three steps, including "writing sample", "loading sample" and "engraving". Wherein, Song typeface is adopted for "writing sample", which was taught by personal example as well as verbal instruction from master to apprentice and remembered with mind. There are six writing pithy formulas on writing sample, that is, "the horizontal stroke should be even, the vertical stroke should be straight, the dot should look like a melon seed, the left-falling stroke should look like a knife, the turning stroke should look like a Chinese Honey locust Spine and the right-falling stroke should look like a shovel". The powered ink used for writing samples is made from ash of burnt pine tree, flour, glue and vinegar. After the characters are written, selected Tangli wood (Tangli wood of Anhui is the best) will be cut into several sections and fire-cured in water for one day so as to remove the sugar in the wood and preventing damage by worms, and then being dried and trimmed. Soak the wood block with water and then cover it with paper. When the paper is half-dried, slightly rub the paper with fingers, the black ink characters will be shown on the wood blocks. This procedure is called "sample loading". The last procedure is "engraving". Character engraving is an important technical procedure in the whole printing process as well as a unique skill of Jinling Sutras Office. It has profound cultural and technical connotation. The engraver will firstly brush the wood block with a layer of vegetable oil, which will loose the wood and make it easy to engrave. The amount of oil usually depends on the experience of the engraver. Then the left and right sides of the characters will be engraved, and the pithy formula for that is "deep for left side and fast for right side".

Manual printing is adopted, which can be divided as flying print and pressing print (a small part is printed with machine). The printing by Jinling Sutras Office focuses on "application of ink should be even, with four angles being printed, and the fold line shall be black." The amount of ink will be increased or reduced according to the wearing status of the printing block. Generally speaking, more ink will be used for new block and less for old block. Brush made of palm pieces is used to evenly and smoothly print with hands with sufficient force. Different from other printing methods, the book layout printed with traditional methods is more elegant, beautiful and full of artistic quality compared with that made of movable-type printing. Compared with books printed with movable-type printing in the early period, the layout is more tidy, even, bright and clear; compared with modern printed books, the layout also has an artistic of manual skill. From the aspect of Buddhism, such layout is more peace, quiet and solemn.

Binding includes procedures, i.e. paging, folding, pinching aligning, bundling up and compaction, page aligning, string twists and turns, front cover and back cover pasting, page ordering, page cutting, drilling and binding, pasting title label, matching folding case, etc. Although the binding procedures look simple, it is in fact a complicated process. Only the procedure of paper twisting will usually need several months of training. To my surprise, in this simple and repeating printing work, the standards are as precise as modern printing equipment: the head margin shall be 2 cun and the lower margin shall be 1 cun, that is, the lower margin shall be 1/2 of the head margin. (The head margin is the upper part of the Buddhist sutras, and the lower margin is the lower part of the Buddhist sutras.) The precision of manual printing at Jinling Sutra Printing House is comparable to modern printing equipment (Fig. 2).

It is worth mentioning that in the whole process of woodblock printing, most of the tools are manufactured by the craftsmen, and the manufacturing methods are taught by the masters by personal example as well as verbal instruction.

After preliminary research, the writer finds that the aesthetic value embodied by manual engraving is the precious aspect of the Jinling Sutras Printing Skill as well as a shortage for the passing on of the woodblock printing art. For instance, the difficulty in cultivating professional talents, the accurate requests on one-time molding of engraving skills, the labor and time-consuming in product output efficiency, increasing space requirements on storage of woodblocks, technical requirements on long-term preservation of woodblocks (anti-damping, anti-moth, fire proofing) etc. Besides, there are only

Fig. 2. Procedures of Jinling Sutras Printing Skill

four masters and apprentices of three generations in Jinling Sutra Printing House, and two of whom are the only apprentices of their masters, talent training and technology inheritance are confronted with a great risk of uncertainty. Although woodblock printing plays an important role in the development and inheritance of China's traditional culture and artistry, it still has equally prominent technical limitations. Therefore, how to conduct effective and living research on such intangible cultural heritage and use digital technology for its comprehensive protection and inheritance in the digital times has become a particularly necessary proposition.

3   New Vision of Intangible Cultural Heritage in Digital Times

Digital protection refers to the protection of intangible cultural heritage based on digitization, which combines the science and technology with culture and use a series of digital and network technology to collect, save, analyze, process, display and communicate and turn the intangible cultural heritage into sharable and reproducible digital forms through multi-media and virtual reality techniques such as transition, representation, recovering, etc.

Nowadays, digital technology has played an important role in the protection of intangible cultural heritage, and the intangible cultural heritage could be displayed with sound image and technique of human, and becomes a "living" culture. As it were, the protection and inheritance of intangible culture heritage in the times of "internet +" is a new trend. However, there are also many difficulties to be overcome. For instance, digital data of intangible cultural heritage is mostly in the stage of simple filing, and it is hard to structure. Besides, due to the characteristics of intangible culture, the "flowage of human" and its living state, it is difficult to comprehensively display the innovation characteristics, changes in heart, aesthetic consciousness, etc. of the inheritor that takes human as the core.

In the past, the work on intangible cultural heritage mainly focused on "protection"; now, we need to consider the development of intangible cultural heritage under modern living methods; and in the future, we even need to consider how to avoid losing intangible cultural heritage as well as the new embodiment of its cultural value under the globalization context. Therefore, the writer proposes to withdraw the cultural gene and innovation index from the body of the intangible cultural context from the design aspect and carry out living state study and practice to intangible cultural heritage and attach importance to the innovation development of intangible cultural heritage in the digital times and under new production methods and living methods. It is a new vision and effort to transfer from protection to focusing on inheritance and innovation.

4 Living State Study and Practice on Intangible Cultural Heritage – Design and Development of Jinling Sutras Typeface

4.1 Withdrawing of Innovation Factor of Intangible Cultural Heritage – "Jinling Edition" and Jinling Sutras Typeface

Over the past year, the writer's team has deeply cooperated with the national-level inheritor Master MA Mengqing and the provincial-level inheritor Master DENG Qingzhi of woodblock printing intangible cultural heritage, and we deeply realized that aesthetic consciousness, living background as well as personal understanding to the professional techniques of the inheritors will directly promote the living evolvement of the intangible cultural heritage. Through our comprehensive research to Jinling Sutra Printing House, the writer finds that since the great aspiration of YANG Renshan to compile the Tripitaka is to make it easy to read and study, while, based on the problems such as the binding methods for ancient books and volumes are difficult to turnover the page, new typeface and ancient books and volumes are selected to adapt to the need of the times, and efforts are made to enhance the quality and the famous "Jinling Edition" was then created: "the paper quality of "Jinling Edition" is soft, the character is as large as a coin, the layout is clear, peace and solemn; the figure of the Buddha is engraved with delicate way of cutting, the composition is careful and precise, combining of form and sprit and with clear layer"; it has perfectly combined the traditional Chinese wood-block printing technique with the Buddhist culture and Buddhist art, forming a unique engraving printing style with religiousness, artistry, nature of cultural relics (Fig. 3).

The typeface adopted by Jinling Sutra Printing House is mutually created by the writer and the engraver, which is characterized by "the horizontal stroke being even, the vertical stroke being straight, the dot shaped like a melon seed, the left-falling stroke shaped like a knife, the turning stroke shaped like a Chinese Honey locust Spine and the right-falling stroke shaped like a shovel", which are more suitable for engraving. This typeface not only accelerates the speed of the engraver but also looks beautiful, neat and uniform. With the development of society, and the invasion of digitalization to the people's daily life, the writer finds that the Printing House is lacking of "sample writers" (In the early period of the Printing House, one writer shall work with sever engravers, from which we can see the importance of writer). At present, among these three generations of masters and apprentices, two of them are the only apprentices to their masters. Wherein, Master MA Mengqing mainly works on repairing ancient books, and only Master DENG Qingzhi can write samples. However, if it needs to cut new blocks, most of the time they will adopt the existing Xisong or Small Standard Song as the typeface. So the writer's team decides to start with the Song typeface in the "Jinling Edition", which embodies the style of peace, quiet and solemn and systematically tidy, to analyze,

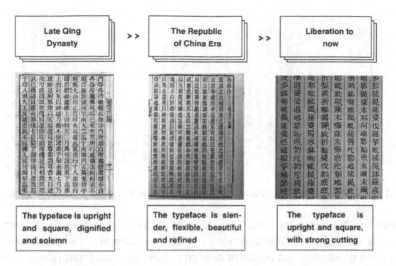

Fig. 3. Typeface style of Jinling edition in different historical periods

compare, withdraw and construct, and cooperate with Beijing Hanyi Fonts to develop the "Jinling Sutras Typeface" through mutual cooperation of "scientific research of universities and colleges – intangible cultural heritage inheritors of the Printing House – Font Enterprise". The original "peace, quiet and solemn" style Song typeface is the innovation factor of intangible cultural heritage withdrawn from "Jinling Edition", while the systematically development and design of the "Jinling Sutras" typeface is the solution to innovation design.

4.2 Innovation Practice that Drives the Intangible Cultural Heritage with Design – Design of "Jinling Sutras" Typeface

Selection of Block-Printed Edition – *Biography of Buddhism.* The key to the design of Jinling Sutras Typeface is the selection of model. Jinling Edition has experienced the practice of eight generations of inheritors in different periods. Each Buddhist Sutras has its own manual style and aesthetic feeling. Through four times of field investigations and several times of communication with the inheritor DENG Qingzhi, the writer finally selected the Biography of Buddhism as the research object. There are two reasons to select this book: firstly, the Biography of Buddhism was completed in the period of Lay Buddhist YANG Renshan, and it has greatly embodied the style and look of "Jinling Edition", with square and upright, elegant, peace, quiet and solemn typeface; this block-printed edition has not been circulated in the market for too many times, so it is well kept and can better display the original appearance of the engraved typeface, and reduce the wearing and mellow edges and angles of typeface caused by repetitive printing (Fig. 4).

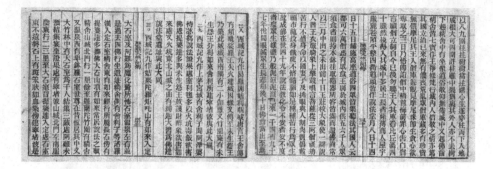

Fig. 4. Biography of Buddhism in the period of Lay Buddhist YANG Renshan

Depiction of Character Pattern. Depiction of pattern is a process of re-learning. In the process of computer depiction, we can feel the deep and fast engraving of the engraver and unadorned and power of handcraft from the rising and falling of strokes; characteristics of the strokes, radicals and font structures are summarized and extracted to sum up the styles and characteristics of the fonts. This is a process of re-engraving, although the tools are different, the purpose of this process is to restore the original form of the typeface to the most extent (Fig. 5).

Fig. 5. Depiction of character pattern

Determination of Styles and Analysis on Competitive Products. Re-engraving is not the results for design of Jinling Sutras Typeface. Through the depiction of over 200

characters, the writer's team has gradually extracted the style of the typeface: quiet and solemn, honest and unadorned. The design positioning is: fonts of main body.

Next, the writer's team has analyzed the developed competitive products in the market. A similar font is Yue Song, a square and upright Qing Dynasty block-printed edition, which takes the movable type block printed Chapters of the Four Books of Hall of Martial Valor as the source of creation. It pursues the beauty of primitive simplicity and nature, with slender font. The strokes can embody the artistic conception of writing while demonstrating the power of engraving, exercising a combination of inflexibility and yielding by combining the writing and engraving. The other font is the folk book engraving font in Zhejiang, which is a computer movable character font that reproduces the engraving fonts of ancient books. It adopts local block-printed edition of Zhejiang, with both thick and thin strokes and simulates the original block-printed characters, to keep the unique style of each character to the most extent while presenting consistent style (Fig. 6).

Fig. 6. Determination of style of Jinling Sutras Typeface and analysis on competitive products

The innovation factor – pattern and appearance of characters of Jinling Edition extracted from the world-level intangible culture heritage - China woodblock printing technique, what the writer needs to do is to carry out innovation design on the basis of maintaining its original nature and style. After systematically straightening single character and summarizing its design style, the writer has systematically designed the whole set fonts of 9,169 characters. In this process, the writer's team has deeply cooperated with Master DENG Qingzhi and experienced the understanding of the engravers to the characters from each stroke. The presentation of the inheritor's personal aesthetic consciousness in the process of the engraving is expressed and analyzed with design language. The importance of this process is to grasp the "living state evolvement" of the technique and the innovation characteristics, psychological changes and aesthetic consciousness of the inheritors that takes human as the core, and then, start from design and reflect and re-create it with design language.

Characteristics of Strokes. Except for maintaining the characteristics of "the horizontal stroke being even, the vertical stroke being straight, the dot shaped like a melon seed, the left-falling stroke shaped like a knife, the turning stroke shaped like a Chinese Honey locust Spine and the right-falling stroke shaped like a shovel" of original fonts of Jinling Edition, in the process of font evolvement in the development of the times, the aesthetic intention of modern engravers is analyzed to stretch and highlight the left-falling stroke, make the turning stroke look like the goose neck boom, and the round angles are protruded when dealing with details, thus the temperature of the handcraft is manifested. A 45° corner cut is adopted for the intersection of two lines, which can not only display the cutting trace but also avoid weakening of strokes in computer fonts (Fig. 7).

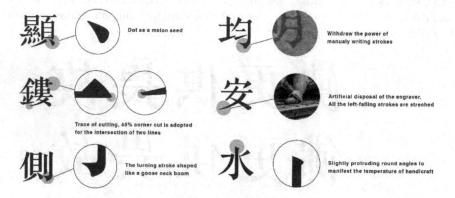

Fig. 7. Characteristics of strokes

Standards for Strokes and Radicals. Strokes and radicals are basic parts as well as the basic elements for font design. In the process of comparison and coordination, the strokes and radicals are gradually extracted, unified and standardized (Figs. 8 and 9).

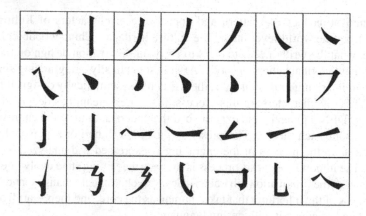

Fig. 8. Standards for design of strokes

Fig. 9. Standards for design of radicals

Analysis on Font Structure. Depiction of pattern is a process of re-learning. In the process of computer depiction, we can feel the deep and fast engraving of the engraver and unadorned and power of handcraft from the rising and falling of strokes; characteristics of the strokes, radicals and font structures are summarized and extracted to sum up the styles and characteristics of the fonts. This is a process of re-engraving, although the tools are different, the purpose of this process is to restore the original form of the typeface to the most extent (Fig. 10).

Fig. 10. Analysis on font structure

Presentation of Foundation Characters of Jinling Sutras Typeface. For woodblock engraving characters, the engravers will engrave the characters on the wood blocks, and the size of type face is flexible. The strokes are of different degree of weights and poorly standardized, which lead to a poor reading effect. However, at the same time, the alternation of words and avoidance among strokes will better remedy its shortcomings in reading effect. It is impossible to make the type face of printing fonts differ with the character pattern under existing technical conditions, and therefore, in the process of manufacturing, it is necessary to keep the characters of the same typeface, even stroke, standard and uniform style, and the type face frame is adopted to define the size of the characters and the body frame is adopted to define the distance between characters.

The writer's team has developed 9,169 characters in the past 10 months and formed a complete peace and solemn style "Jinling Sutra Typeface", which is the first step of practice; then, the digital presentation of Jinling woodblock printing technique and the APP production will make more people understand this world level intangible cultural heritage through network and digital platforms, so as to realize globally sharing of culture, and make the culture of China shared by the world; in the process, deep and careful interview and research are carried out on inheritors through pictorial records and book design, which have recorded the understanding, inspiration and living evolvement, etc. of the inheritors to Jinling Sutra technique in the past two years when we closely cooperate with the inheritors; finally, we have cooperated with the government departments to build and construct Jinling Sutra intangible brand, and let the innovation design enter the world combining with the city culture and image of Nanjing and through the platforms such as Nanjing Design Week, 100% Design London, Paris Design Week, New York Design Week, etc., so as to realize driving the innovation development of intangible culture with design, and further step forward from the protection layer to the inheritance and innovation layers to realize more social value of culture and produce economic value (Fig. 11).

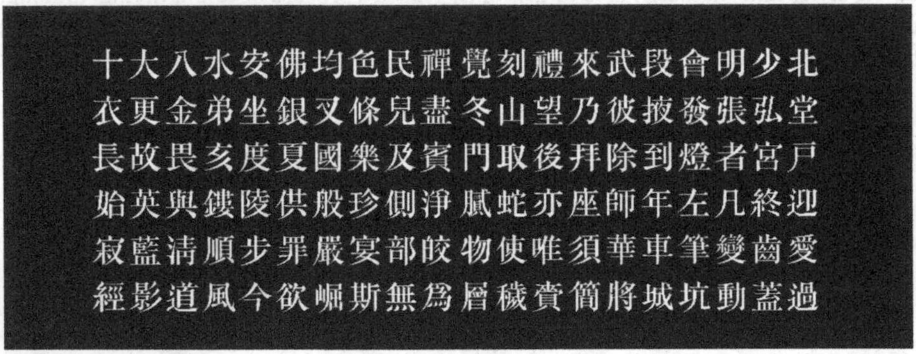

Fig. 11. Foundation words of Jinling Sutras Typeface

5   Approaches and Measures to Drive the Innovation Development of Intangible Cultural Heritage with Design

5.1   People-Oriented – Core of Living State Research

The characteristic of intangible cultural heritage is "intangible", that is, people-oriented living state cultural heritage. It takes people-oriented technique, experience and spirit as the core and is characterized by living evolvement. The "people" mentioned above refer to the inheritors of the intangible cultural heritage. With the transformation of the production and living methods and the changes of environment, their understanding to the technique will have the impression of the main body, and therefore, their mental activity, aesthetic consciousness, living experience, etc. shall be taken as the objects of research. Generally speaking, during the deep cooperation with the inheritors, we will usually find the innovation factor of intangible cultural heritage.

5.2 Withdrawing of Innovation Factor of Intangible Cultural Heritage – Key to Living State Research

It is important to protect the intangible cultural heritages, but it is more important to obtain the resources and motive power for innovation from the heritages, so as to provide materials, inspiration, etc. for our innovation. As it is said by Mr. FEI Xiaotong, "we need to study the seeds of our culture and how to maintain the seeds and meanwhile keep the healthy gene." For withdrawing of innovation factor of intangible culture, we need to withdraw the most distinct characteristics and deeply research the living experience, behaviors, sentiments, aesthetics of the inheritors according to the resources collected; consider the development of the intangible culture in existing living method; avoid the lost and change of intangible cultural heritage; integrate it with the culture combining with the new technology in the digital times; and seek the new embodiment of cultural value in the global context.

5.3 Driving the Innovative Development of Intangible Cultural Heritage with Design – Approaches and Measures for Living State Research

With the traditional perspective, one inspects the origins and development of things and concepts from the dimension of history in order to master the past and know better about the present. In the design thinking, the traditional perspective requires us to take in the wisdom from traditions, through traditional forms to observe the thinking mode, traditional culture, reading habits, living styles, traditional design ideas, craft skills and materials, and communication media, and to design based on it so as to enlighten the modern innovative design. Meanwhile, we need to make it clear that thinking with the traditional perspective is not to fully follow and conservatively copy traditions and transplant symbols, but to discard what has outlived its time and develop the new, to follow the tide of the times, and to explore the interaction between inheritance and innovation, nationalization and internationalization, traditional methods and modern science and technology based on the current living style, so as to revitalize the design.

From the aspect of evolution of human civilization, human has entered the knowledge and network age from the agrarian age and the industrial age, and the corresponding economic form has entered the knowledge and network economy to natural economy and market economy. In this evolution process, the design has always promoted the alteration production and living methods, indicated the degree of evolution of material civilization, and reflected the evolution level of spiritual civilization. The innovation development is driven by design and led with design thought (treat the intangible cultural heritage innovation problem with the "traditional and future perspective" of the complementary design thought); the living state evolvement of intangible cultural heritage as is taken as an research object; approaches and measures such as network platform, intangible cultural heritage products, experience service, publicizing channel, system construction, brand building, profit pattern, audience interaction, etc. are adopted to carry out systematic research; finally, through complicated innovation and design process, it is transformed to corresponding innovation design program of intangible cultural heritage.

5.4 Construction of a Sustainable Development Ecological System with Coordinately Developed "Inheritor- Intangible Cultural Heritage - Environment" that Takes Design as the Cohesion-Social Value of Living State Research

Nowadays, living evolvement is an important inheriting characteristic of the intangible cultural heritage of China. Therefore, the development of intangible heritage shall effectively enter the market and become a circulating commodity with high added value and cultural value, and soundly interact with the market and promote each other, so as to become the force and motive power that drive the development of social culture. Nowadays, mature market operation system is required to bring traditional cultural heritage into the modern lives, and it requires the participation and cooperation of parties such as proper artists, designers, craftsmen, research institute of college and universities, enterprises, governments, etc., and it needs to be connected to proper commercial platforms. It needs to select proper moment to carry out media release and market transmission to build a mature intangible cultural heritage. On the basis of maintaining the original pattern and vision characteristics of intangible handicraft, we should adopt modern aesthetic consciousness and lifestyle to carry out cross-field innovation design for intangible handicrafts, so as to inject innovative products with traditional aesthetic and process features for modern life.

6 Conclusion

In conclusion, the writer's team takes Jinling Sutra Printing House as an example to carry out living state research on intangible cultural heritage in the digital times, and explore the "innovation factor" of intangible culture based on people-oriented theory. We propose to drive the innovative development of intangible cultural heritage with design, and construct the sustainable development ecological system of "inheritor – intangible cultural heritage - environment". It has provided effective application methods for national intangible cultural heritage in the new era, created more social value, cultural value, even economic value.

Acknowledgements. The authors are grateful for the financial support provided by "the Fundamental Research Funds for the Central Universities". (No. 30915013107).

References

1. Liu, W.: Jinling Sutra Printing Technique. Nanjing Publishing House (2012)
2. Song, J.: Research on Protection of Intangible Cultural Heritage. Sun Yat-Sen University Press, Zhongshan (2013)
3. Wang, X.: Ten Years for Protection of Intangible Cultural Heritage of China. Intellectual Property Right Press, Beijing (2015)
4. Song, J.: Report on Protection and Development of Intangible Cultural Heritage of China (2015). Social Science Academic Press, Beijing (2015)
5. Wu, B.: Theory and Methods for Protection of Intangible Cultural Heritage. Culture and Art Publishing House, Hong Kong (2016)
6. Shen, F.: Yuanli – YANG Renshan and Jinling Sutra Printing House. Phoenix Fine Arts Publishing LTD, Nanjing (2016)
7. Lu, C.: Research on Key Problems on Protection and Inheritance of Intangible Cultural Heritage of China in New Trend. China Social Science Press, Beijing (2017)
8. Wang, L., Wan, B.: Intangible Cultural Heritage of Nanjing in Different Periods. Nanjing Publishing House, Nanjing (2016)
9. Yang, H.: Leading Edge for Displaying and Transmission of Intangible Cultural Heritage. Tsinghua University Press, Beijing (2017)
10. Zhang, Z., Qi, R., Shu, H.: Research on Social Power in the Field of Protection of Intangible Cultural Heritage. China Social Science Press, Beijing (2017)
11. Xiao, Y., Chai, L.: Report on Development of Intangible Cultural Heritage of China's Ethnic Minority. China Social Science Press, Beijing (2017)

Formation and Influence of New Media Art Form in Public Space

Lili Zhang[1(✉)] and Yunqiao Su[2]

[1] University of Jinan College of Fine Arts, No. 336, Nanxinzhuang West Road,
Shizhong District, Jinan, People's Republic of China
Cuiweiwei1976@126.com
[2] Shandong College of Arts and Design, No. 1255, College Road,
Changqing District, Jinan, People's Republic of China
630492407@qq.com

Abstract. The unique interactive form of new media art has a subversive influence on design practice and aesthetic perception of public space. Presently, it is an effective way to communicate with the public applying the new media technology as a means of expression. The diversity of new media arts, the diversified interaction modes and interactive forms blend together art and life, thereby achieving the ideals state of "poetic dwelling".

Keywords: New media art · Public space · Interaction

1 Introduction

The pursuit of a better living environment has never ceased from the beginning of human civilization.

The famous environmentalist Sigurd Olsen once said: "If we can move to a vast and open land, where we can enjoy the convenience of modern life while not losing the spiritual dream that we've been long pursuing about from the old times. Then we've made it!" This peaceful and ideal state with the harmonious of natural and human, and the connection with natural world is people's pursuit. Holderlin once heckleda: in this whole world, what is the scale? Heidegger replied: When people are dwelling in peace, the earth will become the earth. "Man, dwells poetically on the earth" – Heidegger particularly fond of Holderlin's poem, for it reveals the depth and elegance of life [1].

Heidegger believed that people should explore the truth through art. He said: "The art essence that all art works and artists are based upon is the integration of truth in the works… Art opens a vast land among people, where everything exists in an extraordinary manner". The natural artistic life he had envisioned was no longer out of reach due to the development of science and technology. New media art forms, especially the rapid updating of digital technologies, the integration of technology and art have transformed interpersonal communication into three-dimensional and multi-dimensional man-machine interaction, and people's lifestyles have also changed quietly. Popular art

© Springer International Publishing AG, part of Springer Nature 2018
A. Marcus and W. Wang (Eds.): DUXU 2018, LNCS 10920, pp. 550–560, 2018.
https://doi.org/10.1007/978-3-319-91806-8_43

aesthetic, social experience interaction, application and perception have been integrated into the city's public space. As a result, new media art has also gradually developed toward the trend of "audience emancipation". For example, give up the concept of "exhibitions" and "artworks", encourage the routinization of art, and break the inherent notion that "artworks" are created by artists and exhibited in museums. The role of the general public has been smoothly transformed from the "objective examination of art" into "subjective participation".

2   The Source of New Media Art Concept in Public Space

Public space concept of new media art's connotation and aesthetics can be traced back very early. Every progress of science and technology in human society provides an opportunity for the development of new horizons and concepts of art. Such as photography gave birth to "technical aesthetics"; movies and animation pioneered the "world of art"; machinery and power inspired the "installation art"; television and video bred "video art" and so on. Whenever the new technology emerges or matures, a variety of art schools and new concepts of aesthetics will come into being. The development of new media art is almost a history of modern science and technology.

The breeding ground for new media art is closely related to the "aesthetic" design needs of industrial and information products. From the late 19th century to the early 20th century, the development of science and industry made the functional changes of traditional arts such as painting and sculpture form three independent art states, that is, modern art, video art and design art. The three infiltrate each other and have formed a new art centering interaction and penetration. At the same time of deconstruction of western classical aesthetics, the postmodernist thinking gradually formed and constantly set off the impact on traditional aesthetic concepts. The latter reached its peak in the 1960s. As a result, the new media art centering on "aesthetic appreciation of life" and "popularization of art" come into being. Since the 1950s, various art movements such as power and light effects art, video installation technology, digital synthesis technology were expanded into urban spaces, and the creation of artists revitalized the city; such as the "Ballet of Light" and "Sky Art" (Fig. 1) created by Otto Piene from German, and the "Art of Earth" created by Christo and Jeanne Claude (Fig. 2). They built a new relationship between art and nature, turning nature into a creative artist. With its unique entity digital display and interactive means, the audiences are immersed in the art world, of which the reality and the virtual world are hard to distinguish; the interaction of real space and virtual space can deliver a unique experience of artistic visual effects, which greatly promoted the development of new media art in public space.

Fig. 1. "Ballet of Light" and "Sky Rainbow" from Otto Piene

Fig. 1. (*continued*)

3 Integration and Convergence of New Media Art and Technology; Jointly Create the Public Space of Multiple-Sense Experience

Public space and new media art have the social attributes of "interaction" and "communication", while also sharing the spirit that "art and culture shall serve the society." The diversity and multi-elements of new media art have enriched the composition of public space. Firstly, the art form of new media is based on the artistic expression of the comprehensive presentation of digital technologies. During the process of communication, the information is exchanged and updated in real time to effectively communicate and exchanges between the works of art and the audience, wherein the presentation of details and sensory experience are attached great importance. Secondly, the new media art actively utilizes various we-media, the Internet and so forth to actively participate in mass culture, which, to a certain extent, eliminates the boundary between the communicator and the audience.

The manifestations of new media art in public space mostly artistically interpret the material elements, which have been consumed or not yet touched in daily life, in a specific space-time environment. It focuses on field atmosphere and cultural environment. The audience can take part of it and become the environmental carrier that promote the information exchange and transmit the dynamic messages between individual information and public information,

Fig. 2. "Pack up the New German Parliament" from Christo and Jeanne Claude

3.1 Spatial Intersection and New Sensory Experience

New media technology brings about more changes in terms of the extension and expansion of creative space. From the formation of ideal graphics and colors, to the reconstruction of the most basic design elements, ideas are expressed with dual language of art and technology, so as to achieve "man-machine communication"; and the changes brought to urban public space is the breakthrough of time and space, as well as multi-dimensional sensory experience. The emergence of new experiences and new horizons promotes the diversified development of new media art forms in public spaces. Meanwhile, the dissemination of new media arts in public spaces also guides the public's aesthetic taste and aesthetic requirements. The "virtual" environment is in sync with the sense of "reality". This new cognitive experience turns the public from a passive receiver to an active participant, so that the artwork can be changed and recreated. Audiences are no longer passively onlookers, but are key elements that trigger the work to come into effect, or directly act as a part of the work.

3.2 The Dual Characteristics of Art and Technology Reflected

First of all, the lead of art is the dominance and core of technology realization. The concept and creativity of new media art in public space stems from the subjective accomplishments of creators and participants, which includes the creators and participants' view to beauty and ugliness in the objective world, and the expression of aesthetic values. Secondly, technology is a tool that conveys artistic ideas. The progress and development of technology bring a brand new space of thinking in terms of artistic form, creation, aesthetics, design means and eventually visual communication effect of public space's new media art. When it comes to the forms of manifestations, traditional art, artistic means of computer virtual technology, and all material media can become the constituent elements of the new media art form in public space, and further serve as the way for creators and the public to interact with each other and participate in aesthetic.

3.3 People Interact More Frequently with the System

Compared with the one-way information transmission of traditional media, the transmission, feedback, collision, integration and stimulation of new media art and multi-dimensional two-way information make it easier to form "exchange and interactive" content in public space. Such as The Cloud, a large-scale interactive installation created by Caitlind r.c. Brown in 2014, which is publicly displayed in the first White Night festival in Calgary, consists of 6,000 new or old Light bulbs. The creator collects local burn-out incandescent bulbs from homes, businesses, museums and eco-stations. Numerous bulbs make up a huge set of clouds and each light bulb is fitted with a pull string that enables the viewer control the lighting of the bulb cloud. The viewer interacts with the work through an impromptu pull switch, allowing him to interact as an individual in the installation art. And Maurice Benayoun's The Tunnel under the Atlantic, a virtual reality interactive device that connects hundreds of thousands of miles between Paris and Montreal, letting hundreds of people to meet through the device. The works look like pipes protruding from ground, reminiscent of the real tunnel that lies in the bottom of the ocean (Fig. 3).

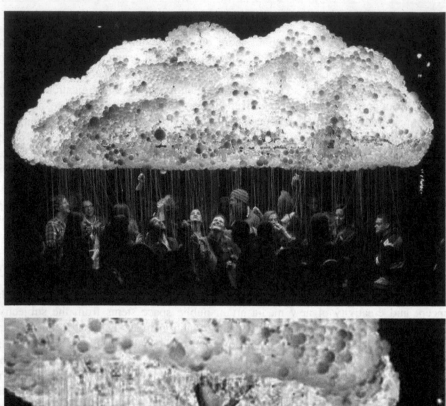

Fig. 3. Caitlind r.c. Brown's "cloud"

These interactive installation works fully embody the design of human "interaction" in complex systems. The "interaction" of new media art in public space not only focuses on the form and content, but also is an "interactive" behavior design (Fig. 4).

Fig. 4. Maurice Benayoun's The Tunnel under the Atlanti

Fig. 4. (*continued*)

4   Visual Language Expansion of New Media Art; Public Space Highlights Cultural Identity

The interactive forms and interactive behaviors brought about by the innovation and application of diversity of new media arts and technologies are visually closer to the public. In the sociological sense, public space has publicity and public domain attributes, and all kinds of new media art works are also social and cultural image representations. The new media art, to a large extent, influences or even constructs the dwelling environment of public space through its interactive form, which directly narrows the distance between art culture and life, and thus influencing and molding the city's personality and space atmosphere. At the same time, the artist's and designer's actions have virtually reinforced the city's activation [2].

The essence of art includes reveals the aesthetic relationship between man and society. The conceptual expansion and adjustment are also an important aspect of the interaction between the new media art form and the public space. Firstly, compared with traditional art, the form of new media art, and the realization of its interaction and virtual technology allow more aesthetic experience into life, so that the public environment and space are of better coordination and cohesion. Secondly, public space is the main venue for the general public to participate in social activities. The new media art form's interactive and easily disseminated features are effective means and platforms of cultivating the public to strengthen communication, to exchange and to actively participate in social activities. Affected by the regional culture of space, art works usually contain specific humanistic information. Audiences unconsciously use the unique geographical vision and life experience as the basis for judgment. New media art works are no exception [3]. Another example is Beggar Robot 2.0: A Robot for the Materially Deprived in Tokyo, a new media art project completed by the IAMAS (Institute of Advanced Media and Science) Deprived in Tokyo) is a beggar robot consisting of vintage electronic components and computer accessories. It can beg passers-by in the streets and put various facial expressions. Arguably, this robot is a messenger that conveys the message that the world is getting poorer instead of wealthier. The works, which were displayed on the streets of Slovenia and Tokyo, received feedback that when the exchange through begging was at a safe distance or via an electronic interface, the well-off group in the society shows more sympathy for the marginalized and disadvantaged [4].

Another example is the work "FLICK_KA", which is one of the interactive installation works collected by the media museum of Zentrum für Kunst und Medientechnologie in Karlsruhe, German. It is an art project based on photo sharing portal. Visitors can create their own portrait photos at ZKM's installed Photo Booth and add it to the FLICK_KA internet platform. As part of the ZKM's data collection, user portraits are updated every second and permanently displayed in the gallery space via large-scale projection on the web. The work presents the details of the portrait, thereby expressing the moral meaning of citizens' equal use of image communication. This work commemorates the 20th anniversary of liberal photography and invites all the citizens of Karlsruhe were invited.

In view of this, it can be seen that the new media art form in public space has gradually become an indispensable art form in modern life, allowing the public to gain more perceptual pleasure on the basis of material environment. Through the cultural care and distinctive public space created by the new media art, a brand new cultural interpretation and expansion to urban life are displayed, so as to integrate and generate more meaningful and valuable forms of new media art. It also makes people look forward to the cultural language developed on the basis of their combination. While using special artistic language to demonstrate the space environment and humanities concept, the new media art form of public space should attach more importance to the innovation of design forms and pay attention to and study the interactive ideology of social aesthetic and culture.

5   Conclusion

For thousands of years, artists have been using brushes to depict the natural world in their eyes. Whether it is the gorgeousness and idealism of the classical period or the romanticism and lyricism of Impressionism, the natural world has always been the source of inspiration for the artists. In the era of new media, nature is no longer the object of art, but the creator of art. And public space is an excellent vehicle for new media art. Public space and new media art have great potential in design and practice. With the change and progress of the society, new media art in public space will derive more vivid and diversified art forms. It not only enriches the visual culture, aesthetics concept, and public life, but also enables the public to set up convenient channels between artistic appreciation and daily life, so as to blend art in life, thereby realize the joyful and aesthetic "Poetic Dwelling" that people's been dreaming about.

References

1. Zhang, L.: Landscape Architecture in Jinan, China from the Perspective of Chinese Garden Aesthetics. Tianjin University, Tianjin (2017)
2. Chen, L.: Outline of New Media Art. Tsinghua University Press, Beijing (2007)
3. Bradley, W., Escher, C.: Art and Social Change: A Critical Reader. Tate: Publishing in association with Afterall, London (2007)
4. Wang, L.: Overview of New Media Art Development. Tongji University Press, Shanghai (2009)

DUXU Case Studies

Compliance with Static vs. Dynamic Warnings in Workplaces such as Warehouses: A Study Using Virtual Reality

Ana Almeida[1,2,3(✉)], Francisco Rebelo[1,2(✉)], and Paulo Noriega[1,2(✉)]

[1] Faculdade de Arquitetura, Centro de Investigação em Arquitetura, Urbanismo e Design, Universidade de Lisboa, Rua Sá Nogueira, Pólo Universitário, Alto da Ajuda, Lisbon, Portugal
almalmeida01@gmail.com
[2] Faculdade de Motricidade Humana, Laboratório de Ergonomia, Universidade de Lisboa, Estrada da Costa – Cruz Quebrada, Lisbon, Portugal
[3] CAPES Foundation, Ministry of Education of Brazil, Brasília – DF, 70040-020, Brazil

Abstract. The static nature of traditional warnings cannot always capture the user's attention. The effectiveness of a warning refers to the way in which it prompts the user to engage in safe behavior. It is known that behavioral compliance is the "golden measure" for evaluating the effectiveness of a warning. Several studies have shown that traditional warnings are not effective in an emergency. Several researches indicate that dynamic safety warnings are more effective than static ones. However, these studies are mostly in critical situations such as emergency evacuations. Literature is not clear about the existence of research on warnings in warehouse operating environments. However, it is known that warehouses are environments where employees often work under pressure and are often involved in accidents. This study objective was to compare the effectiveness of static safety warnings with dynamic ones. This kind of study in real-life is a difficult issue. So, we used an immersive virtual environment for this purpose. Virtual Reality (VR) can be assumed as the most adequate methodology to use in this context, as it overcomes methodological, financial and ethical limitations. Fourteen volunteers participated in the experience. Main results confirmed that dynamic warnings produce greater behavioral compliance even in less dynamic situations such as workplaces such warehouses .

Keywords: Warnings · Virtual reality · Warehouse

1 Introduction

Safety warnings are communication tools that are intended to inform people of hazards in the environment or in products. For a warning to achieve its purpose it is essential that it is effective. If the warning is effective, it leads the user to adopt a safe behavior [1]. Literature shows some characteristics that the warning must present to be effective, such as the presentation type. Consistent findings indicate that static warnings produce less compliance than dynamic warnings [2–5], namely in emergency situations [6–8]. However, there is a near absence of studies in less dynamic situations such as daily work

© Springer International Publishing AG, part of Springer Nature 2018
A. Marcus and W. Wang (Eds.): DUXU 2018, LNCS 10920, pp. 563–572, 2018.
https://doi.org/10.1007/978-3-319-91806-8_44

in warehouses. Thus, this work aims to compare the effectiveness of static vs. dynamic safety warnings in workplaces such as warehouses.

A warehouse is a commercial building used by companies for storage of goods and raw materials. Activities in a warehouse generally include goods loading and unloading, where you can easily identify several risks that can cause great damage. Some risks to which workers are exposed include: (1) Fall of goods, collapse of structures; (2) Vehicles movement on the environment; (3) Electrical hazards; (4) Adverse thermal environments; (5) Hazardous substances handling; (6) Fall on same level [9–14].

1.1 Warnings Effectiveness Evaluation

The occurrence of safe behavior is the primary measure that a warning works. Therefore, measuring behavior is critical to determining whether a warning is effective and contributes to safety and change user's attitude [15]. However, this kind of study may involve high risks and costs [16, 17] because:

- Participants should not be exposed to real risks due to ethical and safety issues;
- In a real scenario dangerous events are rare and unpredictable;
- Developing a scenario where there is a danger that looks real, but at the same time is safe, requires high financial costs, time and effort.

A solution to these limitations is the use of virtual reality (VR), because it allows the simulation of almost real critical situations, without exposing the participant to real risks. The creation of a virtual environment enables the repetition of the experience, as many times as necessary and the manipulation of the characteristics of the environment without so great financial and time costs.

VR is an advanced computer interface that involves real-time simulation where the user can interact, view and manipulate objects in a three-dimensional virtual environment. It creates in the user the illusion of being in an environment even though not physically present [18, 19]. It allows users to examine from different angles, three-dimensional spaces using three unique features of the VR, the so-called three "I's": Imagination, Interaction and Immersion [20].

- Imagination – is related to involvement, meaning the degree of motivation for the engagement of a person with a certain activity. This involvement can be passive, where there is only the exploitation of the environment; or active, where there is environment interaction.
- Interaction – or manipulation, which is the system's ability to detect user input and respond to its real time commands.
- Immersion – is the feeling of being inside the virtual environment.

Thus, the present paper aims to compare the effectiveness of static vs. dynamic safety warnings in warehouses using VR.

2   Method

The objective of this study was to compare the effectiveness of static vs. dynamic safety warnings. This variable was measured by participant behavior observation during the simulation, if he/she had a compliance behavior when faced to static or dynamic warnings.

2.1   Participants

Fourteen volunteers participated in this study, ranging from 18 to 34 years old (M = 22.3; SD = 4.2), eight females and six males.

2.2   Apparatus

Tasks were performed on a Desktop Station with an Intel[R] Core[TM]i7 – 4790 K CPU processor, 8 GB, NVIDIA GeForce GTX 980 video card. Virtual environment interaction was performed using a gamepad, Head Mounted Display (HMD), model DKII, OCULUS Rift (OLED display, resolution 960 X 1080 per eye, 100° field of view) and wireless PHILIPS earphones, model SHC5102/10.

2.3   Virtual Environment

The VE was created according to a desired workplace context. The prototype consisted of a reception room and eight warehouses (Fig. 1). In four of the warehouses there were warnings that were developed in consonance with the ANSI Z535.2 [21] standards, with respect to signal word, color, use of a pictogram and hazard nature, consequences and actions messages. Additionally, the location of the warning was also taken into consideration. Based on previous studies [22], the warning was placed in an uncluttered site

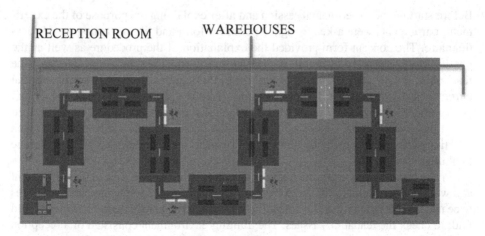

Fig. 1. VE floor plan

and within the individual's field of view. Regarding the environmental modeling, the 3D 4.3 software Unity was used.

2.4 The Warnings

The warnings used in this study (Fig. 2) considered the common risks found in warehouses and the possibility of being deployed in the developed virtual environment. The four warnings used in the experiment were related to the risks: fall of goods, fall on the same level, vehicles movement and hazardous substances. Dynamic (visual) warnings consisted of the same messages surrounded by flashing lights.

Fig. 2. Warnings used in the experiment: (1) Warning! Falling objects, serious injury, go down corridor C; (2) Caution! Wet floor, may result in injury, go down corridor B; (3) Warning! Truck traffic, danger of being hit, wait for the green light; (4) Danger! Toxic substances, danger of contamination, mandatory use of safety equipment. (Color figure online)

2.5 Procedure

Before starting the experimental session and after explaining the purpose of the experiment, participants were asked to sign the consent form and fill the demographic questionnaire. The consent form provided the explanation of the procedure as well as the possibility of risks and discomfort, such as nausea, during the simulation, and stated the feasibility of quit the experience at any time. Participants were unaware of the real purpose of the experiment, it was only said that the aim was to evaluate the virtual environment for recording human behavior data. The experimental session was divided into 3 parts: (1) training session; (2) VR simulation session and (3) response to some questionnaires, among them the Simulator Sickness Questionnaire (SSQ). The average total time was 30 min.

In the training session, participants were invited to explore a virtual environment and walk through rooms and corridors. They were introduced to the interaction devices to be used and the training session began. They were asked to read the posters they would find, to check the readability issues. The training environment consisted of a reception room and two storage rooms. At the reception was posted a placard with instructions on handling the navigation device in the virtual environment. Six more placards were added, along the warehouses, with instructions of directions to be followed by the participants. In the last warehouse, a trigger-activated script was used to display a message board with a positive or negative feedback depending on the behavior of the participant. In Fig. 3 it is possible to observe the location of the placards. Once the participants stated that they felt comfortable to continue with the experience, they should begin the experimental session.

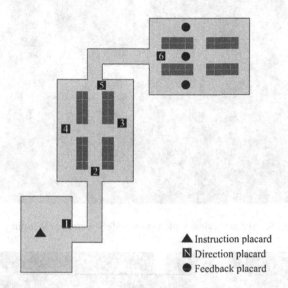

Fig. 3. Location of the placards in the training environment

The experimental session began in the reception room where the participant received information, through the headphones, about tasks that would be performed during the

Fig. 4. Scenario view with a static safety warning (Warning 1)

simulation (Fig. 4). This communication was activated by the investigator through the keyboard. In each warehouse the participant was asked to execute a type of task (i.e., go to the left corridor and say how many units a given box had) (Fig. 5). As they performed the tasks they received new tasks until the simulation was complete (Fig. 6). In the figures below, you can see the warehouses and the location of the warnings (Fig. 7).

Fig. 5. Scenario view with a static safety warning (Warning 2)

Fig. 6. Scenario view with a static safety warning (Warning 3)

Fig. 7. Scenario view with a dynamic safety warning (Warning 4)

2.6 Experimental Design

We used a between subject design for the warning type. Five participants made the procedure with the static warning (3 male and 2 female) and nine (3 male and 6 female) was used in the dynamic warning condition.

3 Results

It is possible to verify in Table 1 and Fig. 8, the results of the behavioral compliance with static and dynamic safety warnings.

Table 1. Behavioral compliance with warnings.

	Static	Dynamic
Warning 1	0%	66,7%
Warning 2	20%	77,8%
Warning 3	20%	77,8%
Warning 4	20%	77,8%

Table shows that the behavioral compliance with the static safety warnings rate was low, on the other hand, dynamic warnings produced high rate levels of compliance (Fig. 8). This result can be justified by the type of warning. According to Duarte and colleagues [7], static warnings may not be effective when they are inserted in contexts where users are involved in complex tasks. In these cases, the use of dynamic warnings produced a greater behavioral compliance.

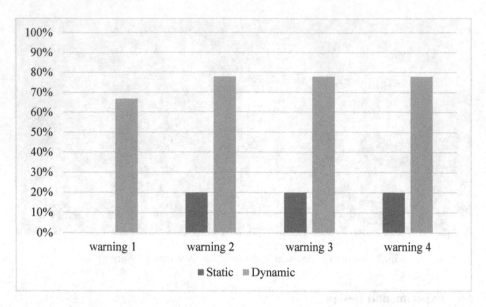

Fig. 8. Behavioral compliance in % for static vs. dynamic safety warnings

4 Discussion and Conclusions

The present paper aimed to compare the effectiveness of static vs. dynamic safety warnings in warehouses using VR. Thus, it was possible to observe that the static warnings were not sufficiently robust to change or influence the behavior of the individual. It is known that the static nature of traditional warnings cannot always capture the user's attention. In this sense, technology-based warnings can compensate for this limitation. Wogalter e Conzola [23], describe some ways in which technology can improve the effectiveness of warnings. Technology can be used to tailor the presentation of warnings to particular groups or individuals. Studies show that the compliance rate increases when the information is directed to the individual through a personalized warning, with the name of the participant [4, 24].

The technology can help to present a warning at a time when it is necessary through the use of sensors to detect the presence of people or a danger [25]. In addition, the technology facilitates the development of dynamic warnings, which in contrast to static warnings, allow the flexibility of changes in physical characteristics as well as in the content of the displayed messages, thus reducing the effects of habituation. According to Laughery e Wogalter [26], people's perceptual and cognitive systems are less attuned to non-changing stimuli. For example, in emergency situations static warnings are not enough to direct people to a safe place [6], on the other hand, when the warning is presented dynamically, it captures attention, raises the consonance rate, helps and increases the speed of the evacuation process [7, 8].

A limitation in this study could be sample dimension, however, as the results are very robust with such few sample, for ethical reason of not disturb unnecessarily participants we opt to stop the study with only this sample.

Later in future researches, it will be necessary to teste the robustness of dynamic warning with more work demanding conditions such as the simultaneous task execution and the compliance with warnings.

Acknowledgements. This work was supported by grants BEX 0660-13/2 to Ana Almeida from CAPES Foundation Ministry of Education of Brazil and CIAUD Research Center from School of Architecture from Universidade de Lisboa through Portuguese Foundation of Science and Technology (FCT).

References

1. Ayres, T.J.: Evaluation of warning effectiveness. In: Karwowski, W. (ed.) International Encyclopedia of Ergonomics and Human Factors, 2nd edn, pp. 1094–1097. Taylor & Francis, Abingdon (2006)
2. Schall, D.L., Doll, D., Mohnen, A.: Caution! warnings as a useless countermeasure to reduce overconfidence? An experimental evaluation in light of enhanced and dynamic warning designs. J. Behav. Decis. Mak. **30**(2), 347–358 (2017)
3. Wogalter, M.S., Laughery, K.R., Mayhorn, C.: Warnings and hazard communications. In: Handbook of Human Factors and Ergonomics, 4th edn, pp. 868–894 (2012)
4. Duarte, E., Rebelo, F., Teles, J., Wogalter, M.S.: A personalized speech warning facilitates compliance in an immersive virtual environment. In: Proceedings of the Human Factors and Ergonomics Society Annual Meeting, vol. 56, no. 1, pp. 2045–2049 (2012)
5. Wogalter, M.S.: Technology will revolutionize warnings. In: Proceedings of the Solutions in Safety through Technology Symposium (2006)
6. Vilar, E.D.P.: Using virtual reality to study the influence of environmental variables to enhance wayfinding within complex buildings. Universidade Técnica de Lisboa (2012)
7. Duarte, E., Rebelo, F., Teles, J., Wogalter, M.S.: Behavioral compliance for dynamic versus static signs in an immersive virtual environment. Appl. Ergon. **45**(5), 1367–1375 (2014)
8. Langner, N., Kray, C.: Assessing the impact of dynamic public signage on mass evacuation. In: Proceeding of the International Symposium on Pervasive Displays - PerDis 2014, pp. 136–141 (2014)
9. Coutinho, C.F.G.: Identificação de perigos e avaliação de riscos num armazém. Escola Superior de Tecnologia do Instituto Politécnico de Setúbal, 22 October 2014
10. Matos, J.: 5 Most Overlooked Warehouse Hazards. http://www.reliableplant.com/Articles/Print/29933. Accessed 07 Jan 2016
11. G. of Ontario: Fact Sheet: Warehouse Hazards
12. OSHA: OSHA Pocket Guide - Worker Safety Series Warehousing - Supply Chain 24/7 Paper. http://www.supplychain247.com/paper/osha_pocket_guide_worker_safety_series_warehousing/osha. Accessed 07 Jan 2016
13. Portal Empresarial da Maia: Riscos e perigos comuns em armazéns — Portal Empresarial da Maia. http://negocios.maiadigital.pt/hst/sector_actividade/armazenagem/riscos_armazenagem/riscos_armazenagens. Accessed 07 Jan 2016
14. Segurança Online: Segurança Online. http://www.segurancaonline.com/gca/?id=1045. Accessed 07 Jan 2016

15. Adams, A.S.: Warning design. In: Karwowski, W. (ed.) EdInternational Encyclopedia of Ergonomics and Human Factors, vol. 3, 2nd edn, pp. 1517–1520. Taylor & Francis, Abingdon (2006)
16. Duarte, E., Rebelo, F., Teixeira, L.: Warnings research methods: where are we now and where are we headed? In: Proceeding of the 5th UNIDCOM/IADE International Conference - "40 IADE 40, from 1969 to 2049", 1–3 october 2009, Lisbon, Portugal, pp. 414–422 (2009)
17. Wogalter, M.S., Laughery, K.R.: Warnings. In: Karwowski, W. (ed.) International Encyclopedia of Ergonomics and Human Factors, 2nd edn, pp. 1367–1373. Taylor & Francis, Abingdon (2006)
18. Gutiérrez, M.A.A., Vexo, F., Thalmann, D.: Stepping into Virtual Reality. Springer, London (2008). https://doi.org/10.1007/978-1-84800-117-6
19. Rebelo, M., Duarte, F., Noriega, E., Soares, P.: Virtual reality in consumer product design: methods and applications. In: Karwowski, N., Soares, W., Stanton, M. (eds.) Handbook of Human Factors and Ergonomics in Consumer Product Design: Methods and Techniques, pp. 381–402. CRC Press, Boca Raton (2011)
20. Burdea, G., Coiffet, P.: Virtual Reality Technology. Presence Teleoper. Virtual Environ. 12(6), 663–664 (2003)
21. American National Standards Institute: American National Standard for Environmental and Facility Safety Signs. ANSI Z535.2: 2011. National Electrical Manufacturers Association, Rosslyn (2011)
22. Duarte, E.M.C.: Using Virtual Reality to Assess Behavioral Compliance with Warnings. Universidade Técnica de Lisboa (2011)
23. Wogalter, M.S., Conzola, V.C.: Using technology to facilitate the design and delivery of warnings. Int. J. Syst. Sci. 33(6), 461–466 (2002)
24. Wogalter, M.S., Racicot, B.M., Kalsher, M.J., Noel Simpson, S.: Personalization of warning signs: the role of perceived relevance on behavioral compliance. Int. J. Ind. Ergon. 14(3), 233–242 (1994)
25. Wogalter, M.S., Kalsher, M.J., Racicot, B.M.: Behavioral compliance with warnings: effects of voice, context, and location. Saf. Sci. 16(5), 637–654 (1993)
26. Laughery, K.R., Wogalter, M.S.: Designing Effective Warnings. Rev. Hum. Factors Ergon. 2(1), 241–271 (2006)

Blue-Collars/Tough Designs: UX Within Fire Service Occupational Safety and Health Programs

Timothy R. Amidon[✉] and Tiffany Lipsey

Colorado State University, Fort Collins, CO 80521, USA
{tim.amidon,tiffany.lipsey}@colostate.edu

Abstract. We discuss a set of ongoing participatory design projects where participants are working to adapt a physiological monitoring prototype for use within the fire service. These projects include members of the fire service community, the director of a comprehensive firefighter medical and fitness program called the Firefighter Testing Program (FTP) located in the Human Performance Clinical Research Laboratory (HPCRL) at Colorado State University (CSU), a user-experience researcher, and a team of developers. The original AvidCor prototype (AC-1) is an affordable physiological monitor that pairs with a smartphone, allowing a user to independently record data about their electro-cardiogram (EKG), pulse oximetry, and body temperature. The purpose of one of these participatory design projects is to identify barriers and envision opportunities where the AC-1 prototype and smart-phone app could be used to increase firefighters' access to information and care that can be used to manage cardio-vascular risk. Similarly, the purpose of the second project is to develop and test a second prototype, the AvidCor Fire-ground (AC-FG), capable of streaming real-time information about firefighters' physiological performance which can enrich the types of decisions making processes that EMS professionals, firefighters, fire officers, and incident commanders engage in while operating within hazardous work environments.

Keywords: Community-based research · Occupational safety and health
Participatory design

1 Introduction

Fire service organizations such as the National Fallen Firefighters Foundation (NFFF), the United States Fire Administration (USFA), International Association of Fire Chiefs (IAFC), International Association of Fire Fighters (IAFF), National Volunteer Fire Council (NVFC), and National Fire Protection Agency (NFPA) devote extensive resources to firefighter occupational safety and health programs (OSHPs). The NFFF, for instance, advances the *Everyone Goes Home* program, a set of 16 initiatives that promote life safety in the fire service [1]. Similarly, the NFPA promulgates industry standards, which include a set that address the design and implementation of occupa-tional safety and health programs [2], comprehensive occupational medical programs

© Springer International Publishing AG, part of Springer Nature 2018
A. Marcus and W. Wang (Eds.): DUXU 2018, LNCS 10920, pp. 573–588, 2018.
https://doi.org/10.1007/978-3-319-91806-8_45

[3], health-related fitness programs [4], and processes for firefighter rehabilitation during certain operations [5]. While *NFPA 1500* deals broadly with OSHPs within the fire service, *NFPA 1582, NFPA 1583,* and *NFPA 1584* focus on moments when physicians, health care providers, fitness professionals, emergency medical services (EMS) personnel, and fire officers evaluate whether prospective and current firefighters are medically or physically qualified for duty. If a cardiac dysrhythmia that only presents when a firefighter's heart rate is elevated is not detected, a crew member could sustain a cardiac injury while performing operations on a fire-ground. If symptoms of cardiac disease are left undiagnosed or unexplained, opportunities for a firefighter to develop plans for managing or ameliorating those symptoms are lost. If a firefighter begins an exercise regimen without the support of fitness professionals, s/he might practice those activities in ways that cause or exacerbate injuries. If an incident manager initiates a rehab process during a structure fire, but a line officer tells a crew that they can return to work without having their vital signs checked by EMS personnel, a firefighter exhibiting symptoms of hydrogen cyanide poisoning could collapse on scene. These examples not only emphasize the critical role that information plays within firefighter comprehensive medical and fitness programs (CMFPs), but also illuminate how user experience (UX) research can be used to improve firefighters' interactions with and access to the types of care and information offered within such programs.

One comprehensive firefighter health and fitness program is the Firefighter Testing Program (FTP) housed within the Human Performance Clinical Research Laboratory (HPCRL) at Colorado State University (CSU). As a longstanding CMFP that has been in existence for over ten years, the FTP has served over 2,000 Coloradan firefighters affiliated with 30 participating agencies. Like other firefighter medical and fitness programs, the FTP seeks to identify behavioral and physiological health risks in firefighters. Yet, the FTP is distinctive because it utilizes *a literate care model* where firefighters are provided with information and support to develop actionable, evidence-based plans for self-managing their health, fitness, and wellness [6–8]. Recent studies have demonstrated that participating in CMFPs like the FTP has a variety of positive benefits that range from reduced injury rates and early detection of treatable diseases to extended career longevity and increased awareness of the ways dietary, exercise, and lifestyle choices impact a firefighter's health and fitness [9–11]. Unfortunately, compliance with NFPA standards is voluntary, and 60-70% of U.S. firefighters do not participate in a comprehensive medical and fitness program [12]. Moreover, little is known about the degree to which existing CMFPs conform to NFPA standards, and CMFPs are only one context when firefighters might benefit from access to health and fitness information that enriches decision making about the ways firefighters practice work. Put simply, one strategy that fire service leaders could leverage to improve firefighter occupational health and safety outcomes is increasing firefighters' access to the types of care and information that are offered within CMFPs such as the FTP.

In this paper, we sketch a set of ongoing participatory design projects where members of the fire service community, the director of the FTP, a UX researcher, and a team of developers are working to adapt a physiological monitoring platform for use within the fire service. The original platform, designed by a team of developers at AvidCor, consists of a physiological monitoring prototype (AC-1) that uses Bluetooth to pair with a smartphone and allows a user to independently record data about their electrocardio-grams (EKGs), pulse oximetry, and body temperature. We begin by providing back-ground on the ways socioeconomic factors influence occupational safety and health outcomes in the fire service and discuss concepts that influence our approach to occu-pational safety and health research. Next, we trace the genesis of our collaborative work within a larger transdisciplinary research team and sketch how the values, tools, and practices we have adapted from community-based research and participatory design methodologies inflect our stance as researchers [13]. We then turn toward a detailed discussion of two ongoing participatory design projects. While the purpose of the first project is to identify barriers and envision opportunities where the AC-1 prototype and smart-phone app could be used to facilitate increased firefighter access to information and care that can be used to manage cardiovascular risk, the purpose of the second project is to develop a second prototype, the AvidCor Fire-ground (AC-FG), which could stream real-time information about individual firefighters' physiological performance while they are working in arduous environments to EMS professionals, firefighters, fire offi-cers, and incident commanders. We conclude by considering the implications our ongoing work may have for other UX researchers who are working to improve systems where stakeholders offer and receive medical information and care.

2   Background

2.1   Socioeconomic Status and Occupational Safety and Health in Blue-Collar Industries

Research has demonstrated that a worker's occupational class and socioeconomic status (SES) directly corresponds to rates in morbidity and mortality [14–16]. "Lower-status jobs," Adler and Newman note, "expose workers to both physical and psychosocial risks" and "carry a higher risk of occupational injury and exposure to toxic substances" [14]. Like other blue-collar workers, firefighters are more likely to sustain injuries than individuals working in white-collar occupations. However, firefighting ranks among those occupations with the very highest rates of workplace injury, including injuries that result in lost-time [15–21].

CMFPs are an invaluable tool within firefighting OSHPs, then, because they provide stakeholders with information and care that can be used to make decisions about how, when, and why different individuals within fire service organizations perform certain types of work. Research indicates that firefighters are twice as likely to sustain a fatal cardiac injury than fellow Americans [22], and appear to develop certain types of cancer at higher rates [22, 23]. The diagnostic tests that are performed within CMFPs are espe-cially critical because they are one of the few moments when firefighters have oppor-tunities to identify medical and health conditions such as cardiac dysrhythmias or heart disease that can be treated before they manifest as injuries or fatalities within operational contexts.

Over the past decade, an annual average of 71,000 firefighters have sustained injuries on duty [24]. It appears that the growing emphasis that national and international fire service organizations have placed on CMFP participation could be having positive effects, as longitudinal data surrounding safety and health outcomes in the U.S. fire service indicates that the overall number of injuries has been declining [24]. However, NFPA researchers also caution that the rate of injury per incident has remained relatively constant over the same period of time [24]. In other words, there has been a significant decrease in the cumulative total of injuries and fires that occur each year, but the rate of injury per incident appears to be relatively static. While the human costs associated with firefighter injury and fatality are inexpressible, the National Institute for Standards and Technology (NIST) estimates the annual economic impact of firefighter injuries in the U.S. is between $2.8 and $7.8 billion [25]. UX research could be used to better understand how factors such as affordability, culture, and access influence participation rates within firefighter CMFPs. UX research can help identify and improve moments when firefighters experience health and fitness care. UX research can help improve the design of interactions between firefighters and health care providers following a *literate care model* that seeks to provide the types of care, information, and support that empowers these workers to develop realistic plans for managing their health and wellness [8]. UX research, in short, could improve access to the types of care and information that have far-reaching impacts for firefighters, families, fire service organizations, and communities.

2.2 Firefighter Occupational Safety and Health Outcomes: An Adaptive Challenge

Our perspectives toward firefighter occupational safety and health are not only inflected by the research we conduct as part of larger transdisciplinary team, but also our past experiences as practitioners within fire and EMS organizations. We understand that occupational safety and health outcomes in the fire service are directly tied to cardiovascular risk and health. The leading cause of firefighter fatality has been, and continues to be, sudden cardiac death [26]. However, causality is easily complicated when researchers look at the events and confluence of factors that precede a firefighter injury or fatality. NIOSH, for instance, frequently identifies issues in communication, incident management, decision making, risk perception, and situational awareness as contributing factors in investigations of incidents where firefighters sustain fatal or serious injuries [27–29]. In an analysis of over 2,000 incidents, a former assistant chief from Indianapolis Fire Department, found that maydays were more likely to be called when crews were working independently from their supervising officer [30]. Moreover, Smith and colleagues conducted a study at a live-fire training facility where they observed that "psychological and psychological strain…has the potential to impair cognitive function" [31]. Still, there is much unknown about the ways physiological variables relate to cognitive and operational performance during specific firefighting activities. Put simply, while we suspect CMFPs have an important and central role within OSHPs, we want to acknowledge that a firefighter's health and fitness is not the sole factor influencing occupational safety and health outcomes in the industry.

Instead, we see occupational safety and health outcomes as an *adaptive challenge*. According to Heifetz & Laurie *technical problems* can be solved by individuals or teams who possess specialized forms of expertise, whereas *adaptive challenges* require stakeholders "to clarify values, develop new strategies, and learn new ways of operating"

[32]. Treating firefighter occupational safety and health as an *adaptive challenge* is a useful approach from our perspective, because it requires researchers, stakeholders, and designers to account for the broader contexts, actors, and factors that surround firefighting. As noted above, whether individuals perform blue- or white-collar work will impact their rates of exposure to workplace hazards which, in turn, influence health and safety outcomes. However, socioeconomic factors also color the types of decisions that fire service leaders and health care providers must make when determining *who* is medically and physically qualified for duty. Indeed, 800,000 of the 1.1 million firefighters who serve communities in the U.S. work in volunteer fire departments [33]. These types of departments often serve communities that are economically disadvantaged and under resourced. While it is entirely sensible for national or international fire service organizations to devote resources toward prompting OSPH in the industry, it is also sensible that leaders of organizations located in communities where it is difficult to recruit and retain volunteers to resist these efforts, as CMFPs could reveal medical conditions that disqualify existing or prospective members. That is, we think that *NFPA 1582* compliant CMFPs employing *literate care models* could be consistent with the types of stance that are necessary for engendering change in some organizations, but other organizations encounter different barriers which will require stakeholders to envision models of care that are sensitive to types of challenges and tensions that are currently impacting firefighters' participation rates in *NFPA 1582* compliant CMFPs.

3   Methodology

3.1   Transdisciplinary, Community-Based Research (CBR)

For over three years, we have been part of a larger transdisciplinary research collaborative that has been working together toward the broad goal of improving firefighter safety and health outcomes in the fire service. Transdisciplinary approaches to team science, as Moldenhauer and Johnson Sackey describe, are particularly suited for addressing adaptive challenges "that can only be tackled with researchers from a variety of disciplines from the sciences and humanities who are willing to create new ways to work together" [34]. Like Moldenhauer and Johnson Sackey, our approach to transdisciplinary research is also inflected by community-based research (CBR) and participatory design (PD) methodologies [13, 34–37]. While there is significant variance within and between these methodological traditions, Grabill observes, each "draw on the practice of working with people to answer questions and solve problems—as opposed to researching 'on' people and their problems" [13]. Following these researchers, we seek to enact research through practices where we identify and seek to respond to challenges alongside members of the fire service community. As researchers who also identify as practitioners—Tiffany was a medic and Tim was a firefighter and technical rescuer—participation takes on an added dimension of critical importance because it allows us to complicate and enrich our individual experiences and histories in fire and emergency medical services. Moreover, our connections to this community means that the types of "relationship building and maintenance" practices which are so vital for CBR and PD projects [13] are practices that we regularly engage in. Just as Tiffany interacts frequently with members of the fire service, Tim often spends time catching up with firefighters who he's previously worked with as either a firefighter, fire instructor, or researcher. Above and beyond the daily activity associated with directing the FTP, Tiffany also works with fire service leaders to help them align department policies with NFPA standards on occupational safety and health. Similarly, Tim has been mentoring a fire chief in the region who is designing a research project to earn an executive fire officer credential from the National Fire Academy.

3.2   Participatory Design (PD)

Like CBR, PD "emphasizes co-research and co-design: researcher-designers must come to conclusions in conjunction with users" [36]. PD has been especially useful within the projects that we are involved in because it offers a framework for "alternating between *practical work* to support changes…and *systematic data collection and analysis*" [36]. According to Spinuzzi, PD involves three stages where "researcher-designers" employ various methods to envision and realize change by setting objectives for a project, collecting and analyzing data about an organization, and designing or testing prototypes that might be used to ameliorate work conditions or processes, and evaluating the designs (see Table 1) [36].

Table 1.   Spinuzzi's stages of participatory design

Stage 1: Initial exploration of work	Stage 2: Discovery processes	Stage 3: Prototyping
"[D]esigners meet the users and familiarize themselves with the ways in which the users work together. This exploration includes the technologies used, but also includes workflow and work procedures, routines, teamwork, and other aspects of the work."	"[D]esigners and users employ various techniques to understand and prioritize work organization and envision the future workplace. This stage allows designers and users to clarify the users' goals and values and to agree on the desired outcome of the project."	"[D]esigners and users iteratively shape technological artifacts to fit into the workplace envisioned in Stage 2. Prototyping can be conducted on site or in a lab; involves one or more users; and can be conducted on-the-job if the prototype is a working prototype."

In the following section, we use Spinuzzi's stages of participatory design as a heuristic for discussing how participatory design activities that our collaborative has previously participated inform and facilitate the research and design work that we are currently engaged in with fire service stakeholders. The aims of this work are to explore how the AC-1 and AC-FG physiological prototypes might fit into the fire service and to adapt the prototypes accordingly.

4   Iterating Designs to Increase Firefighter Access to Health and Fitness Information

4.1   Initial Exploration of Work

Our team possess deep knowledge of the ways the fire service operates, including the ways that firefighters experience work differently based on jurisdictional, geographic, and organizational factors. Still, we have taken steps to explore work processes and technologies associated with CMPHs with fresh eyes. For example, our team organized and co-hosted *Adaptive Challenges*, a one-day symposium with leaders from the Poudre Fire Authority, to co-construct shared understanding of the factors that influence firefighter safety and health outcomes. We brought in four speakers, Chief Tom DeMint (PFA), Division Chief Scott Heiss (Denver Fire Department), Dr. Ron Timmons (University of North Texas), and Dr. Bill Hart-Davidson (Michigan State University) to speak on issues that range from wearable-technologies and automation to communications, risk perception, and cultures of risk within the fire service. 70 fire service leaders participated, including fire officers responsible for overseeing firefighting training, safety and/or health programs at over distinct 25 fire department and representatives from fire service organizations such as the NVFC, NFFF, IAFC, IAFF, International Association of Black Professional Firefighters, International Association of Women in Fire and Emergency Services, Front Range Fire Consortium, Colorado Division of Fire Prevention and Control, and the Colorado Fire and Police Pension Association. During breakout sessions at the symposium, participants spent time rotating through stations focused on topics that influence occupational safety and health outcomes such as blue collar identity, firefighter education and training, access to CMFPs and mental health care, and emergent technologies. Members of our research team facilitated discussion and recorded notes, as participants envisioned solutions and discussed barriers.

After the symposium, we developed activity system diagrams [37] of OSHPs (see Fig. 1) and mapped out contexts when firefighters might receive feedback about their health or fitness according to NFPA standards (see Fig. 2). These analytical tools allow researcher-designers to visualize how components of CMFPs might fit might within a local OSHP and identify moments when increasing access to the types of information and care provided within CMFPs could enrich decision making processes. For instance, *NFPA 1584* calls on organizational managers to enact firefighter rehabilitation processes during operations and trainings that pose an increased risk to personnel. The standard protocols state that after firefighters have performed work for an extended period of time, they should have their vitals evaluated by EMS personnel before they return to work. In practice, however, there are incidents where rehabilitation processes are rarely, if ever, enacted, which mark missed opportunities for personnel to receive timely care or feedback regarding their health and/or fitness. Firefighters exhibiting symptoms of hydrogen cyanide poisoning at a structure fire, for instance, could miss an opportunity to receive care that is essential for managing those exposures.

Actors

Policy Makers (e.g.,
NFPA; NFFF; NVFC;
Colorado Professional Fire
Fighters

Care Providers (e.g., Physicians; Nurses; Insurance
companies; Fitness professionals; Psychologists and
counselors)

Fire Department (e.g.,
Executive fire officers;
Safety and training officers; Line officers; Incident
commanders; Firefighting
personnel; Family mem-
bers)

Tools

EKG; Pulse oximetry;
Treadmill protocol;
Nutrition; Diet; Sleep;
Exercise; Hydration;
CMFPs; PPE; On-scene
rehab; Fitness programs

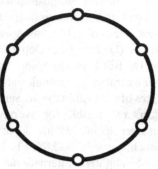

Objective(s)

Reduce workplace injury and
fatality; Limit exposure to
cardiac strain during work and
training; Establish baseline for
each firefighter's respective
fitness and health; Lower
insurance costs; Determine if
candidates and/or firefighters
are medically qualified for
duty; Diagnose and detect
medical conditions that could
result in an injury/fatality
within a candidate or member;
Develop medical treatment
and/or fitness plans to
empower candidate or member
improve health, fitness, and
wellness

Rules NFPA standards
(e.g., 1500; 1582;
1583;1584); Department
policies and guidelines;
Insurance policies; Law
(e.g., HIPPA)

**Community
Stakeholders** Residents
and taxpayers; Politicians;
Business owners;
Workers; Community
leaders; Community
organizations; Visitors.

Division of Labor
Medical and fitness personnel
conduct tests; Executive
officers implement CMFPs;
Fire service leaders,
researchers, and industry
members develop standards.

Fig. 1. Activity system diagram of firefighter occupational safety and health programs

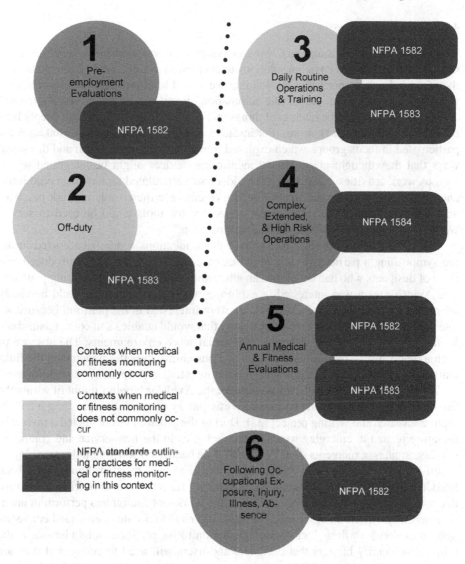

Fig. 2. Contexts when firefighters might receive feedback about their health and fitness

Moreover, these tools enable researcher-designers to approach CMFPs as systems that are enacted through situated practices and identify elements or stakeholders that might be overlooked within them. For example, mental health care providers are often not discussed as stakeholders who could play important roles with OSHPs and CMFPs. By mapping these systems, researcher-designers illuminate moments and locations within these systems when firefighters, line officers, executive fire officers and care providers might benefit by receiving the types of care and information necessary for maintaining fitness or developing health intervention strategies.

4.2 Discovery Processes

The primary aim of the *Adaptive Challenge* symposium was to bring stakeholders from the industry together to envision solutions to occupational safety and health challenges they face today. One particular tension that we hoped to investigate with stakeholders was how emerging technologies like automation, physiological wearables, augmented and virtual reality, and the internet of things might fit into a profession with deeply held blue-collar traditions and cultures. For instance, during breakout sessions, stakeholders participated in focus groups which explored trends in fitness and health and discussed ways that they thought physiological monitoring devices might be integrated within various work activities. However, stakeholders also articulated factors that could influence whether firefighters are likely to adopt or embrace these tools in work practices and sketched examples of problematic ways that the tools could be used to surveil workers or compromise private medical information.

While our collaborative has since built on the foundational work that occurred during the symposium, a particularly serendipitous outcome is that we were introduced to a team of designers who had developed an affordable physiological monitoring platform. The AvidCor team was interested in exploring whether the platform could be viably adapted for use in the fire service; and, we were interested in the platform because we had unable to locate an affordable technology that would enable us to collect data about firefighters' physiological performance in actual work environments. The absence of such a device was a barrier that has impeded our ability to better understand the links that might exist between physiological, communicative, and operational performance.

To further explore if and how a device like the AvidCor monitor might fit within the fire service, we continued the process of participatory discovery by pursuing a collaborative research and writing project [38]. During the project, we conducted a review of literature related to emerging wearable technologies in the fire service and composed two case studies of moments when (what had once been) two new wearable technologies —self-contained breathing apparatus (air tanks) and heat resistant hoods—had been introduced to the industry. This inquiry enabled our team to better appreciate how introducing new tools to the industry can impact the work that firefighters perform in unanticipated ways. Thereafter, we used the case studies to facilitate open-ended conversations to explore how firefighter physiological monitoring platforms might be used in the future and identify barriers that designers and users will need to consider if they are going to avoid the types of unintended consequences that have accompanied the introduction of new protective designs in the past.

4.3 Prototyping

Having developed a broad sense of how physiological wearables could be integrated in the fire service, our team of researcher-designers has since moved on toward prototyping and usability testing. This stage connects back directly to work we have performed during earlier stages, as we have identified a number of contexts (see Fig. 2) where we believe the prototype could be adapted to enrich firefighters' access to feedback about their health and fitness.

Rurally and Geographically Remote Communities (AV-1). Many of the fire depart-ments located outside of the I-25 and I-70 corridors of Colorado—identified as rural and geographically remote communities—do not participate in the FTP. We suspect that the AC-1 could be used to increase these firefighters' access cardiac monitoring, because using the device is fairly simple and provides a reliable means for gathering data about an individual's health (e.g., EKG; oxygen saturation; heart rate and rhythm) that can be signs of heart disease or life-threatening dysrhythmia. The smart-phone app enables individuals to share the tracing with a care provider s/he trusts and, if the tracing indicates any abnormalities, sends an alert message that the user should seek medical care. To further explore if the AC-1 exists as a viable prototype, we are working with firefighters to investigate how the existing hardware, software, and documentation can be rede-signed to facilitate usability. To perform this design-research, we have partnered with three fire departments located in three rurally or geographically remote areas of the state. At each department, we have recruited or seek to recruit 7-20 participants to complete a series of tasks where they set up the device, place electrodes on their body, pair the monitor with an app, and follow the user documentation to acquire an EKG tracing. As firefighters attempt to take a tracing, researcher-designers observe and note moments when the individuals completing the task appear to struggle with the app, hardware, or documentation.

Thereafter, we recruit 4–7 of the phase-one participants to provide feedback on the design of the AC-1 platform and offer feedback on barriers to its use in the fire service during focus group interviews that span 30–45 min. There are two prompts that partic-ipants respond to during a focus group interview. The first prompt asks participants to share feedback on their experiences using the hardware, app, or documentation and to offer solutions that would improve the design of platform components. The second prompt asks participants to consider socioeconomic and cultural factors that could impact whether firefighters in a department located in a community similar to their own might be reluctant to participate in CMFPs or use a platform like the AC-1. In order to encourage co-research and co-design, the focus group facilitator encourages firefighters to forward follow-up questions to one another, to collaboratively envision solutions to the types of barriers they have identified, and to expand on points that other participants have forwarded during previous points in the discussion.

Real-Time Physiological Monitoring of Personnel in Work Environments, Including Firefighter Rehabilitation Processes (AV-FG). One of the major factors that we suspect impacts occupational safety and health outcomes in the fire service is that information and data that provides feedback about a firefighter's health or fitness is sporadic. In some departments, firefighter candidates participate in an agility test and complete a physical—that may or may not be rise to the standard of care outlined in *NFPA 1582*—before they are officially hired. However, they might never be required to complete a physical or participate in an agility test again by their department. Thus, *NFPA 1584* has been an invaluable tool for some jurisdictions, because it has enabled incident commanders to ensure that personnel who have been working for extended periods of time are evaluated by EMS personnel before returning to work during high risk incidents or trainings. While all incidents or trainings in the fire service carry some degree of risk, extended and high-risk operations inherently increase the likelihood of sudden cardiac events because firefighters often work up to and beyond their cardio-vascular threshold.

Developing technologies that provide real-time physiological monitoring could have a powerful impact on occupational safety and health outcomes in the industry because the tools could provide incident commanders, fire officers, firefighters, and EMS with opportunities for the early identification of medical problems or emergencies, which may happen at any time. The data and information that these tools provide could not only be used to intervene if a firefighter or crew is under extreme physiological duress during firefighting or rescue operations, but could also engender firefighters, officers, and incident commanders to develop "data-driven science-based tactics" that reduce or lessen firefighters' exposure to extreme physiological- and heat-stress [39]. Predicting when a life-threatening event could occur is, of course, challenging in a high-risk mission-oriented profession like firefighting, but developing tools that facilitate contin-uous real-time physiological monitoring could eliminate the perception that cardiac events can only happen in high risk environments. That is, these tools might engender opportunities for passively monitoring a firefighters' physiological performance throughout their duty tours rather than sporadically enacting active surveillance as part of firefighter rehabilitation processes during high risk incidents and trainings.

To further explore how a device like the AV-FG might fit within the fire service, we are currently in the process of rapidly iterating prototypes and performing usability testing at the HPCRL. AvidCor developers have designed a prototype that uses two-leads to take an EKG tracing. During the first phase of usability testing, 30 firefighters visiting the FTP as part of periodic screening are being recruited. While participants complete a maximal treadmill protocol wearing the 12-lead gold-standard that is part of the regular screening test at the FTP, they also don two additional leads and a small puck-like device. EKG tracings are taken and compared. Comparative analysis of the 12-lead and 2-lead EKGs tracings gathered during the first 15 usability tests conducted by an AvidCor cardiologist suggested that the device is taking accurate measurements of heart rate and rhythm. During usability tests, clinicians also take notes of the technical difficulties they encounter while operating the platform and communicate them to one of the project managers responsible for passing information to developers. Currently, the developers are addressing technical issues that clinicians have identified before a second sequence of 15 usability tests is performed. Plans for field testing the device are in place, where we will iterate back through the *discovery process* and *prototyping* stages of participatory design using observational methods and focus groups.

Clinical Settings for Performing CMFP Evaluations (AV-FG). While there are many clinical settings that could accommodate CMFP evaluations, less common are physician practices that embrace these types of evaluations as standard practice. We suspect that firefighters may experience versions of CMFPs that do not administer many of the types of tests that *NFPA 1582* proscribes. Within the industry, there are two moments when firefighters typically have their medical health and physical fitness eval-uated as part of a CMFP: When prospective firefighter candidates are hired, or when an existing firefighter returns to work following an injury, illness, or extended leave (See

Fig. 2). In both cases, these types of CMFP evaluations may be viewed by firefighters and care providers as either preventative care or within the realm of the primary care practice. As such, executive fire officers or fire officers vested with the responsibility of administrating OSHPs for a fire department may not encourage these evaluations or place significant weight on whether the evaluations conform to the types of processes *NFPA 1582* sees as necessary for reaching a determination about a firefighter's medical and physical fitness for duty.

As previously mentioned, the FTP at CSU is housed within a clinical research laboratory. This facility is not a point of care. However, it provides the ability for firefighters to participate in the tests that comprise a CMFP evaluation within a fee-for-service model. While there are several agencies that promote annual physicals for firefighters including the NFPA and IAFC, many firefighters do not complete an annual physical or participate in CMFPs that mandate annual physicals. In fact, firefighters who "feel fine" may not see the value in these types of screenings. While we believe that leaders of fire departments and communities have a responsibility to ensure members participate within annual CMFP evaluations that follow the standard of care outlined in *NFPA 1582*, we want to stress that we think that evaluations which are conducted through a *literate care model* that empowers firefighters to develop strategies and concrete plans for managing their long-term health, fitness, and wellness are needed in the occupation.

At this point, we have not yet started a systematic exploration of how the AV-FG could be integrated within clinical settings. However, we are aware there are many jurisdictions that have difficulty accessing clinics like the HPCRL where tests like a maximal treadmill protocol can be administered as part of a CMFP that is *NFPA 1582* compliant. If the AV-FG can be adapted to take EKG tracings for firefighters as they complete the maximal treadmill protocol that mirror the quality and accuracy of those performed using 12-lead in clinical settings, it might be possible for fire departments or healthcare providers to administer these tests independently and send the results to a physician for analysis. Ultimately, these types of evaluations are an investment in a fire department's most valuable asset: the firefighter.

5   Conclusion

Looking across the various contexts where firefighters might have access to care and feedback about their fitness and health (see Fig. 2) suggests that there are a multitude of ways that firefighters might experience CMFPs as end users. Whereas one firefighter might have an entry physical over the course of her career, another might undergo fitness and medical testing annually. Like Opel and Hart-Davidson [8], we think UX research is a useful tool for improving how health care experiences are designed, enacted, and maintained. UX researchers have a great deal to offer these systems, as the robust set practices, tools, and perspectives this discipline uses can be adapted to explore the ways that humans experience care and interact with information within these settings. For instance, firefighters who participate in CMFPs where the sole aim of interactions between care providers and firefighters is to reach a determination about fitness for duty differ markedly from those that are also accompanied by the information and insight offered by fitness professionals at the FTP. CMFPs which follow a *literate care model* can be used to empower firefighters by positioning them as active participants within these programs. Moreover, *literate care models* approach health, fitness, and wellness as a dynamic constellation of factors, many of which hinge on behavioral and lifestyle choices that can be adapted.

The quality of experiences firefighters have within CMFPs matters not only because these programs are tools that fire departments use to improve occupational safety and health outcomes, but because firefighters' access to the types of care and information provided within these programs can identify conditions that determine whether a mother, father, son, daughter, or community member goes home alive when they leave the fire station. We believe that access to quality medical care, quality CMFPs, and quality OSHPs should be understood as a social justice issue because firefighters—and other blue-collar workers—are exposed to risk in occupational settings at disproportionate rates in comparison to white-collar workers. UX researchers—especially those who adapt community-based research and participatory design methodologies—can improve the ethical quality of interactions that occur within OSHPs and CMFPs by working alongside stakeholders to account for the types of experiences that blue-collar workers have within them, by envisioning technological or process improvements that could increase access to the types of care and information that are provided within them, and by advocating for designs that position workers as stewards of their own safety, health, and wellness.

Acknowledgments. Funding for the *Adaptive Challenges* symposium was provided by the Office of Vice President for Research at CSU as part of the Pre-Catalyst for Innovative Partnerships (PRECIP) program. Funding for the promoting access to baseline cardiovascular health in rurally and geographically remote communities project is provided by the National Institution for Occupational Safety and Health via the Center for Work, Health, and Environment as part of a Total Worker Health Pilot Grant (U19OH011227-02). Funding for the fire-ground project physiological monitoring project is provided by the National Science Foundation under a SBIR Grant (1722014). We thank Dr. Genesea Carter for providing feedback on a draft of this paper.

References

1. NFFF: Everyone Goes Home. https://www.everyonegoeshome.com/. Accessed 21 Feb 2018
2. NFPA: NFPA 1500: Standard on Fire Department Occupational Safety, Health, and Wellness Program, 2018 edn. NFPA, Quincy (2018)
3. NFPA: NFPA 1582: Standard on Comprehensive Occupational Medical Program for Fire Departments, 2018 edn. NFPA, Quincy (2018)
4. NFPA: NFPA 1583: Standard on Health-Related Fitness Programs for Fire Department Members, 2015 edn. NFPA, Quincy (2015)
5. NFPA: NFPA 1584: Standard on the Rehabilitation Process for Members During Emergency Operations and Training Exercises, 2015 edn. NFPA, Quincy (2015)
6. Office of Disease Prevention and Health Promotion: Health Literate Care Model. https://health.gov/communication/interactiveHLCM/. Accessed 21 Feb 2018

7. Koh, H., Brach, C., Harris, L.M., Parchman, M.L.: A proposed 'health literate care model would constitute a systems approach to improving patients' engagement in care. Health Aff. **2**, 357–367 (2013)

8. Opel, D.S., Hart-Davidson, W.: Challenges to patient experience: documenting evidence-based practice in the family health center. In: Marcus, A., Wang, W. (eds.) DUXU 2017. LNCS, vol. 10290, pp. 702–712. Springer, Cham (2017). https://doi.org/10.1007/978-3-319-58640-3_50

9. Winter, F.D., Seals, N., Martin, J., Russell, B.: Implementation of first wellness-fitness evaluation for the Dallas Fire-Rescue Department. Proc. Bayl. Univ. Med. Cent. **23**(3), 235–238 (2010)

10. Smith, D.L.: Firefighter fitness: Improving performance and preventing injuries and fatalities ties. Curr. Sports Med. Rep. **10**(3), 167–172 (2011)

11. Leffer, M., Grizzell, T.: Implementation of a physician-organized wellness regime (POWR) enforcing the 2007 NFPA standard 1582: Injury rate reduction and associated cost savings. J. Occup. Environ. Med. **52**(3), 336–339 (2010)

12. NFPA: Fourth Needs Assessment of the U.S. Fire Service. NFPA, Quincy (2016)

13. Grabill, J.T.: Community-based research and the importance of research stance. In: Nickoson, L., Sheridan, M.P. (eds.) Writing Studies Research in Practice: Methods and Methodologies, pp. 210–219. Southern Illinois University Press, Carbondale (2012)

14. Adler, N.E., Newman, K.: Socioeconomic disparities in health: Pathways and policies. Health Aff. **21**(2), 60–76 (2002)

15. Piha, K., Laaksonen, M., Marrtikainen, P., Rahkonen, O., Lahelma, E.: Socio-economic and occupational determinants of work injury absence. Eur. J. Public Health **23**(4), 693–698 (2012)

16. World Health Organization: Environment and Health Risks: A Review of the Influence and Effects of Social Inequalities. WHO, Copenhagen (2010)

17. Griffin, S.C., Regan, T.L., Harber, P., Lutz, E., Chengcheng, H., Peate, W., Burgess, J.: Evaluation of a fitness intervention for new firefighters: injury reduction and economic benefits. Inj. Prev. **22**(3), 181–188 (2016)

18. Macquire, B.L., Hunting, K.L., Guidotti, T.L., Smith, G.S.: Occupational injuries among emergency medical services personnel. Prehosp. Emerg. Care **9**(4), 405–411 (2005)

19. Reichard, A.A., Marsh, S.M., Moore, P.H.: Fatal and nonfatal injuries among emergency medical technicians and paramedics. Prehosp. Emerg. Care **15**(4), 511–517 (2011)

20. US Department of Labor, Bureau of Labor Statistics: Workplace Injury and Illness Summary (2013). https://www.bls.gov/news.release/osh.nr0.htm. Accessed 21 Feb 2018

21. Fahy, R.F., LeBlanc, P.R., Molis, J.L.: Firefighter Fatalities in the United States (2016)

22. LeMasters, G.K., Genaidy, A.M., Succop, P., Deddens, J., Sobeih, T., Barriera-Viruet, H., Dunning, K., Lockey, J.: Cancer risk among firefighters: a review and meta-analysis of 32 studies. J. Occup. Environ. Med. **48**(11), 1189–1202 (2006)

23. Daniels, R.D., Bertke, S., Dahm, M.M., Yiin, J.H., Kubale, T.L., Hales, T.R., Baris, D., Zahm, S.H., Beaumont, J.J., Waters, K.M., Pinkerton, L.E.: Exposure-response relationships for select cancer and non-cancer health outcomes in a cohort of US firefighters from San Francisco, Chicago, and Philadelphia (1950-2009). Occup. Environ. Med. **72**(10), 699–706 (2015)

24. Haynes, H.J.G., Molis, J.L.: United States Firefighter Injuries—2016. NFPA, Quincy (2017)

25. TriData Corporation: The economic consequences of firefighter injuries and their prevention (NIST GCR 05-874). NIST, Gaithersburg (2004)

26. Yang, J., Teehan, D., Farioli, A., Baur, D.M., Smith, D., Kales, S.N.: Sudden cardiac death among firefighters < 45 years of age in the United States. Am. J. Cardiol. **112**(12), 1962–1967 (2013)
27. NIOSH: Career probationary fire fighter and captain die as result of rapid fire progression in a wind-driven residential structure fire—Texas (F2009-11). Death in the line of duty: A summary of a NIOSH fire fighter fatality investigation. NIOSH, Morgantown (2010)
28. NIOSH: Career lieutenant and fire fighter killed and two fire fighters injured by wall collapse at a large commercial structure fire (F2012-13). Death in the line of duty: A summary of a NIOSH fire fighter fatality investigation—Pennsylvania. NIOSH, Morgantown (2013)
29. NIOSH: Career fire fighter dies during fire-fighting operations at a multi-family fatality investigation—Massachusetts (F2011-31). Death in the line of duty: A summary of a NIOSH fire fighter fatality investigation. NIOSH, Morgantown (2013)
30. Abbot, D.: Project mayday. http://projectmayday.net/. Accessed 21 Feb 2018
31. Smith, D.L., Manning, T.S., Petruzzello, S.J.: Effect of strenuous live-fire drills on cardiovascular and physiological responses of recruit firefighters. Ergonomics **44**(3), 244–254 (2001)
32. Heifetz, R.A., Laure, D.L.: The work of leadership. Harv. Bus. Rev. **75**(1), 124–134 (1997)
33. NIOSH: Fire Fighter Fatality Investigation and Prevention. https://www.cdc.gov/niosh/fire/default.html. Accessed 21 Feb 2018
34. Moldenhauer, J.A., Sackey, D.J.: Transdisciplinarity, community-based participatory research, and user-based information design research. In: Marcus, A. (ed.) DUXU 2016. LNCS, vol. 9746, pp. 323–332. Springer, Cham (2016). https://doi.org/10.1007/978-3-319-40409-7_31
35. Blythe, S., Grabill, J.T., Riley, K.: Action research and wicked environmental problems: Exploring appropriate roles for researchers in professional communication. J. Bus. Tech. Commun. **22**(3), 272–298 (2018)
36. Spinuzzi, C.: The methodology of participatory design. Tech. Commun. **52**(2), 163–174 (2005)
37. Spinuzzi, C.: Topsight: A Guide to Studying, Diagnosing, and Fixing Information Flow in Organizations. Amazon Createspace, Austin (2013)
38. Amidon, T.R., Williams, E.A., Lipsey, T., Callahan, R., Nuckols, G., Rice, S.: Sensors and gizmos and data, oh my: Informating firefighters' personal protective equipment. Commun. Des. Q. **5**(4), 15–30 (2017)
39. Grant, C., Hamins, A., Bryner, N., Jones, A., Koepke, G.: Research Roadmap for Smart Fire Fighting: Summary Report. NIST Special Publication 1191. NIST (2015)

Peruvian Public Universities
and the Accessibility of Their Websites

Fanny Dolores Benites Alfaro
and Claudia María Del Pilar Zapata Del Río[✉]

Pontificia Universidad Católica del Perú, Lima, Peru
{fanny.benites,zapata.cmp}@pucp.edu.pe

Abstract. The educational field is not unrelated to the growing use of information and communication technologies (ICTs), due to this, Higher Education institutions publish on their websites the most relevant information and services they provide. On the other hand, access to information systems by people with disabilities is a right and to achieve it, it is important that they are designed with accessibility standards. Knowing this problem, a diagnosis was made of a set of Peruvian public universities, in order to know the problems of web accessibility that they present at a global level and provide adequate recommendations. To this end, a set of web pages of Peruvian public universities was selected to be evaluated considering the recommendations of the Web Accessibility Initiative (WAI) of the World Wide Web Consortium (W3C) and its Methodology for the Evaluation of Web Accessibility in its version 2.0. Based on the accessibility studies, the way of carrying out the evaluation method was defined, which was applied to the study domain, obtaining low levels of accessibility in the contents of the pages: home and academic offer, as well as a list of common problems. Finally, general recommendations were made.

Keywords: Accessibility · University · Web site

1 Introduction

The growing change in the development and use of information and communication technologies (ICT) and the need to create information services from a broad perspective, has led to a large part of these services being provided through Web portals [27]. In the educational field, the institutions of Higher Education University publish on their websites the most relevant information and services they provide [1].

Access to communications by persons with disabilities is a right, which is covered by the UN convention, in order to eliminate the discrimination to which they are subject [1]. Therefore, in order to allow more people to access the Web, it is important to develop features that allow accessibility [1].

In Peru, the legislation on accessibility on the web consists of:

- Law No. 28530 - Law on the promotion of Internet access for people with disabilities and the adaptation of the physical space in public Internet booths [5].
- Ministerial Resolution 126-2009-PCM [1] of the Presidency of the Council of Ministers, which approved the guidelines for accessibility to web pages and mobile

© Springer International Publishing AG, part of Springer Nature 2018
A. Marcus and W. Wang (Eds.): DUXU 2018, LNCS 10920, pp. 589–607, 2018.
https://doi.org/10.1007/978-3-319-91806-8_46

telephony applications for public institutions of the National Computing System. The purpose of the document is that the public institutions of the Peruvian State apply the Web Content Accessibility Guidelines 1.0 (WCAG 1.0) [27].

The Ministerial Resolution is still deficient in terms of accessibility, since it is also necessary to adopt WCAG 2.0. It is also important to note that it is only directed to the web pages of public institutions [26].

Knowing this problem, this evaluation work seeks to make a current and uniform diagnosis of a set of Peruvian Public Universities, which will allow to know the web accessibility problems they present and provide appropriate recommendations [18].

For this purpose a set of web pages of Peruvian public universities were selected considering the recommendations of the Web Accessibility Initiative (WAI) of the World Wide Web Consortium (W3C) and its methodology Conformity Assessment Web Accessibility version 2.0 [13, 14], which is considered an international standard adopted by many countries and is already an ISO called ISO/IEC (ISO/IEC 40500: 2012) [36].

1.1 Web Accessibility

Web accessibility can be defined as a universal access to the Web, regardless of hardware, software, language, culture, geographical location or the physical or mental abilities of users [30].

The goal of web accessibility is to ensure that the information or services delivered through web sites are available and can be used by the widest possible audience [22].

1.2 WCAG Web Accessibility Guidelines

The WCAG guidelines are aimed at those who generate content for the Web and consist of specific recommendations whose focus is on making the content presented in an accessible form. WAI elaborated annexed guides that exploit each point and detail the steps to follow to implement them [21].

WCAG version 1.0

WCAG version 1.0 was an important advance in making the Internet more accessible for people with disabilities. Completed in 1999, WCAG 1.0 provides 14 guidelines and 65 verification points that can be used to determine if the accessibility of a web page is met, through 3 priorities and 3 levels of compliance or adequacy levels [38, 31]:

- Priority 1: Must be fulfilled. It is a basic requirement. It refers to those requirements of the verification points that a Web page must comply with in order not to hinder or prevent access to a large group of users.
- Priority 2: It should be fulfilled. Remove certain barriers. That is, those elements that "must" be grouped to eliminate important barriers in access by different groups are grouped.
- Priority 3: It could be fulfilled. It would improve accessibility for certain groups. It refers to certain characteristics that the Website must comply with in order to reduce the difficulties that some groups of users may encounter when accessing it. These

are recommendations that affect a smaller number of potential users, but that improve the accessibility and usability of the page in general.

In accordance with these priorities, there are 3 levels of compliance in the accessibility assessment:

- Level A. All the checks of priority 1 have been met.
- Level AA. All the checks of priority 1 and 2 have been met.
- Level AAA. All the checks of priority 1, 2 and 3 have been satisfied.

WCAG version 2.0

WCAG 2.0 improves the initial standard by applying to more advanced technologies, being more flexible, detailing in a more precise way which are the checks to be carried out and incorporating better documentation [22].

Unlike the WCAG 1.0 developed exclusively for web technologies that existed in 1999 (HTML, CSS and JavaScript), the WCAG 2.0 was developed in a technologically neutral way. However, sufficient techniques were also developed that provide guidance and examples to meet the guidelines using specific technologies.

he WCAG 2.0 guidelines are composed of 4 principles, 12 guidelines and 61 criteria, each of which will have different levels of compliance (A, AA, AAA), in addition to a set of sufficient techniques and advisory techniques [35, 39]:

- Principle 1: Perceptible: The information and the components of the user interface must be presented in the way they can be perceived. It consists of 4 guidelines and 22 compliance criteria.
- Principle 2: Operable: The components of the user interface and navigation must be operable. It consists of 4 guidelines and 20 compliance criteria.
- Principle 3: Understandable: Information and user interface management must be understandable. It consists of 3 guidelines and 17 compliance criteria.
- Principle 4: Robust: The content must be robust enough to rely on its interpretation by a wide variety of users. It consists of 1 guideline and 2 compliance criteria.

1.3   Tools for Automatic Review of Accessibility

Tools for automatic review of accessibility are programs or online services that check the level of accessibility of a web site using a variety of tools. Using these automatic testing tools helps minimize time and seems less complicated [25]. Some of these automatic tools are described on the W3C website [37].

The use of these accessibility tools will depend on the size and scope of the websites. Some tools are easier to use, others allow to evaluate a page at a time, some provide only a quick scan and evaluation, while others offer a greater focus on the details and are able to review a website with multiple pages [32].

It is a fact that automated tests save time and labor, but manual tests (performed by humans) give greater precision [40]. According to Saleem's review [25] there are 3 categories of results when evaluating websites. First, the real positives are real problems discovered by these tools. Secondly, false positives are errors reported by tools, but when human judgment is used, errors do not occur. Finally, false negatives are defined as errors that cannot be detected by tools [29].

It is for this reason that studies indicate that when performing an accessibility evaluation, a combination of manual and automatic evaluations should be used as much as possible [25].

2 WCAG 2.0 Web Accessibility Evaluation on University Websites

In the study by Zaphiris et al. [20] an accessibility assessment work was carried out on the websites of 7 universities in Cyprus (3 public and 4 private), for which an evaluation was carried out that combined manual and automatic tests. In addition, questionnaires were carried out to determine whether the university authorities knew about the provisions and regulations for web accessibility within their study centers.

In the study by Hilera et al. [12] describes an evaluation of accessibility of the contents of the Web portals of some of the most important foreign and Spanish universities according to three university rankings, checking compliance with WCAG 2.0.

On the other hand, Kane et al. [16] conducted an accessibility study using a multi-method analysis on the homepages of the top 100 universities at the international level, where each site was analyzed by reviewing compliance with WCAG 2.0 accessibility standards and using automatic tools and manual tests.

In the paper Pendergast et al. [24], an examination is made of the requirements of accessibility laws, the formation of the accessibility initiative and the consequent WCAG 2.0. The accessibility testing tools for web sites and web content are discussed and then used to measure the level of compliance of several universities in the United States, finding that in all the websites of the universities had multiple accessibility errors.

In both Navarrete and Lujan Mora [22] perform an evaluation work through which is verified through software tools, the level of compliance with the guidelines on web accessibility and the observance of the syntax of markup languages and style sheets, in the web portals of the main universities of Ecuador. From the results of the analysis a series of guidelines is established to improve the design of the web portals of the universities. The study finds its motivation in the regulations on web accessibility in Ecuador that is part of the declaration of the National Plan for Good Living, 2013–2017.

On the other hand, Laitano [18] presents a study where he makes a first diagnosis of web accessibility carried out in 2012 on a sample of pages of the Argentine public university space. The evaluation verifies the compliance of the WCAG 2.0, contemplating the methodological recommendations of the W3C. The results suggest that the web accessibility barriers found are mostly serious (level A). The most frequent are related to the syntax of the markup language, with the presentation of the content, with the non-textual content and with the visual readability of the text. It also shows that certain groups of people could be particularly favored by the solution of these barriers.

In as much Cordova Solís [6] makes a comparative study of web accessibility in portals of Peruvian universities that offer distance education at the undergraduate level, following the fulfillment of the priorities of the web accessibility contemplated in the Peruvian legislation based on the directives of the W3C. To this end, evaluations are carried out using accessibility assessment tools (HERA and TAW), showing a high degree of non-compliance with the priorities, which constitute information barriers and access to people with a disability who wish to study in a distance mode.

In the work of Ismail and Kuppusamy [15], an exploratory study was conducted on the accessibility of the web pages of 320 universities in India. For this evaluation, automatic tools were used, and a classification was made considering the compliance guidelines of WCAG 2.0. After this evaluation, a comparative classification was made in 3 layers depending on the level of accessibility. The results of the analysis present proposals for the improvement of the websites.

In the work of Kesswani and Kumar [17] an accessibility assessment is carried out to prestigious universities in India using automatic tools, as well as evaluating the websites of prestigious universities in Germany, China and Russia. The results indicate that most of these study centers follow less than 50% of the WCAG 2.0 accessibility guidelines.

While in the work of Acosta-Vargas et al. [23] a web accessibility assessment is carried out using the content accessibility guidelines of WCAG 2.0 and for this they chose 20 universities that are within the Webometrics ranking. These universities are from North America, Latin America, Asia, Africa and Oceania. For this, automatic tools were used with which they obtained different results.

In conclusion it can be said that the largest number of studies on web accessibility evaluation with the WCAG 2.0 guidelines have been carried out in European universities and in North American universities

With regard to studies in Latin American universities, there is a growing interest in improving the web accessibility of websites both for online and face-to-face education, taking into account that many of these countries have regulations that indicate the use of guidelines of web accessibility based on WCAG 2.0 and even on WCAG 1.0, which are mostly ignored due to lack of knowledge, making the websites of their universities have a very low level of accessibility.

It is also observed that a large part of the studies is carried out with automatic tools, because many of them are quite reliable and provide information that can be evaluated and analyzed quickly without the need for manual tests.

On the other hand, there is very little work on evaluation of web accessibility in Peruvian universities, only found a work on universities that provide distance education, these universities being only private.

3 Methodology

We analyzed a set of web pages of Peruvian public universities that are within the Webometrics Ranking of 2016 considering the WCAG 2.0 [39] and the Methodology of Evaluation of Web Accessibility Conformance (WCAG-EM) [11].

Taking these recommendations into account and what is indicated in the accessibility evaluation works on the websites of the Universities of Lujan-Mora et al. [1, 22], and Laitano [18], the following steps are proposed:

1. Selection of Universities for analysis.
2. Definition of the web pages of the selected universities.
3. Definition of the level of compliance.
4. Selection of the tools for the analysis.
5. Execution of the evaluation.
6. Analyze the results.

3.1   Selection of Universities for Analysis

Based on the work of Hilera et al. [12], the main objective of this work is to perform an accessibility evaluation of web pages of a selection of Peruvian universities that are in an international academic university ranking, in this case the Ranking of Universities of Webometrics, which has a great academic reputation. This ranking, called "Webometrics Ranking of World Universities", is a portal of the Cybernetics Laboratory of the Spanish CSIC [8], which considers the productivity and effect of academic products placed on the Internet.

Before selecting universities, it was revised in Peru there are 51 public universities recognized by the National Superintendence of Higher Education University (SUNEDU) [28], of which 11 are from Lima and 40 other departments. Of this group only 30 public universities are in the Webometrics Portal Ranking 2016 [7]. From this group of 30 public universities it was decided to choose the first 14 of the Ranking as a sample and shown in Table 1.

3.2   Web Pages of the Selected Universities

A preliminary step to the evaluation of accessibility is the selection of the web pages of each university, whose accessibility will be analyzed [12]. That is why different works use different amounts of pages per university, among them we have: Laitano [18], Lujan-Mora et al. [3] and Mohamad and Ahmi [4] who used only the main page (home), in the works of Hilera et al. [12], Lujan-Mora and Acosta [2] were evaluated 3 pages and Navarrete and Luján Mora [22] evaluated 6 pages.

For the present work we have selected 2 sufficiently representative pages that are common for each of the 14 public universities selected in the sample, according to the following criteria:

1. The main page of the website (home), being the most important page in terms of accessibility, because if the main page is not accessible, users may have problems to reach other pages of the site.
2. Academic Offer, Careers. For this case, only one informative web page of an undergraduate program should be taken.

In this way when analyzing 2 web pages of each of the universities you can obtain more balanced results than if we only analyze the main page, and there is a high probability that between the 2 include a larger number of problematic components compared to accessibility.

Table 1. 14 public universities selected for the study

Nro.	Position in Webometrics	University	City	URL	Undergraduate students (*)
1	2	Universidad Nacional Mayor de San Marcos	Lima	http://www.unmsm.edu.pe/	32,131
2	3	Universidad Nacional de Ingeniería Lima	Lima	http://www.uni.edu.pe/	12,174
3	4	Universidad Nacional Agraria La Molina	Lima	http://www.lamolina.edu.pe/	5,828
4	5	Universidad Nacional de San Antonio Abad del Cusco	Cusco	http://www.unsaac.edu.pe/	18,760
5	10	Universidad Nacional de Trujillo	Trujillo	http://www.unitru.edu.pe/	16,657
6	14	Universidad Nacional de San Agustín de Arequipa	Arequipa	http://www.unsa.edu.pe/	27,934
7	19	Universidad Nacional Federico Villarreal	Lima	http://www.unfv.edu.pe/site/	24,135
8	21	Universidad Nacional de la Amazonía Peruana	Iquitos	http://www.unapiquitos.edu.pe/	8,781
9	24	Universidad Nacional del Callao	Lima	http://www.unac.edu.pe/	15,749
10	27	Universidad Nacional del Altiplano	Puno	http://www.unap.edu.pe/web/	20,589
11	28	Universidad Nacional Agraria de la Selva Tingo María	Huánuco	http://www.unas.edu.pe/web/	3,301
12	29	Universidad Nacional de Cajamarca	Cajamarca	http://www.unc.edu.pe/	9,414
13	33	Universidad Nacional de Piura	Piura	http://www.unp.edu.pe/ Universidad/index.html	18,112
14	37	Universidad Nacional San Cristóbal de Huamanga	Ayacucho	http://www.unsch.edu.pe/	11,815

(*) 2015.

It is true that a more exhaustive study of all the web pages of the university would lead to more precise results, but it would be very expensive, and it is probable that most pages of a site follow the same pattern.

3.3   Level of Compliance

After having defined the set of web pages that should be evaluated for the 14 selected public universities, the WCAG 2.0 accessibility assessment indicators are defined, taking into account that WCAGs have a high degree of acceptance at international level, and that they constitute the fundamental indicator in the works of Laitano [18], Lujan-Mora et al. [2, 3, 22], Mohamad and Ahmi [4] and Hilera et al. [12].

Even though the Peruvian regulations establish version 1.0 of the WCAG [9], for the WCAG 2.0 version it has been chosen because of the advantage of being technologically neutral and on the presumption that Peruvian legislation will soon adopt the new standard [18].

There are 3 compliance criteria (A, AA, AAA) for the WCAG guidelines so the conformance levels A and AA were applied, since that is what the WCAG-EM conformity assessment methodology [10] advises and recommends for a good evaluation. The AAA level is desirable, so it is not considered. The use of this level of compliance is supported by the works of Laitano [18], Mohamad and Ahmi [4] and Lujan-Mora et al. [2, 3, 22].

3.4   Tools for the Analysis

There are numerous web accessibility evaluation tools, of which 92 are recommended by the W3C through a list [40], which fulfill several functions:

- Tools for automatic evaluation using various types of standards such as WCAG 2.0, WCAG 1.0, Sect. 508, etc.
- Support tools for manual evaluation that will be used by experts in accessibility evaluation, using WCAG 2.0, WCAG 1.0, Sect. 508, etc.
- Tools for HTML, CSS (or grammar) markup validation.
- Tools for color and contrast evaluation.
- Tools for epilepsy detection.
- Tools for the readability evaluation, etc.

That is why, following the suggestions of the WAI [32] evaluations were made using automatic tools. They can only check compliance criteria that support automation.

Because be evaluated accessibility of websites universities, it has made a summary of accessibility evaluation tools that are listed in the Table 2, considering web evaluation work at universities and government entities:

3.5   Evaluation

In this stage it was verified that each web page complies with the requirements of conformity and with the adequacy level AA of the WCAG 2.0. using the selected automatic evaluation tools, which will check those compliance criteria that support automation, in this case the tools: Achequer, TAW and Examinator.

In addition, grammar validation tests were carried out, which included a review of the proper use of the valid HTML and CSS code. For this, two W3C services were used: Markup Validation Services that verifies the validity of the marking of web

Table 2. Tools for accessibility evaluation

Tool	Guidelines	URL
Achecker	WCAG 2.0—W3C Web Content Accessibility Guidelines 2.0, WCAG 1.0, Section 508, US federal procurement standard, Stanca Act, Italian accessibility legislation, BITV, German government standard	http://achecker.ca
TAW	WCAG 2.0—W3C Web Content Accessibility Guidelines 2.0	http://www.tawdis.net/
Examinator	WCAG 2.0—W3C Web Content Accessibility Guidelines 2.0	http://examinator.ws/

documents in HTML, XHTML, etc. [34] and CSS Validator Service that checks the style of the pages of a web page for the specifications of the CSS [33].

3.6 Results

In this stage, the specific details of the evaluation of each web page of the selected universities were registered, in the following way:

- The summary results of the evaluations using automatic tools, in templates where the type of web page is specified (in this case the main page and the academic information page), the tool with which it was evaluated and the result of this evaluation according to the criteria and guidelines of the WCAG 2.0, with their respective scores. With the analysis of these scores you can have a preliminary result of the level of compliance level A and AA.
- The results of grammar assessments (validation of web documents in HTML, XHTML, CSS), by means of automatic tools.
- Tables and graphs of the problems found by compliance criteria A and AA, in units and percentages, were prepared.

4 Accessibility Evaluation

After defining the tools for evaluating the web pages of the selected public universities, the evaluation was carried out.

4.1 Grammar Validation Evaluation

The results obtained from the validation of HTML and CSS for the home of the selected universities are shown in Table 3 and in Table 4. the range of errors used. With respect to the evaluation of the undergraduate program page, the results obtained by the grammar assessment tools are shown in Table 5.

Table 3. HTML y CSS

Home	HTML		CSS	
University	Errors	Warnings	Errors	Warnings
Universidad Nacional Mayor de San Marcos	71	41	1346	506
Universidad Nacional de Ingeniería	64	5	69	640
Universidad Nacional Agraria La Molina	218	40	8	145
Universidad Nacional de San Antonio Abad del Cusco	27	1	108	849
Universidad Nacional de Trujillo	75	26	27	197
Universidad Nacional de San Agustín de Arequipa	8	26	127	134
Universidad Nacional Federico Villarreal	32	30	75	89
Universidad Nacional de la Amazonía Peruana	99	5	27	348
Universidad Nacional del Callao	2	0	0	0
Universidad Nacional del Altiplano	43	0	251	185
Universidad Nacional Agraria de la Selva Tingo María	36	10	110	241
Universidad Nacional de Cajamarca	143	20	12	88
Universidad Nacional de Piura	4	0	--	--
Universidad Nacional San Cristóbal de Huamanga	39	3	239	805

Table 4. Range of errors by color

Color	Description	Range
Dark green	Less number of errors	0-49
Yellow	Intermediate number of errors	50-144
Dark red	Large number of errors	150>
Red	Not evaluated - Abnormal situation	

4.2   Web Accessibility Evaluation Through Automatic Review

To carry out this evaluation, 3 automatic evaluation tools were used: AChecker, eXaminator and Taw 2.0.

AChecker

The first evaluation was carried out with AChecker using WCAG 2.0 guidelines up to level AA. AChecker classifies accessibility problems into three broad categories: Know Problem, which are problems that have been identified as accurate barriers; Likely problems, which are problems that have been identified as probable barriers and require human judgment; and Potential problems that also require human judgment [19].

For this evaluation, only Known Problems have been taken into account, since according to AChecker are the problems that should be repaired immediately [19].

The problems encountered using AChecker of type A (celestial bar) and AA (green bar) when evaluating the home page are shown in Fig. 1 and in Fig. 2 when evaluating undergraduate program page.

Table 5. HTML y CSS

Undergraduate program page	HTML		CSS	
University	Errors	Warnings	Errors	Warnings
Universidad Nacional Mayor de San Marcos	13	13	4	18
Universidad Nacional de Ingeniería	31	8	69	620
Universidad Nacional Agraria La Molina	51	28	7	30
Universidad Nacional de San Antonio Abad del Cusco	10	4	48	566
Universidad Nacional de Trujillo	19	6	3	344
Universidad Nacional de San Agustín de Arequipa	8	14	127	134
Universidad Nacional Federico Villarreal	15	5	77	64
Universidad Nacional de la Amazonía Peruana	24	5	26	451
Universidad Nacional del Callao	5	2	91	670
Universidad Nacional del Altiplano	4	1	251	193
Universidad Nacional Agraria de la Selva Tingo María	14	11	110	241
Universidad Nacional de Cajamarca	67	6	7	72
Universidad Nacional de Piura				
Universidad Nacional San Cristóbal de Huamanga				

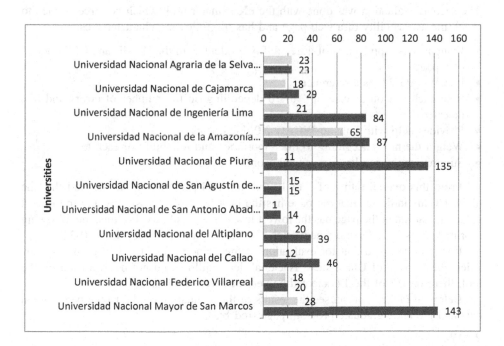

Fig. 1. Evaluation of level A and AA of the home with AChecker (Color figure online)

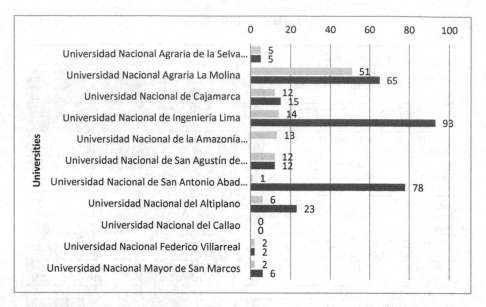

Fig. 2. Level A and AA assessment of the undergraduate program page (Color figure online)

eXaminator

The second evaluation was done with the eXaminator tool, which is a free service to check the accessibility of a web page and has the following characteristics:

- Evaluates the application of accessibility guidelines in the HTML and CSS content of a page.
- Use WCAG 2.0 as a reference.
- Rate each test on a scale of 1 to 10 depending on the number of errors and hits detected.
- Provides help with links to WCAG 2.0 documents.
- Weight the notes according to the importance and reliability of each test.
- Summarize the results in a general score.

From this overall rating of 1 to 10 that the tool performs, it can be said that the highest value indicates that the page has the best level of accessibility and the lowest value indicates that the page has the lowest level of accessibility. For this, the following scoring ranges have been defined: High (7-10), Medium (6.9-4.0), Low (0-3.9).

It should be noted that for evaluation of the home pages of the 14 public universities, the website of Universidad Nacional de Trujillo could not be evaluated by the tool, therefore 13 of the 14 selected universities were evaluated.

Below in Fig. 3 you can see the results of the evaluation on the Home page (green bar) and the undergraduate program page (red bar).

TAW

The third evaluation was made with the Taw 2.0 tool, which is an online tool that analyzes the page, based on WCAG 2.0 and generates a report.

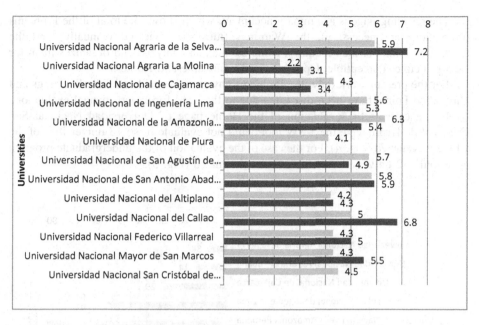

Fig. 3. Evaluation using eXaminator (Color figure online)

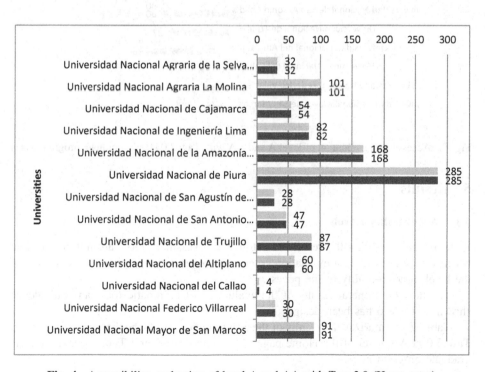

Fig. 4. Accessibility evaluation of level A and AA with Taw 2.0 (Home page)

The resulting page is a summary document, which shows the total of the Problems (corrections are necessary), the Warnings (must be reviewed manually) and the Unverified Points (which require a complete manual analysis) and organizes them for each principle (Perceptible, Operable, Understandable and Robust).

For the present work only, the Problems have been considered. The Warnings and Unverified Points have been discarded due to the need for expert manual evaluation.

In the case of the evaluation of the Home page of Universidad Nacional San Cristobal de Huamanga, the TAW tool could not evaluate it, so 13 universities of the 14 were evaluated (Fig. 4). For the case of the evaluation of the undergraduate program page, only 12 universities of the 14 were evaluated (Fig. 5).

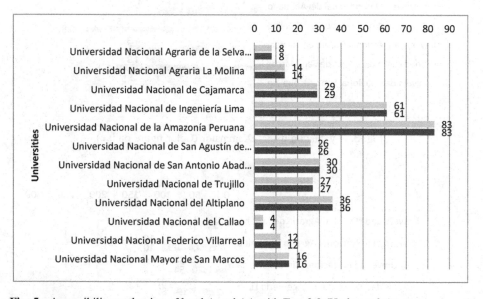

Fig. 5. Accessibility evaluation of level A and AA with Taw 2.0 (Undergraduate program page)

5 Results

5.1 Accessibility Levels

It should be noted that the results of automated assessment tools are not comparable because they use different evaluation criteria, however they can give a similar view of the level of accessibility of the pages.

To show the general results of the evaluation of automatic tools an equivalence shown in Table 6 has been designed.

Table 7 summarizes the results of the 3 automatic tools aChecker, eXaminator and Taw 2.0 at AA level of the Home page of the universities and Table 8 of the undergraduate program page.

Table 6. Ranges by error and score

Color	Description	Errors (AChecker and Taw)	Score (eXaminator)
Dark green	Less number of errors / High accessibility score	0-49	8-10
Yellow	Intermediate number of errors / Medium accessibility score	50-144	4-7.9
Dark red	Large number of errors / Low acccessibility score	150>	0-3.9
Red	Not evaluated - Abnormal situation		

Table 7. Accesssibility results (Home page)

University	Achecker (AA)	eXaminator	Taw 2.0 (AA)
Universidad Nacional Mayor de San Marcos	143	4.3	91
Universidad Nacional de Ingeniería	84	5.6	82
Universidad Nacional Agraria La Molina		2.2	101
Universidad Nacional de San Antonio Abad del Cusco	15	5.9	47
Universidad Nacional de Trujillo			
Universidad Nacional de San Agustín de Arequipa	15	5.7	28
Universidad Nacional Federico Villarreal	20	4.3	30
Universidad Nacional de la Amazonía Peruana	87	6.3	168
Universidad Nacional del Callao	12	5	4
Universidad Nacional del Altiplano	39	4.2	60
Universidad Nacional Agraria de la Selva Tingo María	23	7.2	32
Universidad Nacional de Cajamarca	29	4.3	54
Universidad Nacional de Piura	135	4.1	285
Universidad Nacional San Cristóbal de Huamanga		4.5	

Table 8. Accessibility results (undergraduate program page)

University	Achecker (AA)	eXaminator	Taw 2.0 (AA)
Universidad Nacional Mayor de San Marcos	6	5.5	16
Universidad Nacional de Ingeniería	93	5.3	61
Universidad Nacional Agraria La Molina	65	3.1	14
Universidad Nacional de San Antonio Abad del Cusco	78	5.9	30
Universidad Nacional de Trujillo			27
Universidad Nacional de San Agustín de Arequipa	12	4.9	26
Universidad Nacional Federico Villarreal	2	5	12
Universidad Nacional de la Amazonía Peruana		5.4	83
Universidad Nacional del Callao	0	6.8	4
Universidad Nacional del Altiplano	23	4.3	36
Universidad Nacional Agraria de la Selva Tingo María	5	7.2	8
Universidad Nacional de Cajamarca	15	3.4	29
Universidad Nacional de Piura			
Universidad Nacional San Cristóbal de Huamanga			

In general, none of the university pages achieves the AA compliance level of WCAG 2.0 and therefore would not meet the minimum level recommended by the WCAG-EM Conformity Assessment Methodology to indicate that a Website is accessible.

5.2 Most Common Accessibility Problems

Using the tools TAW 2.0 and AChecker, it has been possible to classify the most common accessibility problems, based on non-compliance with WCAG 2.0 criteria at levels A and AA for the 14 selected universities. It must be borne in mind that each tool does not necessarily evaluate the same criteria, so some differences will be found.

5.2.1 Processing (Level A)

The error in the compliance criterion 4.1.1 is presented due to the duplication of type ID values. Duplication can be problematic for user applications that depend on this attribute to correctly present relationships between different parts of the content. Also presented by misuse of labels attribute start and end markers, which would prevent assistive technology to interpret the page.

5.2.2 Purpose of the Links (Level A)

The error in criterion 2.4.4 is shown because the Title attribute does not provide additional information to clarify in more detail the purpose of the link. To do this, it must be verified that the Title attribute, together with the link text, described the purpose of the link.

If the supplementary information provided by the title attribute is something that the user must know before following the link, as a warning, then it must be provided in the link text and not in the title attribute.

5.2.3 In-Formation and Relationships (Level A) and 1.4.4 - Change of Text Size (Level AA)

It is recommended to use CSS to control the visual presentation of the text.

5.2.4 Non-Text Content (Level A)

The failure of criterion 1.1.1 arises due to the omission of the alt attribute in elements img, area, and input of type "image". Alternative texts are the main means to make information accessible, since they can be interpreted through any sensory modality (visual, auditory or tactile) that best meets the needs of the user.

5.2.5 Contrast (Level AA)

The error in criterion 1.4.3 is due to the specification of colors of the front without specifying background colors or vice versa. It is recommended that the foreground and background color be defined in the same CSS rule. In this way, users with loss of vision or cognitive ability, with language and learning problems, are given access to a web page.

5.2.6   Keyboard (Level A)

It is recommended, to comply with criterion 2.1.1, to enable all the functionalities for the use of the keyboard, in this way users who use the keyboard and the wide variety of technical aids that emulate the pressure of the keys will be able to access them.

5.2.7   Language of the Page (Level A)

It is recommended, to comply with criterion 3.1.1, that the content developers provide on the page the information to correctly present the texts and other linguistic contents, with the purpose that applications such as screen readers can load the pronunciation rules, or the Media players can display subtitles correctly.

5.2.8   Labels or Instructions (Level A)

It is recommended, to comply with criterion 3.3.2, to design user interfaces that provide simple instructions for entering information, such as label associated with visually connected input.

6   Conclusions and Future Works

The WCAG-EM methodology has been applied to analyze the degree of compliance with guidelines 2.0 because it is a known international standard. Two pages of each of the 14 public universities were evaluated: the home page (or home) and a page of undergraduate program, in order to have more balanced results and because in the two pages have found more of problematic components.

The grammatical level evaluation of the 14 pages with the tools W3C Markup Validation Service and W3C CSS Validation Service, indicated that all pages show errors at the level of HTML and CSS, and even universities present a high number of errors on homepage, which would indicate that the code should be reviewed.

The result of the evaluation with the tools Taw 2.0 and AChecker indicates that all the evaluated pages of the public universities, present breaches in the criteria of the WCAG 2.0, both at level A and AA, which is mostly serious. The most frequent are related to the syntax of the markup language, with the presentation of the content, with the non-textual content, with the purpose of the links and the readability of the text. This makes it impossible to guarantee the perception of the contents by most people and the reliable interpretation of them by a wide range of user assistance applications.

Regarding the evaluation carried out by the eXaminator tool, the average evaluation of home pages and undergraduate programs are 4.8 and 5.2 of accessibility level respectively, which would indicate that there is no substantial difference in level of accessibility between the sites. And indicate that both pages have a fairly low level of accessibility.

As it has been possible to demonstrate through this work, the Peruvian public universities do not reach the minimum level of compliance required by WCAG 2.0. This positions Peru in a situation like that of other countries in Latin America. As shown by a study in Chile, where it was shown that none of the 58 university portals reached the minimum level of WCGA 2.0, similarly in Ecuador a study showed that none of the pages are accessible.

Regarding the lines of future work, the following are identified:

Extend the study to the total of Peruvian public universities, and even involve private universities, with the purpose of knowing more widely the level of accessibility of Peruvian universities. Also consider increasing the study of pages by university.

Involve users of universities in the evaluation, as suggested by WCAG-EM, to better understand the use of the evaluated web pages.

References

1. Acosta, T., Luján-Mora, S.: Analysis of the accessibility in websites of Ecuadorian universities of excellence. Enfoqute. **8**(1), 46–61 (2017)
2. Acosta, T., Luján-Mora, S.: Errores de accesibilidad más comunes en los sitios web de las universidades ecuatorianas Most common accessibility errors in websites of Ecuadorian universities.
3. Acosta-Vargas, P., et al.: Evaluación de la accesibilidad de las páginas web de las universidades ecuatorianas (2016)
4. Ahmi, A., Mohamad, R.: Evaluating accessibility of Malaysian public universities websites using achecker and wave. J. ICT. **15**(2), 193–214 (2016)
5. Congreso de la República: Perú- Ley 28530: Ley de promoción de acceso a Internet a las personas con discapacidad (2004)
6. Córdova Solís, M.Á.: Estudio comparativo de accesibilidad web en portales informativos de universidades peruanas de educación a distancia. In: Actas del III Congreso Iberoamericano sobre Calidad y Accesibilidad de la Formación Virtual: CAFVIR 2012, pp. 63–73. Servicio de Publicaciones, Madrid (2012)
7. CSIC: Perú | Ranking Web de Universidades. http://www.webometrics.info/es/Latin_America_es/Per%C3%BA
8. CSIC: Ranking Web de Universidades. http://www.webometrics.info/es
9. Cuervo, J.: Resolución Ministerial n° 126-2009-PCM de 25 marzo 2009, aprueba lineamientos para Accesibilidad a páginas web y aplicaciones para telefonía móvil para instituciones públicas del Sistema Nacional de Informática (2014) http://www.informatica-juridica.com/anexos/resolucion-ministerial-no-126-2009-pcm-de-25-marzo-2009-aprueba-lineamientos-para-accesibilidad-a-paginas-web-y-aplicaciones-para-telefonia-movil-para-instituciones-publicas-del-sistema-nacional-de-in/
10. Velleman, E., et al.: Website Accessibility Conformance Evaluation Methodology (WCAG-EM) 1.0. https://www.w3.org/TR/WCAG-EM/
11. Figueroa Valdés, F.: Desarrollo de sitios Web: la ley, el orden y los estándares (2007). http://eprints.rclis.org/10190/
12. Hilera, J.R., et al.: Evaluación de la accesibilidad de páginas web de universidades españolas y extranjeras incluidas en rankings universitarios internacionales. Rev. Esp. Doc. Científica. **36**(1), 004 (2013)
13. Initiative (WAI), W.W.A.: WAI Guidelines and Techniques | Web Accessibility Initiative (WAI) | W3C. https://www.w3.org/WAI/guid-tech
14. Initiative (WAI), W.W.A.: Web Accessibility Initiative (WAI) - home page | Web Accessibility Initiative (WAI) | W3C. https://www.w3.org/WAI/
15. Ismail, A., Kuppusamy, K.S.: Accessibility of Indian universities' homepages: an exploratory study. J. King Saud Univ. - Comput. Inf. Sci. **30**, 268–278 (2016)

16. Kane, S.K., et al.: A web accessibility report card for top international university web sites. In: Proceedings of the 2007 International Cross-Disciplinary Conference on Web Accessibility (W4A). pp. 148–156. ACM, New York (2007)
17. Kesswani, N., Kumar, S.: Accessibility analysis of websites of educational institutions. Recent Trends Eng. Mater. Sci. **8**, 210–212 (2016)
18. Laitano, M.I.: Accesibilidad web en el espacio universitario público argentino. Rev. Esp. Doc. Científica **38**(1) (2015) 2015DO - 103989redc201511136
19. Luján-Mora, S., et al.: Egovernment and web accessibility in South America. In: 2014 First International Conference on eDemocracy & eGovernment (ICEDEG), pp. 77–82 (2014)
20. Michailidou, E., et al.: eInclusion@ cyprus universities: provision and web accessibility. In: CHI 2012 Extended Abstracts on Human Factors in Computing Systems, pp. 1637–1642. ACM (2012)
21. Naftali, M.R.: Análisis e Integración de métricas para la Accesibilidad Web. Universidad de Buenos Aires (2010)
22. Navarrete, R., Luján Mora, S.: Accesibilidad web en las Universidades del Ecuador. Análisis preliminar (2014)
23. Acosta-Vargas, P., et al.: Evaluation of the web accessibility of higher-education websites. In: 2016 15th International Conference on Information Technology Based Higher Education and Training (ITHET), pp. 1–6 (2016)
24. Pendergast, M.O.: Evaluating the Accessibility of Online University Education. Int. J. Online Pedagogy Course Des. IJOPCD **7**(1), 1–14 (2017)
25. Saleem, M.: Web accessibility compliance for e-Government websites in the Gulf region. Edith Cowan University (2016)
26. Sam-Anlas, C.A., Stable-Rodríguez, Y.: Evaluación de la accesibilidad web de los portales del Estado en Perú. Rev. Esp. Doc. Científica **39**(1) (2016). 2016DO - 103989redc201611213
27. Sam-Anlas, C.A., Stable-Rodríguez, Y.S.: Evaluación de la Accesibilidad: Web del Portal de la Biblioteca Nacional del Perú. Bibl. An. Investig. **11**, 224–231 (2015)
28. SUNEDU: Universidades Públicas. https://www.sunedu.gob.pe/universidades-publicas/
29. Vigo, M., et al.: Benchmarking web accessibility evaluation tools: measuring the harm of sole reliance on automated tests. In: Proceedings of the 10th International Cross-Disciplinary Conference on Web Accessibility, pp. 1:1–1:10. ACM, New York (2013)
30. W3C: Accessibility - W3C. https://www.w3.org/standards/webdesign/accessibility
31. W3C: Checklist of Checkpoints for Web Content Accessibility Guidelines 1.0. https://www.w3.org/TR/1999/WAI-WEBCONTENT-19990505/full-checklist
32. W3C: Selecting Web Accessibility Evaluation Tools | Web Accessibility Initiative (WAI) | W3C. https://www.w3.org/WAI/eval/selectingtools
33. W3C: The W3C CSS Validation Service. https://jigsaw.w3.org/css-validator/validator.html. en
34. W3C: The W3C Markup Validation Service. https://validator.w3.org/
35. W3C: Understanding WCAG 2.0. https://www.w3.org/TR/UNDERSTANDING-WCAG20/
36. W3C: W3C Web Content Accessibility Guidelines 2.0 approved as an ISO/IEC International Standard. https://www.w3.org/2012/07/wcag2pas-pr.html
37. W3C: Web Accessibility Evaluation Tools List. https://www.w3.org/WAI/ER/tools/
38. W3C: Web Content Accessibility Guidelines 1.0. https://www.w3.org/TR/WCAG10/
39. W3C: Web Content Accessibility Guidelines (WCAG) 2.0. https://www.w3.org/TR/WCAG20/
40. W3C: WebAIM: Accessibility Evaluation Tools. https://webaim.org/articles/tools/

Co-design with Raspberry Pi: Developing and Hosting Sustainable Community Application

Salomao David[1($\boxtimes$)] and Esperança Muchave[2]

[1] Research and Development Department,
Communications Regulatory Authority of Mozambique,
Praça 16 de Junho 340, Maputo, Mozambique
sdavid@incm.gov.mz

[2] Research and Development Department, Business School, University of Saint Thomas,
Sommerchield II, Parcela 242/02 Rua Beijo Da Mulata, Maputo, Mozambique

Abstract. The recent financial crisis forced the developing context to embrace economic and social sustainability as an agenda to be considered throughout the conception and deployment of ICT initiatives. This article presents the implications of merging both communities knowledge and information system professional practices to produce application while addressing affordability in the early rounds of design. The developers used Raspberry Pi for hosting the application, Raspberry Pi is a credit card-sized Single-Board Computer (SBC), can be carried in the pocket, handbag, and it is lightweight and does consume less power and energy as compared to traditional computers.

Keywords: Co-design · Raspeberry Pi · Communities · Application · Hosting
ICT

1 Introduction

The recent sub-Saharan financial crisis has drawn attention to the role of affordability in Information and Communication Technology (ICT); unfortunately, affordability has a devastating effect on growth and diffusion of ICT in the developing context (Udo et al. 2008). However, with affordability dilemmas, the sub-Saharan region embraced financial and social sustainability as an agenda to be considered throughout the conception and deployment of ICT initiatives.

Since 2015, Mozambican developers hosted most of the non-profit applications, content and media produced in Mozambique in open access servers hosted elsewhere. Needless to say, that developers known the limitations, and technical implications provided by open access servers. The impact of this action was soon noticed by the users adopting international applications to access content and media produced in Mozambique and being exposed to an overwhelming amount of ads and media produced elsewhere.

According to David et al. (2013), co-design refers to the conception or creation of artefacts drawing on a shared vision, social learning and mutual understanding among all key stakeholders, taking into account that all those involved in the design process

© Springer International Publishing AG, part of Springer Nature 2018
A. Marcus and W. Wang (Eds.): DUXU 2018, LNCS 10920, pp. 608–619, 2018.
https://doi.org/10.1007/978-3-319-91806-8_47

have somehow different perspectives and expectations which should be adequately considered.

The recent popularity of Internet of Things (IoT) and the growth of bandwidth-hungry applications, it does turn down the cost of ICT (Guo et al. 2012). IoT is a new communication paradigm that envisions a near future, in which the object of everyday life will be equipped with microcontrollers, transceivers for digital communication, and suitable protocol stacks that will allow IoT to communicate with users, becoming an integral part of the Internet (Krishna 2017).

Bearing in mind the advancement of IoT and design approaches that nurture users perception and context; a group of Mozambican developers, active users and promotors of Mozambican content and media, set on a journey to adopt co-design as an approach to address affordability and development of non-profit applications.

In this study, co-design was used to infuse communities knowledge and developers practices to produce an application for the local commuter while addressing affordability in the early rounds of design. Furthermore, affordability and sustainability constraints where addressed by adopting Raspberry Pi and by imbuing developers practices with communities knowledge.

The study presents on the first instance thoughtful interaction design actions conducted by a well-structured and selected group of individuals to co-design an application, and on a secondary instance, the human-computer interactions are evaluated to provide understanding about the impact of contextual interaction design.

2   Research Background

In Mozambique, software development has been gaining space and acceptance since the introduction of the subject in the higher education curriculum. The field has also gained acceptance in industries such as entertainment, education, health and banking, as result of the urban diffusion of the Internet.

The Internet commercial growth and diffusion created favourable conditions for the emergence of third-party domain services providers and hosting companies with prices ranging from free to a couple of US dollars (Rabinovich and Aggarwal 1999).

The free hosting is a limited service that provides limited bandwidth, storage and memory, in most cases space and bandwidth provided is not enough for hosting web applications. With this type of service, ads from the hosting provider or other third-party vendors are part of the free hosting package.

The paid hosting services are provided in package bundles from which the developer can select the required bandwidth, storage and memory. For developers in the sub-Saharan region, the main limitation is the price and method of payment. Hence free hosting, which only required a mail registration with all limitations becomes the first selected hosting.

The high cost of hosting it does not only affects developers, but it also affects the users and people who produce content and media. The Internet provided in the sub-Saharan region in most cases covers urban areas, there are few exceptions where the service reaches the rural areas. There exists in the region a digital divide which creates a significant disparity between the has and has not. With developers aiming at hosting services in free hosting sites, there will be a social group within communities which will have difficulties to access content and media created in the country mainly because internet services providers who are not limited to urban areas charge high sums. The problem here addressed are not faced only by users but also to producers of content who are geographically located in the rural areas, they will face the unpleased reality of not being able to upload local content.

3   Literature Review in Co-design

The practice of collective creativity in design has been around for nearly 40 years, going under the name of participatory design (Northern European) or user-centred design (United States) (Sanders and Stappers 2008). In 1995, Edworthy and Stanton (1995) presented user-centred as the approach that identifies and capitalises upon the knowledge of the relevant user-population (e.g. medics, pilots, control room operators), moreover Nesset and Large (2004) emphasised that the user-centred approach "had been typical to position users as a testing or evaluation services for designers to ensure those users needs are met". Furthermore, Nesset and Large (2004) mentioned that the methods employed in user-centred design involve participant observation, system logs, qualitative written surveys or interviews to determine likes, unlike and difficulties.

Kensing and Blomber (1998) described the participatory design as an approach to the assessment, design, and development of technology and organisation systems. Following Nesset and Large (2004) participatory design concept, users change out roles from simple observers to the source of knowledge on their domain, their participation takes a role of peer co-designers, in which users design their expertise and context information.

Sanders et al. (2010) described the participatory design in early 2010 as an emerging design practice that involved different non-designers in various activities throughout the design process.

The terms co-creation and co-design have often been confused and treated synonymously with one another Sanders and Stappers (2008), and Sanders and Simons (2009) pointed out that co-design is directly related to co-creation, in other words, co-design is a specific instance of co-creation Sanders and Stappers (2008).

Russo-Spena and Mele (2012) highlighted that many scholars (Ramaswamy and Gouillart, 2010; Chesbrough, 2011; Russo-Spena and Colurcio, 2010) use the term co-creation to address how social, cultural, economic and technological changes enable organisations, groups and individuals to interact, collaborate, and solve problems by jointly generate solutions and create sustainable artefacts.

Since the past decade researchers (Kleinsmann and Valkenburg 2008; Sanders and Stappers 2008; Steen et al. 2011; Russo-Spena and Mele 2012; David et al. 2013) presented different definitions and approaches for co-design, each with its particularity vision and understanding but all the definitions and approaches pointed to the same fundamental approach.

Kleinsmann and Valkenburg (2008) defined co-design as the process in which actors from different disciplines share their knowledge about both the design process and the design content. They added mentioning that co-designing was done to create shared understanding on both aspects, to be able to integrate and explore their knowledge and to achieve the broader common objective: the new product to be co-designed.

Sanders and Stappers (2008) described co-design as broader sense to refer to the creativity of designers and people not trained in design working together in the design development process.

Steen et al. (2011) perceive co-design, as an approach in which diverse experts (researchers, practitioners, designers and developers) come together to create an artefact cooperatively.

Russo-Spena and Mele (2012) presented their view of co-design as a wide range of practices based on the engagement of many actors linked by a shared context, interest, and it is aimed at a more specific purpose: to bridge the gap between identified ideas or needs and the possibility of finding a solution. Russo-Spena and Mele (2012) went forward showing that the distinguishing characteristic of co-design practices was the high level of interactive learning content, and that co-design was not only seen as an output from inspiration but also as a thought process that involved various activities, such as speaking, writing, drawing, showing, modelling, constructing and documenting.

The approach suggested by David et al. (2013), it circles the co-creation of artefacts drawing on a shared vision, social learning and mutual understanding among all key stakeholders. The approach adopted by David et al. (2013) takes into consideration that all those involved in the design process have somehow different perspectives and expectations which should be adequately addressed. This approach allows researchers to infuse different social and design perspectives to create a solution that would nurture both community and developer's knowledge.

4 Study Methodology

To bound the population of people interested in media and content for entertainment, a group of developers from the University of Saint Thomas of Mozambique benchmarked most of the websites who promote Mozambican events and media (music, cinema, arts). From the exercise were located sixteen (16) active promoters from Maputo, three from Beira and two from Nampula.

Survey questionnaires consisting of demographic items and 20 primary coded questions integrated with 10 secondary coded and open-ended questions were provided online through survey monkey. The survey resulted in 19 valid responses of which 17 were willing to participate physically in the design process, and the remaining two were willing to participate using Skype.

The second phase was to look for active users of content and media produced in Mozambique, to do so were searched online users who had more than 10 downloads and stream of music per week. This search was done on social medias of websites such as musicafresca.com and musicaboa.net.

Where identified three active users, from them it was possible to understand that most of these users are located in schools such as Josina Machel and Francisco Many-anga. Hence five surveyors scaled the schools where there were selected students from grade eight, nine and ten. The surveyors scaled approximately three classes per grade and were located approximately 30 active users. The 30 active users were divided into two groups with two team leaders that would be speaking for each group.

At this stage, three groups were formed to co-design the solution, one group of developers, the other of active users and a group of events promoters who understand about the online and physical promotion of events and media.

The active users were entrusted with the responsibility to select at least five things they like on websites and five things they do not like seeing when they are trying to access content and media. The developers were entrusted with the responsibility of coming up with low-cost technical aspects to develop and host a geo-contextualised solution. Promoters were responsible for specifying the categories to be promoted and provide information about how they promote each category. To evaluate the usage and adoption of the application, google analytics was the selected tool, as it is free for most analysis and to provide real-time data.

5 Design and Development

During the early process of designing the solution, developers requested that all the participants (promoters and active users) review additional websites for benchmarking purposes or provided a sample of websites or platforms used for downloads and promotion of music, cinema information and events, and provided at least three positive aspects and negative aspects of the selected websites. Moreover, developers had to evaluate technological infrastructure and explain to the participants the financial implications. At the end of both processes, each group had to present the outcomes of their task and later brainstorm on the implementation process.

The promoters focus on defining the name of the application "+Musica" (www.musica.co.mz) a web-based application, device independent which aims to provide information about entertainment, cinema for entire Mozambique. The platform is feed by the community, with individual accounts able to upload content to be displayed to people who are looking for entertainment information, the application should not have international, or Google Ads instead it should have contextualised and well-structured ads from local companies or business.

The active users addressed the application layout, emphasising the results of the benchmark about the likes, dislikes and needs of a user on a platform. The active users reported that there are five things that the whole group agreed that are unnecessary and unsatisfactory in applications:

- Google Ads, which according to them are annoying and inappropriate;
- Contents are displayed without any regard for users age. Hence material on the website should be censored before making public;
- Content should not contain ads on the website where it was downloaded;
- To access the content and media, there are several redirections;

- Most of the information in a website must be organised chronologically to avoid accessing old content.

The application was developed in three months (October-November 2016), it was taken into consideration the design perspectives of active users, developers and promoters. The application was hosted under the domain www.musica.co.mz, with no ads and where created conditions for any person within the community being able to insert content and media. The application created had (3) categories namely: (1) music, (2) cinema; and (3) events.

Developers turned attention to IoT devices; they are expected to substantially support the sustainable development of future smart cities (Vlacheas et al. 2013). The IoT has been widely adopted due to the urgent solutions sought for viable living conditions and sustainable development. The IoT is inbuilt with a dynamic global and self-configuring network infrastructure where physical, virtual things are identifiable and communicate with interoperable standard and protocols.

The developers were bearing in mind the hosting limitations and the financial benefits IoT devices have to the developers community. Raspberry Pi was adopted to host the application; this is a credit card-sized Single-Board Computer (SBC) developed in the United Kingdom (UK) by the Raspberry Pi Foundation with the intention of promoting the teaching of basic computer science in schools (Wachira 2015). It is interesting to note that Raspberry Pi has a wide range of utilities and can be easily converted to work in any environment.

The Raspberry Pi Foundation developed numerous versions (Raspberry Pi Zero, Zero W, 1 model A+, 1 model B+, 2 model B, 3 model B) of the device since the beginning of the foundation to the present.

In this study, the version used was the Raspberry Pi 1 model B+, which comes with 512 MB of RAM, HDMI port, four USB ports, micro-SD card socket, audio part, camera and DSI display connector, built into a single component. The processor of the model B+ is 32 bit, it has a system chip of 700 MHz, which is built on an ARM11 architecture the same Cambridge-based company that develops processors used in many smart-phones (HTC Dream, iPhone 3G, Nokia N97, HTC Hero) (Forhad Symon et al. 2017).

Similar to any other computer the Raspberry Pi 1 model B+ use an OS in our case we adopted the Raspian, an open source OS that kept the price of the platform low (Maksimovic et al. 2015).

Developers took into consideration other gadgets taking into analyses affordability, power consumption and size. In all three categories the Raspberry Pi 1 model B+ came on top with four main advantages:

- It is portable, it has a credit card size, can be carried in the pocket, handbag, and it is lightweight;

- Consume less power and energy as compared to traditional computers as showed in Table 1 Anwaar and Shah (2015), Raspberry Pi 1 model B+ consumes 11664 (eleven thousand and six hundred and sixty-four) Megajoule (MJ) of energy per year, a very lower amount compared (desktop computer, ProLiant Server);

Table 1. Energy consumption

Devices	Per day	Per month	Per year
Raspberry Pi	48.6 MJ	972 MJ	11664 MJ
Smartphone	108 MJ	2160 MJ	25920 MJ
Laptop	1080 MJ	21600 MJ	259200 MJ
Desktop	1771.2 MJ	35424 MJ	425088 MJ
HPE ProLiant DL580 Gen 10 520 2P	38400 MJ	4147200 MJ	50457000 MJ

- The most interesting feature is affordability; the cost vary between the 25 to 35 USD, very cheaper compared with standard computers; and
- It is suitable for new application development, testing application, debugging, hardware development, play games and hacking.

6   Results and Discussion

The data evaluated in this study was from February to October 2017; during this period the application had 2801 (two thousand and eight hundred and one) visitors from which 48% were new visitors, and the remaining 52% were returning visitors. The quasi-half and half percentage of returning and new visitors it is an indicator that the application has a significant probability to double the number of visitors, as data demonstrates that those who visited the application at least once, tend to become regular visitors and act as application refers.

The 2801 sessions resulted in 12698 (twelve thousand and six hundred ninety-eight) page views with an average duration of 7 minutes per session, from which most of the pages viewed were about music, followed by videos. It means that visitors are more interested in music than any other category.

From the music category where streamed approximately 53197 (fifty-three thousand and one hundred ninety-seven) songs, and were downloaded 6700 (six thousand and seven hundred) songs.

The video category had approximately 3400 (three thousand and four hundred) video views.

The above-mentioned high discrepancy between the streamed times and the number of downloads indicate that most of the visitors prefer to stream than to download, and this can be caused by the type of device, operating system or storage space. The devices used to access the platform where most mobile phones (55.9%) and desktop computers (35.8%) and tablets (8.3%). The operating system (OS) most used by visitors is Android OS, Apple iOS and Windows OS.

The data demonstrate that the majority of application visitors in Mozambique use devices with low storage capacity rounding between 2–4 Gigabytes (GB). Hence, the researchers assumes that the space required to run the OS and mobile content limits the space to store media and content from the application. The iOS users differently from those with low storage capacity, they cannot download music from the application due to Apple restrictions.

An interesting point to notice was that the more extended sessions were done via computers, which leads the researcher to believe that those visitors have been streaming. Further, the researchers could notice that visitors using personal computers access the website via a national network, free access points of internet and home network, differently from those who used mobile phones which in most of the cases used mobile operators network.

The number of megabytes spent by each visitor during the streaming is directly connected with the application server configuration. The streaming bitrate varies from 20 Kilobits (kbps) to 320 kbps; applications with high-quality such as Google Player, Beats Music and Spotify use up to 320 kbps for streaming and consequently increase the amount of data spent by the visitors when streaming compared with those using 64 kbps such as Pandora.

In one hour the amount of data spent by a visitor in an application with a configuration of 320 kbps is 115.2 Megabytes (MB), and with a lower configuration such as 64 kbps, visitors spend in an hour 28.8 MB.

Considering the context of the application users, and taking into consideration the financial constraints, developers configured the server with a lower bitrate (64 kbps). Furthermore, it was adopted a deductive method to calculate the amount of data spent by the visitors in +Musica (www.musica.co.mz). Therefore, it was made an estimative of hours used for streaming, using the average session duration (7 min) times the number of sessions (2801) which resulted in approximately 327 h.

The estimates mentioned above-allowed developers to calculate the quantity of data and traffic generated by visitors, where:

$$xMB = \frac{327\,h \,*\, 28.8\,MB}{1h} = 9417.6\,MB$$

The xMB was converted to GB and Gigabits (Gbps) as shown in the calculation below and the results for the traffic generated with audio streaming was of 75.3 Gbps and visitors spent approximately 9.2 GB.

$$xGB = \frac{9417.6\,MB}{1024} = 9.2\,GB$$

$$xGbps = \frac{9.2\,GB \,*\, 8\,Gbps}{1\,GB} = 73.6\,Gbps$$

The average size of each music downloaded was 6 MB, and the total of downloads was of 6700, with that the researchers were able to calculate the approximated quantity of data (39.3 GB) spent with downloads which resulted in traffic of approximately 314.1 Gbps.

In the first months, the application only received traffic from direct access, and by the end of the evaluated period, the scenario changed, with 37% of the visitors being from sources such as organic search 21%, 15% from social media and 1% from referral searches. Direct access amounts up to date to 63% of traffic generated.

The application was designed to allow users to be informed about all kind of event, visitors of this category were not tracked, because there is a missing link between actual visitors and people who did attend the event.

The internet frequently has been characterised as male-dominated service (Padilla-Walker et al. 2010; Tsai and Tsai 2010), in this study, the results are not different and indicate that the majority of visitors are male with 68% of visitors but with a lower average time spent in the site of approximately 7 min. The female users who are 32% of visitor access the application from developing countries such as Mozambique, South Africa and India with an average double time online than male users.

The visitors age varies between under 15 to over 45; there has been a high promotion of the application in social media (Facebook, WhatsApp and Instagram), most of the promotion is performed by people who visit the application. The highest age group which visited the application range 18 to 24 (45%) followed by the range 25 to 34 (40%) and the remaining 15% were from visitors with age over 35 years.

For the surprise of co-designers (developers, active users and promoters) social media made the application known around the globe in countries where the primary language is not Portuguese such as United States of America, India, Russia, South Korea and China.

Most of the website sessions are from Mozambique with 2398 (85.61%) followed by the United States of America with 193 sessions (6.89%), South Africa 40 (1.43%) and India 37 (1.32%) sessions.

During the analysis period the application was inactive during 3 h for six (6) scheduled maintenance sessions. The maintenance consisted of updating some functionalities and perform upgrades. The functionalities upgraded were related to album upload, and album streaming, the release of each upgrade allowed the co-designers to add new ideas and conceptions.

7 Conclusion

Co-design sustainable ICT solutions, became an emerging form of societal-scale computer supported cooperative activity which challenges communities and developers knowledge of information system. Not only due to the peer-to-peer interaction a phenomenon of sociological and technological design but also to the practices of skilled professionals that have to be infused into community ideas, perceptions and expectations.

The peer-to-peer communication activity anticipated contextual implications on the cultural and political point, and it concluded by becoming the driving force to solve complex critical pieces to deploy and register the application domain. During the development stage public participation had to be assured by allowing the application to work with mobile devices to allow communities the opportunity to interact further with the artefact.

The segregation of tasks between the promoters, active users and developers was the critical success of the co-design process and the application adoption. There were a clear perception and imaginary boundary in which each organisational structure was open to explain the twists and approaches that could be used to produce an application capable of solving the existing problems.

Active users stressed that ads in a foreign language make browsing experience complicated, the application should be easy to browse and capable of delivering content and media. This concern was taken in consideration by designers, by not allowing ads to be hosted in the platform under any circumstance.

The use of low cost and processing devices in this case study allowed developer to perceive that quality can be provided by using Raspberry Pi without reducing or impacting quality. Nevertheless, being a community application, the capability to have more than 50 users simultaneously connected, is a technology limitation due to unavailability of resources required by the hosting device to provide the same quality of service. Moreover, developers believe that such limitation will be solved with the next version of the application.

In this study interactions became imbued with participant activity, discussion from the social to cultural and technical perspective, reflecting on the practices of the social organisation and possible application users.

The release of this application changed the entertainment market in Mozambique directly and indirectly. The introduction of a new application changed the way things were done, after the release of the application, the co-designers continued to benchmark the application, and it was possible to notice competing platforms have been adopting the same design approach. Competing applications such as *musicaFresca* have reduced the number of ads and implemented direct download links while new platforms began to advertise events and local ads.

It is not known if this behaviour changes is related with the appearance of competition in the market or not, what is certain is that the market is becoming competitive which paves the way for more interaction design and collaborative approach to application development.

In this study, it was noticed that language is not a barrier to access a specific type of content, as in the application the portuguese language was used to display content. The information and the structure of the application are written in Portuguese which was not an obstacle for visitors that are non-Portuguese speakers, approximately 60% of the visitors were English speakers, the double percentages over the Portugues speakers and other language speakers.

Furthermore, it is not only about sustainability, or designing an application or putting something in the market, it is about the desire that the market has to use an application that will save bandwidth and result in the better use of technology. While the actual market is hanged on ads, users get frustrated because due to the time required to load the pages.

References

Anwaar, W., Shah, M.A.: Energy Efficient Computing: A Comparison of Raspberry PI with Modern Devices (2015)

David, S., Sabiescu, A., Cantoni, L.: Co-design with communities. A reflection on the literature (2013). https://doi.org/10.13140/RG.2.1.2309.9365

Edworthy, J., Stanton, N.: A user-centred approach to the design and evaluation of auditory warning signals: 1 Methodology. Ergonomics **38**(11), 2262–2280 (1995). https://doi.org/10.1080/00140139508925267

Forhad Symon, A., Hassan, N., Rashid, H., Ahmed, I., Reza, S.: Design and Development of a Smart Baby Monitoring System based on Raspberry Pi and Pi Camera (2017). https://doi.org/10.1109/ICAEE.2017.8255338

Guo, B., Yu, Z., Zhou, X., Zhang, D.: Opportunistic IoT: exploring the social side of the internet of things. In: 2012 IEEE 16th International Conference on Computer Supported Cooperative Work in Design (CSCWD), pp. 925–929. IEEE (2012)

Kensing, F., Blomberg, J.: Participatory design: issues and concerns. Comput. Support. Coop. Work (CSCW) **7**(3–4), 167–185 (1998). https://doi.org/10.1023/A:1008689307411

Kleinsmann, M., Valkenburg, R.: Barriers and enablers for creating shared understanding in co-design projects. Des. Stud. **29**(4), 369–386 (2008). https://doi.org/10.1016/j.destud.2008.03.003

Krishna, P.A.V.: Exploring the Convergence of Big Data and the Internet of Things. IGI Global (2017)

Maksimovic, M., Vujovic, V., Davidović, N., Milosevic, V., Perisic, B.: Raspberry Pi as internet of things hardware: performance and constraints (2015)

Nesset, V., Large, A.: Children in the information technology design process: a review of theories and their applications. Libr. Inf. Sci. Res. **26**(2), 140–161 (2004). https://doi.org/10.1016/j.lisr.2003.12.002

Padilla-Walker, L.M., Nelson, L.J., Carroll, J.S., Jensen, A.C.: More than a just a game: video game and internet use during emerging adulthood. J. Youth Adolesc. **39**(2), 103–113 (2010). https://doi.org/10.1007/s10964-008-9390-8

Rabinovich, M., Aggarwal, A.: RaDaR: a scalable architecture for a global Web hosting service. Comput. Netw. **31**(11), 1545–1561 (1999). https://doi.org/10.1016/S1389-1286(99)00043-2

Russo-Spena, T., Mele, C.: "Five Co-s" in innovating: a practice-based view. J. Serv. Manag. **23**(4), 527–553 (2012). https://doi.org/10.1108/09564231211260404

Sanders, E.B.-N., Brandt, E., Binder, T.: A framework for organizing the tools and techniques of participatory design. In: Proceedings of the 11th Biennial Participatory Design Conference, pp. 195–198. ACM, New York (2010). https://doi.org/10.1145/1900441.1900476

Sanders, E.B.-N., Stappers, P.J.: Co-creation and the new landscapes of design. CoDesign **4**(1), 5–18 (2008). https://doi.org/10.1080/15710880701875068

Sanders, L., Simons, G.: A social vision for value co-creation in design. Open Source Bus. Resour. December 2009

Steen, M., Manschot, M., De Koning, N. Benefits of co-design in service design projects. Int. J. Design **5**(2), 53–60 (2011). http://resolver.tudelft.nl/uuid:eefaaa3c-cc7d-408e-9e00-883c6f2ccb03

Tsai, M.-J., Tsai, C.-C.: Junior high school students' internet usage and self-efficacy: a re-examination of the gender gap. Comput. Educ. **54**(4), 1182–1192 (2010). https://doi.org/10.1016/j.compedu.2009.11.004

Udo, G., Bagchi, K.K., Kirs, P.J.: Diffusion of ICT in developing countries: a qualitative differential analysis of four nations. J. Glob. Inf. Technol. Manage. **11**(1), 6–27 (2008)

Vlacheas, P., Giaffreda, R., Stavroulaki, V., Kelaidonis, D., Foteinos, V., Poulios, G., Demestichas, P., Somov, A., Biswas, A.R., Moessner, K.: Enabling smart cities through a cognitive management framework for the internet of things. IEEE Commun. Mag. **51**(6), 102–111 (2013)

Vujović, V., Maksimović, M.: Raspberry Pi as a sensor web node for home automation. Comput. Electr. Eng. **44**, 153–171 (2015). https://doi.org/10.1016/j.compeleceng.2015.01.019

Wachira, K.: Use of Emergent Mid-Level Computational Devices in the Creation of Robust and Affordable Auxiliary Infrastructure Subsystems (2015). https://doi.org/10.13140/RG.2.1.4510.6722

Research on the Adaptability of Underground Soft Guidance and Culture Based on Memorability

Yang Du[1], Chao Liu[2], and Ye Zhang[1(✉)]

[1] School of Architecture and Art Design, Beijing Jiaotong University,
Beijing 100044, China
531892226@qq.com

[2] Baidu User Experience Department, Baidu, Beijing 100085, China
Liuchao05@baidu.com

Abstract. Make research on the influence of relevance between various soft guidance factors and regional culture of the underground space on the user memory through 50 subway station samples. Firstly, mark out 9 categories and 45 sub elements in extension and connotation aspects of every sample, and preliminarily obtain the rule of the soft guidance of subway station in 9 categories; secondly, analyze every category in accordance with the image scale method. Then, according to the investigation on user memory of various soft guidance, acquire the memory score of every soft guidance. Later, utilize the quantification analysis method to make category score and partial correlation coefficient calculation, and obtain the positive and negative correlation between various sub-factors and memory, so as to get the main categories and factors influencing the soft guidance memory, and give the suggestions for reference for the future soft guidance design.

Keywords: Soft guidance · Memory · Cultural adaption
Quantification theory type I · Kansei engineering

1 Introduction

Following the constant development of road traffic, city expansion and modernization process, the intricate roads in city result in the "difficulty to find the road" for many people [1], while the underground space is easy to get the people in a sense of pressure and insecurity due to its closeness [2]. Meanwhile, the direction recognition of underground space may decrease largely, so that some humanized design is required to improve such situations. The soft guidance, also known as the landmark orientation, is the devices and ornaments or the space and environment change factors (other than the routine orientations) with orientation function formed through the crowd memory based on the differentiated landmark characteristics. The research plans to make surveys on memory strength of multiple soft guidance samples, be aware of which factors have significance influence on their memory among the soft guidance samples of underground spaces, and excavate the correlation between them and the culture.

Firstly by searching the photos in the internet and other ways, the researchers finally decide to take the soft guidance of subway station with rule to follow and in abundant sample number as the research subject, to make preliminary network photo collection. According to the data collected, in the soft guidance of subway station, the soft guidance of public arts is the most significant one in large number, especially the murals and plane decorations oriented to the plane design. Mainly focused on the soft guidance of plane decorations, by collecting the photos of soft guidance of multiple stations, the research plans to partition the categories on the soft orientation through the extension and connotation, of which the extension includes the foreground element type, primary vision type and secondary vision type, as well as the layout and background pattern and color; the connotation comprises the relation of soft guidance and station name, propagation objective and style. Combined with the user's memory strength on the soft guidance of every station, discuss the influence of the correlation, between these categories & sub-factors and the culture, on the soft guidance memory, and find the memory rule of soft guidance. The research will be carried out from two aspects: firstly, make the unrelated category separation on the soft guidance of various stations, and make the factor matching over every soft guidance according to 9 separated categories; secondly, according to the result obtained from the user memory experiment, make memory score calculation and memory strength sequencing for 50 soft guidance samples; finally, utilize the quantification theory type-I algorithm, calculate the partial correlation coefficient of 9 categories, research out which factors among the memory strengths of soft guidance play a driving role and which factors backfire, and research the correlation between the promotion sub-factors and culture.

2   Collection of Soft Guidance Samples

Gather the completion time of Beijing metro line and cultural & historical information of various stations through the internet, finally determine the stations in 9 metro lines, mainly focusing on Beijing Metro Line 4, 6, 8 and 10, as the research subjects, and make photo collection on station. Then, screen the collected photos, and finally select 50 soft guidance point locations of 46 stations among them as the research objects, to mainly research the influence of the relation, between the soft orientation category and culture, and its difference in expression way on memory (Table 1).

3   Core Factor Analysis

3.1   Core Factor Category Division and Sub-factor Demarcation

Firstly, study all factors possibly influencing the soft guidance memory by the focus group method, and select out the generally recognized factors possibly influencing the memory, to obtain 9 main categories after consolidation, and divide them into several characteristic factors in accordance with the non-correlation principle, then make rough matching for the collected photos and various characteristic factors, eliminate or consolidate the factors in small and no number, and finally obtain 45 accurate factors (Table 2).

Table 1. 50 soft guidance picture samples

No.	Subway Station	Picture	Theme	No.	Subway Station	Picture	Theme	No.	Subway Station	Picture	Theme
1	JIANGUOMEN		Chinese Astronomy History	18	YONGHEGONG Lama Temple		Tibetan Buddhism Culture	35	SHICHAHAI		Image of Autumn Lotus
2	DONGSI SHITIAO I		Lofty Spirit of China	19	CHAOYANGMEN		Phoenix Dancing Toward the Sun	36	GULOUDAJIE		Evening Drum & Morning Bell
3	DONGSI SHITIAO II		Go to the World	20	JINTAILU		Talent Seeking at Gold Dias	37	PANJIAYUAN		Happy Treasure Shopping in Beijing
4	ZAOYUAN		Pastoral Sonata	21	BEIHAI North		Wonderful Scene Viewing in Beihai Park	38	FENZHONGSI		Walk Together in Common Language
5	YUANMINGYUAN Park		Fourteen Scenes of the Old Summer Palace	22	NANLUOGUXIANG I		Drawing of Time	39	JIJIAMIAO		Land of Colorful Flower
6	XIDAN I		Old Famous Shop	23	NANLUOGUXIANG II		City Memory	40	FENGTAI Railway Station		Rainbow Changji
7	XIDAN II		Old Beijing	24	CHEGONGZHUANG		Color Charm + Chinese Style	41	LIANHUAQIAO		Deep in Lotus Bloom
8	Beijing Zoo		Animal Paradise	25	CHEGONGZHUANG West		Facing the World	42	ZHICHUNLI		vertical and horizontal
9	PINGANLI		Four Peaceful Seasons	26	HUAYUANQIAO		Youth Trace	43	JIAOMEN East		In front the Stage and Behind the Scenes
10	XIYUAN I		Longevity Hill	27	CISHOUSI		Magnificent Ancient Towers	44	CAOQIAO		Blossom Age
11	XIYUAN II		Mountain and Sea of Happiness & Longevity	28	HUJIALOU		Pleasure, Anger, Sorrow and Joy	45	SHOUJINGMAO		Story of Dream
12	HUANGCUN Railway Station		Span	29	DONGDAQIAO		Ancient Charm of Dongyue Temple	46	GONGZHUFEN		Birds Adoring the Phoenix
13	GAOMIDIAN South		Sound of Nature	30	DONGSI		Dongsi Memory	47	CHEDAOGOU		Harmonious Mutualism
14	XUANWUMEN		Xuanman Culture	31	Happy Valley Scenic Area		Happy Sea	48	CHAOYANG Park		Realm of Nature
15	National Library		Four Treasures of National Library of China	32	CIQIKOU		The Story of the Stone	49	QINGHUADONGLUXIKOU		Memory of Students
16	East Gate of Peking University		Peking University	33	HUFANGQIAO		Huguang Guild Hall	50	Olympic Green		Olympic Dream of China
17	XISI		Old Joy of Beijing	34	BEITUCHENG		Tradition & Modernity				

(1) Extension characteristic factors

In the soft guidance of mural-oriented subway plane decoration, the foreground is an element of great significance, in general, it is divided into the element type, primary vision type, secondary vision type and general layout, while the background consists of pattern and color.

X1 element type: According to the preliminary sample screening, it is divided into unitary, binary and polynary, of which the polynary refers to that the main elements are

Table 2. Table of categories and sub elements

			1	2	3	4	5	6	7
Extension	Foreground	X1 element type	Unitary	Binary	Polynary				
		X2 primary vision type	Nature	Traditional patterns	Buildings	Scenes	Artificiality and others	Human	None
		X3 secondary vision type	Nature	Traditional patterns	Buildings	Scenes	None		
		X4 layout	Centered	Symmetric	Tiled	Shift			
	Background	X5 pattern	Nature	Traditional patterns	Geometric	Others	None		
		X6 color	Bluish violet	Red orange	Yellowish brown	Multi-color	Black, white and gray	Natural color of wall	Metal
Connotation		X7 correlation to station name	Direct correlation	Partial correlation	Correlation in connotation	Adjacent correlation	Non-correlation		
		X8 propagation objective	Geographic information culture	Historical information	Characteristics of the times	Industry characteristics			
		X9 style	Cute	Avant-garde	Classical	Magnificent	Natural		

more than or equal to three kinds of different elements in general, and the elements in the same type but different shape can be concluded into the unitary type.

X2 primary vision type: It basically includes everything we can get in our daily life, which is classified as seven kinds of elements under the premise of not affecting each other. Nature contains the animals, plants, mountains and water in natural, the sun, universe and other non-artificial matters; The traditional patterns refer to the patterns with cultural deposits or mythological color inheriting from the ancient time, including the moiré, phoenix and peony, etc.; The building is the generalization of independent buildings; The scene is constituted by multiple buildings, characters and articles; The artifacts and others refer to artifacts, like ceramics, etc.; the elements with the single human as the primary vision and with the primary vision unable to be identified is classified to be none.

X3 secondary vision type: It refers to the vision subject only next to the primary vision, as the setoff of subject or having certain relation with the subject, not appearing as the shading, or in case the primary vision cannot be found for the whole soft guidance, the relatively prominent element is identified as the secondary vision.

X4 layout: The layout type is divided based on the picture composition. The centered type refers to that the primary vision is in the middle of the picture; The symmetric type refers to the vision symmetry or physical symmetry; The tiled type refers to that the vision element spreads all over the whole picture; The shift type refers to that the primary vision is not in the middle of the picture, but shifts to other direction.

X5 pattern: The pattern can be divided into five categories, of which the grouping of the nature and traditional patterns is the same as that of the primary vision, and the geometry refers to the background patterns constituted by the geometric lines or patterns throughout the whole picture.

X6 color: Firstly divided into the red, orange, yellow, green, blue and violet section as per the color cycle, and then simplify the integration principle in accordance with the factors [3], and we further classify the color into the bluish violet, red orange, yellowish brown, multi-color, black and white and gray; besides, name the situation in which marble and cement are directly used as the background as the natural color of wall; and the situation in which the metal is used as the background as the metal color.

(2) **Connotation characteristic factors**

Soft guidance connotation is mainly to research the way of internal relation between the soft guidance and its regional culture and referential meaning, which is divided into three categories: correlation between the station soft guidance and station name, propagation objective and overall style.

X7 correlation with station name: It refers to the relation between the content and station name, which is divided into five categories: Direct correlation refers to that the content directly manifests the existing station look, and the station is named on this account; The partial correlation is divided into two categories, of which the first category refers to that the part in the picture is directly correlated to the station style, while the another part shows the derivational concept of station name. The another category does not directly show the station style, but shows the sub-factor in the style; The correlation in connotation refers to that the meaning, extended concept and background situation are related to the station concept, like the station history and culture, etc.; The adjacent correlation refers those not directly correlated to the station name, but their referential soft guidance content in geographically adjacent relation. Non-correlation refers to the soft guidance failing to form any relation.

X8 propagation objective: It refers to the division as per the objective type of propagating information through soft guidance. The geographic culture information refers to the relevant culture information for communicating station building or its region; The historical information refers to the relevant historical events, background, legends and stories, etc.; Characteristics of the times refers to that the soft guidance mainly shows the social human style and features at a specific historic time; Industry characteristic shows the main industries at the region.

X9 style: Refer to the style shown by the whole picture, which is divided into the cute lively type, avant-garde type, classical type, magnificent type and natural type.

3.2 Explanation on Substitution of Sample Characteristic Element and Its Rules

After confirming 45 kinds of elements of 9 categories based on two directions of extension and connotation, 50 samples are reviewed one by one and judgment and type division is implemented and corresponding codes are filled into X1–X9 characteristics sequence of Table 3. By reviewing distribution quantity occupation condition of each category in table, type explanation is implemented initially from the following aspects:

Generally speaking, the quantity of soft guidance with polynary element types is the most, unitary soft guidance taking the second place. Background color of unitary soft guidance is generally single color and polynary element adopts plain technique on overall layout and yellowish-brown color is selected for background color.

Table 3. Category analysis of sample

No	X1	X2	X3	X4	X5	X6	X7	X8	X9	No	X1	X2	X3	X4	X5	X6	X7	X8	X9
1	3	4	4	4	1	1	2	3	4	26	3	6	3	3	5	2	5	3	3
2	3	2	4	3	2	3	4	3	3	27	3	3	5	3	2	6	1	1	3
3	3	4	5	3	2	1	4	4	5	28	2	5	5	2	5	6	5	3	1
4	3	2	1	2	1	4	3	2	4	29	3	4	4	2	5	5	4	1	3
5	1	3	2	2	5	3	1	1	3	30	3	6	5	3	4	5	3	3	3
6	2	3	2	4	3	4	2	4	4	31	3	4	5	3	1	5	1	4	1
7	3	4	2	3	5	7	5	3	3	32	2	6	5	3	3	4	4	2	3
8	3	1	4	3	5	3	2	4	1	33	3	4	4	3	2	3	3	1	3
9	1	5	5	2	2	5	3	1	3	34	1	2	5	4	3	1	5	3	3
10	3	1	2	4	5	3	4	1	3	35	1	1	4	3	5	6	2	1	5
11	3	7	4	3	2	2	4	1	3	36	1	5	2	2	3	3	3	3	3
12	1	5	5	3	4	5	3	4	3	37	3	4	5	3	5	1	3	1	5
13	3	5	5	3	5	3	5	3	2	38	3	5	1	3	5	6	3	3	1
14	3	4	5	3	2	3	3	3	3	39	3	1	5	1	1	1	3	4	1
15	3	7	2	3	2	6	2	4	3	40	1	1	5	3	5	6	5	4	1
16	3	4	4	3	5	3	1	1	3	41	1	1	1	1	5	1	1	1	5
17	3	4	4	3	5	5	3	1	4	42	2	7	4	3	5	1	4	4	2
18	3	4	2	2	5	7	2	1	4	43	3	1	1	1	5	3	4	2	3
19	3	2	3	1	5	3	2	1	4	44	3	6	4	4	3	2	5	3	5
20	3	4	4	2	2	3	3	2	4	45	3	1	1	2	1	5	5	4	5
21	3	4	1	2	1	3	1	4	4	46	1	2	4	1	2	1	3	1	4
22	3	4	5	3	5	3	3	3	3	47	1	1	5	1	1	5	5	3	5
23	3	4	5	3	5	5	3	3	4	48	1	1	5	3	1	5	2	1	5
24	3	2	4	2	2	6	4	1	3	49	1	4	5	3	5	6	2	3	3
25	3	1	1	2	2	7	5	3	2	50	1	6	2	4	2	2	3	4	2

Because polynary elements of primary vision are more, scenes and nature account for the majority, where expression method of primary vision of scene is plain without redundant background pattern and with most of classical and magnificent style; primary vision is nature coordinating with it, of which expression technique is mostly of nature style; there is no secondary vision for artificiality and other types; overall layouts without primary vision all adopt plain technique.

Elements of the secondary vision are mostly none and scenes and elements of nature type are polynary, and primary visions are also nature in symmetry layout; background-free pattern of traditional type is classical in style; main purpose of scene element is to introduce station culture, which is classical in style; where there is no secondary vision, background colors are mostly black, white and gray, related to station connotation.

Layout is mainly tiled and the styles are mostly classical to express station culture or industry characteristics.

Background patterns are dominated by none or traditional patterns and nature elements mainly express industry characteristics, and primary visions are scenes; overall payout of traditional pattern is plain, related to station connotation to introduce station culture with classical style; where there is background-free pattern, it takes scene or nature as primary vision, without secondary vision, focusing on yellowish-brown color, more related to station culture.

Colors are mainly yellowish-brown, black, white and gray; yellowish-brown background is selected for polybasic elements of background-free pattern and metal bottom color can be taken for background wall with avant-garde, classical and magnificant styles.

Station name relevancy is mainly connotation correlation and non-correlation and direct correlation is all related to geographic information of station and industry characteristics of station. Part of correlation is focused on station culture and industry characteristics, however, a small part of correlation expresses modern age characteristics or age characteristics related to modern society in all ages, magnificant in style; connotation correlation is mainly to highlight station culture and ancient age characteristics, which is focused on stations in tourist area and stations adjacent to accommodation groups with historical profundity; non-correlation is mainly to express age characteristics of modern society, such as fashion, etc.

Proportion of main purpose of soft guidance setting to express geographic information culture is equal to that of to express age characteristics and has occupied the majority, secondly, industry characteristics, lastly history information kind and these to express age characteristics basically occur in metro station adjacent to living quarters.

Styles are mainly classical, magnificant style ranking the second and then nature and cute style and avant-garde style is least. Classical styles are mostly polybasic elements, which express geographic information culture and ancient age characteristics; nature style mainly takes harmony of human and nature as subject and is mainly installed at present station adjacent to parks or where the royal hunting ground was located in ancient times.

Conclusion in this part is only to describe obvious phenomenon in data of Table 3, but positive and negative correlation function to memory in these factors cannot be known and we will get its principle by further experiment.

4 Influence of Type Factor on User Memory

Next, we will test whether these type factors will exert influence on users and what factors will greatly influence memory by quantification research method. Therefore, two key problems will be led to here: firstly, in 9 kinds of categories, which category is key point to influence user on soft guidance memory? What is influence force ranking of these categories to user memory? Secondly, in various categories, what influence do specific factors exert to strong and weak degree of users?

The research seeks for contact principle between culture adaptivity degree of soft guidance and memory of user to soft guidance by relevant research method of kansei engineering.

4.1   User Test

Photo acquired shall be selected in the principle as follows: (1) try to eliminate surrounding environment influence and cut out soft guidance as core factor and remove information that may have hinting function to soft guidance matching in nearby environment. (2) To ensure test effect, we will match soft guidance photo bottom with four options that are similar to geography of metro station or station name form or connotation for selection of users. Before test, a PDF document of accurate metro names matching with soft guidance shall be provided and testers will memorize within the same time and matching of station and soft guidance shall be implemented in correlation. After inner test, the whole test process is relatively smooth and users can know test purpose and will not be interfered with uncertain factors and display interface screen shot of questionnaire mobile phone is as shown Fig. 1.

Fig. 1. Survey questionnaire form of mobile-phone soft guidance matching

We issue questionnaire to several users on mobile social platform and these users all live in Beijing for more than one year and are relatively familiar with metro lines of

Beijing. Data statistics form adopts network survey questionnaire form and is characterized by fast propagation speed and high recycle efficiency, etc. Before testee answers questionnaire, he will get prompt of answering process of questionnaire and single item selection shall be implemented to metro station name matching with photo in process according to evidence. Finally, questionnaires are taken back and invalid questionnaires are eliminated. The follows are data statistic result of summary and memory score has been calculated (Table 4) and NO is high-low order of memory of metro station and X1 to X9 are main nine kinds of category codes and Score is memory score code (ranking has been implemented according to memory score).

Table 4. Memory degree score

No	X1	X2	X3	X4	X5	X6	X7	X8	X9	Score	No	X1	X2	X3	X4	X5	X6	X7	X8	X9	Score
1	1	6	2	4	2	2	3	4	2	0.76	26	3	6	4	4	3	2	5	3	5	0.44
2	1	2	4	1	2	1	3	1	4	0.76	27	3	2	4	2	2	6	4	1	3	0.44
3	3	7	2	3	2	6	2	4	3	0.76	28	3	1	1	2	2	7	5	3	2	0.44
4	3	3	5	3	2	6	1	1	3	0.72	29	2	5	5	2	5	6	5	3	1	0.44
5	3	4	5	3	2	3	3	3	3	0.72	30	3	4	4	2	2	3	3	2	4	0.44
6	1	3	2	2	5	3	1	1	3	0.68	31	3	4	5	3	5	1	3	1	5	0.44
7	1	5	5	3	4	5	3	4	3	0.64	32	3	1	2	4	5	3	4	1	3	0.44
8	1	1	1	1	5	1	1	1	5	0.64	33	1	2	5	4	3	1	5	3	3	0.4
9	3	4	5	3	5	3	3	3	3	0.64	34	1	1	5	3	1	5	2	1	5	0.4
10	3	5	1	3	5	6	3	3	1	0.6	35	3	2	3	1	5	3	2	1	4	0.4
11	3	4	5	3	1	5	1	4	1	0.6	36	3	4	4	2	5	5	4	1	3	0.4
12	1	4	5	3	5	6	2	3	3	0.6	37	3	6	3	3	5	2	5	3	3	0.4
13	3	4	2	2	5	7	2	1	4	0.6	38	3	1	1	1	5	3	4	2	3	0.4
14	3	4	1	2	1	3	1	4	4	0.56	39	1	1	5	1	1	5	5	3	5	0.36
15	3	2	4	3	2	3	4	3	3	0.56	40	1	5	5	2	2	5	3	1	3	0.36
16	1	1	4	3	5	6	2	1	5	0.56	41	1	1	5	3	5	6	5	4	1	0.32
17	2	6	5	3	3	4	4	2	3	0.52	42	1	5	2	2	3	3	3	3	3	0.32
18	2	3	2	4	3	4	2	4	4	0.52	43	3	4	4	3	2	3	3	1	3	0.28
19	2	7	4	3	5	1	4	4	2	0.52	44	3	1	5	1	1	1	3	4	1	0.28
20	3	4	5	3	2	1	4	4	5	0.48	45	3	4	2	3	5	7	5	3	3	0.28
21	3	1	4	3	5	3	2	4	1	0.48	46	3	4	4	3	5	5	3	1	4	0.28
22	3	4	4	4	1	1	2	3	4	0.48	47	3	2	1	2	1	4	3	2	4	0.28
23	3	4	5	3	5	5	3	3	4	0.48	48	3	7	4	3	2	2	4	1	3	0.24
24	3	1	1	2	1	5	5	4	5	0.48	49	3	6	5	3	4	5	3	3	3	0.16
25	3	4	4	3	5	3	1	1	3	0.44	50	3	5	5	3	5	3	5	3	2	0.16

Memory score of users to soft guidance of all metro can be obtained by questionnaire inquiry (full score: 1), where the highest score is 0.76, referring to 76% correction rate. The lowest score is 0.16 and it means that memory is high where value is larger than 0.5. Herein, memory of Olympic Green, Gongzhufen and National Central Library is the highest, but memory of Dongsi and Southern Gaomidian is the minimal. Next, influence of category and characteristics factors to user memory shall be further analyzed.

4.2   Correlation Analysis of Soft Guidance and User Memory

The research is applied to linear recession analysis and its principle is to use quantification-I theory and is applied to kansei engineering. Coefficient of partial correlation is calculated by SPSS software based on it. Regression equation can be defined as follows [4]:

$$y = \sum_{j=1}^{m} \sum_{k=1}^{r_j} \delta(j, k) \hat{b}_{jk} \qquad (1)$$

Where, $\delta(j, k)$ represents reaction of any sample at category j characteristics factor k; $\hat{b}_{jk}$ represents score of category j characteristics factor k. In form language analysis, standard treatment shall be implemented to $\hat{b}_{jk}$; at that time, forecast equation shall be written as [4]:

$$y = \bar{y} + \sum_{J=1}^{m} \sum_{k=1}^{r_i} \delta(j, k) \hat{b}_{jk}^* \qquad (2)$$

Where, $\bar{y}$ represents constant term, $\bar{y} = \frac{1}{n} \sum_{i=1}^{n} y_i; \hat{b}_{jk}^*$ is standard coefficient, $\hat{b}_{jk}^* = \hat{b}_{jk} - \frac{1}{n} \sum_{k=1}^{r_j} n_{jk} \hat{b}_{jk};$

n_jk represents reaction times of the kth characteristics factor of category j in all samples with the number of n.

Partial correlation coefficient calculation shall be implemented by SPSS software and multiple correlation coefficient is calculated. By taking 45 characteristics factor as independent variable and memory score as dependent variable for analysis, result is obtained as Table 5 [3, 11]:

Partial correlation coefficient has represented high-low influence degree, which can be known from table:

X1. In element type: unitary and binary elements have positive performance, which shows that in this type, the fewer the element is, the more beneficial it will be for soft guidance memory by user, but element increase will cause interference effect on user memory, thus causing negative correlation. However, as a whole, partial correlation of element type is lowly ranked, which shows that under effect of numerous elements, main element type quantity is not the focus concerned by users for memory.

X2. In primary vision type: five elements, i.e. traditional pattern, building, artifact and other, human and none, affect memory positively, which shows that people are more likely to resonate and generate memory for things that contain human factors, and especially, traditional pattern and single figure subject affect memory greatly while nature or scene containing various complex elements has a negative impact on memory. But partial correlation of primary vision is relatively lowly ranked, so it cannot be used as main type affecting soft guidance memory.

Table 5. Quantification I-theory analysis result

Project		Category	Category invocation point		Partial correlation coefficient	Partial correlation ranking
Extension	X1 element type	Unitary		0.0003	0.4447	8
		Binary		0.1545		
		Polynary	−0.0446			
	X2 primary vision type	Nature	−0.0534		0.5721	6
		Traditional patterns		0.1543		
		Buildings		0.0851		
		Scenes	−0.1068			
		Artificiality and others		0.0616		
		Human		0.1359		
		None		0.0221		
	X3 secondary vision type	Nature	−0.0239		0.4042	9
		Traditional patterns	−0.1369			
		Buildings	−0.0583			
		Scenes		0.0283		
		None		0.0517		
	X4 layout	Centered	−0.0027		0.504	7
		Symmetric	−0.0155			
		Tiled	−0.0407			
		Shift		0.2103		
	X5 pattern	Nature	−0.0950		0.6612	3
		Traditional patterns		0.0413		
		Geometric	−0.2111			
		Others	−0.4582			
		None		0.0998		
	X6 color	Bluish violet	−0.1066		0.6016	5
		Red orange	−0.0588			
		Yellowish brown	−0.0078			
		Multi-color	−0.2131			
		Black, white and gray		0.0171		
		Natural color of wall		0.0611		
		Metal		0.3930		

(continued)

Table 5. (*continued*)

Project		Category	Category invocation point	Partial correlation coefficient	Partial correlation ranking
Connotation	X7 correlation to station name	Direct correlation	0.2079	0.764	1
		Partial correlation	0.0331		
		Correlation in connotation	0.0965		
		Adjacent correlation	−0.0673		
		Non-correlation	−0.2485		
	X8 propagation objective	Geographic information culture	−0.1796	0.6764	2
		Historical information	0.0184		
		Characteristics of the times	0.0179		
		Industry characteristics	0.2229		
	X9 style	Cute	−0.2324	0.6186	4
		Avant-garde	−0.2104		
		Classical	0.0512		
		Magnificent	−0.0189		
		Natural	0.1622		
Constant item			0.472		
Multiple correlation coefficient			0.8053		

X3. In secondary vision type: scene and none have positive correlation effect, while nature, traditional pattern and character and building have negative correlation effect. But partial correlation of the type is last ranked, which means that it has the least effect on user memory.

X4. In overall layout: only offset has positive correlation effect on memory, because position offset of primary vision or main memory point in overall layout can cause visual impact to user, which is beneficial to memory strengthening, while centering, symmetry and plain have negative correlation effect.

X5. In pattern: traditional pattern and background-free pattern have positive effect on memory, background-free pattern makes the whole frame quite regular, and there is no surplus element mixing memory point, which makes visual subject more prominent, and traditional pattern can be positive correlation to memory. Uncertainty and complexity of nature, geometry and other background pattern element may mislead the people and cause memory misleading easily, and especially, other elements are irregular, so they have the largest negative effect on memory. Partial correlation of pattern is thirdly ranked, which shows that background pattern has relatively great effect on the whole soft guidance frame, so it has relatively great effect on memory.

X6. In colors: black, white and gray, natural color of wall and metal have played the role of positive correlation to memory, that is to say, natural color of material is taken as background color and black, white and gray belong to color-free color and all are positive correlation. Therefore, no outstanding background color will play positive influence on memory, especially, metal bottom color because it is not only just a kind of color, but also embody to material; when the two are combined. Style is more outstanding and memory strength is the highest. However, negative influence of multicolor on memory is the most strong, therefore, background with color will influence memory of users on soft guidance, what's more, the more the colors are, the greater the influence will be.

X7. Relation with station name: partial correlation coefficient is 0.764, ranking the first, which means that influence of relation between soft guidance and station name on memory strength of users is the maximal. Herein, influence of direct correlation and positive correlation is the most strong, but part of correlation and connotation correlation belongs to type that can exert correlation between soft guidance and station name, which is favorable to user memory. Adjacent correlation and non-correlation will exert negative influence on user's memory, where negative function of non-correlation is the strongest, which means that it only reflects age characteristics or certain concept, without any correlation with station name and soft guidance cannot express characteristics of the station and memory is the lowest.

X8. In propagation objective: history information, age characteristics and industry characteristics are all in positive correlation, especially industry characteristics, because of its specialty, it does not exist in neighborhood of all metro stations generally, therefore, it is easier to be known and memorized by users. Geographic information culture is in negative correlation. Overall ranking of the type is No.2, of which memory influence on users is only inferior to station name contact.

X9. In style: classical style and nature style play the role of promotion to soft guidance of user memory, but cute, avant-garde and magnificent styles are unfavorable to soft guidance of user memory; especially, category invocation point of cute and avant-garde styles are relatively low, which will weaken memory of users to soft guidance.

5 Conclusion

The research compares and analyzes soft guidance of 50 metro stations in 9 lines and discusses correlation between soft guidance of memory with culture by statistics result of user tests, of which results show that memory is higher if it is directly related to station or the correlation with industry characteristics is closer. Other background patterns, multicolor background colors and cute and avant-garde modern design styles have generated relatively strong negative correlation function. Besides, users mostly recognize soft guidance containing classical element or soft guidance with relatively classical overall style and the higher the memory of users is, the better effect of soft guidance that is closely related to traditional culture will be obtained.

Foresaid conclusion will provide valuable theory and design guidance to soft guidance of future metro station in several aspects of visual subject, element selection, color and materials, relationship with station name and culture connotation, etc. In the future, we will further research how each category will be applied to design of soft guidance reasonably according to 9 categories of the research. Thereby, a set of complete soft guidance of underground space will be promoted as important theoretical support of soft guidance design of future metro station.

Acknowledgments. It is a project supported by the Youth Team Project, Fundamental Research Funds for the Beijing Jiaotong University (A17JB00040). The corresponding author of this article is Ye Zhang.

References

1. He, J.: City Guide - Research on static visual guidance system of urban public space, School of architecture and urban planning, Tongji University, pp. 1–315 (2008)
2. Ma, X.: Guidance-orientated System Design of Urban Underground Space, Tianjin University, pp. 1–70 (2009)
3. Zhang, Y., Lou, H., Yu, H.: Morphology elements research on chinese small-sized liquor bottle design. pp. 1–12 (2015)
4. Li, Y.: Research on product image style design based on quantification-I Theory.Lin. Mach. Des. **4**, 41–43 (2010)
5. Mao, H., Jing, S.: Application of guidance-oriented system in urban culture — urban image research by taking guidance-oriented system of jingdezhen for example. Beauty Times City **11**, 104–105 (2016)
6. Wang, X., Zhao, L.: Urban landmark design and urban tourism development. Urban Probl. **4**, 7–10 (2007)
7. Hu, X.: Application method research of urban context inheritance in landmark landscape building design. Buil. Mater. Decor. **46**, 67–68 (2015)
8. Li Chenglai, L., Yan, S.: Concrete and anti-rationalism design aesthetics tendency in landmark building design. Sichuan Archit. **6**, 69–73 (2014)
9. Yang, H., Yang, Y., Yang, H.: Soft orientation design of metro transfer station space – take Tianjin Yingkoudao metro station for example. J. Tianjin Urban Constr. Univ. **3**, 227–231 (2016)
10. Huang, S.-W., Yang, M.-C., Liao, C.-H., Lin, Y.-C.: A kansei study of beverage packaging form with coffee image. Res. Des. **16**, 1–14
11. Lin, Y.-C., Yeh, C.-H., Wei, C.-C.: How will the use of graphics affect visual aesthetics? A user-centered approach for web page design. Int. J. Hum.-Comput. Stud. **71**, 217–227 (2013)
12. Daar, I.O.: Guidance Molecules in Cancer and Tumor Angiogenesis, vol. 114, pp. 1–274. Academic Press, Cambridge (2012)
13. Roberson, R.: Guidance and Control, vol. 8 (1961)
14. Cho, N., Kim, Y., Shin, H.-S.: Generalization of linearly parametrized trajectory shaping guidance laws. IFAC-PapersOnLine **50**, 8285–8290 (2017)

15. Chu, J.C., Chen, A.Y., Lin, Y.-F.: Variable guidance for pedestrian evacuation considering congestion, hazard, and compliance behavior. Transp. Res. Part C: Emerg. Technol. **85**, 664–683 (2017)
16. Vaz, D.V., Kay, B.A., Turvey, M.T.: Effects of visual and auditory guidance on bimanual coordination complexity. Hum. Mov. Sci. **54**, 13–23 (2017)
17. Morana, S., Schacht, S., Scherp, A., Maedche, A.: A review of the nature and effects of guidance design features. Decis. Support Syst. **97**, 31–42 (2017)
18. Lentzakis, A.F., Ware, S.I., Su, R., Wen, C.: Region-based prescriptive route guidance for travelers of multiple classes. Transp. Res. Part C: Emerg. Technol. **87**, 138–158 (2018)

A Preliminary Study on Design for Different Social Classes

Jiong Fu[✉] and Chenhui Shi

Institute of Design Trend, Design School, Shanghai Jiao Tong University, Shanghai, China
redfox78@sjtu.edu.cn

Abstract. In the 40 years since the implementation of the reform and opening up policy (the Chinese economic reform), China's economy has developed at an unprecedented rate, and the social division of labor has become increasingly complex. As a result, Chinese society has discernibly diverged into a number of new social classes. As these newly emerged social classes continue to grow, their social impacts are becoming more significant. In addition, the existing social classes are undergoing continuous changes, as their values and lifestyles become increasingly differentiated; the structural gaps among classes have become wider. Consequently, people from different social classes have an increasingly poorer understanding of one another. Product and service designers are thus faced with the same problem, because they are no longer able to apply their own life experiences to identify with the needs of consumers from different social classes. Through teaching processes in a graduate course, this study attempts to explain the values and lifestyles of the new social classes in China with suitable theories and methodologies. This is done to investigate representative individuals of each class and to find the pain points that inhibit their lives in order to design products and services suitable for them.

Keywords: Social differentiation · Social class
Illustration of representative individuals · Product and service design

1 Introduction

Over the course of China's modernization, the establishment and improvement of the socialist market economy, the continuous changes in economic structure, the adjustment of industrial structure, and the reform of the income distribution policy have driven continuous social differentiation. As a result, the social-class structure has become increasingly complex and diversified. Changes to the existing social classes and the emergence of new social classes correspond to changes in the values, lifestyles, and consumption behavior of social groups. Such dynamic changes have generated great challenges for product and service designers. How should they overcome the limitations and biases of their own social class to develop an in-depth and accurate understanding of the needs and pain points of consumers from unfamiliar social groups? This study attempts to answer these questions on the basis of the teaching process in a graduate course.

A. Marcus and W. Wang (Eds.): DUXU 2018, LNCS 10920, pp. 635–647, 2018.
https://doi.org/10.1007/978-3-319-91806-8_49

Social Differentiation and Changes in Class Structure. Some scholars have pointed out that there are fewer academic studies focused on social differentiation than on social integration. In China, social differentiation is either directly used as a fuzzy and abstract concept or seen as an equivalent to the stratification of social classes or the interests of social classes [1]. Social differentiation in this study refers to the continuous decomposition of the social structure into new social elements and the formation of a new social structure constituted by new divisions and the reorganization of social relationships. The changes in class structure are an important dimension and specific manifestation of social differentiation.

Social class is a concept commonly used when studying social stratification. Numerous theories and research designs utilize a variety of methods and criteria to categorize social classes such as economic relations, income, political status, lifestyle, and consumption behavior. At present, the most influential social stratification method in China is the theoretical framework proposed by Lu and his team that uses occupation and possession of organizational, economic, and cultural resources as criteria for the determination of social class [2]. Changes in class structure usually involve two forms of social mobility: horizontal and vertical. Vertical mobility refers to the movement of individuals and groups, either up or down, between social-economic levels. The essence of such social mobility is a change in social status. Horizontal mobility refers to the derivation of a new social class on the same level as the preceding social class. The essence of such mobility is the diversity and complexity of class structure.

Although the pace of reform and economic growth in China has slowed down, the social, political, and economic conditions remain favorable. With the changes in the social division of labor and the diversification of values, the old class structure has gradually broken down and the overall social mobility exhibits a vertical and upward trend.

2   The New Social Classes and Illustration of Representative Individuals

Rather than explore the theory and method of class segmentation, the research focus of this study was to identify representative individuals of the emerging social classes and investigate their differentiating characteristics in order to discover potential break-throughs that may lead to better product and service design. The exploration process selected three archetypal emerging social classes that were identified during the teaching process of a university graduate course, namely, the political and cultural elite, the new industrial working class, and new farming professionals.

2.1   The Political and Cultural Elite

The political and cultural elite comprise a small part of the core of society. Since members of this class tend to be distant from the public, designers are less familiar with their needs and demands. Therefore, investigating the political and cultural elite has research value. Because of the lack of existing research data and exposure to this population group, the present author utilized information shared by correspondents on major social media platforms as research data and integrated it with relevant studies. The author then summarized the shared social-class characteristics of the individuals, in terms of values, lifestyle, consumption behavior, and aesthetic preferences. An illustration of the representative individual was then provided on the basis of the compiled features.

Definition. In this context, the political and cultural elite is defined as individuals who possess greater organizational resources and political status. The majority of the people in this group are engaged in fields related to the formation of culture and ideology. They tend to have greater social influence and decision-making power. An example may be officials from the Department of Culture or from the press and publication bureau of local government or artists who are members of the Chinese People's Political Consultative Conference (CPPCC).

The majority of the political and cultural elite graduated from Party Schools or art schools. Aged between 45 and 60 years old, they are at a prosperous stage of life with rich experience in politics or artistic expression. Research has also shown that the political elite in China has become "younger." The composition of the class has been gradually institutionalized to ensure the vitality of the group [3].

Values. The values pursued by the political and cultural elite are mainly concentrated on social status, health, and family. Organizational resources are usually the primary factor affecting their social status. They attach great importance to recognition by individuals from the same class as an important component of their organizational resources. As members of the political and cultural elite have an advantage in power, wealth, and prestige, they tend to place more emphasis on accountability, tolerance, and respect. Their attitude toward family is usually more traditional than that of others, with an emphasis on order and a sense of ritual.

Lifestyle. Members of the political and cultural elite tend to purposely downplay their political status and present themselves as cultural figures. In addition to engaging in meetings, political reports, and creative activities, they also participate in social activities with the corresponding stakeholders to maintain and expand their social network. In addition, accumulating a wider range of organizational resources is an important part of their daily lives. Moreover, because they are usually in middle age, healthcare has become an integral part of their life. In their leisure time, they also enjoy landscape photography, occasionally sharing their perceptions of life and commenting on current affairs. A passion for traditional calligraphy and painting appears to be a norm of the group. They tend to show enthusiasm for arts appreciation; antiques, incense, tea, and Buddhist studies are among their favorites. Typically, they also utilize the Internet to increase their visibility and establish their personal image.

Consumption Tendencies. Respectability lies at the core of the pursuits of the political and cultural elite in terms of consumption; it is also the external basis for maintaining their social relations and accumulating organizational resources. They tend to attach more significance to the cultural attributes and values of products and services, in order to embody their identity as the cultural elite. However, their consumption behavior still has a utilitarian tendency, and they are insensitive to fashions and trends. Many are more inclined to use flagship China-made cellphone brands, such as Huawei, and to wear semi-formal and semi-casual shirts or polo shirts.

Aesthetic Preferences. The aesthetic preferences of the political and cultural elite usually correspond with that of the traditional Chinese literati. Such preferences are not only the direct manifestation of their role as the cultural elite but also an important channel of communication and identification with other individuals in this class. They are usually passionate about objects that convey deep meanings or reflect natural beauty, such as traditional Chinese calligraphy and paintings of flowers, birds, insects, and fish, and they are actively engaged in the practice and creation of such artistic work.

Representative Description. On the basis of the aforementioned characteristics of the political and cultural elite, coupled with demographic factors and contextual descriptions, this study illustrated a representative individual of this group as follows:

Mr. Lin, 54, is the head of the printing department at the press and publication bureau in City A. After entering the workplace, he studied for an MBA at University B in Shanghai. His work keeps him busy and, as a leading member of the bureau, he is often required to attend business dinners. Mr. Lin has a typical family of three with abundant wealth. His daughter has gone to study in the United States, while he and his wife live in an apartment in the city center. His wife is a professor of literature at University C. Mr. Lin likes to spend his spare time practicing calligraphy in his study or engaging in small talk with his wife over a tea tasting. Occasionally, Mr. Lin will go out with several friends to collect artistic inspirations.

2.2 The New Industrial Working Class

With the rise of China's economy following the implementation of the economic reform, a new industrial working class has gradually emerged in society, known as "migrant workers." Second-generation migrant workers have emerged to become the dominant force of the new industrial working class. Born and raised during the reform period, they moved from villages to the urban labor market at the turn of the century because of the substantial urban-rural income gap brought about by rapid industrialization and globalization. At present, this new generation has carried on the relay from its predecessors and become an important force in the construction of urban economies. According to the "2016 National Monitoring Survey Report on Migrant Workers," the number of migrant workers reached 280 million at the end of 2016. Many of this population group are workers migrating from rural to urban areas. Their average monthly income is 3,275 yuan. They are mainly engaged in the construction, wholesale, and retail industries, as well as the transportation, storage, postal, and hospitality industries. The values and lifestyles of second-generation migrant workers are substantially different from those of the first generation, but they face issues in their sense of identity and social exclusion that are strikingly similar to those of the previous generation. Some scholars refer to the second generation of migrant workers as "the ruptured" due to their lack of any sense of belonging to urban life; furthermore, because they moved to the city at a young age, it is difficult for them to return to the rural areas. This dilemma makes the new industrial working class (represented by second-generation migrant workers) a research focus for many sociologists.

Definition. The new industrial working class in this study refers mainly to second-generation migrant workers born after 1980. The majority of them migrated to urban areas for work at an early age; some of them were even born and grew up in the city. As a major source of young labor, second-generation migrant workers have supported the rapid development of secondary and tertiary industries as well as the rapid rise of some emerging industries in urban areas. Since they have spent a substantial amount of time working in the city, they are very familiar with urban consumer culture. However, problems such as income inequality, a lack of relatability with urban life, and a lack of protection of basic human rights have pushed them to the margins of urban life. Second-generation migrant workers are considered a lower level in the social hierarchy in terms of their possession of organizational, economic, and cultural resources.

Values. For second-generation migrant workers, social acceptance, income growth, and the maintenance of close family relationships are their key value pursuits. Second-generation migrant workers have a better growth environment and education background than first-generation migrant workers did, as well as a broader scope of vision; hence, they have a more modern and more open mind, with stronger individualist characteristics. They are more attracted by the sense of independence and freedom granted by working in cities than by life in rural areas. However, they are also deeply aware of the gap between themselves and other social classes in the cities. For this reason, they are highly motivated to pursue personal development and elevate their social status. They are eager to be accepted by urban society and actively safeguard their rights and interests. Furthermore, years of working away from their rural hometown have led to the absence of family life; consequently, second-generation migrant workers attach great importance to the maintenance of a close family relationship, particularly emotional bonds with their children.

Lifestyle. Second-generation migrant workers are often engaged in relatively tedious and repetitive jobs. Although their class consciousness has gradually come into being and they have started protecting their rights and interests through group movements, the system for protecting their rights and interests remains underdeveloped. As a result, migrant workers often take on heavy workloads with no guarantee of basic paid leave for national holidays or rest breaks. In their limited spare time, they tend to take pleasure in social activities and shopping and to relieve stress along the way. Their activities include pursuing fashion and trends, wearing stylish outfits, and using smartphones. To a large extent, their social efforts help to overcome their incomplete sense of identity as migrant workers and to generate self-affirmation. More often, however, they tend to immerse themselves in the online world and video games to relax and escape the pressures of work and feelings of social exclusion.

Due to their lack of competitiveness, they are forced to change jobs and places of residence frequently and are often compelled to live in poorer living conditions. Some surveys show that because of the high education costs for children without a corresponding urban *hukou* (household registration document) and difficulties in finding a school, 61.7% of the children of migrant workers are forced to remain in their hometowns. The sense of loneliness caused by separation from their home and family intensifies under their harsh living conditions and exclusion from urban life. Furthermore, the difficulties faced in achieving personal goals have also generated a sense of helplessness and insecurity among many migrant workers.

Consumption Tendencies. According to the existing statistics, the growth in the living expenses of second-generation migrant workers has sped up, which indicates that their consumer desires have also intensified. Nevertheless, a large proportion of spending is still concentrated on daily necessities, particularly food and clothing. It is worth noting that as their income rises, a greater number of migrant workers are beginning to pay more attention to their physical and mental health. The situation has changed substantially from earlier times, when a minimum amount of money was spent on treating serious illnesses, while the treatment of minor illnesses was often ignored. In addition, the proportion of consumption devoted to self-development and personal enjoyment is also increasing.

Aesthetic Preferences. Years of working in cities have equipped the new generation of migrant workers with the ability to recognize and grasp changes in urban culture quickly. In the same way that cities embrace multiple cultures, the aesthetic preferences of this class are also diverse. In general, they tend to appreciate youth and energy and to emphasize individual personality. However, they often lack sufficient wealth to express and pursue their aesthetic preferences.

Representative Description. Ms. Wang, 35, is a handler in the logistics industry. She and her husband left their small village and came to work in City S five years ago. Over the past five years, they have changed their jobs several times and ended up working at the same logistics company. They share a dormitory room with their coworkers. In their spare time, they usually watch TV in their room or chat with their friends on their cellphones. At weekends, Ms. Wang goes shopping for things like clothing and living essentials with female friends she met at work. Ms. Wang has a daughter who lives with her grandparents and who has just started studying at a junior high school in their hometown. Every Chinese New Year, she returns to her hometown and brings her daughter snacks and new clothes, which she buys with money saved from her daily expenses, as a form of compensation for her daughter. When she works in the city, she can only keep up with her daughter's progress at school and in life through her cellphone.

2.3   New Farming Professionals

In the early stage of the economic reform, the rural areas acted as a reservoir of industrial development, as a large amount of labor was supplied from the rural areas to support urban construction. With the arrival of the post-industrial era, the emerging tertiary industries, such as services and logistics industries, have also attracted a large number of young migrant workers. The massive loss of rural labor during this process has led to the decreased efficiency of overall agricultural production. In addition, urban residents, represented by the middle-class population, have attached greater importance to healthier living, creating a huge demand for high-quality agricultural and sideline products and many business opportunities. As a result, a new type of farmer, known as the "new farming professional," has begun to emerge. This new social group has received substantial political support from the government.

Definition. The new farming professionals in this study were defined on the basis of three criteria: (1) individuals who engage in agricultural production and management; (2) the purpose of their participation in corresponding activities is to pursue economic profit; and (3) they consider agricultural production and management as their only profession. Generally, there are four types of new farming professional: individuals who manage and operate agricultural production, as in large specialized households or family farms; individuals with professional farming knowledge and skills, such as agricultural workers; individuals engaged in social activities, such as agricultural equipment operators; and a new generation of farmers who have received an agricultural education from the relevant colleges or technical secondary schools.

The first type of new farming professional is usually born in a traditional farming family. The age of the individuals in this population group ranges from 20 to 60 years. Their level of engagement in agricultural production tends to be deep, and the entire family is usually involved in relevant agricultural activities. They may have a certain amount of land, but they often possess limited resources, such as organizational, economic, and cultural resources. Nevertheless, thanks to increasing government support, members of this group are able to increase their income gradually by improving the traditional agricultural production methods with the aid of scientifically rational methodologies for agricultural production and operation and the rules of the market mechanism. This population group has thus infused vitality into agricultural development in China. Given that the average age of the new farming professional has been decreasing, this study mainly focused on the first type of new farming professionals aged between 20 and 35.

Values. The main value pursuit of new farming professionals is to maximize earnings from agricultural production and create better living conditions. Coming from traditional farming families, they still attach great importance to simplicity, practicality, and self-dependence. As witnesses of the advantages of new technology and management methods in the information era, they have a strong desire to enhance their knowledge and management skills. Moreover, since they are still living in rural areas, they also long for more open and diversified urban lifestyles and hope to narrow the gap between their lives and urban life through hard work.

Lifestyle. Although, to the new farming professionals, life appears to be relatively monotonous, it is positive and provides a sense of fulfillment. In addition to daily production management, they tend to invest a great deal of time and effort into learning new technologies and management skills due to their lack of the relevant knowledge and their goal of increasing their earnings. Moreover, they are highly sensitive to changes in the market and technology and are willing to accept these changes while actively applying their newly acquired knowledge and skills to their production practices. Apart from being engaged in work, they are also involved in recreational activities to release stress and relax. Furthermore, family life is often of significant importance to them.

Consumption Tendencies. Due to their life experience, even though the income of the new farming professionals has significantly increased, like traditional farmers, they are still inclined to spend money on functional and practical products. However, as their expenditure on products that suit their basic needs increases, the proportion of expenses for enjoyment also gradually increases, and the products that they consume have thus become more diverse. As a result, their living standards have improved significantly. Furthermore, with a growing number of e-commerce providers beginning to shift their focus toward rural markets, the consumption behaviors and habits of the new farming professionals are greatly affected.

Aesthetic Preferences. The aesthetic preferences of the new farming professionals often carry the imprint of the traditional aesthetics of rural villages. In addition, their aesthetic preferences are greatly influenced by the Internet. As the younger generation, their desire for self-expression and embodiment of individuality is strong. However, the absence of education and an aesthetic-based environment makes it difficult for them to express themselves properly. Instead, they can only give their own interpretations of the fragmented information acquired online. This results in misinterpretations of the original information and inappropriate self-expression, giving them a "grotesque" image.

Representative Description. Mr. Chen, 24, was born and raised in a village in Hainan. After graduating from senior high school, he helped his parents to manage their betel-nut farm. He has now replaced his parents and become the head of the farm. He visits the farm every day, mainly to check the growth of the crops and the safety of the fields. When he is not busy with farming activities, he regularly attends agricultural training organized by the village to expand his relevant knowledge and skills. He also goes to town to get a better understanding of market conditions. In his spare time, he enjoys fishing and dining with several friends from the same village. In addition, he travels with his family each year.

3 Pain Points Identification and Targeted Design

3.1 Pain Points of the Political and Cultural Elite

Members of the political and cultural elite attach great importance to their social status and have a strong awareness of the significance of healthcare. Maintaining their social status, accumulating organizational resources, and keeping a healthy and cultural lifestyle are goals of the utmost importance to them.

Maintaining Social Status. Members of the political and cultural elite tend to seek recognition from individuals of the same social class through extensive and frequent participation in social activities. Being identified as members of the "cultural elite" is an important card when they wish to establish and maintain social relations with one another. Similarly, calligraphy and traditional painting, which are believed to have a strong cultural connotation, have become their common topics of association. Although they tend to use off-line communication channels, with their growing understanding of Internet culture, high-end online communities that allow cultural exchange with the elite will gradually become their new social networking hubs.

Management of Healthy Diet. Since the majority of the political and cultural elite are in their middle age and their work inevitably exposes them to unbalanced diets, the majority of the political and cultural elite have a suboptimal health status, which contradicts their attitudes toward health and healthy lifestyles. For that reason, diet management that suits their age and physical condition has become a primary need in daily life.

Online Ordering and Delivery Service Application. When users first log in to the application, they can create a personalized health database by importing their health information from other mobile applications or entering their data manually. If necessary, the application platform also allows for professional one-on-one improved diet consultancy services that are more targeted. When users order online, the system will reference their health information in their profile and automatically recommend nutritious and healthy recipes. Users can also choose dishes based on their actual needs. There is a variety of search options in terms of the amount of oil and salt used in each dish. In addition, the nutritional content of the dishes will be presented to users in real time. On the basis of the actual dishes that have been ordered, the system will generate a diet health report on a regular basis to encourage users to maintain or adjust their eating habits.

Once an order is placed, the nearest kitchen of the supplier will prepare fresh semi-cooked dishes accordingly, with individually packaged seasoning, and deliver them to the user, together with a set of disposable, environmentally friendly tableware, to save the user from the trouble of having to clean the implements after meals. The user simply needs to finish cooking the dishes on the basis of the tutorials in the order interface of the application. If the user does not have time to cook the dishes, he/she can also opt for fully prepared dishes.

The system also allows users to customize their own dishes in advance by paying an extra fee if they have any dietary needs beyond the basic menu. The nearest kitchen of the supplier will purchase the corresponding ingredients to satisfy users' specific needs (Fig. 1).

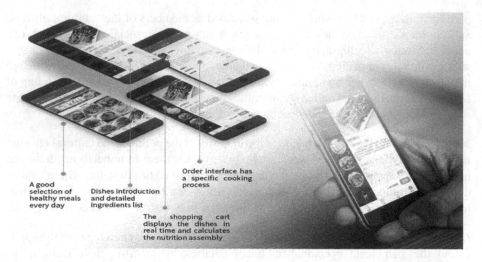

A good selection of healthy meals every day

Dishes introduction and detailed ingredients list

Order interface has a specific cooking process

The shopping cart displays the dishes in real time and calculates the nutrition assembly

Fig. 1. The interface prototype of the online ordering and delivery service application designed for the political and cultural elite

3.2 Pain Points of the New Industrial Working Class

Second-generation migrant workers attach the greatest importance to their sense of identity and emotional bonds with their family. They have an urgent need to obtain better working and living conditions and concrete protection of their rights and interests in order to enhance their social status and sense of identity. In addition, they seek to maintain a close relationship with their parents and children in their hometown and to minimize their absence from their children's personal growth.

Protection of Rights and Interests. Although second-generation migrant workers are increasingly aware of their rights and interests through participation in certain group activities, they are still considered an underprivileged group because of their insufficient legal knowledge and lack of channels to protect their rights. They believe that improving their working environment and living standards is the first step to ensuring the protection of their rights and interests as well as to obtaining a sense of identity. In order to save money on accommodation, for instance, many migrant workers choose to share the rental of an apartment. However, shared housing with other individuals usually means a lack of privacy; as a result, embarrassing situations become inevitable.

Private Space Expansion and Privacy Protection Furniture Set for Dormitories. The furniture set consists of a foldable curtain and a closet installed next to the user's bed. When fully unfolded, the set can effectively protect the user's privacy in bed. In addition, the closet serves as an excellent storage area. The curtain is even more flexible, because it serves as an easy "switch" between "private" and "open." When the set is folded at approximately 90 degrees, it creates a triangular, private space next to the bed, allowing the user to enjoy time on his/her own when sitting on the edge of the bed (Fig. 2).

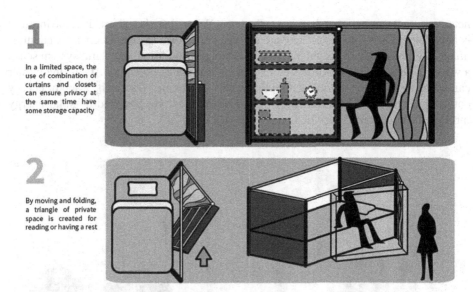

1

In a limited space, the use of combination of curtains and closets can ensure privacy at the same time have some storage capacity

2

By moving and folding, a triangle of private space is created for reading or having a rest

Fig. 2. The usage scenarios of private space expansion and privacy protection furniture set for dormitories designed for the new industrial working class

Absence From Family. As the population of second-generation migrant workers continues to grow, the problems of "left-behind children" become more prominent. Second-generation migrant workers believe that working in cities is their best option. Only through that can they improve their material conditions to afford better education for their children and allow them to change their fate. However, maintaining close relationships and full communication with their "left-behind" children, supervising their progression in study, as well as minimizing the negative impact on their children's physical and mental development caused by the absence of parents have become the most notable pain points for the social group.

3.3 Pain Points of New Farming Professionals

The core pursuit of the new farming professionals is to increase income in order to improve living standards and enrich their lives. Consequently, during daily agricultural production and operations, they are mainly concerned with how to improve their management effectively, increase yields and sales, and enrich their leisure life.

Crop Security Management. The protection of cash crops during large-scale cultivation and timely detection and suppression of theft and vandalism have always been managerial challenges for new farming professionals who specialize in producing and managing cash crops. With the technological advancement of the Internet of Things, solutions to this problem that are more convenient and effective are developing.

Intelligent Electronic Security Fence. The system comprises several independent infrared fences; the intelligent electronic security fence creates an invisible protective net to ensure the safety of cash crops on the farm. When there is an intrusion, the infrared beams detect the location and activate the nearest embedded camera, which captures images of the intruder(s) as photographic evidence. In addition, the alarm system sends a warning directly to the farmer's cellphone via a mobile application. Thus, the farmer can arrive at the scene in time and minimize any economic losses. The issue of energy consumption is solved because the infrared beam posts are powered by solar energy through the solar panels installed on the top face (Fig. 3).

Intelligent electronic security fence
In order to ensure the safety of cash crops on the farm, an invisible fence is formed by multiple independent electronic fences. When an outsider intrusion is detected, the orientation is determined by the infrared fence and the photo taken by the most recent camera to get the evidence and an alarm is made directly to the farmer via the mobile APP. Farmers can be timely information based on the information to avoid economic losses. The top of the product has solar panels, enough to solve the problem of energy consumption.

Fig. 3. The usage scenarios of intelligent electronic security fence designed for the new farming professionals

Enrichment of Life. Although highly efficient and professional production has brought considerable income growth to the new farming professionals, corresponding and direct changes to their consumption structure and lifestyle are more difficult to introduce. The rich and varied lifestyles and products in cities remain inaccessible for them, which is exactly why the second-generation migrant workers left their hometowns to work in the cities in the first place. With the new farming professionals becoming more financially capable than the previous generations of farmers, satisfying their growing consumer demand and desire for cultural and recreational life has become an imminent issue.

4 Conclusions and Reflection

By exploring the changes in the social-class structure that have occurred as a result of social differentiation, this study selected three emerging social classes (the political and cultural elite, the new industrial working class, and new farming professionals), analyzing and summarizing their values, lifestyles, consumption tendencies, and aesthetic preferences. The results of the analysis were then condensed and refined to create the image of a representative individual corresponding to each class. This study then identified their main pain points, one of which was selected for targeted product and service designs.

The findings of the study were compiled on the basis of the teaching content of a graduate course. Limited by the course duration, the information collected was not exhaustive. Specifically, the designs in Sect. 3 were completed in a rush; hence, they lacked sufficient refinement. Nevertheless, it is hoped that the findings of this study can provide designers with novel insights for the design of products and services for population groups with which they are unfamiliar. They would then be able to approach the design process from a social-class perspective and develop a comprehensive and an in-depth understanding of the target population quickly at general and individual levels. They would then be able to apply design methods incrementally, such as the illustration of a representative individual to the concrete pain points of the target population, in turn providing guidance for their actual designs.

References

1. Li, H.-S.: Xiandaihua Jincheng zhong de Shehui Fenhua yu Shehui Zhenghe (Social differentiation and social integration in the process of modernization). Doctoral dissertation, the Party School of the Central Committee of the Communist Party of China (2015). (in Chinese)
2. Lu, X.-Y.: Dangdai Shehui Jieceng Yanjiu Baogao (Report on contemporary social classes in China). Social Science Academic Press, Beijing (2002). (in Chinese)
3. Lu, J.: Gaige Kaifang hou Woguo Zhengzhi Jingying Yanbian Yanjiu (Research on the evolution of the Chinese political elite following the implementation of the reform and opening-up policy). Masters' Thesis, Anhui University (2013). (in Chinese)

Investigation on the Correlation Model Between Display Height and Tilt Angle

Huimin Hu[1], Yahui Bai[2], Chaoyi Zhao[1(✉)], Yinxia Li[2], Na Lin[1], and Zhongting Wang[1]

[1] Ergonomics Laboratory, China National Institute of Standardization, Beijing, China
{huhm,zhaochy,linna,wangzht}@cnis.gov.cn
[2] School of Mechanical Engineering, Zhengzhou University, Zhengzhou, Henan, China
1298687634@qq.com, liyxmail@126.com

Abstract. The correlation model about display height and tilt angle on standing posture was proposed based on the analysis of man-machine relationship. The experiment about display height and tile angle was designed to verify the correction of the model. 12 participants had evaluated the different heights of display and adjusted the preferred display tile angle at each height. The experiment data shows the preferred display height is below the eye height of people within 60 cm and the preferred display tile angle have a strong relativity with the display height, which is consistent with the data calculated by the model equations. The model can be used for the design of display height and tile angle on standing posture.

Keywords: Standing · Preferred display angle · Man-Machine Matching Model
Comfort · Display

1 Introduction

Displays are widely used in our society, whether it's satellite monitoring or watching VCD. As one of the main human-machine interaction devices, the height and tile angle of display had a significant impact on user experience. The unreasonable design may do harm to user health [1]. The viewing distance and viewing angle were the main research factors on the relationship between human and display when sitting. Many researches on display settings have been done, which provided the theoretical principle for the ergonomic design of display.

International Standards Organization pointed out that the optimum position for the most important visual display is 20°–50° below the horizontal line of sight. Lee [2] showed viewing angle was highly correlated with preferred viewing distance. The more deflected from the direct front view, the shorter the preferred viewing distance was. In conclusion, the preferred viewing angle was a range angle, which was mainly about 20° to 50° below the light of sight that varied according to different research. Furthermore, the viewing distance and viewing posture had an effect on the preferred viewing angle. Shieh and Lee [3] found the preferred screen angle was about 120°–125° horizontally, or about 30° below the light of sight. Ji et al. [4] found that the screen tile angle had an effect on the comfort of head. The screen angle may influence the recognition time and the comfort of head.

© Springer International Publishing AG, part of Springer Nature 2018
A. Marcus and W. Wang (Eds.): DUXU 2018, LNCS 10920, pp. 648–656, 2018.
https://doi.org/10.1007/978-3-319-91806-8_50

All in all, the reality was complicated when people made a reaction to a system, which involves the environment, the machine and themselves. This study proposed a correlation model about display height and tilt angle on standing posture based on the analysis of man-machine matching relationship, which can be used in the ergonomic design of display setting in height and tile angle.

2   The Correlation Model

The subjective comfort evaluation is influenced by the whole human-machine-environment system, which means the experimental environment and the characteristics of the machine can have some effect on people, however, it is complicated to research the system in combined factors [5]. This research mainly focused on the relationship between human and the display on comfort standing posture. The display height and tile angle were the main factors that influence the comfort. Figure 1 shows the human-display relative position on comfort standing watching system, where the complicated human structure is simplified to indicate the major joint.

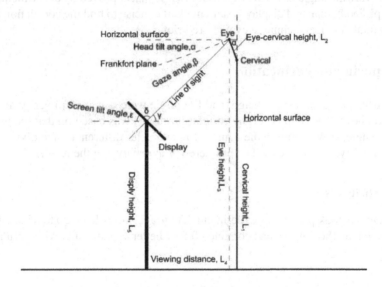

Fig. 1. Human-display relative position diagram

In Fig. 1, Lx is used to represent the sizes and Greek letters indict the angles. L_1 shows the cervical height; L_2 indicates the distance from eye to cervical; L_3 represents the eye height when people interacting with display; L_4 indicates the viewing distance, which means the horizontal distance from eye to display center; L_5 represents the center of display height. α is head tilt angle; β is gaze angle, which represents the angle from the Frankfort plane to the plane formed by the pupils and the visual target; γ is the angle from the line of sight to the horizontal line; δ is the preferred viewing angle, which is the angle from the line of sight to the up line of display; ε is the screen tile angle. In this model, the comfortable range of α was about $0°$ to about $20°$ and β was about $0°$ to about $45°$ [6].

According to geometrical relationship, the following equations can be concluded:

$$\gamma = \alpha + \beta(0°, 65°) \tag{1}$$

$$\gamma + \delta + \varepsilon = 180° \tag{2}$$

$$\tan \gamma = (L_3 - L_5)/L_4 \tag{3}$$

So, the Man-Machine Matching Model is showing as

$$\delta = 180 - \varepsilon - \arctan(L_3/L_4 - L_5/L_4) \tag{4}$$

According to the equations, the preferred display height is related to the head tile angle α, gaze angle β, viewing distance L_4 and eye height L_3. The preferred display tile angle is connected to the display height L_5, viewing distance L_4, eye height L_3 and preferred viewing angle δ. The δ is almost the same that approved by experiment below. The simplified human and display system made it concise to find the correlation and the using of mathematical technique even more brief.

3   Experiment Verification

The experiment about display height and tile angle were designed to verify the model proposed above. The propose of the correlation model was based on that the preferred viewing angle, δ was almost the same. However, the difference of individuals was unpredictability, which need to be considered when analyzing the results.

3.1   Participants

12 participants took part in this experiment. Their age varies from 20 to 32 and heights from 152 cm to 180 cm. All had corrected 0.8 or better visual acuity with normal color vision.

3.2   Environment

Surveys of actual illumination levels showed that the majority of VDT-equipped offices are within the range of 300–500 lx [7]. In this experiment, the average ambient light illumination was set as 460 lx.

3.3   Task and Procedure

Each participant was required to proceed with the following steps:

(1) Measure the participants' eye height, record the results and introduce the procedure to the participants.
(2) Adjust the display height L_5 to 70 cm, which was below the simulation height 99 cm. Set the screen tile angle ε to 0° and play the unified video file.
(3) The participates walked from one meter away from the display to a comfortable viewing distance.
(4) The standard watching posture was natural stance. The participants adjusted the screen tile angle ε to the best watching angle and then evaluated the height of display according to the 7 levels subjective score, see Table 1.

Table 1. 7 levels subjective score

1	2	3	4	5	6	7
Very uncomfortable	Uncomfortable	Less comfortable	General	More comfortable	Comfortable	Very comfortable

(5) Record the screen tile angle ε that the participants adjusted, viewing distance L_4 and the subjective score.
(6) Based on the best watching angle, the participants adjusted the display outwards to the limit angle that can also be watched comfortably. Record the outward limit screen tile angle ε-.
(7) Based on the best watching angle, the participants adjusted the display inwards to the limit angle that can also be watched comfortably. Record the limit screen tile angle ε + .
(8) Increase the display height by every 10 cm each time to the eye height of participant, repeat steps (2) to (7) for the other heights.

According to the eye height of participants, each participant finished 9 to 11 groups heights and all the participants finished 174 heights experiment. According to China Standard [8], L_2 was 12 cm–15 cm, and the max of α in this study was 20°. Max

Table 2. Original data record form

L_5	L_4	ε	ε^-	ε^+	Score	Remarks
70	27	9	4	18	1	–
80	34	13	8	20	3	–
90	31	16	7	21	3	–
100	37	18	14	26	3	–
110	39	26	20	37	4	–
120	44	36	30	46	6	–
130	44	45	39	51	6	–
140	47	57	51	65	7	–
150	48	68	60	74	7	–
160	45	79	74	81	6	–
170	45	84	80	86	4	–

$(L_2 - L2\cos\alpha) = 0.9$ cm, so the difference between L_3 and the measurement of eye height was very small. In this study, the measurement eye height is L_3 for every participant. The experiment data record form was shown as Table 2.

In the example data record form, with the center of display height rising, the viewing distance L_4 varied around 35 cm, the screen tile angle ε rising regularly, the subjective comfort score of display height increasing to the top and then decreasing.

4   Results

4.1   The Preferred Display Height

The eye height L_3 of 12 participants varied from 142 cm to 170 cm, so the $L_3 - L_5$ value of each participant was different when the display height L_5 was the same. The experiment collected 174 comfort score about the display height from 12 participants, which can be divided into 11 groups according to the value of $L_3 - L_5$. The mean score and sample numbers of each group were shown as Fig. 2. The number in the top of bars are the samples in the corresponding group. The height represents $L_3 - L_5$ and the scores are the average comfort score of display height.

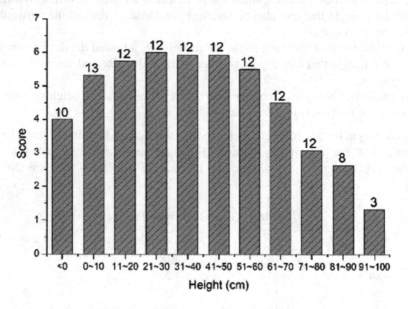

Fig. 2. The comfort score of display height

There was an upward trend when the value of $L_3 - L_5$ increased from -10 cm to 30 cm. The average was 4 (general) when the display height was higher than eye height in 10 cm and it increased over 5 (more comfortable) when the display height was lower than the eye height within 30 cm. There was a slight slide when the value of $L_3 - L_5$ was between 31 cm to 60 cm while the score was still over 5. The decline was notably when the display was lower over 60 cm while the score declined below 5 and gradually diminished. The preferred display height was under the eye height within 60 cm according to the experiment data.

According to the Man-machine correlation model equations, the viewing distance L4 and the eye height L3 need to be given first. The viewing distance ranged from 18 cm to 48 cm and the average was 32 cm. The average of 12 participants eye height L3 was 156 cm. When $L_4 = 32$ cm and $L_3 = 156$ cm, the equation $\tan \gamma = (156 - L_5)/32$ can be got according to Eq. (3). The range of γ was 0° to 65° according to Eq. (1), and so the preferred display heights was 96 cm to 156 cm. The preferred display height was below the eye height within 60 cm according to the model, which was exactly the same with the experiment results.

4.2   The Preferred Display Tile Angle

The preferred display tile angle varied from the height of display height and the changing trend was shown in Fig. 3. The 1 to 12 represented the 12 participants. The chart depicted the preferred display tile angle increased along with the display height become higher. In addition, the preferred display height was different when the display was at the same height. The increasing angle was not absolute, which varied from different people.

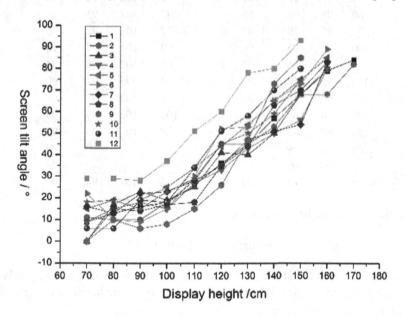

Fig. 3. Display height and tile angle

As the preferred display height above, the value of each participant was different when the display height L_5 was the same. For example, when the display height was 120 cm, the screen tile angle that adjusted by each participant was different but varied from 25° to 55°. The height of each participant was totally different, which was one of the reasons that the screen tilt angle was different. The analysis of the $L_3 - L_5$ value with the display tile angle of all participants was more meaningful than analysis the display height with the display tile angle of each participant.

The main factor that effected the preferred display height was the value of eye height minus the display height according to the model, however, the individual difference can't be neglected either. In order to research the relationship between the $L_3 - L_5$ and the preferred display tile angle, the Pearson correlation coefficient R of this two groups data were calculated, and the results was -0.922 (N = 174, p < 0.01). The preferred display tile angle varied according to the display height and participants, but the correlation was obvious.

According to the experiment data and Eq. (4), the preferred viewing angle δ can be calculated. All the δ of each display height and each participant were shown as the Table 3. The preferred viewing angle δ was mainly ranged from 90° to 103° and the average of δ was 96°.

Table 3. The preferred viewing angles

L_5	δ							
	1	2	3	...	10	11	12	Mean
70	96	95	105	...	92	102	91	98
80	98	99	88		92	107	93	96
90	95	99	83		97	102	98	96
100	100	95	90		99	104	97	98
110	97	86	93		94	107	88	94
120	95	78	77		84	95	92	90
130	93	84	88		91	102	87	91
140	90	86	92		101	102	97	95
150	89	82	91		109	105	99	99
160	88	99	98		–	–	–	99
170	96	99			–	–	–	98
Mean	94	91	91		96	103	94	96

So, the Eq. (4) can be simplified as

$$\varepsilon = 84^\circ - \arctan(x/32) \quad (x = L_3 - L_5) \tag{5}$$

The Eq. (5) shows that the preferred display tile angle was strongly related to $L_3 - L_5$. The simplified correlation model can be used in the height and angles design of display.

The experiment data of 12 participants was shown the scatter diagram, Fig. 4. The Eq. (5) was also shown in the diagram. The line has the same trend with the experiment data. In the preferred range of display height, the experiment data and equation data went through a paired-samples T test for the significance analysis and there was no significant difference (p = 0.559 > 0.05). The preferred display tile angle that got from the model equation accord basically with the experiment data. The Eq. (5) was verified to be a logical way to provide basic references.

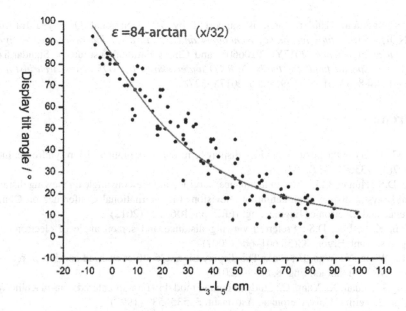

Fig. 4. Preferred display tile angle

In addition, during the experiment, the participants were asked to adjust the display outwards to the limit angle that can also be watched comfortably, and the angle was recorded as $\varepsilon-$. Then the participants adjusted the display inwards to the limit angle that can also be watched comfortably, and the angle was recorded as $\varepsilon+$. The preferred display angle was a particular angle range, not a particular angle. The maximum of the acceptable screen tile angle was 20° up or below the preferred screen tile angle. 10° up or below the equation line is acceptable when using the Eq. (5) to calculate the screen tile angle, because the individual differences.

5 Conclusions

In conclusions, the experiment date verified the logical of the proposed correlation model between display height and tile angle. For display height, the experiment data shown that the preferred display was under the eye height within 60 cm, and the height calculated by the correlation model was exactly the same with the experiment results. For display tile angle, by using the experiment results, the correlation Eq. (4) can be simplified as Eq. (5). The Eq. (3) indicated the relationship between preferred display height and the angle γ, while the Eq. (5) can be used to calculate the preferred display angle when the eye height and the viewing distance were given first. Therefore, the application of the model should be taken with specific circumstance. For instance, this study tested only one ambient illumination level. If the results hold for other ambient illumination level, the parameters may need to be corrected.

Acknowledgement. This research is supported by 2017 National Quality Infrastructure (2017NQI) project *study on the key technology and standard for human-centred design and product user experience* (2017YFF0206603) and China National Institute of Standardization through the "*special funds for the basic R&D undertakings by welfare research institutions*" (522016Y-4488, 522016Y-4679, and 522017Y-5278).

References

1. Jin, C.: Effect of the position of video display terminal on computer vision syndrome. Int. Eye Sci. **7**(5), 1336–1337 (2007)
2. Lee, D.S., Huang, M.L.: Screen luminance, subtitle, and viewing angle on viewing distance of liquid crystal display high-definition television. In: International Conference on Computer Science and Electronics Engineering. IEEE, pp. 106–109 (2012)
3. Shieh, K.K., Lee, D.S.: Preferred viewing distance and screen angle of electronic paper displays. Appl. Ergon. **38**(5), 601–608 (2007)
4. Ji, L., Wang, Y., Wan, H., et al.: The display tilt angle effect on head comfort in reasonable range. Mod. Manufact. Eng. **8**, 67–70 (2016)
5. Wang, L., Yuan, X., Yang, C.: Study of human model in human-entered man-machine system design. J. Beijing Univ. Aeronaut. Astronaut. **5**, 535–539 (1997)
6. BS EN ISO 13406-2: Ergonomic requirements for work with visual displays based on flat panels Part 2: ergonomic requirements for flat panel displays (2002)
7. Laubli, T., Hunting, W., Grandjean, E.: Visual impairments in VDU operators related to environmental conditions. In: Grandjean, E., Vigliani, E. (eds.) Ergonomics Aspects of Visual Display Terminals. Taylor & Francis, London (1982)
8. GB/T 10000-1988: Human Dimensions of Chinese Adults

Short Paper: How Do People Choose a Means for Communication in Disaster Situations?

Surveys After the Great East Japan Earthquake and the Kumamoto Earthquake

Masayuki Ihara[✉] and Hiroshi Watanabe

NTT Service Evolution Laboratories, NTT Corporation, Yokosuka, Japan
ihara@acm.org, watanabe.hi@lab.ntt.co.jp

Abstract. In disaster situations, people try to communicate with acquaintances for a variety of reasons. In general, they try to immediately communicate with family or important friends to confirm their safety. To understand the damage situation, they may try to communicate with neighbors whom they don't often communicate with in daily life. This paper introduces the results of surveys of people who experienced the Great East Japan Earthquake, 2011 and the Kumamoto Earthquake, 2016 in Japan to discover what communication modalities were used and why they were chosen.

Keywords: Disaster · Communication modality · Information grasp · Survey

1 Introduction

In daily life, people communicate with acquaintances in a wide variety of relationships such as family, friends, and colleagues. Indeed, there are many kinds of friends. For example, they may be old friends whom they have not contacted in a long time or those they contact often in daily life. Mothers of young children often join a community based on their child's associations. After a disaster, they may talk to others in an evacuation center. Disasters are fortunately rare but after a disaster it is important to communicate with many kinds of people since the type of information needed is unusual. This paper introduces the results of surveys of people who experienced the Great East Japan Earthquake, 2011 and the Kumamoto Earthquake, 2016 in Japan to discover what communication modalities were used and why they were chosen.

2 Related Work

To grasp information in disaster situations, people use many kinds of communication modalities such as face-to-face, telephone, email, SNS(texting), etc. SNS is one of most effective modalities. For example, Twitter can be used as a post-disaster modality by security extension [4]. Nagar's work [6] analyzed the spread of disaster information by social media. Busa's work [2] discussed trust-building through social media

A. Marcus and W. Wang (Eds.): DUXU 2018, LNCS 10920, pp. 657–663, 2018.
https://doi.org/10.1007/978-3-319-91806-8_51

communications in disaster management. Wohn compared face-to-face and computer-mediated communication in terms of social support [8], but did not focus on disaster situations. Shklovski showed that ICT use could find communities in disaster situations [7].

In this study, we elucidate the information needed and communication targets in disaster situations. To that end, we surveyed people who experienced the Great East Japan Earthquake, 2011 and the Kumamoto Earthquake, 2016 in Japan.

3   Information Needed in Disaster Situations

In disaster situations, it is important to grasp "information". A report on the Great East Japan Earthquake in 2011 noted that 78.5% of evacuees carried their own mobile devices, and at train stations in urban areas, many tried to get disaster information from digital signage displays.

The need to acquire information in disaster situations has three goals. First, people try to obtain information about the safety of family and friends. In this case, they have two psychological desires; one of which is that they want to know their family or friends are alive as soon as possible, and other is that they want to lower their anxiety by the act of communicating with someone special.

Second, they try to grasp information about the disaster. After an earthquake, they want to know its magnitude, areas affected by the disaster, damage to roads or buildings, suspension of public transportation, etc.

Third, they try to obtain information to maintain their life. After safety confirmation, they start thinking of lifelines such as electricity, water, and food. Announcements from the city office about food supplies are critical in stabilizing their emotions. In most cases, these bits of information are acquired by communicating with somebody.

A related work [1] extracted five behaviors in disaster situations. However, as we focus on information, the three goals above are our key concerns.

4   Questionnaire Survey

We conducted a web questionnaire survey to determine how people chose what means of communication in disaster situations. The subjects were 150 people who experienced the Great East Japan Earthquake, 2011 and another 150 from the Kumamoto Earthquake, 2016 in Japan. The affected area of the Great East Japan Earthquake covered many prefectures. In this survey, we determined the affected area as the three prefectures of Miyagi, Iwate, and Fukushima. These three were most heavily damaged prefectures. The earthquake disconnected the Internet in many areas by destroying facilities and/or flow control of the public communication network.

We selected the 300 subjects (in their 20's to 60's) from a database of a web survey company. The survey was conducted from Feb. 24 to 27, 2017. Note that the survey was part of many questionnaires and the question given to the subjects was "What means did you use for communication to obtain information in the disaster situation?" Multiple responses were accepted.

We set eight communication targets to obtain information: family, neighbors, colleagues, old friends, local town communities, new friends at a shelter, mother/father communities of elementary school, and those of kindergarten. The communication modalities targeted in this survey were face-to-face, telephone, email and SNS. The telephone category includes both mobile and fixed phone. The email category includes both mobile and PC email. The SNS category includes many texting applications such as Facebook messenger, etc.

5   Results

We introduce the survey results here. Figures 1 and 2 show the survey results of subjects who experienced the Great East Japan Earthquake and the Kumamoto Earthquake, respectively. Figure 3 displays the total results for both subject groups.

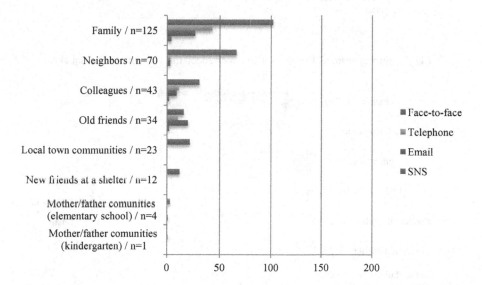

Fig. 1. Survey results of subjects who experienced the Great East Japan Earthquake.

As seen in Fig. 3, regarding communication with family (n = 249), they predominantly used face-to-face (193, 77.5%). This result shows their psychological desire to seek relief in seeing people face-to-face, not online. They also used the telephone (108, 43.4%), email (52, 20.9%) and SNS (36, 14.5%). These communication channels, if working, permit the rapid confirmation of family safety.

Regarding communication with neighbors (n = 139), they used face-to-face (133, 95.7%). Regarding communication among mother/father communities based on children, they communicated face-to-face (5, 71.4%) and SNS (3, 42.9%); note that the number of answers was small (n = 7). The reason for these results is that they are neighbors in the same elementary school area and that those who have children are familiar with SNS.

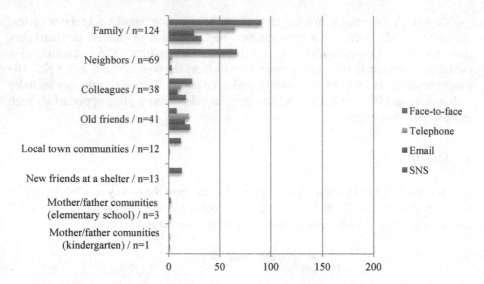

Fig. 2. Survey results of subjects who experienced the Kumamoto Earthquake.

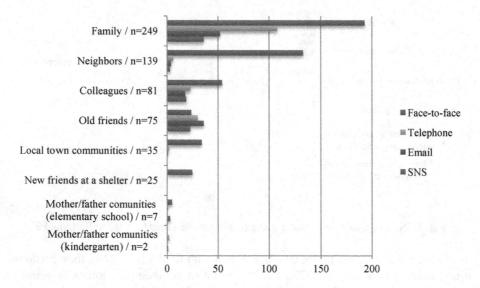

Fig. 3. Total results of the two subject groups.

On the other hand, regarding communication with old friends (n = 75), they used email (36, 48.0%), telephone (30, 40.0%), face-to-face (24, 32.0%) and SNS (23, 30.7%). These are because old friends do not necessarily live in the same area. Regarding communication with colleagues (n = 81), they used face-to-face (54, 66.7%), telephone (23, 28.4%), email (18, 22.2%), and SNS (19, 23.5%).

6   Discussion

One interesting finding from the survey is that parents who have children in the same elementary school used the community network established by those parents. As the parent community network is wider than the neighbor network, they can obtain valuable information that cannot be obtained from neighbors.

For example, they could discover that a supermarket in the next town is open while the one in their home town is closed. Moreover, they can obtain information valuable for parents having children since the parent network is constructed among parents with a common focus on children. For example, they may obtain information as to which roads are safe for the children to use to go to school. Information needed in disaster situations is strongly focused on family safety. Parents with small children try to grasp common information from parent communities.

Figure 4 is a comparison of SNS use between the Great East Japan Earthquake and the Kumamoto Earthquake. The result is that more people used SNS after the Kumamoto Earthquake. This is because SNS applications were not widely used in Japan when the Great East Japan Earthquake occurred, 2011 (See the 2017 WHITE PAPER Information and Communications in Japan [9]).

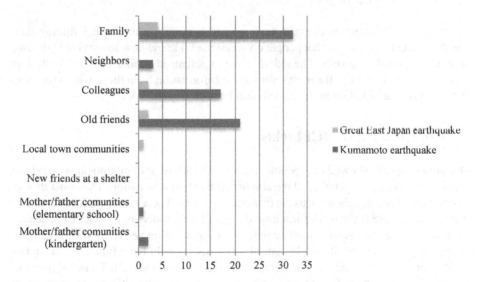

Fig. 4. A comparison between the Great East Japan Earthquake and the Kumamoto Earthquake regarding the use of SNS.

Figure 5 is a comparison between the Great East Japan Earthquake and the Kumamoto Earthquake regarding the use of telephones. The result is many people used telephones in both cases. These results show that SNS use is likely to be very common in future disaster situations as well as the telephone. People have a psychological desire to confirm the safety of their family and friends by hearing their voice.

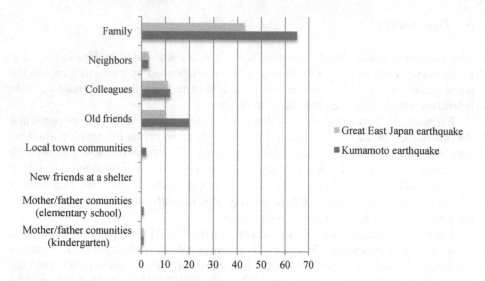

Fig. 5. A comparison between the Great East Japan Earthquake and the Kumamoto Earthquake regarding the use of the telephone.

Regarding information deemed necessary to acquire, an interesting finding from another related interview is that people obtained useful know-how to survive in disaster situations from older people. The elderly have experienced similar disasters in the past and know how to manage the messy situations. Information from those who have experienced a similar situation in the past should be well shared.

7   Contribution to HCI Fields

Our survey results showed that people use a wide variety of communication modality according to the target person and the aim of information acquisition. They also showed that SNS has high likelihood of use in disaster situations. These results will better inform discussions on the framework for a total design of SNS tools and its user experiences. As shown in the use case of parent communities, information needed is strongly related to the geographical conditions. Disaster-biased SNS should have functions to support multi-communities based on its geographical area size and individual aims of information acquisition. Although commercial SNS applications offer multi message thread (any user can create a user group thread), message threads based on communities of geographical areas should be established automatically after a disaster.

Goolsby's study [3] showed that social media provides the means for creating new communities and for reenergizing old communities. This indicates the possibility of existing communities helping people in disaster-affected areas even if the "old friends" live far from the affected area.

Another important aspect is the need for face-to-face. People want to know that their family or friends are alive as soon as possible. In other words, they try to physically move to an evacuation center, etc. in order to confirm the safety of family or friends. A technology that targets this need could be effective. A new technology to assist in safety confirmation in disaster situations could utilize the movement of people among centers. One example is the multi-hop type communication technology based on mobile phone; it supports safety confirmation by using the movement of people among evacuation centers [5].

8   Conclusion

In this study, we detailed a survey we conducted on the means for communication actually used in disaster situations. The results showed that people chose a variety of communication modalities according to psychological factors and distance limitations.

Future work includes a framework for designing more comprehensive SNS tools and making the user experience more effective.

References

1. Asai, D., Sagata, Y., Asano, Y.: On-site information seeking behaviors in earthquake and tsunami. In: CHI 2013 Extended Abstracts on Human Factors in Computing Systems (CHI EA 2013), pp. 1881–1886. ACM, New York (2013)
2. Busa, M.G., Musacchio, M.T., Finan, S., Fennell, C.: Trust-building through social media communications in disaster management. In: Proceedings of the 24th International Conference on World Wide Web (WWW 2015 Companion), pp. 1179–1184. ACM, New York (2015)
3. Goolsby, R.: Social media as crisis platform: the future of community maps/crisis maps. ACM Trans. Intell. Syst. Technol. **1**(1), 11 (2010). Article no. 7
4. Hossmann, T., Carta, P., Schatzmann, D., Legendre, F., Gunningberg, P., Rohner, C.: Twitter in disaster mode: security architecture. In: Proceedings of the Special Workshop on Internet and Disasters (SWID 2011), Article no. 7, 8 p. ACM, New York (2011)
5. Ihara, M., Seko, S., Miyata, A., Aoki, R., Ishida, T., Watanabe, M., Hashimoto, R., Watanabe, H.: Towards more practical information sharing in disaster situations. In: Yamamoto, S. (ed.) HIMI 2016. LNCS, vol. 9735, pp. 32–39. Springer, Cham (2016). https://doi.org/10.1007/978-3-319-40397-7_4
6. Nagar, S., Seth, A., Joshi, A.: Characterization of social media response to natural disasters. In: Proceedings of the 21st International Conference on World Wide Web (WWW 2012 Companion), pp. 671–674. ACM, New York (2012)
7. Shklovski, I., Palen, L., Sutton, J.: Finding community through information and communication technology in disaster response. In: Proceedings of the 2008 ACM Conference on Computer Supported Cooperative Work (CSCW 2008), pp. 127–136. ACM, New York (2008)
8. Wohn, D.Y., Peng, W., Zytko, D.: Face to face matters: communication modality, perceived social support, and psychological wellbeing. In: Proceedings of the 2017 CHI Conference Extended Abstracts on Human Factors in Computing Systems (CHI EA 2017), pp. 3019–3026. ACM, New York (2017)
9. WHITE PAPER Information and Communications in Japan. http://www.soumu.go.jp/johotsusintokei/whitepaper/eng/WP2017/2017-index.html. Accessed 21 Jan 2018

A Platform to Connect Swiss Consumers of Fair Trade Products with Producers in Developing Countries: Needs and Motivations

Julia Klammer and Fred W. G. van den Anker[✉]

University of Applied Sciences Northwestern Switzerland, Riggenbachstrasse 16,
4600 Olten, Switzerland
{julia.klammer,fred.vandenanker}@fhnw.ch

Abstract. The concept of user experience departs from the concepts of usability and usefulness by paying more attention to emotional-affective aspects of use. It also addresses human needs and motivations in a way that goes well beyond the focus on efficient and effective task performance that is central to the concepts of usability and usefulness. In this contribution we report on the basic user needs and motivations we identified for the use of a platform that aimed at establishing a stronger connection between Swiss consumers of fair trade products and producers in developing countries. This resulted in a web-based "access to market-platform" that is based on "crowd ordering" and enables the producers to market bio-farmed products directly to consumers in Europe. Several needs and motivations that have been proposed in the framework of human needs categorizations were shown to be relevant for our case, such as "money"/income and competence development on the part of the producers, "relatedness" or community-building on the part of the consumers and their need for "stimulation", i.e. to learn more about the products, production and producers. The need to "do good for others" that is central to fair trade is discussed to take the paradigm shift from a task- towards a "self"-oriented approach in UX one step further by integrating an "other"-orientation in UX design. Furthermore, the distinction between pragmatic and hedonic components of UX is discussed in the light of the basic need of improving living conditions on the part of the producers and community-building aspects on the part of the consumers.

Keywords: User experience · Usability · User-centered design · User needs
User motivation · Fair trade · Ethical consumption · Crowdfunding
Crowd ordering

1 Introduction

1.1 Context

This contribution arose from a two-year research and development project carried out together with a Swiss fair trade company (in the following called Fairco)[1]. Fairco, whose

---

[1] The project was financed by the Swiss Commission for Technology and Innovation CTI.

© Springer International Publishing AG, part of Springer Nature 2018
A. Marcus and W. Wang (Eds.): DUXU 2018, LNCS 10920, pp. 664–681, 2018.
https://doi.org/10.1007/978-3-319-91806-8_52

roots go back to the 1970s, is specialized in building and maintaining organic and fair trade supply chains from smallholder farmers in southern countries to consumers in European countries, especially Switzerland. Fairco has long-term relationships with producer networks in Brazil, Tunisia, Burkina Faso and Togo. In this relation Fairco does not only act as an import organization, but also partners up with the local producers: it contracts with farming families, advises them on organic cultivation, educates them, organizes certifications and invests in local processing facilities and projects to develop sustainable production structures in developing countries.

The project reported here was initiated by Fairco to establish a stronger relation between the producers in the developing countries and European consumers through a web-based platform. In the end, the platform was supposed to deliver services that would generate more involvement on both sides. One of the results was a web-based "access to market-platform", a website that enables producers in the developing countries to market their bio-farmed products that are not yet part of Fairco's supply chain directly to consumers in Europe (see Fig. 1).

Fig. 1. The "Access to market platform" enabling producers in developing countries to sell their products to consumers based on the principle of crowd ordering. URL: https://www.gebana.com/projects/ch/project.

Using the example of mango production, the term "producers" includes farmers, e.g. mango plantation owners who sell fresh mango, "collectors" (those who collect and sell fresh mango to Fairco or its mango dryers) and mango dryers, who sell dried mango. These producers may already be part of Fairco's network or may be new producers, thus enabling more farmers to bring their products to market through the platform. This is realized through online "crowd ordering": engagement by the consumers based on the principles of crowdfunding. New products will be exported to Switzerland at the moment a previously defined minimum amount of "pre-orders" has been reached.

1.2 Focus of This Contribution

This paper focuses on those parts of the development process that bear a direct relationship to issues of user-centered design, usability and user experience: the phases of (1) context and needs analysis at the beginning of the project and (2) usability testing of prototypes later on in the project[2]. In both these activities we tried to complete our task- and process-oriented approach to analysis and evaluation with the identification and analysis of motivational aspects of use, an integration of components that is core to UX design beyond mere usability (see Sect. 2 for a more extensive discussion). Apart from contextual preconditions that have to be met to enable the producers in the developing countries to participate, the success of the platform (or more general: the connection endeavor) depends for a great deal on the *motivation* of both producers and consumers to participate. For that purpose their individual interests and needs have to be met. In our case, it is the platform application that has to address those interests and needs. One of the central questions was how the platform can help to improve the living conditions of the producers in the developing countries. This requires a solution that fits into the "lifeworld" of the producers. It requires a solution that "makes sense", is sustainable and creates commitment of *all* people involved on the long-term. So, the next question was how the consumers can be sustainably motivated and involved. At the same time, the platform had to meet Fairco's interests and business goals.

In this contribution, we present and reflect our project results in relation to the concept of user experience, highlighting motivational aspects as a central component of user experience and thus moving beyond a narrow usability- and task-related perspective. In connection with that, we reflect the specifics of fair trade business and consumption.

2 UX Design: Building upon Needs and Motivations

The concept of user experience has been conceived as moving beyond usability by incorporating motivational, emotional-affective, enjoyment/fun and aesthetic aspects into the perceived and experienced qualities of products [see e.g. 2–5]. The concept of usability, in contrast, rather focusses on efficient and effective task performance. In his hedonic/pragmatic model Hassenzahl [6] distinguishes between usability and utility (the functionality offered) as pragmatic product qualities and hedonic product qualities such as "stimulation" (e.g. originality or challengingness, e.g. promoting competence development), "identification" (the image communicated by the product, but also the extent to which a product connects with others rather than isolates) and "evocation", which is similar to Norman's "reflective level" [3], and refers to a product's symbolic value, its ability to provoke thoughts, memories and stories. A strict distinction between hedonic and pragmatic product qualities (especially usefulness) may be subject to debate. For example, in the framework of the Technology Acceptance Model [TAM, 7], the hedonic aspect of "identification", specifically "image", has been shown to determine the

---

[2] The technical development and implementation of related "services" have been described elsewhere [1].

perceived usefulness of a product, a "pragmatic" quality in Hassenzahl's model. Furthermore, competence development as a "hedonic" aspect (of "stimulation") in a sociotechnical approach always has been part of developing useful systems for work situations, since "the product of work is people" [8].

However, the main contribution of this distinction between pragmatic and hedonic or "instrumental" and "non-instrumental" qualities [9, 10] within the concept of user experience is that it draws us away from a too strong focus on efficient and effective task performance, which has been predominant in the area of user-centered design for a long time, and instead puts emphasis on the question what a system can do for oneself as a person. Desirable products are said to be those that combine a high task-orientation or good pragmatic qualities with a high self-orientation or hedonic qualities [6, 11]. In this respect Hassenzahl [11, 12] also distinguishes, in line with the different levels of action regulation proposed in e.g. Self-Regulation Theory [13] and Activity Theory [14, 15], between "do-goals" and "be-goals".

"Do-goals" relate to human action, "what" we do (see Fig. 2). "Be-goals" relate to basic human needs, such as being competent, feeling related to others, being popular, being stimulated. They motivate our behavior, make it meaningful, explain why we do things. In product design they shift our focus from *what* a system supports us to do (usefulness/the functionality provided) and *how* we are supported by the product in reaching our task-related goals (usability) to *why* we use or buy a product, what are the underlying reasons, what drives, what motivates us to do so. Although such high-level goals may be of limited use when it comes to concrete systems design [16, p. 680][3], they can be considered as fundamental to an experience-based approach to user-centered design [12]. In this context, hedonic qualities have been put forward as "motivators", pragmatic qualities (usability, usefulness) only as "hygiene factors" [17], a distinction that goes back to Herzberg's two-factor (motivation-hygiene) theory of work motivation [18]. In a similar vein and based on Maslow's hierarchy of human needs [19], Jordan [20] and Hancock et al. [21] propose to move beyond the levels of functionality and usability to generate "pleasurable" user experiences.

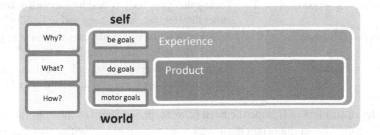

Fig. 2. A three level hierarchy of goals (adapted from [12])

---

[3] Goodwin [16] distinguishes between four goal types at different levels: *basic human goals*, corresponding to basic human needs like being safe and healthy, *life goals*, *end goals*, "something the people can help accomplish" (p. 681) and *experience goals*, which describe how the persona wants to feel using the product or service.

Needs and Motivations in Relation to Fair Trade Consumption. Considering need fulfillment not only as a major source of positive experiences with technology [12, 17] but for technology *acceptance* in the first place, the question raised here is which needs motivate users to participate on a platform connecting fair trade consumers in Europe with producers in Africa. For that purpose we refer to the list of universal psychological needs by Sheldon et al. [22] in Table 1 (below)[4]. "Money" can be expected to be a need motivating the producers in developing countries to participate, not to create "luxury" (see Table 1), which represents a rather Western view, but rather to make a living.

Table 1. Top-ten psychological needs [22], Fig. adapted from [12]

Need	Description
Autonomy - independence	Feeling like you are the cause of your own actions rather than feeling that external forces or pressure cause your action
Competence - effectance	Feeling that you are very capable and effective in your actions rather than feeling incompetent or ineffective
Relatedness - belongingness	Feeling that you have regular intimate contact with people who care about you rather than feeling lonely and uncared of
Self-actualizing – meaning	Feeling that you are developing your best potentials and making life meaningful rather than feeling stagnant and that life does not have much meaning
Security – control	Feeling safe and in control of your life rather than feeling uncertain and threatened by your circumstances
Money – luxury	Feeling that you have plenty of money to buy most of what you want rather than feeling like a poor person who has no nice possessions
Influence – popularity	Feeling that you are liked, respected, and have influence over others rather than feeling like a person whose advice or opinion nobody is interested in
Physical thriving – bodily	Feeling that your body is healthy and well-taken care of rather than feeling out of shape and unhealthy
Self-esteem – self-respect	Feeling that you are a worthy person who is as good as anyone else rather than feeling like a "loser"
Pleasure - stimulation	Feeling that you get plenty of enjoyment and pleasure rather than feeling bored and understimulated by life

For the consumers in Europe the need of relatedness - both to the community and to fair trade - might be an important motivator to participate in activities that connect them with the producers. "Doing good for others" seems to be part of the need structure in fair trade consumption, which is not covered by Sheldon et al.'s [22] categorization of needs. This shows a limited applicability of the basic needs as depicted in Table 1 to the area of fair trade or in general to areas in which moral behavior plays a role. In line with

---

[4] Hassenzahl et al. [17] reduced these to a list of seven: autonomy, competence, relatedness, meaning, security, popularity and stimulation.

the shift to a higher self-orientation in the concept of user experience, the needs as shown in Table 1 are self-oriented. However, the motivation to support fair trade is at least partly related to "the other" as opposed to "the self". For the consumer of fair trade, the need to generate meaning in the sense of creating a deeper purpose also implies the need to improve the living conditions of "the other" i.e. the producers of the fair trade goods. Positive effects of "doing good" on the person's self-image (i.e. "being good", being a morally good person) [23, 24] aside, motivations related to the "social features" of products - such as decent living and working conditions for producers in developing countries - are missing in the above categorization of needs. At this point Schwartz' Value Theory is relevant. In his categorization of "motivationally distinct" human values Schwartz [25] proposes the category of "self-transcendence", which includes values that are concerned with "enhancement of others and transcendence of selfish interests". We might also draw on attitude- and motivation-based approaches in research on fair trade or "ethical" consumption [see 26]. "Ethical obligation", understood as "an individual's internalized ethical rules, which reflect their personal beliefs about right and wrong" has, for example, been proposed as a driver of fair trade consumption [27]. These considerations seem to give cause for taking the "shift" from a task- towards a "self"-oriented approach to considering needs and motivations in UX design one step further by integrating an "other-orientation" into UX design to fulfill user needs in such areas as fair trade.

3 Connecting Consumers and Producers: The Platform Development Process

Needs and motivations for the use of the platform were identified and validated throughout the whole platform development process, which consisted of:

- *the exploration and identification of potentially useful platform applications* together with Fairco
- *analysis:* a context analysis of one of Fairco's producer networks, namely the mango production in Burkina Faso, West Africa, and a consumer needs analysis in Switzerland
- *iterative development*:
  - the creation of user stories for the development of the selected applications
  - UI design and software implementation, and
  - prototype evaluation and usability testing.

First, we conducted interviews and group discussions with five employees from Fairco's central office in Switzerland. Our context and needs analysis in Burkina Faso included 12 interviews with producers and co-workers of the production facility as well as external producers such as dryers, collectors and farm holders (see Fig. 3).

Fig. 3. Impressions from the context and needs analysis with producers and coworkers in Burkina Faso (Mango production)

Furthermore, to investigate the consumers' interests and motivations concerning the platform, a focus group with six typical Fairco customers between the age of 35 and 64 years was conducted in Switzerland. These consumers were representative for Fairco's core customer group, i.e. well-educated persons around the age of 50, as well as younger customers that show a higher online-affinity (e.g. Facebook fans or people who do online purchases).

Following a human-centered design process (ISO 9241-210), the context and needs analysis was used to derive requirements and user stories for platform development. The subsequent development process consisted of two iterations of prototyping and evaluation with 14 Swiss consumers in total.

In the next section, the results of our context and needs analysis with the producers in Burkina Faso and the consumers in Switzerland are described. In Sect. 5 the results of the phase of prototype development and testing are described, focusing on the users' needs and motivations that were elicited rather than the usability findings.

4 Context and Needs Analysis to Identify Meaningful Platform Applications

4.1 Context Analysis in Africa: Producers' Needs and Motivations

The interviews with the producers in Burkina Faso revealed the following needs and motivations for a stronger connection with consumers in the North.

Equipment, Tools and Financing to Support Local Production. The most evident needs that producers mentioned are directly linked to the production itself and how the North could support different steps in the supply chain. Specific problems and needs that the producers mentioned were: (1) the lack of work equipment like weighing machines, transport crates, cutting tools to thin out mango trees (to prevent them from insect infestation) or transport vehicles that can be covered and cooled, (2) computers and other communication tools such as smartphones to have internet access and (3) repairs or investments in bigger projects like water draining or weed control.

Another problem that was identified and that is linked to these needs is that many producers have difficulties with liquidity, e.g. having to rent a transport vehicle instead of buying one, or not having enough cash to pay collectors or buy fresh products. Many of the producers claimed that they could produce far more if they could get loans or prepayment for specific steps in the supply chain. This shows the high potential for participation projects to support the production process.

Know-How Transfer and Consultancy: Need for Professionalization. The producers expressed the need to become more professional in their production. Some of them said that they do not have enough know-how concerning administration and human resources management and that they would profit from more exchange among each other but also with experts from the North to get know-how on agricultural engineering.

Consumer Feedback. The interviews showed that it is very important for the producers to sell high quality products. When asked about the needs regarding the exchange with the consumers in the North, most of them said that they would like to get more information on how their products are further processed (what happens with the mangos? where exactly do they go?) and get feedback on their products from end-consumers (how consumers like their dried mangos, how well the product is received). This is quite similar to the consumers' need for information, as will be described in Sect. 4.2.

Need for Creating a Higher Income Through Access to Market. Producers stated that a platform connecting them with consumers in the North would be a great chance to generate an additional income. By having access to the international organic food market they could sell more products. For example, mango farmers who also grow honey, vegetables or chili or female dryers who produce shea butter on the side would have the opportunity to sell their products. This is especially important in the light of the problem articulated by some of the interviewees that in particular the women have long periods of unemployment between harvesting seasons. One conclusion was that the platform could be a tool to test the need of consumers for specific new products.

4.2 The North Perspective: Consumers' Motivation for Participation

The focus group showed that in particular needs for networking and sharing, participation and information are central to the consumers.

Need for Participation and Community. It turned out that the consumers' main desire is to take part and to get actively involved with Fairco, to be part of a community that participates in Fairco's supply and development activities. According to the focus group, the platform could support the community in their striving to help the producers to work better. Participation projects, such as crowd funding mobile phones and credit, were considered useful on the condition that consumers have enough background knowledge about the project. Consumers appeared to have a negative attitude towards classic donations that are not tied to specific purposes.

Moreover, consumers wish to have more exchange among themselves and they find it important to make the community visible. In particular, collective orders ("bulk orders") by consumers are a central topic here.

Beyond Mere Information: Need for "Stimulation". Similar to the producers' need to know more about where their products go and how they are received by consumers, the consumers themselves would like to have more detailed information i.e. "stories" on the products and production process. They would appreciate knowing more about the manufacturers' work (for example, who processes the raw materials?), the relevance of the product for the fair trade business in the producer's country and differences to other products. Also, the consumers like to follow the progress of their ordered products. Consumers appeared to have the desire to be as close to the activities as possible. To participate in projects, the consumers would like to have background information about the underlying reasons for development projects and support activities (what do local people really need?). Consumers would also like to know the status of ongoing projects and campaigns and what is currently going on in the producer community in the South.

5   Aligning Producers' and Consumers' Needs

5.1   Evaluation of a First Platform Prototype Supporting Consumer Participation

The main idea of the platform was that consumers can participate in several crowd funding projects to support the production in the South. On the basis of the context analysis in Africa and the workshops with consumers in Switzerland, four requirements were formulated together with Fairco's marketing team for designing the participation activities online: (1) give precise information on the concrete need of the producers, (2) focus on the products and give background information on projects, (3) enable clear and "small" activities that consumers can take part in within one larger project and (4) make participants visible as a community. Based on an expert evaluation of a first mockup, an advanced prototype was developed. This prototype (see Fig. 4) was a clickable HTML dummy containing an overview page with four participation projects that a consumer could join, a detailed page of each project and a page where the consumer would specify his or her participation eventually. This prototype was used for the first usability test with seven consumers from Switzerland to find out whether they understand what the projects are all about, how they can contribute to them and which kind of project presentation is optimal for the conversion of visitors to acting consumers. For example, consumers could choose to give money to buy crates ("Crates for Burkina Faso" in Fig. 4), donate their old phone to support communication and mobility ("Smartphones against pests") or an old bike ("Mobility for farmers"). The results of the evaluation are described in detail below.

Crowdfunding projects with different forms of participation (donate goods or money for developmental goals)

Fig. 4. First platform prototype for participation activities

Show Impact and Meaningfulness of Participation Projects to Support Long-Term Motivation. By asking consumers for what reason they selected a specific project (on the overview page) we could identify several reasons what makes projects interesting for consumers. One of them was the personal relationship of the user to the selected project, i.e. finding the project thematically important. This relates to what the consumers said during the evaluation: they appreciate donating money for specific, meaningful purposes (i.e. for bikes). This also corresponds to the need for participation as it was described in Sect. 4.2.

Some consumers said that they like "complete packages", i.e. several project goals within one long-term project, because they want to see the relation between different steps and how their support works out in detail, e.g. what the producers do with the bicycles. Consumers indicated that projects should contain clear and distinctive steps that stand alone and can be realized independently from one another. The evaluation showed that temporary short-term projects are found to be less interesting than projects in which something is developed and produced over a longer period of time (sustainability). Within that light, consumers evaluated the timeline on the detail page (showing the progress of the project) as very important (although it was not easy to comprehend in this first prototype). They want to see what happens on site and how their participation impacts the producers' everyday lives. For example, a "story" could be that twenty farmers can now make daily control visits at their farms because of the bicycles that were provided through a crowdfunding project.

For that reason, projects with multiple goals should be split. This suggestion could be implemented to a certain extent into the second prototype by dividing projects into "progress stages" (see Sect. 5.2).

Provide Precise and Unique Information to Fulfill the Need for *Stimulation* **i.e. Learn More.** The second reason consumers selected a project was to better understand the project or campaign and get more information, out of interest for the project. The participants found it important that project descriptions present a consistent "story" and contain precise details of how the project will be implemented. Information about the exact procedure, in particular showing how donations or other participation activities by consumers influence the producers' life in the developing countries, was found to be very important, especially when the project consists of donating goods.

Consumers said that they would appreciate constant information about the progress of projects, not only on the quantity of what has been achieved but also background information on what is happening on-site. According to the consumers' answers, this information should be unique and distinctive for every project, making it feel like "live" information rather than automatically generated news.

Conclusions on Participation and User Experience: Content Over User Interaction. The results showed that the long-term participation projects as they were represented in the first prototype needed more elaboration to uphold the consumers' motivation for a longer period of time. One idea was to separate different project stages and make the timeline more easy to understand. Moreover, the projects that Fairco had created for the prototype were evaluated as too complicated for consumers to keep track. Also, projects such as collecting "smartphones against pests" were found to be subject to too many risks, e.g. concerning assuring a safe transport, checking if smartphones are working, checking batteries and providing charging cables. On top of that, consumers questioned the goal of the project as well: Would it really help farmers to be provided with a smart-phone? So, beyond usability issues, consumers indicated that the platform's content - the participation projects - should be meaningful and worth realizing in the first place.

5.2   Evaluation of a Second Prototype Supporting Crowd Ordering Activities

In a second prototype (Fig. 5), we had a stronger focus on the impact of the participation projects presented to the consumers. The projects represented through the prototype were more directly related to supporting the production in the South to enable the producers to fulfill one of their basic needs: get better access to the consumer market in the North (see Sect. 4.1). The projects presented to consumers also focused more on Fairco's products, representing a need that was formulated by the consumers in the beginning (see Sect. 4.2). Consequently, the projects were designed as "crowd ordering" activities. In this model, instead of providing indirect support as in the collective funding of bicycles, consumers would collectively pre-order products and thus support producers in getting their products into the international (organic food/fair trade) market. To reach that goal, projects were separated into three project stages that consumers could partic-ipate in:

1. "Establishing a consumer community"/Voting ("red" in Fig. 5): Consumers can help to establish a consumer community by clicking on "interests me", meaning that they support the idea of a new project. This phase should help Fairco to find out which projects are interesting for consumers in the North. If enough consumers support a project, the next phase starts.
2. "Establishing producer community" ("blue" in Fig. 5): After having gathered a consumer community of supporters, a specific crowd funding project starts to support the local production, for example by funding tools and equipment like weighing machines for cashew nuts.
3. "First test export of products/test delivery" ("green" in Fig. 5): Once the production is launched through project stage 2, consumers can pre-order a specific amount of the new product. As soon as a certain quantity has been reached, the according amount of e.g. cacao will be produced and delivered to Switzerland.

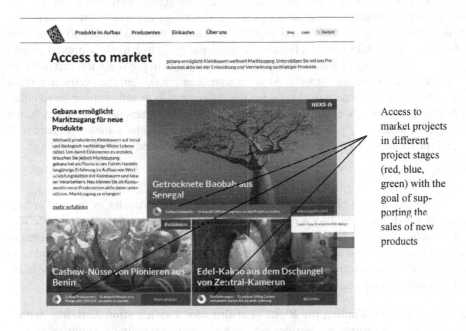

Access to market projects in different project stages (red, blue, green) with the goal of supporting the sales of new products

Fig. 5. Second prototype for access to market projects (Color figure online)

In order to reach more consumers (online coverage) and more diversity of the projects (e.g. the production of fair trade clothes), Fairco decided to partner up with NGOs and other institutions for some of the projects. Moreover, the timeline representing the progress of projects was redesigned to fulfill the need for precise information and explicit presentations of what is going on in the South. This prototype was evaluated with the last and most extensive usability test with seven consumers.

Clear Project Presentation to Support Participation. One of the biggest challenges appeared to be the clear presentation and distinction of the three stages outlined above. Again, throughout the evaluation of the presented projects together with consumers, the need for precise information could be identified as being very important. Many usability problems could be identified that were related to how the progress of projects was visualized in the "timeline" reported earlier. Consumers wanted, out of interest, to have precise information about the project and the idea behind it. This result makes it even clearer that the need for information and the need for participation/being active are two distinctive but strongly related needs that can be addressed for a good user experience. One test participant put it as follows:

«There should be only three things: Project overview, Be active, Progress.» (Customer Quote)

Call to Action: Separating Participation from Information. The consumers' answers during evaluation showed that more thought has to be put into the main calls to action to engage the consumers in supporting projects. Throughout the task scenarios we wanted to know whether the different calls to action were attractive for the consumers. According to the three stages above, the main calls to action within a participation project were (1) to follow a project that has just been launched and get update information (possibility to click button "interests me"), (2) to actively support a project with donating money or goods (button "support") and (3) to pre-order the first delivery of a new product (button "order"). As it became clear throughout the evaluation, there has to be a strong differentiation between the different calls to actions in order to either fulfill the need for only getting information or the need to participate in a project. Some of the calls to action, e.g. to follow a project, were associated by some consumers with social media networks and were consequently being perceived as too less binding:

«The button "interests me" is not binding at all, it just feels like a «Like» on Facebook.» *(Customer quote)*

Furthermore, most of the consumers were confused in particular by the first project stage in which they voted for a project by clicking on the button "interests me". This call to action was somehow in between information and participation and therefore not understood by the consumers. Some of the consumers indicated that they wanted to know about the consequences of choosing a project in each phase and how their interaction impacts the project.

Context Matters: Finding the Right Wordings for Participation Activities within Fair Trade Consumption. Besides getting answers to the main questions relating to the overall idea of the platform and its projects, the evaluation also appeared to be useful for language and wording issues that relate to the context of fair trade, crowd activities and ethical consumption. The consumers identified some examples where content was still formulated too strongly from the company's perspective instead of focusing on what consumers can do.

Some of the consumers noted that they really like the idea of supporting producers from the very beginning:

«I like the idea of taking part from the beginning. It feels like being a pioneer.» (Customer quote)
«I like that you can support a project right from the beginning, this gives you a more personal relation.» (Customer quote)

For that reason, wordings like "be a part from the beginning" or "be a pioneer" were considered being included by the development team. "Product in progress" or "Access to market", for example, were not clear to most of the consumers. Instead, one of them suggested to focus on the products that can be offered in the near future, like "Coming soon"/"What will be offered in the future", to see how consumers can support new products, showing a direct link between their consumption and the producers.

Partnering and Relatedness to Values. The idea that Fairco would work together with NGOs in order to realize access to market projects was well-received by the consumers. However, at first some consumers did not understand the role of partners in relation with the projects and were therefore skeptical whether this fits the company's believes and values. For that reason, the consumers need to have detailed information of who exactly the partners are and what they do in order to be motivated to support a project, which again shows the significance of the values that are inherent to ethical consumption. Furthermore, the consumers' answers showed that project partners would be favored or criticized, depending on how well they fit to the context of the company.

The results show how important it was to include questions and test scenarios within the usability test that contain real-life, and not dummy content. By doing so, an evaluation can go beyond mere usability issues and include aspects of motivation, commitment and relatedness to the product and the company, which are in our case all part of the *experience* of ethical consumption.

6 Discussion

In this contribution we highlighted the need to consider the user's motivations and basic needs, in addition to the tasks and processes to be supported by a new system, as central to user experience design. In our case this concerned the development of a platform connecting consumers of fair trade products with producers in developing countries, especially West Africa. In the end, crowdfunding as well as crowd ordering applications were developed, to generate more involvement from both the consumer and the producer side.

The user needs and motivations that could be identified in the process of development were linked to the basic needs that have been proposed to guide user experience design (see Sect. 2). Several of these basic needs could be shown to be relevant for our case of connecting fair trade consumers with producers in developing countries:

- A central need of the producers in the developing countries is to make a living (*"money"*) by generating additional income through the platform. All their needs concerning the platform were directly related to their food production i.e. improving the quality of the food and the production process and raising sales through access to the international organic food market. This also included their need for *competence development* i.e. becoming more professional by acquiring more know-how in the area of agricultural engineering. In terms of the distinction made in Sect. 2 between hygiene factors and motivators, raising income can be considered as a hygiene factor, competence development as a motivator.

- Swiss consumers appeared to have information needs that can be linked to a need for "*stimulation*" [compare 28; 22]: they want to learn more about and get the stories behind the products, the producers, the production and even the delivery process in order to feel more involved. The access to market platform was designed accordingly with background information on the products, the producers, production and delivery.
- The need of "*relatedness/belonging*" became apparent in the consumers' wish to strengthen community aspects by making the community more transparent i.e. community members more visible and supporting collective ("bulk") ordering, which was then in the end the core idea of the crowd ordering platform.

By comparison, Hassenzahl et al. [17] found *stimulation*, *relatedness*, *competence* and *popularity* to be the most salient needs in their study of positive experiences with interactive products in general. Which needs are most salient in technology adoption and the generation of positive experiences of course depends on the specific product. The need for "relatedness/belonging", for example, clearly plays a significant role in the wide-spread use of and positives experiences with social media. Our study also showed the relevance of this need in online participation and engagement in the area of fair trade consumption. The findings are relevant in relation to the growing popularity of online campaigning using social media, especially in the area of fair trade, ethical consumption and developmental work. NGOs are nowadays competing to reach online coverage. The identification of basic user needs and motivations, as we did in our study, can help to identify and design attractive applications, websites and services that improve user experience and strengthen long-term commitment and participation in such areas.

As has already been pointed out in Sect. 2 our study also gives cause to complement existing needs categorizations with needs, motivations and values that are central to the area of fair trade, or ethical consumption in general. Central in this area is the motivation to "do good for others" out of an ethical obligation that may have become part of the consumers' identity. This may take the paradigm shift from a task- towards a "self"-oriented approach in UX (see Sect. 2) one step further by integrating an "other"-orientation in UX design, at least for those areas in which ethical/moral behavior plays a role. It implies the consideration of the needs of others by taking their perspective. For example, the Swiss consumers indicated that they do not want to donate things that they themselves do not want to use any more (e.g. old mobile phones) perceiving it as disrespectful and as not actively supporting the development of the producers' competences and accomplishments.

Returning to the distinction between pragmatic and hedonic qualities and the concepts of usability, usefulness and user experience, it is the pragmatic aspect of (perceived) usefulness of the platform that turned out to be an influential motivator for the use of the platform. The producers see the platform mainly as an opportunity to connect them to the Western market and sell more and better quality products and thus as an instrument for improving their living conditions. As we saw, improving the living conditions in developing countries was also a need of the Swiss consumers, as part of their social, moral orientation towards the "other" i.e. the producers in the developing countries. Usefulness in this case has a strong connection to and dependence on the living circumstances of the producers. Addressing major concerns or "life needs" is what will make systems in the context of developing countries successful. This fits well to an approach in which the consideration of basic needs is central to creating positive user experiences. In the case of creating added value for the producers, this also means creating a platform that, beyond a narrow task-oriented conception of usefulness [29], is meaningful for the producers' lives in developing countries, a platform that makes sense in the light of their major needs and concerns in daily life.

Furthermore, the distinction between pragmatic and hedonic product qualities doesn't always seem easy to uphold (see also Sect. 2). We think this was shown by the discussion with Swiss consumers concerning community aspects. On the one hand the needs expressed by Swiss consumers were related to the need of "relatedness/belonging/togetherness". On the other hand, this need for stronger community-building was also clearly task-related i.e. supporting the collective ordering of goods. The collective task goal of crowd ordering, as it is now supported by the platform, will probably also help strengthen community aspects and feelings of relatedness. It shows that both task-related or functional and social-emotional aspects have to be considered in close relation in order to develop successful systems that create positive user experiences. This also means that we have to find ways to consider these different elements of UX as an integral part in the different steps from context analysis, through development and testing to implementation. Despite the availability of validated UX measuring instruments (AttrakDiff [28], UEQ [30], meCUE [31]), we are still at the beginning concerning the development of methods that support such an integrated consideration of different UX elements in the different stages of design and development. In the last years, many human-centered design or usability engineering departments have been renamed into "UX" without changing analysis, design and evaluation activities a lot. The mainly academic paradigm shift in orientation does not seem to have had profound consequences for the methods applied in practice [32]. At this point, we are challenged to integrate the different components of UX, including usability and usefulness, into UX analysis, design and evaluation methods that can be used in today's development practices, such as agile development and thus lead to more holistic development practices. This concerns, for example, integrating motivational aspects to a higher extent and more systematically within the early stages of product development, such as context of use analysis and early experience prototyping and testing.

References

1. Hutter, H.-P., Ahlenstorf, A.: New mobile service development process. In: Marcus, A., Wang, W. (eds.) DUXU 2017. LNCS, vol. 10289, pp. 221–232. Springer, Cham (2017). https://doi.org/10.1007/978-3-319-58637-3_17
2. Bargas-Avila, J.A., Hornbæk, K.: Old wine in new bottles or novel challenges? A critical analysis of empirical studies of user experience. In: CHI 2011, pp. 2689–2698 (2011)
3. Norman, D.A.: Emotional Design: Why We Love (or Hate) Everyday Things. Basic Books, New York (2004)
4. Peter, C., Beale, R.: Affect and Emotion in Human-Computer Interaction. From Theory to Applications. Springer, Heidelberg (2008). https://doi.org/10.1007/978-3-540-85099-1
5. Law, L.-C., van Schaik, P., Roto, V.: Attitudes towards user experience (UX) measurement. Int. J. Hum. Comput. Stud. **72**, 526–541 (2014)

6. Hassenzahl, M.: The thing and I: understanding the relationship between user and product. In: Blythe, M.A., Monk, A.F., Overbeeke, K., Wright, P.C. (eds.) Funology: From Usability to Enjoyment. Kluwer (2003)
7. Venkatesh, V., Davis, F.D.: A theoretical extension of the technology acceptance model: four longitudinal field studies. Manag. Sci. **46**(2), 186–204 (2000)
8. Herbst, P.: The product of work is people. In: Davis, L.E., Cherns, A.B. (eds.) The Quality of Working Life: Vol. I: Problems, Prospects and the State of the Art, pp. 439–442. Free Press, New York (1975)
9. Hassenzahl, M.: Hedonic, emotional, and experiential perspectives on product quality. In: Ghaoui, C. (ed.) Encyclopedia of Human Computer Interaction. Idea Group (2006)
10. Thüring, M., Mahlke, S.: Usability, aesthetics and emotion in human-technology interaction. Int. J. Psychol. **42**(4), 253–264 (2007)
11. Hassenzahl, M.: User experience (UX): towards an experiential perspective of product quality. In: IHM (2008)
12. Hassenzahl, M.: Experience Design. Technology for All the Right Reasons. Morgan & Claypool, San Rafael (2010)
13. Carver, C.S., Scheier, M.F.: On the Self-Regulation of Behavior. Cambridge University Press, Cambridge (1989)
14. Kaptelinin, V., Nardi, B.A.: Acting with Technology: Activity Theory and Interaction Design. MIT Press, Cambridge (2006)
15. Nardi, B.A. (ed.): Context and Consciousness. Activity Theory and Human-Computer Interaction. MIT Press, Cambridge (1996)
16. Goodwin, K.: Designing for the Digital Age: How to Create Human-Centered Products and Services. Wiley, Indianapolis (2009)
17. Hassenzahl, M., Diefenbach, S., Göritz, A.: Needs, affect, and interactive products - facets of user experience. Interact. Comput. **22**, 353–362 (2010)
18. Herzberg, F., Mausner, B., Snyderman, B.B.: The Motivation to Work, 2nd edn. Wiley, New York (1959)
19. Maslow, A.H.: Motivation and Personality. Harper & Row, New York (1970)
20. Jordan, P.W.: Designing Pleasurable Products. Taylor & Francis, London (2000)
21. Hancock, P.A., Pepe, A., Murphy, L.L.: Hedonomics: the power of positive and pleasurable ergonomics. Ergon. Des. **13**(1), 8–14 (2005)
22. Sheldon, K.M., Elliot, A.J., Kim, Y., Kasser, T.: What is satisfying about satisfying events? Testing 10 candidate psychological needs. J. Pers. Soc. Psychol. **80**(2), 325–339 (2001)
23. Varul, M.Z.: Ethical selving in cultural contexts: fairtrade consumption as an everyday ethical practice in the UK and Germany. Int. J. Consum. Stud. **33**(2), 183–189 (2009)
24. Varul, M.Z.: Ethical consumption: the case of fair trade. Kölner Zeitschrift für Soziologie und Sozialpsychologie, Special Issue **49**, 366–385 (2009)
25. Schwartz, S.H.: Are there universal aspects in the structure and contents of human values? J. Soc. Issues **50**(4), 19–45 (1994)
26. Andorfer, V.A., Liebe, U.: Research on fair trade consumption - a review. J. Bus. Ethics **106**(4), 415–435 (2012)
27. Shaw, D., Shiu, E., Clarke, I.: The contribution of ethical obligation and self-identity to the theory of planned behaviour: an exploration of ethical consumers. J. Mark. Manag. **16**(8), 879–894 (2000)
28. Hassenzahl, M., Burmester, M., Koller, F.: Der user experience (UX) auf der Spur: Zum Einsatz von www.attrakdiff.de. In: Brau, H., Diefenbach, S., Hassenzahl, M., Koller, M.F., Pessner, M., Rose, K. (eds.) Usability Professionals (2008)

29. Davis, F.D.: Perceived usefulness, perceived ease of use, and user acceptance of information technology. MIS Q. **13**(3), 319–341 (1989)
30. Laugwitz, B., Held, T., Schrepp, M.: Construction and evaluation of a user experience questionnaire. In: Holzinger, A. (ed.) USAB 2008. LNCS, vol. 5298, pp. 63–76. Springer, Heidelberg (2008). https://doi.org/10.1007/978-3-540-89350-9_6
31. Minge, M., Wagner, I., Thüring, M.: Developing and validating an English version of the meCUE questionnaire for measuring user experience. In: Proceedings of the 60th Annual Meeting of the Human Factors and Ergonomics Society, pp. 2056–2060. Sage Publications, New York (2016)
32. Messner, T.: Von Usability zu User Experience. Auswirkungen auf die Praxis. Master thesis University of Applied Sciences Northwestern Switzerland (2016)

Little Big Choices: Customization in Online User Experience

Marco Neves[✉] and Maria Reis

CIAUD – Research Center for Architecture, Urban Planning and Design,
Lisbon School of Architecture, University of Lisbon, Lisbon, Portugal
mneves@fa.ulisboa.pt, mangelica_barros@hotmail.com

Abstract. Customization can be a decisive factor in improving online user experience. It is a procedure that allows users to get involved with an interactive system to obtain results that better match their needs. These results are achieved through a co-design process. To establish the importance of customization in this context, we developed a design project for online customization of lacrosse equipment for Ativo brand. It was intended for users to create their own lacrosse equipment, with the possibility of adapting them to their tastes and requirements. For the tool to become viable it was necessary to consider several interaction tasks. Screens were designed, first trough 11 wireframes and later through 194 visual layouts. The project was evaluated with usability tests, using a support questionnaire to verify tasks were effectively fulfilled. The result is a tool which allows wide customization of various options related to these products, their implementation on the brand website and improvement of its user experience.

Keywords: Customization · Co-design · User experience · Interaction

1 Introduction

Customization is the attempt to transform large scale production into individually tailored objects. This purpose is something difficult to achieve, since what makes an object adjusted to every individual cannot be previously thought in an exhaustive way. Or not at least, if the object is intended for a significant number of people. So, customization came to be understood as a process that increases alternatives, by making available a set of options. In Web environment, product customization has become a major factor in improving user experience.

To better understand this importance and the specific character it has, we must establish differences between customization and personalization. Therefore, customization is considered as the permission given to users, to control interaction with a system or artefact, to achieve results that better match their needs. On the other hand, personalization for Web environment, prepares a system to identify users, to provide them content, experience and functionalities, assumed for their profile.

In this context, factors associated with online customization create an interesting approach with potential commercial application. These factors were considered for Ativo brand, which operates in the field of design and manufacture of lacrosse sports equipment. The main reason was a problem identified by brand managers, in which their customers were not obtaining products the way they needed for their activity. Whether it was by difficulty in expressing their needs to designers, or difficulty in designers understanding what customers wanted, given that this is a very specific market niche.

For this matter a website design project was developed, with a tool for customizing lacrosse equipment for this brand. This tool aims to enable website users to co-create their own lacrosse equipment, adapting products to their needs, from customization options. Users would in this way, perform little choices that would result in big achievements for the brand.

To make the tool usable and feasible, it was necessary to consider interaction design and user experience principles, and to understand the role of usability in the design process. Use of this online customization tool is based on elements that can only be edited, within a limited number of options (colour, texture, patterns, models, among others). We present the process of designing such a tool, including screen wireframes, visual layout and interaction possibilities.

The tool, as well as interaction tasks, were submitted to a small group of potential users to be tested. Such usability tests, were made to check correct understanding, functioning and interaction of the website and allow improvements and corrections.

The overall purpose is to demonstrate the value of customization as a tool for differentiation and distinction, when convincing a customer to choose products. Including for this, permission to participate in the process of choosing options to be included in final products. This distinction of products by placing options for customization and giving permission to each user to become co-creator of the final product being acquired, can be a brand strategy in digital interactive media. Customization, associated with personalization or co-creation, will create a link between consumers, their needs, and products they think are more appropriate to meet such needs.

The approach is based on a transition from the notion of "one size fits most" to "one-to-one", where specific needs of everyone are assumed and will be more likely realized through their participation in final stages of the process. Customization addresses this perspective, moving part of the final responsibility for users, who will decide what they consider to be best for them.

The developed project evidences the concept of customization, in the context of interaction design for Web environment, as essential for development of a tool that matches products to user's requirements.

2   Personalization and Customization

Personalization is a concept that can be defined in several ways, depending on the context in which it is applied [1]. It has, however, been associated with a company's ability to communicate with consumers to provide them with an individualized shopping experience [2]. Particularly when used in e-commerce, where the possibility of personalization is taken as a marketing tool. The Internet came to intensify personalization opportunities, identifying users, collecting information through search history and recommending products [3].

While in this sense personalization is a tool that induces consumers to purchase a mass-produced product or service, but presumably best suits their needs, it can also be understood as modifying products through individual user preferences. For Mugge et al. [4], many users may not be satisfied with standard products because of their individual preferences. One strategy that can give a company competitive advantage is precisely to allow consumers to customize their products.

This notion of customization (word which derives from 'customers'), to make a product more personal, usually includes: (a) a purpose of customization, (b) what is customized (interface, content, etc.), and (c) the target of customization (user, consumer, etc.) [1]. It is therefore a process that modifies functionality, information access, interface or the distinct personality of a system, to give increased importance to a user or group of users. As such, it is the adaptation of products and services developed by a producer, through collected information of consumer behavior, having technology as main facilitator [5].

With more demanding consumers, companies are forced to find new ways to meet their customers' needs, while trying to differentiate themselves from competition. According to Venasen [6] personalization allows creation of products and services that better respond to consumers' needs, especially since the resulting output is achieved by a mutually beneficial bidirectional contact, between supplier and consumer.

For Peppers and Rogers [7] differentiation in this case is achieved because of interaction, which allows a client to feel exclusive, with a will to maintain its relationship and loyalty to a company [8]. By increasing loyalty, the company also increases customer's life time value, fueled by repeated purchases. Mugge et al. [4] argue that by allowing product customization, producers give consumers "design authority", as they accept customers to participate in creating a customized product, from a predefined set. This authority causes customers to take the product as unique and a symbol of their identity. A factor that suggests assigning design authority to customers can increase the likelihood of purchase and the probability of its repetition.

Despite these benefits, it should be considered customization of products is an activity that expends a lot of time for potential consumers, with an extra effort when compared to buying a standard product. Thus, the effort of personalizing a product should represent an additional value for consumers, otherwise time spent in customization may have a negative effect on purchase intention [4].

According to Mugge et al. [9], a personalized product is used as a means of individual expression, which has a positive consequence, an increase of connection to what is acquired. Products are purchased for many reasons, some of them end up becoming special and treasured by their owners. This link is defined as "the emotional bond a person experiences with a product" [10]. When this product-owner link is created, the owner tends to add more care to the product. In this way, he tries to give a longer life to it.

When a consumer wants to customize the appearance of a product, he invests time, effort, attention and makes creative choices [9]. And so, the product ends up reflecting symbolically an individual, for himself and for others.

3   Online User Experience

Online media has been used to create such experiences tailored to users interests and needs, although this goal is achieved in several different ways [11]. According to Lee [12], one can understand a personalization made automatically by computerized systems, of companies and organizations. It is a specific and individual collection of information, made through observation of user behaviors and actions, such as clicks, latest searches, purchase history, among others. The system is designed to identify users and provide them with content, experience, and features that meet their expected needs [13]. Lee [12] also states the major purpose of this personalization of user's online experience is to provide these functions without any effort on the part of the user.

For example, on a travel website, you see certain promotions for places you have been or have searched for. In mobile apps, personalization identifies user's profile so that users can find what they want more easily and quickly. In no situation does a user need to make changes or set something on the system, since all available information is used to create an identity for each user.

On the other hand, possibility of customization starts at companies, which provide users with options for them to choose from. Users proactively specify what they need and require for a product [3]. Users can customize a product or service through actions such as adjusting layout or organizing content, but also changing color or changing design-related factors [13]. The advantage of customization is to allow users to have a better experience by controlling interaction, and thus achieving exactly the results they wanted.

4   Mass Customization of Clothing

There is nowadays a context of mass production, characterized by a brief product life cycle of clothing products, with excess supply at low prices. This serial reproduction corresponds to creation of scale economies.

Mass customization is an alternative to this context. According to Lee et al. [14], mass customization is a hybrid form, understood as mass production of customized individual products or services. Mass customization focuses on the individual and on arranging custom products, maintaining approximately the same price level, while taking advantage of large scale production means. The logic of mass production and technological advances allows companies to reduce development process and product manufacturing cycle [2].

Mass customization of apparel products always involves co-design. Consumers get a unique product, partially designed by themselves, usually through digital media, with the help of tools or platforms designed for this purpose. These platforms present virtual models, so users can see the result of their customization in options companies allow them to edit, such as styles, fabrics, patterns, colours, etc. [14].

Sports companies appear as leaders in development of mass customization, and while some of them make this activity an additional component, others are dedicated exclusively to mass customization through online media, since the Internet has been identified as the most important tool in the production cycle of mass customized products [15].

5 Co-design

Co-design is then a key factor in customizing. Within design processes involving participation, there is sometimes confusion with co-creation and sharing of the creative process. These are often synonymous notions. But for Sanders and Stappers [16], co-creation refers to any act of collective creativity, e.g., creativity shared between two or more people. Co-creation is taking more and more attention from brands, and is being used to complete products, especially in more advanced stages. For instance, Nike ID (www.nikeid.com), which allows its customers to customize footwear, choosing colours, materials and several other details. Co-creation emerges as a solution to give new impetus to the offer of products and services. This trend follows increasing investment of brands in user experience. Not being able to distinguish their products by technical qualities or by price, brands are forced to look beyond the product itself [16].

Co-design also points to collective creativity as Sanders and Stappers [16] refer, but applied to the design process. We can understand it as a specific co-creation. It refers to shared creativity between designers and untrained people who work together during the design development process. Users can then be part of the design team as experts in their own experiences and needs [17].

However, for this opportunity to be made available to users, it is necessary to provide them with the right tools to express themselves. It should be recognized that not all individuals have the same propensity for creativity, and as such, designed experiences should allow individual expression in a simple way [18].

6 Design Project

A design project was developed to address a customization tool for lacrosse equipment within Ativo website, a brand which operates in the field of design and manufacture of lacrosse sports equipment. The project came as a solution to solve a perceived difficulty in communicating with Ativo customers, as they were not able to obtain the type of equipment they wanted. This tool would ease the problem, by creating an online aid for customization of lacrosse equipment. The main goal was to enable Ativo clients to communicate in a simple and direct way, through media where they could configure themselves what they wanted.

This online customization tool has limited options (in terms of visual elements such as colour, texture or patterns), as it is based on graphic language standards and layouts pre-designed for the brand.

First steps conceiving the tool were sketches and wireframes to create a structure that would meet all user requirements. We developed 11 model screens, as exemplified in Fig. 1.

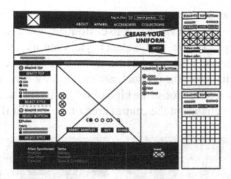

Fig. 1. Initial wireframe screen.

We also identified the need to recreate products in 3D to provide the best possible way, for customers to communicate what they want, obtaining as result a simulation as close as possible to the final product.

6.1 Customization Tool

For the customization tool, visual layouts were developed for 194 options within website browsing and customization tasks. All material was set together in Marvel App to arrange an interactive prototype. We created a structure adapted to users, their expected behaviour and their usage of information levels. In this way, we conceived two lateral columns, one in the left and one in the right, placing an area for visualization of products at the centre. This arrangement would change according to selected options (Fig. 2).

Fig. 2. Customization tool with initial options.

On the left side column, we can choose a product through model, collar, pockets, fabric and style to customize. The tool was created to allow customization of two product categories: apparel and accessories. This column will adapt to product types according to their category.

For the apparel product type, users have the possibility to add or remove a top and bottom. For example, we can choose a vest to customize, and as consequence, in the left column the 'Select Top', 'Fabric' and 'Select Style' options will appear. In the 'Select Top' option we can choose other models from the top. After selecting the option, we can see the resulting change in the product, at the centre, where the vest was.

In 'Fabric' it is possible to choose the kind of fabric and at the same time to visualize the consequent product change at the central area of the screen (Fig. 3a and b).

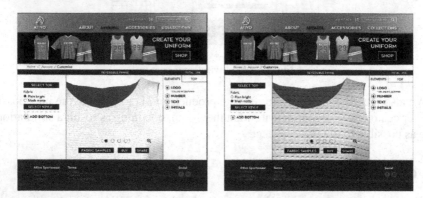

Fig. 3. (a) and (b) Two screens with different fabric options selected: plain bright on the left and Mesh matte on the right.

In the 'Select Style' option, we can choose a style of our preference and edit it (Fig. 4).

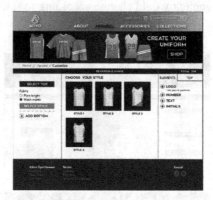

Fig. 4. Screen to choose product style.

Users have the possibility, throughout this path, to add a bottom that allows the same type of options as those described above for the top, such as model, fabric or style. If for instance, a user adds shorts, the system will automatically inform of additional costs.

Within this column, users have always possibility to add products within these types: apparel or accessories. Every change in fabric or style will not imply a loss of previous choices.

Product customization column on the right side is divided into two or three tabs ('elements', 'top' and/or 'bottom') depending on user's choice. In 'elements' tab, users can add multiple elements to a product, whether it is just 'bottom' or 'top' or both. There are four types of elements users can add: 'logo', 'number', 'text', and 'initials'. To add an element like a logo, we can enter one or more logos as well as choose their positions, always allowing to delete or add more logos whenever we want. Before adding, information is given explaining only.jpg and.png files are accepted (Fig. 5).

Fig. 5. Customization tool right side column.

Once a .jpg or .png file is chosen and a position is picked, users can see an image preview on the product. This position can be changed whenever we want.

The next element possible to add is a number, which will allow to change font and its position. However, size will automatically be set, considering regulatory restrictions. For instance, in women's equipment, a number cannot be less than 15 cm (5.9") in front and 20 cm (7.8") at the rear.

In 'text' element, users can add a player or team name, or just one word with the possibility to choose from an available positions list. The last element, 'initials', allows users to add a maximum of two initials, and choose their position according to available places for this element. There are placement limitations for various elements, considering positions advisable or mandatory for each of them.

In 'top' and 'bottom' tabs users can edit colours and patterns of the product, depending on the selection made. They can also do this for elements such as numbers

Fig. 6. Highlight of selected area.

and initials and any chosen style, by selecting areas to change. For users to choose an area to edit, it is necessary to select the desired area directly by clicking on the product. This zone is then highlighted (Fig. 6).

Alternatively, we can also select an editing area by browsing among various available areas. This is possible by clicking arrows that allow to scroll through the different areas. After choosing an area to change, there are three options – 'base colour', 'pattern' and 'outline' – that do not always appear, since not all areas allow all three options. For instance, collars cannot have an outline in production and thus, when users select collar to edit, this option is not presented.

In 'base colour' option, users have a colour palette so they can change base colour of a chosen area. In 'pattern' option users can choose a pattern they want in the selected area. After choosing the pattern, users can choose scale and colour for it (Fig. 7). Finally, in 'outline' a colour palette is also presented in the same way.

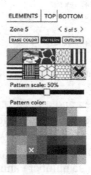

Fig. 7. 'Bottom' tab with 'Pattern' option selected.

In the central area where products are presented, there are three other options: 'fabric samples', 'buy' and 'share'. In 'fabric samples' option, users can request samples, with a message showing cost of sending samples and whether to add that order to the shopping cart. In 'buy' option, users add products to the cart and receive a notification that products have been added to the shopping cart. Finally, in 'share' option, users can share an image of customized product, to show their team or friends.

6.2   Tests and Improvements

Usability tests (n = 12) were performed with the developed prototype. Such tests consisted in providing the interactive prototype of the tool to fulfil a set of 14 tasks. In the scope of these tests a questionnaire was elaborated to confirm or not, usability of created tool, within website context. For all tasks, it was asked what difficulties each user encountered while performing them.

After analysing the results, we concluded it was necessary to give greater visual contrast to 'add bottom', "top" and "elements" tabs because they are functionalities represented in a very subtle way and gone unnoticed. To correct this, an "add bottom" button with a coloured outline was created, to give more prominence to functionality, and to assure it would not be confused with product setting buttons, such as "select style" or "select top". As for "elements" and "top" tabs, which are located on the right side of the tool, an outline was also added around the functions as well as a black background to make selection visible. Both changes are displayed in Fig. 8.

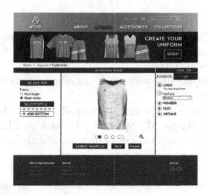

Fig. 8. Customization tool after usability tests.

7   Conclusion

Development of an online customization tool for lacrosse equipment and its evaluation allowed us to understand that combining interaction possibilities with customization, opens a new window on the relationship between a brand and users of their products.

Experience of using Ativo brand website has become more extensive and complete, as the website and the tool incorporated in it, influence interaction final output, as well as final product constitution. We have established a feedback and feedforward relationship, essential for a good interactive experience.

The approach to customization, personalization and co-design allowed us to understand the purpose of each concept and their importance in designing the tool. It was also possible to understand that preparing pre-designed equipment models will speed up creative process of users, and productive process of the brand. The tool eliminates undesirable excessive waste of time in constant modification of proposals, as it passes part of the task to users, which will more easily be able to express their needs.

Introducing customization in sportswear is still a subject with much to explore. However, customization attributes an emotional value to products, leading to an increase of their life time, through higher esteem consumer ends up giving it, due to emotional load.

And so, this project allows Ativo to have an innovative tool in the market in which it operates, gaining a competitive advantage factor to its competitors. At the same time, it creates an emotional connection with its users, so that they themselves perceive they are interacting with "someone". This connection and consequent improvement in user experience is expected to lead to greater satisfaction with products and a desired brand loyalty.

Acknowledgements. The authors would like to thank the funding support by the Foundation for Science and Technology of the Ministry of Science, Technology and Higher Education of Portugal under the project UID/EAT/04008/2013 (CIAUD).

References

1. Fan, H., Poole, M., Vilares, M.: What is personalization? Perspectives on the design and implementation of personalization in information systems. J. Org. Comput. Electron. Commer. **16**(3–4), 179–202 (2006)
2. Cho, H.: Consumer acceptance of online customization for apparel. Ph.D. thesis, The Florida State University (2007)
3. Arora, N., Dreze, X., Ghose, A., Hess, J., Ivengar, R., Jing, B., Joshi, Y., Kumar, V., Lurie, N., Neslin, S., Sajeesh, S., Su, M., Syam, N., Thomas, J., Zhang, J.: Putting one-to-one marketing to work: personalization, customization, and choice. Mark. Lett. **19**, 305–321 (2008)
4. Mugge, R., Schoormans, J.P.L., Lange, A.: 'Consumers' appreciation of product personalization. In: Fitzsimons, G., Morwitz, V. (eds.) NA - Advances in Consumer Research, vol. 34, pp. 339–341. Association for Consumer Research, Duluth (2007)
5. Montgomery, A., Smith, M.A.: Prospects for personalization on the internet. J. Interact. Mark. **23**(2), 130–137 (2008)
6. Vesanen, J.: What is personalization? – A literature review and framework. Helsinki School of Economics. Working Papers (2005)
7. Peppers, D., Rogers, M.: Managing Customer Relationships: A Strategic Framework. Wiley, Hoboken (2004)
8. Ball, A.D., Coelho, P.S., Vilares, M.J.: Service Personalization and Loyalty. Marketing Department Faculty Publications, Paper 13 (2006)
9. Mugge, R., Schifferstein, H., Schoormans, J.: Personalizing product appearance: the effect on product attachment. In: Kortgouzu, A. (ed.) Proceedings of the Fourth International Conference on Design and Emotion, Ankara (2004)
10. Schifferstein, H., Zwartkruis-Pelgrim, E.: Consumer-product attachment: measurement and design implications. Int. J. Des. **2**(3), 1–14 (2008)
11. Babich, N.: The Difference Between Customization and Personalization. https://uxplanet.org/the-difference-between-customization-and-personalization-624ddd70b163. Accessed 12 Sept 2017
12. Lee, M.: Designing personalization in technology-based services. Ph.D. thesis, Carnegie Mellon University, Pittsburgh (2013)
13. Schade, A.: Customization vs. Personalization in the User Experience. https://www.nngroup.com/articles/customization-personalization. Accessed 22 May 2017
14. Lee, S., Kunz, G., Fiore, A., Campbell, J.: Acceptance of mass customization of apparel: merchandising issues associated with preference for product, process, and place. Cloth. Text. Res. J. **20**(3), 138–146 (2000)
15. Ribeiro, L., Miguel, R., Pereira, M., Barata, J., Silva, M.: Implementation of mass customisation: the case of the apparel industry. In: Global Fashion Conference (2014)
16. Sanders, E., Stappers, P.: Co-creation and the new landscapes of design. CoDesign Int. J. CoCreation Des. Arts **4**(1), 5–18 (2008)
17. Visser, F.: Bringing the everyday life of people into design. Ph.D. thesis, TU Delft (2009)
18. Buxton, B.: Sketching User Experiences: Getting the Design Right and the Right Design. Elsevier, London (2010)

The Influence of Short Text Ad. on Consumer Purchase Intention: An Empirical Study

Jia Qu[✉] and Can Huang[✉]

Baidu, Beijing, China
{qujia,huangcan01}@baidu.com

Abstract. Small message service (SMS), as a kind of short text advertisement, is cheaper and has the most users. Therefore, it is very popular in marketing promotion. According to iResearch, the market size of SMS is about 120 billion in 2017, with 50% annual compound growth. Though SMS marketing aroused the interest of the majority of scholars, few people combined Consumer purchase intention with the product features and customer groups on a specific s text. And there is a short of practice guidelines for SMS marketing. Under this background, we systematically studied the importance of the business and marketing of information factors for short texts in different customer groups in credit products. Through experiments, firstly we found that among the credit products, 4–6 information points are the most acceptable for consumers in short texts, which must include the core information, product function and price. That is to say, the credit limit and interest of credit product are the most important things for all customer groups. Secondly, for credit product, enhancing benefits and reducing costs factors, which are marketing of information factors, have positive effect on consumer purchase intention. However, attracting attention, including exaggerated and novelty expression, has negative effects. At the same time, stimulating demand factors have different effects on White-collar and businessman customers, for example, for low-income white-collar workers, giving them some hints of borrowing scene is positive, but for high-income white-collar workers and businessmen it is negative. This study attempts to establish a short text marketing dictionary for credit products to provide guidance for related enterprises.

Keywords: Short text ad · Business and marketing of information factors
Customer group

1 Introduction

Short text service (SMS) as a kind of text message is used in mobile promotions all over the world (Daneshfar et al. 2016). In the Asia, the SMS is a widely adopted mobile phone application (Kim et al. 2008). At the same time, seventy percent of the American mobile advertising is sent via the SMS (Bruno 2006).

With the further development of the big data, each person becomes the source and carrier of information (Manyika et al. 2011), and the short text advertisement can be more precisely put into using (Much and Chung 2015). The target consumers can be identified by their behavior and other basic information, and can be sent the needed products at the correct time to avoid the waste of advertising (Barnes and Scornavacca 2004; Khasawneh and Shuhaiber 2013). Not only does SMS advertising cost little, but also it takes an advantage of unlimited copy and fast transmission. The message can be easily sent to friends, improving the impact of advertising.

Due to the advantages of short text advertisements, it is still widely used in marketing promotion of credit business. So, studying how short text ads attract consumers is crucial for us. Through depth interviews, we found that consumer behavior of reading SMS can be divided into 3 parts, including receiving SMS, reading SMS, willing to try or called consumer purchase intention. From receiving to reading SMS, consumers have their own viewing habits to choose when and how to read a messages. From reading to having a try, the factors of the SMS will impact the consumer purchase intention, as shown below.

Receiving SMS ⟶ Reading SMS   Willing to try ⟶

Viewing habits   the information factors of SMS

When studying the impact of different information factors on consumer purchase intention, due to the different views for consumer groups, this paper will analyze how short text influences the main consumer groups separately. We studied high-income white-collar workers whose salary is more than 10,000 Yuan, low-income white-collar workers whose salary is less than 10,000 Yuan, and businessmen. Therefore, this paper meanly focus on:

(1) The cognitive model for consumers and factors which matter in each period during the process from receiving to reading SMS. That is to say, when and what kinds of short texts will the consumers be more likely to read.

(2) The factors that affect the consumer purchase intention in credit business, which it is the more important question in this study.

• The most acceptable number of factors in one short text. That is to say, the least and the highest amount of factors for one short text.

• How does the different information factors influence the different customer groups respectively?

2 Research Method

The research is divided into two parts. The first step is to understand the process that how consumers read the SMS and the information factors influencing the acceptance of SMS advertising, through the depth interviews and secondary data analysis. The second step is to study the importance of all kinds of informational factors that are collated in the first step through the experiment.

2.1 Depth Interviews and Secondary Data Analysis

2.1.1 Script

From two aspects to understand the consumer's SMS reading habits. On the one hand, when and where will the consumers check the message? And how to read the message, whether there will be other behavior after reading, such as surfing the Internet to get more information or consulting the client service center. On the other hand, we study what kinds of messages they often received and the acceptance of different types of SMS advertising. Further, we want to know what information factors can attract the attention of consumers.

2.1.2 Participants

We interview 45 target consumers in total, including 15 businessmen, 15 high-income white-collar workers and 15 low-income white-collar workers. In order to keep the samples from deviation, we not only researched the consumers who used our products, but also researched the lost consumers. And we are sure the sampling distribution including the age, education, occupation are matched with the overall distribution.

2.2 Experiment

2.2.1 Materials

(1) Information factors (independent variables)

Through depth interviews and secondary data analysis, from which we found the information factors in competitors' short text ads and previous research findings. At last, we found that the factors of short text ads are divided into two parts: business factors and marketing factors. Business factors refer to the factors related to the credit business. Marketing factors refer to the factors not including business factors.

According to the previous understanding of the business, the impact of the business (product) itself on the consumer purchase intention mainly includes financial characteristics and users' experience which are further divided into seven majors.

From receiving to reading the full short text, consumers will experience the following psychological process:

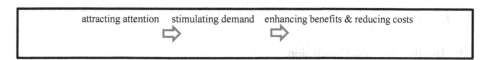

Therefore, marketing factors should be included in the each step of the psychological processes. Through the theory, depth interviews and competitors' advertising, we finally put forward a total of 11 marketing factors.

In the end, information factors in credit business were divided into two types: business factors (7) and marketing factors (11), as shown below (Fig. 1).

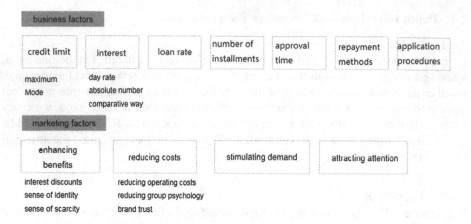

Fig. 1. Information factors in credit business: business factors (7) and marketing factors (11)

2.2.2   Procedure

The experiment about business factors was used within-subjects design. Different business factors were arranged and combined to form a SMS. The experiment about perceived factors was also used within-subjects design. Based on the existing standard short text, we increase each of the perceived factors in it to form the short text. In total, we test more than 300 short texts.

The program was established by software E-prime: Randomly presented the message to consumers through E-prime, each consumer needs to assess the willingness to apply that is seen as consumer purchase intention. And we measured it using a 10-point Likert scale (1–10 points).

2.2.3   Participants

We interview 90 target consumers in total, including 30 businessmen, 30 high-income white-collar workers and 30 low-income white-collar workers. In order to keep the samples from deviation, we are sure the sampling distribution including the age, education, occupation are matched with the overall distribution.

3   Results

3.1   Depth Interview Conclusion

Finally, we found that the process for consumer in reading a short text, firstly, it is to read the short text in a rough way, and then if the core information attracts the consumer, he will read short text in detail.

The main factor that affects click value rate in SMS from "Receiving SMS "to" reading the short text in a rough way" is short text blocking: Most consumers have turned on the intelligent interception function. Due to this function, short texts can be blocked by numbers, keywords and so on.

From "reading the short text in a rough way "to" reading the short text in detail", the main factor that affects click value rate is the time sending the short text, the consumer's judgment about the type of SMS and the sense of trust. In details:

(1) Noon and night are the best time to send short text. But the best time to receive the short text is different for customer groups. High-income and low-income white-collar workers prefer to view short text at noon or at night. But for businessman, there is no difference in the whole day time. The main reason is that white-collar workers are busy at worktime. During the noon and night, they are more available to check the messages. Businessman's leisure time is uncertain, so there is no difference. In addition, we also should consider the policies and regulations when sending the messages.

(2) By means of official number and emphasis on brand, it is possible to prevent the consumer from judging that the message an advertisement and it can enhance the trust of the consumer.

Receiving the text message, a consumer will determine the type of message firstly whether is an advertising or notification. And an advertising is more possible to be ignored directly. After that, the consumer will judge whether the message can be trusted by other information, for example whether the number is the official number segment such as 955.

3.2   The Result About Experiment

3.2.1   The Amount of Information Factors

As Goldhaber (1997) said, information is not scarce - especially on the Net, where it is not only abundant, but overflowing. But attention is scarce and desirable for us. So we should know how much information should be included in a text message firstly?

Our statistical method is to calculate the amount of information contained in each piece of message and the corresponding purchase intention, which may also be called as the intention of application in the credit business. In the experiment, each message contains a different amount of information from one to seven points of information. Regardless of what specific factors represent, each information factor should be calculated. For example, a text message is "a maximum amount of 300,000 yuan, only 3 steps to complete the application," then the message contains two information points.

Statistics show that, when a message contains 4–6 points of information (including business factors and perceived factors), the user has a higher willingness to apply. Information factor is too little to attract the user's interest, so we need to show at least four kinds of points of information. Too many points of information makes users feel impatient and may miss key information. So a short text is better to include 4–6 points of information.

However, due to different cognitive ability of different customer groups, the amount of acceptance to points of information is also different. Compared with the other two groups (low-income white-collar workers and businessmen), High-income white-collar workers can accept more points of information. With the amount of information factors differ from each other, the acceptance of different customer groups are shown as below (Fig. 2).

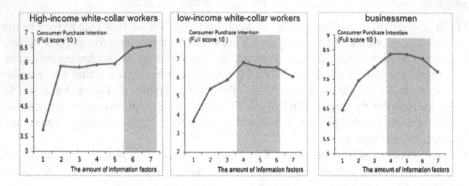

Fig. 2. The acceptance of the amount of information factors for different customer groups

3.2.2 The Business Factors in Information Factors

We studied how these business factors rank as the matter of importance. We studied the importance of the seven business factors in the ranking. We used "the consumer purchase intention when there is A factor in the message" minus the "the consumer purchase intention when there is without A factor in the message". And this is called the importance of A factor. The data found that for all customers, interest and credit limit are the most important factors, much higher than other business factors, including loan rate, number of installments, approval time, repayment methods, application procedures and so on.

At the same time for different customer groups, the importance of various business factors are also different, for high-income white-collar workers and low-income white-collar workers, the introduction of interest is more important. However, for businessmen, credit limit is more important. Getting through qualitative interviews, the main reason is that the credit limit of high-income white-collar workers is generally high and meet their requirements. Therefore, when selecting a new product, high-income white-collar workers will conduct more comparison of interest rates. However, the demand for credit limit is higher for businessmen, so they tend to use a higher credit limit to conduct the business better. In addition to the credit limit and interest, low-income white-collar workers are also concerned about the number of installments, owing to the lower income. Longer installments can reduce the pressure to repay a debt. The importance of different business factors for different customer groups are shown as below (Fig. 3).

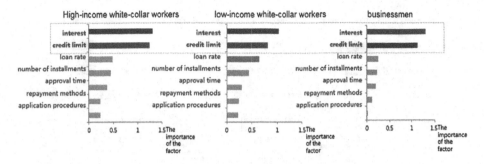

Fig. 3. The importance of the factors for different customer groups (business factors)

Not only did we consider what to introduce, but also we studied how to use different rhetorical methods to introduce the same kind of the product when studying the importance of business factors. We mainly selected the most important factors including interest and credit limit to study the most appropriate way of expression because they are the most important factors for all consumer groups. We found that the message for low-income white-collar workers needs to be easy to understand and easy to express. Nonetheless, for businessmen and high-income white-collar workers professional expressions are required.

More concretely, low-income white-collar workers needs to know the credit limit that the majority can get. While the high-income white-collar workers and businessmen prefer the maximum credit limit. At the same time, low-income white-collar workers also prefer to know interest in comparative way, for example interest is 40% lower than credit card. However, businessmen and white-collar workers accept more specific and professional expression for interest, businessmen prefer day rate. And high-income white-collar workers prefer the expression of absolute numbers, such as if you borrow 1000 yuan, you should pay 0.5 yuan interest per day.

3.2.3   Marketing Factors of Information Factors

On the whole, the factors about "enhancing benefits" and "reducing costs" are positive ones, "attracting attention" are negative ones and "stimulating demand " are differentiated for different customer groups. "Reducing costs" includes reducing operating costs, reducing group psychology, as well as brand trust. "Enhancing benefits" including interest discounts, sense of identity, sense of scarcity etc.

For all customer groups, "attracting attention" factor has a negative impact on consumer purchase intention because novelty and excessively exaggerated will diminish the user's trust.

The "stimulating demand" factors have different impact on different customer groups, which have a greater positive effect on low-income white-collar workers and a more negative impact on high-income white-collar workers and businessmen. The main reason is that high-income white-collar workers and businessmen have higher demand for credit limit and "stimulating demand" factors includes smaller-amount consumption scenarios, resulting in the perceptions of low credit limit (Fig. 4).

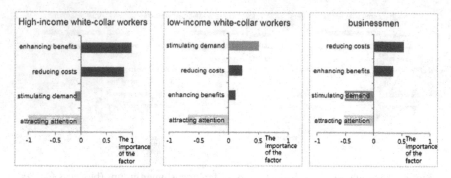

Fig. 4. The importance of the factors for different customer groups (Marketing factors)

More specifically, low - income white-collar workers prefer to take advantage of cheaper prices and choose the products that are used by the public. High income and business people will assess the cost and benefit rationally. On the other hand, the less an advertisement looks like an advertisement, and the more it looks like an editorial, they are more likely to stop, look and read. Different groups have different preferences for promotion. Low income white-collar workers prefer to use the product for free in a short time. However, high income white-collar workers prefer long-term interest incentives, such as interest discounts.

3.2.4   Summary

Overall, credit limit and interest are the most important business factors. At the same time, the influence of marketing factors on different groups are different. The specific sort for each group can be seen in the following figure (Fig. 5).

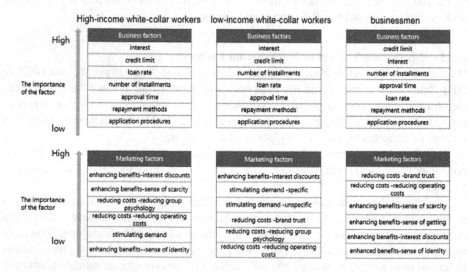

Fig. 5. The importance of the factors for different customer groups (business and marketing factors)

4   Discuss

Accordance to the core findings of the experiment, designers change the promotional pages from the left one to the right one for low-income white-collar workers (Fig. 6).

Fig. 6. The change of the promotional pages

Through depth interviews and experiments, we studied how the short text factor can increase consumer purchase intention, it provides important reference for improving the ability of attracting consumers. However, the shortcoming of this study is that we only tested the factors of short text in credit scenario. In other scenarios, the influence of short text factors on consumer purchasing intention is not clear, and will be followed up in future research.

References

Barnes, S.J., Scornavacca, E.: Mobile Marketing: The Role of Permission and Acceptance. Inderscience Publishers, Geneva (2004)

Bruno, A.: Ads do mobile 2006 (2006). http://www.allbusiness.com. Accessed 15 Feb 2009

Daneshfar, Z., Roshani, A., Sabzali, H.: Investigating the effectiveness of the SMS marketing in increasing the sale of insurance in the bank branches (a case study). In: International Conference on Industrial Engineering and Operations Management Detroit, Michigan, USA, September 2016

Kim, G., Park, S., Oh, J.: An examination of factors influencing consumer adoption of short text service (SMS). Psychol. Mark. **25**(8), 769–786 (2008)

Khasawneh, M.A., Shuhaiber, A.: A comprehensive model of factors influencing consumer attitude towards and acceptance of SMS advertising: an empirical investigation in Jordan. Int. J. Sales Mark. Manag. Res. Dev. **3**(2), 1–22 (2013)

Manyika, J., Chui, M., Brown, B., et al.: Big Data: The Next Frontier for Innovation, Competition, and Productivity. McKinsey, New York (2011)

Much, A., Chung, C.: Applying the technology acceptance model in a two country study of SMS advertising. J. Bus. Res. **68**(2015), 1–6 (2015)

Goldhaber, M.H.: Attention shoppers! The currency of the new economy won't be money, but attention – a radical theory of value. Wired **5**, 1–6 (1997)

Expected User Acceptance of an Augmented Reality Service for a Smart City

Francisco Rebelo[1,2(✉)], Paulo Noriega[1,2], Tiago Oliveira[2],
Daniela Santos[2], and Sabrina Oliveira[3]

[1] CIAUD, Universidade de Lisboa, Rua Sá Nogueira | Pólo Universitário |
Alto da Ajuda, 1349-063 Lisboa, Portugal
`fsrebelo@gmail.com`
[2] Laboratório de Ergonomia, Faculdade de Motricidade Humana,
Universidade de Lisboa, Estrada da Costa, Cruz Quebrada, Portugal
[3] Laboratório de Ergonomia e Usabilidade, Universidade Federal do Pará,
Curitiba, Brazil

Abstract. Despite the existence of automatic systems for collecting information about events in the city, without information sharing by citizens, smart city services concepts can hardly success. Thus, the problem is not the existence of technology solutions for smart cities concepts, but how to develop services that will involve citizens to share information about the events in the city. Social psychology theories point out that sense of bellowing, perceived enjoyment, perceived reciprocal benefits, power of knowledge, outcome expectation and perceived status, provides an involvement for citizens to share information and knowledge. In this paper, we propose to relate those theories, with the intension to use a mobile augmented reality service. We created an online survey, based in a scenario with a video, where the participants visualize a character behavior sharing and getting information in the city, using a mobile augmented reality service. The results confirm that the participants accept and want to use a mobile augmented reality service in a smart city, and have been identify the factors that could be more associated with the intention to use the augmented reality technology in the smart city, namely perceived enjoyment, intention to share experience, intention to get knowledge, perceived value, perceived similarity and perceived reciprocal benefits. Exploring those constructs inside gamification solutions in this mobile augmented reality service, is discussed in the conclusion.

Keywords: Smart city · Technology acceptance · Augmented reality

1 Introduction

This paper outlines a research project, funded under the Portugal 2020 Program, which involves the conceptualization, design and implementation of an information technology platform where the wealth of data collected by citizens (volume, variety and detail), is aggregated with data collected by a variety of other existing sensors in the city, giving in real time, a clearer and more vivid vision of the global "pulse" of the city. The platform will also create an adequate environment (physical and virtual) for cooperation between citizens and city authorities enabling that the information added

© Crown 2018
A. Marcus and W. Wang (Eds.): DUXU 2018, LNCS 10920, pp. 703–714, 2018.
https://doi.org/10.1007/978-3-319-91806-8_55

by one part to be available to all stakeholders. This objective proposes an approach to the concept of Smart Cities that puts the citizen as the focal point of the data collection and information sharing process. The citizen is the most relevant element in this process of sharing information, because humans have the most notably sensory and processing capabilities that allow them to create criteria about city status. Thus, allowing people to be more than a passive information receiver but an active contributor to healthy smart city pulse. Hence, is fundamental that the citizen can be engaged in a virtual community, to consult and share information. Virtual communities (VCs) play an important role in this subject, affecting the way that the citizen uses and share the information in the smart cities.

In this context, it is fundamental that the citizen can share the information and knowledge associated with the events in the city. Some studies have emphasized the importance of knowledge sharing in VCs, to identify the aspects that facilitate the knowledge sharing behavior [1–3].

A good example of sharing knowledge is the *Tripadvisor* application, where users share their experiences about their travels with other potential travelers. Also related with the use of such apps, some studies found that online evaluations of movies or booking might affect the sales [4, 5].

However, in order to people share information in those kind of apps or VCs, first they have to accept technology. In this stud the evaluation of the user acceptance was done according to some social psychology theories: sense of bellowing (familiarity, perceived similarity and trust in other members); perceived and expected reciprocal benefits; perceived value; knowledge power and enjoyment; beside the intension to use a mobile augmented reality service.

Sense of Bellowing
Some researchers studied what factors attract people to the VCs [6]. For those authors, an important factor for the success and survival of a VC is the sense of belonging and participation. According to Hagerty et al. [7], sense of belonging is considered as one specific process of connection between people and an important factor for mental health and social well-being. Sense of bellowing describes an emotional connection of a user to a VC that are related with a sense of identification and membership [8]. Also, sense of bellowing is an important component in online communities [9], contributing to the members' loyalty to VCs [10], and it subsistence [11]. Sense of bellowing can be evaluated with the following variables: familiarity, perceived similarity and trust in other members.

Perceived and Expected Reciprocal Benefits
According to Kankanhalli et al. [12] perceived reciprocal benefit in the context of information sharing is defined as the benefit expectancy of a future request for information being met as a result of current contributions. In this context, in order to the Citizen contribute with information events of the city he must believe that their contribution is worth the effort. Inside the smart city contexts where the Citizen time and energy are limited, by the others stimulus and tasks, they usually unwilling to share scarce resources with others. Earlier research in this area suggested that information sharing in online communities is facilitated by a strong sense of reciprocity [3]. Perceived and expected reciprocal benefits can be evaluated with the intention to share and get information.

Outcome Expectations

Outcome expectations means to the expected consequence of one's own behavior [2, 13], also refer to an individual's belief that activity realization leads to a beneficial outcome [14]. In the smart city context, personal outcome expectation refers to the rewards following the actions of Citizen, who share their information in return for some benefits, such as information that can improve their efficiency. Outcome expectations can be evaluated with the intension to share and to get information.

Knowledge Power

If a person has control over an information that the others need or want, this puts a person in a powerful position. According to Kankanhalli et al. [12], knowledge is considered a source of power and individuals may hide it, because people are afraid that loss of knowledge will cause them to lose their competitive advantage. In this context, people can prefer to retain information than share it. In the same line, Dunford [15] and Grandori and Kogut [16], suggests that some persons have a reluctance do share information due to their insecure feelings, such as the fear to lost career opportunities. In the context of smart city, this power comes when the Citizen is in a position to share or not an important information that can be important for the others.

1.1 Perceived Enjoyment

According to Hsu and Lin [17], perceived enjoyment can be defined as the degree to which an internet user participates in social networks, because the process "yields fun and enjoyment". The authors suggested that enjoyment is a factor that determines the intention of users to participate in social networks. Another complementary definition is proposed by Venkatesh [18], that defined perceived enjoyment as "the extent to which the activity of using a specific system is perceived to be enjoyable in its own right, aside from any performance consequences resulting from system use". From another viewpoint, Kankanhalli et al. [12], defined enjoyment in helping others, as the perception of pleasure obtained from helping others via knowledge contribution. Previous research in the work context, indicated that employees are intrinsically motivated to knowledge contribution because they enjoy helping others [19].

1.2 Intention to Use and Perceived Value

Perceived value refers to the perception that a service would be appropriated for a described situation [20]. Intention to use is influenced by attitudes towards the behavior, subjective norm and perceived behavioral control, that are associated with the technology acceptance model [21]. Both concepts are connected and influences the Citizen decision to use or share information in a particular online platform.

1.3 Objectives

The main objective of this study is to evaluate the expected user acceptance of a mobile augmented reality service for a smart city, using a scenario where a person uses this service. We are also interested to identify the constructs from the previous theories that are more related with intention to use a mobile augmented reality service and explore the existence of relations between the individual characteristics of the participants and the constructs.

2 Methodology

A questionnaire was designed to elicit the expected participant acceptance of an augmented reality service for a smart city, using the following previously described parameters: sense of bellowing (familiarity, perceived similarity and trust in other members); perceived and expected reciprocal benefits; outcome expectations; perceived enjoyment; knowledge power and perceived value and intention to use.

Considering that the interaction with an augmented reality system could be a new experience for many persons, we create a video with a narrative that enables the comprehension of a potential usage of a mobile augmented reality service. This narrative served as script in the development of the video where a protagonist, a citizen of an intelligent city (Maria), uses her smartphone to share and consult information about the city, in different situations during a day when she must go to a medical appointment. During the course, Maria interacts with a mobile augmented reality service to report a problem for citizens safety (a hole in the sidewalk) and to consult two good practices (an restored building and urban art in a building). After each interaction with the mobile augmented reality, Maria receives a feedback with additional information about the events (i.g. number of persons that already reported the event) and a reward.

The illustrations are made in Adobe Illustrator® and placed on the VideoScribe® application. The video lasted 2 min and 39 s.

2.1 Video Narrative

Maria is at home and receives a notification on her smartphone that she has a medical appointment scheduled in 40 min (Fig. 1). Maria starts her journey to the health center where she will have her appointment, but while she walks she finds a hole in the sidewalk that can be a problem for the people safety. She has the idea of sharing this information in the City's Information Sharing Platform, taking a photo. After this action, Maria receives the information that she was the 10th person to report, the repair is expected soon, and she will have a reward for sharing (Fig. 2).

After the appointment, Maria will walk through the city and receive a mobile notification, that she and another 1000 people reported six months ago, the existence of a ruined building. Now, she can use her mobile augmented reality system, to see the building before the restoration (Fig. 3). Later, Maria is surprised by an intervention of urban art in a building, she receives a notification in her mobile augmented reality system saying that she should point the camera of her smartphone, if she wanted to have more information about this urban art. In addition to using the camera of the mobile phone she still shares the information. After, she received the information that was the first person to share and have earned a reward (Fig. 4).

Fig. 1. Maria's presentation, she has a medical appointment in 40 min.

Fig. 2. First situation, Maria finds and reports a hole in the sidewalk.

Fig. 3. Second situation, Mary uses RA to visualize the building before restoration.

Fig. 4. Third situation, Maria is the first to report the existence of an urban art.

2.2 Sample

In total, 194 questionnaires were collected online for analysis. The gender ratio corresponds to 78 men (59.8%) to 116 women (40.2%). The minimum age was 17 years and the maximum age was 70 years, the average was 33.9, with a median of 28.5 and a standard deviation of 13.6 years.

The nationality with the highest frequency was Portuguese (n = 183, 94.4%) followed by Brazilian (n = 9, 4.62%), Guinean (n = 1, 0.5%) and French (n = 1, 0.5%). For the qualification of the sample 5 participants (2.6%) have basic education, 53 (27.3%) high school, 85 (43.8%) graduation, 44 (22.7%) master's degree and 7 (3.6%) PhD.

Responding to the question "weekend occupation", 56 (28.9%) chose to stay home, 120 (61.9%) get out and 18 (9.3%) indecisive or other response. For the question "place for vacations", 107 participants (55.2%) show interest in spending vacations in a city, while 87 (44.8%) prefer to interact with nature.

Twenty-two participants (11.3%) don't use or rarely use social networks while 172 (88.7%) say they frequently use social networks. Of the 194 participants, 17 (8.8%) don't use social networks, 82 (42.3%) use mainly to see information and 95 (49%) use essentially to share information.

2.3 Survey

Based in the previous described references, we developed a questionnaire in the Google Forms online platform, divided into 4 sections: (1) consent terms; (2) video with the scenario to be studied; (3) 12 questions in a seven-point Likert scale ranging from 1 to 7, where 1 was (completely disagree), 2 (disagree), 3 (disagree partially), 4 (don't agree or disagree), 5 (Partially agree), 6 (Agree) and 7 (completely agree); and (4) demographic data (gender, age, nationality, profession, qualifications, place of residence preference, weekend occupation, frequency of use of social networks and reason for use of social networks).

Following the 12 questions for each questionnaire construct:

Familiarity: I became familiar with Maria's interests and behaviors in the city.
Perceived Similarity: I feel that Maria has interests similar to mine.
Trust in Other Members: Maria will do everything within her capacity to help others.
Sense of Belonging: I feel I am part of the city where Maria lives.
Intention to Get Knowledge: I want to get information, shared in the smart city, about the places in the city where Maria lives.
Intention to Share Experience: If I went to Maria city I would like to share events with other people.
Perceived enjoyment: The process of sharing events in the Maria city's is enjoyable.
Perceived reciprocal benefits: If Maria shares events (problems and good thinks of the city), other citizens will also share events with her.

Knowledge power: Maria feels important and special when sharing the events of the city.

Knowledge sharing: Maria uses her smartphone to keep up-to-date on city events.

Perceived value: The way Maria reported events in the city, could help me achieve my goals in the smart city.

Intention to use: I would like to try this kind of interaction with the city.

2.4 Procedures

Participants were recruited through social networks or contacted by email. All participants responded freely and spontaneously to the questionnaire after reading and agreeing to the consent form. The confidentiality of the data collected and its use for research purposes has been ensured.

Participants start by viewing the video before answer the previously described 12 questions and the demographic data.

The data, was processed with IBM SPSS (*Statistical Package for Social Sciences*) software to perform the statistical analysis.

3 Results and Discussion

Table 1 shows the distribution of scores by percentage of participants (N = 194). The first and second columns shows respectively the sentences and the constructs. The third column, the percentages of participants that: 1 (completely disagree), 2 (disagree), 3 (disagree partially). The fourth column, the percentage of participants that: 4 (don't agree or disagree). The fifth column, the percentage of participants that: 5 (Partially agree), 6 (Agree) and 7 (completely agree). All the agreements are related with the sentences.

Considering our main objective, evaluate the expected user acceptance of a mobile augmented reality service for a smart city, using a scenario where a person uses this service, we verify in the Table 1 a distribution tangentially to the right. On average, 68.4% of the participants identifies with the Maria behaviors and want to try this kind of interaction, although most of them, feel that they are not part of this city. Only 39.2% agrees positively with the sentence "I feel I am part of the city where Maria lives". Probably they did not identify themselves with the city in the movie, since we try to not use familiar elements from any particular city.

In order to identify the minimum number of factors representing relationships between the various items from the questionnaire a factorial analysis was performed. The validity tests of factorial analysis (c.f. Pereira [22]) allow to say that the factorial analysis has validity for the chosen variables. Thus, the Keyser-Meyer-Olkin test had a value of 0.891 revealing that the principal components analysis is good. The Bartlet sphericity test allows to reject the null hypothesis of non-correlation between the initial variables ($\chi = 1146$; df = 66; $p < 0.001$).

Table 1. Distribution of scores by participants for each question.

Sentences	Construct	Percentage of responses 1, 2 and 3	Percentage of responses 4	Percentage of responses 5, 6 and 7
I became familiar with Maria's interests and behaviors in the city	Familiarity	16.5%	24.2%	59.3%
I feel that Maria has interests similar to mine	Perceived similarity	18%	26.3%	55.7%
Maria will do everything within her capacity to help others	Trust in other members	4.6%	10.8%	84.6%
I feel I am part of the city where Maria lives	Sense of belonging	45.4%	15.5%	39.2%
I want to get information, shared in the smart city, about the places in the city where Maria lives	Intention to get knowledge	23.2%	17%	59.8%
If I went to Maria city I would like to share events with other people	Intention to share experience	19.1%	16.5%	64.4%
The process of sharing events in the Maria city's is enjoyable	Perceived enjoyment	14.4%	17.0%	68.5%
If Maria shares events (problems and good thinks of the city), other citizens will also share events with her	Perceived reciprocal benefits	10.8%	12.4%	76.8%
Maria feels important and special when sharing the events of the city	Knowledge power	9.3%	16.5%	74.2%
Maria uses her smartphone to keep up-to-date on city events	Knowledge sharing	4.1%	8.2%	87.6%
The way Maria reported events in the city, could help me achieve my goals in the smart city	Perceived value	9.3%	13.4%	77.3%
I would like to try this kind of interaction with the city	Intention to use	13.9%	13.4%	72.7%
Global average		15.7%	15.9%	68.4%

In Table 2, the factor matrix after varimax rotation can be seen. The factor extraction determined three factors. These represent a cumulative percentage of 67% of the variance.

Table 2. Factorial analysis.

Constructs	Factor 1	Factor 2	Factor 3
Evaluated	47.7%	11.6%	7.7%
Intentions to use	**0.85**	0.24	0.11
Perceived enjoyment	**0.77**	0.31	0.13
Intention to share experience	**0.76**	0.17	0.23
Intention to get knowledge	**0.73**	0.13	0.36
Perceived value	**0.64**	0.52	0.20
Perceived similarity	**0.62**	0.06	0.56
Perceived reciprocal benefits	**0.58**	0.51	0.12
Knowledge power	0.00	**0.84**	0.18
Trust in the others	0.28	**0.65**	0.10
Knowledge sharing	0.41	**0.65**	−0.09
Sense of belonging	0.11	0.08	**0.81**
Familiarity	0.25	0.12	**0.77**

The first factor, responsible for 47.7% of the variance, is saturated in descending order by intentions to use, perceived enjoyment, intention to share experience, perceived value, perceived similarity and perceived reciprocal benefits. The second factor, responsible for 11.6% of the variance, is saturated in descendent order by the knowledge power, trust in the others and knowledge sharing. The third factor is saturated by Sense of belonging and familiarity.

Concerning user acceptance off a mobile augmented reality service, the item that is associated with it, is the sentence intention to use this service, that is in the first person, thus ask directly to participants in the study if they would like to try that kind of interaction in the city. Thus, the constructs from the social psychology theories that according to the first factor in the factor analysis are best associated with intention to use are the perceived enjoyment the, intention to share experience, perceived value, perceived similarity and perceived reciprocal benefits.

Related with the other relations between the user acceptance constructs with the individual characteristics of the participants, we used Mann-Whitney U, a non-parametric test for independent samples to analyze the data. We don't found any significant differences between the constructs and the age, gender and habilitation ($p > 0.05$). However, we verified significant differences in the use of networks (people who never, or rarely use social networks, $n = 22$) and (people who use almost always, or always use social networks, $n = 172$) for the following constructs[*]: perceived similarity ($z = -1.8$; $p < 0.05$); intention to get knowledge ($z = -2.4$; $p < 0.05$); Perceived reciprocal benefits ($z = -2.6$; $p < 0.05$); knowledge sharing ($z = -1,9$; $p < 0.05$ and the intention to use ($z = -2.7$; $p < 0.01$). Chart 1 illustrates the scores for each construct and the sentence. This means that for participants who "never or rarely use social networks", and users who "always or almost always use social networks," don't have an interest to use a mobile augmented reality service to get or share information in a smart city (Fig. 5).

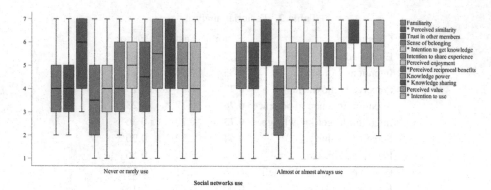

Fig. 5. Scores across constructs by frequency of use of social networks

4 Conclusions

This study reports the result of expected user acceptance evaluation of a mobile augmented reality service for a smart city, using a scenario where a person uses this service. The identification of the acceptance of this kind of technology in an early phase of our project development – Smart City Sense, will be very important to justify the costs involved in the development of a mobile augmented reality service. For this subject we identified that 72.7% of the participants agree with the sentence "I would like to try this kind of interaction with the city". However, 27.3% of the participants disagree (13.9%) or don't have a preference (13.4%) for this kind of interaction. We verify significant differences between the participants that use frequently social networks and the intension to use this kind of technology, particularly to get or share information. In conclusion, those results showed the use of a mobile augment reality service in a smart city is a good option for the participants that have a frequent use of social networks.

In this study we were also interested in identifying the factors that could be more associated with the intention to use the augmented reality technology in the smart city. From factor analysis we can observe that the, perceived enjoyment, intention to share experience, intention to get knowledge, perceived value, perceived similarity and perceived reciprocal benefits, are the factors more associated with the intention to use augmented reality. Exploring those constructs inside gamification solutions in this mobile augmented reality service, could be a good strategy to engage the Citizen in our Smart City Sense Project. In order to citizens use the augmented reality technology in the smart city, the design solutions must include the fun of use, they must allow citizens to share the experience and get knowledge. They must be very well informed and aware of the technology and how the use of technology benefits you and the other members of the community.

Acknowledgements. This work is co-financed by the project LISBOA-01-0247-FEDER-017906: Smart City Sense, FEDER, in the scope of the Program Portugal 2020, through LISBOA2020.

References

1. Chiu, C., Hsu, M., Wang, E.: Understanding knowledge sharing in virtual communities: an integration of social capital and social cognitive theories. Decis. Support Syst. **42**, 1872–1888 (2016). https://doi.org/10.1016/j.dss.2006.04.001
2. Hsu, M., Ju, T., Yen, C., Chang, C.: Knowledge sharing behavior in virtual communities: the relationship between trust, self-efficacy, and outcome expectations. Int. J. Hum. Comput. Stud. **65**(2), 153–169 (2007). https://doi.org/10.1016/j.ijhcs.2006.09.003
3. Wasko, M.M., Faraj, S.: Why should i share? Examining social capital and knowledge contribution in electronic networks of practice. MIS Q. **29**(1), 35–57 (2005). https://doi.org/10.2307/25148667
4. Clemons, E., Gao, G., Hitt, L.: When online reviews meet hyperdifferentiation: a study of the craft beer industry. J. Manag. Inf. Syst. **23**, 149–171 (2006). https://doi.org/10.2753/mis0742-1222230207
5. Duan, W., Gu, B., Whinston, A.: Do online reviews matter? - an empirical investigation of panel data. Decis. Support Syst. **45**, 1007–1016 (2008). https://doi.org/10.1016/j.dss.2008.04.001
6. Zhou, Z., Jin, X.L., Vogel, D.R., Fang, Y., Chen, X.: Individual motivations and demographic differences in social virtual world uses: an exploratory investigation in second life. Int. J. Inf. Manag. **31**(3), 261–271 (2011). https://doi.org/10.1016/j.ijinfomgt.2010.07.007
7. Hagerty, B., Lynch-Sauer, J., Patusky, K., Bouwsema, M., Collier, P.: Sense of belonging: a vital mental health concept. Arch. Psychiatr. Nurs. **6**(3), 172–177 (1992). https://doi.org/10.1016/0883-9417(92)90028-h
8. Hagborg, W.: An investigation of a brief measure of school membership. Adolescence **33** (130), 461–468 (1998)
9. Roberts, T.: Are newsgroups virtual communities? In: CHI 1998 Proceedings of the SIGCHI Conference on Human Factors in Computing Systems, pp. 360–367. ACM Press/Addison-Wesley Publishing, New York (1998)
10. Lin, H.: Determinants of successful virtual communities: contributions from system characteristics and social factors. Inf. Manag. **45**(8), 522–527 (2008). https://doi.org/10.1016/j.im.2008.08.002
11. Koh, J., Kim, Y.: Knowledge sharing in virtual communities: an e-business perspective. Expert Syst. Appl. **26**(2), 155–166 (2004). https://doi.org/10.1016/s0957-4174(03)00116-7
12. Kankanhalli, A., Tan, B.C.Y., Wei, K.: Contributing knowledge to electronic knowledge repositories: an empirical investigation. MIS Q. **29**(1), 113–143 (2005). https://doi.org/10.2307/25148670
13. Bandura, A.: Self-Efficacy: The Exercise of Control. Worth Publishers, New York (1997)
14. Chiu, C., Hsu, M., Wang, E.: Understanding knowledge sharing in virtual communities: an integration of social capital and social cognitive theories. Decis. Support Syst. **42**(3), 1872–1888 (2006). https://doi.org/10.1016/j.dss.2006.04.001
15. Dunford, R.: Key challenges in the search for the effective management of knowledge in management consulting firms. J. Knowl. Manag. **4**(4), 295–302 (2000). https://doi.org/10.1108/13673270010379849
16. Grandori, A., Kogut, B.: Dialogue on organization and knowledge. Organ. Sci. **13**(3), 224–231 (2002). https://doi.org/10.1287/orsc.13.3.224.2774
17. Hsu, C., Lin, J.: Acceptance of blog usage: the roles of technology acceptance, social influence and knowledge sharing motivation. Inf. Manag. **45**, 65–74 (2008). https://doi.org/10.1016/j.im.2007.11.001

18. Venkatesh, V.: Determinants of perceived ease of use: integrating control, intrinsic motivation, and emotion into the technology acceptance model. Inf. Syst. Res. 11(4), 342–365 (2000). https://doi.org/10.1287/isre.11.4.342.11872
19. Wasko, M., Faraj, S.: It is what one does: why people participate and help others in electronic communities of practice. J. Strateg. Inf. Syst. 9(2–3), 155–173 (2000). https://doi.org/10.1016/s0963-8687(00)00045-7
20. Sánchez-Fernández, R., Iniesta-Bonillo, M.A.: The concept of perceived value: a systematic review of the research. Mark. Theor. 7(4), 427–451 (2007). https://doi.org/10.1177/1470593107083165
21. Davis, F.: Perceived usefulness, perceived ease of use, and user acceptance of information technology. MIS Q. 13, 319–340 (1989). https://doi.org/10.2307/249008
22. Pereira, A.: Guia prático de utilização do SPSS: Análise de dados para ciências sociais e psicologia. Edições sílabo, Lisboa (1999)

The Design of the SaiteBooker: An Authoring Tool for E-books for Health Distance Learning Courses in Brazil

Carla G. Spinillo[1(✉)], Claudio H. Silva[1], Ana Emília F. Oliveira[2],
Dilson José L. Rabêlo Jr.[2], and Aldrea M. O. Rabelo[2]

[1] Department of Design, The Federal University of Paraná, Curitiba, Brazil
cgspin@gmail.com
[2] UNASUS, The Federal University of Maranhão, São Luis, Brazil

Abstract. The demand for e-books for distance learning courses in the health field in Brazil has increased. Thus, it is necessary to accelerate the e-book production process. In this regard, this article reports the development and evaluation of saiteBooker, an authoring tool for e-books proposed by the Open University of the Unified Health System (UNA-SUS/UFMA) in Brazil. Within an information design approach, a qualitative evaluation was conducted, with 32 participants, through: (a) Expert assessment (n = 16) by technology and design experts, and information design researchers; followed by (b) Users' assessment (n = 16). The results of the Expert assessment showed deficiencies in the visualization and consistency of components and functions of the tool. Based on these results, the saiteBooker tool was improved for the Users' assessment (online questionnaire prior and post interaction). The results indicated that the improved tool was positively evaluated, meeting users' expectations. To conclude, it is highlighted the importance of an evaluation method that combines technology and information design views with user testing.

Keywords: Authoring tool · E-books · Information design · Health

1 Introduction

The use of digital means to communicate content has increased worldwide, particularly in distance learning. In the health field, in particular, there is a high demand for distance learning courses to train professionals, such as doctors, nurses and pharmacists. E-books have then, become an essential tool in such courses. This is due to the fact that the e-books' production process is faster compared to that of printed books, since the printing and binding stages are not necessary.

Another advantage of e-books over printed books is that e-books allow the use of dynamic and interactive resources. Readers/users can access contents through audio text, videos, animations or kinetic typography. These can be employed to draw users' attention to particular contents and/or to motivate reading. Moreover, e-books can make use of hyperlinks to add complementary content to the main topic. The use of technological resources makes it possible for e-books to break the paradigm of linear narrative [1, 2].

© Springer International Publishing AG, part of Springer Nature 2018
A. Marcus and W. Wang (Eds.): DUXU 2018, LNCS 10920, pp. 715–729, 2018.
https://doi.org/10.1007/978-3-319-91806-8_56

In this sense, Rojeski [3] adds that the popularity of e-books is also due to the fact that they can be easily accessed via digital devices, such as smartphones and tablets; and to their low purchase cost.

Several studies have been conducted on the design and use of e-books. Some of the aspects which have been investigated are users' preference and attitude towards e-book reading; effectiveness and suitability of e-books' graphic interfaces, and their interactivity and usability [4–9]. For instance, Bidarra et al. [7] discuss the effect of interaction and elements of the interface on preference for the graphic interface design by e-book users. Similarly, Huang [2] investigates users' preference for page turning in e-books. Marshall and Bly [10] discuss users' reading experience with e-books, claiming that navigation is strongly affected by components of the graphic interface.

Although the studies conducted have generated a variety of results, the recognition of e-books as a valuable type of publication seems to be a point of convergence among authors.

1.1 The Need of E-book Authoring Tools in Brazil

In Brazil, tools for authoring e-books in Portuguese are scarce, particularly those with open access to users. These are essential to meet the demand for e-books for distance learning courses in the health field. According to the Brazilian Ministry of Health, from 2010 to 2017 a total of 1,097,330 professionals enrolled on the distance learning courses offered by the Open University of the Unified Health System [11]. Thus, there is a need for authoring tools in Portuguese to facilitate e-book production in the health area in Brazil.

By taking this into account, the Open University of the Unified Health System of the Federal University of Maranhão (UNA-SUS/UFMA) has developed a collaborative, open access authoring tool for e-books - the SaiteBooker. SaiteBooker is intended to account for particular editorial aspects of the health field, such as medical images, and health related icons for interface menus. This article reports the process of developing and evaluating the SaiteBooker within an information design approach.

2   Information Design Approach

Information design aims at providing efficient communication through printed and/or digital artifacts/systems [12]. According to the International Institute for Information – IIID [13], information design is concerned with 'the defining, planning and visualization of the contents of a message with the intention of achieving particular objectives in relation to the needs of the target users'. By focusing on the visualization of contents (graphic interface) addressed to users, an information design approach was adopted to the development of the authoring tool for e-books proposed by the UNA-SUS/UFMA. To set the ground for this paper, information and interaction design principles are briefly presented in the next section.

2.1   Information Design Principles

In order to guide the development of graphic artifacts and their interfaces, the literature on information design and related areas presents principles and recommendations regarding users' cognitive aspects, visual perception, attention and motivation [14–17]. A comprehensive view of the aspects to be considered in design processes for information artifacts/systems is provided by Pettersson [14] through a set of principles. These principles are divided into four categories: functional, aesthetic, cognitive and administrative principles. The functional and aesthetic principles concern usability of artifacts/systems and their graphic presentation of information. The cognitive principles refer to aspects of the users' domain, and the administrative principles refer to legal, cost, safety and ethical aspects in the design of artifacts/systems.

Since authoring tools make use of interactivity, it is also important to consider interaction design principles. Blair-Early and Zender [16] present principles to support the development of interfaces in digital artifacts/systems. For the authors 'interface is content', that is, the interface should be part of the content, and the interaction should lead directly to it. The principles proposed by Blair-Early and Zender [16] are in line with those proposed by Nielsen [18] and which have been widely employed by researchers and professionals in the development and evaluation of digital artifacts.

Of the principles proposed by Pettersson [14] and those proposed by Blair-Early and Zender [16], the following were considered pertinent to the design of authoring tools for e-books.

Functional Principles

- Simplicity: the components should be presented in a concise and accurate manner
- Unity/Consistency: the presentation of components, their graphic relations and functions should be consistent throughout the interface
- Proximity/Chunking: related components/functions should be placed closely to allow visual grouping
- Hierarchy: components/functions differing in degree of importance should be ordered accordingly, from broader topics to more specific topics.
- Structure: components and functions should be arranged in a logical and clear manner
- Emphasis: elements which require users' attention (e.g., hyperlinks) should be highlighted
- Alignment: the components of the interface should be lined up
- Clarity in language: plain language should be used for labels and texts.

Aesthetics Principles

- Harmony: the components/functions should be displayed/organized in a sensible way so as to produce a pleasant and coherent interface
- Proportion: the components should be in a balanced ratio to promote harmony.

Interaction Design and Usability Principles

- Interface is content: elements of the interface should be designed to 'minimize interface and maximize content'

- Obvious start: a starting point of the interaction should be easily spotted in the interface
- Clear reverse: the interaction design should make reversing any actions possible (e.g., end a section)
- Conventions: components/functions which are conventions for interaction should be employed as they are familiar to users (except when they impose difficulties/limitations to users)
- Feedback: tasks should produce prompt and noticeable feedback to inform users of the effects of their actions.
- Landmarks: way showing components should be provided to inform users of their location in the interface space.
- Adaptation: the interface should be flexible/adaptable to users' needs and/or to patterns of interaction
- Help: supporting resources to assist users should be made available on the interface
- User control and freedom: interface should be designed to empower users to freely achieve their goals during interaction
- Error prevention/management: the system/interface should be designed to avoid errors.

The above-mentioned principles were considered in the evaluation of the saiteBooker tool. Before presenting the evaluation process, aspects of the authoring tool design process are introduced together with information about UNA-SUS/UFMA.

3   The UNA-SUS/UFMA and the SaiteBooker Tool

The Open University of the Unified Health System (UNA-SUS) was created in 2008 by the Brazilian Ministry of Health. UNA-SUS aim is to broaden the access to health education through distance learning courses offered by university partners. Fourteen universities are currently part of the UNA-SUS system, and provide doctors and nurses, among other professionals, access to courses in a number of areas (e.g., family health, environmental health surveillance, maternal and child health, mental health, and management of pharmaceutical assistance). The Federal University of Maranhão - UFMA is the university partner with the highest production of courses. From 2014 to 2017 the UNA-SUS/UFMA offered a total of 60 distance learning courses to health professionals throughout the country.

The saiteBooker authoring tool has been developed to accelerate the design process of e-books produced by the UNA-SUS/UFMA, making it a more efficient and accessible process to non-computing/programming specialists. Previously, the process to create an e-book involved three teams of professionals: instructional designers, graphic designers and information technology experts.

The instructional design team was responsible for the pedagogical contents and for defining the draft of the visual structure of the e-books. The graphic designers were responsible for the production of images (e.g., infographic, drawings, motion graphics) and for the typesetting. The information technology team was responsible for programming the e-book features/functions.

The e-book development process is an iterative process, requiring approval rounds by the instructional designers until the e-book is considered ready to be made available in the Virtual Learning Environment. The approval round process can be time-consuming for the graphic design and information technology teams as well as for the instructional designers. The authoring tool has improved this process by providing graphic and technological resources to the instructional design team. This has made it possible to skip two stages of the process: the typesetting/image production and the programming.

A diagram illustrating how the development process for e-books has improved with the saiteBooker authoring tool is shown in Fig. 1. The dotted arrows indicate the possible iterations during the process before the authoring tool. The full arrows indicate the flow.

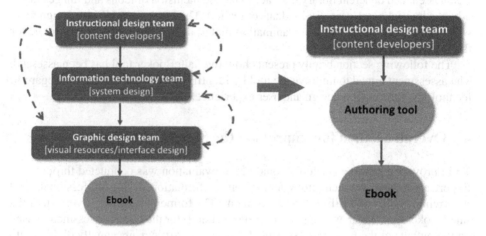

Fig. 1. On the right, the improved design process of e-books with the saiteBooker authoring tool, in relation to the conventional process (on the left).

3.1 Characteristics of the SaiteBooker Tool

The saiteBooker tool was designed according to the following criteria:

- to be an easy-to-use and intuitive tool to enable ordinary users to create their e-books;
- to be used online by users of different operating systems (e.g., Android, IOS);
- to be open access, requiring only a user registration;
- to be simple and compact with specific features for creating e-book designs;
- to allow previews for desktops, tablets and smartphones during the e-book design process; and
- to be used by a single user or by a team of users (collaborative tool), since it offers autonomy for the former, and may fit into a workflow for the latter.

The saiteBooker has five main areas:

1. The Project area is for entering general information about the e-book project;
2. The Theme area is for creating the layout features of the e-book (e.g., color, font size, line spacing) and/or for choosing from a range of themes available;
3. The Media area is for uploading, storing and for adding images to an ongoing project;
4. The Canvas area is for typesetting the e-book pages and;
5. The Export area is for uploading/exporting the created e-book.

Regarding healthcare professionals, the saiteBooker offers specific functions/ features to support the design of e-books, such as the library of icons and images on health-related topics. It was developed by information technology professionals and information designers, as well as researchers and health professionals. As a result, it is a consistent and coherent library that facilitates the inclusion of icons and images in the e-books by healthcare users (individuals or teams). The UNA-SUS/UFMA design team will soon include audio and video/animation materials to broaden the library scope for the saiteBooker users.

The following section briefly presents how the SaiteBooker tool has been assessed. The assessment aimed to improve the tool by identifying its weaknesses with regard to technology, information design and user experience.

4   Overall Method for Improving the SaiteBooker Tool

To improve the saiteBooker tool, a qualitative evaluation was conducted through: (a) Expert assessment by technology and graphic/information design professionals and researchers, followed by (b) Users' assessment. The former used a Beta1 version of the saiteBooker tool, which was enhanced (Beta2 version) for the Users' assessment, based on the outputs of the Expert assessment. A total of 32 participants equally divided into Expert assessment and Users' assessments, evaluated the tool. Figure 2 shows a synthesis of the evaluation process.

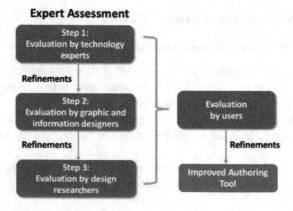

Fig. 2. Synthesis of the evaluation process of the saiteBooker authoring tool.

4.1 Expert Assessment

The Expert evaluation was conducted in three consecutive steps. The information obtained in each step led to refinements in the saiteBooker tool, as briefly explained below.

Step 1: Evaluation by Technology Experts
This step consisted of a hands-on-workshop to identify problems related to the system design. It was conducted with three experts in web development. An explanation of the features of the authoring tool was provided to participants, who were then asked to develop an e-book for a given medical content: "Public Health Management". The outputs of this step were analyzed qualitatively. The problems/difficulties encountered by the participants when creating the e-book were adjusted in the system design of the saiteBooker tool which was then, assessed in the next step.

Step 2: Evaluation by Graphic and Information Design Experts
This step aimed at identifying problems regarding the graphic interface and interaction design of the saiteBooker. The same procedures for Step 1 were adopted, but now participants could choose the theme of the e-books to be created. Participants were requested to use all available features of the authoring tool. The hands-on-workshop was conducted with 10 experts in graphic and information design. At the end of the workshop, participants were asked to fill in an online questionnaire on the usability of the tool. The outputs of this step were also analyzed qualitatively, taking into account the problems/difficulties pointed out by the participants in order to improve the tool.

Step 3: Evaluation by Design Researchers
This step was carried out by three design researchers. The aim here was to rank the improvements to be made in the authoring tool based upon the drawbacks pointed out in the previous steps. For this, the FIP - Frequency, Impact, and Persistence - technique [9, 18] was used to measure the frequency of occurrence of the identified problems, their impact on usability, and their persistence. A score (1–10) was assigned to each aspect of the problems (frequency, impact and persistence) by the researchers, individually. Then, the scores were discussed by the researchers. Next, the agreed scores were put into the formula (1) for calculating each problem's severity. The scores varied from 0 to 100: 70–100 high severity problems, 30–69 medium severity problems, 0–29 low severity problems.

$$\text{severity} = \frac{\text{score (frequency)} \times \text{score (impact)} \times \sqrt{\text{score (persistence)}}}{\sqrt{10}} \tag{1}$$

Improvements made in the authoring tool according to the outputs of this step resulted in the Beta2 version of the tool for users' assessment.

4.2 Users' Assessment

The evaluation by users aimed at verifying their experience when interacting with the Saite-Booker tool (Beta2 version). The evaluation was conducted individually with 16 volunteer attendees during a national conference on telemedicine and tele-health, held in Brazil. Participants were invited to answer an online questionnaire prior and post interaction. Before interacting with the tool, participants were asked to state their expectations regarding authoring tools to create e-books on health education/training (online question). Next, participants were briefly introduced to the tool and invited to freely interact with it. Participants then, answered a number of online questions with Likert-type scale, each question with seven levels of agreement (1 = disagree to 7 = agree). The questions regarded satisfaction with the tool, its usability, navigation and graphic interface. The online questionnaire ended with an open question asking for suggestions for further improvements to the saiteBooker tool. The results were analyzed qualitatively.

5 Synthesis of the Results of Expert Assessment

5.1 Step 1: Evaluation by Technology Experts

The results of the assessment showed that the saiteBooker tool greatly improved the production process of a 30-page long e-book on "Public Health Management". There was a reduction in the development time of the e-book. In general, creating 30-page e-books would take around eight hours, but with the authoring tool the process took four hours or less. Another positive aspect was the grouping of functions and of interface components of the saiteBooker, which were also hierarchically presented in the menus. This was considered a facilitating aspect of the authoring tool interface by the participants.

However, some problems were pointed out by the technology experts when using the tool. The main difficulty was to place elements (images, texts, titles) on the pages using the available grid system (rows and columns). Based on these results, some adjustments were made in the Beta1 version of the saiteBooker tool for the next step of the evaluation.

5.2 Step 2: Evaluation by Experts in Graphic and Information Design

In general, participants evaluated their experience with the authoring tool positively. All of them were able to develop e-books using the various functions of the saiteBooker tool. The evaluation questionnaire had a total of 109 responses, regarding how easy or how difficult it was to use the authoring tool, as well as suggestions for improvements.

However, most responses were on participants' difficulties (N = 46 out of 109) in using the tool. They mainly regarded the interface (N = 15) and functions of the system design (N = 19). The most recurrent problems were related to: poor/lack of visualization of functions and components of the interface, unclear/ambiguous labels for buttons and icons, unnecessary actions to add an image to a page, inappropriate relation between buttons/icons and their functions. These problems were compiled for evaluation by design researchers so as to identify their severity in the next step.

5.3 Step 3: Evaluation by Design Researchers

For the evaluation of the problems/deficiencies pointed out in Step 2, the researchers considered the criteria used in a previous evaluation study of the graphic interface of virtual learning objects of the distance learning courses offered by UNA-SUS/UFMA [9]. These were:

1. Inadequate aspects of the interface,
2. Probable usability problems as a consequence; and
3. Negative implications on usability. These refer to effectiveness, efficiency and satisfaction with the use of the tool.

A total of 44 problems/deficiencies in the authoring tool were identified. These were then hierarchized: 22 were considered of high severity, 18 of medium severity, and four of low severity. The interface of the authoring tool presented problems of greater severity which were related to the visualization and consistency of components and functions, particularly with regard to icons and buttons. The typographic resources for page creation were considered as of medium and low severity, while those referring to the production and inclusion of images (e.g., graphics, timeline) were considered as of high and medium severity. These results were taken into account in order to generate the recommendations to improve the saiteBooker tool (Beta2 version).

The recommendations for the SaiteBooker tool were ranked according to their degree of severity, and grouped into the following categories: interface design, system design and task execution. To facilitate the visualization of the recommendations proposed, a spreadsheet was created with visual examples of the problems and possible alternatives for adjustments. The graphic interface and functions of the saiteBooker tool were then properly adjusted by the team of developers. As a result, a Beta2 version of the saiteBooker was designed to be assessed by users in the final stage of the evaluation process.

5.4 Synthesis of the Results of Users' Assessment

The results of participants' experience with authoring tools for e-books showed that most of participants (n = 9 out of 16 participants) were familiar with such tools, but only four of them had previously created e-books. Participants' expectations of e-book authoring tools (n = 59 responses) prior to the interaction with the saiteBooker were mainly: to publish in various formats such as HTML, ePub, and PDF (n = 14); to speed the design process (n = 13); to allow inserting photos, videos, audio and other interactive resources (n = 12); and to have online publishing facility (n = 11). Participants' responses after interaction indicated that the saiteBooker is likely to match their expectations.

In general, the tool was positively assessed by the participants. They found the experience of interacting with the saiteBooker quite satisfactory (n = 12 out of 16 participants). The tool was considered ease to use (n = 12), to learn (n = 11) and to navigate (n = 11). The graphic interface was considered intuitive and friendly (n = 10) with a clear sequence of screens (n = 13), and with an adequate number of elements/information. The icons (n = 11) and color (n = 9) were also positively assessed. Nevertheless, only half of the participants (n = 8) found that interface layout facilitates interaction.

This suggests that adjustments should be made to enhance interaction design in the saiteBooker tool.

Finally, when asked to indicate whether they believe people would be interested in using the saiteBooker, 14 out of 16 participants considered it to be of interest by marking 6 and 7 in the Likert scale (1 = non-interested to 7 = very interested).

Although generally satisfied with the tool, participants considered that the saite-Booker tool could be further improved by: providing an online tutorial, showing history of (track) adjustments in the e-book project, and broadening the image library.

6 Discussion and Improvements in the SaiteBooker Tool

The results of the Expert evaluation indicated that some design principles were not properly met. The problems identified on the graphic interface showed disagreement with the functional principles (Proximity, Chunking, Hierarchy, and Structure) and the interaction principles (Interface is content, User control and freedom). This seems to be due to the fact that principles are general in nature, so that they can be applied in different

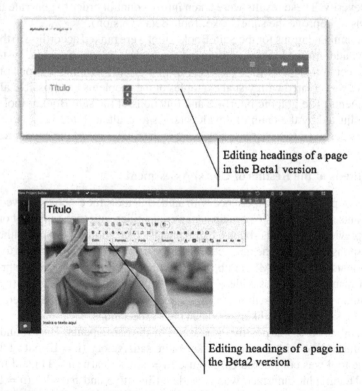

Editing headings of a page in the Beta1 version

Editing headings of a page in the Beta2 version

Fig. 3. In the improved version (Beta2 version) of the saiteBooker visual emphasis is employed to allow identification of the selected object. The object's properties are grouped and placed near the object to be edited. These resources were not made available as such in the Beta1 version of the tool.

contexts and design processes. Therefore, they must be adapted by the developers to the particular demands of each project/artifact. For that reason, the authoring tool developers may have made specific decisions (e.g., position of buttons, visualization of functions) based on their knowledge and experience, which may not have been the most appropriate ones for the authoring tool users.

Considering this, the users' evaluation of the saiteBooker tool after the assessment by technology and design experts/researchers was of prime importance. The evaluation allowed the identification of deficiencies which were not perceived by the developers during the design process of the tool. This made it possible to improve the usability and efficiency of the saiteBooker tool, ratifying the importance of an interdisciplinary approach to the design of digital artifacts/systems to support distance learning in the health field.

Thus, based on the results of the expert and users' assessments, improvements were made to the SaiteBooker tool, which were also aligned with the principles of information design, interaction design and usability, earlier mentioned in this paper. The following figures show examples of the improvements made. These are mainly related to the following principles: Interface is Content, Adaptation, User control and freedom, Emphasis, Hierarchy, Proximity/Chunking (Figs. 3, 4, 5 and 6).

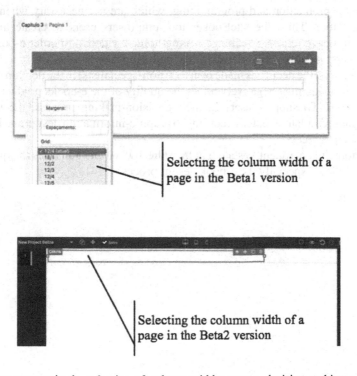

Fig. 4. Improvement in the selection of column widths to ease decision making on the page column layout by users. In the Beta1 version the selection of column widths was made through menu options, whereas in the Beta2 version users can freely select the area for a column.

Adding pages in the Beta1 version   Adding pages in the Beta2 version

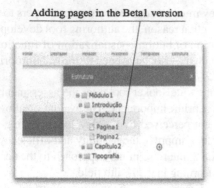   

Fig. 5. Improvement in the way pages are added to facilitate visualization of the number of pages of an e-book section.

The saiBooker tool also improved the development process of e-books by making it shorter/faster, therefore more efficient. The conventional process involves steps of type-setting/image production and programming, which are not necessary when using the saiteBooker tool. Thus, the siteBooker tool empowers users to create and display elements of a page (e.g., texts, images, infographics, videos), to order e-book content (e.g., chapters, sections), and to publish the produced e-book.

Nevertheless, the decisions made by users (non-specialists) in the domain of graphic-information design may negatively affect the quality of the e-books produced with the authoring tool. To support users in their decision-making process, the siteBooker provides page templates created according to graphic-information design and interaction design good practices. ·

Therefore, it is pertinent to state that the saiteBooker tool enhances the quality of e-book production, especially the e-book design process.

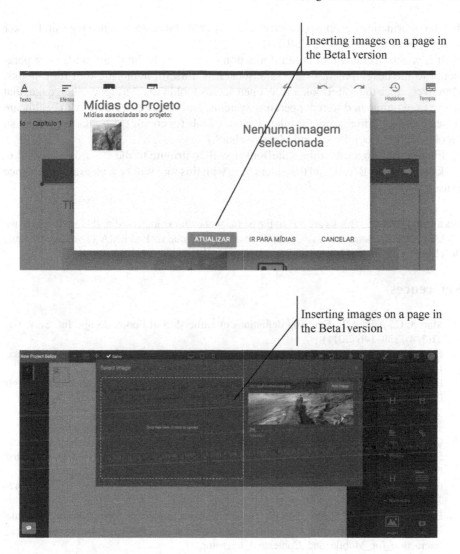

Fig. 6. Improvement in the insertion of images on an e-book page, making the task of importing images from the web and from computer files easier.

7   Conclusion and Final Comments

This article reported an information design approach to the development of the saite-Booker, an authoring tool for e-books produced by the Open University of the Unified Health System (UNA-SUS/UFMA) in Brazil. Principles and design criteria were presented, as well as the features of the tool and its evaluation process (Expert and Users' assessments). Based upon the results of the evaluation process, it is pertinent to conclude that the information design approach effectively contributed to enhance the saiteBooker tool proposed by the UNA-SUS/UFMA.

It is worth stressing that both information design and technology fields were paramount to the development of the saiteBooker as a useful authoring tool for e-books. Moreover, since the saiteBooker is an open access tool in the Portuguese language, that can be used online in different operating systems, and is addressed mainly to healthcare professionals, it differs from the other available tools for creating e-books (e.g., Atavist, iBooks Author, LucidPress, and Maestro ebook).

Finally, it is hoped that the saiteBooker will contribute to the creation of useful e-books on health in Brazil, and that interacting with this tool will be a pleasant experience to users.

Acknowledgement. Thanks are due to the participants who volunteered to this study and to the UNA-SUS/UFMA team of developers. Thanks are also due to FAPEMA (The Research and Development Agency of Maranhão State, Brazil) for their financial support.

References

1. Martin, C., Aitken, J.: Evolving definitions of authorship in Ebook design. Inf. Serv. Use **31**(3–4), 139–146 (2011)
2. Huang, J.: How Interface Elements for Page Turning in eBooks Affect Reader Preference. Unpublished Master Dissertation, The University of Waikato (2017)
3. Rojeski, M.: User perceptions of ebooks versus print books for class reserves in an academic library. Ref. Serv. Rev. **40**(2), 228–241 (2012)
4. Wilson, R.: Ebook readers in higher education. Educ. Technol. Soc. **6**(4), 8–17 (2003). https://strathprints.strath.ac.uk/2510/6/Wilson_ETS_2003_Ebook_readers_in_higher.pdf
5. González, J.C., Guzmán, J.L., Dormido, S., Berengel, M.: Development of interactive books for control education. In: Proceedings of the 10th IFAC Symposium Advances in Control Education. The International Federation of Automatic Control, pp. 150–155 (2013)
6. Fojtik, R.: Ebooks and mobile devices in education. Procedia – Soc. Behav. Sci. **182**, 742–745 (2015)
7. Bidarra, J., Natálio, C., Figueiredo, M.: Designing ebook interaction for mobile and contextual learning (2015). https://www.researchgate.net/publication/268446567_Designing_eBook_Interaction_for_Mobile_and_Contextual_Learning
8. Yalman, M.: Preservice teachers' views about e-book and their levels of use of e-books. Procedia – Soc. Behav. Sci. **176**, 255–262 (2015)
9. Spinillo, C.G., Padovani, S., Smythe, K.C.A.S., Bueno, J., Figueiredo de Oliveira, A.E.: The open university of the unified health system in Brazil (UNA-SUS/UFMA): identification and hierarchization of problems in distance learning courses. In: Marcus, A., Wang, W. (eds.) DUXU 2017. LNCS, vol. 10290, pp. 724–739. Springer, Cham (2017). https://doi.org/10.1007/978-3-319-58640-3_52
10. Marshall, C., Bly, S.: Turning the page on navigation. In: Proceedings of the 5th ACM/IEEE-CS Joint Conference on Digital Libraries, pp. 225–234. ACM (2005)
11. UNA-SUS. The Open University of the Unified Health System. unasus.gov.br/page/una-sus-in-numbers/arouca-offers-educational-and-matriculas. Accessed 12 Nov 2017
12. SBDI - Sociedade Brasileira de Design da Informação. http://sbdi.org.br/. Accessed 12 Nov 2017

13. IIID - International Institute for Information. http://www.iiid.net/home/definitions/. Accessed 12 Nov 2017
14. Pettersson, R.: It Depends: ID – Principles and Guidelines. Institute for Infology, Tullinge (2007)
15. Lipton, R.: The Practical Guide to Information Design. Wiley, Hoboken (2007)
16. Blair-Early, A., Zender, M.: User interface design principles for interaction design. Des. Issues **24**(3), 85–107 (2008)
17. Frascara, J.: Communication Design: Principles, Methods and Practice. Allworth Press, New York (2004)
18. Nielsen, J.: Usability Engineering. Academic Press, Boston (1993)

Tourism and Virtual Reality: User Experience Evaluation of a Virtual Environment Prototype

Yanick Trindade[1(✉)], Francisco Rebelo[1,2], and Paulo Noriega[1,2]

[1] CIAUD, Faculdade de Arquitetura, Universidade de Lisboa, Rua Sá Nogueira,
Pólo Universitário, Alto da Ajuda, 1349-063 Lisboa, Portugal
lamberttrindade@hotmail.com

[2] Ergonomics Laboratory, Faculdade de Motricidade Humana, Universidade de Lisboa,
Estrada da Costa, 1499-002 Cruz Quebrada, Portugal

Abstract. Tourism is one of the largest industries and one of the fastest growing sectors in the world. At present and due to accessibility and improvement of technology, the tourism industry has been using experiences based on Virtual Reality, because they offer immersive experiences that absorb the user through sensory stimulation like sight and sound. The game, plays an essential role in the imaginary constructive process. By engaging fascination through interactivity, digital games introduce a sense of experimentation that facilitates immersion. In this context, the present preliminary study sought to assess the user experience through development of an immersive virtual reality game, to share the cultural aspects of São Tomé island and engaging the participants to visit the island. The goal of this study is to evaluate usability and user experience in a three-dimensional virtual reality environment prototype of a beach place, in a traditional hostel. Concerning usability, we evaluated the participants interaction in virtual world through their behavior, and responses to questionnaires of presence and simulator sickness. To evaluate the user experience, we evaluated emotions through use of a scale of valence and arousal (SAM) and categories of emotions elicited by the VR simulation using the Geneva Emotion Wheel. The results reveal that the three-dimensional virtual reality environment prototype provided high level of immersion, the control and sensory factors also present high value, while the distraction factors recorded reveal that they were not significant, and participant also felt that the experience had a high level of realism. No significant simulator sickness problems were reported. User experience was emotionally positive with high values of pleasure and contentment. In conclusion, the 3D virtual reality environment prototype was able to engage the participants and provide interactive experiences capable to seducing and arousing interest in the São Tomé and Príncipe islands.

Keywords: Usability methods and tools · Virtual reality · Tourism · Design

1 Introduction

The development of new communication and interactive strategy aiming a new look at the legacy of collective memories of a region, state or country, can be a relevant factor

© Springer International Publishing AG, part of Springer Nature 2018
A. Marcus and W. Wang (Eds.): DUXU 2018, LNCS 10920, pp. 730–742, 2018.
https://doi.org/10.1007/978-3-319-91806-8_57

for enhancement of cultural aspects of the islands of São Tomé and Príncipe. One of the strategies, can be through by the development of interactive experiences based on digital games that involve users, arousing they interest in another culture and its intrinsic cultural aspects. The historical roots of São Tomé and Príncipe culture, are closely linked to reciprocal acculturation between Europeans from Portugal and Africans from the African coast south of the Sahara [1]. In this sense, the establishment of relations between the concepts of Digital Games, interactivity, culture, emotion and empathy, traditional aspects, internal and globalized space, adds value, difference and fosters reciprocal exchange between different cultures.

Tourism has emerged as a major economic sector and source of social and environmental change since the 1950s. It has also become a field of serious research and scholarship in many academic disciplines since 1970s [2]. Its characteristics should be defined: intangibility – it is a service, not a product, and as a result it cannot be touched, just experienced; heterogeneity – each customer experiences a service in a different way; inseparability – it cannot be taken home like a product and has to be consumed at the place of the destination; perishability – once the opportunity of selling a service at a certain point has forgone, it cannot be resold at a later point in time; lack of ownership – a service that cannot be owned [3]. The essence of travel and tourism experience is tourists' encounters with the destination environments, the "realities" of others. Tourists are tempted by the allure of places and landscapes; some mainly driven by desire to experience the visual sensations of distant territories [4], others by the deeper meaning behind interacting with the sociocultural aspects of tourism destinations [5]. Due to technological advances, some studies have highlighted the use of Virtual Environments as a promising tool for tourism field [6]. Successfully supporting actions such as sightseeing in a virtual tourism destination will lead users to perceive a sense of presence, of him/herself as being in the destination. Consequently, presence explains the effectiveness of VR as substitute to and/or simulation of travel [7]. When compared to conventional methods, the advantages of using VR tools for tourism context, relate to the ability to create low-cost experimental (in some case) interactive and realistic environments, as well enhanced control of the variables.

1.1 Current Study

Understanding how potential travelers/tourists respond to various VR stimuli, the attitudinal consequences of "having been" in a destination, is of practical importance as destination managers are increasingly faced with strategic decisions to invest in various technology platforms and modalities [8]. In this context, this preliminary study emerged as an antechamber of the main research project itself (PhD thesis), through the development of a virtual reality immersive game prototype, with the aim of disseminating the cultural aspects (material/immaterial) of São Tomé and Príncipe islands, with the purpose to providing interactive experiences capable of seducing and arousing interest in the islands as a tourist destination, either by emanating intrinsic aspects characteristic of the islands or by the idyllic atmosphere as a vacation spot, using a three-dimensional virtual reality environment prototype of a beach place, through traditional hostel. Consequently, the current preliminary study is divide in two key moments: Analyze the participants interaction in virtual world, through their behavior in one side and in the other side to analyze user experience, by assessing their subjective perceptions as: Sense of presence, Simulator sickness but also using the Self-Assessment Manikin (SAM) and Geneva Emotion Wheel to access emotional state and reaction of participant, to assess its feasibility (i.e., protocol, content, equipment, data system) to achieve the main goal of this study.

1.2 Goals

The main goal of this research work is to evaluate a virtual reality three-dimensional prototype of a beach place, through traditional hostel, on São Tomé Island. In particular, we want to know if this virtual environment is capable of emotionally involve participants and provide interactive experiences capable to seducing and arousing interest in the islands. In addition, we also want also to evaluate the VR environment and equipment (HTC VIVE) concerning immersion factors and participants simulator sickness.

2   Method

2.1 Participants

Thirteen university students participated in this preliminary study, whose age range was between 26 and 45 years old. Of these, seven were men and six were woman. as the characteristics, they focused on those who: play regularly (4 participants), occasionally play (2 participants) and those who are not "players" (7 participants), but also in the fact that they have already used the virtual reality devices, (4 have already used and the rest have not).

2.2 Game Apparatus

An immersive Virtual Reality (VR) system set-up was used to evaluate 3D virtual reality environment prototype. Participants interact with a "mystery game" genre called SOIA, which was created using the UNITY® game engine version 5.5.0 (see Fig. 1).

Fig. 1. Images of the prototype developed game (SOIA).

To perform VR experience, the participants used the Virtual Reality HTC VIVE® Development Kit with one Head-Mounted Display (HMD), two controllers and two motion sensors/bases (see Fig. 2). This game was divided into three parts: initial logos, training zone (tutorial) and Hostel (gaming experience). The objects and virtual 3D environment were developed in Autodesk Maya®, and later attached to the UNITY® game engine. As for gameplay, actions and movements within the virtual environment, we use features developed in our laboratory - ErgoVR, as well as the VRTK features made available by Sysdia Solutions Ltd and Steam VR® at UNITY ASSET STORE for free.

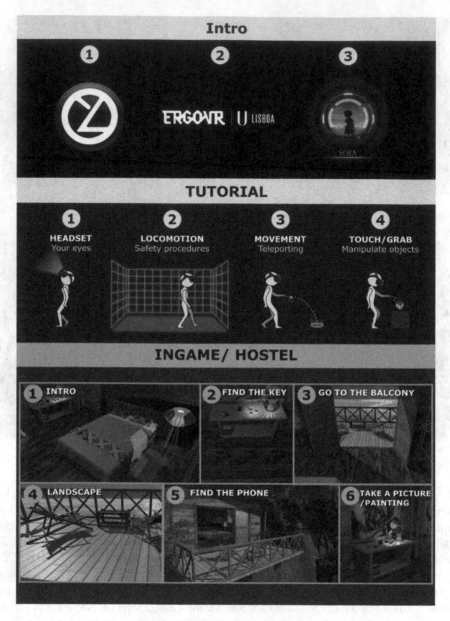

Fig. 2. Sequence of game moments.

The game was run on an ASUS® computer, with Intel® Core ™ i7 processors, 16 GB RAM and NVIDIA® GeForce® GTX 1080 M graphics.

The simulation's image frame rate, i.e., number of rendered frames per second (FPS), oscillated between 100 and 60 Hz per second.

2.3   Virtual Environment Prototype

In the first moment of the game, participants visualize the logos "Yanick Lambert" and "ERGO-VR-ULisboa". Participants are then virtually transported to the training zone where they will interact and view visual and sound information, to accomplish tasks and appreciate the VR experience:

- **Information about the use of HMD**, (his eye in the virtual world).
- **Locomotion area and limits**, as well as safety procedures (avoid colliding with objects and walls in the real world).
- **Movement** and information regarding the way he can move in the virtual world using teleporting, as well the areas which it can move or not using the HTC VIVE controller.
- **Touch, grab and manipulate** objects in the virtual world using the HTC VIVE controller.

The tutorial takes approximately 10 min to be accomplished.

After completing the tutorial, the participant is teleported to the Hostel located on the São Tomé island. At the beginning, it will have a sound introduction with a voice so that he can get a sense of where he is. As for the interactions and moments of the gaming experience, the user will have to perform the following tasks:

- **Find the gold key on the table.**
  After finding the key, an opening animation of the balcony door that is closed at the beginning will be triggered.
- **Move to the balcony.**
  On the balcony, a collision box was placed and will trigger the next sound information related with the landscape and the place (São Tomé island).
- **Find the phone.**
  In the balcony, the participant will have to locate the mobile phone that is on top of the bamboo table. He will have to grab it using one of the interaction controller and go back into the room.
- **Take a picture of the painting.**
  Again, inside the room, the user will have to position the phone as if it were taking the picture, and will immediately receive feedback corresponding to the action, through the highlight the painting frame in green tones and with a countdown so that it has the feeling that he's shooting something.
- **Information concerning the painter will be presented in 3D space as an information hologram.**
- **End of the experience.**

2.4   Measures

One usability test was conducted, to gather behavioral and subjective measures. This usability test, sought to analyze the participants' overall user experience and satisfaction with the game prototype, by assessing their subjective perceptions about their interaction with the virtual environment. To achieve the evaluation goal, the following steps were accomplished:

Self-Assessment Manikin (SAM): A non-verbal pictorial assessment technique to measures the pleasure and arousal, associated with the participants affective reaction to a wide variety of stimuli [9] in three moments (tutorial zone, in game/hostel bedroom and the balcony). The Geneva Emotion Wheel (GEW): Discrete emotion terms corresponding to emotion families that are systematically aligned in a circle. Underlying the alignment of the emotion terms are the two dimensions valence (negative to positive) and control (low to high), separating the emotions in four quadrants: Negative/low control, negative/high control, positive/low control, and positive/high control. Also, in the very center of the wheel, the response options "no emotion" and "other emotion" is offered [10]. These two methods (SAM ad GEW), was used for more accuracy in the results. The Simulator Sickness Questionnaire (SSQ): in order to evaluate to what extent, the VE prototype could be satisfactorily used by the participants and the occurrence of any Virtual Reality Induced Symptoms and Effects [6] Participants were asked to score 23 symptoms on a four-point scale. The Presence Questionnaire (PQ): this questionnaire, which was applied at the end of the simulation, intended to evaluate to what extent the participants felt present inside the VE [6]. Participants were asked to score the quality of their VE experience according to their sense of presence, and a number of factors pertaining to the VE's characteristics/system set-up, namely: sensory factors; level of realism; interaction factors; distraction factors; and display image quality. Each question was ranked using a 7-point scale, where participants indicated the strength of their agreement with the questions' statements. The last two questionnaires were applied at the end of experience after the SAM and GEW questionnaires.

2.5 Procedure

All participants will respond to a written consent form and the entire game experience will be held in the same place and under the same conditions. The experiment was performed in a room using a desktop computer, with the presence of two researchers, the head research and another that belonging to the ERGOVR laboratory. A few moments before the game experience, each participant receives the essential information about the game. Soon after, the participant will perform a pre-test using SAM and Geneva to measure the emotional state, through generic examples in order to familiarize himself with the two methods that will be applied at the end of his VR experience. Each participant will perform their game experience in approximately 20 min. After finishing the game experience, the participant will respond first to the SAM questionnaire, where we will use two scales: affective valence scale (Pleasure/Unpleasure) and the activation scale(Calm/Excited) in three different moment of the virtual experience (Tutorial, Hostel/bedroom and Hostel/balcony). For accuracy of data collected, they also will respond to the Geneva Emotion Wheel to access emotional state in a particular moment of the game experience. Then the participant will respond to the questionnaire survey, Questionnaire (A): PRESENCE and the Questionnaire (B): Simulator Sickness, and the participant will not be able to tell the next participants what happened in their experience to not affect the next and future participants.

3   Results and Discussion

The data collected for SAM emotional measures reveal that the average pleasure score was 7,7 and the average arousal was 4,5 (values between 1–9). If we look to the values in specifics moments of the game experience (see Fig. 3), we can see that the Hostel zone (bedroom and balcony) present highest value of pleasure when compared with tutorial zone. Regarding the arousal, the excitement level was higher in the tutorial zone, and in the hostel, participants presented values closer to the middle.

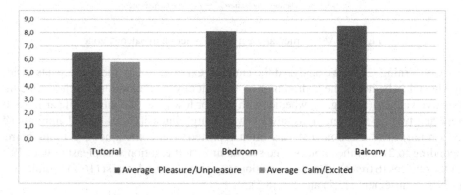

Fig. 3. SAM: average-pleasure and arousal.

Analyzing the results at specific moments in the game (see Fig. 3), we can provide a more detailed analysis. In the tutorial zone, the arousal values were close to 6 (Arousal Average = 5.8, Standard Deviation = 2.5), this is due to the fact that it is the first moment using virtual reality, is a moment of discovery, experimentation and learning. The tutorial is a practical and demanding exercise, so it activates users. The pleasure presented values close to seven (Pleasure Average = 6.5; Standard Deviation = 1.9). When teleported to the hostel/bedroom, some participants verbalized their reaction or nodded in approval (Arousal Average = 3.9; Standard Deviation = 3.1), (Pleasure Average = 8.1; Standard Deviation = 1.3). Analyzing the values of the three moments evaluated, the balcony was the one in which the values of excitement were the lowest, that is, the participants felt more calm and relaxed. This can be justified by the fact that they are contemplating the landscape and the view of the beach in line with the sound of the sea water. These results are in coherence with other studies using SAM to evaluate VR user experience [11]. In this same place the participants also chose as the area where the level of pleasure was the highest (Arousal average = 3.8, Arousal Standard Deviation = 3.3) (Pleasure Average = 8.5; Pleasure Standard Deviation = 1.1). Figure 4, shows results of the 13 participants in the balcony zone.

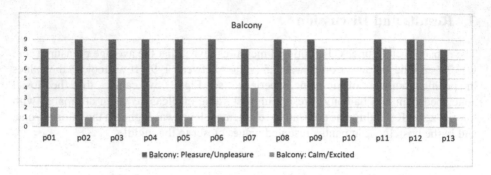

Fig. 4. SAM: participants emotional reaction in balcony zone.

Concerning GEW, we analyzed the emotion experienced by the participants inside the hostel (whether in the bedroom or on the balcony). All emotions circumscribe the positive valence (see Fig. 5), whether with high or low level of control. All participants reported two types of emotions, always with a high intensity of 4 or 5 (1 minimum/5 maximum). The emotion that was often reported was contentment, 7 times corresponding to 27% of the choices. The second most felt emotion was pleasure with 19% of the choices (6 times). The other emotions registered were: Interest (16%), Admiration (15%), Amusement (15%) and Joy (8%).

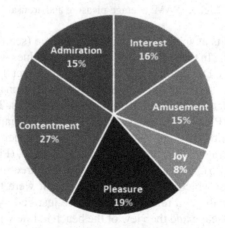

Fig. 5. Emotions reported by participants in the hostel using GEW.

As for the SSQ's, the data gathered exposes few numbers of occurrence. The presence of symptoms in SSQ is reported in four levels. Absent, light, moderate or severe. Six from the thirteen participants reported a total absence of symptoms. No one presented moderate or severe symptoms. Seven participants reported slight symptoms. Two of them reported 1 symptom, two, 2 symptoms, one 3 symptoms and 2, 7 symptoms. The Table 1 reports the frequency of each symptom for the reported light symptom. The three symptoms more often reported are difficulty concentrating.

Table 1. Reported light symptoms in SSQ.

Symptom	Light
General discomfort	1
Fatigue	2
Headache	
Salivation increasing	1
Sweeting	1
Nausea	1
Difficulty concentrating	4
"Fullness of the head"	2
Dizziness with eyes open	1
Dizziness with eyes closed	1
Vertigo	1
Stomach awareness	1
Burping	
Eyestrain	1
Difficulty focusing	3
Blurred vision	1
Eye pain	1
Eye irritation	
Watery eyes	
Dry eyes	
Burning eyes	
Double vision	
General discomfort	1

In what concerns the Presence questionnaire (PQ) the scale ranged from 1 to 7, the data gathered reveals that: (1) the participants felt highly present/immersion (Average = 5.5, Standard Deviation = 0.7); (2) the VE's sensory factors were very compelling (Average = 5.9, Standard Deviation = 0.7); (3) the VE's overall realism was also high (Average = 6.1, Standard Deviation = 0.6); (4) the VE's interaction factors were fairly good (Average = 6.1, Standard Deviation = 0.4); (5) overall, the participants were not distracted by the system set-up's devices (Average = 2.8, Standard Deviation = 0.7) and could easily concentrate on the task. If we looked at the first question related to the immersion level, "During the simulation, did you feel that you were" inside "the virtual environment?" we found that the responses tended to "always" (score 1–7), we found that most participants felt "always" "inside" the virtual world (Fig. 6).

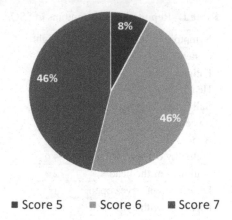

Score 5   Score 6   Score 7

Fig. 6. Most scored: first question related to the immersion level.

4   Conclusions

This paper emerged as part of the constructive process of a methodology that allows us to create an experience in virtual reality in order to seduce and arouse interest on the São Tomé and Príncipe island and some cultural aspects associated with it. As for the goal we proposed for the elaboration of this study, it was successfully achieved with feedback on the virtual environment very positive, not only from the point of view of the virtual environment created, but also from the curiosity about the island and some elements present in the virtual world. For example, one of the participants showed an interest in one of the paintings present in the bedroom, asking questions about where it could be seen and if it was for sale. The results were very positive, either from the point of view of emotional data collection through SAM and Geneva, as well as the more technical aspects related to the interaction and the virtual environment created and some aspects related to the state after the simulation.

As for the emotional aspects, the valence (pleasure) reached values close to the highest value in the scale, as well as the arousal scale revealed that the environment created a state of calm and contentment in the hostel area, especially when the participant it was in the balcony area. Regarding presence, the results show that the participants were very involved in the experience/immersion, the level of realism was also good, and the sound and visual effects present in the VR provided an even more immersive experience. Regarding the general state after the simulation, few factors were reported and even those reported were not more than slight symptom. This means that in general the interaction strategies, quality of the visual image presented as well as the actions realized in the virtual world by the user were quite fluid and with few delays in the actions performed.

Concerning the tutorial zone, two participants mentioned that the tutorial is too long. We also noticed that in some cases the participants would move their heads out of the game field. The delimitation of the area of locomotion not so close to the walls can help us to get around this problem. Already in the hostel and standing inside the bedroom with the doors closed and when the initial animation start, three participants touched the key in the inverse position to expectable, and so the animation of the key (flying) going to the door lock was not to desirable, since the participant was on his back to the door, not seeing the animation and in some cases was crossed by the key. To get around this position problem, instead of a single trigger, we can place two collision boxes, one of which triggered animation in one position and the other in another. Another method would be through a path, that is, after touching the key it would follow a path and when there was some object in its path it would bypass that object and then return to the path (a bit like the mechanics used in some car games). One of the participants also mentioned that the fact that the key has a fanciful and not a realistic animation, took some realism from its experience inside the bedroom at the beginning. On the balcony, one of the users complained about the reflection of sea water ("hurt the eyes"). Although this problem was not reported by anyone else, is necessary to consider in a next phase of this research work, by incorporating a new shader for the water reflection. Also, two participants reporting a little delay when moving the phone. This is related to the frames per second (fps) that in the future we can increase through the optimization of the virtual environment. One participant put into action a dilemma that may or may not have been reckless to the other participants, due to the fact that it had some difficulty in differentiating the emotional state on the balcony, since at the same time the user felt very calm, but at the same time he was also very excited, thus having some difficulty in choosing the corresponding emotion.

In the next stages, it will be necessary to develop a more complex game narrative, involving the creation of characters and short stories, as well the introduction of more objects in order to spread cultural aspects of São Tomé Island. The incorporation of characters and environments from the traditional tales of the São Tomé island within the virtual world, is one of the great challenges/ objectives of the main research work, as it will help to share one of the intrinsic cultural aspects of the islands, the traditional tales that were handed down from generation to generation by the elders.

Acknowledgements. A Ph.D. scholarship (SFRH/BD/129105/2017) granted to Yanick Trindade, from FCT: Fundação para a Ciência e Tecnologia (the Portuguese Science Foundation), supported this study.

Research Center-CIAUD School of Architecture ULisboa.

References

1. Seibert, G.: Camaradas, Clientes e Compadres: Colonialismo, Socialismo e Democratização em São Tomé e Príncipe, 2nd edn. Vega Editora, Lisboa (2002)
2. Robinson, P., Lück, M., Smith, S.: Tourism, 1st edn. CABI, Wallingford, Oxfordshire (2013)
3. Benea, I.: Influences of Social Media on the Tourism and Hospitality Industry. Modul Vienna University, Vienna (2014)
4. Steenjacobsen, J.: Nomadic tourism and fleeting place encounters: exploring different aspects of sightseeing. Scand. J. Hosp. Tour. **1**(2), 99–112 (2001)

5. Gibson, A., O'Rawe, M.: Virtual reality as a travel promotional tool: insights from a consumer travel fair. In: Jung, T., tom Dieck, M.Claudia (eds.) Augmented Reality and Virtual Reality. PI, pp. 93–107. Springer, Cham (2018). https://doi.org/10.1007/978-3-319-64027-3_7
6. Reis, L., Duarte, E., Rebelo, F.: Older workers and virtual environments: usability evaluation of a prototype for safety sign research. In: Soares, M., Rebelo, F. (eds.) Ergonomics in Design, pp. 279–295. CRC Press, Boca Raton (2016)
7. Zahorik, P., Jenison, R.: Presence as being-in-the-world. Presence: Teleoperators Virtual Environ. **7**(1), 78–89 (1998)
8. Tussyadiah, P., Wang, D., Jung, T., Dieck, M.: Virtual reality, presence, and attitude change: empirical evidence from tourism. Tour. Manag. **66**, 140–154 (2018)
9. Bradley, M., Lang, P.: Measuring emotion: the self-assessment manikin and the semantic differential. J. Behav. Ther. Exp. Psychiat. **25**, 49–59 (1994)
10. Sacharin, V., Schlegel, K., Scherer, K.: Geneva Emotion Wheel Rating Study. Swiss Center for Affective Sciences, University of Geneva (2012)
11. Oliveira, T., Noriega, P., Rebelo, F., Heidrich, R.: Evaluation of the relationship between virtual environments and emotions. In: Rebelo, F., Soares, M. (eds.) AHFE 2017. AISC, vol. 588, pp. 71–82. Springer, Cham (2018). https://doi.org/10.1007/978-3-319-60582-1_8

Evaluating the Benefit of Accordion Web Elements for Low Literacy Populations

Shannon Tucker[1], Kathryn Summers[2([⊠])], Tim McGowan[2], and Chris Klimas[1]

[1] University of Maryland School of Pharmacy, Baltimore, MD 21201, USA
{stucker,cklimas}@rx.umaryland.edu
[2] University of Baltimore, Baltimore, MD 21201, USA
ksummers@ubalt.edu, tim_mcgo@gmail.com

Abstract. Online applications for benefit programs typically feature large blocks of text and complicated forms, often simply converted from paper forms. While initiatives like plain language promote information accessibility, long, complicated applications can severely limit program accessibility for the populations they intend to help. In the general population, the use of optimized forms can reduce user errors and lead to shorter fixations. The use of accordion web elements has been promoted as a way to condense lengthy page content. However, there is some debate regarding the increased interaction cost to the casual user. Prior research indicates that accordion interface elements may constitute a barrier to users with low literacy skills. This eye tracking study compares accordion-based text and forms with non-accordion text and forms to measure task engagement, reading persistence, time on task, and form completion errors.

Keywords: Usability · Low literacy · Accordion web elements · Form design

1 Introduction

The National Assessment of Adult Literacy (NAAL) is designed to measure the literacy level of adults in the United States through a series of real-world activities. Results from the most recent assessment in 2003 highlight little change from previous assessments, with 43% of participants performing at the lower end of the literacy spectrum on prose literacy tasks, and 33% on document literacy tasks[1]. Adults in this range can perform only the most basic activities online, which can affect their ability to understand and complete web forms. Low literacy often appears disproportionately among the elderly, the poor, the undereducated, and racial minorities [1].

Applying for means-tested government assistance programs such as subsidized housing requires participants to read program requirements and fill out applications. People applying to these programs are more likely to be poorer and less educated than the overall population [2]. Online applications for these programs often feature large

---

[1] Prose literacy is focused on the knowledge and skills needed to complete tasks related to using information in continuous text, whereas document literacy focuses on non-continuous text [1].

© Springer International Publishing AG, part of Springer Nature 2018
A. Marcus and W. Wang (Eds.): DUXU 2018, LNCS 10920, pp. 743–755, 2018.
https://doi.org/10.1007/978-3-319-91806-8_58

blocks of text and complicated forms, simply scanned from their paper counterparts and modified for use on a web page. Long, complicated applications may severely limit accessibility for the very people these programs intend to help [3].

Low-literate web users often rely on different strategies than stronger readers when searching for information on complex web pages and forms, often leading to increased confusion, errors, and task abandonment [4, 5]. Best practices in form optimization can reduce the occurrence of errors and improve successful completion of the desired task for all users [6]. Additional research with low-literacy populations has identified design recommendations that can improve performance for this population, including larger buttons and form fields, simplifying labels, using supporting imagery, minimizing the need for scrolling, and incorporating indicators that track user progress [5, 7, 8].

Research has also shown that low-literate users are best served through the use of a linear navigation structure in web pages and forms [5, 7]. Users of all reading levels demonstrate a preference for forms that are provided in a series of chunks as opposed to a long, scrollable page [9]. Similar to chunking content in a linear sequence of pages, accordions have become a more commonly used web element for condensing lengthy pages. Accordions provide the user with a selection of headings on a single page that they can choose to expand and read. However, there is some debate about their effectiveness, suggesting they may instead increase interaction costs [10, 11]. A recent 2014 study focused on optimizing form instructions also observed lower form completion rates for low-literate users when utilizing accordion elements; these were attributed largely to the users' unfamiliarity with this type of web element [12].

While there are questions to be explored about the effectiveness of accordions in web forms, their value to potentially improve reading comprehension on standard web pages has not been examined. Research has been conducted on replacing large blocks of information with an incremental series of smaller chunks, with demonstrated benefits to a variety of users [4, 12]. It may be possible that an accordion element that is optimized for low-literate users can prove beneficial to this population.

2   Methods

2.1   Design

A mixed method observational study using eye tracking was conducted to evaluate the barrier effect and increased interaction costs of web-based accordion interfaces on text-based and form interfaces in low-literacy populations. Research goals focused on the effect of accordion web elements on:

- task persistence and success of reading and form-based tasks
- reading persistence
- minimizing peripheral distraction
- the reduction of user errors

Publicly accessible web-based instructions and public assistance forms from the Baltimore County, Maryland Housing and Urban Development Family Self Sufficiency Program (HUD) were redesigned to use an accordion interface and selected web-based form usability guidelines [9]. Initial evaluation of text instruction readability using the Flesch Reading Ease Score (FRES = 42.8) and Flesch-Kincaid Grade Level (FKGL = 12.7) indicated text was difficult to read and at a 12th US grade level [14–16][2]. While government agencies recommend using caution when assigning grade level scores and readability formulas, use of FRES and FKGL suggests difficulty for low literacy populations that could be impacted by the use of accordion web elements [15].

To reduce the context effect due to variations in literacy level between participants, a within-subjects design was used. Since this design would require the exposure of both the original and improved interface, carryover effect was a concern to researchers. To counterbalance these effects, participants were randomly assigned to one of two condition schedules (a) original interface-improved interface or (b) improved interface-original interface, with a planned two-week gap between the initial interface condition and the secondary interface exposure.

2.2 Participants

Participants were recruited for this study from a participant database maintained by the University of Baltimore. To ensure participants qualified as low literate, the Rapid Estimate of Adult Literacy in Medicine (REALM)[3] was used to ensure participants were at or below an eighth grade reading level (maximum score = 60) [14]. A total of 10 qualified participants were recruited based on historical REALM scores. Nine participants (n = 9) completed all study required observation sessions for study inclusion and met the minimum REALM threshold (<60). REALM ranges for participants in this study ranged between 36 and 57 (M = 48).

Of the 9 participants, 67% identified as female (n = 6) and 33% as male (n = 3). Of the nine participants, eight identified as African American and one as Caucasian. All reported living in the greater Baltimore-metro region. While one participant did not provide age data, reporting participants ranged from 29 to 59 (M = 50).

---

[2] The Flesch Reading Ease Score (FRES) and Flesch-Kincaid Grade Level Score (FKGL) are one of several common measures to evaluate text for readability. Calculating a score based on the total words/sentences and total syllables/words FRES and FKGL scores provide a level of difficulty and US school grade level respectively. Where FRES is measured on a range of 0–100 with 100 considered "very easy" and 0 "very confusing," scores in the 70–80 range would be considered equivalent to a 7th US school grade. The FKGL formula provides a more direct calculation of school grade equivalency by directly indicating the reading level of an equivalent US school grade. Both the FRES and FKGL are available as tools within Microsoft Word and website text analysis tools [17].

[3] The Rapid Estimate of Adult Literacy in Medicine (REALM) provides researchers a short, easy to administer assessment of literacy level. During REALM administration test participants are presented with a printed sheet of 66 words and then asked to read each word aloud. Pronunciation and comprehension is scored by a facilitator. Scores are reliably converted to a score mapped to a US grade level equivalency. While REALM is reliable in grade level mapping through 8th grade [19, 20], there is little discrimination in grade level beyond this level.

2.3 Procedure

Following recruitment via phone, participants were invited to the research location to give informed consent. Upon giving informed consent, a REALM test was administered by a research assistant to confirm literacy level was within the acceptable study limits. Participants were then invited into an observation room with one-way glass and asked to sit at a workstation with a Tobii T60 monitor for interaction with the text-based instructions and form.

Prior to the presentation of each interface, participants were presented with a 9 dot calibration screen from Tobii Pro 3.4.8 to determine the appropriate placement of eye tracking equipment and evaluate the use of corrective eye wear if present. Participants with bifocals or correctable vision without appropriate eye wear were provided access to single vision reading glasses. Following calibration, participants were given oral instructions on reading text-instructions or completing the web-based form as appropriate. Participants were instructed that they could view text-based instructions as long as they preferred. When completing the associated form, participants were instructed to complete the form to the best of their ability and indicate when they had completed the task.

2.4 Analysis

Qualitative Analysis. Qualitative analysis was conducted in a two-step process. Initial coding of observation notes and session video recordings was performed by the primary and secondary researchers [21]. This identified individual participant patterns and themes related to study research questions, including: (1) task success, (2) participant behavior, (3) reading patterns, and (4) form response patterns. Initial coding was followed by pattern coding by the secondary researcher to identify themes between participants for further analysis and discussion.

Text Instruction Interface. Evaluating task duration and end of task was determined primarily by the participant's verbal indication of task completion. However, an early end of task was indicated by the participant clicking on a page element that would prematurely end their session in real-world conditions (e.g. visiting another web page). Criteria for task success for the text instruction stimuli was based on recorded gaze data for each text instruction segment covering 90% of text area.

Form Interface. The end of the task was determined primarily by the participant's verbal indication of task completion or clicking "submit" in the case of the "improved" form interface. Criteria for task success for both the original and improved stimuli was based on a participant viewing and completing form fields in each form section as appropriate. Total time spent on form field segments was recorded for each form section.

Quantitative Analysis. Quantitative data was exported from Tobii Studio Pro 3.4.8 and analyzed in IBM SPSS v25. Measures included: (1) task success, (2) total time on task, (3) time on task by section, (4) reading persistence (text instructions), and (5) area visit duration (text instructions). Task success as defined in the qualitative review of session recordings was determined as "true" or "false" and transcribed for evaluation. Time on task and time on task by segment was recorded based on participant video timestamp codes in Tobii Studio Pro. Areas of Interest (AOIs) were created for text instruction interfaces with 5 AOIs covering page layout components (header, footer, left and right sidebars, and center content) and 11 AOIs covering section headers and section text content and paragraph sub-elements.

3 Results

3.1 Text Instruction Comparison

Task Success. Task success is divided into two components: (1) content review and (2) reading persistence. Participants who visited/fixated on all instructional content sections were considered to have successfully completed content review. Participants who fixated on paragraph text instructions within a section, were considered to have completed the reading task associated with the stimulus.

Content Review. There is no significant difference between "original" and "improved" interface content review rates (Table 1. Content review completion by participants). It is important to note that in both conditions, participants visited few sections beyond "Overview" (Table 2. Section content review by participants). This section appeared before the page fold as a default with no user intervention, making it difficult to skip under general conditions. In practical terms, this suggests that the accordion interface is no better than a plain text interface for reading tasks. However, it is important to note that the "next" button in the "improved" interface appeared below the page fold. This would require participants to scroll down the page to access this information. Since very few participants scrolled in the plain text interface, it is a reasonable assumption that they would not scroll in an accordion interface.

Table 1. Content review completion by participants (text instructions)

Condition	N	Completion	Partial completion
Original	9	22.2% (2)	77.8% (7)
Improved	9	33.3% (3)	66.7% (6)

Table 2. Section content review by participants

Condition	Overview	Eligibility	Benefits	Savings	Program
Original	9	2	2	2	2
Improved	9	4	3	3	3

Reading Persistence. Evaluating reading persistence was performed using text associated AOIs in Tobi Studio Pro. Due to an error in fixation recording, only eight (n = 8) participants were evaluated for reading persistence. Focusing specifically on the "Overview" section, participants spent less than one minute reading in the "original" (M = 25.37 s) and "improved" (M = 59.14 s) AOI fixation durations associated with header, paragraph, and bullet text. While reading time is more than double in the "improved" interface, the difference was not statistically significant t(5) = 1.29, p = 0.25).This may be due to the small sample size. However, evaluation of heat map visualizations counters any argument for a practical difference between conditions. A visual inspection of heat maps for individual participants reveals no observable density change across text for individual participants (see Figs. 1 and 2 for representative examples).

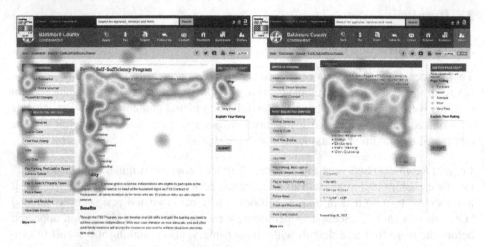

Fig. 1. Reading persistence comparison (P01)

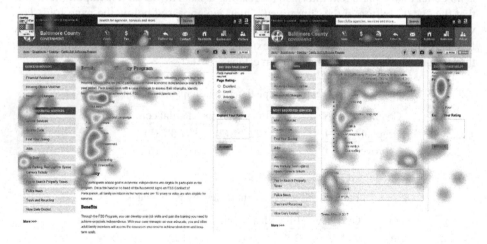

Fig. 2. Reading persistence comparison (P10)

3.2   Form Comparison

Task Success. To establish the criteria for task success in this interface group, researchers first identified all required form inputs within the form. Since no form data was collected during research sessions, participant form input was analyzed from session recordings. Participants who completed all required fields was considered as a successful completion of the form. Not visiting a section or partially completing a section was recorded as partial completion for the condition form task. While there was a marked difference between individuals who completed the improved form over the original form (Table 3. Task completion by participants), this was not statistically significant. However, in practical terms, the quality of life benefits associated with completing such forms would likely provide stronger motivation than was apparent in the lab.

Table 3. Task completion by participants (form)

Condition	N	Completion	Partial completion
Original	9	55.6% (5)	44.4% (4)
Improved	9	88.9% (8)	11.1% (1)

Time on Task. On average participants took approximately 17–21 min to complete the "original" form and 10–15 min to complete the "improved" form (Table 4. Total time on task). While this represented a 31.69% reduction in total form completion time, this difference was not statistically significant $t(8) = 1.967$, $p = 0.085$.

Table 4. Total time on task (seconds)

Condition	N	Mean	Median	Std. deviation	Std. error mean	Min	Max	Mean percent improved
Original	9	879.00	824.00	349.17	116.39	348	1302	
Improved	9	600.44	450.00	289.99	96.66	264	1019	−31.69%

Observed Form Issues. The increased rate of partial completion by individuals in the "original" form condition, raises questions regarding form attributes that may contribute non-completion. Further examination of performance in more detail (Fig. 3) within each subsection confirms the presence of form issues when compared with the "improved" condition.

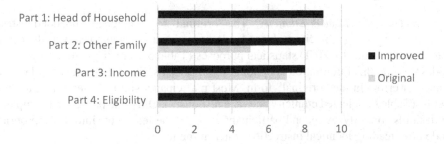

Fig. 3. Participants completing form sections

Computer Skills. As is often the case with participants with low literacy skills, there appeared to be a lack of familiarity with basic computing tasks. Eight out of 9 participants had form completion errors associated with computer skills. Seven of 9 participants had inconsistent or no use of capitalization throughout the form. Ability to back space and correct errors was an issue for two participants. Mouse issues also resulted in moderator intervention for four participants due to clicking the right mouse button or having difficulties clicking into form fields. Additionally, two participants used the browser BACK button in an attempt to navigate through the "improved" form. This suggested the accordion interface may have been a new feature that they did not understand. Thus, they may have previously encountered a form that allowed use of the back button to traverse form sections, or it may reflect a general mental model that the "back" button should return you to a previous screen in a web interface. Due to the stimulus design using Tobii Studio, use of the browser BACK button resulted in a blank screen, requiring moderator assistance to return to the test session.

Skipped Questions/Sections. When presented with the "original" interface, participants were presented with the entire first page of the fillable PDF form, presenting sections for head of household, other family members, and income. This is contrasted with the "improved" interface, presenting only the head of household section. Manual review of participant behavior during this task revealed that two participants (one in each task condition) stopped progress on the form after they completed all on-screen elements. While the "original" form included the word "over" in the page footer and the Adobe Acrobat interface listed this page as 1 of 2, these elements did not provide enough indication that an additional page was present. The common practice of converting a paper form into a fillable PDF appeared to be problematic for other participants as well, since at least two participants clicked on the "over" text to advance to page two before proceeding to scroll the page manually.

Similarly, in the "improved" condition, the presence of the "next" button and clickable accordion headings provided no indication to one participant that additional data was required in the form. Despite looking at the headings for additional accordion sections, this participant did not look at or click the "next" button. It should also be noted that only one participant clicked the headers in the accordion-based form to navigate between each section. All other participants used the "next step" button to progress linearly through the form.

Unclear Question: Race & Ethnicity. The "original" form included embedded instructions for completing ethnicity and race fields, requiring applicants to convert their input into numeric codes for HUD statistical purposes (Table 5. Statistical ethnicity and race codes). While this information is optional for applicants, these fields generated significant user errors in the "original" form. Most participants simply entered text in these fields. (Table 6. Selected ethnicity and race responses). Only one participant completed both fields correctly. A second participant changed the text entry into the appropriate code after reading identical instructions later in the form.

This issue was eliminated in the "improved" form by the inclusion of drop down fields. Thus, the improvement in accuracy between the "original" and "improved" forms for these fields reflects a difference between a converted paper form and a web form, rather than a full-length form versus an accordion layout.

Table 5. Statistical ethnicity and race codes.

Ethnicity	Race
1 - Hispanic	1 - White
2 - Not hispanic	2 - African American
	3 - American Indian
	4 - Asian
	5 - Hawaiian Native/Pacific Islander

Table 6. Selected ethnicity and race responses

Ethnicity	Race
"n/a"	"black"
"noneb"	"b"
"e"	"a m"
"baptist"	"bNo"

Unclear Question: Other Members of Household. Two participants misunderstood the purpose of this section. Instead of entering family members (or leaving blank), they filled in their own information into the form for a second time.

4 Discussion

4.1 Text Instructions

Overall, results indicate there is no difference between plain text and accordion web pages for text-based information in low literacy users. While there are numeric differences in time spent in sections and reading behavior, the lack of significance and short time spent reading raises questions regarding the reading behavior of the participants in general and in relation to this study. With the small population it is difficult to determine trends and behaviors based on REALM scores and reading behavior. It is likely that some participants with REALM scores below 45 typically avoid reading tasks [22]. While not a part of the research aims of this study, participant time spent searching off task areas of the interface (e.g. header, sidebars, etc.) was observed, as is consistent with previous research into online navigational and reading behaviors associated with low literacy [5, 12, 22].

4.2 Form

Similar to the text instructions there was no significant differences between stimuli conditions. However, the increase in successful application completion is notable, and the stakes for successful completion of this type of form are high. Given the small sample size, it is difficult to say if this improved success rate was attributed to the use of accordions or was simply the result of a native web-based form rather than a PDF, but other research confirms the benefit of "chunking" information for this population [5, 22].

Our analysis shows that utilizing drop down fields as a substitute for text fields for race/ethnicity improves data entry speed and accuracy of user data entry for fields that require standardized input. While not discussed in depth in this study, other form improvements that would be easy to implement in a web-based form are likely to improve task speed. For example, clear separation between the optional form fields and required fields is likely to improve task speed. Including a radio button on the first accordion section that skips the other members of household section if it is not relevant to the user would further increase form completion speed. Additionally, ensuring application or database level validation and data transformation routines would compensate for various data formatting issues without burdening end users.

5   Implications

Despite the lack of significant findings, this study does confirm the lack of reading in this population that underscores the need for continued investigation, as part of the effort to find structures that support and motivate low literacy populations to read without disenfranchising others.

The intentionally limited application of best practices for form design was intended to highlight the potential impact of minimal improvements to the (unfortunately frequent) deployment of long PDF forms converted from paper. However, additional work should compare forms divided accordion sections versus a division into a series of short pages. Similarly, a long but more web-optimized form could be compared to an accordion form with similar optimizations.

6   Limitations

6.1   Participant Motivation

Based on participant behavior during sessions, it is unclear if participant motivation was a factor in task performance. During observation sessions, 2 participants stopped to take phone calls during the session with one participant claiming "I'll be out in 15 or 20 min" despite only just beginning the text-based instruction task. One participant appeared to fall asleep momentarily in an observation session. While this may be behavior that would occur naturally outside of the laboratory setting when completing similar tasks, it is unclear if the motivation of applying for needed benefits would increase attentiveness and persistence.

6.2   Comparable Designs

Text-Based Design. While the "improved" text-based instruction interface included header, footer, and sidebar elements, the lack of interactive features (e.g. active links and a working feedback form) changed the participant interaction with the web interface. This required researchers to closely monitor participant behavior and make a determination when a task ended.

Form Design. While the aim of the study was to evaluate the impact accordion interfaces have on reading and form completion in low-literacy populations, the creation of the "improved" web-based form also incorporated some improvements based on web-based form usability guidelines [13]. Specifically, the use of drop down menus for ethnicity and race fields and visual formatting imperfections in the "improved" form limit the ability to attribute improvements to the accordion interface.

6.3 Eye Tracking Configuration

Areas of Interest. While Tobii Studio Pro 3.4.8 supports both static and dynamic areas of interest (AOIs), the ability of the software to adapt to scrolling web-based content is limited to static areas of interest using a consistent interface. However, the use of accordion web elements introduces dynamic interface changes within a single page. The changing interface requires the use of either dynamic AOIs to encapsulate changes in the interface or changing static AOIs to account for page scrolling. Since one format of AOIs could not universally capture interface components, approaches were stimulus specific.

Text Instruction Interfaces. The short text passages within each accordion section resulted in an interface that required no scrolling to read text instructions at 100% magnification. Despite the ability for participants to scroll and view footer information, only 1 out of 8 participants did so. This required re-adjustment of AOI placement for one participant, creating a slight mismatch of comparison data for header AOIs across interfaces.

Form Interfaces. The close spacing of the "original" PDF text form and the close proximity of AOI areas did not provide enough spacing between header and form input elements to reliably distinguish fixations between sections. Additional consideration is needed establishing protocols for comparison between divergent stimulus sources.

Supporting Magnification. Eye tracking best practices necessitates the use of web stimulus at 100% magnification level to allow comparable interfaces across a range of participants. Undiagnosed vision issues and lack of appropriate eye wear in aging low literacy populations may contribute to lack of motivation or attention during reading tasks. However, limiting participants only to individuals with normal or correctible to normal vision with single vision lenses would almost eliminate the ability to research in this population. This raises questions about appropriate protocol for eye tracking in low literacy and older populations. While qualitative and other observational approaches provide an avenue for user research with populations, limiting the use of eye tracking only to populations that "track well" ultimately limits the transferability of data to general populations. Finding new approaches that moderate the technical limitations of eye tracking equipment with procedures that allow for more flexible evaluation of screen-based interfaces efficiently is an area for future exploration.

Acknowledgements. The authors would like to thank Rachel Sherard and Anna Haraseyko for assistance with data collection and participant management. Additional thanks are made to Eric Wronsky, Kate Coats, Rachel Sherard, Morgan Denner, Suzanne Royer, Cheryl Lynn Daniel, and Walt Livingston for their work on preliminary pilot studies leading this research.

References

1. Kutner, M., Greenberg, E., Jin, Y., Paulsen, C.: The health literacy of America's adults: results from the 2003 national assessment of adult literacy (NCES 2006-483). U.S. Department of Education. National Center for Education Statistics, Washington, D.C. (2006)
2. Irving, S.K., Loveless, T.A.: Dynamics of economic well-being: participation in government programs, 2009–2012: who gets assistance. Household Economic Studies, pp. 1–29 (2015)
3. Posada, R.H., Cano, T.C., Rodríguez, J.A.: Accessibility in eGovernment, pp. 1–2. ACM Press (2014). https://doi.org/10.1145/2662253.2662327
4. Kodagoda, N., Wong, W., Kahan, N.: Behaviour characteristics: low and high literacy users information seeking on social service websites. In: Proceedings of the 10th International Conference NZ Chapter of the ACM's Special Interest Group on Human Computer Interaction, pp. 13–16. ACM (2009). https://doi.org/10.1145/1577782.1577785
5. Summers, K., Wu, J., Abela, C., Souza, R., Langford, J.: Designing web-based forms for users with lower literacy skills. In: Proceedings of the American Society for Information Science and Technology, pp. 1–12 (2007). https://doi.org/10.1002/meet.14504301174
6. Seckler, M., Heinz, S., Bargas-Avila, J.A., Opwis, K., Tuch, A.N.: Designing usable web forms: empirical evaluation of web form improvement guidelines, pp. 1275–1284. ACM Press (2014). https://doi.org/10.1145/2556288.2557265
7. Chaudry, B.M., Connelly, K.H., Siek, K.A., Welch, J.L.: Mobile interface design for low-literacy populations. In: Proceedings of the 2nd ACM SIGHIT International Health Informatics Symposium, pp. 91–100. ACM (2012). https://doi.org/10.1145/2110363.2110377
8. Hill, J., Simha, R.: Designing a literacy-based mobile application for adult learners, pp. 3076–3083. ACM Press (2016). https://doi.org/10.1145/2851581.2892397
9. Wang, Y.C., Yueh, H.P.: The effect of length in employment sites' web form design on user preferences. J. Libr. Inf. Stud. **12**(1), 109–134 (2014). https://doi.org/10.6182/jlis.2014.12(1).109
10. Appleseed, J.: Form usability: the pitfalls of inline accordion and tab designs, 21 October 2014. https://baymard.com/blog/accordion-and-tabdesign
11. Loranger, H.: Accordions for complex website content on desktops, 18 May 2014. https://www.nngroup.com/articles/accordions-complex-content/
12. Alton, N.T., Rinn, C., Summers, K., Straub, K.: Using eye-tracking and form completion data to optimize form instructions. In: IEEE International Professional Communication Conference (IPCC), pp. 1–7. IEEE (2014). https://doi.org/10.1109/ipcc.2014.7020389
13. Bargas-Avila, J.A., Brenzikofer, O., Roth, S.P., Tuch, A.N., Orsini, S., Opwis, K.: Simple but crucial user interfaces in the world wide web: introducing 20 guidelines for usable web form design. In: User interfaces. InTech (2010)
14. Kincaid, J.P., Fishburne Jr., R.P., Rogers, R.L., Chissom, B.S.: Derivation of new readability formulas (automated readability index, fog count and flesch reading ease formula) for navy enlisted personnel (No. RBR-8-75). Naval Technical Training Command Millington TN Research Branch (1975)

15. Si, L., Callan, J.: A statistical model for scientific readability. In: Proceedings of the Tenth International Conference on Information and Knowledge Management, pp. 574–576. ACM, October 2001. https://doi.org/10.1145/502585.502695
16. Awal, D.H., Mills, C.: Cosmetic facial surgery: are online resources reliable and do patients understand them? Br. J. Oral Maxillofac. Surg. 6(2), 124–128 (2018). https://doi.org/10.1016/j.bjoms.2017.12.011
17. READABLE. https://readable.io
18. Centers for Medicare & Medicaid Services Tool Kit Part 7 - Using Readability Formulas. https://www.cms.gov/Outreach-and-Education/Outreach/WrittenMaterialsToolkit/ToolkitPart07.html
19. Davis, T.C., Long, S.W., Jackson, R.H., Mayeaux, E.J., George, R.B., Murphy, P.W., Crouch, M.A.: Rapid estimate of adult literacy in medicine: a shortened screening instrument. Fam. Med. 25, 391–395 (1993)
20. Alqudah, M., Johnson, M., Cowin, L., George, A.: Measuring health literacy in emergency departments. J. Nurs. Educ. Pract. 4, 1–10 (2014). https://doi.org/10.5430/jnep.v4n2p1
21. Saldaña, J. (2015). The Coding Manual for Qualitative Researchers, p. 118. Sage, Thousand Oaks
22. Summers, K., Summers, M.: Reading and navigational strategies of web users with lower literacy skills. In: Proceedings of the American Society for Information Science and Technology, vol. 42 (2005). https://doi.org/10.1002/meet.1450420179

Research on Interface of Large-Scale Equipment Network Management System Based on User Experience

Lei Wu[⊠], Lijun Mou, and Yao Su

School of Mechanical Science and Engineering,
HuaZhong University of Science and Technology,
Wuhan 430074, People's Republic of China
lei.wu@hust.edu.cn

Abstract. This paper reports on an experimental study on interface design to measure the mechanism of user experience in large-scale equipment network management system. Based on human factors and cognitive psychology theory, we conducted a comparative research study. Prototypes of the interface were designed based on the two types of information layout which were undergoing 5-point Likert questionnaire method to evaluation the user experience of the users. The main findings of this study were as follows: (1) we found that the interface improvement before (material A) and improved interface (material B) had significant differences on user experience in each level; (2) the improved interface (material B) has a significant better effect on user experience compare to improvement interface before (material A) ($P < 0.05$). (3) The user background has no significant difference on user experience ($P > 0.05$). The research results can help us to deeply understand the design of user interface in the complex industrial interface scenarios.

Keywords: User interface · Information visualization
Experimental evaluation · User experience

1 Introduction

With the rapid increase in the large amount of information and the explosive growth of large amounts of data, this has begun to give us more information to choose from, which has also led to dramatic changes in our information needs. First of all, the aesthetic needs of information were more pressing. The aesthetic of information is related to the pleasures of the user's reading of information. Secondly, the information content needs to attract users, allowing users to be attracted by the information during the reading process. The information needs to be distinctive and attractive so that the user can more deeply understand the information and reflect the information expressed in the process of cognition. In this paper, information visualization research is mainly from the user experience and psychology theory, how to provide users with the better information visualization. Human-computer interaction design should fully consider the problem from the perspective of the user, so it is very important to define the role of the user in the communication of information and the needs of the user in the information transmission.

© Springer International Publishing AG, part of Springer Nature 2018
A. Marcus and W. Wang (Eds.): DUXU 2018, LNCS 10920, pp. 756–767, 2018.
https://doi.org/10.1007/978-3-319-91806-8_59

Faced with such a huge user needs and market competition, intelligent industrial monitoring systems urgently need to be innovative design to attract users in terms of function, aesthetic and interaction. User Experience is the subjective experience of a product or information system when the user is using it. For the user group of intelligent industrial monitoring and control system, the commonalities of the user experience are that the user can use the clear semantics while having the aesthetic. User-centered design and evaluation is to put the user in the first place in every stage of the design, in order to achieve maximum service for target users.

This paper discusses the role of user experience in equipment management system and how to improve user experience. Through the research and analysis, the paper summarizes the user requirements and the design points, through the visual design and experimental evaluation to improve human-computer interaction system of the equipment management. As shown in Fig. 1.

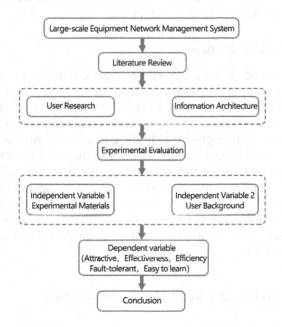

Fig. 1. The theoretical framework of this study.

2   Literature Review

2.1   User Experience

In the development of user experience, the research began in the 1990s by American psychologist Cognis Norman [1]. He thinks a good product should meet the user's without boring the user and the product should be simple, elegant and pleasant to the user. Alben (1996) argues that user experience has permeated all aspects of users and interactions, including how users feel at the process of using, understanding of interactions or products [2]. Wikipedia (2009) point on that all emotions and experiences that users generate when using a product or system are called user experiences [3]. Nielsen Norman Group believes that user experience actually covers the needs of users in all aspects of engineering, marketing, graphic, industrial design and interactive design. The design of product and service interactions should be tailored to meet the needs of users in all aspects. We want to make users feel satisfied with the use and possession of a product, it must be combined with the elements of multiple areas to consider and design, and ultimately can be presented to the user's design. The IOS (2010) standard defines user experience as "people's perceptions and responses to products or systems or services that they use or expect to use [4]. The earliest user experience concept is mainly for the user experience of the product [5]. However, with the development of the Internet and the advent of the big data era, the user experience has gradually been applied to the Internet design. Product development and design must meet the needs of the vast majority of users. How to make users feel satisfied, first of all we should recognize who is the target user.

2.2 Information Visualization

Information visualization is mainly to provide users with a way to quickly access and understand the information [6]. Visualization realizes the visualization of abstract data through the combination of the color levels of the graphic icons. The abstract data includes both numerical values and non-numeric numerical values [7]. With the continuous development of information visualization, it has now permeated many industries, such as scientific research, internet interface design, data mining and digital library [8].

In the human-computer interaction interface, the basic principles of interaction design are formed by refining the common features of different interfaces [9]. Excellent design must follow the basic principles of interactive design. Larry Tesler argues that there are always some complications in the design. These complications exist in every aspect of the design. These complications cannot be simplified and must be converged in a reasonable way [10].

3   User Research and Information Architecture

3.1   User Research

Each product should have its own target user groups, delineated a relatively fixed part of the group, it is necessary to conduct their research analysis, the main purpose of the product is to meet the needs of the users. Building a reasonable persona is an important part of the design process. When using a product, there are usually novices, skilled and general types of users. Most of the users are general level. Design should follow the general level of users. In this paper, two-character roles are constructed through user research and analysis. persona 1(Xiao Xiao) is a student, the main requirement is to make an appointment and use the device, persona 2(Zhang Lin) is an administrator, the main requirement is to process student appointment and handle machine faults, as shown in Fig. 2.

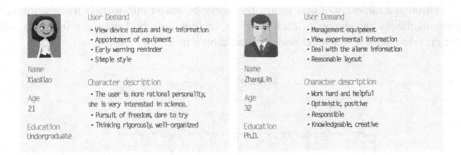

Fig. 2. Persona cards

Through the construction of user roles, the needs of different groups of users are clarified so as to facilitate the construction of subsequent system function frameworks.

3.2   Information Architecture

Through literature review and character cards establishment, the research can clarify the user's problems encountered in various stages of use, in view of these issues for equipment management system interface design, the system is divided into four major functional modules, reservation management, equipment management, data management, system settings. The main function of the reservation management is to provide a reservation for students, the administrator can deal with the reservation information and a view of the history reservation information. The equipment management function can monitor the status of the device, and it can view the device fault information and the running log. Data management functions can be used for data retrieval and uploading reports. System setting functions can manage the information of equipment and personnel, as shown in Fig. 3.

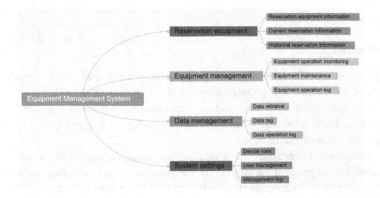

Fig. 3. Information architecture of the equipment management system

Through a summary of user needs, this paper builds an information framework and presents the layout features of each function, including each of the main interface and the corresponding lower level interface, as shown in Fig. 4.

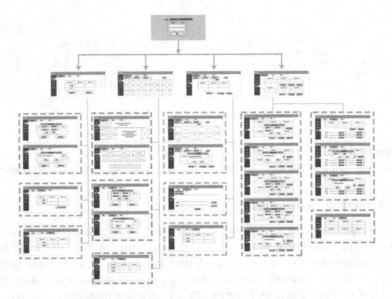

Fig. 4. Wireframe of the equipment management system

This paper summarizes the function and style of the system interface design based on literature review, user research and information architecture. In order to evaluate the difference between interface improvement before (material A) and improved interface (material B), this paper carried out the experimental evaluation, through the experimental analysis to evaluate the user experience.

4   Research Method

4.1   Definition

The experiment was a within-group design, all participants were tested the two experimental materials. We counterbalanced the experiment stimuli using a random method to compensate for learning effects. Participants were asked to complete tasks in random order. Each task was conducted one time for each participant. During each task, there are 15 s of break time.

The independent variables in this research were information layout and user background. The dependent variable is user experience which was measured in 5-point Likert questionnaire. Independent variables: (1) The information layout: the experimental materials had two levels: interface improvement before (material A) and improved interface (material B). (2) User background: user background had two levels: mechanical background group and design background group. Dependent variables: The user experience score used the five evaluation indexes of IOS9241-11 which were attraction, effectiveness, efficiency, fault tolerance and easy to learn.

4.2 Hypotheses

The hypotheses of this study are as follows:

H1: Information layout significantly affects the user experience.
H2: User background significantly affects the user experience.

4.3 Participants

A total of 30 undergraduate and graduate students at School of Mechanical Science and Engineering of HuaZhong University of Science and Technology were randomly selected to participate in this experiment, 13 male and 17 female and aged 18–35, which female of subjects accounted for 56.7%, male subjects were 43.3%. The mechanical background group and design background group each consisted of 15 people. All participants were the right-hand user. All participants had normal or corrected-to-normal color vision, 4 participants wore glasses and 3 of them wore contact lenses. None of the participants had prior eye surgeries or eye problems.

4.4 Material

The experiment used the HUST advanced manufacturing and technology experiment center equipment network management system as the experimental material, the materials were shown in a 14 in. LCD Monitor (16:10, 1366 * 768 pixels), the experimental material was designed by Axure interaction prototype, as shown in Fig. 5.

Material A   Material B

Fig. 5. Interface improvement before (material A) and improved interface (material B)

4.5 Procedure

Participants sat in front of the monitor in chairs set at a distance of about 40–50 cm. Desk and monitor position and height was fixed. The chair was adjustment to fit participant's natural angles of elbow and knee. Test environment was a quiet laboratory without interference and noise. The room was artificially illuminated and only a minimum of objects was contained inside. Participants were instructed to switch off their mobile phones to reduce possible distractions during the experiment. Before the experiment began, participants were asked to read an introduction of the experiment requirements and then sign the "experimental consent". Next, they read a short manual about the experiment stimuli to insure they were able to understand and solve the given task. Then, participants were asked to operate on the experimental material for typical tasks. After the experiment, participants were asked to complete the questionnaire immediately. A total of 60 questionnaires were collected after the experiment.

4.6   Experiment Task

Task 1: First, the user logs in to the system, and then enter the device status page, click device A-00001 to enter the device parameter page, and confirm the temperature of the device at the third node, as shown in Fig. 6.

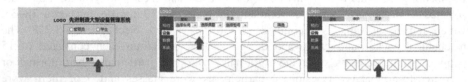

Fig. 6. Flow chart of task 1

Task 2: The user switches the main menu page, enters the data management page, clicks the data tag, enters the upload data page, and uploads the experimental data, as shown in Fig. 7.

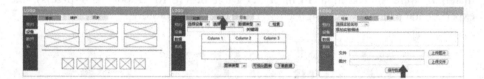

Fig. 7. Flow chart of task 2

5   Results and Discussion

Using IBM SPSS Statistics analysis, the results were as follows:

5.1   The Descriptive Analysis

Using descriptive analysis of SPSS, the following data results are obtained. Through the data and the graph, it can be seen that in the case of different independent variables, the variables of attractiveness, effectiveness, efficiency, fault tolerance, all showed significant differences. The score of the improved interface (material B) was higher than that of the interface improvement before (material A) in all indexes. Among them, the difference between attractiveness and easy-to-learn scores is the largest, indicating that the aesthetic level of the improved interface (material B) is obviously better than that of the interface improvement before (material A); the improved layout of the interface is reasonable and the descriptive text is added which makes it easier for users to learn and use the interface as shown in Table 1 and Fig. 8.

Table 1. Descriptive analysis of dependent variables of experimental materials

		N	Mean	SD	Lower limit	Upper limit
Attractive	Improvement before	30	1.567	.6261	1.333	1.800
	Improved	30	4.333	.6609	4.087	4.580
	Total	60	2.950	1.5341	2.554	3.346
Effectiveness	Improvement before	30	2.533	.8996	2.197	2.869
	Improved	30	4.267	.7849	3.974	4.560
	Total	60	3.400	1.2101	3.087	3.713
Efficiency	Improvement before	30	2.267	.9072	1.928	2.605
	Improved	30	4.233	.7279	3.962	4.505
	Total	60	3.250	1.2839	2.918	3.582
Fault-tolerant	Improvement before	30	1.667	.6609	1.420	1.913
	Improved	30	3.133	.8193	2.827	3.439
	Total	60	2.400	1.0448	2.130	2.670
Easy to learn	Improvement before	30	1.567	.7279	1.295	1.838
	Improved	30	4.167	.8339	3.855	4.478
	Total	60	2.867	1.5235	2.473	3.260

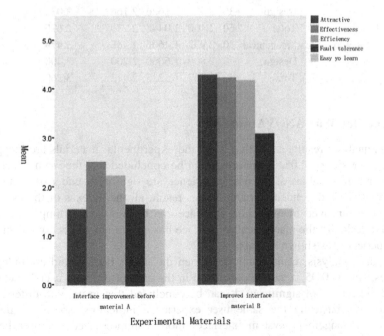

Fig. 8. Bar chart analysis of experimental material independent variables (Color figure online)

It can be seen from the data and the graph that under the circumstances that the users' background variables are different, the variables of attractiveness, effectiveness, efficiency, fault tolerance and easy to learn have corresponding changes. In the circumstances of different users' background, The variables in the indicators of the score difference is not obvious, the difference is small, which attractiveness, effectiveness, efficiency and easy to learn the four scores, the design professional scores were lower than the mechanical professional score, we can see that the design professionals are more demanding in aesthetics, effectiveness, efficiency and easy to learn, and mechanical professional have higher requirements for fault tolerance as shown in Table 2 and Fig. 9.

Table 2. Descriptive analysis of dependent variable in user experience

		N	Mean	SD	Lower limit	Upper limit
Attractive	Mechanical	30	3.000	1.3391	2.500	3.500
	Design	30	2.900	1.7291	2.254	3.546
	Total	60	2.950	1.5341	2.554	3.346
Effectiveness	Mechanical	30	3.467	1.1366	3.042	3.891
	Design	30	3.333	1.2954	2.850	3.817
	Total	60	3.400	1.2101	3.087	3.713
Efficiency	Mechanical	30	3.300	1.1788	2.860	3.740
	Design	30	3.200	1.3995	2.677	3.723
	Total	60	3.250	1.2839	2.918	3.582
Fault-tolerant	Mechanical	30	2.200	.8867	1.869	2.531
	Design	30	2.600	1.1626	2.166	3.034
	Total	60	2.400	1.0448	2.130	2.670
Easy to learn	Mechanical	30	2.933	1.4606	2.388	3.479
	Design	30	2.800	1.6060	2.200	3.400
	Total	60	2.867	1.5235	2.473	3.260

5.2 The One-Way ANOVA Analysis

The data analysis results show that when the experimental materials are independent variables, the sig $\leq$ 0.05. Therefore, it can be concluded that the main effects of the five dependent variables of the user experience are significant under different experimental material independent variables. As a result, all the indexes of the user experience of the improved man-machine interface can be significantly improved, and the improved design of the man-machine interface has a significant effect of enhancing the user experience, as shown in Table 3.

The data analysis results show that when the user's background are independent variables, sig $\geq$ 0.05, it can be concluded in the case of different users' background, the main effect is not significant. It can be concluded that users with different backgrounds have basically the same user experience indicators, so in the design of equipment management system interface, more common needs in user behaviors should be considered, as shown in Table 4.

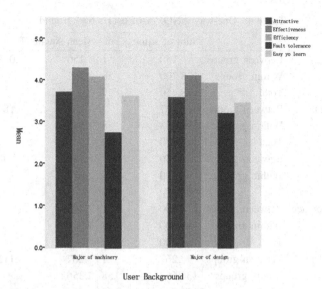

User Background

Fig. 9. Bar chart analysis of user background variables (Color figure online)

Table 3. One-way ANOVA of experimental materials

		Sum of squares	df	Mean square	F	sig
Attractive	Between groups	114.817	1	114.089	277.089	.00
	Within groups	24.033	58	.414		
	Total	138.850	59	45.067		
Effectiveness	Between groups	45.067	1	.713	63.239	.00
	Within groups	41.333	58			
	Total	86.400	59			
Efficiency	Between groups	58.017	1	58.017	85.768	.00
	Within groups	39.233	58	.676		
	Total	97.250	59			
Fault-tolerance	Between groups	32.267	1	32.267	58.241	.00
	Within groups	32.133	58	.554		
	Total	64.400	59			
Easy to learn	Between groups	101.400	1	101.400	165.512	.00
	Within groups	35.533	58	.613		
	Total	136.933	59			

Table 4. One-way ANOVA of user's background

		Sum of squares	df	Mean square	F	sig
Attractive	Between groups	.150	1	.150	.063	.803
	Within groups	138.700	58	2.391		
	Total	138.850	59			
Effectiveness	Between groups	.267	1	.267	.180	.673
	Within groups	86.133	58	1.485		
	Total	86.400	59			
Efficiency	Between groups	.150	1	.150	.090	.766
	Within groups	97.100	58	1.674		
	Total	97.250	59			
Fault-tolerance	Between groups	2.400	1	2.400	2.245	.139
	Within groups	62.000	58	1.069		
	Total	64.400	59			
Easy to learn	Between groups	.267	1	.267	.113	.738
	Within groups	136.667	58	2.356		
	Total	136.993	59			

6 Conclusions

Through quantitative analysis of user experience and descriptive analysis and one-way analysis of variance, this paper draws the following conclusions:

(1) The experimental material independent variables have significant differences in five evaluation indexes of user experience, with sig values both less than or equal to 0.05. Therefore, it can be concluded that the user experience score of the improved interface (material B) is significantly different from that interface improvement before (material A). At the same time, with the descriptive analysis of the chart can be learned, improved interface (material B) score of each index was significantly higher than interface improvement before (material A).

(2) The user background variables have no significant differences in the five evaluation indexes of user experience, sig $\geq$ 0.05, therefore, it can be concluded that there is no significant difference in the user interface between the user ratings. Therefore, the design of equipment management system interface should pay more attention to the common design of the user's cognitive behavior.

(3) There are some limitations in this paper. The number of participants in the questionnaire is Inadequate, and most of them are students of HuaZhong University of Science and Technology, so the data are limited. In this experiment, two tasks are carried out, and the tasks are not comprehensive enough, and some of the functions of the system have not been evaluated. In future research, eye movement and electroencephalogram can be added to the experiment to obtain more accurate results.

Acknowledgments. The research financial supports from the Natural Science Youth Foundation of Hubei Province (2017CFB276) and CES-King Far Excellent Young Scholar Joint Research Funding (CES-KF-2016-2018).

References

1. Norman, D., Miller, J., Henderson, A.: What you see, some of what's in the future, and how we go about doing it: HI at Apple Computer. In: Conference Companion on Human Factors in Computing Systems, p. 155. ACM (1996)
2. Alben, L.: Quality of experience. Interactions **3**, 11–15 (1996)
3. Wikipedia Homepage. https://en.wikipedia.org/wiki/User_experience_design. Accessed 11 Jan 2018
4. ISO 9241-210:2010: Ergonomics of human-system interaction—Part 210: human-centered design for interactive systems. Directly by ISO (2010)
5. Rosenfeld, L., Moville, P.: Information Architecture for the World Wide Web, 2nd edn. O'Reilly Media, Inc., Sebastopol (2002)
6. Lewis John, L., Casello Jeffrey, M.: Effective environmental visualization for urban planning and design: interdisciplinary reflections on a rapidly evolving technology. J. Urban Technol. **19**(3), 85–106 (2012)
7. Ware, C.: Information Visualization Perception for Design, 2nd edn. Morgan Kaufmann Press, San Francisco (2004)
8. Manovich, L.: The Language of New Media. MIT Press, Massachusetts (2001)
9. Rouse, W.B., Morris, N.M.: On looking into the black box: prospects and limits in the search for mental models. Psychol. Bull. **100**(3), 349 (1986)
10. Tesler, L.: Law of conservation of complexity. http://en.wikipedia.org/. Accessed 7 Jan 2018

Design of Human-Machine Interface System in Inverter Spot Welding

Yancong Zhu[✉] and Wei Zhou

Beijing Normal University, Beijing, China
Yancong.zhu@bnu.edu.cn

Abstract. With the rapid development of chip technology, the control demand increasingly complex in the field of digital inverter welding power. Researches on precise control of energy conversion are developed and can meet the needs of a variety of welding process. But with the continuous improvement of user experience, the early HMI (Human Machine Interface) has been unable to meet the demands. Aiming at high frequency inverter spot welding, a human-machine interface system, with PIC32MX764F128L microprocessor as the main chip is designed. The system includes communication interface, data storage interface, monitor and alarm interface. It can realize the setting, modification, monitor and storage for welding parameters by the LCD touch screen. All the design is based on the inverter spot welding current and welding technology. It proves that the human-machine interface system is stable, easy-input and strong anti-interference ability.

Keywords: HMI · Inverter spot welding · Human-machine interface
PIC32MX764F128L microprocessor · LCD touch screen

1 Introduction

Resistance spot welding (RSW) is a very important material welding technology, which is widely used in various industrial sectors. The assembly method has the characteristics of high production efficiency, low cost, material saving and easy automation [1]. It is widely used in aerospace, electronics, automobile and other industrial fields. Within a short span of time for the nugget formation the weldment material undergoes expanding, yielding and melting process, and diverse disturbing factors and their interactions influence the welding process, so it is difficult to accurately control the quality of spot welding. For these problems above, high frequency inverter spot welding is applied. The inverter spot welding power supply is one of the important directions for the development of resistance spot welding power supply [2].

High power high frequency resistance spot welding is widely used in automobile industry. It is estimated that there needs 4000–6000 resistance welding spots in one car produced [3, 4]. More and more of the resistance welding machine has been in the direction of digital development. It makes the welding quality more reliable on the one hand. On the other hand the application of the human-machine interaction interface makes resistance welding machine been easier and more intuitive to use [5].

© Springer International Publishing AG, part of Springer Nature 2018
A. Marcus and W. Wang (Eds.): DUXU 2018, LNCS 10920, pp. 768–777, 2018.
https://doi.org/10.1007/978-3-319-91806-8_60

In the research field of digital inverter spot welding machine, the man-machine interface is an important part of the welding machine, and the digitalization of interface is very important for the whole spot welding system. The main function of the interaction is to accomplish the input and display of welding parameters of the spot welding control system, which can accomplish energy conversion and technological requirements better [5]. At present in the human-machine interaction system, the main input method of welding parameters is using dial switch, keyboard with LED and LCD. The dial switch fits the condition of less parameters. Now mainly interface use the keyboard with LED or use LCD. There are various problems in these designs. For example, the design above of human-machine interaction interface is single but with complex operation, low portability, long learning process, etc. A software development of the resistance spot welding man-machine interface based on DSP is introduced in literature [3], and the hardware adopted the official development board. The design of the man-machine interactive system based on phase dc spot welding is illustrated in the paper [4], with the keyboard and 8-color LCD.

With the rapid development of chip technology and accuracy improvement of spot welding, the control demand become increasingly complicated, and the user experience become constantly improved. Early embedded control system cannot meet the present higher requirements, which are simpler, more convenient, more beautiful and real-time operated. Now, many companies have designed a series of welders, which are characterized with pure text display and graphical user interface for welding parameters.

2   Hardware Design of Human-Machine Interaction System

2.1   The Overall Structure of High Frequency Inverter Spot Welding System

The spot welding equipment is composed of servo pressurization system, inverter power system, control system and human-machine interface.

The electrode pressure has an important influence on the quality of spot welding. The electric force is usually regulated by the solenoid switch valve and the pressure reducing valve. The servo pressure system, which composed of servo driver and servo motor, can control the pressure of the electrode through the torque of the motor. And the speed of the electrode is controlled by the motor speed. The servo system can ensure the quality of resistance welding.

The power supply system is mainly composed of IGBT inverter, transformer and rectifier. The inverter process of welding machine is as follows: the three-phase or single-phase alternating current are rectified, after filtering, and get a relatively smooth straight. The inverter circuit composed of IGBT inverts the current into alternating current at different frequencies, which is reduced by the transformer. After the pressure, the rectifying filter can obtain a smooth dc output welding current.

2.2   The Structure of Human-Machine Interaction System

Human-machine interaction system consists of man-machine interface and software program. The hardware parts are controlled by the microprocessor, the touch screen and the man-machine interface. The software program adopts modular structure, including communication module, data storage module, monitor and alarm module, etc. Communication module accomplishes the communication between the resistance welder and the touch screen in the system. The data storage module accomplishes to read, record and the store the parameters and the results of welding. Monitor module controls the welding process and gives an alarm with the failure data. The overall structure of human-machine interaction system is shown in Fig. 1.

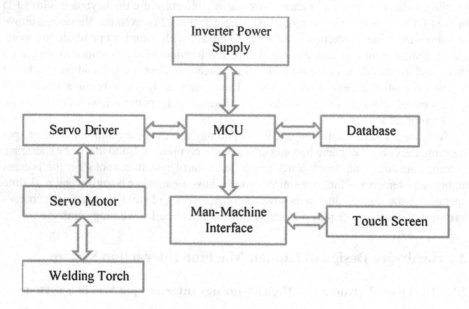

Fig. 1. General frame of human-machine interaction

2.3   The Hardware Structure of Human-Machine Interaction System

The core controller of the human-machine interaction interface is PIC32MX764F128L, which is manufactured by Microchip Technology Incorporated. It is a 32-bit microprocessor, and has been enhanced in the image, image processing, peripherals and industrial interface options. The processor has high speed and enough memory, which has very good electrical performance. The MCU core contains [6]:

- 80 MHz/105DMIPS, 32-bit MIPS M4 K® Core
- USB 2.0 On-The-Go Peripheral with integrated PHY
- 10/100 Ethernet MAC with MII/RMII Interfaces
- 2 x CAN2.0b modules with 1024 buffers
- 8 Dedicated DMA Channels for USB OTG, Ethernet, and CAN
- MIPS16e mode for up to 40% smaller code size
- 32 × 32-bit Core Registers
- 32 × 32-bit Shadow Registers
- Fast context switch and interrupt response

- 512K Flash (plus 12K boot Flash)
- 64K RAM (can execute from RAM)
- 8 Channel General Hardware DMA Controller
- Flash prefetch module with 256 Byte cache

The parameters can meet the design requirements.

The LCD touch screen is mainly used to set welding parameters, choose welding technology and issue welding commands. The touch screen choose XG104STC01N/R series products, which is designed and manufactured by Shenzhen X.R.D LCD Technology Co. Ltd. The screen is carried by SGUS (Super Graphics Utility Software) system, which can easily implement the touch function by SGUS serial intelligent display terminal, such as data text entry, return value of the key, regulation incremental, pop-up menus, etc. It has UART communication, which can support 921600 BPS rate of communication. It can store pictures and fonts, and can be updated via a serial or SD card. It supports UNICODE character display and RTC clock function. The instruction set is simple and easy to develop.

It can also quickly implement display functions such as dial clock, icon variable, art word, curve display, list display, text display, etc.

The communication between the main control chip and the SGUS touch screen is accomplished through RS232 serial port.

2.4 Design Basis of Human-Machine Interaction Interface

The appearance of the man-machine interface is designed according to the welding procedure. The basic welding process of inverter spot welding power source is: the preloading - welding - maintain   stop, four stages. In the welding process, the welding current can be divided into the following phases: gently preheating current-welding current—heat treatment transition—heat treatment current—cold current [7]. The welding time and current are set, regulated and displayed through the man-machine interface. A sequence diagram of spot welding process, which shows the change of welding pressure and current over time is showed in Fig. 2.

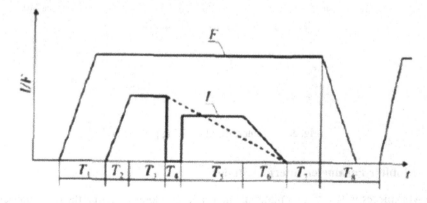

Fig. 2. Technics sequence chart of spot welding

3   Man-Machine Interface Design

The design of the interface is simple by using the touch screen. Considering the actual operation requirements of the industry, the design of interface consists of welding parameters, monitoring parameters, electrode step length, electrode pressure, real-time curve and so on. Only welding parameters and monitoring parameters are described in this paper.

3.1   Welding Parameter Interface Design

The interface of welding parameter is designed according to the welding procedure, which is to set the current and corresponding time of the welding process. The operator can manually enter the required parameters according to the actual situation. This design pattern can ensure the wide technological adaptability of welding process. In a parameterized welding mode, the relevant parameters will be automatically saved after each welding. And next time, the CPU read the last saved welding data first after system initialization so as to achieve the purpose of power-fail protection and welding parameters reproduce last time.

The mode selection of spot welding is also designed in the interface, and the user can choose the mode between single point welding and continuous welding according to different weld assemblies. The entire interface design is shown in the Fig. 3.

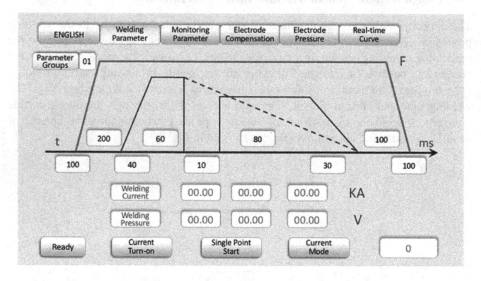

Fig. 3. The interface of welding parameter

3.2   Monitor Parameter Interface Design

The workpieces with different material and thickness determine that the operator needs to adjust the welding current after electing electrode pressure and welding time. Operator should check the weld nugget diameter which is produce by different samples with different welding current, until the solder joint quality fully meets the requirements of the technical conditions. Based on experimental results, users input the upper and lower limit of corresponding welding current, voltage and power, through the touch screen. At the same time, the monitoring module will perform the real-time monitoring, which will generate alarm when detect the abnormal state, to ensure the safety of the welding production. The design is shown in Fig. 4.

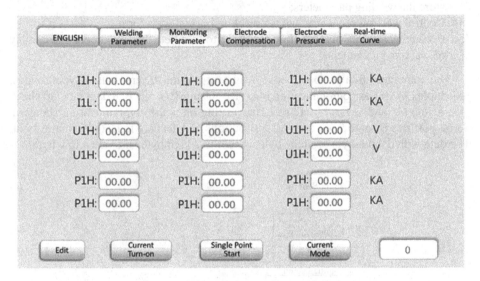

Fig. 4. The interface of monitor parameter

4 Software Design of Human-Machine Interaction System

4.1 Welding Working Process

Following is the working process of the welding machine. The parameters of the man-machine interface are set and sent to the MCU controller before the start of spot welding. After receiving the starting signal, the servo motor will operate according to the spot welding control. The controller will check the mechanical origin when starting the machine and keep each electrode moving from the same position. The electrode drops a certain distance first, and then slowly close to the welding part. This way can realize the soft contact between the workpiece and the electrode.

After the electrode get the suitable place, the motor is controlled. The motor torque controls electrode pre-pressure. The motor torque changes into the pressure after the preloading, and then the welding power supply begins to output current. At the end of welding, the point welding power supply sends an end signal to the MCU. The motor is reversed and the electrode is back to the origin point after the pulse signal controlling. Then the whole system waits for the next instruction controlled by the MCU.

4.2 Software Design of Whole System

Design of the software system adopts hierarchical structured thinking. Modularization of the entire software and simplification of module function, can improve reliability and stability of the software, and facilitate maintenance and debugging. The software mainly completed the following functions [7]:

(a) Accomplish the initialization of the system program, and set the storage units to store the welding parameters;

(b) Control welding sequence, and set welding current waveform;

(c) Communicate with man-machine interface to complete the adjustment and display of welding parameters.

The communication protocol between system and touch screen use asynchronous, full-duplex UART as communication interface. Using 8N1 mode, 8 data bits, n0 check bits, a stop bit, and a start bit are set. The starting bit is the communication standard. Serial port rate is set to 9600 bps. All instructions and data are in hexadecimal format. The data with double-byte or multi-byte, is sent in a high byte and then a low byte.

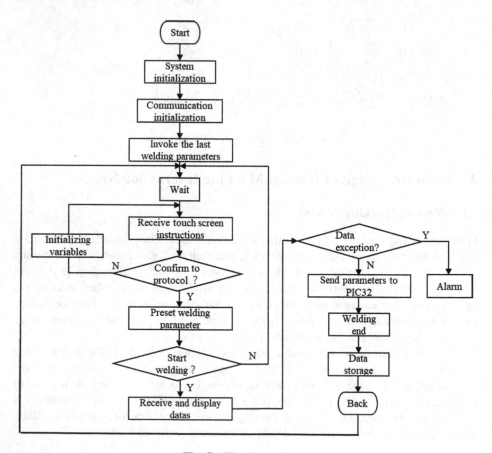

Fig. 5. The program flow

With the development of each module, a whole function program based on the process, is written to carry out the predetermined function of human-machine interface. The procedure flow is shown in Fig. 5.

4.3 Software Design of Touch Module

When the touch screen is touched, the jitter must be eliminated first. Then interrupt pin sends interrupt request to the CPU, which will jump into interrupt service program after receiving the request, and shut off external interrupt. Then the CPU collects X, Y coordinate, takes A/D conversion, reads the conversion result, and gets the position coordinates of the touch point. Then the CPU compare the position coordinates with the set key boundary coordinates, and determine the touch key. The flow chart is shown in Fig. 6.

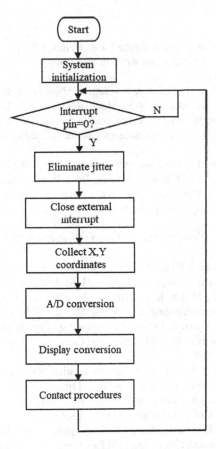

Fig. 6. The touch module flow

5   Conclusion

A human-machine interaction system of inverter spot welding was introduced based on PIC microprocessor and touch screen control. The system implements the inverter spot welding parameter setting and display of the welding current in different stages, welding mode, monitor mode, selection of welding process and setting. The control system communicates with the man-machine interface. The parameters are sent to the power control system as the welding machine current. It is proved that the interface is simple, clear, easy to operate and high in practical value.

Funding. The publication of this research project was supported by the Fundamental Research Funds for the Central Universities (No. 01900-310422110).

References

1. Xi, Z.: Pressure Welding. China Machine Press, Beijing (2001)
2. Wang, F.: Development of resistance welding equipment at home and abroad. Electric Weld. Mach. **35**(2), 1–4 (2005)
3. Wang, X., Meng, G., Xie, W.: Software development based on DSP of resistance spot welding human-machine interface. Electric Weld. Mach. **40**(4), 57–62 (2010)
4. Chen, D., Cao, B., Ye, W.: The design of human-machine interaction system in the digital three-phase secondary rectifier resistance spot welding. Electric Weld. Mach. **37**(1), 11–13 (2007)
5. Sun, X., Khaleel, M.A.: Dynamic strength evaluations for self-piercing rivets and resistance spot welds joining similar and dissimilar metals. Int. J. Impact Eng. **34**(10), 1668–1682 (2006)
6. PIC32MX764F128L in Production. http://www.microchip.com/wwwproducts/cn/en552078
7. Shayan, A.R.: Study of dynamic performance of advanced high strength (AHSS) resistance spot-welds (2006)
8. Hua, F., Ma, M., Li, J., Wang, G.: State of the art of impact testers for spot welds. Engineering (05) (2014)
9. Pouranvari, M., Marashi, S.P.H.: On the failure of low carbon steel resistance spot welds in quasi-static tensile–shear loading. Mater. Des. **31**(8), 3647–3652 (2010)
10. Chao, Y.J., Wang, K., Miller, K.W., Zhu, X.-K.: Dynamic separation of resistance spot welded joints: Part I—experiments. Exp. Mech. **50**(7), 889–900 (2010)
11. Chao, Y.J., Wang, K.: Dynamic failure of resistance spot welds-issues, problems and current research. In: Proceedings of the XI International Congress & Exposition on Experimental & Applied Mechanics (2008)
12. Wang, H., Ma, J., Wang, C.: Study on the classification of multi-spectral images based on a FSVM multi-class classifier with the binary tree. Optoelectron. Lett. **6**(1), 61–64 (2010)
13. Fugate, G., Felty, J.: Automation of solder joint inspection procedures utilizing laser induced infrared. IEEE Trans. Compon. Hybrids Manuf. Technol. **10**, 374–378 (1987)
14. Li, C.-H., Kuo, B.-C., Lin, C.-T., Huang, C.-S.: A spatial–contextual support vector machine for remotely sensed image classification. IEEE Trans. Geosci. Remote Sens. **50**, 784–799 (2012)
15. Bayram, I., Selesnick, I.W.: Frequency-domain design of overcomplete rational-dilation wavelet transforms. IEEE Trans. Signal Process. **57**, 2957–2972 (2009)

16. Yue, Z., Zhou, K., Cai, L.: Mathematical description of AC resistance spot welding control problem and limits of its controller design. In: American Control Conference (ACC) Washington, no. 6, pp. 17–19 (2013)
17. Tang, H.: Machine mechanical characteristics and their influences on resistance spot welding quality. Michigan University (2000)

Author Index

Abascal-Mena, Rocío III-218
Abnousi, Freddy II-447
Abujarad, Fuad III-149
Aguillar, Daniel Antonio Midena I-593
Aljohani, Maha I-608
All, Anissa I-277
Almada, Juan Felipe II-403
Almeida, Ana III-563
Alton, Noel II-653
Amidon, Timothy R. III-573
Aquino Jr., Plinio Thomaz I-593
Arciniegas, Jose L. I-223
Arenas, Juan I-673, III-375

Baca, Julie I-628
Baccus, Wendy L. I-356
Backhaus, Nils II-527
Bai, Yahui III-648
Baños Díaz, Gloria I-327
Baranauskas, M. Cecilia C. I-153
Barattin, Daniela I-367
Barroso Castañon, Jose Alberto II-73
Battaiola, André Luiz I-165
Bell, John III-185
Benites Alfaro, Fanny Dolores III-589
Bie, Bingmei III-459
Blustein, James I-608
Böhm, Patricia III-247
Bonin, Renan III-3
Branham, Stacy II-51
Braun, Philip III-247
Breyer, Felipe Borba II-543
Burmester, Michael I-306
Buzzi, Maria Claudia III-94

Cain, William III-185
Candello, Heloisa II-414
Canedo, Edna Dias I-379, I-642
Cao, Qi III-158, III-170
Cao, Sha II-513
Cao, Simin II-200
Cardarelli Leite, Leonardo III-67
Carlson, Kristina III-149
Carruth, Daniel I-628

Cezarotto, Matheus I-165
Chang, Danni I-3
Chen, Jie III-415
Cheng, Bo III-342
Cheng, Cui III-185
Cheng, Xiandong III-503
Choi, Chang-Beom I-417, II-39
Choi, Jaewoong II-39
Chunpir, Hashim Iqbal I-658
Clark, Jarrett W. I-346
Collantes, Luis I-496
Collina, Luisa I-14
Conrad, Jan I-27, I-560
Conradie, Peter I-277
Conrado, Daniel B. F. III-231
Creager, Alaina I-741
Cui, Tong III-41

da Silva, Fabio Q. B. II-338
Dam, Peter III-67
David, Salomao III-608
Davis, Elijah I-628
de Araujo, Daniel Paz III-3
de Assumpção Macedo, Jefté II-543
de Castro Andrade, Rafael II-187
de Freitas Guilhermino Trindade,
    Daniela III-490
de Godoi, Tatiany Xavier III-490
De Letter, Jolien I-277
De Marez, Lieven I-277
De Oliveira Heidrich, Regina II-403
de Paula Barretto, Francisco III-471
De Ruyck, Olivia I-277
De Vos, Ellen II-3
Deng, Rong I-256
Desloge, Allissa III-149
Desurvire, Heather I-40
Di Sabatino, Peter I-14
Dickey-Kurdziolek, Margaret II-51
Ding, MuRong III-435
Ding, Xiaoguo III-329
Ding, Yu-Yi III-158, III-170
Döllinger, Nina I-573
Dong, Xueyan III-257

Dong, Yumei   I-256
Dong, Zhanjun   II-498
Dornig, Jan   II-427
Dou, Jinhua   II-513
Drew, Mandy R.   I-356
Du, Yang   III-620

Emmanouil, Marina   II-3
Espinoza, Carlos   I-673
Espinoza, Jorge   I-673

Fackert, Sven   I-560
Falcone, Brooke   I-356
Fernandes, Farley   I-693
Ferranti, Marcelo P.   III-67
Filgueiras, Ernesto   I-693
Filippi, Stefano   I-367
Fischer, Holger   I-711, I-758
Fraga, Tania   II-437
Freer, Daniel   III-185
Fronemann, Nora   I-509, III-52
Fu, Jiong   III-635
Fu, Rongrong   III-459

Galluzzo, Laura   I-14
Gatis Filho, Sílvio José Vieira   II-543
Geerts, David   I-223
Giraldo, William J.   I-223
Gobena, Dagmawi Lemma   II-614
Gonçalves da Silva e Souza, Priscilla   I-379
Gong, Chao   I-60
Gong, Qian   II-297
Gong, Xiaodong   II-297, II-557
Granollers, Toni   I-396
Gu, Jiafeng   II-586
Gu, Qunye   I-77
Gu, Xiusheng   III-285
Gu, Zhen Yu   III-406
Guan, Xiaolei   III-133
Guerino, Guilherme Corredato   III-490
Guimarães, Cayley   III-16
Guo, Xinwei   II-575

Haasler, Kristin   I-306
Han, Daseong   III-270
Han, Jing-Hua   III-158, III-170
Han, Ting   III-389
Hao, Zeyu   III-363
Haraseyko, Anna   II-653

Hawkey, Kirstie   I-608
He, Canqun   II-586
He, Hao   III-503
He, Jun-en   III-285
Helgath, Jana   III-247
Henriques do Amaral, Wilian Daniel   II-73
Henschel, Julian   I-306
Hu, Huimin   III-648
Huang, Can   III-693
Huang, Shi   I-406, III-158
Huang, Zhao   I-91
Hurtienne, Jörn   I-528

Ihara, Masayuki   III-657
Isemann, Daniel   III-247
Isherwood, Paul   I-429
Israr, Ali   II-447

Ji, Yong Gu   III-124
Ji, Zhangyu   II-586
Jia, Jingpeng   III-257
Jiang, Bin   II-258, III-41
Jiang, Lijun   II-200, III-285
Jiao, Yang   II-447
Jin, Yi   III-299, III-314, III-329
Jo, HyunJae   I-417
Jordan, Philipp   II-19
Jung, In-Ho   II-39
Jung, Jaehong   II-447

Kelner, Judith   II-543
Kepplinger, Sara   I-546
Khan, Nawaz   II-313
Kim, Daehoon   II-39
Kim, Hyejin   III-270
Kim, Jung Hyup   III-424
Kim, Young Woo   III-124
Klammer, Julia   III-664
Klautke, Hannah   III-185
Klimas, Chris   III-743
Kock, Simon   I-573
Koehler, Christian   I-27
Konnestad, Morgan   I-185
Kreminski, Max   I-40
Krüger, Anne Elisabeth   III-52
Kuge, Jeremias   I-528

Laib, Magdalena   I-306
Lau, Frances   II-447

Laurentiz, Silvia   III-28
Lazaro, Danielly J. P.   III-16
Lee, Carman   I-3
Lee, Chia-Chieh   II-603
Lee, Hyowon   II-623
Lee, Joon Suk   II-51
Lee, Kun   II-327
Lei, Tian   II-218
Leung, Lo Kwok   I-3
Li, Dawei   II-389
Li, Wei   III-196
Li, Xiaohua   III-285
Li, Yinxia   III-648
Li, Zhelin   II-200
Li, Zhengquan   III-285
Li, Ziyang   III-503
Lim, Jungsub   III-270
Lima, João Paulo   II-338
Lin, Na   III-648
Lipsey, Tiffany   III-573
Liu, Chao   II-62, III-158, III-170, III-351,
    III-620
Liu, Chunrong   III-299, III-314, III-329
Liu, Gang   II-158
Liu, Hao   III-535
Liu, Maoqi   II-557
Liu, Sicong   II-158
Liu, Song   II-472
Liu, Wei   I-795, II-148, II-461
Liu, Yanlin   I-101
Liu, Zhen   II-200, III-285
Loarte, Pamela   I-673
López, Diego M.   I-546
López-Ornelas, Erick   III-218
Loures Brandão, Guilherme Valle   II-73
Lu, Song   III-515
Lu, Yanjuan   III-257
Lu, Zhaolin   III-342
Luedeke, Tobias   I-27
Lv, Meiyu   II-227

Ma, Dede   III-110
Maguire, Martin   I-429
Man, Qianhe   II-83
Marchetti, Emanuela   II-110
Martens, Jean-Bernard   I-141
Martinez, Santiago Gil   I-185
Mastrantoni, Claudia   I-14
Mazzocchi, Maddalena   I-14
McGowan, Tim   III-743

McKilligan, Seda   I-725
Meléndez, Roy   II-247
Meng, Yifan   III-285
Merlin, José Reinaldo   III-490
Miao, Yingying   II-258, III-41
Michalski, Rafał   I-439
Minge, Michael   I-451
Moquillaza, Arturo   I-496
Mou, Lijun   III-756
Mubin, Omar   II-19
Muchave, Esperança   III-608
Munkvold, Bjørn Erik   I-185
Murillo, Braulio   I-470

Namoun, Abdallah   II-271
Nascimento, Carla   II-338
Nawar, Haytham   II-285
Neris, Vânia P. A.   III-231
Neves, André   I-693
Neves, Marco   III-682
Nguyen, Ngoc Thi   II-623
Ni, Nan   II-218
Ning, Bing   I-112
Noriega, Paulo   II-379, III-563, III-703,
    III-730

Obaid, Mohammad   II-19
Oberthür, Simon   I-758
Ognjanovic, Svetlana   I-125
Oliveira, Ana Emília F.   III-715
Oliveira, Sabrina   III-703
Oliveira, Tiago   III-703
Olivera Cokan, César   I-479

Pan, Weiying   II-258
Paraguai, Luisa   II-640
Parente da Costa, Ruyther   I-642
Park, Hye   I-725
Patkar, Nitish   I-758
Paz, Freddy A.   I-496
Paz, Freddy   I-470, I-479, I-496, I-673,
    I-782, II-247, III-375
Peissner, Matthias   III-52
Peng, Qiong   I-141
Peng, Shi   III-351
Pereira de Aguiar, Michelle   I-165
Pereira Jr., Clorisval   III-67
Pereira, Guilherme C.   I-153
Pillan, Margherita   II-127
Pinhanez, Claudio   II-414

Pinho, Helder   II-338
Pollmann, Kathrin   I-509, III-52
Pow Sang, Jose   I-470
Pritschet, Andreas   III-247
Promann, Marlen   I-741

Qian, Yingjie   III-257
Qin, Jingyan   II-389, II-513, II-575, III-363
Qin, Long   III-415
Qiu, Yue   I-60, II-297
Qu, Hequn   II-227
Qu, Jia   III-693
Queiroz, Francisco   III-67
Quinde, Mario   II-313

Rabelo, Aldrea M. O.   III-715
Rabêlo Jr., Dilson José L.   III-715
Rabite de Almeida, Caio Augusto   II-73
Radianti, Jaziar   I-185
Ramírez, Juan José   III-375
Rasche, Nancy   I-741
Rebelo, Francisco   II-379, III-563, III-703,
    III-730
Reed, Charlotte M.   II-447
Reinhardt, Daniel   I-528
Reis, Maria   III-682
Ren, Siyu   III-389
Ribeiro, Carlos Eduardo   III-490
Rico-Olarte, Carolina   I-546
Riedmann-Streitz, Christine   I-203
Rittmeier, Florian   I-711
Rodrigues, Kamila R. H.   III-231
Ruíz, Alexandra   I-223

Saenz, Michael   I-741
Saldien, Jelle   I-277
Sánchez, Manuel   I-496
Santos, Andre L. M.   II-338
Santos, Daniela   III-703
Saraiva, Marília Moraes   II-543
Sauer, Stefan   I-711
Schindler, Kristina   I-573
Schippert, Katharina   I-306
Schubert, Maximilian   III-247
Search, Patricia   I-241
Seifu, Addis   II-614
Senette, Caterina   III-94
Senft, Björn   I-711, I-758
Severgnini, Frederico M.   II-447

Sgarbi, Ederson Marcos   III-490
Sherard, Rachel   II-653
Shi, Chenhui   III-635
Shi, Di   I-256
Shin, Han Sol   II-327
Silva, Claudio H.   III-715
Silva, Paula Alexandra   II-19
Sinram, Victoria   I-509
Song, Jee Ho   II-327
Souza, Jean Elder Araújo   II-543
Souza, Tancredo   II-338
Spinillo, Carla G.   III-715
Spinillo, Carla Galvão   II-187
Spitz, Rejane   III-67
Staniów, Marta   I-439
Steigleder, Ana Paula   II-403
Steimle, Toni   I-560
Stephane, A. Lucas   I-346
Stigberg, Susanne Koch   I-771
Su, Yao   III-756
Su, Yunqiao   III-524, III-550
Summers, Kathryn   II-653, III-743
Sun, Jian   I-268
Sun, Xiaohua   II-427
Sun, Xu   II-673
Swierenga, Sarah J.   III-149

Tan, Hong Z.   II-447
Tang, Chen   III-80
Tang, Dai   III-257
Tang, Fang   II-96
Tao, Xinyi   III-389
Teichrieb, Veronica   II-338
Thüring, Manfred   I-451, II-527
Tian, Xiaoying   I-141
Tian, ZhuoYu   I-91
Tong, Xueting   II-353
Trapp, Anna Katharina   II-527
Traupe, Ole   I-573
Trindade, Yanick   III-730
Trujillo, Amaury   III-94
Tucker, Shannon   III-743

Urssi, Nelson J.   II-365

Valente, Andrea   II-110
van den Anker, Fred W. G.   III-664
Van Hove, Stephanie   I-277
Varella Gomes, Péricles   I-165

Venturelli, Suzete III-471
Vilar, Elisângela II-379
Vilcapoma, Max I-782
Vukelić, Mathias I-509

Waddell, Daniel I-628
Wallach, Dieter I-27, I-560
Wang, Bing Jing III-406
Wang, Cong III-435
Wang, Lei II-472
Wang, Wentao II-62, III-351
Wang, Xiaohui II-389
Wang, Xiaoxian III-535
Wang, Xuesong I-795
Wang, Zhi II-483
Wang, Zhongting III-648
Watanabe, Hiroshi III-657
Weslley Sant'Anna de Paula Lima,
    Tércio III-490
Wienrich, Carolin I-573
Winn, Brian I-165
Wu, Fong-Gong II-603
Wu, Lei III-756
Wu, Menghan II-148
Wu, Qiong III-415
Wu, Shaoxin III-285
Wu, Yichen II-127
Wu, Zhanwei II-353

Xie, Yang III-314, III-329
Xin, Xin I-256, II-3, II-148
Xiong, Zhiyong II-200
Xu, Di III-285
Xu, Jun II-158
Xu, Lemeng III-110
Xu, Raoshan II-158
Xu, Shaobing III-342

Yang, Cheng Hung III-406
Yang, Jianming I-268

Yang, Xiaonan III-424
Yang, Xu II-586
Yao, Yongjie II-200
Ye, Feng I-294
Yoon, Sol Hee III-124
Yu, DanDan III-435
Yu, Tae Jun II-327

Zancan, Breno Augusto Guerra III-490
Zapata Del Río, Claudia María
    del Pilar I-327
Zapata Del Río, Claudia María
    Del Pilar III-589
Zeiner, Katharina M. I-306
Zhang, Guangshuai I-77
Zhang, Lanyun II-673
Zhang, Lili III-550
Zhang, Liqun III-80, III-133
Zhang, Mu II-498
Zhang, Pengyi III-110
Zhang, Shujing II-513, III-363
Zhang, Sijia II-218
Zhang, Xuan III-196
Zhang, Ye III-459
Zhang, Ye III-620
Zhang, Yi Shen III-196
Zhang, Yin Shuai III-415
Zhao, Bin I-60, II-169
Zhao, Chao II-62
Zhao, Chaoyi III-648
Zhao, Shifeng I-795
Zhao, Yunjing II-427
Zheng, Yangshuo II-483
Zhong, Ke III-80, III-133
Zhou, Wei III-768
Zhou, Yuanming I-795
Zhu, Di III-445
Zhu, Qiumeng II-218
Zhu, Xu III-299
Zhu, Yancong III-768

Printed in the United States
By Bookmasters